Nepal

Bradley Mayhew
Lindsay Brown
Wanda Vivequin

LONELY PLANET PUBLICATIONS
Melbourne • Oakland • London • Paris

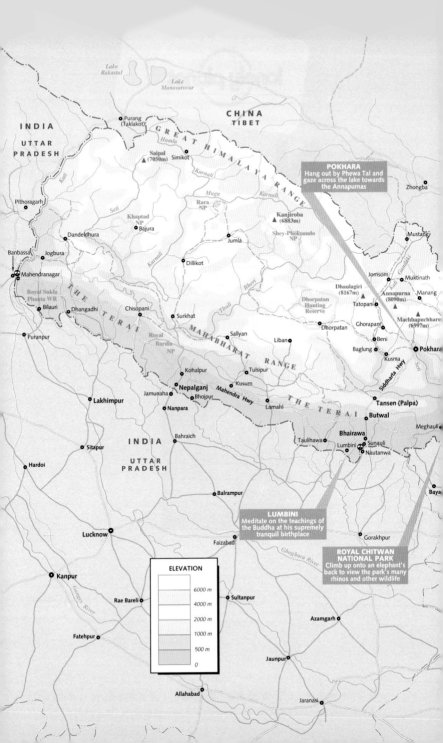

INDIA

UTTAR
PRADESH

Lake
Rakastal

Lake
Manasarovar

CHINA
TIBET

Purang
(Taklakot)

GREAT HIMALAYA RANGE

Humla

Saipal
(7050m)   Simikot

Karnali

Karnali

Zhongba

POKHARA
Hang out by Phewa Tal and
gaze across the lake towards
the Annapurnas

Pithoragarh

Dandeldhura

Banbassa

Jogbura

Mahendranagar

Royal Sukla
Phanta WR

Bilauri

Dhangadhi

Puranpur

Seti

Khaptad
NP

Bajura

Karnali

Chisapani

Sarju

THE   TERAI

Jumla

Dillikot

Bheri

Surkhat

Rara
NP

Mugu

Kanjiroba
(6883m)

Shey-Phoksundo
NP

Thuli

Sallyan

Liban

Dhorpatan
Hunting
Reserve

Royal
Bardia
NP

MAHABHARAT

Kohalpur

Tulsipur

Kusum

RANGE

Jomsom

Dhaulagiri
(8167m)

Tatopani

Dhorpatan

Ghorapani

Baglung

Beni

Kusma

Mustang

Muktinath

Gandaki

Manang

Annapurna
(8090m)

Machhapuchhare
(6997m)

Pokhara

Siddharta Hwy

Seti

Lakhimpur

Jamunaha

Nanpara

Nepalganj

Bhojpur

Mahendra Hwy

Lamahi

THE   TERAI

Tansen (Palpa)

Butwal

Meghauli

Sitapur

Bahraich

Taulihawa

Bhairawa

Lumbini   Sunauli

Nautanwa

Baya

Hardoi

INDIA

UTTAR
PRADESH

Balrampur

LUMBINI
Meditate on the teachings of
the Buddha at his supremely
tranquil birthplace

Gorakhpur

**ROYAL CHITWAN
NATIONAL PARK**
Climb up onto an elephant's
back to view the park's many
rhinos and other wildlife

Lucknow

Faizabad

Ghaghara River

Kanpur

Ganges River

Rae Bareli

Sultanpur

ELEVATION

6000 m

4000 m

2000 m

1000 m

500 m

0

Azamgarh

Fatehpur

Jaunpur

Allahabad

Jaranasi

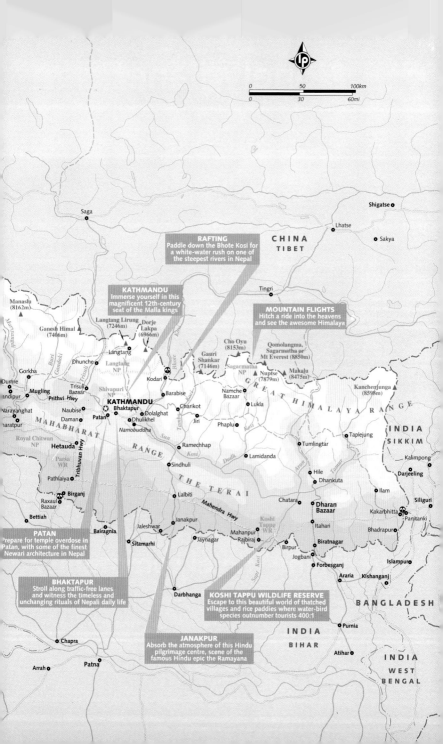

RAFTING
Paddle down the Bhote Kosi for a white-water rush on one of the steepest rivers in Nepal

KATHMANDU
Immerse yourself in this magnificent 12th-century seat of the Malla kings

MOUNTAIN FLIGHTS
Hitch a ride into the heavens and see the awesome Himalaya

PATAN
Prepare for temple overdose in Patan, with some of the finest Newari architecture in Nepal

BHAKTAPUR
Stroll along traffic-free lanes and witness the timeless and unchanging rituals of Nepali daily life

KOSHI TAPPU WILDLIFE RESERVE
Escape to this beautiful world of thatched villages and rice paddies where water-bird species outnumber tourists 400:1

JANAKPUR
Absorb the atmosphere of this Hindu pilgrimage centre, scene of the famous Hindu epic the Ramayana

www.lonelyplanet.com

your online travel community

Contents – Text

AROUND THE KATHMANDU VALLEY

KATHMANDU TO POKHARA

POKHARA

THE TERAI & MAHABHARAT RANGE

TREKKING 306

MOUNTAIN BIKING 342

RAFTING & KAYAKING 350

LANGUAGE 359

GLOSSARY 363

THANKS 368

INDEX 377

MAP LEGEND back page

METRIC CONVERSION inside back cover

Contents – Maps

MAPS

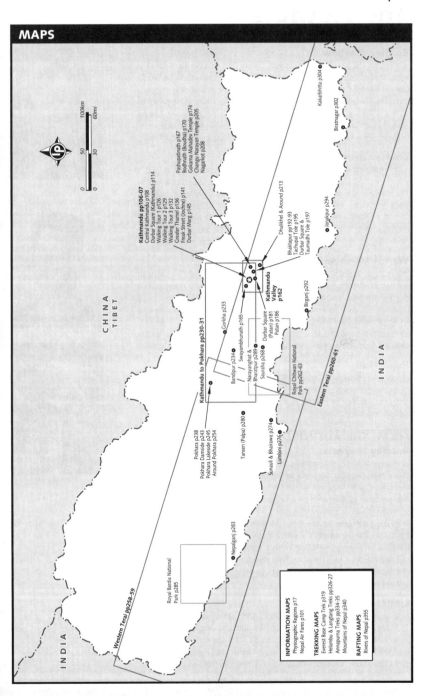

0   50   100km
0   30   60mi

The Authors

Bradley Mayhew
Bradley started travelling in southwest China, Tibet and northern Pakistan while studying Chinese at Oxford University. Upon graduation he fled to Central America for six months to forget his Chinese and now regularly travels to China's borderlands in a futile attempt to get it back. He is the co-author or author of Lonely Planet's *Pakistan, Karakoram Highway, Central Asia, Mongolia* and *Shanghai* guides, among others. He splits his time between Sevenoaks in southeast England and obscure parts of Montana.

Lindsay Brown
After completing a PhD on evolutionary genetics, and a short stint as a science editor, Lindsay started at Lonely Planet as a guidebook editor. There followed duties as Senior Editor and Series Publishing Manager of Walking Guides. He is now ensconced as Publishing Manager, Outdoor Activity Guides, responsible for the Walking, Cycling, Diving & Snorkeling and Watching Wildlife series. As an LP author he has contributed to *Australia, South India, Sri Lanka,* and *Thailand's Islands & Beaches.*

Wanda Vivequin
Wanda was brought up in Holland, Kenya, Lebanon and Canada, and her family eventually settled in New Zealand where she completed a degree in politics and a post-graduate diploma in journalism. Five years reporting for daily newspapers were followed by six years working as a spin-doctor for the New Zealand Department of Conservation. Wanda is a Nepalophile and she returns to her favourite country every year to run trekking trips and explore. Wanda currently lives in Edmonton, Canada.

Hugh Finlay
Hugh joined Lonely Planet in 1985 and has written *Jordan & Syria*, and co-authored *Morocco, Algeria & Tunisia* and *Kenya*; he was the co-ordinating author of the 9th edition of *Australia* and the 9th edition of *Africa on a shoestring.*

FROM THE AUTHORS

Bradley Mayhew
Lots of people helped out with this edition. Rajeev Shrestra was a life-saver with his help on transport information and festival dates. Ram Hamugain took time out to show me around Balthali. Bharat Bhasnet was gracious as ever with his time and passion for ethical tourism. Best of wishes to all of you and the many other Nepalis who were generous with their time and knowledge during hard times in Nepal. Thanks as always to Stan Armington of Malla Treks who helped with many tricky details and is always unfailing in his support of this title.

Final thanks and love to my wife Kelli for her support, patience and the enormous shopping list of things to bring home from Kathmandu. Thanks honey.

Lindsay Brown
First and foremost I thank Stan Armington (author of Lonely Planet's *Trekking in the Nepal Himalaya*) for his practical help, hospitality and great knowledge of Nepal. Thanks also to Peter Stewart and Megh Ale for their invaluable updates. Their expert help was greatly appreciated; however, I take full responsibility for any errors in the text.

I don't have enough space to adequately thank the following people: Bharat Basnet, Durga Bhandari, Wade Campbell, Crispin Conroy, Lyall Crawford, Dinesh Giri, Dawa Lama, Surendra Malla, Bruce Moore, Marco Peter, Pushpa KC, Rajendra Shrestha, Deepak Thapa and Gangaram and his Corolla. Finally, I thank the incomparable Bradley Mayhew for sharing his favourite Chinese restaurant in Kathmandu, and Jenny, Patrick and Sinead for everything else.

Wanda Vivequin

I would like to thank Kanak Mani Dixit (Himal South Asia) for answering my all questions and Meera Bhattarai (Association for Craft Producers, Fair Trade Group Nepal) for information on crafts and culture. Heartfelt thanks also go to Rajendra Dhamala (Langtang Ri Trekking) for his wisdom, company and infinite patience. Trish Batchelor (CIWEC medical clinic) gets a mention, as does Kerry Moran. Thanks also to Marc for being such a good sport about my addiction to Nepal.

THIS BOOK

The five editions of Lonely Planet's *Kathmandu & the Kingdom of Nepal* guide were the work of Nepali writer Prakash A Raj. In 1989 Tony Wheeler and Richard Everist completely rewrote the book, renaming it *Nepal*. In 1992 Richard Everist researched the 2nd edition, and the next three editions were written by Hugh Finlay. This is the 6th edition of *Nepal*.

Bradley Mayhew coordinated this edition of *Nepal*, and wrote the Facts for the Visitor, Getting There & Away, Getting Around, Kathmandu and Around the Kathmandu Valley chapters; Lindsay Brown researched the Kathmandu to Pokhara, Pokhara, The Terai & Mahabarat Range, Trekking, Rafting & Kayaking and Mountain Biking chapters; Wanda Vivequin wrote Facts about Nepal. Thanks to Deepak Thapa for his update on Nepal's political situation.

The Mountain Biking chapter was originally written by John Prosser, and updated for the 4th, 5th and current editions by Peter Stewart, owner of Himalayan Mountain Bikes. David Allardice, operations manager for Ultimate Descents International and co-author of *White Water Nepal*, originally wrote the Rafting & Kayaking chapter; it was updated by Megh Ale of Ultimate Descents Nepal. Stan Armington, author of Lonely Planet's *Trekking in the Nepal Himalaya*, has updated the Trekking chapter for the last two editions.

From The Publisher

This edition of *Nepal* was commissioned by Janine Eberle. Amanda Sierp and Suzannah Shwer coordinated the mapping and editing respectively, and Ray Thomson managed the project. Thanks to Pete Cruttenden, Anne Mulvaney, Craig MacKenzie, Susannah Farfor, Brigitte Ellemor and Barbara Delissen for their editorial assistance, and Simon Tillema for his GIS-mapping expertise. Quentin Frayne updated the Language chapter.

The layout of this book was designed by Steven Cann, who also chose the colour images. The cover was designed by Maria Vallianos and the final artwork was prepared by James Hardy. Pepi Bluck selected the illustrative material. Thanks to Tasmin Wilson, Vicki Beale, Sally Darmody and Katrina Webb for their invaluable last-minute assistance. Many thanks to Himal Books, Nepal for use of content from Toni Hagen's *Nepal* (1998).

Foreword

ABOUT LONELY PLANET GUIDEBOOKS

The story begins with a classic travel adventure: Tony and Maureen Wheeler's 1972 journey across Europe and Asia to Australia. There was no useful information about the overland trail then, so Tony and Maureen published the first Lonely Planet guidebook to meet a growing need.

From a kitchen table, Lonely Planet has grown to become the largest independent travel publisher in the world, with offices in Melbourne (Australia), Oakland (USA), London (UK) and Paris (France).

Today Lonely Planet guidebooks cover the globe. There is an ever-growing list of books and information in a variety of media. Some things haven't changed. The main aim is still to make it possible for adventurous travellers to get out there – to explore and better understand the world.

At Lonely Planet we believe travellers can make a positive contribution to the countries they visit – if they respect their host communities and spend their money wisely. Since 1986 a percentage of the income from each book has been donated to aid projects and human rights campaigns, and, more recently, to wildlife conservation.

Although inclusion in a guidebook usually implies a recommendation we cannot list every good place. Exclusion does not necessarily imply criticism. In fact there are a number of reasons why we might exclude a place – sometimes it is simply inappropriate to encourage an influx of travellers.

UPDATES & READER FEEDBACK

Things change – prices go up, schedules change, good places go bad and bad places go bankrupt. Nothing stays the same. So, if you find things better or worse, recently opened or long-since closed, please tell us and help make the next edition even more accurate and useful.

Lonely Planet thoroughly updates each guidebook as often as possible – usually every two years, although for some destinations the gap can be longer. Between editions, up-to-date information is available in our free, monthly email bulletin *Comet* (W www.lonelyplanet.com/newsletters). You can also check out the *Thorn Tree* bulletin board and *Postcards* section of our website, which carry unverified, but fascinating, reports from travellers.

Tell us about it! We genuinely value your feedback. A well-travelled team at Lonely Planet reads and acknowledges every email and letter we receive and ensures that every morsel of information finds its way to the relevant authors, editors and cartographers.

Everyone who writes to us will find their name listed in the next edition of the appropriate guidebook. The very best contributions will be rewarded with a free guidebook.

We may edit, reproduce and incorporate your comments in Lonely Planet products such as guidebooks, websites and digital products, so let us know if you don't want your comments reproduced or your name acknowledged.

How to contact Lonely Planet:
Online: e talk2us@lonelyplanet.com.au, W www.lonelyplanet.com
Australia: Locked Bag 1, Footscray, Victoria 3011
UK: 72-82 Rosebery Ave, London, EC1R 4RW
USA: 150 Linden St, Oakland, CA 94607

RICHARD I'ANSON

Title Page: Swayambhunath Stupa, Kathmandu Valley (Photograph by Richard I'Anson)
Above: Rice terraces, Jhelibrang
Left: Bridge across the Marsyangdi Khola, Bhulebule, Annapurna region
Below: Man and bullock cart ford a river, the Terai

BRETT SHEARER

CHRIS MELLOR

PAUL DYMOND

Above: Elephants and their trainers cross the Rapti River, Sauraha, Royal Chitwan National Park
Right: Raft on the Sun Kosi River
Below: Bungy jumping at the Last Resort, Bhote Kosi

ANDERS BLOMQVIST

ANDERS BLOMQVIST

GREG ELMS

RICHARD I'ANSON

Above: Durbar Square, Kathmandu
Left: Traditional clay pots, Potter's Quarter, Bhaktapur
Below: Bronze statues for sale, Durbar Square, Patan

PAUL DYMOND

PAUL DYMOND

Above: Hari Shankar Temple, Durbar Square, Patan
Right: Street vendor, Pushnupati, Kathmandu
Below: Rani Pokhari (Queen's Pond), Kathmandu

CAROL POLICH

JEFF CANTARUTTI

GARETH MCCORMACK

Above: Trekkers, Langtang
Left: Snowfields and Ama Dablam, Everest region
Below: Trekkers near Chirwa, Kanchenjunga Trek

JEFF CANTARUTTI

SCOTT DARSNEY

MARK ANDREW KIRBY

Above: Boats on Phewa Tal, Pokhara
Right: Canyoning near the Last Resort (Bhote Kosi)
Below: Hot-air balloon, Kathmandu Valley

ALISON WRIGHT

ANDERS BLOMQVIST

ANDERS BLOMQVIST

Above: Tej Festival, Balephi
Left: Nuns, Tibetan New Year festival, Bodhnath Stupa, Kathmandu Valley
Below: Pilgrims, Nepali New Year festival, Asan Tole

KRAIG LIEB

RICHARD I'ANSON

Introduction

Draped along the greatest heights of the Himalaya, the kingdom of Nepal is a land of eternal fascination, a place where the ice-cold of the mountains meets the steamy heat of the Indian plains. It's a land of ancient history, colourful cultures and people, superb scenery and some of the best trekking on earth.

Nepal's history is shaped by its geographical location, between the fertile plains of India and the desert-like plateau of Tibet. Its position between India and China has meant that Nepal has at times played the role of intermediary – a canny trader between two great powers – while at other times it has faced the threat of invasion. Internally its history is just as dynamic, producing the Himalaya's most sophisticated cultures, centred on the three great minikingdoms of the Kathmandu Valley – Kathmandu, Patan and Bhaktapur. Here, in the winding alleys and hidden courtyards scattered with temples and shrines, traders and holy men conduct their affairs among ancient beauty and modern-day squalor. The evocative power of these surroundings enables one to mentally turn back the clock to the medieval era.

Behind the time-worn temples and palaces of the Kathmandu Valley, above and beyond the hills that ring the valley, rises the 'Abode of Snows' (in Sanskrit: Himalaya), a natural kingdom and a magnet for trekkers, mountaineers and adventurers from around the world. Fortunately, these days your surname doesn't have to be Hillary, Messner or Bonington for you to venture into the realm of the world's grandest mountains. With a dash of enterprise and a modicum of fitness most travellers can walk the trails that lead into the roadless heights of the Himalaya.

Whether you get your adrenaline kicks from some of the world's premier white-water rafting, kayaking and mountain biking, or from the sight of your first tiger or rhino through the dawn mist atop an elephant in Chitwan National Park, Nepal will leave countless impressions. Many visitors, drawn to Nepal by the promise of adventure, leave equally bewitched by the friendliness and

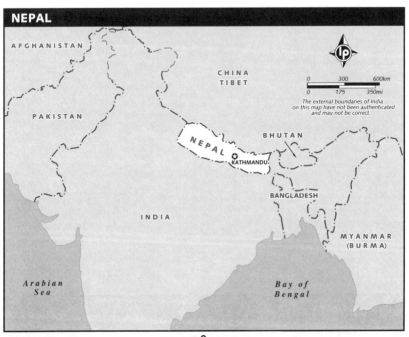

openness of the Nepali people and their amazingly rich and diverse culture.

From the natural rhythm you ease into on a trek to the rhythm of a tabla drum at one of Kathmandu's palace restaurants, Nepal is an amazingly diverse country that offers something for everyone. One journey through this land is rarely enough. The first thing many people do after a visit to Nepal is to start planning the next one.

Facts about Nepal

HISTORY

The history of Nepal began in, and centres on, the Kathmandu Valley. Over the centuries Nepal's boundaries have extended to include huge tracts of neighbouring India, and contracted to little more than the Kathmandu Valley and a handful of surrounding city-states.

Nepal's founding father, Prithvi Narayan Shah, referred to Nepal as 'a yam between two boulders' – namely China and India. It was the meeting point between the Mongoloid peoples of Asia and the Caucasoid peoples of the Indian plains. In earlier times, Nepal prospered from its location as a convenient resting-place for traders, travellers and pilgrims moving between these countries.

The Kiratis & Buddhist Beginnings

Recorded history begins with the Kiratis, who were Hindu and worshipped Shiva. Arriving from the east around the 7th or 8th century BC, these Mongoloid people are the first known rulers of the Kathmandu Valley. King Yalambar (the first of their 29 kings) is mentioned in the Hindu epic the Mahabharata but little more is known about them.

Buddhism also arrived during Kirati times and it is claimed that the Buddha, together with his disciple Ananda, visited the Kathmandu Valley and stayed for a time in Patan. Around the 2nd century BC, the great Indian Buddhist emperor Ashoka is said to have also visited the Kathmandu Valley. It is believed he erected four stupas (pagodas) around Patan and enlarged the great stupas at Bodhnath and Swayambhunath.

Early Indian Influences

Buddhism faded and Hinduism reasserted itself with the arrival from Northern India of the Licchavis. In AD 300 they overthrew the last Kirati king and brought into Nepal the caste divisions and some social and religious traditions that continue today; the Kiratis resettled in the east and are ancestors of the Rai and Limbu people. The Licchavis also ushered in a golden age of Nepali art and architecture, and their strategic position allowed them to prosper from trade between India and

China. Some of Nepal's earliest historical records can be dated back to this time including a lengthy inscription from 476 at the beautiful Changu Narayan Temple in the eastern part of the Kathmandu Valley.

The Thakuris, then Darkness

Amsuvarman, the first Thakuri king, came to power in 602, thus succeeding his Licchavi father-in-law. He consolidated his power to the north and south by marrying his sister to an Indian prince and his daughter to a Tibetan prince.

From the late 7th century until the 13th century Nepal slipped into its 'dark ages', of which little is known. Tibet invaded in 705 and Kashmir invaded in 782. The Kathmandu Valley's strategic location, however, ensured the kingdom's growth and survival. King Gunakamadeva is credited with founding Kantipur, today's Kathmandu, around the 10th century.

The Golden Age of the Mallas

The first of the Malla kings came to power in the Kathmandu Valley around 1200. The Mallas had been forced out of India and their name can be found in the Mahabharata and in Buddhist literature. This period was a golden one which stretched over 550 years, though it was peppered with fighting over the valuable trade routes to Tibet.

The earlier years (1220–1482) were largely stable under Jayashithi Malla. Hinduism had a strong influence over society and culture. Agricultural techniques improved and more people worked and lived in the hill country.

The first Malla rulers coped well despite disastrous earthquakes and disease. A massive Muslim invasion from Bengal swept through the valley leaving damaged Hindu and Buddhist shrines in its wake. In India the damage was even more widespread and many Hindus were driven into the hills and mountains of Nepal, where they established small Rajput principalities. The Nepal we know today consisted of 46 separate small states, each minting their own coins and maintaining standing armies.

After the death of Jayashithi Malla's grandson, Yaksha, the Kathmandu Valley was broken up among his children into the three kingdoms of Bhaktapur, Kathmandu and Patan, all of which fought over the right

to control the rich trading routes with Tibet. The rest of the country remained a patchwork of tiny independent kingdoms.

The rivalry between the three kingdoms of the Kathmandu Valley extended to include arts and culture, which flourished in the competitive climate. The outstanding collections of exquisite temples and buildings in each city's Durbar Square are evidence of the huge amounts of money spent by the rulers to outdo each other. The 15th century in particular saw massive amounts of activity. Money for these works came from trade with Tibet, and evidence of it stands in the form of gilded pagodas and stunning wooden carvings.

Unification under the Shahs

It took more than two and a half decades of conquest and consolidation, but Prithvi Narayan Shah, founder of the Shah dynasty, finally realised his dream of a unified Nepal in 1769. Originally ruler of the tiny kingdom of Gorkha, halfway between Pokhara and Kathmandu, Prithvi Narayan conquered the Kathmandu Valley and then moved his capital to Kathmandu. A strong sense of nationalism, the need to protect Nepal's lucrative trade position and a desire to create a strong, unified defence against the British in India were behind his mammoth efforts.

The kingdom's power continued to grow until a 1792 clash with the Chinese in Tibet led to an ignominious defeat. In the ensuing treaty the Nepalis had to cease their attacks on Tibet and pay tribute to the Chinese emperor in Beijing; the payments continued until 1912.

British power on the subcontinent was growing at this time and a British envoy arrived in Kathmandu in 1792. The expanding Nepali boundaries, stretching all the way from Kashmir to Sikkim by the early 19th century, caused tensions with the Raj and, despite treaties with the British, disputes over the Terai (the lowlands south of the Himalayan foothills) led to war.

By 1810 Nepal had almost doubled its size, but the 1816 Sugauli treaty with the British ended its growth. Britain took Sikkim and most of the Terai, and Nepal's present-day eastern and western borders were established. Some of this land was restored to Nepal in 1858 in return for support given to the British during the Indian War of Independence.

The Sugauli treaty opened the door for Indian business influence in Nepal. A century later, when new direct trade routes were established between India and Tibet, the Nepalis began to lose their influence as an intermediary between the two countries. A British resident was sent to Kathmandu to keep an eye on things. Nepal's borders were cut off to all foreign contact from 1816 until 1951. The British residents in Kathmandu were the only westerners to set eyes on Nepal for more than one hundred years.

Many Nepali eyes were, however, viewing the outside world. The British were so impressed by the fighting abilities of the Nepalis that they brought mercenaries, known as Gurkhas, into the British army. Gurkha mercenaries have fought in the British army ever since (see the boxed text 'Bravest of the Brave' later in this chapter).

The Ranas

Politics, power struggles and palace intrigue in the royal household created a volatile mix that led to the Kot Massacre in 1846. This bloody night was engineered by the young Chhetri noble, Jung Bahadur; it catapulted his family into power and side-lined the Shah dynasty.

Ambitious and ruthless, Jung Bahadur organised for his soldiers to massacre several hundred of the most important men in the kingdom – noblemen, soldiers and courtiers – while they were assembled in the Kot courtyard adjoining Kathmandu's Durbar Square. Jung Bahadur took the title of Prime Minister and changed his family name to the more prestigious Rana. Later, he extended his title to maharaja (king) and decreed it hereditary. The Ranas became a second 'royal family' within the kingdom and held the real power while the Shah kings were kept as figureheads.

The hereditary family of Rana prime ministers held power for more than a century. Development in Nepal stagnated, although the country did manage to preserve its independence during a time when European colonial powers were snatching up virtually every country unable to defend itself. Only on rare occasions were visitors allowed into Nepal.

Jung Bahadur Rana travelled to Europe in 1850 and brought back a taste for neoclassical architecture, examples of which can be seen in Kathmandu today. To the Ranas' credit, *suttee* (the Hindu practice of casting widows on their husband's funeral pyre) was abolished, forced labour was ended, and a school and a college were established in Kathmandu. But while the Ranas and their relations lived luxuriously, the peasants in the hills were locked in a medieval existence.

Elsewhere in the region dramatic changes were taking place. After WWII, India gained its independence and the communist revolution took place in China. Tibetan refugees fled into Nepal when the new People's Republic of China annexed Tibet, and Nepal became a buffer zone between the two Asian giants. At the same time King Tribhuvan, forgotten in his palace, was being primed to overthrow the Ranas.

Restoration of the Shahs

In late 1950 Tribhuvan escaped from his palace to the Indian embassy and from there to India. Meanwhile, the Nepali Congress party, led by BP Koirala, managed to take most of the Terai from the Ranas and established a provisional government that ruled from the border town of Birganj. India exerted its influence and negotiated a solution to Nepal's turmoil, and Tribhuvan returned to Nepal in 1951 to set up a new government composed of Ranas and commoners from the Nepali Congress party.

Although Nepal gradually reopened its long-closed doors and established relations with many other nations, dreams of a new democratic system were not permanently realised. Tribhuvan died in 1955 and was succeeded by his son Mahendra. A new constitution provided for a parliamentary system of government and in 1959 Nepal held its first general election. The Nepali Congress party won a clear victory and BP Koirala became the new prime minister. In late 1960, however, the king decided the government wasn't to his taste and had the cabinet arrested. Political parties were banned and Mahendra swapped his ceremonial role for real control.

In 1962 Mahendra decided that a partyless, indirect *panchayat* (council) system of government was more appropriate to Nepal. Local *panchayats* chose representatives for district *panchayats*, which in turn were represented in the National Panchayat. The real power, however, remained with the king who chose 16 members of the 35-member National Panchayat, and appointed the prime minister and his cabinet. Political parties continued to be banned.

Mahendra died in 1972 and was succeeded by his British-educated son Birendra. Popular discontent with slow development, official corruption and rising costs simmered in the 1970s. In 1979 the smouldering anger finally exploded into violent riots in Kathmandu, and King Birendra announced a referendum to choose between the *panchayat* system and one that would permit political parties to operate. The result was 55% to 45% in favour of the *panchayat* system; however, the king maintained the direct appointment of 20% of the legislature, which in turn was responsible for the election of the prime minister.

On the surface, the *panchayat* system, which allowed a secret vote and universal suffrage, did not appear to be dictatorial: the constitution theoretically guaranteed freedom of speech and peaceful assembly, as well as the right to form unions and associations (if they were not motivated by party politics).

The reality was somewhat different. Nepal's military and police apparatus were among the least publicly accountable in the world and there was strict censorship. Mass arrests, torture and beatings of suspected activists are well documented, and the leaders of the main opposition, the Nepali Congress, spent the years between 1960 and 1990 in and out of prison. The aristocracy, in general, managed to retain its influence and wealth. It is also widely accepted that a huge portion of foreign aid was routinely creamed off into royal and ministerial accounts.

People Power

In 1989 the opposition parties formed a coalition to fight for a multiparty democracy with the king as constitutional head; the upsurge of protest was called the Jana Andolan, or People's Movement. Popular support was motivated in part by economic problems caused by an Indian government blockade, and in part by widespread discontent with blatant corruption.

In February 1990 the government responded to nonviolent protest meetings with bullets, tear gas, thousands of arrests and torture. However, after several months of intermittent rioting, curfews, a successful strike, and pressure from various foreign aid donors, the government was forced to back down. The people's victory did not come cheaply; it is estimated that more than three hundred people died.

On 9 April King Birendra announced he was lifting the ban on political parties. On 16 April he asked the opposition to lead an interim government, and announced his readiness to accept the role of constitutional monarch.

Democracy & the Maoist Uprising

In May 1991, 20 parties contested a general election for a 205-seat parliament. The Nepali Congress won power with around 38% of the vote. The Communist Party of Nepal-Unified Marxist-Leninist (CPN-UML) won 28%, and the next largest party, the United People's Front, 5%.

In the years immediately following the election, the political atmosphere was uneasy. In April 1992 a general strike degenerated into street violence between protesters and police, and resulted in a number of deaths.

In late 1994 the Nepali Congress government, led by GP Koirala (brother of BP Koirala) called a midterm election. No party won a clear mandate, and a coalition formed

Revolutionary Tourism

In March 2002, at a time of heavy fighting between the Maoists and government forces, the chief ideologue of the Maoists, Dr Baburam Bhattarai published an 'open letter to foreign tourists'. In it he stated that the Maoists welcomed tourism and tourists since they 'are all for making maximum utilisation of the natural and cultural resources for the rapid economic development and well-being of the country and the people'. But he also warned that 'the unassuming traveller can be caught between the crossfire of the contending armies' and advised them 'not to venture into areas where active fighting is going on' even though 'they are most welcome into the revolutionary base areas, which are firmly under the control of the revolutionary forces'.

A cease-fire has since been reached between the Maoists and the Government, but the warning contained within Bhattarai's message should still be heeded. Check on the current political situation before venturing into remote areas.

between the CPN-UML and the third major party, the Rastriya Prajatantra Party (RPP), the old *panchayats*, with the support of the Nepali Congress. This was one of the few times in the world that a communist government had come to power by popular vote.

Political stability did not last long and in the late 1990s coalitions were formed and broken with alarming frequency, governments came and went with startling regularity, and opportunism and corruption were rife.

In 1996 the Maoists (of the Communist Party of Nepal), fed up with government corruption and by the failure of democracy to deliver improvements to the people, declared a 'people's war'. The insurgency began in the poor regions of the far west and gathered momentum, but was generally ignored by the politicians. The repercussions of this nonchalance finally came to a head in November 2001 when the Maoists broke their cease-fire and an army barracks was attacked west of Kathmandu. After a decade of democracy it seemed increasing numbers of people, particularly young Nepalis and those living in the countryside, were utterly disillusioned.

The beginning of the 21st century has seen the political situation in the country take a turn for the worse. By the end of 2002 nearly 8000 people, including many civilians, had been killed in the Maoist uprising. At that time Amnesty International accused the army and police of human rights abuses in connection with their role trying to control the uprising, while the Maoists were accused of recruiting children as soldiers.

The Royal Massacre & Aftermath

On 1 June 2001 the Nepali psyche was dealt a huge blow when Crown Prince Dipendra gunned down almost every member of the royal family during a get-together in Kathmandu. Among the 10 victims were King Birendra and Queen Aishwarya. In the months that followed, several versions of events were spawned. The palace was quick to release an official report that concluded Dipendra had shot his family, but there were plenty of conspiracy theories pointing the finger at the new king Gyanendra, the Maoists, or some other sinister element. A monarch who had served the country through some extraordinarily difficult times was gone. When the shock of this loss subsided the uncertainty of what lay ahead hit home.

Shortly after the massacre there were more internal problems in the ruling party and another prime minister – Sher Bahadur Deuba – was appointed. In April 2002 a five-day strike called by the Maoists paralysed

The Royal Massacre – for the Love of a Woman?

It was meant to be a pleasant family gathering at Narayanhiti Royal Palace but the night of 1 June 2001 turned into one of Nepal's greatest tragedies.

In a hail of bullets 10 members of Nepal's royal family including King Birendra and Queen Aishwarya were gunned down by a deranged, drunken Crown Prince Dipendra who eventually turned a weapon on himself. Dipendra did not die straight away and, despite being in a coma, was pronounced the king of Nepal. His rule ended two days later, when he too was declared dead. The real motive behind the massacre will never be known, but many believe Dipendra's murderous rage was prompted by his parents' disapproval of the woman he wanted to marry.

The object of his love was Devyani Rana, a beautiful aristocrat. The pair had often been seen together in public. However, the king and queen had allegedly told him that were he to ever marry Devyani, the crown would go to his younger brother Nirajan.

In the days that followed the massacre, a tide of emotions washed over the Nepali people – shock, grief, horror, disbelief and denial. A 13-day period of mourning was declared and in Kathmandu impromptu shrines were set up for people to pray for their king and queen. About 400 shaven-headed men roamed the streets around the palace on motorbikes carrying pictures of the monarch. All over the city, barbers were shaving the heads of other men, a mark of grief in Hindu tradition.

The initial disbelief and shock gave way to suspicion and conspiracy theories that are still being debated. The new king, Gyanendra, who had been in Pokhara at the time of the massacre, has much to do to gain the love and respect of the people. Several books have been published speculating about what exactly provoked this devastating royal drama, though doubtless the truth will never be known.

the country and intense clashes between the military and rebels continued.

In October 2002 King Gyanendra, frustrated with the political stalemate and the continued delay in holding national elections, dissolved the government and appointed Lokendra Bahadur Chand as prime minister. Not surprisingly, this move was labelled unconstitutional. Several large protest rallies were held in Kathmandu by the political parties and the Maoists continued to call for mass strikes.

On January 29 2003 the Nepali government and the Maoists reached a cease-fire agreement in which they agreed to solve their differences through controlled negotiation. An April 2003 media poll found that Nepalis were generally optimistic about the chances of the Maoists demands being resolved in a peaceful manner. Given the precarious political situation with the Maoists, the palace and the political parties arrayed against each other, complete stability may be a long time in coming.

GEOGRAPHY

Nepal may be a small country, but when it comes to height it is number one in the world. Mountains cover 80% of Nepal, providing huge challenges in a country where 80% of people live off the land. Nepal measures about 800km east–west and 230km at its widest point north–south, making a total area of around 147,181 sq km.

Within that small area, however, is the greatest range of altitude on earth – starting with the Terai, only 100m or so above sea level, and finishing at the top of Mt Everest (8848m), the world's highest point.

Physiographic Regions

Nepal consists of several physiographic regions, or natural zones: the plains in the south, four mountain ranges, and the valleys lying between them. Most people live in the fertile lowlands or on the southern sunny slopes of the mountains where farming is easier and life less harsh.

The Terai The only truly flat land in Nepal is the Terai (sometimes written Tarai). Seen from the air, this part of the Gangetic plain's monotonous expanse comes to a sudden halt as it turns into mountainous relief. The last of this landscape, about 100m above

sea level, extends up to 40km into Nepal. The region is a montage of paddy fields, oases of mango groves, bamboo stands and villages beneath scattered palms.

A lowland area, about 150m above sea level, known as the Inner Terai or the Dun, is between the Chure Hills and the foothills of the Mahabharat Range.

Chure Hills Known as the Siwalik Hills in India, the Chures are the first of the four mountain ranges and run the length of the country. They have an average height of 900m, reaching 1350m in places. This range separates the Terai from the Inner Terai and harbours the fossilised remains of many mammals no longer typical of Eurasia.

Mahabharat Range North of the Inner Terai, the next range of foothills is the Mahabharat Range, or the 'Middle Hills'. These vary between 1500m and 2700m in height, and though quite steep, are characterised by water-retentive soils that allow cultivation and extensive terracing. On the lower slopes, remnants of subtropical forests can be found. On the upper reaches, above cultivation, temperate elements begin. These mountains are severed by three major river systems: the Karnali, the Narayani and the Sapt Kosi.

Pahar Zone Between the Mahabharat Range and the Himalaya lies a broad belt called the midlands, or the Pahar zone. This includes fertile valleys (previously large lakes) such as Kathmandu, Banepa and Pokhara and supports nearly half of Nepal's population. The central and eastern parts of this zone have been extensively cultivated. Lying between 1000m and 2000m, subtropical and lower temperate forests (damaged by fuel and fodder gathering) are found here.

The stunningly located Pokhara area, right at the foot of the Annapurna massif, is unique because there is no formidable barrier directly to the south to block the path of spring and monsoon rain clouds. As a result Pokhara receives an exceptionally high level of rainfall, limiting cultivation to below 2000m.

At the other extreme, the Humla-Jumla area in the west is protected to the south by ranges over 4000m in height; these stop much of the region's monsoon moisture. The area is characterised by wide, uneroded valleys, snowless peaks and drier vegetation.

PHYSIOGRAPHIC REGIONS

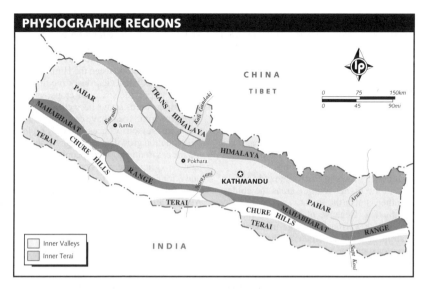

CHINA

TIBET

PAHAR

TRANS - HIMALAYA

MAHABHARAT

Karnali

Kali Gandaki

Jumla

TERAI

CHURE HILLS

RANGE

HIMALAYA

Marsyani

Pokhara

KATHMANDU

TERAI

CHURE HILLS

TERAI

MAHABHARAT

PAHAR

Arun

RANGE

Sapt Kosi

Inner Valleys

Inner Terai

INDIA

0   75   150km
0   45   90mi

The Himalaya Nepal's borders contain about one-third of the total length of the Himalaya. This includes 10 of the world's 14 tallest mountains which tower over 8000m. These mountains are terraced and cultivated up to about 2700m, or to the level of cloud and mist. As a result, the high-temperate forest above this to the tree line is fairly well preserved.

The inner valleys are those cradled within the Himalayan ranges. The higher parts of these broad, glacier-worn valleys, which are found in the Everest, Langtang and upper Kali Gandaki areas, are not affected by the strong winds that desiccate the valley floors. The partial rain-screen of these high valleys creates ecologies that are different again.

The Trans-Himalaya North of the Himalaya is a high desert region, similar to the Tibetan plateau. This area encompasses the arid valleys of Mustang, Manang and Dolpo, as well as the Tibetan marginals.(the fourth range of mountains, which sweeps from central to northwestern Nepal, averaging less than 6000m in height). The trans-Himalaya is in the rain-shadow area and receives significantly less precipitation than the southern slopes. Uneroded crags, spires and formations like crumbling fortresses are typical of this stark landscape.

GEOLOGY

About 60 million years ago, the Indo-Australian tectonic plate collided with the Eurasian continent. As the former was pushed under Eurasia, Earth's crust buckled and folded and mountain building began.

The upheaval of mountains caused the temporary obstruction of rivers that once flowed unimpeded from Eurasia to the sea. However, on the southern slopes of the young mountains, new rivers formed as trapped moist winds off the tropical sea rose and precipitated. As the mountains continued to rise and the gradient became steeper, these rivers cut deeper and deeper into the terrain.

The colossal outcome was the formation of four major mountain systems running northwest by southeast. These were cut in places by the north-south gorges of both new rivers, and the original rivers whose watersheds in Tibet are older than the mountains themselves. In conjunction with the innumerable rogue ridges that jut out from the main ranges, the terrain can be likened to a complex maze of ceilingless rooms.

The mountain-building process continues today, not only displacing material laterally, but also sending the ranges even higher and resulting in natural erosion, landslides, silt-laden rivers, rock faults and earthquakes.

CLIMATE

Nepal has a typical monsoonal, two-season year. There's the dry season from October to May and there's the wet season (the monsoon) from June to September.

In summer (May to September) Kathmandu can get very hot, with temperatures often above 30°C (May and early June, the months before the monsoon, are the hottest). Even in the winter months (October to April) the bright sunny days often reach 20°C, although with nightfall the mercury may plummet to near freezing.

It never snows in the Kathmandu Valley, and in the higher altitude areas the coldest weather is also the driest weather, so snow is unusual. Because of its lower altitude, Pokhara is warmer and more pleasant than Kathmandu during winter, but hotter before the monsoon and wetter during it.

For information about the importance of climatic factors in planning a visit to Nepal, see When to Go in the Facts for the Visitor chapter.

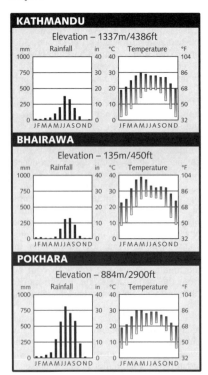

ECOLOGY & ENVIRONMENT

The ecology and environment of Nepal are fragile and a rapidly growing population is constantly putting more pressure on the land. Much of the land between the Himalaya and the Terai has been vigorously modified by humans to provide space for crops, animals and houses. Forests have been cleared, towns have grown and roads have eaten into valleys that were previously accessible only on foot.

Population growth is the biggest issue facing the environment. More people need more land for agriculture; trees continue to be cut down for housing and firewood. Although in places like the Annapurna Conservation Area, Kangchenjunga Conservation Area and Sagarmatha National Park efforts have been made to promote alternatives and support reforestation.

Grazing animals and deforestation have meant that during each monsoon huge chunks of hillsides devoid of trees are washed away. These often-massive landslides leave gigantic scars and wash valuable soil downriver that is eventually dumped in the Bay of Bengal. In 2002 virtually the entire village of Khobang in eastern Nepal was washed away in a landslide.

Air and water pollution in the Kathmandu Valley are severe. But during a Maoist strike when the valley shuts down and the streets are not choked with vehicles, the views of the Lamjung himal are crystal-clear.

Agriculture

The Terai is considered the 'rice bowl' of Nepal, although rice is usually grown at altitudes up to 2000m, and higher in western parts of the country. It is usually planted before the monsoon, transplanted soon after and harvested in the autumn. If possible, wheat is planted in the cleared rice fields and harvested in spring.

Fields of yellow-flowering mustard are planted for making cooking oil. Corn is grown on the hillsides, while millet is grown above the rice zone. Barley is sown in the higher altitudes, as is buckwheat with its pink and white flower cluster. The Sherpas grow potatoes at altitudes of up to 4000m.

Various other food crops are grown on the berms dividing the plots, including soya beans, lentils, chilli peppers and sesame.

There are numerous trees planted around villages and fields, whether for shade, fruit, animal fodder or medicine. Bananas, mangoes, papaya, citrus fruits, peaches and apples are all new sources of income for people in the remote hill areas. In the west, plots of tobacco are commonly seen in villages, as are fields of cannabis, grown for hemp. In addition, stinging nettles are picked with tongs, rendered harmless by boiling and eaten as greens. A variety of fig trees provide shade for pilgrims and travellers. The magnificent mushrooming canopies of banyan and pipal trees are unmistakable, usually found together atop a stone dais designed for accommodating porters' loads.

FLORA

There are 6500 known species of trees, shrubs and wildflowers in Nepal. The height of floral glory can be witnessed in March and April when rhododendrons burst into colour (there are 30 species in Nepal). The huge magnolias of the east with their showy white flowers on bare branches are also spectacular, as are the orchids (more than 300 species in Nepal).

In the postmonsoon season, the flowers of summer are all but gone. However, in the subtropical and lower temperate areas, some wildflowers that have survived environmental degradation include pink luculia, mauve osbeckia and yellow St John's wort. Flowering cherry trees, and blue gentians in the temperate areas, add autumnal colour to the villages. Otherwise, one can enjoy the autumn yellows of withering maples and ginger, and the reds of barberry shrubs.

In the Kathmandu Valley, silky oak with its spring golden inflorescence, and bottlebrush and eucalyptus, are planted as ornamentals, along with cherry, poplar and jacaranda. Historically, the Nepalis have been avid gardeners of such exotics as hibiscus, camellia, cosmos, salvia and marigold.

Tropical Zone
Up to 300m
Sal, a broad-leaved, semideciduous hardwood, dominates here. The leaves are used for 'disposable' plates, and the wood is used for construction. There is also a deciduous moist forest of acacia and rosewood in this zone, as well as open areas of tall elephant grass. These forest types are typical of the Chure hills and the Inner Terai.

Subtropical Zone
1000m to 2000m
The dominant species east of the Kali Gandaki are the true chestnuts and a member of the tea family, *schima*. Because of the popularity of chestnut wood as a source of fuel, it is often depleted. In the west, the chir pine is found on all aspects.

Lower Temperate Zone
1700m to 2700m
Evergreen oaks are indigenous to this zone. In the east, the oaks of the wet forests are festooned with moss and epiphytes and have dense understoreys. A wet forest occurring mostly on western Nepal's north and west faces comprises horse chestnut, maple and walnut. Alder and birch are prevalent along watercourses. Many homogeneous blue-pine forests occur in the west, mostly on south faces, and range to the tree line.

Upper Temperate Zone
2400m to 4000m
Another evergreen oak, widespread throughout the dry forests of the west, exhibits two types of leaves: the young ones are spiny, while the older ones have leaf margins. In the east this species is confined to southern slopes but is heavily cut for fodder and fuel.

The spectacular wet rhododendron forests are interspersed with hemlock and fir. *Rhododendron arboreum,* the national flower, reaches heights of 18m and ranges in colour from red to white.

Subalpine Zone
3000m to 4000m
Silver fir mixed with oak and birch extends to the tree line in the west. East of the Kali Gandaki, only birch is found to the tree line.

Alpine Zone
4000m to Snow Line
Above the tree line, vegetation must cope with extremes, both in ground temperatures and moisture levels. Only the most tenacious of wildflowers thrive here. In the trans-Himalaya, the vegetation is restricted to the arid-adapted species of the Tibetan plateau.

FAUNA
Birds
More than 800 bird species are known in Nepal, or nearly 10% of the world's species.

Resident bird numbers are augmented by migratory species, as well as winter and summer visitors.

Eight species of stork have been identified along the watercourses of the Terai. Similar in appearance are the cranes, though these are not as well represented, save for the demoiselle cranes that fly down the Kali Gandaki and Dudh Kosi for the winter, before returning in spring to their Tibetan nesting grounds. Herons and egrets are quite common in the tropics and subtropics.

Most of the waterfowl are migratory. Many can be seen at the Kosi Barrage in the eastern Terai and in the Chitwan and Bardia areas. The bar-headed goose has been observed flying at altitudes near 8000m.

Lammergeier *(Gypaetus barbatus)*

Raptors or birds of prey of all sizes are found in the Himalaya, and are especially prevalent with the onset of winter. Raptors include the small Eurasian kestrel, the Himalayan griffon and the lammergeier. The latter two, with a wingspan of nearly 3m, are carrion eaters. There are also true eagles present, including the resident golden eagle common in the Khumbu.

There are six species of pheasant in Nepal, including the national bird, the impeyan pheasant, the male of which has a plumage of iridescent colours. These birds are 'downhill fliers', – they do not fly, per se, and must walk uphill! The cheer and koklas pheasants live west of the Kali Gandaki, while the kalij pheasant is common throughout Nepal.

Nepal hosts 17 species of cuckoo, which are characterised by their distinctive calls.

Arriving in March, they herald the coming of spring. The Indian cuckoo is recognised by its '*kaphal pakyo*' call, which announces in Nepali that the fruit of the box myrtle is ripe. The common hawk cuckoo has a repetitious call that rises in a crescendo and sounds like 'brain fever' – or so it was described by British sahibs as they lay sweating with malarial fevers. Most cuckoos are social parasites, meaning they lay their eggs in the nests of other species.

One of the most colourful, varied and vocal families is the timalids, or babblers and laughing thrushes, common from the tropical Terai to the upper temperate forest. They range in length from 8cm to 33cm, and live in both terrestrial and arboreal habitats. They can often be identified by their raucous calls. The black-capped sibia with its constant prattle and ringing song is an integral part of the wet temperate forests. The spiny babbler is Nepal's only endemic species.

Nepal is home to 15 members of the crow family. The two species of blue magpies are similar in appearance, but each occupies a different altitudinal range: the red-billed blue magpie is a resident of the subtropical zone, while the yellow-billed blue magpie is found in the temperates. Likewise the Indian treepie prefers the tropics, while the Himalayan species lives in the subtropics and temperates. Above the tree line, two species of chough, congregating in large flocks in winter, are prevalent. Though the two species often overlap in range, the yellow-billed chough is found higher and is known to enter mountaineers' tents high on Everest. Another member of the crow family, also conspicuous in the trans-Himalayan region, is the large raven.

Besides such families as kingfishers, bee-eaters, drongos, minivets, parakeets and sunbirds, there are a host of others including 30 species of flycatchers and nearly 60 species of thrushes and warblers.

In the Kathmandu Valley, sparrows and pigeons demonstrate adaptability to urban centres by their sheer numbers. Dark kites, hawk-like birds with forked tails, are common over the city. At sunset loose groups of crows, mynahs, egrets and kites fly to their respective roosts. Pulchowki, Nagarjun and Shivapuri are excellent areas for finding birds of subtropical and temperate habitats.

In the Pokhara region, the Indian roller is conspicuous when it takes flight, flashing the iridescent turquoise on its wings. Otherwise, while perched, it appears as a plain brown bird. Local superstition has it that if someone about to embark on a journey sees a roller going their way it is a good omen. If they see a crow, however, it is a bad omen and the trip is aborted. Many trips must be destined for delay thanks to the presence of the common crow!

Mammals

Due to habitat degeneration from both natural and human causes, opportunities for viewing mammals are usually restricted to national parks, reserves and western Nepal, where the population is sparse. Wildlife numbers have also been thinned by poaching for pelts, and other animal parts that are considered to be delicacies or medicinally valuable. Animals are also hunted because of the damage they inflict on crops and domestic animals.

At the top of the food chain is the royal Bengal tiger, which is solitary and territorial. Males have territorial ranges that encompass those of two or three females and may span as much as 100 sq km. Royal Chitwan National Park in the Inner Terai and Royal Bardia National Park in the western Terai protect sufficient habitat to sustain viable breeding populations.

The spotted leopard is an avid tree climber and, in general, more elusive than the tiger. Like the tiger, this nocturnal creature has been known to prefer human flesh when it has grown old or been maimed. Local people have likened the spotted leopard to an evil spirit because its success at evading hunters suggests it can read minds.

The snow leopard is often protected from hunters, not only in national parks, but also because it inhabits inhospitable domains above the tree line and sensitive border regions. Its territory depends upon the ranges of ungulate (hoofed) herds, its prey species. Packs of wolves compete directly and when territories overlap, the solitary snow leopard will be displaced.

The one-horned rhinoceros is the largest of three Asian species and is a distinct genus from the two-horned African rhino. It has poor eyesight, and though it weighs up to two tonnes, it is amazingly quick. Anyone who

encounters a mother with its calf is likely to witness a charge, which is disconcertingly swift, even if you are on an elephant. The rhino is a denizen of the grasslands of the Inner Terai, specifically the Chitwan Valley, although it has also been reintroduced to Royal Bardia National Park and Royal Sukla Phanta Wildlife Reserve.

The Indian elephant is different from its African relative; belonging to a separate genus. The only wild elephants known to exist in Nepal are in the western part of the Terai and Chure hills, though individuals often range across the border from India. Elephants are known to maintain matriarchal societies, and females up to 60 years of age bear calves. Though elephants are able to reach 80 years of age, their life spans are determined by dentition. Molars are replaced as they wear down, but only up to six times. When the final set is worn, the animal dies of starvation.

There are several species of deer, but most are confined to the lowlands. The spotted deer is probably the most beautiful, while the sambar is the largest. The muntjac, or barking deer, which usually makes its presence known by its sharp, one-note alarm call, is found at altitudes up to 2400m, while the unusual musk deer, which has antelope-like features and is only 50cm high at the shoulder, ranges even higher.

There are two primates: the rhesus macaque and the common langur. The rhesus is earth-coloured, with a short tail and travels on the ground in a large, structured troop, unafraid of humans. The langur is arboreal, with a black face, grey fur, and long limbs and tail. Because of Hanuman, the monkey god in the Hindu epic the Ramayana, both species are considered holy and are well protected. The rhesus ranges from the Terai up to 2400m, while the langur goes up to 3600m.

Two even-toed ungulate mammals are found in the alpine regions. They are the Himalayan tahr, a near-true goat, and the blue sheep, which is genetically stranded somewhere between the goat and the sheep. The male tahr with its flowing mane poses on the grassy slopes of inner valleys, while the blue sheep turns a bluish-grey in winter and is found in the trans-Himalayan region.

The Himalayan black bear is omnivorous and a bane to corn crops in the temperate

Himalayan black bear

forests. Though it rarely attacks humans, its poor eyesight may lead it to interpret a standing person as making a threatening gesture and to attack. If so, the best defence is not to run, but to lie face down on the ground – particularly effective when one is wearing a backpack. Nepal's bears are known to roam in winter instead of hibernating.

There are some prominent canines, though they are fairly shy. The jackal, with its eerie howling that sets village dogs barking at night, ranges from the Terai to alpine regions. It is both a hunter and a scavenger, and will take chickens and raid crops.

The pika, or mouse hare, is the common guinea-pig-like mammal of the inner valleys, often seen scurrying nervously between rocks. The marmot of western Nepal is a large rodent; it commonly dwells in the trans-Himalaya.

Noisy colonies of flying foxes or fruit bats have chosen the trees near the Royal Palace in Kathmandu and the chir pines at the entrance to Bhaktapur as their haunts. They are known to fly great distances at night to raid orchards. They have adequate eyesight for their feeding habits and do not require the sonar system of insectivorous bats.

Pulchowki, Nagarjun and Shivapuri are good areas for sighting small mammals.

Reptiles
There are two indigenous species of crocodile: the gharial and the marsh mugger. The gharial inhabits rivers and is a prehistoric-looking fish-eating creature with bulging eyes and a long, narrow snout. The marsh mugger prefers stagnant water and is omnivorous, feeding on anything within reach. Because of the value of its hide and eggs, the gharial was hunted to the brink of extinction, but has increased in numbers since the establishment of a hatchery and rearing

centre in Chitwan. Both crocodiles inhabit the Terai.

Though venomous snakes such as cobras, vipers and kraits are present, the chance of encountering one is small, not only because of their evasive tactics, but also because they are indiscriminately slaughtered. The majority of species are found in the Terai, though the mountain pit viper is known higher up, along with a few other nonvenomous species.

NATIONAL PARKS & CONSERVATION AREAS
Despite Nepal's small size and heavy demand for land, it has managed to set aside an impressive 18% of its landmass for protection. In 2002 there were nine national parks, four conservation areas, three wildlife reserves and one hunting reserve protecting every significant ecological system in the country. The innovative and creative land protection mechanisms in Nepal focus on accommodating people and their needs, not evicting them. They promote sustainable development and the preservation of culture and work to balance the needs of conservation with resource development, including tourism.

Most people visit at least one of the Nepal's protected areas. The majority head to the Annapurna Conservation Area, Sagarmatha National Park, Royal Chitwan National Park or Langtang National Park. Some other conservation areas are in hard-to-reach places, where roads are bad and transportation difficult, or in the Maoist-affected regions of the far west and east of the country.

Entry fees vary. The cheapest is Rs 250 and the most expensive is US$700! Citizens of SAARC (South Asian Association for Regional Cooperation) countries pay less than other visitors. Trekking permits are no longer required (see the Trekking chapter for details).

GOVERNMENT & POLITICS
In April 1990, the Jana Andolan, or the People's Movement, forced King Birendra to abandon the *panchayat* system under which the king enjoyed virtually sole power (see People Power under History earlier).

The new constitution adopted in November 1990 provided for a constitutional monarchy,

National Parks & Conservation Areas

name	location	features	best time to visit	entry fee (Rs)
Annapurna CA	north of Pokhara, central Nepal	most popular trekking area in Nepal, extremely diverse landscapes and cultural groups, high Annapurna peaks	Oct-Apr/ May	2000
Dhorpatan HR	central Nepal	Nepal's only hunting reserve (access is difficult)	Mar-Apr	500
Kangchenjunga CA	eastern Nepal	third-highest mountain in the world, 30 species of rhododendron, many endemic flower species, snow leopard	Mar-Apr, Oct-Nov	2000
Khaptad NP	far western Nepal	core area is important religious site	Mar-April, Oct-Nov	1000
Koshi Tappu WR	eastern Nepal	grasslands, often flooded during monsoon, 280 species of birds, wild buffalo	Oct-Apr	500
Langtang NP	northwest of Kathmandu	culturally diverse, varied topography, important location on migratory route for birds travelling between India and Tibet	Mar-Apr, Sept–mid-Dec	1000
Makalu-Barun NP & CA	eastern Nepal	rugged steep remote wilderness areas. Rich diversity of plant and animal life	Oct-May	1000
Manaslu CA	central Nepal bordering Annapurna CA	rugged terrain, 11 types of forest, snow leopard, musk deer	Oct-Nov, Mar-Apr	2000
Mustang CA	central Nepal, bordering Tibet	Tibetan culture, walled city of Lo Monthang, arid landscapes	Mar-Nov	* (see below)
Parsa WR	south of Kathmandu	sal forests, wild elephants, about 300 species of birds, many snake species	Oct-Apr	500
Rara NP	northwest Nepal	Nepal's biggest lake, little visited, many migratory birds	Oct-Dec, Mar-May	1000
Royal Bardia NP	far western Terai	sal forest, tiger, one-horned rhinoceros, over 250 species of birds	Oct-early Apr	500
Royal Chitwan NP	southwest of Kathmandu, bordering India	tropical and subtropical forests, rhinoceros, tiger, gharial crocodile, 450 species of birds, World Heritage Site	Oct-Feb	500
Royal Sukla Phanta WR	southwestern Nepal	riverine flood plain, grasslands, endangered swamp deer, wild elephants	Oct-Apr	500
Sagarmatha (Everest) NP	northeast of Kathmandu	highest mountains on the planet, home of the Sherpa people, stunning monasteries, World Heritage Site	Oct-May	1000
Shey Phoksundo NP	northwest Nepal	trans-Himalayan ecosystem, alpine flowers, high passes, snow leopard, musk deer	June-Sept	1000
Shivapuri NP	Kathmandu Valley	accessible from Kathmandu, many bird and butterfly species, leopards	Oct-May	250

* US$700 per week, US$70 each additional day

NP = National Park CA = Conservation Area WR = Wildlife Reserve HR = Hunting Reserve universal adult franchise and a multiparty parliamentary system. Members of the 205-seat Pratinidhi Sabha (House of Representatives) are elected every five years.

Members of the 60-seat Rastriya Sabha (National Assembly) have six-year tenure; a third retire every two years. Thirty-five members are elected by proportional representation, 15 by government representatives, and 10 by the king.

Nepal's 12-year experiment with democracy faced a major setback when King Gyanendra dissolved the government in 2002. By the end of 2002, Nepal had been through more than a dozen governments, many of them frail coalitions that lasted less than a year. In early 2003 Gyanendra made a statement, reassuring Nepali people their hard-won democracy was not under threat, and that new elections would be held later in the year.

For an account of the Maoist insurgency that has dominated Nepali politics since 1996 see History earlier in this chapter.

ECONOMY

By Western standards, Nepal is one of the poorest countries in the world, with an estimated GDP of only US$220 per person (although many people operate outside the cash economy). Undernourishment is a problem in some areas. Reliance on foreign aid has grown and with current levels of corruption in government, development schemes are unlikely to address Nepal's extreme poverty.

Agriculture

Around 40% of GDP is accounted for by agriculture (including fisheries and forestry). At present, most farmers succeed in meeting their basic needs and producing a small surplus for cash sales.

In the late 1970s Nepal exported large quantities of rice. The development of the Terai opened up new land, temporarily relieving some of the population pressure in the hills, and the so-called green revolution (utilising improved seeds, artificial fertilisers and pesticides) led to increased productivity. The population, however, is again growing more rapidly than production, and Nepal has to import much more food than it can produce.

Population growth has caused the average size of landholdings to continue to drop; it now stands at around 0.7 hectares in the hills and a little over one hectare in the Terai. In a good year, half a hectare in the hills around Kathmandu might produce around 1000kg of rice and 500kg of mixed vegetables, but if the farmer does not own the land up to 50% of this production will go to the owner as rent.

Where possible, crops are supplemented with livestock (especially in the mountain areas), but the animals are often of poor quality, partly because there is a serious shortage of animal fodder. Nepal's remaining forests are used as a source of fodder, and this can also lead to environmental damage.

Manufacturing

Although it employs a small number of people, manufacturing is an important source

Tibetan Carpets

An amazing success story of the last few decades is that of Tibetan carpets. Although weaving is an indigenous craft, in 1960 the Nepal International Tibetan Refugee Relief Committee, with the support of the Swiss government, began encouraging Tibetan refugees in Patan to make and sell carpets.

Tibetan and New Zealand wool are used to make the carpets. The exuberant colours and lively designs of traditional carpets have been replaced with more muted hues for the international market, but the old ways of producing carpets remain the same. The intricacies of the senna loop method are hard to pick out in the blur of hands that is usually seen at a carpet workshop; each thread is looped around a gauge rod that will determine the height of the carpet pile, then each row is hammered down and the loops of thread split to release the rod. To finish it off the whole expanse is clipped to bring out the design.

The carpet industry has declined somewhat over recent years, largely because of negative publicity about the exploitative use of child labour and the use of carcinogenic dyes (practices that continue, despite their illegality). Still, today Nepal exports more than 244,000 sq metres of rugs (down from a peak of 300,000 sq metres in the 1990s), valued at around US$135 million. The industry accounts for around 50% of the country's exports of manufactured goods to countries other than India, and employs more than 250,000 workers.

of income for those forced to seek seasonal work because there is not enough food where they live. Up to half a million Nepali men seek seasonal work in Indian cities.

Manufacturing and industry account for around 30% of GDP, up from around 20% a decade ago. These include grain-processing, and the manufacture of building products, textiles and soap. Still, the manufacturing industries (mainly in the Terai) and service sector are unable to meet the demand for work, so there is significant underemployment.

Tibetan carpets contribute significantly to foreign exchange earnings and are exported around the world (see the boxed text 'Tibetan Carpets' earlier in this chapter).

Tourism

For many people the only accessible source of income is the tourist trade, either as a market for handicrafts and other small-scale businesses such as lodges, shops, travel agencies, or as a receiver of services such as hotel staff and porters. At its peak the tourist industry employed about 200,000 people directly and indirectly. Yet the government has failed to devise a coherent tourism plan.

The industry suffers from chronic oversupply and is highly vulnerable to political instability. The hijacking of an Indian Airlines flight out of Kathmandu in 1999, the royal massacre in June 2001, the bombing of the New York World Trade Centre in September 2001, the growing Maoist insurgency and the general downturn in global tourism contributed to a massive decline in tourist numbers in 2002. The slump has had a painful effect on hotel owners, many of whom can no longer afford to even pay the interest on their hotel loans.

Foreign Exchange & Trade

Nepal's trade is dominated by India, and many activities within the country are Indian-owned or controlled. In the first quarter of 2002 foreign exports fell by 10.5%, despite India increasing its demand for goods. In March 2002 the all-important bilateral Trade and Transit Treaty with India was renewed, reviving exports to India.

Some cynics claim that the real mainstays of the Nepali economy are smuggling and foreign aid. There are no official figures for the smuggling, but foreign aid accounts for 14% of hard-currency receipts.

Development

Nepal has made encouraging economic advances since the country was opened up to foreigners in 1950, but there is still progress to be made. There is a better road system, greater access to electricity, safer drinking water, more doctors and improved irrigation, yet nearly half the population lives below the poverty line. Adding to the problem is Maoist insurgency, which has targeted bridges and hydroelectric power stations.

The challenges facing Nepal are immense. Health services, especially outside the Kathmandu Valley, are limited – the ratio of doctors to people was one to 18,439 in 2001, and the hospital bed ratio one to 2349 people. For many peasant families the fragile state of the environment means life will become even more difficult in the future. More people are moving into the crowded Kathmandu Valley, the Terai and to India. The Maoist insurgency and food shortages have emptied valleys in western Nepal of people who have moved southward to escape the violence and hunger. In Kathmandu, the gulf between rich and poor is extreme. The aristocracy wields considerable power and influence, and many of its members lead lives that are extraordinarily privileged.

On the positive side, those living in distant valleys have better access to educational services. Literacy rates are now up to 65% for males and 47% for females. A telephone system links all major towns, although phone installations have become targets for Maoists and locals are not keen to repair installations until the insurgency subsides. Roads continue to extend into distant parts of the country.

Nepal's physical resources are extremely limited. There are few accessible minerals and little unexploited arable land. There are great hydroelectric power resources, although the market for them is likely to be found in India and the capital and ecological costs involved in construction are huge.

Foreign Aid

Foreign aid is vital to the Nepali economy: 58% of the government's total development budget in 2001 came from foreign grants and loans. In the four decades since 1960, about US$4 billion has been pumped into the country. Unfortunately, not nearly enough of this money reaches the people or places it should, due to poorly designed programmes, high administration costs and corruption.

The flow of foreign aid first began in 1951 in the form of bilateral aid from India and the USA. In 1970 multilateral aid became the norm and organisations such as the Asian Development Bank (ADB) and United Nations became primary moneygivers and lenders. International nongovernmental organisations now provide huge amounts of money in aid.

This sector has come under increased criticism for failing to generate the economic and social development that had been expected. Two recent reports released by multilateral donors, the UN Development Programme (UNDP) and the ADB, state Nepal has not made proper use of the multibillion dollar aid it receives and that it should rely less on government to reduce poverty.

Charlie Pye-Smith's book *Travels in Nepal* provides an interesting insight into some aid projects visited by the author in Nepal during the 1980s. (See Books in the Facts for the Visitor chapter.)

POPULATION & PEOPLE

Nepal has just over 23 million people (2001 census) and this number is increasing at the rapid rate of 2.45% annually. The country faces the challenge of balancing the needs of the environment with the requirements of this growing population. There are equal numbers of men and women, and life expectancy is just under 60 years. Rates of infant mortality (64 per 1000 live births) and maternal mortality (415 per 100,000 live births) are high compared with Western figures.

One million people live in the entire Kathmandu Valley, 500,000 of whom live in Kathmandu. Nepal remains predominantly rural; 85% of people live in the countryside. Life on the flat fertile lands of the Terai is relatively easy, so the population here is increasing more rapidly.

The human geography of Nepal is a remarkable mosaic of peoples who have not so much assimilated as learned to tolerate one another. Kathmandu is the best place to see diverse ethnic groups, including Limbu, Rai, Newar, Sherpa, Tamang or Gurung.

Simplistically, Nepal is the meeting place of the Indo-Aryan people of India and the Tibeto-Burmese of the Himalaya. There are three main cultural zones running east–west:

the north including the high Himalaya; the middle hills; and the Terai. Each group has adapted its lifestyle and farming practices to its environment, but has retained its own traditions. Social taboos, especially among the caste Hindus, have meant little mixing between groups.

Nepal's diverse ethnic groups speak somewhere between 24 and 100 different languages and dialects depending on how fine the distinctions made are. Nepali functions as the main language.

Himalayan Zone

The hardy people that inhabit the high mountainous regions of the Himalaya are known as Bhotiyas. These people are of Tibeto-Burmese origin and crossed the high passes to settle in Nepal. Each group remained basically separate from the others although their languages are all Tibetan-based and, with a few exceptions, they are Buddhist.

The Bhotiyas are named after the region they come from by adding the suffix *pa* to their name. These include the Sherpas of the Everest region, the Manangpa of the Manang region north of the Annapurna himal, and the Lopa of the Mustang region.

The difficulty of farming and herding at high altitude drives these people to lower elevations during winter. Here they continue to graze their animals or supplement their incomes with trade.

Thakalis Originating along the Kali Gandaki Valley in central Nepal, the Thakalis have emerged as the entrepreneurs of Nepal. They once played an important part in the salt trade between the subcontinent and Tibet and today are active in many areas of commercial life. Originally Buddhist, many pragmatic Thakalis have now adopted Hinduism. Most Thakalis have small farms, but travellers will regularly meet them in their adopted roles as hoteliers, especially on the Jomsom Trek.

Tamangs The Tamangs make up one of largest groups in the country. They live mainly in the hills north of Kathmandu although you will find a sprinkling of small settlements in the east and far west.

According to some accounts, the Tamang ancestors were horse traders and cavalrymen from an invading Tibetan army who settled in Nepal. They are well known for their independence and suspicion of authority, probably caused by the fact that in the 19th century they were relegated to a low status and seriously exploited, with much of their land distributed to Bahuns and Chhetris. As bonded labour they were dependent on menial work such as labouring and portering – a familiar sight in Kathmandu today is that of a Tamang man in his short-sleeved woollen shirt pushing a cart or pulling a rickshaw. In the hills they work mainly as farmers and labourers; and many of the 'Tibetan' souvenirs, carpets and *thangka* (religious paintings on cotton) you see in Kathmandu are made by Tamangs.

Their religion is closely associated with Tibetan Buddhism and the approach to a Tamang village is usually marked with a *mani* wall made up of prayer stones engraved with mantras. The entrance of the village is sure to have a *chorten* (pagoda).

Tibetans About 12,000 of the 120,000 Tibetans in exile around the world live in Nepal. The heavy hand of the Chinese during the 1950s and the flight of the Dalai Lama in 1959 gave rise to waves of refugees who settled mainly in Kathmandu or Pokhara.

Although their numbers are small, Tibetans have a high profile, partly because of the important role they play in tourism. Many hotels and restaurants in Kathmandu are owned or operated by Tibetans. They have also been responsible for the extraordinary success story of the Tibetan carpet industry.

Tibetans are devout Buddhists and their arrival in the valley has rejuvenated a number of important religious sites, most notably the stupas at Swayambhunath and Bodhnath. A number of large, new monasteries have been established.

Sherpas The Sherpas who live high in the mountains of eastern and central Nepal are probably the best known Nepali ethnic group. These nomadic Tibetan herders moved to Nepal 500 years ago, bringing with them their Buddhist religion and building the beautiful *gompas* (monasteries) that dot the steep hillsides. Their homeland is the high altitude Solu Khumbu region where many people head to catch a glimpse of Mt Everest.

Bravest of the Brave

'Bravest of the brave, most generous of the generous, never had the country more faithful friends than you.' – Sir Ralph Turner after WWI on the Gurkha soldiers who fought in the British army.

The Gurkhas are indeed known for being tough, spirited and loyal, with battle skills that have won them a place among the world's fighting elite. Their trademark symbol is the viciously curved *khukuri* knife which, according to those who fought with them, they were adept at using.

Contrary to some misconceptions, Gurkhas are not an ethnic group. They are a fighting force that originated in Gorkha and are made up mainly of Gurung and Magar people as well as some Rai and Limbu from the east, and Chhetri. After the Sugauli treaty was signed in 1816, the Gurkhas became a regular part of the British army. Over 300,000 Nepalis fought in WWI and WWII, garnering a total of 13 Victoria Crosses – the highest military honour in Great Britain – for their efforts.

Since 1948, as a result of a signed agreement between Great Britain and Nepal, Gurkhas serve in the military of both the UK and India. For a long time the money earned by them was a major source of foreign exchange in Nepal. But this is now decreasing because both the Indian and British governments are not recruiting as many Nepali soldiers.

In November 2002 three former Gurkhas, all in their 80s, who had fought with the British in WWII, challenged a British Ministry of Defence decision that had excluded them from compensation payments. They claimed racial discrimination by the British government and asked for £10,000 each in compensation for brutal treatment they suffered as prisoners of the Japanese. In March 2003 the British Government withdrew its appeal against a ruling that gave the retired Gurkhas a right to claim compensation. The ruling has paved the ways for more than 300 other Gurkhas to claim the same compensation. Some 3500 Gurkhas still serve in the British forces. Most recently, many of them took part in peacekeeping operations in Afghanistan.

The **Gurkha Welfare Trust** (☎ 020-7251 5234; Ⓦ www.gwt.org.uk) is a UK-based charity that provides pensions and medical care for 11,500 former soldiers and war widows.

The Sherpa name is synonymous with mountaineering and trekking and they have achieved worldwide fame for their skill, hardiness and loyalty in these pursuits. Sherpas have cornered the trekking market. Many visitors think that a Sherpa and a porter are the same thing and are surprised when the first Sherpa they meet is their trekking agency manager or Kathmandu guesthouse owner.

Midlands Zone

The middle hills of Nepal are the best places to witness village life at its most rustic. In the east are the Kirati who are divided into the Rai and Limbu groups. The Newari people dominate the central hills around the Kathmandu Valley, while the Magars and Gurungs inhabit the hills of the Kali Gandaki.

Moving west, the Bahun and Chhetri are the dominant groups, although the lines between castes have become blurred over time.

Rais & Limbus The Rais and Limbus are thought to have ruled the Kathmandu Valley in the 7th century BC until defeated around AD 300. They then moved into the steep hill country of eastern Nepal, where many remain today. Others have moved to the Terai or India to find work.

The Kirati are easily distinguishable by their beautiful Mongolian features. They are of Tibeto-Burmese descent, and their traditional religion is distinct from either Buddhism or Hinduism, although the latter is exerting a growing influence. They are excellent soldiers and are well represented in the Gurkha regiments.

Many of the men still carry a large *khukuri* (curved knife) tucked into their belt and wear a *topi* (Nepali hat).

Newars The Newars of the Kathmandu Valley number about 1.1 million and make up 6% of the population. Their language, Newari, is distinct from Tibetan, Nepali or Hindi, and they follow a version of Hinduism with Buddhist overtones. The Newars are excellent farmers, as well as skilled artists; the Kathmandu Valley is filled with spectacular examples of their artistic work.

Their origins are shrouded in mystery: most Newars have Mongoloid physical characteristics, but there are others who haven't. It is generally accepted that the Newars' ancestors were of varied ethnicity and all set-tled the Valley – possibly originating with the Kiratis, or an even earlier group.

Newars lead a communal way of life, but some other of their traditions are on the wane. Living so close to the centre of power and higher education has also meant there are many Newars in the bureaucracies of Kathmandu. See the boxed text 'Newari Customs' later in this chapter, and the Kathmandu Valley chapter for more on this group.

Gurungs The Gurungs, a Tibeto-Burmese people, live mainly in the central midlands, from Gorkha and Baglung to the southern slopes of the Annapurnas. One of the biggest Gurung settlements is Ghandruk, with its sweeping views of the Annapurnas and Machhapuchhare. The Gurungs have made up large numbers of the Gurkha regiments and army incomes have contributed greatly to the economy of their region.

Many Gurungs are farmers, growing rice, wheat, maize and millet on steeply terraced hillsides. Their villages are often perched on the tops of ridges and their fields can be up to an hour's walk below. They also keep herds of sheep and goats – sometimes as a large village flock. During the summer months the sheep are herded to higher pastures; at the end of the monsoon, they are herded back down to the villages.

Magars The Magars, a large group (around 8% of the total population), are a Tibeto-Burmese people who live in many parts of the midlands zone of western and central Nepal. They are also farmers and tend to work the lower parts of the hills.

The Magars are also excellent soldiers and fought with Prithvi Narayan Shah to help unify Nepal. Their kingdom of Palpa (based at Tansen) was one of the last to be incorporated into the unified Nepal. They make up the biggest numbers of Gurkhas, and army salaries have greatly improved Magar living standards.

The Magars generally live in two-storey, rectangular or square thatched houses washed in red clay. They have been heavily influenced by Hinduism, and in terms of religion, farming practices, housing and dress, they are hard to distinguish from Chhetris.

Bahuns & Chhetris The Hindu caste groups of Bahuns and Chhetris are dominant in the middle hills, making up 30% of the country's population.

Even though the caste system was abolished in 1963 these two groups remain at the top of the hierarchy. In Hinduism there is no relationship between caste and ethnicity, so Bahuns (or Brahmins as they are also known) and Chhetris are simply the two highest castes (Brahmin priests and Kshatriya warriors respectively).

Bahuns and Chhetris played an important role in the court and armies of Prithvi Narayan Shah, and after unification they were rewarded with tracts of land. Their language, Khas Kura, then became the national language of Nepal, and their high-caste position was religiously, culturally and legally enforced. Ever since, Bahuns and Chhetris have dominated the government in Kathmandu.

Outside the Kathmandu Valley, the majority of Bahuns and Chhetris are simple peasant farmers, indistinguishable in most respects from their neighbours. Sometimes their wealth is reflected by relatively large houses. Most live in two-storey stone or mud-brick thatched houses that are washed with lime or red ochre. Many had roles as tax collectors under the Shah and Rana regimes, and to this day many are money-lenders with a great deal of power.

The Bahuns tend to be more caste-conscious and orthodox than other Nepali Hindus, sometimes creating difficulties in relationships with 'untouchable' westerners. Many are vegetarians and do not drink alcohol; marriages are arranged within the caste.

There is no particular cultural dress by which they can be recognised but men in both castes wear a sacred thread – the *janai*.

Terai Zone

Until the eradication of malaria in the 1950s, the only people to live in the valleys of the Inner Terai, and along much of the length of the Terai proper, were Tharus and a few small associated groups. Since the Terai was opened for development, it has also been settled by large numbers of people from the midlands – every group is represented and more than 50% of Nepali people live in the region.

A number of large groups straddle the India–Nepal border. In the eastern Terai, Mithila people dominate; in the central Terai, there are many Bhojpuri-speaking people; and in the western Terai, Abadhi-speaking people are significant. All are basically cul-

tures of the Gangetic plain, and Hindu caste structure is strictly upheld. In various parts, notably around Nepalganj and Lumbini, there are also large numbers of Muslims.

Tharus One of the most visible groups is the Tharus, who are thought to be the earliest inhabitants of the Terai (and they're even thought to be immune to malaria). About one million Tharu speakers inhabit the length of the Terai, including the Inner Terai around Chitwan, although they mainly live in the west. Caste-like distinctions exist between different Tharu groups or tribes. Most have Mongoloid physical features.

Nobody is sure where they came from, although some believe they are the descendants of the Rajputs (from Rajasthan), who sent their women and children away to escape Mughal invaders in the 16th century. The women later married into local tribes. Others believe they are descended from the royal Sakya clan, the Buddha's family, although they are not Buddhist. Their beliefs are largely animistic, and increasingly influenced by Hinduism, and they live a life that is well adapted to their environment. Apart from farming, Tharus also hunt and fish.

More recently, the Tharus were exploited by *zamindars* (landlords), and many Tharus fell into debt and entered into bonded labour. In 2000 the *kamaiyas* (bonded labourers) were freed by government legislation, but little has been done to help these now landless and workless people. Consequently, in most Terai towns in western Nepal you will see squatter settlements of former *kamaiyas*.

EDUCATION

Education was the first 'development project' of post-Rana Nepal in the 1950s and huge numbers of schools were built all over the country. Today there are over 40,000 schools in Nepal. This has no doubt helped to raise the literacy rates to 65% for men and 47% for women, although quality of education remains woefully inadequate for most children.

Children stay at school for up to 12 years and the lucky ones will go on to one of the country's four universities. Out of every 1000 children born, 700 will begin school. Only 70 of these will reach their 10th school year, when they sit their School Leaving Certificate (SLC) board examination. Rote learning and chanting out long lists of facts is a favoured

Temple Architecture

Newar Pagoda Temples

The distinctive Newar pagoda temples are a major feature of the Kathmandu Valley skyline. While strictly speaking they are neither wholly Newari nor pagodas, the term has been widely adopted to describe the temples of the valley.

The temples are generally square in design, and may be either Hindu or Buddhist (or both in the case of mother goddesses). On rare occasions temples are rectangular or octagonal. This depends on the god being worshipped; Krishna, for example, can occupy octagonal temples, whereas Ganesh, Shiva and Vishnu can only inhabit square temples.

The major feature of the temples is the tiered roof, which may have one to five tiers, with two or three being the most common. In the Kathmandu Valley there are two temples with four roofs and another two with five (Kumbeshwar at Patan and Nyatapola at Bhaktapur). The sloping roofs are usually covered with distinctive *jhingati* (baked clay tiles), although richer temples will often have one roof of gilded copper. The *gajur* (pinnacle of the temple) is usually bell-shaped and made of baked clay or gilded copper.

The temples are usually built on a stepped plinth, which may be as high as, or even higher than, the temple itself. In some cases the number of steps on the plinth corresponds with the number of roofs on the temple.

The temple building itself has just a small sanctum, known as a *garbha-griha* (literally 'womb room') housing the deity. Worshippers practise individually, with devotees standing outside the door to make their supplications. The only people permitted to actually enter the sanctum are *pujari* (temple priests).

Perhaps the most interesting feature of the temples is the detailed decoration, which is only evident close up. Under each roof there are often brass or other metal decorations, such as *kinkinimala* (rows of small bells) or embossed metal banners. The metal streamer that often hangs from above the uppermost roof to below the level of the lowest roof (such as on the Golden Temple in Patan) is called a *pataka*. Its function is to give the deity a means of descending to earth.

The other major decorative elements are the wooden struts that support the roofs. The intricate carvings are usually of deities associated with the temple deity or of the *vahana* (deity's vehicle) but quite a few depict explicit sexual acts.

ALL ILLUSTRATIONS BY KELLI HAMBLET

Nyatapola Temple, Taumadhi Tole, Bhaktapur

Temple Architecture

Stupas

The Buddhist *stupas* of the Kathmandu Valley – particularly the *stupas* of Swayambhunath and Bodhnath – are among the most impressive and most visited monuments in Nepal. The earliest *stupas* in India were merely domed burial mounds, but they have evolved over the centuries to become complex structures that represent the Buddha and Buddhist philosophy.

The lowest level of the *stupa* is the plinth, which may be simply a square platform, but may also be terraced, as at Bodhnath. On top of the plinth is the hemispherical *kumbha* (dome; kumbha literally means 'pot'), which is usually whitewashed each year.

Atop the dome is a spire, which always consists of a number of elements. Immediately on top of the dome is a *harmika*, a square base usually painted on each side with a pair of eyes, which most people believe represents the all-seeing nature of the Buddha. There is a third eye between and above the two normal eyes and the 'nose' is not a nose at all but the Nepali number one, which signifies the unity of all life.

Topping the *harmika* is a tapering section of 13 stages, which are said to represent the 13 stages of perfection. At the very peak is a gilt parasol, symbolising royalty.

The five elements are represented in the *stupa*'s structure: the base symbolises earth; the dome water; the spire fire; the umbrella air; and the pinnacle ether.

Swayambhunath Stupa, Kathmandu Valley

Shikhara Temples

The second-most common temples are the *shikhara* temples, which have a heavy Indian influence. The temples are so named because their tapering tower resembles a *shikhara* (in Sanskrit, a mountain peak). Although the style developed in India in the 6th century, it first appeared in Nepal in the late Licchavi period (9th century).

The main feature is the tapering, pyramidal tower, which is often surrounded by four similar but smaller towers, and these may be located on porches over the shrine's entrances. The tower is usually built on a square stepped plinth.

Occasionally the *shikhara* temple follows the same basic design but is much more elaborate, with porches and small turrets seemingly all over the place. The Krishna Mandir and the octagonal Krishna Temple, both in Patan's Durbar Square, are excellent examples.

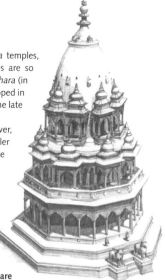

Krishna Mandir, Patan Durbar Square

method of teaching. Many students leave school literate, and with a little English, but with few job- or life-skills.

Many villages only have a primary school, meaning children either have to walk long distances each day or board in a bigger town to attend secondary school. The ratio of boys to girls at both primary and secondary schools is almost 2:1 in favour of boys.

The country's 150,000 teachers are poorly paid and the majority are untrained. Classrooms are basic and often over-crowded, with few books or resources.

Private schools cater to about 20% of students. However, allegations of profit-making at the expense of the students' education have dogged this sector, and in recent years it has been a target for Maoist protest action.

Those who can afford to, travel overseas for their education, traditionally to India but increasingly to the USA, Australia or New Zealand.

ARTS
Wander around the Kathmandu Valley and you will appreciate Nepal's wonderful connection between art and architecture. It often feels as though you are in a vibrant open-air museum where fine woodcarving and sculptures can be found in surprisingly accessible places. By simply casting your eyes upward at a temple you'll see a series of centuries-old roof struts carved with intricate figures. Crafts also reflect the Nepali melting pot where religious art has Tantric, Hindu and Buddhist overtones and the dividing line between the religions is blurred.

Architecture & Sculpture
The oldest architecture in the Kathmandu Valley has faded with history. Grassy mounds are all that remain of Patan's four Ashoka stupas and the magnificent stupas of Swayambhunath and Bodhnath have undoubtedly changed many times over the centuries. Magnificent stonework is one of the lasting reminders of the Licchavi period (4th to 9th centuries AD). Many of the valley's temples have beautiful Licchavi stone pieces in their courtyards; the temple of Changu Narayan in the east is a particularly good example, as is the statue of Vishnu asleep on a bed of serpents at Budhanilkantha.

Unfortunately, no wooden buildings and carvings are known to have survived from these early days. The valley's earliest wood-carving dates from the 12th and 13th centuries. This craft flourished during the Malla period and fine examples are the roof struts of two buildings in Kathmandu's Durbar Square – the great Basantapur Tower in Hanuman Dhoka (the old Royal Palace) and the Kasthamandap building. To see one of the oldest and finest survivors of this period you should visit the Indreshwar Mahadev Temple in Panauti, near Banepa.

The artistic skills of the valley's Newar people flourished under the Mallas. Their skills extended far beyond the woodwork for which they are so well known and included fine metalwork, terracotta, brick-work and stone sculptures. The finest metalwork includes the stunning images of the two Tara goddesses at Swayambhunath, and the river goddesses Ganga and Jamuna in Patan's Mul Chowk.

The Nepali architect Arniko visited Tibet in the late 13th century and showed off the multiroofed Nepali pagoda design that became popular in China and eastern Asia. Contact with Tibet also influenced Nepali artists, with vivid Tibetan colours and fantastic Tibetan creatures appearing in their art and architecture.

The end of the Malla period saw temples appearing all over the Kathmandu Valley. Squabbling and competition between the city-states of Kathmandu, Patan and Bhaktapur fuelled the building boom; each tried to outdo the other with magnificent palaces and temples. The multiroofed Nepali pagoda remained the style of the day, although there was a strong Indian influence, as seen in the Krishna Mandir of Patan's Durbar Square, the spires of the Mahabouddha Temple in Patan, and the two temples at the top of the stairway to Swayambhunath.

The great age of Nepali architecture came to a dramatic end when Prithvi Narayan Shah invaded the valley in 1769. The magnificent wood-carved temples and palaces that remain are mostly from before unification, but traditional building skills are still evidenced in extensive restoration projects such as the Hanuman Dhoka in Kathmandu and the Tachupal Tole buildings in Bhaktapur, which were completed in the 1970s. Today some young architects are attempting to incorporate traditional features into their buildings.

Tamang child, Langtang

Man wearing a traditional *topi* (hat)

Woman lighting butter lamps, Kathmandu Valley

Limbu girl from far eastern Nepal

CHRIS KLEP

Yak, Langtang Valley

CHRIS KLEP

Himalayan tahr

ANDERS BLOMQVIST

Making molasses and rice for the elephants

JEFF CANTARUTTI

Monkey at Swayambhunath, Kathmandu Valley

Painting

Chinese, Tibetan, Indian and Mughal influences can all be seen in Nepali painting styles over the centuries. The earliest Newari paintings were illuminated manuscripts bound in ornate covers dating from the 11th century. Of interest is the absence of perspective in many paintings and the fact that colour was used less for definition or shading than for religious symbolism. Unfortunately, much art has left the country or is hung in temples where it is rarely seen, but Bhaktapur's art gallery has a fine collection.

Modern Nepali artists struggle to make a living, although there are many small galleries around Kathmandu featuring local work. Some artists are fortunate enough to get a sponsored overseas exhibition or a posting at an art college outside the country to teach their skills. Commissioning a painting by a local artist is a way to support the arts and take home a unique souvenir of your trip.

Music & Dance

The last few years has seen a revival in Nepali music and songs, both folk and 'Nepali modern'. Staple Hindi film songs have been supplanted by a vibrant local music scene thanks to advances made in FM radio (which blares out of many shops and taxis in Kathmandu).

Dancing and traditional music enliven festivals and family celebrations when streets or entire villages will erupt with the energetic sounds of flutes, drums and cymbals, or sway to the moving soulful sounds of devotional singing and the gentle twang of the four-stringed *saringhi*.

Nepali dance styles are as numerous and varied as the ethnic groups in Nepal, with something for just about every occasion. They range from the subtle foot stomping, quasi line-dancing style of the Sherpa people and the religious Cham dancing performed by Tibetans to the complex, sometimes very melodramatic interpretive Hindi dances. Joining in with an enthusiastic group of porters from different parts of the country at the end of a trekking day is a great way to learn some of the moves.

A good introduction to modern Nepali folk music is the trio Sur Sudha, whose evocative recordings such as *Festivals of Nepal* and *Images of Nepal* (Domo Records) will take you back to the region long after you've tasted your last dal bhaat and flown home. You can listen to track excerpts at ⓦ www.amazon.com.

Film

The Nepali film industry has come a long way since the 1980s and early 1990s when only four or five films were produced annually. More recently the local film industry was making up to 70 films per year, although this bubble burst in 2001 when government-imposed curfews caused audience numbers to plummet and finances to dry up. There are 20 cinemas in Kathmandu.

Recent scandal has both helped and rocked the industry. After a Bollywood heart throb made incendiary anti-Nepal comments in December 2000, Kathmandu streets erupted in violence. The incident prompted a backlash against Indian films, while local films enjoyed a massive rise in popularity buoyed by cheaper production, marketing and distribution costs.

Literature

Nepal's literary history is amazingly brief, dating back to just the 19th century. The written language was not used much before then, although religious verse, folklore, songs and translations of Sanskrit and Urdu dating back to the 13th century have been found.

One of the first authors to establish Nepali as a literary language was Bhanubhakta Acharya (1814–68) who broke away from

Tika

A visit to Nepal is not complete without being offered a *tika* by one of the many sadhus (Hindu holy men) that wander the streets dusty, barefoot, and carrying a tin can and walking staff. The ubiquitous *tika* is a symbol of blessing from the gods worn by both women and men. It can range from a small dot to a full mixture of yogurt, rice and *sindur* (a red powder) smeared on the forehead. The *tika* represents the all-seeing, all-knowing third eye and receiving this blessing is a common part of most ceremonies. It is an acknowledgment of a divine presence at the occasion and a sign of protection for those receiving it. Shops carry a huge range of tiny *tikas* that women have turned into a fashion statement.

Newari Customs

The Newars are divided into castes, whether they nominally consider themselves Hindu or Buddhist. Caste rules are not quite as rigid as in some parts of India, but intermarriage is rare and untouchables are still grossly disadvantaged.

The usual dress for a Newari woman is a sari and blouse, often with a shawl. The men wear *surwal* (trousers with a baggy seat that are tighter around the calves, like jodhpurs), a *daura* (thigh-length double-breasted shirt), a vest or coat and the traditional *topi* (Nepali cap). The most distinctive caste is the Jyapu, who are farmers. Jyapu women wear a black sari with a red border, while the men often wear the traditional trousers and shirt with a long piece of cotton wrapped around the waist. They prefer to carry goods on a shoulder pole.

Newari children undergo a number of *samskara* (rites of passage) as they grow up. The *namakarana* (naming rite) is performed by the priests and chief of the clan, and the family astrologer gives the child its public and secret name. The next rite is the *machajanko* (rice feeding), which celebrates the child's presence on earth and wishes them a smooth life. Next for boys comes the *busakha*, performed between the ages of three and seven, when the head is shaved, leaving just a small tuft. This is followed by the fixing of a *kaitapuja* (loincloth), which marks a commitment by the boy to bachelorhood and self-control. Girls undergo *Ihi* (a symbolic marriage to Vishnu) between the ages of five and 11, and at this time she begins to wear a thick cotton thread. The *Ihi samskara* venerates chastity and guarantees the girl a choice of husband. This is followed by a *barha* (menarche rite), which protects the girl's virginity and safeguards against passion.

Weddings are usually negotiated through a *lami* (mediator), and take place at times deemed auspicious by the family astrologer. The bride is taken in a noisy procession to the groom's house where she is received with an oil lamp and the key to the house. The *chipka thiyeke samskara* involves the serving of 84 (!) traditional dishes and is a symbol of the couple's union.

The first *janko* (old-age *samskara*) takes place at 77 years, seven months and seven days, the second at 83 years, four months and four days and the third at 99 years, nine months and nine days. The final *samskara* is *sithan* (cremation), which marks the body's move to its final destination.

the influence of Indian literature and recorded the Ramayana in Nepali; this was not simply a translation but a 'Nepali-ised' version of the Hindu epic. Motiram Bhatta (1866–96) also played a major role in 19th-century literature.

The country later supported a small, hardy and dedicated literary community that struggled to have their works published in a country where literacy levels were extremely low. During the isolationist time of the Ranas, publishing was state-controlled and some writers moved to India to publish their work.

Today a vibrant and enthusiastic literary community exists, meeting in teashops, brew houses and bookstalls in Kathmandu and other urban centres. Funding comes from small prizes and writers' families – sales are often so low they barely cover the cost of the paper. Magazines of contemporary literature provide another opportunity to be published; these include the Royal Nepal Academy's *Samakalin Sahitya* and *Kabita*, and the private journals *Bagar* and *Unnayan*.

SOCIETY

Nepal's location between India and China, the combined influence of Hinduism and Buddhism, and its diversity of ethnic groups have resulted in a complex blend of customs and beliefs.

At the centre of Nepali life is the family. Loyalty to one's family and the practice of customs associated with one's ethnic group are non-negotiable. To break these rules is to risk being isolated from one's family and community. While young Nepali people, especially in urban areas, are being influenced by Western values and practices, the vast majority of people live by traditional customs and principles. In most ethnic groups, joint and extended families live in the same house or share several homes. In some smaller villages extended families make up the entire community. Growing and harvesting food is the main focus of village life and everyone helps out.

Children are much loved and are an important part of the family. Not to have children is almost unheard of and a Nepali woman will pity you if you are childless. Children are entertainment, an extra set of hands for the farm and someone to look after you as you grow older.

Arranged marriages remain the norm although there are a growing number of 'love marriages'. There are several ways marriages can be arranged. A family will either have one person already chosen or a selection of suitable men will be presented and the girl may choose her husband. Child marriages have been illegal since 1963. Today the average age of marriage for girls is just under 19 years old. Family connections generated by marriage are important considerations and marriages between ethnic groups are rare.

Having a son is still an important achievement within marriage, especially for Hindu families, where there are religious rites that can only be performed by the eldest son. Girls are regarded by some groups as a burden who will not earn an income to support her elders and needs to be married off.

Older people are respected members of the community and are cared for by their children. Old age is a time for relaxation, prayer and meditation.

Puja

Every morning women all over Nepal can be seen walking through the streets carrying a plate, usually copper, filled with an assortment of goodies. These women are not delivering breakfast but are taking part in an important daily ritual called *puja*. The plate might contain flower petals, rice, yoghurt, fruit and sweets and is an offering to the gods made at the local temple. Each of the items is sprinkled onto a temple deity in a set order and a bell is rung to let the gods know an offering is being made. Once an offering is made it is transformed and a small portion returned to the giver as a blessing from the deity. Upon returning home from her morning trip, the woman will give a small portion of the blessed offerings to each member of the household. *Puja* describes a vast array of acts of Hindu worship, ranging from a simple offering to animal sacrifice for some of the more terrifying gods that need a little extra to be appeased.

RELIGION

From early morning until evening everywhere in Nepal there is evidence of the importance of religion in everyday life. From the simple early morning *puja* (ritual offerings) of a Kathmandu housewife at a local Hindu temple to the chanting of Buddhist monks in a village monastery, religion is a mainstay of Nepali life.

In Nepal, Hinduism and Buddhism have mingled wonderfully into a complex, syncretic blend. Nowhere is this more evident than in Kathmandu where spectacular Buddhist and Hindu temples stand side by side. Nepal is said to be the only Hindu kingdom in the world and the king is revered as an incarnation of the god Vishnu.

The Buddha was born in Nepal but the Buddhist religion first arrived in the country around 250 BC, introduced, it is said, by the great Indian Buddhist emperor Ashoka. Buddhism gave way to Hinduism although a Tantric form of Tibetan Buddhism made its way into Nepal in the 8th century AD. Today Buddhism is practised mainly by the people of the high Himalaya, such as the Sherpas and Tamangs, and by Tibetan refugees.

Officially Nepal is a Hindu country but in practice the blend of Hindu and Buddhist beliefs offers a pantheon of Tantric deities tagged on to the list of Hindu gods or, in many cases, blended with them. The vast majority of the population are Hindu with the next biggest group being Buddhist followed by small groups of Muslims, Christians and Shamanists.

Hinduism

Hinduism is a polytheistic religion that has its origins in the Indian subcontinent about 2000 years ago.

Hindus believe in a cycle of life, death and rebirth with the aim being to achieve *moksha* (release) from this cycle. With each rebirth you can move closer to or farther from eventual *moksha*; the deciding factor is *karma*, which is literally a law of cause and effect. Bad actions during your life result in bad *karma*, which ends in a lower reincarnation. Conversely, if your deeds and actions have been good you will reincarnate on a higher level and be a step closer to eventual freedom from rebirth.

Hinduism has a number of holy books, the most important being the four Vedas, the 'divine knowledge' that is the foundation of Hindu philosophy. The Upanishads are contained within the Vedas and delve into the metaphysical nature of the universe and soul. The Mahabharata is an epic 220,000-line poem that contains the story of Rama. The famous Hindu epic, the Ramayana, is based on this.

The Hindu religion has three basic practices. These are *puja* (worship; see the boxed text), the cremation of the dead, and the rules and regulations of the caste system.

There are four main castes: the Brahmin, or priest caste; the Kshatriya, or soldiers and governors; the Vaisyas, or tradespeople and farmers; and the Sudras, or menial workers and craftspeople. These castes are then subdivided, although this is not taken to the same extreme in Nepal as in India. Beneath all the castes are the Harijans, or untouchables, the lowest, casteless class for whom the most menial and degrading tasks are reserved.

Despite common misconceptions, it is possible to become a Hindu, although Hinduism itself is not a proselytising religion. Once you are a Hindu you cannot change your caste – you're born into it and are stuck with your lot in life for the rest of that lifetime.

A guru is not so much a teacher as a spiritual guide, somebody who by example or simply by their presence indicates what path you should follow. A sadhu is an individual male on a spiritual search and is easily recognised, usually wandering around half-naked, smeared in dust, with his hair and beard matted.

Buddhism

Strictly speaking, Buddhism is not a religion, as it is centred not on a god but on a system of philosophy and a code of morality. Buddhism was founded in northern India in about 500 BC when prince Siddhartha Gautama achieved enlightenment. According to some, Gautama Buddha was not the first Buddha but the fourth; nor is he expected to be the last 'enlightened one'. Buddhists believe that the achievement of enlightenment is the goal of every being, so eventually we will all reach buddhahood (nirvana).

The Buddha never wrote down his *dharma* (teachings), and a schism that developed later means that today there are two major Buddhist schools. The Theravada (Doctrine of the Elders), or Hinayana, holds

that the path to *nirvana* is an individual pursuit. In contrast, the Mahayana school holds that the combined belief of its followers will eventually be great enough to encompass all of humanity and bear it to salvation. To some, the less austere and ascetic Mahayana school is considered a 'soft option'. Today it is practised mainly in Vietnam, Japan and China, while the Hinayana school is followed in Sri Lanka, Myanmar (Burma) and Thailand. There are still other, sometimes more esoteric, divisions of Buddhism, including the Tantric Buddhism of Tibet, which is the version found in Nepal.

The Buddha renounced material life to search for enlightenment but, unlike other prophets, found that starvation did not lead to discovery. He developed his rule of the 'middle way' (moderation in all things). The Buddha taught that all life is suffering – suffering comes from our sensual desires and the illusion of their importance. By following the 'eightfold path' these desires will be extinguished and a state of *nirvana*, where our desires are extinct and we are free from their delusions, will be reached. Following this process requires going through a series of rebirths until the goal is reached and no more rebirths into the world of suffering are necessary. The path that takes you through this cycle of births is *karma*, but this is not simply fate. *Karma* is a law of cause and effect; your actions in one life determine the role you will play and what you will have to go through in your next life.

Tibetan Buddhism There are four major schools of Tibetan (Vajrayana) Buddhism and all of them are represented in the Kathmandu Valley: Nyingmapa, Kargyupa, Sakyapa and Gelugpa. The Indian sage Padmasambhava (known to Tibetans as Guru Rinpoche) is credited with establishing Buddhism in Tibet in the 8th century. The Nyingmapa order traces its origins back to Padmasambhava. The Kargyupa (Whispered Transmission) order was established by Marpa in the 11th century and has a strong Tantric influence. Marpa's most famous disciple was Milarepa, Tibet's most revered poet.

The Sakyapa was also founded in the 11th century and rose to a position where it ruled Tibet (with the support of the Mongols) until it came into conflict with the

Gelugpa (Virtuous) order, which had been founded in the 14th century by Tsongkhapa.

The Gelugpa were celibate and advocated monastic discipline. The school introduced the system of reincarnated spiritual leaders and ultimately came to power – again with the support of the Mongols – in the late 17th century. It was a Mongol ruler who conferred the title Dalai Lama (Ocean of Wisdom) on its leader. The Gelugpa completely isolated Tibet and maintained a strict theocratic state.

In some texts, Tibetan Buddhism may be referred to using the old-fashioned term Lamaism, and the Gelugpa are known as the Yellow Hats, while the other schools are sometimes collectively identified as the Red Hats.

Islam
Nepal's small population of Muslims (about 3.5% of the total population) originated in different parts of Asia, and today are mainly found close to the border with India and in a handful of isolated villages.

The first Muslims, who were mostly Kashmiri traders, arrived in the Kathmandu Valley in the 15th century. A second group arrived in the 17th century from Northern India, and they primarily manufactured armaments for the small hill states. The descendants of these early immigrants today speak Nepali and are indistinguishable from upper-caste Hindus.

The largest Muslim group are the Terai Muslims, many of whom arrived before unification. Others gradually drifted north from India, especially following the War of Independence in 1857. Many of them still have strong ties with the Muslim communities in the Indian states of Bihar and Uttar Pradesh. A number of Tibetan Muslims arrived in Nepal following the 1959 Chinese takeover of Tibet.

Unlike in India, where communal tension is a major problem, Nepal's Hindu and Muslim communities coexist peacefully.

Shamanism
Shamanism in practised by a number of Gurung people and is thought to date back some 50,000 years. The ancient healing traditions of shamanism are still taught in the Himalayas of Nepal, Bhutan and Northern India and are based on a cosmology that divides the world into three main levels: the Upper World where the sun, moon, stars, planets, deities and spirits important to the shaman's healing work abide; the Middle World of normal human life; and the Lower World, where powerful deities and spirits exist that can cause problems in the Middle World. During ceremonies the shaman will call on the deities and spirits, which he or she wishes to assist in the ritual. At the end of the ceremony the shaman will send these spirits and deities back to their appropriate worlds.

GODS OF NEPAL

Westerners may have trouble understanding Hinduism principally because of its vast pantheon of gods. In fact you can look upon all these different gods simply as pictorial representations of the many attributes of a god. The one omnipresent god usually has three physical representations: Brahma is the creator, Vishnu is the preserver and Shiva is the destroyer and reproducer. All three gods are usually shown with four arms.

Each god has an associated animal known as the 'vehicle' on which they ride, as well as a consort with certain attributes and abilities. Generally each god also holds symbols. You can often pick out which god is represented by identifying either the vehicle or the symbols.

Most temples are dedicated to one or another of the gods, but most Hindus profess to be either Vaishnavites (followers of Vishnu) or Shaivites (followers of Shiva). A variety of lesser gods and goddesses also crowd the scene. The cow is, of course, the holy animal of Hinduism.

The definitions that follow include the most interesting and most frequently encountered 'big names', plus associated consorts, vehicles and religious terminology.

Brahma

Incarnations, Manifestations & Aspects

There's a subtle difference between these three possibilities. Vishnu has incarnations – 10 of them in all. They include Narsingha the man-lion, Krishna the cowherd and the Buddha: the teacher. Shiva, on the other hand, may be the god of 1000 names, but these are manifestations – what he shows himself as – not incarnations. When you start to look at the Buddhist 'gods' their various appearances are aspects rather than incarnations or manifestations.

Brahma

Despite his supreme position, Brahma appears much less often than Shiva or Vishnu. Like those gods, Brahma has four arms, but he also has four heads, to represent his all-seeing presence. The four *Vedas* (ancient orthodox Hindu scriptures) are supposed to have emanated from his mouths.

Saraswati

The goddess of learning and consort of Brahma, Saraswati rides upon a white swan and holds the stringed musical instrument known as a *veena*.

Saraswati

Shiva

As creator and destroyer, Shiva is probably the most important god in Nepal – so it's important to keep on his good side! Shiva is often represented by the phallic lingam, symbolic of his creative role. His vehicle is the bull Nandi and you'll often see this figure outside Shiva temples. The symbol most often seen in Shiva's hand is the trident.

Shiva is also known as **Nataraja**, the cosmic dancer whose dance shook the cosmos and created the world. Shiva's home is Mt Kailash in the Himalaya and he's also supposed to be keen on smoking hashish. He takes various forms including peaceful Pashupati and destructive Bhairab.

Pashupati

In the Kathmandu Valley Shiva is most popularly worshipped as Pashupati, the lord of the beasts. As the keeper of all living things, Pashupati is Shiva in a good mood, and the temple of Pashupatinath is the most important Hindu temple in the country.

Shiva

Bhairab

In Nepal, Shiva appears as Bhairab when he is in his fearful or 'terrific' form. Bhairab can appear in 64 different ways, but none of them

is pretty. Typically he has multiple arms, each clutching a weapon; he dances on a body and wears a headdress of skulls. More skulls dangle from his belt, and his staring eyes and bared fangs complete the picture. Usually Bhairab is black, carries a cup made from a human skull and is attended by a dog. The gruesome figure of Bhairab near the Hanuman Dhoka palace entrance in Kathmandu is a good example of this fearsome god at his worst.

Tara

Another deity who appears in both the Hindu and Buddhist pantheons is the Tara goddess. There are actually 108 different Taras, but the best known are Green Tara and White Tara. These Taras are two of the *shaktis* (female consorts) to the Dhyani Buddhas.

Bhairab

Shakti

While Shakti the goddess is Shiva's consort, shakti is the creative or reproductive energy of the gods, which often manifests in their consorts. A Hindu god's shakti is far more than just a companion. A shakti often symbolises certain parts of a god's personality, so while Shiva is the god of both creation and destruction, it is often his shakti, Parvati, manifesting as Kali or Durga, who handles the destructive business and demands the blood sacrifices.

The Kathmandu Valley has numerous shrines and temples dedicated to the great goddesses, including four shrines dedicated to the Joginis, the mystical goddesses who are the female counterpart to the Bhairabs. These shrines are found near Sankhu at the eastern end of the valley, at Guhyeshwari near Pashupatinath, at Pharping and at Vijeshwari.

Parvati

Shiva's shakti is Parvati the beautiful, and she is the dynamic element in their relationship. Just as Shiva is also known as Mahadev, the Great God, so she is Mahadevi, the Great Goddess. Just as Shiva is often symbolised by the phallic lingam, so his shakti's symbol is the yoni, representing the female sex organ. Their relationship is a sexual one and it is often Parvati who is the energetic and dominant partner.

Parvati

Shiva's shakti has as many forms as Shiva himself. She may be peaceful Parvati, but she may also be fearsome **Kali**, the black goddess, or **Durga**, the terrible. In these terrific forms she holds a variety of weapons in her hands, struggles with demons and rides a lion. As Kali, the fiercest of the gods and goddesses, she demands sacrifices and wears a garland of skulls.

Machhendranath

A strictly Nepali Hindu god, Machhendranath has power over the rains and the monsoon and is regarded as protector of the Kathmandu Valley. It's typical of the intermingling of Hindu and Buddhist beliefs in Nepal that, in the Kathmandu Valley at least, Machhendranath has come to be thought of as an incarnation of

Durga

Seto (white)
Machhendranath

Avalokiteshvara, the Bodhisattva of our era. In actual fact the connection from Avalokiteshvara to Machhendranath is not quite so direct. Purely Buddhist Avalokiteshvara is linked with Shiva through Lokeshvara, the lord of the world. Machhendranath is then a manifestation of Lokeshvara.

There are two forms of Machhendranath based on colour and features: Seto (White) Machhendranath of Kathmandu and Rato (Red) Machhendranath of Patan. Some scholars say that they are the same god, but for others they are different.

Ganesh

With his elephant head, Ganesh is probably the most easily recognised of the gods and also the most popular. Ganesh is the god of prosperity and wisdom and there are many Ganesh shrines and temples in Nepal. Ganesh's parents are Shiva and Parvati and he obtained his elephant head thanks to his father's notorious temper. Coming back from a long trip, Shiva discovered Parvati in bed with a young man. Not pausing to think that their son might have grown up a little during his absence, Shiva lopped his head off! Parvati then forced him to bring his son back to life, but he could only do so by giving him the head of the first living thing he saw – which happened to be an elephant.

Hanuman

The monkey god Hanuman is the important character from the Ramayana who came to the aid of Rama – he helped to defeat the evil Rawana and release Sita from his grasp. Hanuman's trustworthy and alert nature is commemorated by the many statues of Hanuman seen guarding palace entrances. The best known in Nepal is the image of Hanuman that stands beside the old Royal Palace entrance in Kathmandu, and indeed gives the old palace its name of Hanuman Dhoka.

Hanuman also has an important medicinal connection in Nepal and other Hindu countries. The Ramayana recounts a legend of how Rama desperately needed a rare herb grown only in the Himalaya region, and sent Hanuman to procure it for him. Unfortunately, by the time he finally arrived in the mountains, Hanuman had

Ganesh

forgotten which particular herb he had been asked to bring back to Rama, but he got around the problem by simply grabbing a whole mountain, confident that at least somewhere on the mountain would be the required plant.

On the walls of the Bir Hospital in Kathmandu you can see a large illustration of Hanuman flying through the air, tightly clasping a whole mountain.

Vishnu

Although in Nepal (where he often appears as Narayan) he also plays a role in the creation of the universe, Vishnu is the preserver. Narayan is the reclining Vishnu, sleeping on the cosmic ocean, and from his navel appears Brahma, who creates the universe.

Vishnu has four arms and can often be identified by the symbols he holds: the conch shell or *sankha*, the disc-like weapon known as a *chakra*, the stick-like weapon known as a *gada*, and a lotus flower or *padma*. Vishnu's vehicle is the faithful man-bird

Hanuman

Garuda, and a winged Garuda will often be seen kneeling reverently in front of a Vishnu temple. Garuda has an intense hatred of snakes and is often seen destroying them. Vishnu's shakti is Lakshmi, the goddess of wealth and prosperity.

Vishnu has 10 incarnations, starting with Matsya, the fish. Then he appeared as Kurma, the tortoise on which the universe is built. Number three was his boar incarnation as Varaha, who bravely destroyed a demon who would have drowned the world. Vishnu was again in a demon-destroying mood in incarnation four as Narsingha (or Narsimha), half-man and half-lion. (See the boxed text 'Narsingha' in the Around the Kathmandu Valley chapter for an explanation of the legend behind this incarnation.)

Still facing difficulties from demons, Vishnu's next incarnation was Vamana, the dwarf who reclaimed the world from the demon-king Bali. The dwarf politely asked the demon for a patch of ground upon which to meditate, saying that the patch need only be big enough that he, the dwarf, could walk across it in three paces. The demon agreed, only to see the dwarf swell

Vishnu

into a giant who strode across the universe in three gigantic steps.

In his sixth incarnation Vishnu appeared as Parasurama, a warlike Brahman who proceeded to put the warrior-caste Chhetris in their place.

Incarnation seven was as Rama, the hero of the Ramayana who, with help from Hanuman the monkey god, rescued his beautiful wife Sita from the clutches of Rawana, evil king of Lanka. Sita is believed to have been born in Janakpur, and this is also where she and Rama married.

Incarnation eight was the gentle and much-loved **Krishna**, the fun-loving cowherd, who dallied with the *gopis* (milkmaids), danced, played his flute and still managed to remain devoted to his wife Radha.

For number nine Vishnu appeared as the teacher, the Buddha. Of course, Buddhists don't accept that the Buddha was just an incarnation of some other religion's god. But perhaps it was just a ploy to bring Hindu converts back into the fold.

Incarnation 10? Well, we haven't seen that one yet, but it will be as Kali the destroyer, when Vishnu wields the sword that will destroy the world at the end of the Kaliyuga, the age we are currently in.

Krishna

The artwork for the Gods of Nepal special section was drawn by Professor TC Mafapuria.

Facts for the Visitor

SUGGESTED ITINERARIES

While many people come to Nepal just to trek in the Himalaya, there is indeed a great deal more to the country. The Kathmandu Valley is worth devoting at least a week to in itself, although most people miss its highlights as they rush off to the mountains as quickly as possible. The temple squares in Kathmandu, Patan and Bhaktapur, and the stupa (Buddhist religious structure) complexes of Swayambhunath and Bodhnath are world-class sites and should not be missed.

The Terai, the lowland strip that runs the width of the country, is a fascinating area that is often completely overlooked by foreign visitors but which has a great deal to offer. Visiting the Royal Chitwan and Royal Bardia National Parks in the Terai offers visitors a chance to ride elephant-back and view an incredible variety of bird and animal life, including the royal Bengal tiger and the rhinoceros. Other Terai towns, such as Janakpur and Lumbini, are significant religious sites and are also worth a visit, particularly if you are travelling overland to/from India.

One Week

With a week you could get to grips with the highlights of the Kathmandu Valley, though you'd have to make an effort to prise yourself out of the comforts of Thamel. Take day trips to Swayambhunath and Patan and consider staying overnight in Bhaktapur and (if you have an interest in Tibetan culture) Bodhnath. Hire a mountain bike for a day's pedalling out to the sacred sites around Pharping or the traditional village and countryside of Bagmati. Get a final Himalayan kick from the mountain views at Nagarkot or Dhulikhel, only a couple of hours' drive from Kathmandu.

Two Weeks

With two weeks up your sleeve you really have to choose between sightseeing and trekking. You could visit the relaxing lakeside town of Pokhara as well as Kathmandu; or the Royal Chitwan National Park in the Terai, where you will hopefully catch sight of (among other wildlife) a rhinoceros and a royal Bengal tiger. It would be possible to fly out to Jomsom or Manang and do some

day hikes on the Annapurna Circuit but that would be a potentially frustrating rush. Take a couple of days to try canyoning, rafting or kayaking at The Last Resort or Borderlands, half a day's drive from Kathmandu.

One Month

One month is a good amount of time to get a good feel for Nepal. The Kathmandu Valley is really worth a week. You could then do an extended trek (such as the Everest Base Camp Trek) or a shorter trek and slot in a visit to Pokhara and Royal Chitwan National Park.

Two Months

Those lucky souls with two months at their disposal should have no difficulty in spending that time in Nepal, particularly if trekking is on the agenda. The longer treks, such as the Annapurna Circuit and the Everest Base Camp Trek, take around three weeks; four when you include transport from Kathmandu. This leaves another four weeks to explore Kathmandu and Pokhara, and also gives you the chance to discover the flora and fauna of the Terai at Royal Chitwan and Royal Bardia National Parks and Koshi Tappu Wildlife Reserve.

PLANNING
When to Go

Climatic factors are very important in planning when to visit Nepal. October to November, the start of the dry season, is in many ways the best time. With the monsoon only recently finished, the countryside is green and lush and Nepal is at its most beautiful – the air is sparkling clean, visibility is excellent and the Himalayan views are near perfect. Furthermore, the weather is still balmy. There are some important and colourful festivals to enjoy, though bear in mind that these festivals can be disruptive if you are on a tight schedule (see Public Holidays later in this chapter). For obvious reasons, this is also the high tourist season.

In December and January the climate and visibility are still good, though it can get very cold. Trekkers need to be well prepared, as there may be snow on high-altitude routes. Heading for the Everest Base Camp at this time of year can be a real feat of endurance and the Annapurna Circuit is often closed by snow on the Thorung La. Down in Kathmandu, the cheaper hotels – where there is no heating – are often chilly and gloomy in the evenings.

February to April, the tail end of the dry season, is the next-best time to visit. The weather gets warmer so high-altitude treks are not as arduous, although by the end of the dry season, before the monsoon breaks, it starts to get too hot for comfort. Visibility is not as good as earlier in the dry season but Nepal's wonderful rhododendrons and many other flowers are in bloom, so there's plenty of colour to be seen along the trekking trails.

May and early June are not the best times to visit as it is extremely hot and dusty and the coming monsoon seems to hang over you like a threat.

Mid-June to September, when the monsoon finally arrives, is the least popular time to visit Nepal. The rains wash the dust out of the air, but the clouds obscure the mountains so you're unlikely to enjoy more than a rare glimpse of the Himalaya. Although it doesn't rain all day it usually rains every day and the trails and roads are muddy and plagued by leeches; rivers are high; and landslides on the roads often hold up transport. The latter part of the monsoon (August and September) is a time of festivals, which will certainly enliven a visit to Kathmandu.

Maps

Remote Nepali villages often have diverse names and their exact location can be open to interpretation. You may find reality varies considerably to what appears on your map.

The best maps in Nepal are those produced by Karto-Atelier. These locally made maps are a result of German-Nepali collaboration and are simply outstanding. Currently available are maps to Kathmandu, Pokhara and a route map for Kathmandu to Everest, for Rs 800 each.

There are many locally produced and cheaper maps available in Nepal which for most trekkers prove quite adequate. The main series is produced by Himalayan Maphouse and these include the brand Nepa Maps. See the website ⓦ www.himalayan maphouse.com for an online catalogue, which includes Kathmandu and Pokhara maps, as well as Chitwan and rafting route maps. They are decent quality and reason-

ably priced at Rs 200 to Rs 400 each but they definitely aren't reliable enough to use for off-route trekking. These and other maps are sold at a string of glossy map shops throughout Thamel and elsewhere in Kathmandu.

Lonely Planet produces a *Kathmandu City Map*. As well as detailed maps of Kathmandu, this handy fold-out laminated map also features maps of Patan and Bhaktapur, a walking tour and comprehensive index.

For details of trekking maps see the Trekking chapter.

What to Bring

Nepal's climatic variations due to altitude mean that at certain times of year you'll have to come prepared for almost any weather. If you're in Nepal during the winter you'll find it's T-shirt weather in the Terai, but up at the Everest Base Camp you'll want the best down gear money can buy.

In the Kathmandu Valley the daytime weather is pleasant year-round, but in winter the temperature drops as soon as the sun sets, or even goes behind a cloud. It never reaches freezing in the valley, however, so it's sweater or warm-jacket weather, nothing worse. Climb higher to the valley edge at Nagarkot and it gets much colder. If you plan to ride a bicycle, or you have a respiratory problem, Kathmandu's air pollution is sufficiently bad to justify a mask.

During the monsoon you'll need an umbrella or a raincoat, particularly in Pokhara where the rainfall is much heavier than in Kathmandu.Sunglasses, a hat and covering for unprotected skin are all necessary on high-altitude treks or for prolonged exposure in the Terai (see the Trekking chapter for more information on trekking necessities).

Clothing is easily and cheaply available in Nepal so if there's any question about bringing a particular item, leave it behind – you can always buy one if you need it. The one exception to this is small-size or large-size trekking boots.

Most toiletries are readily available, including toilet paper. Women should, however, bring tampons if needed.

If you plan on staying in cheap hotels a padlock can be useful to prevent theft from your room (hotels in this category often lock the doors with a latch and their own padlock, rather than a lock set into the door). Ear plugs are recommended if you sleep lightly – cheap hotels and lodges are often very noisy. Resealable plastic bags can be useful for carrying everything from washing powder to peanuts.

If you're visiting Royal Chitwan National Park or other places in the Terai a good insect repellent is a necessity. Bring a torch (flashlight) for trekking and frequent power cuts ('load-shedding').

TOURIST OFFICES

The Ministry of Tourism doesn't overdo things; there is very little printed information available and the handful of tourist offices around the country are of limited use.

The **Nepal Tourism Board** (☎ 01-4256909; **w** *www.welcomenepal.com*) operates an office in Kathmandu's Tribhuvan airport, and has leaflets and maps. The tourist office in the Tourist Service Centre, east of Tundikhel in central Kathmandu, has government publications and an information counter.

There are also tourist offices in Pokhara, Bhairawa, Birganj, Janakpur and Kakarbhitta. Again, these are virtually useless unless you have a specific inquiry. See the relevant sections for contact details.

VISAS & DOCUMENTS
Visas

All foreigners, except Indians, must have a visa. Nepali embassies and consulates overseas issue visas with no fuss. You can also get one on the spot when you arrive in Nepal, either at Kathmandu's Tribhuvan airport or at road borders: Biratnagar, Birganj/Raxaul Bazaar, Sunauli, Kakarbhitta, Mahendranagar, Dhangadhi, even the funky Kodari checkpoint on the road to Tibet. This system has been in place for years and is unlikely to change soon, nonetheless it's safest to get a visa before you arrive.

A Nepali visa is valid for entry for three to six months from the date of issue. You can download a visa application form from the websites of the Nepali embassy in Washington, DC (**w** www.nepalembassyusa.org) or London (**w** www.nepembassy.org.uk). Children under 10 require a visa but are not charged a visa fee. Your passport must have at least six months validity.

To obtain a visa on arrival by air in Nepal you must fill in an application form and provide a passport photograph. Visa application forms are available on a table in the arrivals hall, though some airlines (like Thai) provide this form on the flight. To get a jump on the immigration queue, you can download the visa-on-arrival form from **w** www.treks.com .np/visa. A single-entry visa valid for 60 days costs US$30. At Kathmandu's Tribhuvan airport the fee is payable in any major currency but it's a good idea to have enough small bills to cover the equivalent cost. At land borders, officials will probably require payment in cash US dollars. Only single-entry visas are routinely available on arrival.

If you have already visited Nepal during the same calendar year the visa fee is the same but you'll only get a 30-day visa. Much of the time you spend in the visa-on-arrival queue is waiting while officers scour your passport for previous entry stamps.

At Nepali embassies abroad it's possible to get a multiple-entry visa (US$80 or equivalent), which gives you multiple trips into Nepal for a year, with each stay valid for 60 days, up to a total of 150 days in any calendar year. Multiple-entry visas are useful if you are planning a side trip to Tibet, Bhutan or India. You can change your single-entry visa to a multiple-entry visa at Kathmandu's Central Immigration Office for US$50.

If you are just planning a lightning visit to Kathmandu it's possible to get a 48-hour transit visa at Kathmandu airport for US$5, as long as you have an air ticket out of the country within 48 hours.

If you stay in Nepal for longer than the duration of your initial 60-day visa, you will require a visa extension (see following). Transit visas are nonextendable.

Don't overstay a visa. You can pay a fine of US$2 per day at the airport if you have overstayed less than 30 days (plus in theory US$3 per day between 30 and 90 days and US$5 per day for over 90 days). If you've overstayed more than a week get it all sorted out at Kathmandu's Central Immigration Office *before* you get to the airport, as a delay could cause you to miss your flight.

Visa Extensions It costs US$30 (payable in rupees) for a 30-day visa extension. These are available from immigration offices in Kathmandu and Pokhara only. You get a 30-day extension whether you are staying for an extra day or an extra 30 days.

Every visa extension requires your passport, money, photos and an application form. Collect all these before you join the queue. There are several instant photo shops near the immigration offices. If you plan ahead, there are many photographers in Kathmandu and Pokhara who will provide passport photos more cheaply, within a day.

Visa extensions are normally available the same day. At peak times the queues are long and the formalities are tedious. For a fee, trekking and travel agencies can assist with the visa extension process and can usually save you the time and tedium of queuing.

You can extend your visa up to a total stay of 120 days without undue formality. You should be able to get a further 30 days extension but you may need to show a flight ticket proving that you are leaving the country during that time period, since you are only allowed to stay in Nepal for a total of 150 days in a calendar year on a tourist visa.

You can get up-to-date visa information at the website of the Department of Immigration (W www.immi.gov.np).

For more details on getting a visa extension in Kathmandu see Information in the Kathmandu chapter.

Trekking Permits

Trekking permits are not required for the main trekking areas of Everest, Annapurna and Langtang but you'll need to pay national park and conservation fees. Permits are still required for all remote regions.

Trekking permits are only issued (and extended) at the immigration offices in Kathmandu and Pokhara. See Trekking Permits in the Trekking chapter for more details.

Travel Insurance

A travel insurance policy to cover theft, loss and medical problems is a good idea. There is a wide variety of policies available, so check the small print. Some policies exclude 'dangerous activities', which may include trekking (and definitely bungy jumping and rafting). Choose a policy that covers medical and emergency repatriation, including (for trekkers) helicopter evacuation fees, which run to US$1500 per hour in Nepal.

You may prefer a policy that pays doctors or hospitals directly rather than you having to pay on the spot and claim later. If you have to claim later make sure you keep all documentation. Some policies ask you to call back (reverse charges) to a centre in your home country where an immediate assessment of your problem is made.

Other Documents

If you think you might drive a car or ride a motorcycle while in Nepal then it is worth having an international driving permit.

It's a good idea to keep a number of passport photos with your passport so they are immediately handy for trekking permits, visa applications and other official documents.

EMBASSIES & CONSULATES
Nepali Embassies & Consulates

For embassies and consulates not listed below check out the websites of Nepal's Ministry of Foreign Affairs (W www.mofa.gov.np) or Department of Immigration (W www.immi.gov .np/location.php).

Australia
Honorary Consulate-General: (☎ 9328 7062, fax 9340 1084) Suite 501, Level 5, Edgecliff Centre, 203–233 New South Head Rd, PO Box 474, Edgecliff, Sydney, NSW 2027. Open 9.30am to 11.30am Monday to Thursday.
Consulate General: (☎ 3220 2007, fax 3211 9885) Level 7, 344 Queen St, Brisbane, Queensland 4000
Consulate General: (☎ 9386 2102, fax 9836 3087) Suite 2, 16 Robinson St, Nedlands, WA 6009
Honorary Consulate: (☎ 9676 3154, fax 9681 9899, e nepalconsulate@simplytravel.com.au) 1/40 Beach St, Port Melbourne, Vic 3207

Bangladesh
(☎ 02-601890, fax 882 6401, e rnedhaka@bd mail.net) United Nations Rd, Road 2, Baridhara, Dhaka

Canada
(☎ 416-865 0200, fax 416-865 0904) Royal Bank Plaza, South Tower, 32nd floor, PO Box 33, Toronto, Ontario M5J 2J9

China
(☎ 6532 1795, fax 6532 3251, e rnebc@public .netchina.com.cn) No 1, Xi Liu Jie, Sanlitun Lu, Beijing 100600 (see also Tibet)

France
(☎ 01 46 22 48 67, fax 01 42 27 08 65, e nepal@ worldnet.fr) 45 bis rue des Acacias, 75017 Paris

Germany
(☎ 3435 9920, fax 3435 9906, W www.nepal embassy-germany.com) Guerickestrasse 27, 10587 Berlin-Charlottenburg

India
Embassy: (☎ 332 7361, fax 332 6857, e ram janki@del.2.vsnl.net.in) 1 Barakhamba Rd, New Delhi 110001

Consulate-General: (☎ 479 1117, fax 479 1410, ⓔ rncg@cal.vsnl.net.in) 1 National Library Ave, Alipore, Kolkata (Calcutta) 700027

Japan
(☎ 3705 5558, fax 3705 8264, ⓔ nepembjp@big.or.jp) 14–19 Todoroki 7-chome, Setagaya-ku, Tokyo 158-0082

Myanmar (Burma)
(☎ 545 880, fax 549 803, ⓔ rnembygn@datseco.com.mm) 16 Natmauk Yeiktha (Park Ave), PO Box 84, Yangon (Rangoon)

Netherlands
(☎ 6241 530, fax 6246 173, ⓔ nepal.consulate@inter.nl.net) Keizersgracht 463, 1017 DK, Amsterdam

Thailand
(☎ 2-391 7240, fax 2-381 2406, ⓔ nepembkk@asiaaccess.net.th) 189 Soi 71, Sukhumvit Rd, Prakanong, Bangkok 10110

Tibet
(☎ 682 2881, fax 683 6890, ⓔ rncglx@public.ls.xz.cn) Norbulingka Rd 13, Lhasa, Tibet Autonomous Region

UK
(☎ 020-7229 1594, fax 7792 9861, Ⓦ www.nepembassy.org.uk) 12A Kensington Palace Gardens, London W8 4QU

USA
Embassy: (☎ 202-667 4550, fax 667 5534, Ⓦ www.nepalembassyusa.org) 2131 Leroy Place NW, Washington, DC 20008
Consulate-General: (☎ 370 3988, fax 953 2038) 820 2nd Ave, 17th Floor, New York, NY 10017
Honorary Consulate: (☎ 434 1111, fax 434 3130, ⓔ skelly@blumcapital.com) Suite 400, 909 Montgomery St, San Francisco, CA 94133; other honorary consulates in Chicago and Boston

Embassies & Consulates in Nepal

Travellers continuing beyond Nepal may need visas for Bangladesh, China, India, Myanmar (Burma) or Thailand. The only visas for Tibet (actually a Chinese visa and a travel permit for Tibet) dished out in Kathmandu are for organised groups; individuals wishing to travel to Tibet should get a visa before arriving in Nepal (Delhi is a good place to get one). See Tibet under Land in the Getting There & Away chapter for advice about travelling independently in Tibet.

Many foreign embassies in Kathmandu are clustered around the northeast of the centre and include the following:

Australia (☎ 01-4371678, fax 4371533) Bansbari, just beyond the Ring Rd in Maharajganj.

Your Own Embassy

It's important to realise what your own embassy – the embassy of the country of which you are a citizen – can and can't do to help you if you get into trouble. Generally speaking, it won't be much help in emergencies if the trouble you're in is remotely your own fault. Remember that you are bound by the laws of the country you are in. Your embassy will not be sympathetic if you end up in jail after committing a crime locally, even if such actions are legal in your own country.

Officials of all embassies in Nepal stress the benefits of registering with them, telling them where you are trekking, and reporting in again when you return. The offices of KEEP and the Himalayan Rescue Association (see Information in the Kathmandu and Trekking chapters for details) have forms from most embassies, so it's simple to provide the information.

In genuine emergencies you might get some assistance, but only if other channels have been exhausted. For example, if you need to get home urgently, a free ticket home is exceedingly unlikely – the embassy would expect you to have insurance. If you have all your money and documents stolen, it might assist with getting a new passport, but a loan for onward travel is out of the question.

Bangladesh (☎ 01-4372843, fax 4373265) Maharajganj. Open 9am to 1.15pm and 2pm to 5pm Monday to Friday. Visa application mornings only; tourist visas are not issued here, but are available on arrival in Dhaka.

Canada (☎ 01-4415398) Lazimpat

China (☎ 01-4411740, fax 4414045) Baluwatar. Open 9am to noon and 3pm to 5pm Monday to Friday. Visa applications are accepted Monday, Wednesday and Friday 9.30am to 11.30am; passports are generally returned the next working day between 4pm and 4.30pm, though same-day express services are possible. If applying yourself you will need to have proof (such as an air ticket to Shanghai) that you are not travelling via Tibet.

France (☎ 01-4413332, fax 4419968) Lazimpat

Germany (☎ 01-4412786, fax 4416899) Gyaneshwar

India (☎ 01-4410900, fax 4413132, Ⓦ www.south-asia.com/Embassy-India) Lainchhaur. Open 9.30am to noon and 1.30pm to 5pm Monday to Friday. Visa applications 9.30am to 12.30pm, collect visas 4pm to 5pm. Allow seven to 10 days for processing of tourist visas, which are valid for six months. Transit visas (Rs 350; valid for 15 days from date of issue) are issued the same day, start from that date and are nonextendable. One photo is required. The cost for a tourist visa varies according to nationality, but is around Rs 2400. US citizens pay an extra fee of around Rs 1500.

Japan (☎ 01-4426680, fax 4414101) Pani Pokhari

Myanmar (Burma) (☎ 01-5521788, fax 5523402) Chakupath, near Patan Dhoka (City Gate), Patan. Open 9.30am to 1pm and 2pm to 4.30pm Monday to Friday. Visa applications mornings only. Fourteen-day visas are available, four photos are required, 24-hour turnaround; the cost is US$20.

New Zealand (☎ 01-4412436, fax 4414750) Dilli Bazaar; honorary consulate only

Pakistan (☎ 01-4374024, fax 4374012) Narayan Gopal Chowk, Ring Rd, Maharajganj. Open 9am to 5pm Monday to Friday.

Thailand (☎ 01-4371410, fax 4371408) Bansbari. Open 8.30am to 12.30pm and 1.30pm to 4.30pm Monday to Friday. Visa applications accepted 9.30am to 12.30pm, two photos required, 24-hour turnaround; the cost is about US$10, though most nationalities don't need a visa for stays of less than 30 days.

UK (☎ 01-4410583, fax 4411789, W www.britain .gov.np) Lainchhaur. Open 8.30am to noon and 2pm to 3.30pm Monday to Thursday, 8.30am to 11.30am Friday.

USA (☎ 01-4411179, fax 4419963, W www.south-asia.com/USA) Pani Pokhari. US citizen services 1pm to 4pm Monday, Wednesday and Friday, 8am to 4.30pm Tuesday and Thursday.

CUSTOMS

All baggage is X-rayed on arrival and departure. In addition to the import and export of drugs, customs is concerned with the illegal export of antiques. You may not import Nepali rupees, and only nationals of Nepal and India may import Indian currency. There is no restriction on bringing in either cash or travellers cheques, but the amount taken out at departure should not exceed the amount brought in. Officially you should declare cash or travellers cheques in excess of US$2000, or the equivalent, but no-one seems to bother with this.

Visitors are permitted to import the following articles for their personal use (and we quote):

Cigarettes, 200 sticks; cigars, 50 sticks; alcoholic liquor, one bottle not exceeding 1.15 litre; one binocular; one movie camera with 12 rolls of film;

one video camera; one ordinary camera with 15 rolls of film; one tape recorder with 15 tape reels or cassettes; one perambulator; one bicycle; and one stick.

Antiques

Customs' main concern is preventing the export of antique works of art, with good reason, as Nepal has been a particular victim of international art theft in the last 20 years (see the boxed text 'Nepal's Stolen Heritage').

It is very unlikely that souvenirs sold to travellers will be antique (despite the claims of the vendors), but if there is any doubt, they should be cleared and a certificate obtained from the **Department of Archaeology** (*☎ 01-4250683; Ramshah Path, Kathmandu*) in the National Archives building. If you visit between 10am and 1pm you should be able to pick up a certificate by 5pm the same day. These controls also apply to the export of precious and semiprecious stones.

Nepal's Stolen Heritage

In the last 20 years Nepal has seen a staggering amount of its artistic heritage spirited out of the country by art thieves – 120 statues were stolen in the 1980s alone. Much of the stolen art languishes in museums or private collections in European nations and in the United States, while in Nepal remaining temple statues are, sadly, increasingly kept under lock and key.

One of the reasons that photography is banned in some temples in Nepal is that international thieves often use photos of temple images to publish underground 'shopping catalogues'. Pieces are then stolen to order, often with the aid of corrupt officials, to fetch high prices on the lucrative Himalayan art market. UN conventions against the trade exist but are weakly enforced.

Several catalogues of stolen Nepali art have been produced in an attempt to locate these stolen treasures and put pressure on museums and private collectors to return the located pieces.

In 2000 one piece was returned from a museum in Berlin and in 2002 several more were returned to the Kathmandu Museum, hopefully marking the slow return of Nepal's heritage to its rightful home.

MONEY
Currency

The Nepali rupee (Rs) is divided into 100 paisa (p). There are coins for denominations of five, 10, 25 and 50 paisa, and for one, two, five and 10 rupees, although as the rupee coins are not in wide circulation and prices are generally rounded to the nearest rupee, you often don't come across any coins at all. This is a great contrast to a time not long ago, when outside the Kathmandu Valley, it was rare to see any paper money. Mountaineering books from the 1950s often comment on the porters whose sole duty was to carry the expedition's money – in cold, hard cash.

Bank notes come in denominations of one, two, five, 10, 20, 25, 50, 100, 500 and 1000 rupees. Away from major centres, changing a Rs 1000 note can be very difficult, so it is always wise to keep a stash of small denomination notes. Even in Kathmandu, many small businesses – especially rickshaw and taxi drivers – simply don't have sufficient spare money to allow them the luxury of carrying a wad of change.

Exchange Rates

country	unit		rupee
Australia	A$1	=	Rs 43
China	Y1	=	Rs 9
Euro zone	€ 1	=	Rs 76.6
India	INRs 100	=	Rs 160
Japan	¥100	=	Rs 63
UK	UK£1	=	Rs 121
USA	US$1	=	Rs 77

For the latest exchange rates try w www .oanda.com.

Exchanging Money

Major international currencies, including the US dollar and pounds sterling, are readily accepted. In Nepal the Indian rupee is also like a hard currency – the Nepali rupee is pegged to the Indian rupee at the rate of INRs 100 = Rs 160. Be aware that INRs 500 notes are not accepted anywhere in Nepal, apparently due to forgeries.

When you change money officially, you are required to show your passport, and you are issued with a foreign exchange encashment receipt showing your identity and the amount of hard currency you have changed. Hang onto the receipts as they have a number of potential uses.

Many upmarket hotels and businesses are obliged by the government to demand payment in hard currency; they will also accept rupees, but only if you can show a foreign exchange encashment receipt that covers the amount you owe them. In practice this regulation seems to be widely disregarded and you are rarely asked to prove the source of your rupees. Airlines are also required to charge tourists in hard currency, either in cash US dollars, travellers cheques or credit cards, and this rule is generally followed.

If you leave Nepal via Kathmandu's Tribhuvan airport, the downstairs exchange counter will re-exchange the amount shown on 'unused' exchange certificates. The bank keeps the receipts used for re-exchange so make sure you have photocopies if you need them for other purposes. Be warned that official re-exchange is not possible at any bank branches at the border crossings.

ATMs Standard Chartered Bank (formerly Grindlays Bank) has ATMs in Kathmandu and Pokhara; you can get cash advances on both Visa and MasterCard 24 hours a day, though travellers have reported that these machines don't take cards that run on the Cirrus system. See the Kathmandu and Pokhara maps in their respective chapters for locations.

Some other banks, such as the Himalaya Bank, also have ATMs but these only accept local cards.

Credit Cards Major credit cards are widely accepted at mid-range and better hotels, restaurants and fancy shops in the Kathmandu Valley and at Pokhara. Elsewhere it's safer to assume that credit cards won't be accepted, and so you will need to carry enough cash or travellers cheques to cover your costs.

Branches of Standard Chartered Bank and some other banks such as Nabil Bank and Himalaya Bank give cash advances against Visa and MasterCard in Nepali rupees only (no commission), and will also sell you foreign currency travellers cheques against the cards with a 2% commission.

The American Express (AmEx) agent is Yeti Travels in Kathmandu (see Money under Information in the Kathmandu chapter). It advances travellers cheques to cardholders for a standard 1% commission.

International Transfers Bank transfers from overseas can be time-consuming, though major Nepali banks have switched from telex to the computerised Swift system these days. Pin down every possible detail, ensure that you know which bank the money is going to, make sure they have your name exactly right and if possible ensure that you are notified of the transfer at the same time as the bank.

In general it's easier to send money through a private company such as Western Union (w www.westernunion.com) or Moneygram (w www.visitnepal.com/moneygram), which can arrange transfers within minutes. Western Union's agents in Nepal include Yeti Travels, Sita World Travel (see Money in the Kathmandu chapter) and Nabil Bank; Moneygram uses Easylink, with offices in Thamel, Bodhnath, Butwal and Pokhara.

Note that money can often only be received in Nepali rupees, not US dollars.

Banks & Moneychangers Official exchange rates are set by the government's Nepal Rastra Bank. Rates at the private banks vary, but are generally not far from the official rate. The daily newspapers list the Nepal Rastra Bank's rate, providing a useful reference point.

There are exchange counters at the international terminal at Kathmandu's Tribhuvan airport and banks and/or moneychangers at the various border crossings. Pokhara and the major border towns also have official moneychanging facilities, but changing travellers cheques can be difficult elsewhere in the country, even in some quite large towns. If you are trekking try and take enough small denomination cash rupees with you to last the whole trek.

The usual banking hours are 10am to 2pm Sunday to Thursday, and until noon on Friday.

The best private banks are the Nepal Bank Ltd, Standard Chartered Bank and Himalaya Bank. Some hotels and resorts are also licensed to change money, though their rates are often lower. Rates and commissions also vary slightly from bank to bank.

In addition to the banks there are licensed moneychangers in Kathmandu, Pokhara, Birganj, Kakarbhitta and Sunauli/Bhairawa. The rates are often marginally lower than the banks, but there are no commissions. The big advantages of the moneychangers over the banks is that they have much longer opening hours (typically from 9am to 7pm seven days a week) and they are also much quicker, the whole process often taking no more than a few minutes.

Most licensed moneychangers will provide an exchange receipt; if they don't you may be able to negotiate better rates than those posted on their boards.

Costs

If you stay in rock-bottom accommodation and survive on a predominantly Nepali diet you could live in Nepal for less than US$5 a day. On an independent 'village inn' or 'teahouse' trek your living costs are likely to be around that level.

If you stay in comfortable, lower midrange hotels, sit down to eat in popular tourist-oriented restaurants, rent bicycles and take taxis from time to time your living costs could be around US$14 to US$20 a day. Move to a mid-range hotel, hire a car between towns and spend much time rafting or on an organised trek and you are looking at US$40 to US$50 per day. The tourist centres of Kathmandu and Pokhara seem to suck money out of you by osmosis, primarily because there are so many ways to spend it. The current slump in tourism has resulted in widespread discounting.

Most of the major upmarket tour and trekking operators offer significant discounts for residents, so make your resident status clear when you ask for prices and make bookings.

Tipping & Bargaining

Tipping is prevalent in Kathmandu. In expensive establishments you should tip up to 10%, while in smaller places some loose change or Rs 25 will be most appreciated (don't worry about it in the really cheap restaurants). Taxi drivers don't expect to be tipped.

Before bargaining, try to establish a fair price by talking to local people and other travellers. Paying too much feeds inflation, while paying too little denies the locals a reasonable return for their efforts and investments. Not everything is subject to bargaining: You should respect standard food, accommodation and entry charges, and follow the going rate for services.

Bargaining is usually regarded as an integral part of a transaction and is, ideally, an enjoyable social exchange. Nepalis do not ever appreciate aggressive behaviour. A good deal is when both parties are happy. Try to remember that Rs 10 might make quite a difference to the seller, but in hard currency it amounts to very little (less than US$0.15).

Taxes

Most hotels and restaurants in the mid to upper range charge 10% VAT tax, on top of which is slapped a 2% Tourism Service Charge. The VAT tax is often (incorrectly) charged on the tourism tax, meaning that you are actually charged 12.2% tax.

POST & COMMUNICATIONS
Post

The postal service to and from Nepal is, at best, erratic but can occasionally be amazingly efficient. Most articles do finally arrive at their destination, but they can take weeks.

Poste restante services are quite well organised, but ask people writing to you to print your family name clearly and underline it. Misfiled mail often results from confusion between family names and given names. In general, poste restante is fast losing out to Web-based email accounts (see Email & Internet Access later).

American Express cardholders can have mail sent to: American Express, Yeti Travels Pty Ltd, Hotel Mayalu, Jamal Tole, PO Box 5376, Durbar Marg, Kathmandu. The Kathmandu Guest House will hold mail for its guests.

Airmail rates for a letter (up to 20g)/postcard are Rs 2 within Nepal, Rs 15/12 to South Asian Association for Regional Cooperation (SAARC) countries, Rs 25/15 to Europe and the UK and Rs 30/18 to the USA and Australia.

Parcel Post Having stocked up on souvenirs and gifts in Nepal, many people take the opportunity of sending them home from Kathmandu. Parcel post is not cheap or quick, but the service is reliable. Sea mail is much cheaper than airmail, but it is also much slower (packages take about 3½ months) and less reliable.

The contents of a parcel must be inspected by officials before it is wrapped so do not take it to the post office already wrapped. There are packers at the Kathmandu foreign post office who will package

it for a small fee. The maximum weight for sea mail is 20kg; for airmail it's 10kg.

Some specialised shipping companies (see the Kathmandu chapter for examples) offer air freight, which is considerably cheaper than airmail and not that much more expensive than sea mail. It still goes by air; the catch is that it has to be picked up at an international airport and you'll have to deal with customs paperwork and fees there.

If an object is shipped to you, you may find that customs charges for clearance and collection at your end add up to more than the initial cost of sending it. Often it would have been worth paying extra to take it with you on the plane in the first place. The airlines can provide details of their excess baggage rates.

Courier For a 500g package of documents DHL and FedEx charge around US$40 to the US and UK and US$43 to Australia. FedEx was offering a 40% discount to the US and UK at the time of research. Nondocuments cost up to 50% more for the same weight.

Telephone

The telephone system works pretty well, and it's easy to make local, STD and international calls. Reverse-charge (collect) calls can only be made to Canada, Japan, the USA and the UK.

The cheapest and most convenient way to make calls is through one of the hundreds of private call centres that have sprung up across the country. Look for signs advertising STD/ISD services. It's really only worth using the government telegraph offices if you need to make a call in the middle of the night when other places are closed.

With the private operators, expect to pay around Rs 120 to Rs 130 per minute to most countries. Many of the hotels also have direct-dial facilities, but always check their charges before you make a call.

Internet phone calls are cheapest of all. These are available in Kathmandu and Pokhara, and are technically illegal. Nevertheless, they are the preferred option these days as it means calls to just about anywhere cost around Rs 30 to Rs 50 per minute. There is some delay (echo) in the line when making Internet calls, but it is fine for most purposes.

The international country code for Nepal is ☎ 977. For outgoing international calls the international access number is ☎ 00, which is followed by the country code. For domestic telephone information call ☎ 197.

An extra digit was added to telephone numbers nationwide in March 2003. Kathmandu, Patan and Bhaktapur numbers are now seven digits; all others are six digits. The numbers listed in this book have been revised but you may still see old numbers listed on hotel cards, websites etc in Nepal.

Email & Internet Access

Consider opening a free email account such as ekno (Ⓦ www.ekno.lonelyplanet.com), Hotmail (Ⓦ www.hotmail.com) or Yahoo! (Ⓦ www.mail.yahoo.com). You can then access your mail from any Web-connected computer worldwide.

Email and Internet services are offered by dozens of places in Kathmandu (Rs 20 to Rs 30 per hour) and Pokhara (Rs 2 per minute). Internet access is also available in most other towns, but connections are usually slow and relatively expensive, as connection may involve an STD call to Kathmandu.

DIGITAL RESOURCES

A good place to start your Web explorations is the Lonely Planet website (Ⓦ www.lonely planet.com). Here you'll find succinct summaries on travelling to most places on earth, postcards from other travellers and the Thorn Tree bulletin board, where you can ask questions before you go or dispense advice when you get back. You can also find travel news and updates to many of our most popular guidebooks, and the subwwway section links you to the most useful travel resources elsewhere on the Web.

The following sites have information on Nepal and lots of links to other sites:

Catmando.com (Ⓦ www.catmando.com) A hip gateway site with lots of ads as well as a link to Radio Nepal

Explore Nepal (Ⓦ www.explorenepal.com) Another good gateway information site with many links set up by category

Food Nepal (Ⓦ www.food-nepal.com) Excellent introduction to Nepali food and ingredients; with recipes from a mango lassi to chicken chilli

Go to Kathmandu (Ⓦ www.go2kathmandu.com) Good travel site with a comprehensive range of topics and links

Himalayan Explorers Club (HEC) (Ⓦ www.hec .org) This nonprofit Western and Nepali organisation facilitates good environmentally sound experiences for travellers. Whether it's volunteer teaching you're after or you just want to hang in the clubhouse, check out this site.

Muktinath Foundation International (Ⓦ www .muktinath.org) Information on the sacred site of Muktinath on the Annapurna Circuit, with useful, up-to-date travel information on the region

Nepal.Com (Ⓦ www.nepal.com) Another gateway site with mostly commercial links, though finding info can be a bit laborious

Nepal Home Page (Ⓦ www.info-nepal.com) A site with good information, yellow pages, festival dates, recipes and a FAQ page

Nepal News (Ⓦ www.nepalnews.com) An excellent site with daily news items which also carries links to all major online news media in Nepal

Nepal Now (Ⓦ www.nepalnow.com) Excellent news site with an overview of foreign media coverage of Nepal

Nepal Tourism Board (Ⓦ www.welcomenepal .com) The official site, with tourism news, promotional and some glossary pics

Trekinfo.Com (Ⓦ www.trekinfo.com) You guessed it – all the trekking information about the region that you'll need to get started

Trekking Agents Association of Nepal (TAAN) (Ⓦ www.taan.org.np) Offers trekking information, regulations and news, with links to the association's 300 trekking company members

Visit Nepal (Ⓦ www.visitnepal.com) A comprehensive site with detailed information for travellers and many links to organisations and companies within the country

BOOKS

There is no shortage of good books about Nepal – the Himalaya and heroic mountaineers, colourful religions and temples, the history, and brave Gurkhas have all inspired writers and photographers; the results are piled high in numerous bookshops in Nepal, of which there is a surprisingly good selection. Most are in Kathmandu and Pokhara.

The following are only some of the more interesting titles and include books that are long out of print and others that may only be available in Nepal.

Lonely Planet

There are a number of Lonely Planet books that are of interest to visitors to Nepal.

Trekking in the Nepal Himalaya, by Stan Armington, covers everything you need to know before setting out on a trek in Nepal. The book includes day-by-day coverage of all the main trekking routes, with an excellent medical section covering the problems likely to be encountered in the mountains.

Read This First: Asia & India is invaluable for first-time travellers to the region, while *Healthy Travel Asia & India* is a detailed health guide to the subcontinent and beyond.

Travel with Children, by Cathy Lanigan, is a handy reference for travellers who want to take the kids; and for an introduction to the language try the *Nepali phrasebook*.

Shopping for Buddhas, by Jeff Greenwald, is a funny, astute book about the author's travels in Nepal, motivated by the obsessive pursuit of a perfect statue of the Buddha, and perfect Buddhist stupas are depicted in his hard-cover, colour-illustrated *Buddhist Stupas in Asia: The Shape of Perfection*.

A Season in Heaven: True Tales from the Road to Kathmandu, by David Tomory, documents a series of oral histories recalling the heady overland days of the late '60s and early '70s. Two chapters concentrate on Nepal.

Guidebooks

Nepal Namaste, by Robert Rieffel, is an excellent locally produced English-language book with all sorts of odd titbits of information.

The Himalaya Experience, by Jonathan Chester, provides an interesting, colourful appetite-whetter for the entire Himalayan region. It has a great deal of information about trekking and climbing as well as some wonderful photographs.

White Water Nepal, by Peter Knowles, is a must for anyone seriously interested in rafting and kayaking, and especially anyone contemplating a private expedition – it's widely available in Kathmandu. It has detailed information on river routes, 60 maps, river profiles and hydrographs, plus advice on equipment and health.

Mountaineering

Every first ascent of a Himalayan peak seems to have been published, including, naturally, numerous accounts of climbing Everest.

The history of the sport is described in several books. *Himalaya*, by Herbert Tichy, describes the author's journeys in the region from the 1930s, including his ascent of Cho Oyu, the third-highest peak climbed at that time. *The Conquest of Everest*, by Sir John Hunt, is the official account of the first successful climb of the world's highest moun-tain, while *Everest*, by Walt Unsworth, is probably the best history of Everest mountaineering.

Annapurna, by Maurice Herzog, is a mountaineering classic. Herzog led the first group to reach the top of an 8000m peak, but the descent turned into a frostbitten nightmare taking them to the very outer edges of human endurance. *Annapurna South Face*, by Chris Bonington, describes in detail the planning that goes into a major expedition, the complicated logistics of the actual climb, and makes an authoritative account of a highly technical assault on a difficult face.

Everest the Hard Way, also by Bonington, describes his expedition's first ascent of the southwestern face in 1975. Bonington did not reach the top of Everest until 1985, when he set a record as the oldest Everest summiteer. He was 50 years old at the time but just nine days later his record fell to 55-year-old American climber Dick Bass.

The bestseller *Into Thin Air*, by Jon Krakauer, is an emotionally gripping story of the disastrous Everest expedition of 1996 in which eight climbers died. This was a controversial expedition as there were a number of inexperienced, paying climbers.

The Trekking Peaks of Nepal, by Bill O'Connor, is a complete description of the climbing routes up Nepal's 18 'trekking peaks'.

Many People Come, Looking, Looking, by the late renowned mountain-photographer Galen Rowell, is a thought-provoking study of the impact of trekking and mountaineering on the Himalayan region. There's a good description of the Annapurna Circuit and a quick side trip to knock off a little 6000m peak.

On a lighter note *The Ascent of Rum Doodle*, by WE Bowman, is a classic spoof of these often all-too-serious tomes; and *Nepal Himalaya*, by HW Tilman, gives an often-amusing account of some early trekking expeditions together with the odd mountain assault which had, by today's standards, an amazing lack of advance planning. Although Tilman was a Himalayan mountaineering pioneer he has probably contributed even more to the current popularity of trekking. His book has been republished together with other Tilman classics in *The Seven Mountain-Travel Books*. Tilman's dry wit is quite delightful.

History & Politics

End of the Line (subtitled 'The Story of the Killing of the Royals in Nepal'), by Associated Press correspondent Neelesh Misra, pieces together the night in 2001 when Prince Dipendra massacred most of his immediate family, including the king (see the boxed text 'The Royal Massacre' in the Facts about Nepal chapter). Misra's previous book *173 Hours in Captivity* chronicles the hijacking of the Indian Airlines flight from Kathmandu in December 1999.

Massacre at the Palace: The Doomed Royal Dynasty of Nepal, by Jonathan Gregson, takes a wider look at Nepal's royal family; the first half slogs through 200 years of royal intrigue before the recent massacre is examined. It's published in some countries as *Blood Against the Snows*. Gregson's previous book *Beyond the Clouds: Journeys in Search of the Himalayan Kings* is a portrait of the royal kings of the Himalaya, including the kings of Nepal and Mustang, as well as Bhutan and Sikkim.

Fatalism & Development – Nepal's Struggle for Modernization, by Nepali anthropologist Dor Bahadur Bista, is an often controversial analysis of Nepali society and its dynamics. It has a very good historical introduction, and the author looks especially critically at the role of the caste system.

Travels in Nepal, by Charlie Pye-Smith, is a travel account with an interesting theme; the author travelled Nepal studying the impacts and benefits of foreign aid to the country, and his conclusions are incisive and thought-provoking.

Culture & People

People of Nepal, by Dor Bahadur Bista, describes the many and diverse ethnic groupings found in the country. *High Religion*, by Sherry B Ortner, is probably the best introduction to Sherpa history, culture, religion and traditional society. Changes in trading patterns and cultures among Nepal's Himalayan people are examined in *Himalayan Traders*, by C Von Furer Haimendorf.

Nepal – the Kingdom in the Himalaya, by Toni Hagen, is one of the most complete studies of Nepal's people, geography and geology. Hagen has travelled extensively through Nepal since the 1950s, and the book reflects his intimate knowledge of the country and also has fine colour plates. This is one of the best and most up-to-date references available.

Tiger for Breakfast, by Michel Peissel, is a biography of the colourful gentleman who was probably the best-known resident expatriate in the kingdom: Boris Lissanevitch of the Royal Hotel and Yak & Yeti Restaurant in Kathmandu.

The lives and roles of women in Nepal are examined in the insightful *The Violet Shyness of Their Eyes: Notes from Nepal*, by Barbara J Scot and *Nepali Aama*, by Broughton Coburn, which details the life of a remarkable Gurung woman.

Natural History

The Heart of the Jungle, by KK Gurung, details the wildlife of Royal Chitwan National Park.

Birds of Nepal, by Robert Fleming Sr, Robert Fleming Jr & Lain Singh Bangdel, is a field guide to Nepal's many hundreds of birds, while the book of the same by Richard Grimmett & Carol Inskipp is a comprehensive paperback with line drawings. *Birdwatchers' Guide to Nepal*, by Carol Inskipp, is slightly older and thus harder to get outside Nepal. Inskipp is also the author of *A Popular Guide to the Birds & Mammals of the Annapurna Conservation Area* and *Nepal's Forest Birds: Their Status and Conservation*.

The flora of Nepal is described in *Himalayan Flowers & Trees*, by Dorothy Mierow & Tirtha Bahadur Shrestha – the best available field guide to the plants of Nepal, and *Flowers of the Himalaya*, by Oleg Polunin & Adam Stainton, also available in a concise version that covers 1000 flowers with 700 colour plates.

Art & Architecture

The Art of Nepal, by Lydia Aran, is readily available in Nepal and concentrates on the art that can actually be seen in the country, and *Nepal – Art Treasures from the Himalaya*, by Waldschmidt, describes and has illustrations of many Nepali works of art. *Himalayan Art*, by Madanjeet Singh, covers the art of the whole Himalayan region and features excellent photographs.

Kathmandu Valley Towns, by Fran Hosken, looks at the temples, people, history and festivals of the towns of the Kathmandu Valley. The book is illustrated with a great many black-and-white and colour photographs.

Nepal, by Michael Hutt, is an excellent guide to the art and architecture of the Kathmandu Valley. The book outlines the main forms of art and architecture, and then goes on to describe specific sites within the valley, often with layout plans. It features excellent colour plates, and black-and-white photos.

Also featuring great photography is *Power Places of Kathmandu*, by Kevin Bubriski & Keith Dowman. Bubriski provides photos of the valley's most important sacred sites and temples, while noted Buddhist scholar Dowman provides the interesting text.

Tibetan Rugs, by Hallvard Kåre Kuløøy, is a fascinating and well-illustrated introduction to the subject. If you enjoy the Tibetan rugs made in Nepal you may be disappointed to find that the author summarily dismisses modern rugs as doing 'very little justice to a very splendid tradition'.

Travel & Literature

The Snow Leopard, by Peter Matthiessen, is, on one level, an account of a trek to Dolpo in the west of Nepal, keeping an eye open for snow leopards on the way. On another level, however, this moving and beautiful book pursues 'the big questions' of spirituality, nature and Buddhism, with the Himalaya as a constant background. This is one of our favourite books.

Stones of Silence is by Matthiessen's companion on the trek, George Schaller. The work depicts the same journey, along with an account of various journeys in the Himalaya.

Arresting God in Kathmandu, by Samrat Upadhyay, is an engaging, evocative and very readable series of short stories set in Kathmandu, by an author billed as the first Nepali writer writing in English (now living in the US). The author's new novel *Guru of Love* is due out soon.

Chomolungma Sings the Blues: Travels Around Everest, by Ed Douglas, is an interesting portrait of the communities that live in the shadow of Everest and how they continue to deal with the social and environmental problems brought by trekkers and mountaineers attracted to the world's most enigmatic peak. It's a good alternative to the blinding testosterone of most climbing books.

Himalayan Voices, by Michael Hutt, subtitled 'An Introduction to Modern Nepali Literature', includes work by contemporary poets and short-story writers.

To the Navel of the World, by Peter Somerville-Large, is an amusingly written account of a saunter around Nepal and Tibet. The author does some deep-winter trekking, using yaks, in the Solu Khumbu region and up to the Everest Base Camp. His encounters with tourism in remote locations are very funny.

Travelers' Tales Nepal, edited by Rajendra Khadka, is a collection of 37 interesting and wide-ranging stories from a variety of writers, including Peter Matthiessen and Jimmy Carter. It is one in a series published by Travelers' Tales Inc.

Video Night in Kathmandu, by Pico Iyer, gallivants all around Asia, but the single chapter on Nepal has some astute and amusing observations on the collision between Nepali tradition and Western culture, particularly video culture.

The Waiting Land: A Spell in Nepal, by Dervla Murphy, is an interesting account of a visit to Nepal at a time when great changes were at hand. The author tells of her time spent in a Tibetan refugee camp near Pokhara, and of her travels in the Langtang region.

FILMS

Despite its stunning scenery, Nepal is used as a film location surprisingly rarely. Perhaps the best-known film shot here is Bertolucci's *Little Buddha* which was filmed at Bhaktapur's Durbar Square. The Imax film *Everest* has proved very popular and is credited by some as having significantly boosted the number of people wanting to trek in the Everest region.

More recently, Oscar-nominated, Nepali-French co-production *Caravan*, directed by Eric Valli, has been a huge success. It was renamed for distribution abroad as *Himalaya*, and has some magnificent footage of the Nepali landscape. It was shot mostly in the Upper Dolpo district of western Nepal.

Basantpur by Neer Shah, the co-producer of *Caravan*, is a recent Nepali film depicting the intrigues and conspiracies of life at the Rana court. It owes something to Bollywood 'masala movies' (a little bit of everything) and is based on a historical novel written nearly 60 years ago.

Another recent Nepali film to look out for is *Mukundo* (Mask of Desire) directed by Tsering Rita Sherpa, which explores secular and spiritual desires in Kathmandu.

NEWSPAPERS & MAGAZINES

Nepal's main English-language daily paper, *Rising Nepal*, is basically a government mouthpiece. For a more balanced view of local issues there's the daily *Kathmandu Post* or the weekly *Nepali Times*, which really tackles the main issues in depth and gives some interesting insights into local politics. *Spotlight* is a local weekly current affairs magazine that is also worth a look.

For international news you'll have to look farther afield. The *International Herald Tribune* and *Le Monde* are widely available in Kathmandu, as are *Time* and *Newsweek* – for the bargain price of Rs 70. Indian dailies such as the *Statesman* or the *Times of India* can also be found.

Himal South Asia is a bimonthly magazine mainly devoted to development and environment issues. It's an excellent publication with top-class contributors.

The glossy *Travellers Nepal* and *Nepal Traveller* are competing free monthly tourist magazines distributed at many hotels. They often have articles about sightseeing, festivals, trekking and other activities in Nepal, in addition to directories of airlines, embassies etc.

A number of Nepali newspapers and magazines are online. The best sites are ⓦ www.nepalnews.com, ⓦ www.nepalnews.net and ⓦ www.kantipuronline.com (the latter has the online *Kathmandu Post*).

RADIO & TV

Radio Nepal has news bulletins in English at 8am, 1.05pm and 8pm daily (for a text version 'tune in' online at ⓦ www.catmando .com).

In the Kathmandu Valley, two popular commercial FM radio stations playing contemporary Western and local music are Kantipur FM (96.1 MHz) and Hits FM (92.1 MHz). A station that plays a bit of everything, from John Lennon to Ravi Shankar, is HBC FM (104 MHz).

In Kathmandu you can listen to the BBC World Service (in English and Nepali) on Radio Sagarmatha (102.4FM).

Nepal Television is the local station, which has an English news bulletin at 10pm. Satellite TV is common. Most mid-range and top-end hotels have dishes, and you can watch everything from the BBC World Service to American wrestling.

PHOTOGRAPHY & VIDEO

Bringing a video camera to Nepal poses no real problem, and there are no video fees to worry about. The exception to this is in Upper Mustang and Langtang border regions where an outrageous US$1000 fee is levied.

Film & Equipment

There are numerous camera and film shops in Kathmandu and Pokhara and good-quality film is readily available. Do check, however, that the packaging has not been tampered with, and that the expiry date has not been exceeded. Out in the smaller cities and towns there is little choice and even greater chance of coming across expired film.

Colour-print film can be processed rapidly, competently and economically in Kathmandu and Pokhara, and there are numerous places offering a same-day service for print film.

Typically, Fujicolor 100 36-exposure colour print film costs about Rs 150. Developing is typically Rs 40 plus around Rs 5 to Rs 10 for each print.

Slide film costs Rs 410 to Rs 450 for Provia or Sensia (100 or 200 ASA) and Rs 300 for Elitechrome (100 ASA), though Sensia film can be in short supply. Slide processing costs between Rs 300 and Rs 360 for 36 shots.

New camera equipment is surprisingly cheap in Nepal. The range of cameras and lenses is also good, although digital cameras have yet to come on the scene. New Rd in central Kathmandu is the best place to look. Just be sure to ascertain whether what you are buying has an international warranty.

Technical Tips

Nepal is an exceptionally scenic country so bring plenty of film. To photograph Nepal's diverse attractions you need a variety of lenses, from a wide-angle lens if you're shooting inside compact temple compounds to a long telephoto lens if you're after perfect mountain shots or close-ups of wildlife. A polarising filter is useful to increase contrast and bring out the blue of the sky.

Remember to allow for the intensity of mountain light when setting exposures at high altitude. At the other extreme it's surprising how often you find the light in Nepal is insufficient. Early in the morning, in dense jungle in Royal Chitwan National Park, or in gloomy temples and narrow streets, you may often find yourself wishing you had high-speed film. A flash is often necessary for shots inside temples or to 'fill in' shots of sculptures and reliefs.

Restrictions

It is not uncommon for temple guardians to disallow photos of their temple, and these wishes should be respected. Don't photograph army camps, checkposts or bridges.

Photographing People

Most Nepalis are content to have their photograph taken, but always ask permission first. Sherpa people are an exception and can be very camera shy. Bear in mind that if someone poses for you (especially sadhus – holy men), they may insist on being given *baksheesh* (donations).

Respect people's privacy; most Nepalis are extremely modest. Although people carry out many activities in public (they have no choice), it does not follow that passers-by have the right to watch or take photographs. Riverbanks and village wells, for example, are often used to wash at, but the users expect consideration and privacy.

Religious ceremonies are also often private affairs, so first ask yourself whether it would be acceptable for a tourist to intrude and take photographs at a corresponding event in your home country – then get explicit permission from the senior participants. The behaviour of many photographers at places such as Pashupatinath in the Kathmandu Valley (the most holy cremation site in Nepal) is deeply embarrassing. Imagine the outrage a busload of scantily clad, camera-toting tourists would create if they invaded a family funeral in the West.

Airport Security

All luggage (including carry-on cabin baggage) is X-rayed at Kathmandu's Tribhuvan airport on the way in and the way out of the country; signs on the X-ray equipment state that the machines are not film-safe for undeveloped film. Have exposed film inspected manually when leaving the country.

TIME

Nepal is five hours and 45 minutes ahead of GMT; this curious time differential is intended to make it very clear that Nepal is a separate place to India, where the time is five hours and 30 minutes ahead of GMT! There is no daylight saving time in Nepal.

When it's noon in Nepal it's 1.15am in New York, 6.15am in London, 1.15pm in Bangkok, 2.15pm in Tibet, 4.15pm in Sydney and 10.15pm the previous day in Los Angeles, not allowing for daylight saving or other local variations.

ELECTRICITY

Electricity is only found in major towns and some odd outposts such as Namche Bazaar in the Solu Khumbu. When available it is 220V/50 cycles – 120V appliances from the USA will need a transformer.

Sockets usually take the three-round-pin plugs, sometimes the small variety, sometimes the large. Some sockets take plugs with two round pins. Local electrical shops sell cheap adapters.

Outside Kathmandu blackouts ('load-shedding') are a fact of life and can be random or regular. In winter, power shortages are endemic, especially if there has been low rainfall in the previous monsoon (which means water flow is reduced and the hydro-electric resources have to be rationed).

Power surges are also likely. If you are using expensive equipment such as a computer it is worth buying a volt guard with spike suppressor (automatic cut-off switch). These are available from most electronic shops for around Rs 1000.

LAUNDRY

There are no public laundrettes in Nepal. Hotels generally discourage guests from doing their own laundry, especially in Kathmandu where water shortages are common. Most hotels (and some dry-cleaners) have a laundry service, and this is generally very reasonably priced at Rs 10 to Rs 20 per item.

TOILETS

Throughout the country, the 'squat toilet' is the norm except in hotels and guesthouses geared towards tourists.

Next to the typical squat toilet is a bucket and/or tap. This water supply has a two-fold function: flushing the toilet and cleaning the nether regions (with the left hand only) while still squatting over the toilet. More rustic toilets in rural areas may simply consist of a few planks precariously positioned over a hole in the ground.

Public toilets are rare, but can usually be found in bus stations, larger hotel lobbies and airports, although the worst of these will leave you gagging for days. While on the road between towns and villages, it is acceptable to go discreetly behind a tree or bush.

HEALTH

Travel health depends on your predeparture preparations, your daily health care while travelling and how you handle any medical problem that may develop. While the potential dangers can seem quite frightening, in reality few travellers experience anything more than an upset stomach – usually just travellers diarrhoea. Taking care over water and food can minimise your chances.

Kathmandu's pollution levels can very quickly give you a sore throat, a cold and a hacking cough. Fresh ginger is good for sore throats, but the only real way to recover is to get out of the city and the pollution.

In summer and in particular when trekking make sure you drink enough – don't rely on feeling thirsty to indicate when you should drink. Always carry a water bottle with you on long trips.

Predeparture Planning

Make sure you're healthy before you start travelling. If you are going on a long trip make sure your teeth are OK. Always take a spare pair of glasses and your prescription.

If you require a particular medication take an adequate supply, as it may not be available locally. Take part of the packaging showing the generic name rather than the brand, which will make getting replacements easier. Have a legible prescription or letter from your doctor to show that you legally use the medication to avoid any problems.

Anyone with known heart disease should carry a recent copy of their ECG. This is useful in aiding quick diagnosis of problems that may arise.

Immunisations Plan ahead for getting your vaccinations; some of them require more than one injection, while some vaccinations should not be given together. Note that some vaccinations should not be given during pregnancy or to people with allergies – discuss this with your doctor.

It is recommended you seek medical advice at least six weeks before travel. Be aware that there is often a greater risk of disease with children and during pregnancy.

Discuss your requirements and itinerary in detail with your doctor, but vaccinations you should consider for this trip include the following (for more details about the diseases themselves, see the individual disease entries later in this section).

Diphtheria & Tetanus Vaccinations for these two diseases are usually combined and are recommended for everyone. After an initial course of three injections (usually given in childhood), booster injections are necessary every 10 years.

Hepatitis A The hepatitis A vaccine (eg, Avaxim, Havrix 1440 or VAQTA) provides long-term immunity (possibly for more than 10 years) after an initial injection and a booster at six to 12 months. Alternatively, an injection of gamma globulin can provide short-term protection against hepatitis A for two to four months. It is not a vaccine, but is a ready-made antibody collected from blood donations. It is reasonably effective and, unlike the vaccine, it is protective immediately. Hepatitis A vaccine is also available in a combined form (Twinrix) with hepatitis B vaccine. Three injections over a six-month period are required, the first two providing substantial protection against hepatitis A.

Hepatitis B Travellers who should consider vaccination against hepatitis B include those on a long trip, as well as those visiting countries where there are high levels of hepatitis B infection, where blood transfusions may not be adequately screened or where sexual contact or needle sharing is a possibility. Vaccination involves three injections over six months.

Japanese B Encephalitis Consider vaccination against this mosquito-borne disease if spending a month or longer in the Terai during the monsoon (August to October). This vaccination involves three injections over 30 days.

Malaria Medication Antimalarial drugs do not prevent you from being infected, but do kill the malaria parasites during a stage in their development and significantly reduce the risk of you becoming very ill or dying. Expert advice on medication should be sought, as there are many factors to consider, including the area to be visited (there is virtually no risk of contracting malaria in Nepal outside of the Terai region), the side effects of medication, your medical history, your age and whether you are pregnant.

Meningococcal Meningitis Centers for Disease Control (CDC) in the USA has removed its recommendation for this vaccine for travel to Nepal, but it is a very safe, cheap and highly effective vaccine that should be considered by long-term travellers and expats.

Polio Although virtually nonexistent in the West these days, polio is still prevalent in Nepal. Keep up to date with this vaccination, normally given in childhood, with a booster (drops of vaccine) once as an adult.

Rabies This is a viral brain infection transmitted to humans from animals, usually dogs. Vaccination should be considered by those who will spend a month or longer in a country where rabies is common, especially if they are cycling, handling animals, caving or travelling to remote areas, and particularly for children (who may not report a bite). Pretravel rabies vaccination involves having three injections over 21 to 28 days. If someone who has been vaccinated is bitten or scratched by an animal, they will require two booster injections of vaccine; those not vaccinated require more. The human rabies immune globulin (HRIG) is available in Kathmandu.

Typhoid Vaccination against typhoid is never 100% effective but it does offer good protection. It is advisable for travel to Nepal, and is available either as an injection or as capsules to be taken orally.

Yellow Fever A yellow fever vaccine is the only vaccine that is a legal requirement for entry into many countries, including Nepal, but this only applies when coming from an infected area (parts of Africa and South America).

Health Guides Lonely Planet's *Healthy Travel Asia & India*, by Dr Isabelle Young, is packed with answers to all the common health questions.

Follow the Health link on the Lonely Planet site (**w** www.lonelyplanet.com) for links to the World Health Organization (WHO) and the US Centers for Disease Control and Prevention (CDC).

Kathmandu's **CIWEC Clinic Travel Medicine Center** has an excellent interactive website at **w** www.ciwec-clinic.com for medical advice on travel in Nepal. Email advice is available.

Basic Rules

Food Vegetables and fruit should be washed with purified water or peeled where possible. Beware of ice cream that is sold in the street or anywhere it might have been melted and refrozen; if there's any doubt (eg, if there's been a power cut in the last day or two), steer well clear.

Water The number one rule is *be careful of the water*, especially ice, and don't drink the tap water.

In actual fact, the relative safety of the water varies with the season. During the dry season (November to April) you will probably get away with drinking the tap water, in Kathmandu at least. During the monsoon, however, when the heavy rains wash all sorts of stuff into the water supply, don't even think about it. Drinking boiled and filtered water is the best idea at any time of year and absolutely imperative in the wet season.

At high altitudes the water is generally safer than it is lower down and in more densely populated areas. Nevertheless, trekkers should never drink water from springs or streams unless they are absolutely positive they are at a higher level than any villages or cattle. In Nepal that is a very hard thing to guarantee and it is always wiser to prepare your drinking water carefully.

Bottled water is available everywhere and is safe to drink, but the unrecyclable plastic bottles are creating a huge litter problem. The best alternative is to have your own water bottle and to treat the water with iodine. This is 100% safe and has the added benefit of not requiring a fire. There are some people for whom iodine is unsuitable, notably pregnant women and those with iodine allergies or thyroid problems.

Take care with fruit juice, particularly if water may have been added. Milk should be treated with suspicion, as it is often unpasteurised, though boiled milk is fine if it is kept hygienically. Tea or coffee should be OK, since the water should have been boiled.

Water Purification The simplest way of purifying water is to boil it. Vigorous boiling is enough to kill most pathogens, even at an altitude where the boiling point is lower (at Everest Base Camp water boils at 83°C).

Consider purchasing a water filter for a long trip. When buying a filter read the specifications, so that you know exactly what it removes from the water and what it doesn't as simple filtering will not remove all dangerous organisms. Chlorine and iodine will kill many pathogens, including parasites such as Giardia and amoebic cysts, but cyclospora and cryptosporidium cysts are both highly resistant to chemical treatment.

Environmental Hazards
Acute Mountain Sickness Lack of oxygen at high altitudes (over 2500m) affects

most people to some extent. As less oxygen reaches the muscles and the brain, the heart and lungs compensate by working harder, resulting in acute mountain sickness (AMS) or altitude sickness. Symptoms usually develop during the first 24 to 48 hours at high altitude. Mild symptoms include headache, lethargy, dizziness, difficulty sleeping and loss of appetite. AMS may become more severe without warning and can be fatal. Severe symptoms include breathlessness, a dry, irritable cough (which may progress to the production of pink, frothy sputum), severe headache, lack of coordination and balance, confusion, irrational behaviour, vomiting, drowsiness and eventually unconsciousness. There is no hard-and-fast rule as to what is too high; 3500m to 4500m is the usual range, but AMS has been fatal at 3000m. More important than absolute altitude is the rate of ascent – problems are more likely to occur as a result of ascending too fast and a lack of acclimatisation.

Treat mild symptoms by resting at the same altitude until recovery, usually a day or two. Paracetamol or aspirin can be taken for headaches. If symptoms persist or become worse, however, *immediate descent is necessary*; even 500m can help. Drug treatments should never be used to avoid descent or to enable further ascent.

The drugs acetazolamide and dexamethasone are recommended by some doctors for the prevention of AMS; however, their use is controversial. They can reduce the symptoms, but they may also mask warning signs – severe and fatal AMS has occurred in people taking these drugs.

To help prevent AMS:

- Ascend slowly – have frequent rest days, spending two to three nights at each rise of 1000m. If you reach a high altitude by trekking, acclimatisation takes place gradually and you are less likely to be affected than if you fly directly to high altitude.
- It is always wise to sleep at a lower altitude than the greatest height reached during the day if possible. Also, once above 3000m, care should be taken not to increase the sleeping altitude by more than 300m per day.
- Drink extra fluids. The mountain air is dry and cold, and moisture is lost as you breathe.
- Eat light, high-carbohydrate meals
- Avoid alcohol as it may increase the risk of dehydration
- Avoid sedatives

Heat Exhaustion Dehydration and salt deficiency can cause heat exhaustion. Take time to acclimatise to high temperatures, drink sufficient liquids and do not do anything too physically demanding.

Salt deficiency is characterised by fatigue, lethargy, headaches, giddiness and muscle cramps; salt tablets won't help – adding extra salt to your food is better.

Anhidrotic heat exhaustion is a rare form of heat exhaustion that is caused by an inability to sweat. It tends to affect people who have been in a hot climate for some time, rather than newcomers. It can progress to heatstroke. Treatment involves removal to a cooler climate.

Heatstroke This serious, occasionally fatal, condition can occur if the body's heat-regulating mechanism breaks down and the body temperature rises to dangerous levels. Long, continuous periods of exposure to high temperatures and insufficient fluids can leave you vulnerable to heatstroke.

The symptoms include a sense of feeling unwell, not sweating very much (or at all) and a high body temperature (39° to 41°C or 102° to 106°F). Where sweating has ceased, the skin becomes flushed and red. Severe, throbbing headaches and lack of coordination will also occur, and the sufferer may be confused or aggressive. Eventually the victim will become delirious or convulse. Hospitalisation is essential, but in the interim get victims out of the sun, remove their clothing, cover them with a wet sheet or towel and then fan continually. Give fluids if they are conscious.

Hypothermia In Nepal's mountain regions you should always be prepared for cold, wet or windy conditions, whether you are trekking at high altitudes, out walking or hitching, or simply taking a long bus trip over mountains, particularly at night.

Hypothermia occurs when the body loses heat faster than it can produce it and the core temperature of the body falls. It is surprisingly easy to progress from very cold to dangerously cold due to a combination of wind, wet clothing, fatigue and hunger, even if the air temperature is above freezing. It is best to dress in layers; silk, wool and some of the new artificial fibres are all good insulating materials. A hat is important, as a lot of heat is lost through the head. A strong, waterproof outer layer (and a 'space' blanket for emergencies) is essential. Carry basic supplies, including fluid and food containing simple sugars, to generate heat quickly.

Symptoms of hypothermia are exhaustion, numb skin (particularly toes and fingers), shivering, slurred speech, irrational or violent behaviour, lethargy, stumbling, dizzy spells, muscle cramps and violent bursts of energy. Irrationality may take the form of sufferers claiming they are warm and trying to take off their clothes.

To treat mild hypothermia, first get the person out of the wind and/or rain, remove their clothing if it's wet, and replace it with dry, warm clothing. Give them hot liquids (not alcohol) and some high-kilojoule, easily digestible food. Do not rub victims; instead, allow them to slowly warm themselves. This should be enough to treat mild hypothermia and is the only way to prevent severe hypothermia, which is a critical condition.

Prickly Heat This is an itchy rash caused by excessive perspiration trapped under the skin. It usually strikes people who have just arrived in a hot climate. Keeping cool, bathing often, drying the skin and using a mild talcum or prickly heat powder or resorting to air-conditioning may help.

Sunburn At high altitude you can get sunburnt surprisingly quickly, even through cloud. Use a sunscreen, a hat, and a barrier cream for your nose and lips. Calamine lotion or a commercial after-sun preparation are good for mild sunburn. Protect your eyes with good-quality sunglasses, particularly if you will be near water, sand or snow.

Infectious Diseases

Diarrhoea Simple things such as a change of water, food or climate can all cause a mild bout of diarrhoea, but a few rushed toilet trips with no other symptoms is not indicative of a major problem.

Dehydration is the main danger with any diarrhoea, particularly in children or the elderly, as it can occur quite quickly. Under all circumstances *fluid replacement* (at least equal to the volume being lost) is the most important thing to remember. Weak black tea with a little sugar, soda water, or soft drinks allowed to go flat and diluted 50% with clean water are all good. With severe diarrhoea a rehydrating solution is preferable to replace lost minerals and salts. Commercially available oral rehydration salts (ORS) are very useful and available in pharmacies across Nepal (Rs 6); add them to boiled or bottled water. In an emergency you can make up a solution of six teaspoons of sugar and a half teaspoon of salt to a litre of boiled or bottled water. Stick to a bland diet as you recover.

Gut-paralysing drugs such as loperamide or diphenoxylate can be used to bring relief from the symptoms, although they do not actually cure the problem. Only use these drugs if you do not have access to toilets, eg, if you *must* travel. Note that these drugs are not recommended for children under 12 years.

In certain situations antibiotics may be required: diarrhoea with blood or mucus (dysentery), any diarrhoea with fever, profuse watery diarrhoea, persistent diarrhoea not improving after 48 hours and severe diarrhoea. In these situations, having paid attention to maintaining your hydration, it would be wise to be assessed by a doctor. Severe diarrhoea is usually bacterial in origin and this should be confirmed by a stool test.

Where this is not possible the recommended drugs for the treatment of bacterial diarrhoea are norfloxacin 400mg twice daily or ciprofloxacin 500mg twice daily for three days. However, these are not recommended for children or pregnant women, and should be avoided by those with diarrhoea and fever or bloody diarrhoea. The drug of choice for children would be naladixic acid, with the dosage dependent on weight. A five-day course is given.

Giardiasis & Amoebic Dysentery Giardiasis is caused by a common parasite, *Giardia lamblia*. Symptoms include stomach cramps, nausea, a bloated stomach, watery, foul-smelling diarrhoea and frequent gas. Giardiasis can appear several weeks after you have been exposed to the parasite. The symptoms may disappear for a few days and then return; this can go on for several weeks.

Amoebic dysentery, caused by the protozoan *Entamoeba histolytica*, is characterised by a gradual onset of low-grade diarrhoea, often with blood and mucus. Cramping, abdominal pain and vomiting are less likely than in other types of diarrhoea, and fever may not be present. It will persist until treated and can recur, causing other health problems.

You should seek medical advice if you think you have giardiasis or amoebic dysentery, but where this is not possible, tinidazole or metronidazole are the recommended drugs. Treatment is a 2g single dose of tinidazole or 400mg of metronidazole three times daily for five to 10 days.

Hepatitis This is a general term for inflammation of the liver, the most common cause of which is an infection with one of the hepatitis viruses. Viral hepatitis is a worldwide problem and is particularly prevalent in Asia. The symptoms are similar in all forms of the illness, and include fever, chills, headache, fatigue, feelings of weakness and aches and pains, followed by loss of appetite, nausea, vomiting, abdominal pain, dark urine, light-coloured faeces, jaundiced (yellow) skin and yellowing of the whites of the eyes.

Hepatitis A is transmitted by contaminated food and drinking water. You should seek medical advice, but there is not much you can do apart from resting, drinking lots of fluids, eating lightly and avoiding fatty foods.

Hepatitis E is transmitted in the same way as hepatitis A; it can be particularly serious in pregnant women, and is a common cause of hepatitis in Nepal.

There are almost 300 million chronic carriers of **hepatitis B** in the world. It is spread through contact with infected blood, blood products or body fluids, eg, through sexual contact, unsterilised needles and blood transfusions, or contact with blood via small breaks in the skin. Other risk situations include having a shave and tattooing or body piercing with contaminated equipment. The symptoms of hepatitis B may be more severe than type A and the disease can lead to long-term problems such as chronic liver damage, liver cancer or a long-term carrier state. Hepatitis C and D are spread in the same way as hepatitis B and can also lead to long-term complications.

There are vaccines against hepatitis A and B, but there are currently no vaccines against the other types of hepatitis. Following the basic rules about food and water (hepatitis A and E) and avoiding risk situations (hepatitis B, C and D) are important preventative measures.

AIDS & Prostitution in Nepal

HIV/AIDS has become a major problem in Nepal. Official figures reveal that over 2500 people in Nepal died from AIDS-related illnesses in 1999. There are an estimated 60,000 Nepalis infected with the virus, and more than 30,000 intravenous drug users in Nepal who are at risk of contracting the virus. A public education programme has been implemented, and along roadsides throughout the country you'll see billboards with cartoon pictures of condoms.

Although prostitution exists in Nepal, particularly in the border towns and along the main truck routes, it is virtually invisible to Western visitors. It is believed that over 100,000 Nepali women (many abducted from Nepal as children) work in Indian brothels, often in conditions resembling slavery, and over 30,000 of these women are estimated to be HIV positive. When obvious AIDS symptoms force these women out of work, some manage to return to Nepal. However, they are shunned by their families and there is virtually no assistance available to them or their children.

HIV/AIDS Infection with the human immunodeficiency virus (HIV) may lead to the fatal disease, acquired immune deficiency syndrome (AIDS). Any exposure to contaminated blood, blood products or body fluids may put the individual at risk. The disease is often transmitted through sexual contact or dirty needles – thus vaccinations, acupuncture, tattooing and body piercing can be as dangerous as intravenous drug use. It can also be spread through infected blood transfusions; in Nepal, blood is screened for HIV but the test may miss the disease in the 'window period' when it is not easily detected.

If you do need an injection, ask to see the syringe unwrapped in front of you, or take a needle and syringe pack with you (available from pharmacies in Nepal).

Fear of HIV infection should never preclude treatment for suspected serious medical conditions.

Meningococcal Meningitis This serious disease can be fatal. Epidemics occurred in Nepal in the 1980s but none have occurred since.

Trekkers to rural areas of Nepal should be particularly careful, as the disease is spread by close contact with people who carry it in their throats and noses and spread it through coughs and sneezes; they may not be aware that they are carriers of the disease. Lodges in the hills where travellers spend the night are prime spots for the spread of infection.

Treatment for meningitis is large doses of penicillin given intravenously, or chloramphenicol injections.

Typhoid Contaminated water and food cause this dangerous gut infection, and medical help must be sought.

In its early stages sufferers may feel they have a bad cold or flu on the way, as early symptoms are a headache, body aches and a fever which rises a little each day until it is around 40°C (104°F) or more. The victim's pulse is often slow relative to the degree of fever present – unlike a normal fever where the pulse increases. There may also be vomiting, abdominal pain, diarrhoea or constipation.

In the second week the high fever and slow pulse continue and a few pink spots may appear on the body; trembling, delirium, weakness, weight loss and dehydration may occur.

Insect-Borne Diseases

Malaria This serious and potentially fatal disease is spread by mosquitos. It is not found in the tourist areas of Nepal – the Kathmandu Valley, Pokhara and the Himalaya – but is known to exist in the lowland Terai region, particularly during the monsoon months. The risk in Royal Chitwan National Park is extremely low except in the hot months of June, July and August, when the risk is simply low.

If you are travelling in endemic areas it is extremely important to avoid mosquito bites and to take tablets to prevent this disease. Symptoms range from fever, chills and sweating, headache, diarrhoea and abdominal pains to a vague feeling of ill-health. Return to Kathmandu and seek medical help immediately if malaria is suspected. Most health facilities in Nepal are not able to diagnose malaria adequately. Without treatment malaria can rapidly become more serious and can be fatal.

Travellers are advised to avoid mosquito bites at all times by observing the following advice:

- wear light-coloured clothing
- wear long trousers and long-sleeved shirts
- use mosquito repellents containing the compound DEET on exposed areas (prolonged overuse of DEET may be harmful, especially to children, but its use is considered preferable to being bitten by disease-transmitting mosquitoes)
- avoid perfumes or aftershave
- use a mosquito net impregnated with mosquito repellent (pyrethrin) – it may be worth taking your own

Japanese B Encephalitis This viral infection of the brain is transmitted by mosquitoes. Most cases occur in rural areas as the virus exists in pigs and wading birds. Symptoms include fever, headache and alteration in consciousness. Hospitalisation is needed for correct diagnosis and treatment. There is a high mortality rate among those who have symptoms; of those who survive, many are intellectually disabled.

Bedbugs & Lice

Bedbugs mainly live in dirty mattresses and bedding, evidenced by spots of blood on bedclothes or on the wall. Bedbugs leave itchy bites in neat rows. Calamine lotion or a sting relief spray may help.

Lice cause itching and discomfort, making themselves at home in your hair (head lice), your clothing (body lice) or in your pubic hair (crabs). They are caught through direct contact with infected people or by sharing combs, clothing and the like. Powder or shampoo treatment will kill the lice. Infected clothing should then be washed in very hot, soapy water and dried in the sun.

Leeches

During the monsoon, trekkers often get these on their legs or in their boots; they attach themselves to your skin to suck your blood. Salt or a lit match will make them fall off. Don't pull them off, as the bite is more likely to become infected. Clean and apply pressure if the point of attachment is bleeding. Insect repellent may keep them away.

WOMEN TRAVELLERS

Generally speaking, Nepal is a safe country for women travellers. However, women

Ama Dablam, Everest region

BILL WASSMAN

Gosainkund Lake, Langtang National Park

STAN ARMINGTON

Machhapuchhare, near Pokhara

CHRIS MELLOR

Mustard field, the Terai

Manang, Annapurna Circuit Trek, with Gangapurna in the background

Lo Monthang, Mustang Conservation Area

should still be cautious. Nepali men may have peculiar ideas about the morality of Western women, given Nepali men's exposure to Western films portraying 'immodest' clothing and holiday flings with locals. Dress modestly, which means wearing clothes that cover the shoulders and thighs – take your cue from the local people if you need to gauge what's acceptable.

Sexual harassment is low-key but does exist. Trekking guides have been known to take advantage of their position of trust and responsibility. It's very difficult to insure against this, but the best advice is to not trek alone. The Chhetri Sisters trekking agency in Pokhara is run by women and specialises in providing women staff for treks (see Guides & Porters in the Trekking chapter for contact details).

The best chance of making contact with local women is to go trekking, as it is really only here that Nepali women have a role that brings them into contact with foreign tourists – as often as not, the man of the house is a trekking guide or porter, or is away working elsewhere, which leaves women running the lodges and the many teahouses along the routes.

GAY & LESBIAN TRAVELLERS
There's little of an open gay scene in Nepal. Homosexuality is officially illegal and gay Nepalis are subject to police harassment and blackmail. Gay couples holding hands in public will experience no difficulties, as this is socially acceptable, but public displays of intimacy *by anyone* are frowned upon.

The Blue Diamond Society (☎ 01-4427608; e cspsb@yahoo.com) is the first gay organisation in Kathmandu. It provides education, support and advice to Nepal's gay male community, and runs the country's only AIDS/HIV prevention programme. Contact Sunil Pant.

DISABLED TRAVELLERS
Wheelchair facilities, ramps and lifts (and even pavements!) are virtually nonexistent throughout Nepal and getting around the packed, twisting streets of traditional towns can be a real challenge. It is common for hotels to be multilevel, with most guest rooms on the upper floors, and many places – even mid-range establishments – do not have lifts. This being said, many lodges are built on ground level. Bathrooms equipped with grips and railings are not found anywhere, except perhaps in some of the top-end hotels.

There is no reason why a visit and even a trek could not be custom-tailored through a reliable agent for those with reasonable mobility.

Navyo Nepal (☎ 01-4280056; w www.navyonepal.com) has some experience in running cultural tours and treks for people with disabilities in Nepal and neighbouring Tibet.

A couple of useful general websites are Access-Able Travel Source (w www.access-able.com) and Accessible Journeys (w www.disabilitytravel.com).

SENIOR TRAVELLERS
Older travellers will find that their age will probably command them a certain amount of respect, but on a practical level there are no discounts or other concessions available. It's possible to hire a car and driver to get around if crowded public transport no longer appeals; see Car & Motorcycle in the Getting Around chapter for more details. Porters and guides make the trekking experience feasible for those who are unable (or unwilling) to carry huge backpacks up steep paths; see Guides & Porters in the Trekking chapter.

TRAVEL WITH CHILDREN
Few people travel with children in Nepal, yet with a bit of planning it is remarkably hassle-free. As always, children are great ice-breakers, and the local hospitality and friendliness shines through even more when you throw a couple of kids into the equation.

In the main tourist centres (Kathmandu and Pokhara), most hotels will have triple rooms, and quite often rooms with four beds, which are ideal for families with young children. Finding a room with a bath tub can be a problem at the bottom end of the market. Garden space is at a premium in Kathmandu hotels, but many places have a roof garden, and some of these can be good play areas for kids. Check thoroughly, however, as some are definitely not safe for young children.

One of the hardest parts about life on the road with kids in Nepal is eating out at restaurants. While the food is excellent and there's always something on the menu which will appeal to kids – even if it's only chips or banana porridge – service is usually quite slow.

By the time the food arrives your kids will be bored stiff and ready to leave. You can minimise the hassles by eating breakfast at your hotel, having lunch at a place with a garden (there are plenty of these) where the children can let off steam, and in the evening going to the restaurant armed with pencils, colouring books, stories and other distractions to keep them busy for half an hour. Pilgrims Bookstore in Kathmandu has a fine collection of kid's books, including colouring books. Away from the tourist areas highchairs are virtually nonexistent and finding nonspicy food children will eat may be more of a problem.

Walking the crowded and narrow streets of Kathmandu can be a hassle with young kids unless you can get them up off the ground – a backpack is ideal, but a pusher or stroller would be more trouble than it's worth unless you bring one with oversize wheels.

One of the most rewarding things to do with kids is to take them trekking in the mountains – see the 'Independent Trekking with Children' boxed text in the Trekking chapter for more details.

Disposable nappies are available in Kathmandu and Pokhara, but for a price – better to bring them with you if possible. Cloth nappies can be a headache, but remember that disposable nappies are almost indestructible, and waste disposal in Nepal is already a major problem.

Check out Lonely Planet's *Travel With Children* for handy hints and advice about the pros and cons of travelling with children.

DANGERS & ANNOYANCES
Theft
While petty theft is not on the scale that exists in many countries, reports of theft from hotel rooms in tourist areas (including along trekking routes) are fairly commonplace, and theft with violence is not unheard of. Never store valuables or money in your hotel room.

One of the most common forms of theft is the rifling of backpacks on the roofs of buses. Try to make your pack as theft-proof as possible – small padlocks and cover bags are a good deterrent. It is also not unheard of for things to go missing out of backpacks at Kathmandu's Tribhuvan airport.

There's little chance of ever retrieving your gear if it is stolen, and even getting a police report for an insurance claim can be difficult. Try the tourist police, or if there aren't any, the local police station. If you're not getting anywhere, go to **Interpol** (☎ 01-4412602) at the Police Headquarters in Naxal, Kathmandu. The documentation requires a passport photo and photocopies of your passport and visa; the process takes two days.

Safety while Trekking
Fired up by the gung-ho stories of adventurous travellers, it is also easy to forget that mountainous terrain is always potentially dangerous. Rescue services in foreign countries are limited and medical facilities are often primitive or nonexistent. Only a tiny minority of trekkers end up in trouble, but accidents can often be avoided or the risks minimised if people have a realistic understanding of trekking requirements. See the Trekking Safely section in the Trekking chapter for more advice.

There have been a couple of cases of trekking lodges burning to the ground after a kerosene stove explosion. It pays to scope out a possible exit route from all hotels and lodges you stay in.

Government Travel Advice

Most governments publish travel advisories: Consular Information Sheets include entry requirements, medical facilities, and areas of general instability; travel warnings highlight areas with health and safety risks, civil unrest or other dangers; and public announcements may have late-breaking information.

You can view travel advisories at the following sites:

Australian Department of Foreign Affairs (travel advice line ☎ 06-6261 3305/1111, [W] www.dfat.gov.au/consular/advice)
British Foreign Office Travel Advice Unit (☎ 020-7008 0232/3, travel advice line 0374-500900, fax 020-7008 0155, [W] www .fco.gov.uk/travel) Old Admiralty Building, London SW1A 2PA, UK
New Zealand Ministry of Foreign Affairs and Trade (☎ 04-439 8000, [W] www.mft .govt.nz/travel/index.html)
USA Dept of State (24-hour travel warnings ☎ 202-647 5225, fax 202-647 3000, [W] www .travel.state.gov/travel_warnings.html)

Maoists

The seven-year Maoist 'people's war' has cost nearly 8000 lives so far (for details see History in the Facts about Nepal chapter). The Maoists are more of a threat to the tourist industry than to individual tourists who have never been specifically targeted. Bombs have been exploded in areas of Kathmandu and Patan visited by tourists, however, and there have been several high-profile examples of trekking groups who have been forced by armed gangs to pay protection money of hundreds of dollars. Several groups have had cameras stolen. Night curfews are in effect in many towns across Nepal.

Various governments offer advice on which areas they deem unsafe; most of these are remote and in mid-western Nepal. At the time of research, the Kathmandu Valley, the Annapurna region, the Everest Base Camp Trek and the Mahendra Hwy in the Terai were all unaffected, except for the occasional tedious checkpoint. Lukla airport (the main gateway to the Everest region) was attacked by Maoist rebels in 2002. The Dolpo, Jumla, Jiri and Kanchenjunga trekking regions were off limits in early 2003.

Most travel warnings focus on administrative districts, which aren't shown on many maps. For an administrative map of Nepal, go to W www.ncthakur.itgo.com/map04.htm. Travelling through these districts on major highways should not be a problem, but you'll be quizzed at checkpoints – don't travel at night. The situation is very fluid so you should always check the government travel advisories listed in the boxed text 'Government Travel Advice' before travelling.

It is hoped that the current cease-fire between the government and the Maoists will lead to a meaningful peace.

Strikes & Demonstrations

Nepal's political process involves frequent demonstrations and strikes, and these have become even more prevalent in the last couple of years. They are generally peaceful, but any large gathering of people can cause problems. Often there are processions in the street and meetings in Tundikhel, the parade ground in the centre of Kathmandu. It's best to avoid large groups of slogan-chanting youths, in case you end up on the downstream side of a police *lathi* charge (a team of police wielding bamboo staves) or worse.

A normal procession or demonstration is a *julus*. If things escalate there may be a *chakka jam* (jam the wheels), when all vehicles stay off the street, or a *bandh*, when all shops, schools and offices are closed as well. If you've booked a flight during one of these events, you may end up travelling in a bicycle rickshaw at an outrageous price. When roads are closed the government runs blue buses with armed policemen from the airport to major hotels, departing from the Sanchaya Kosh Bhawan Shopping Centre at the east end of Greater Thamel.

Traffic, Pollution & Hassle

Traffic on Kathmandu's streets is a rumpus of pollution-belching vehicles with two, three and four wheels wending their way around a mass of people and animals. The combination of ancient vehicles, low-quality fuel and lack of emission controls makes the streets of Kathmandu particularly dirty, noisy and unpleasant. Traffic rules exist, but are rarely enforced; be especially careful when crossing streets or riding a bicycle – traffic is supposed to travel on the left side of the road, but many drivers simply choose the most convenient side, which can make walking in Kathmandu a highly stressful experience.

Dasain Stoppages

Dasain (15 days in September or October) is the most important of all Nepali celebrations. Tens of thousands of Nepalis hit the road to return home to celebrate with their families. This means that while villages are full of life if you are trekking, buses and planes are fully booked and overflowing, porters may be hard to find (or more expensive than usual) and cars are hard to hire. Many hotels and restaurants in regional towns close down completely, and doing business in Kathmandu (outside Thamel) becomes almost impossible.

The most important days, when everything comes to a total halt, are the ninth day (when thousands of animals are sacrificed), and the 10th day (when blessings are received from elder relatives and superiors). Banks and government offices are generally closed from the eighth day of the festival to the 12th day. The final day of Dasain is on the full moon in September or October.

Consider bringing a face mask to filter out dust and emission particles if you plan to ride a bicycle or motorcycle in Kathmandu.

A minor hassle in Thamel comes from a barrage of irritating flute sellers, tiger balm sellers, chess set sellers, musical instrument sellers, hashish sellers, travel agency touts and rickshaw drivers. In Kathmandu's and Patan's Durbar Squares you'll also come across a string of would-be guides whose trade has been badly hit by the downturn in tourism. There's less hassle in Bhaktapur, though there are some persistent *thangka* (Tibetan paintings on cotton) touts.

Scams

Be aware if offered deals by gem dealers (especially in Thamel, Kathmandu) that involve you buying stones to sell for a 'vast profit' at home. The dealers' stories vary, but are usually along the lines of the dealer not being able to export the stones without paying heavy taxes, so the idea is you take them and meet the dealer when you get home, he will sell them to his local contact and you both share the profit. Falling for this ruse is not as unusual among travellers as you might expect.

Other scams include young kids asking for milk; you buy the milk at a designated store at an inflated price, the kid then returns the milk and pockets some of the mark-up (you can prevent this by opening the milk).

Credit card scam is not unusual; travellers have bought some souvenirs only to find thousand of dollars worth of Internet porn subscriptions chalked up on their bill.

LEGAL MATTERS

Hashish has been banned since 1973, but illegal or not, it's readily available in Nepal. Thamel is full of shifty, whispering dealers. Possession of a small amount involves little risk, although potential smokers should keep the less-than-salubrious condition of Nepali jails firmly in mind. Don't try taking any out of the country either – travellers have been arrested at the airport on departure.

If you get caught smuggling something serious – drugs or gold – chances are you'll end up in jail, without trial, and will remain there until someone pays for you to get out. Jail conditions in Nepal are reportedly horrific. Bribery may be an option to avoid jail in the first place, but this is an extremely

sensitive area in which to dabble and unless you can do it in a way which is deniable, you may just end up in deeper strife.

A handful of foreigners currently languish in jails in Kathmandu. If you want to pay a humanitarian visit you can contact your embassy for a list of names and their locations. Take along items of practical use, such as reading matter, blankets, and fresh fruit.

BUSINESS HOURS

Most government offices in Kathmandu are open from 10am to 5pm Monday to Saturday during summer and 9am to 4pm during the winter (roughly mid-November to mid-February). Offices close at 3pm on Friday. Sunday is the weekly holiday and most shops and all offices and banks will be closed. Museums are generally closed on Sunday and Monday. See also Public Holidays following.

PUBLIC HOLIDAYS

Many holidays and festivals affect the working hours of government offices and banks, which close for the following public holidays and some or all of the days of the following festivals (note this list is not exhaustive). See the Major Festivals Calendar in the special section 'Festivals of Nepal' for the exact dates of the festivals, which vary annually.

Prithvi Narayan Shah's Birthday 10 January
Basant Panchami January/February
Democracy Day 18 February
Maha Shivaratri February/March
Bisket Jatra (Nepali New Year) 13/14 April
King's Birthday 7 July
Janai Purnima July/August
Teej August/September
Indra Jatra September
Dasain September/October
Tihar October/November
Constitution Day 9 November

ACTIVITIES

Nepal is one of the world's top destinations for **trekking**; offers spectacular **mountain biking**; and has some of the world's best **white-water rafting**.

We have dedicated chapters to each of these activities: see the Trekking, Mountain Biking and Rafting & Kayaking chapters for detailed explanations of how to make the most of these sports in Nepal.

[Continued on page 76]

RESPONSIBLE TOURISM

Tourism, in particular trekking, is having a great environmental and social impact in Nepal. The local communities in or around popular tourist routes have been hugely affected by tourism, for both better and worse, but usually without having a say in the matter.

It is an irony that we as travellers often inadvertently damage the very things we came to see: we crave to get off the beaten track and end up creating another beaten track; we want to experience traditional culture but don't want to lose our foreign comforts; and we are often disappointed when traditional villages adopt modern housing, transport and dress – things we would not question in our own culture. These are among the many contradictions – inherent in travel – you will face when visiting Nepal.

A few tour operators, both abroad and in Nepal, are making conscious efforts to address these problems, but it's slow going. The best companies are those that have a serious commitment to protecting the fragile ecosystems in these and other areas, and which direct at least some portion of profits back into local communities. Although these won't always be the cheapest trips, the extra money you spend is an important way to contribute to the future of the areas you visit.

There are several good examples of how tourism can act as a positive force. **Explore Nepal** (☎ 01-4248942; W www.xplorenepal.com.np) in Kamaladi, Kathmandu operates a number of 'clean-up treks', where participants are involved in helping clean up villages along the trekking routes. The company's director was at the forefront of the campaign to have polluting three-wheeler Vikram tempos banned from the Kathmandu Valley. Its Hotel Kantipur Temple House in Kathmandu recycles its water and has banned plastic goods from the hotel.

The gorgeous **Dwarika's Village Hotel** in Kathmandu funds a large workshop where craftspeople patiently repair and restore fretwork windows and carvings that would otherwise almost certainly be lost in Kathmandu's rush to survive and modernise. These pieces are then incorporated into the hotel decor.

One important contribution you can make is to reduce the growing mountains of waste plastic in village rubbish heaps by not buying bottles of mineral water; instead carry a water bottle and filter or treat the water with iodine. If you absolutely *must* buy bottled water at least buy one 2L bottle, rather than two 1L bottles.

Your very presence in Nepal will certainly have an effect – some people say an increasingly negative one. The challenge for you as a visitor to Nepal is to respect the rights and beliefs of the local people, and to minimise your impact – culturally and environmentally. The further you venture off the beaten track, the greater your responsibility as a visitor becomes. As the cliche goes, 'the Himalaya is there to change you, not for you to change the Himalaya.'

Economic Choices

As the country's third-largest money earner and an employer of up to a quarter of a million Nepalis, tourism is vital to Nepal, but it often wields a double-edged sword. While visitors can instil local pride with their interest in Nepal's traditional arts and crafts, for example, the resulting souvenir trade often warps the very nature of these traditional crafts, robbing religious items like *thangkas* (religious paintings on cotton) and Hindu statuary of their sacred significance. Few tourism-related problems, it seems, have solve-all solutions.

Don't underestimate your power as an informed consumer, however. You can maximise the beneficial effects of your expenditure by frequenting locally owned restaurants and fair trade craft stores, and by using environmentally aware trekking agencies. 'Ecotourism' in Nepal's national parks and conservation areas has encouraged local governments to make environmental protection a priority. Hiring a guide on a trek also helps; it adds to your safety and understanding and provides direct employment and infuses money into the hill economy. Entry fees to historical sights contribute to their preservation.

Pay a fair price for goods or services but don't get carried away. Haggling down the last Rs 10 like a pit bull terrier chewing on a dog toy will only result in hardship and disrespect; yet paying over the odds will drive up local inflation (especially for the next tourist).

Fair Trade The principles of fair trade emphasise an exchange that benefits both parties, through supporting safe working environments, sustainable and traditional methods of production, profit sharing, supporting the work of low-income women and discouraging child labour.

A number of shops specialise in handicrafts produced by low-income women. These are nonprofit development organisations and the money goes to the craftspeople in the form of fair wages (not charity). They also provide training, product development, and rehabilitation programmes. Your purchasing power can help low-income and low-status women and at the same time support traditional craft-making skills.

One of the best of these organisations is **Mahaguthi** (W *www.maha guthi.org/EN/0.html*), which was established with the help of Oxfam. Its shops in Kathmandu and Patan sell a wide range of crafts that support a programme to rehabilitate destitute women and children.

Sana Hastakala (W *www.peoplink.org/hastakala*) in Kathmandu, **Dhankuta Sisters** and **Dhukuti** in Patan (established with the help of Unicef), are similar organisations based on the principles of fair trade.

The **Maheela** shop in Thamel is operated by the **Women's Foundation** (W *www.womenfoundation.org*), which runs a shelter for women and children who have suffered abuse, domestic violence, forced labour or have been victims of trafficking, as well as offering training in handicraft production. You can sponsor children through the organisation and you'll receive regular updates on their progress.

For details on all these organisations and their crafts, see Shopping in the Kathmandu chapter and Shopping under Patan in the Kathmandu Valley chapter. See also the Janakpur Women's Development Centre under Janakpur in The Terai & Mahabharat Range chapter.

More information on fair trade can be found on the website of the International Federation of Alternative Trade at W www.ifat.org.

Ethical Shopping Unfortunately, there is still a thriving trade in endangered animal furs and trophies in Nepal, despite the fact that this is also officially prohibited.

Be aware that *shahtoosh* (or *shartoosh*) shawls are illegal both in Nepal and abroad. *Shahtoosh* comes from the wool of the protected *chiru*, or Tibetan antelope, which are killed for their superfine hair (a 2m shawl requires the death of three antelopes). *Shahtoosh* shawls are often referred to as 'ring shawls', as they are fine enough to pass through a finger ring, but this term is also used for perfectly legal *pashmina* (where the hair is merely sheared from a living mountain goat). If in doubt check with the dealer, though you can also tell by the price; *shahtoosh* is four or five times more expensive than *pashmina* (see Shopping in the Facts for the Visitor chapter).

Begging Various kinds of begging are relatively common in Nepal, partly because both Hinduism and Buddhism encourage the giving of alms. This presents many visitors with a heart-rending moral dilemma. Should you give? Sometimes, especially if you've just spent Rs 500 on drinks, it seems grotesque to ignore someone who is genuinely in need. It is often worth checking to see how the local Nepalis react; if they give, it's a reasonably safe assumption that the beneficiary is genuine.

Around the main religious shrines, especially Pashupatinath, there are long lines of beggars. Pilgrims customarily give a coin to everyone in the line (there are special moneychangers nearby who will change notes for small-denomination coins). Sadhus (holy men) are another special case, and are usually completely dependent on alms. There are plenty of con artists among their ranks, but equally, plenty of genuine holy men.

In the countryside, visitors will quickly be discovered by small children who chant a mantra that sounds something like: 'bonbonpenone-rupeeee?' Someone, somewhere, started giving children sweets, pens and money, and it sometimes seems that every child in Nepal now tries their luck. Don't encourage this behaviour. Most Nepalis find it offensive and demeaning (as do most visitors), and it encourages a whole range of unhealthy attitudes.

An excellent way to help villagers become involved in development activities is to carry a few *Trekkers Educational Gift Packs*. This is a collection of books in Nepali produced by the Himal Association and available in Kathmandu bookshops. If you present these books to teachers and village elders, you are contributing more to long-term progress than you would by giving a cash donation or passing out pens.

Thamel attracts many of Kathmandu's estimated 1000-plus street kids. The lure of easy money attracts many kids onto the streets in the first place, and gives them a powerful incentive to remain. It's also a dog-eat-dog world: children seen receiving money may well be beaten up and have it stolen. By giving to beggars you are in many ways encouraging a further influx of people into Kathmandu where very few facilities exist for them. There are signs up around Thamel asking visitors not to do so. If you want to give money, several organisations operate shelters in Kathmandu, including the UK-based **Street Children of Nepal Trust** (☎ 1722-416340; ⓦ www.streetchildrenofnepal.org).

Although the blind and people with leprosy are probably genuinely dependent on begging for their survival, long-term solutions are offered by organisations like Kathmandu's Leprosy Hospital and See Nepal. **See Nepal** (☎ 01-4475927; ⓦ www.hollows.com.au; PO Box 501, Kathmandu) is an innovative and effective programme well known to most Australians because of the involvement of the late Professor Fred Hollows. Many forms of blindness are dealt with in rural clinics and, often, relatively simple treatments and surgical techniques can restore people's sight. See Nepal has opened a factory in Nepal that manufactures the plastic lenses used in cataract operations. The organisation accepts donations.

Cultural Considerations

An important dimension of responsible tourism is the manner and attitude that visitors assume towards local people. You'll get more out of your visit by learning about Nepali life and culture and by travelling with an open mind.

One of travel's great gifts is that it allows you to re-examine your own culture in a new light. Life for many is extremely hard, but despite the scarcity of material possessions, Nepal has many qualities that shame the so-called 'developed' world.

Most Nepalis make allowances for the odd social gaffe, even if it does embarrass them, but they do appreciate it when a genuine effort is made to observe local customs. Following is a collection of simple suggestions that will help you to avoid offence.

Behaviour

- Dress appropriately – shorts, Lycra and revealing clothes are unsuitable for women. Shorts are acceptable for men only when trekking; going without a shirt anywhere is not. Nudity is unacceptable anywhere.
- Public displays of affection are frowned upon. Nepali men often walk around hand in hand, but this does not have the same implication as it does in San Francisco.
- Raising your voice or shouting show extremely bad manners and will not solve your problem, whatever it might be. Always try to remain cool, calm and collected.
- Bodily contact is rarely made, even for shaking hands, although among Nepali men with frequent Western connections it is becoming more accepted. The namaste greeting (placing your palms together in a prayer position) is a better choice.
- A sideways tilt of the head, accompanied by a slight shrug of the shoulders, conveys agreement in Nepal, not a 'no' (visitors from India will be used to this)
- Never touch anything or point at anything with your feet, the 'lowest' part of the body. If you accidentally do this, apologise by touching your hand to the person's arm and then touching your own head.
- It's bad manners to step over someone's outstretched legs, so avoid doing that, and move your own legs when someone wants to pass. In contrast, the head is spiritually the 'highest' part of the body, so don't pat children on the head.
- When handing money to someone (or receiving) pass (or receive) with your right hand and touch your right elbow with your left hand, as a gesture of respect.
- When addressing someone, particularly elders, it's a good idea to add -ji at the end of the name (eg, Danny-ji) to convey respect.
- Nepalis do not like to give negative answers or no answer at all. If you are given a wrong direction or told a place is much nearer than it turns out to be, it may be through fear of disappointing you.

Visiting a Temple
- Always walk clockwise around Buddhist stupas, *chortens* and *mani* walls
- Always remove your shoes before entering a Buddhist or Hindu temple or sanctuary.
- You may also have to remove any items made from leather, such as belts and bags.
- Many Hindu temples do not permit Westerners to enter
- It's customary to give a *khata* (white scarf) to a lama when you are introduced. The scarves can easily be found in Tibetan shops. A small donation to a temple or monastery will always be appreciated.
- Don't step over a shrine or offering, don't smoke in a holy place and definitely don't urinate on a *chorten* (yes, we actually saw that one!)

Visiting a Nepali Home
- Fire is sacred, so do not throw rubbish into it. In a Nepali home the kitchen is off limits to strangers.
- Avoid 'polluting' food by inadvertently touching it or bringing it into contact with a used plate or utensil. Using your own fork or spoon to serve more food is not acceptable; always wait to be served. Putting your used plate on a buffet table risks making the food still on the table *jutho* (polluted). (A high-caste Brahmin simply cannot eat food prepared by a lower-caste individual.)
- Notice how Nepalis drink from a cup or water vessel without letting it touch their lips
- Guests are generally expected to wash their hands and mouth before dining
- Always remove your shoes before entering a Nepali home

Photography
- Do not intrude with a camera, unless it is clearly OK with the people you are photographing
- Ask before entering a temple compound whether it is permissible to enter and take photographs
- Do not exchange addresses or offer copies of photos unless you definitely intend to follow it up

Responsible Trekking

Popular trekking areas like the Annapurna and Everest regions have seen their fine ecological balance upset and pre-existing environmental problems intensified in recent years. Trekkers' demands for heating and hot water have led to increased deforestation, there are litter and sanitation problems, and wildlife has been driven away from many regions. You can help by choosing an environmentally and socially responsible trekking company and heeding some of the following advice.

Trekking Gently in the Himalaya, a booklet by Wendy Brewer Lama, is an excellent resource which has essential tips for trekkers. It's available at the Kathmandu Environmental Education Project (see Useful Organisations later in this section) offices in Thamel and Pokhara.

Firewood & Forest Depletion Minimise the use of firewood by staying in lodges that use kerosene or fuel-efficient wood stoves and solar-heated hot water. Avoid using large open fires for warmth – wear additional clothing instead. Keep showers to a minimum, and spurn showers altogether if wood is burnt to produce the hot water.

Consolidate cooking time (and wood consumption) by ordering the same items at the same time as other trekkers. *Dal bhaat* (rice and lentils) is usually readily available for large numbers of people, does not require special lengthy cooking time and is nutritious and inexpensive. Remember that local meals are usually prepared between 10am and 11am, so eating then will usually not require lighting an additional fire. Treat your drinking water with iodine rather than boiling it.

Those travelling with organised groups should ensure kerosene is used for cooking.

Garbage & Waste You can do several things to reduce the amount of rubbish and pollution in the hills. Purifying your own water instead of buying mineral water in nonbiodegradable plastic bottles is the most important of these.

Independent trekkers should always carry their garbage out or dispose of it properly. You can burn it, but you should remember that the fireplace in a Nepali home is a sacred institution and throwing rubbish into it would be a great insult. Take out all your batteries, as they will eventually leak toxins.

Toilet paper is a particularly unpleasant sight along trails; if you must use it, carry it in a plastic bag until you can burn it. Better yet, carry a small plastic trowel to bury your faeces (well away from any streams) and a small plastic water container so that, like the vast majority of people in the world, you can clean yourself with water instead of toilet paper.

Those travelling with organised groups should ensure that toilet tents are properly organised and that rubbish is carried out. Check on the company's policies before you sign up.

Water Do your bit to minimise pollution and don't soap up your clothes in the streams. Instead use a bowl or bucket and discard the dirty water away from water courses.

On the Annapurna Circuit, the Annapurna Conservation Area Project (with New Zealand government assistance) has introduced the Safe Water Drinking Scheme – a chain of 16 outlets selling purified water to trekkers. Its aim is to minimise the demand for plastic mineral water bottles. An estimated one million plastic bottles are brought into the Annapurna Conservation Area each year creating a serious litter problem. The outlets are found in Tal, Bargarcchap, Chame, Pisang, Hongde, Manang, Letdar, Thorung Phedi, Muktinath, Kagbeni, Jomsom, Marpha, Tukuche, Khobang, Lete and Ghasa.

Useful Organisations

Gift for Aid (☎ 01-4259122; W www.giftforaid.org) is a Dutch initiative that aims to connect foreign travellers with local small-scale tourism-funded development projects. It can often link visitors with volunteer opportunities.

If you have any clothes or medicines left at the end of your trip, why haul them home when you can donate them to a useful cause? Several organisations accept clothes, including **Porters Progress** (☎ 01-4410020;

W *www.portersprogress.org)* in Thamel. The organisation campaigns for the ethical treatment of porters, porter safety and medical relief, and offers free English tuition and medical training to porters. It operates a clothes and kerosene stove bank in Lukla and currently has clothes for 700 porters. See the boxed text 'Porters, Exploitation & IPPG' in the Trekking chapter for more on the fair treatment of porters.

If you have time it's well worth checking out the BBC video *Carrying the Burden*, which plays daily at 4pm (or on request) at **Porters Progress**, and daily at 2pm at the **Himalayan Explorers Connection**, next to KEEP.

Sometimes contributing to a charity just involves kicking back in a good guesthouse. Nature's Grace Lodge in Pokhara (see Places to Stay in the Pokhara chapter) is run by the **Child Welfare Scheme** (W *www.childwelfarescheme.org)*, which operates development programmes, a clinic and a vocational centre in the region. Administrative costs are directly covered by profits from the guesthouse.

If you want tips on how you can lessen your environmental impact, you can visit the **Kathmandu Environmental Education Project** *(KEEP;* ☎ *01-4259275, 4259567;* W *www.keepnepal.org; open 10am-5pm Sun-Fri)* in Thamel (see Information in the Kathmandu chapter for details). KEEP also accepts donations of medical supplies and other equipment.

The **Annapurna Conservation Area Project** *(ACAP;* ☎ *01-4225393, ext 363; Tridevi Marg; open 9am-5pm daily, 9am-4pm daily winter)* is a nongovernmental, nonprofit organisation that exists to improve local standards of living, to protect the environment and to develop more sensitive forms of tourism. ACAP has started work on a number of projects, such as forestry nurseries, introducing wood-saving technologies (eg, efficient stoves), banning fires altogether in certain areas, and building rubbish tips and latrines.

In the Khumbu region the similar **Sagarmatha Pollution Control Committee** (SPCC) works on waste reduction and recycling and helped banned glass bottles from the Everest region. Also in the Khumbu, the **Himalayan Foundation for Integrated Development** (W *www.hima layafoundation.org)* assists the local community with small-scale ecotourism and education projects.

For more on the general issues behind responsible tourism, check out **Tourism Concern** (W *www.tourismconcern.org.uk)*, the **Centre for Environmentally Responsible Tourism** (W *www.c-e-r-t.org)* or **Partners in Responsible Tourism** (W *www2.pirt.org/pirt/)*.

For details on organisations that offer volunteer opportunities, see Volunteer Work in the Facts for the Visitor chapter.

[Continued from page 68]

Ultra Marathons

Those insane enough to consider a normal 24km marathon warm-up stroll might want to consider Nepal's two ultra marathons. The annual Annapurna Mandala Trail is a nine-day foot race around the Annapurna Circuit from Besisahar, over the 5400m Thorung La and down the Kali Gandaki valley to Dhampus, near Pokhara. If that doesn't sound challenging enough for you, go for psychological testing and then consider the Himal Race, a 955km, 22-day run from Annapurna to Everest Base Camps, won in 2002 in a time of 108 hours.

Canyoning

This new sport is an exciting combination of rappelling, caving and even swimming that has been pioneered in the canyons and waterfalls near Last Resort and Borderlands resorts. See those entries in the Around the Kathmandu Valley chapter for details.

Hot-Air Ballooning

For a different view of the Himalaya and the Kathmandu Valley, try from a basket suspended 1km above the valley! A company in Kathmandu operates balloon flights every morning during the high season, and while not cheap, they are spectacular. See Activities in the Kathmandu chapter for details.

Paragliding, Gliding & Bungy Jumping

Pokhara is the place to head for if you feel the need to throw yourself off a cliff, either on a tandem paragliding flight with an instructor or solo after a multiday course. Glider and ultralight flights are also available. See Activities in the Pokhara chapter for details.

One of the world's longest bungy jumps is set up on a bridge which straddles the Bhote Kosi gorge near the Tibetan border. See the Last Resort entry in the Around the Kathmandu Valley chapter for details.

COURSES
Yoga, Buddhist Meditation & Massage

Nepal is a popular place for people to take up spiritual pursuits, particularly around the Kathmandu Valley, although Pokhara is becoming increasingly popular.

Check the notice boards in Thamel for up-to-date information about yoga and Buddhism courses, and shop around before you commit yourself. A number of courses are regularly advertised, some very much at the New Age end of the spectrum ('Making Your Own Inner Mandala').

Ananda Yoga Center (☎ 01-4311048, ⓔ ananda@ yoga.wlink.com.np) PO Box 1774, Kathmandu Valley (see Central Kathmandu map). On the edge of the valley at Satungal, overlooking Matatirtha Village, 8km west of Kathmandu, this is a nonprofit yoga retreat offering courses in reiki, hatha yoga and teacher training. Six-day live-in courses cost US$80.

Centre for Buddhist Studies (ⓦ www.cbs.edu.np) The centre offers longer university-accredited courses that students can attend part-time.

Himalayan Buddhist Meditation Centre (☎ 01-4221875, ⓦ www.dharmatours.com/hbmc) PO Box 817, Kamaladi, Kathmandu. This place has talks, meditation courses (three to five days US$50-85, plus dorm accommodation US$3 or private rooms US$6/9), classes on yoga, *thangka* and mandala painting courses, twice-weekly guided meditations and reiki treatments (Rs 1500 for 1½ hours). There are guided meditations Monday and Thursday at 6pm and occasional day-long *dharma* teachings on Saturdays. Tibet-related videos are shown every Tuesday at 6pm in the attached restaurant (Rs 50 or free if you eat there) and there's a small bookshop. This centre is affiliated with the Kopan Monastery.

Kathmandu Center of Healing (☎ 01-4425946, ⓦ www.ancientmassage.com & ⓦ www.kath manduhealing.com) PO Box 8975, Maharaj-ganj, Kathmandu. This place offers one-month professional courses in Thai massage. These cost around US$600 and include lunch and dormitory accommodation. There are also five-day (US$120) and 10-day (US$240) introductory courses. Other activities, such as yoga, a one-month (1½ hours a day) tai chi course (US$100), a two-day reiki course and various 'healing seminars' are available depending on who is at the centre at the time.

Kopan Monastery (☎ 01-4481268, fax 441267, ⓦ www.kopan-monastery.com) PO Box 817, Kathmandu. This monastery, at Kopan north of Bodhnath, is affiliated with the Himalayan Buddhist Meditation Centre (see earlier in this list). It offers very reasonably priced and popular courses for seven days (US$54) or 10 days (US$80), generally given by foreign teachers. There's also an annual one-month course (US$320) held in November, followed by an optional seven-day retreat (US$40). You must be prepared to follow monastery regulations. See Around Bodhnath in the Around Kathmandu Valley chapter for more details.

Nepal Vipassana Center (Kathmandu office ☎ 01-4250581, e nvc@htp.com.np, PO Box 12896, Kathmandu; in Budhanilkantha ☎ 4371655).10-day retreats are held twice a month at this centre northeast of Kathmandu, just north of Budhanilkantha, as well as occasional shorter courses. These are serious meditation courses that involve rising at 4am every morning, not talking or making eye contact with anyone over the entire 10 days, and not eating after midday. The fee is donation only. For students who have already completed at least one 10-day course, hour-long meditation sessions are held twice a week in the city meditation centre in the Jyoti Bhawan building on Kantipath.

Patanjali Yoga Center (☎ 01-4278437) Kathmandu map. A recommended place for yoga west of Kathmandu's city centre. Five-day courses start every Monday, and these involve attending the centre for three hours per day, and include lunch.

Rangjung Yeshe Institute (W www.shedra.com) At Bodhnath's Ka-Nying Sheldrup Ling Gompa. The institute offers a fairly advanced two-week course on Tibetan Buddhist teachings, practice and meditation, led by the monastery's abbot Chokyi Nyima Rinpoche. The course is held in mid-November and costs US$100.

Sadhana Yoga (W www.sadhana-yoga.org.np) Pokhara. One to 21 days are offered here at the cost of Rs 1100 per day, which includes accommodation, meals and steam and mud baths. See the Pokhara chapter for details.

Music & the Arts

The **Kalamandapa Institute of Classical Nepalese Performing Arts** at the Hotel Vajra (see Places to Stay – Mid-Range in the Kathmandu chapter) offers private dance tuition. Contact Rajendra Shresthra through the hotel.

Kathmandu's **Gandharba Association** (see Entertainment in the Kathmandu chapter for details) offers lessons in the *saranghi* and you may be able to find teachers for other instruments too.

Language

Nepali is not a difficult language to learn, and there are a number of courses available. You will see signs and notices around Kathmandu advertising language courses, some of them conducted by former Peace Corps workers. Embassies should be able to recommend a course that they themselves attend.

Most schools offer courses (often around two weeks long) or individual tuition. Expect to pay about US$50 for a two-week course and around US$3 for private hourly tuition.

Places to try in Kathmandu include:

Intercultural Training & Research Centre (ITC) (☎ 4414490, e itc@mos.com.np) Just off Tridevi Marg. This well-respected language centre works with many aid agencies, including the UK's VSO. It offers crash courses (three hours), 60-hour beginner courses in two- to four-week and six-week-long intermediate courses. All tuition is one-on-one and costs around Rs 300 per hour.

Kathmandu Institute of Nepali Language (☎ 422 0295, e namrata@mos.com.np) Jyatha, by Café des Trekkers. The institute offers a week course of five hours for Rs 1250.

Thamel Nepali Language Institute (☎ 4442949, 4426116, e view@wlink.com.np) Thamel, opposite Pilgrims Book House, upper floor. This tiny place offers an intensive course of 20 hours a week or a more relaxed six-hours-a-week course, for roughly Rs 200 per hour for one-on-one tuition, plus Rs 800 for learning materials. You stay with a local family.

There are often flyers around Bodhnath advertising Tibetan language tuition and apartments to rent, as well as opportunities to volunteer-teach Tibetan refugees.

WORK

For Western visitors, finding work in Nepal is very difficult, though not impossible. The easiest work to find is teaching English, as there are many private schools and a great demand for English-language lessons. However, at less than US$100 a month the pay is very low. Other remote possibilities include work with airline offices, travel and trekking agencies, consultants or aid groups.

Officially you need a work permit if you intend to find employment (even unpaid) in Nepal and you are supposed to have this before you arrive in the country. Changing from a tourist visa once you are in the country is rarely permissible. The work permit has to be applied for by your employer and you are required to leave the country while the paperwork is negotiated. The process can take months.

Volunteer Work

It's possible to get work as a volunteer, and this can be a rewarding experience and one which gives you the opportunity to put something back into the community. Volunteer programmes were scaled back in 2001 and 2002 due to Maoist activity in the rural areas that form the Maoist heartland. Contact the agencies below to see if programmes have been restored (there are many more).

Educate the Children (W www.etc-nepal.org) Three-month teaching stints in rural Nepal offered by this Nepali organisation. There's a US$100 placement fee and living costs around US$30 per week.

Global Action Nepal (☎ 01403-864704, W www .gannepal.org) British organisation that helps volunteers train Nepali teachers for six-month stints. No experience is required. The £2000 includes flights, insurance, accommodation and food and you are expected to assist in fundraising.

Himalayan Explorers Connection (HEC) (W www .hec.org) The HEC publishes the annual *Nepal Volunteer Handbook*, which outlines the opportunities for volunteering in Nepal. It is available for US$10 from the HEC office in Thamel (where you can also flick through a copy – see Information in the Kathmandu chapter) or online to members.

Insight Nepal (W www.insightnepal.org) Pokhara-based programme that runs three-month volunteer programmes for US$800, which includes training, food, accommodation, trekking and a Chitwan safari excursion.

I-to-I (UK ☎ 0870-333 2332, USA ☎ 800-985 4864, W www.i-to-i.com) Three-month volunteer stints cost £1400.

KEEP (W www.keepnepal.com) Arranges volunteer work on location at villages, including at Shermanthang in Langtang, or you can offer to teach English to porters and guides in Kathmandu for one month. See Information in the Kathmandu chapter for details.

Volunteer Work Opportunity Programs (VWOP; ☎ 01-4416614, e vwop2000@hotmail.com) Nepali organisation that coordinates teaching, agricultural and environmental volunteers to work on projects and live with a local family in various parts of the country. There's a one-off administration fee of US$220.

ACCOMMODATION

In Kathmandu and Pokhara there is a wide variety of accommodation from rock-bottom flea pits to five-star international hotels where rooms of US$150 a night cost almost the nation's average annual per capita income! The intense competition between the many cheaper places keeps prices down and standards up – Kathmandu has many fine places with pleasant gardens and rooms for less than US$10 a night including private bathroom and hot water. At peak times, rooms in the four- and five-star places used to be in short supply but the recent downturn in tourism has left many of these places languishing.

A Note on Hotel Prices

Nepal's hotel prices have always been seasonal and, shall we say, flexible, with peak season running from October to November and February to April. The current drop in tourism has had a deepening effect on hotel discounting rates, so much so that currently there's hardly a hotel in Kathmandu that charges full tariff.

The exact room rate you will be quoted depends partly on the season and partly on general tourist numbers. At the time of research the slump in tourism meant that many mid-range hotels were offering discounts of up to 60% even in the high season, particularly in Kathmandu and Pokhara where competition is fiercest. In this guide we have generally given the high-season room rates shown on hotel tariff cards, followed, as a guide, by the maximum discount we were offered during high-season research. You may find even lower rates during the monsoon (June to September). If, however, tourist numbers pick up during the lifetime of this book, you may find that smaller discounts are offered. In reality prices are highly negotiable all the time.

At most hotels the printed tariffs are pure fiction, published partly in the hope that you might be silly enough to pay them, partly to fulfil government star rating requirements; 20% to 50% discounts are par for the course anywhere these days. If business is slow you can often negotiate a deluxe room for a standard room rate. Some mid-range hotels offer discounts for booking online but you'll get at least this much on the spot, if not more.

You can also negotiate cheaper rates for longer stays. In the cool of autumn and spring you get a further discount on air-conditioned rooms simply by agreeing to turn off the air-con.

The main towns of the Terai have hotels of reasonable standard, where rooms with fans and mosquito nets are around Rs 400, down to grimy, basic places catering to local demand from around Rs 50. Some of the cheap places will only have tattered mosquito nets, if any at all.

Elsewhere in the country the choice of hotels can be very limited, but you will find places to stay along most of the major trekking trails. It's quite possible to trek from lodge to lodge rather than camp site to camp site. On some trails places may be spartan – the accommodation may be dorm-style or simply an open room in which to unroll your sleeping bag. Smoke can be a real problem in places where the chimney has yet to make an appearance. At the other extreme, some trails such as the popular Pokhara to Jomsom route have excellent lodges and guesthouses at every stopping place.

The recent dramatic drop-off in visitor numbers to Nepal means that many places outside of the main tourist centres remain deserted. Managers and even chefs may be absent from off-the-beaten-track resorts so phone ahead to these places. Hotels with only one or two guests may be reluctant to turn on the hotel heating or hot water. On the plus side (for travellers at least) there are plenty of discounts available, you'll have an excellent choice of rooms and you'll often have smaller towns completely to yourself.

All mid-range and top-end hotels charge a VAT tax of 10% plus a tourism service charge of 2%. Almost all quote their prices in US dollars. Budget places usually quote prices in rupees and generally forget about the tax.

FOOD & DRINKS
Nepali Food
Generic Nepali food is distinctly dull. Hindu Nepalis are vegetarian and most of the time meals consist of a dish called *dal bhaat tarakari*, literally 'lentil soup', 'rice' and 'curried vegetables'. If you are lucky it will be spiced up with a bowl of *achar* (pickles) and maybe some *chapati* (unleavened Indian bread), *dahi* (curd or yoghurt) or *papad* (pappadam – crispy fried thin pancake). The occasional dal bhaat tarakari, prepared to tourist tastes in Kathmandu restaurants, can be just fine. Strictly local

versions, eaten day in and day out while trekking, can get very boring indeed.

Most Nepalis round off a meal with a *digestif* of *pan* (betel nut). Those little spots of red on the pavement that look like little pools of blood are (generally) *pan*.

Newari Food In contrast to the generally bland Nepali food, Newari food is varied, spicy and interesting. There is a wide range of interesting dishes available in the increasing number of Kathmandu restaurants serving Nepali food, although these usually serve a somewhat modified version suitable to tourists' tastes.

Newaris are great meat eaters. *Buff* (water buffalo) is the meat of choice (cows, and thus beef, are sacred and never eaten) but pork (often called 'wild boar' on Newari menus) is also popular. Very little is wasted when a beast is slaughtered, and in true Newari eateries you can find dishes made from just about every imaginable body part or fluid – from fried brains to braised tongue and steamed blood! Spices are heavily used, with chilli being at the forefront.

Many Newari dishes are only eaten at particular celebrations or family events and for these (and the best Newari food in general) you need to be invited to a Newari home. For a rundown of Newari dishes see the Nepali Menu Reader later in this chapter.

Restaurants
There are a number of 'rules' and customs relating to eating and drinking in Nepal and following them can make life much easier. For a start, the Nepali eating schedule is quite different from that in the West. The morning usually begins with little more than a cup of tea. The main meal is not taken until late morning. In areas where Western visitors are not often seen and even more rarely catered for, finding food will be much simpler if you go along with this schedule.

You can also save yourself a lot of time and frustration if you pay attention to what you order as well as when you order it. In small local restaurants the cooking equipment and facilities are often very limited.

Places with some experience of catering to Western tastes will often offer amazingly varied menus, but just because they offer 20 different dishes don't expect them to be able to fix two of them at the same time.

Nepali Menu Reader

Nepali & Newari Food

aloo tahmah – stew-like dish made from potatoes, bamboo shoots and beans

aloo tareko – fried potato with cumin, turmeric and chilli

bandhel tareko – fried wild boar (or pork) with onions, tomatoes and spices

chatamari – rice-flour pancake topped with meat and/or egg, sometimes over-optimistically called a 'Newari pizza'

choyla – roasted, diced *buff* (buffalo) meat, usually heavily spiced and eaten with *chura*

chura – beaten rice (think of flat Rice Bubbles!), served in place of rice

chyau ko tarkari – mushrooms with peas, tomatoes and spices

dayakula – meat curry

gundruk – traditional Nepali sour soup with dried vegetables

gurr – made from raw potatoes ground and mixed with spices and then grilled like a large pancake and eaten with cheese

kachila – raw *buff* mince mixed with oil, ginger and spices

khasi kho ledo – lamb curry

kwati – soup made from sprouted beans and eaten during festivals

momoch – Newari version of Tibetan *momo*

samay baji – ritual feast of *chura*, *choyla*, boiled egg, black soybeans, diced ginger and *wo*

sandeko – cold pickles

sekuwa – barbecued meat: *buff*, pork, fish or chicken

sikarni – sweet whipped yoghurt dessert that may include nuts, cinnamon and dried fruit

sukuti – spicy nibble of dried roasted meat

tama – traditional Nepali soup made from dried bamboo shoots

tawkhaa – a jelly of curried meat, served cold

wo – lentil-flour pancake

Tibetan Dishes

gacok – a hotpot extravaganza named for the pot it's cooked in, normally for a minimum of two or three people; order an hour or two in advance

kothey (kothe) – fried *momos*

momo – typical Tibetan dish made by steaming meat or vegetables wrapped in dough; similar to Chinese dim sum or Italian ravioli

phing – glass noodles, vermicelli

pingtsey – wontons

richotse – *momos* in soup

sha-bhalay (sya-bhakley) – meat in a deep-fried pancake or pastie

shabrel – meat balls

talumein – egg noodle soup

thentuk – similar to *thugpa* but with noodle squares

thugpa – traditional thick Tibetan meat soup

tsampa – ground roasted barley, mixed with tea, water or milk and eaten dry either instead of rice or mixed with it; a staple dish in the hill country

tserel – vegetable balls

Indian Dishes

aloo – potatoes

bhaji – vegetable fritter

biryani – steamed rice with meat or vegetables

channa masala – chickpea curry

chicken tikka – skewered chunks of marinated chicken, often displayed with a noticeable lack of refrigeration in restaurant windows

gobi – cauliflower

korma – curry-like braised dish, often quite sweet

makani – any dish cooked with butter, often dal or chicken

malai kofta – vegetable dish of potato and nut dumplings in a rich gravy

matter paneer – unfermented cheese with peas

murgh – chicken

nan – baked bread

palak paneer – unfermented cheese with spinach in a gravy

pakora – fried vegetables in batter

pilau – rice cooked in stock and flavoured with spices

rogan josh – Kashmiri lamb curry

samosa – pyramid-shaped, deep-fried and potato-filled pasties

sag – spinach

If you and your five friends turn up at some small and remote café and order six different dishes you can expect to be waiting for dinner when breakfast time rolls around the next day. In that situation it makes a lot of sense to order the same dish six times!

[Continued on page 91]

STAN ARMINGTON

Masked dancer, Mani Rimdu festival

KRAIG LIEB

Traditional Nepali New Year's chariot

RYAN FOX

Masked character, Dasain celebrations, Patan

RICHARD I'ANSON

Nepali New Year festival

Nepal's colourful holidays and festivals occur virtually year-round and a visit to Nepal is almost certain to coincide with at least one, particularly in the Kathmandu Valley. Certain times of year, particularly August and September towards the end of the monsoon, are packed with festivals. They go a long way towards compensating for the less-than-ideal weather at this time of year. Nepal's most spectacular festivities are its chariot processions, similar to the epic processions of India. These tottering 20m-tall chariots of the gods are often chronically and comically unstable (imagine hauling a 60ft-tall jelly through the streets of Kathmandu) and moving them requires hundreds of enthusiastic devotees.

Major Festivals Calendar

As the actual holidays aren't declared more than a year in advance, many of the following dates are estimates only, but should be correct to within a day or so. Check in Nepal for exact dates.

festival	place	2003	2004	2005
Magh Sankranti	Narayanghat, the Terai	mid-Jan	mid-Jan	mid-Jan
Basant Panchami	Swayambhunath, Kathmandu	6 Feb	26 Jan	13 Feb
Losar	Bodhnath & all Tibetan communities	1 Feb	20 Feb	9 Feb
Maha Shivaratri	Pashupatinath Temple	1 Mar	18 Feb	8 Mar
Holi	countrywide	18 Mar	6 Mar	24 Mar
Chaitra Dasain	countrywide	10 Apr	29 Mar	17 Apr
Bisket Jatra	Bhaktapur	14 Apr	14 Apr	14 Apr
Buddha Jayanti	Swayambhunath, Kathmandu	16 May	4 May	23 May
Naga Panchami	countrywide	3 Aug	22 Jul	10 Aug
Janai Purnima	countrywide	12 Aug	31 Jul	19 Aug
Gai Jatra	Kathmandu, Bhaktapur	13 Aug	1 Aug	20 Aug
Krishna Jayanti	Patan	19 Aug	6 Sep	26 Aug
Teej	Pashupatinath	29 Aug	16 Sep	6 Sep
Indra Jatra	Kathmandu	9 Sep	27 Sep	17 Sep
Dasain				
Fulpati	countrywide	2 Oct	20 Sep	10 Oct
Vijaya Dashami	countrywide	5 Oct	23 Sep	12 Oct
Kartika Purnima	countrywide	10 Oct	28 Sep	16 Oct
Tihar				
Deepawali	countrywide	25 Oct	12 Nov	1 Nov
Bhai Tika	countrywide	27 Oct	14 Nov	3 Nov
Haribodhini Ekadashi	Budhanilkantha Temple, Kathmandu Valley	5 Nov	25 Oct	12 Nov
Bala Chaturdashi	Pashupatinath	23 Nov	12 Dec	30 Nov
Sita Bibaha Panchami	Janakpur	28 Nov	17 Nov	6 Dec

Title Page: Monk performing a ritualistic dance, Mani Rimdu festival (Photo: Richard I'Anson)

Lunar Calendar

Nepali holidays and festivals are principally dated by the lunar calendar, falling on days relating to new or full moons. The lunar calendar is divided into bright and dark fortnights. The bright fortnight is the two weeks of the waxing moon, as it grows to become *purnima* (the full moon). The dark fortnight is the two weeks of the waning moon, as the full moon shrinks to become *aunsi* (the new moon).

The Nepali New Year starts on 13 or 14 April with the month of Baisakh, and is 57 years ahead of the Gregorian calendar used in the West. Thus the year 2002 in the West is 2059 in Nepal. The Newars, on the other hand, start their New Year from the day after Deepawali (the third day of Tihar), which falls on the night of the new moon in late October or early November. Their calendar is 880 years behind the Gregorian calendar, so 2002 in the West is 1122 to the Newars of the Kathmandu Valley.

See Public Holidays in the Facts for the Visitor chapter for more information on business closures and interruptions during the festival times.

January–February

Magh Sankranti The end of the coldest winter months is marked by this festival and ritual bathing, despite the cold, during the Nepali month of Magh. The festival is dated by the movement north of the winter sun and is one of the few festivals not timed by the lunar calendar. Soon after, on the new-moon day, the Tribeni Mela (a mela is a fair) is held at various places including Devghat, on the banks of the Narayani River near the town of Narayanghat in the Terai.

Basant Panchami The start of spring is celebrated by honouring Saraswati; since she is the goddess of learning this festival has special importance for students. The shrine to Saraswati just below the platform at the top of Swayambhunath is the most popular locale for the festivities. This is also a particularly auspicious time for weddings.

Losar The New Year for the Tibetan and Bhotiya people commences with the new moon in February and is welcomed with particular fervour at the great stupa of Bodhnath (Boudha). Ceremonies are also performed at Swayambhunath and in the Tibetan community at Jawlakhel, near Patan. The Sherpa people of the Solu Khumbu region also celebrate at this time.

February–March

Maha Shivaratri Shiva's birthday falls on the new-moon day of the month of Falgun. Festivities take place at all Shiva temples, but most particularly at the great Pashupatinath Temple, and devotees flock there from all over Nepal and India.

Many sadhus make the long trek to Nepal for this festival and the king of Nepal will also make an appearance late in the day. The crowds bathing in the Bagmati's holy waters at this time are a colourful and wonderful sight.

Holi This exciting festival (also known as Fagu) is closely related to the water festivals of Thailand and Myanmar and takes place on the full-moon day in the month of Falgun. By this time, late in the dry season, it is beginning to get hot and the water which is sprayed around so liberally during the festival is a reminder of the cooling monsoon days to come. Holi is also known as the Festival of Colours and as well as spraying water on everything and everyone, coloured powder (particularly red) and coloured water are also dispensed. Foreigners get special attention, so if you venture out on Holi leave your camera behind (or keep it well protected) and wear old clothes that can get colour-stained.

A pole supporting a three-tiered umbrella is set up in front of the Basantapur Tower in Durbar Square in the centre of Kathmandu and on the final day the umbrella is taken down and burnt.

Guru Mapa, the demon of the Itum Bahal in Kathmandu (see Kilgal Tole to Itum Bahal in the Walking Tours special section), has his annual feed on Holi night. The inhabitants of Itum Bahal sacrifice a buffalo on the banks of the Vishnumati River, cook it in the afternoon in their great courtyard and in the middle of the night carry it in huge cauldrons to the Tundikhel where the demon is said to live.

March–April

Chaitra Dasain Also known as Small Dasain, this festival takes place exactly six months prior to the more important Dasain celebration. Both Dasains are dedicated to Durga and once again it's a bad day for goats and buffaloes who are sacrificed early in the morning in Kot Square (north of Durbar Square in central Kathmandu).

Seto Machhendranath The Chaitra Dasain sacrifices also signal the start of the Seto (White) Machhendranath festival, a month prior to the much larger and more important Rato (Red) Machhendranath festival in Patan (see the April–May section later). The festival starts with removing the image of Seto Machhendranath from the temple at Kel Tole (see the Walking Tours special section) and placing it on a *rath* or towering and creaky wooden temple chariot. For the next four evenings, the chariot proceeds from one historic location to another eventually arriving at Lagankhel in the south of Kathmandu's old town. There the image is taken down from the chariot and carried back to its starting point in a palanquin while the chariot is disassembled and put away until next year.

Bisket Jatra Nepali New Year starts in mid-April, at the beginning of the month of Baisakh; the Bisket festival in Bhaktapur is the most spectacular welcome for the New Year, and one of the most exciting annual events in the valley (see the boxed text 'Bisket Jatra at Khalna Tole' in the Around the Kathmandu Valley chapter).

Bisket is Bhaktapur's great chariot festival, but while in Kathmandu and Patan it is Machhendranath who gets taken for a ride, here it is

Bhairab, accompanied by Betal and the goddess Bhadrakali, all on huge ponderous chariots.

The New Year is also an important time in the valley for ritual bathing, and crowds of hill people visit the Buddhist stupas of Swayambhunath and Bodhnath.

Balkumari Jatra The small town of Thimi also welcomes the New Year with an exciting festival instituted by King Jagat Jyoti Malla in the early 1600s in which Balkumari, one of Bhairab's consorts is honoured. All through the first day of the New Year devotees crowd around the Balkumari Temple in Thimi and as dusk falls hundreds of *chiraqs* (ceremonial oil lamps) are lit. Some devotees lie motionless around the temple all night with burning oil lamps balanced on their legs, arms, chests and foreheads.

The next morning men come from the various toles or quarters of Thimi and from surrounding villages, each team carrying a *khat* (palanquin) with images of different gods. As the 32 *khats* whirl around the temple, red powder is hurled at them and the ceremony reaches fever pitch as the *khat* bearing Ganesh arrives from the village of Nagadesh. The crowds parade up and down the main street until late in the morning when Ganesh, borne by hundreds of men, makes a break for home, pursued by the other *khats*. Sacrifices are then made to Balkumari.

In the nearby village of Bode another *khat* festival, with just seven *khats* rather than 32, takes place. Here a volunteer spends the whole day with an iron spike piercing his tongue. Successful completion of this painful rite brings merit to the whole village as well as the devotee.

April–May

Rato Machhendranath Although Seto and Rato Machhendranath may be the same deity, the Rato or Red Machhendranath festival of Patan is a much more important occasion than the Kathmandu event. Machhendranath is considered to have great powers over rain and, since the monsoon is approaching at this time, this festival is a plea for good rain.

As in Kathmandu, the Rato Machhendranath festival consists of a day-by-day temple chariot procession through the streets of the town, but here it takes a full month to move the chariot from the Pulchowki area – where the image is installed in the chariot – to Jawlakhel, where the chariot is dismantled.

The main chariot is accompanied for most of its journey by a smaller chariot, which contains the image of Rato Machhendranath's companion, which normally resides in the nearby Minanath Temple (see Patan in the Around the Kathmandu Valley chapter for details).

The highlight of the festival is the Bhoto Jatra, or showing of the sacred vest. Machhendranath was entrusted with the jewelled vest after there was a dispute over its ownership. The vest is displayed three times in order to give the owner the chance to claim it – although this does not actually happen. The king of Nepal attends this ceremony, which is also a national holiday.

From Jawlakhel, Rato Machhendranath does not return to his Patan temple, however. He is conveyed on a *khat* to his second home in the village of Bungamati where he spends six months of each year. The main chariot is so large and the route is so long that the Nepali army is often called in to help transport it.

May–June

Buddha Jayanti (the Buddha's Birthday) Siddhartha Gautama (the Buddha) was born at Lumbini and a great fair is held here on his birthday. Swayambhunath is the centre for the celebrations around Kathmandu, although events also take place at Bodhnath and in Patan.

A constant procession of pilgrims makes its way around the stupa at Swayambhunath. The stupa's collection of rare *thangkas* (Tibetan paintings on cotton) and *mandalas* (geometrical representations of the world) is shown on the southern wall of the stupa courtyard on this single day each year. There are also colourful monk dances.

Kumar Sasthi The birthday of Shiva's son Kumar (or Kartikkaya), the god of war and brother of Ganesh, is also known as Sithinakha. The festival also marks the start of the rice-planting season and is an annual occasion for cleaning wells.

July–August

Naga Panchami On the fifth day after the new moon in the month of Saaun, *nagas* (serpent deities) are honoured all over the country. Numerous legends are told about snakes; they are considered to have all sorts of magical powers including special powers over the monsoon rains. Pictures of the *nagas* are hung over doorways of houses; this not only appeases the snakes, but also keeps harm from the household.

Various foods are put out for snakes. A bowl of rice is offered because of an incident at the Siddha Pokhari pond just outside Bhaktapur which, legend has it, was once inhabited by an evil *naga*. A holy man determined to kill the *naga* himself by taking the form of a snake, and told his companion to be ready with a bowl of magic rice. If, after he entered the pond, the water turned white then the *naga* had won and it was all over. If, on the other hand, the water turned red then he had defeated the *naga* and although he would emerge from the pond in the form of a snake, the magical rice could restore his original form. Sure enough the water turned red, but when the holy man in the form of a hideous serpent emerged from the water his horrified companion simply turned tail and ran, taking the rice with him. The holy man tried to catch him, but failed, and eventually decided to return to the pond and remain there.

To this day the inhabitants of Bhaktapur keep well clear of the Siddha Pokhari pond and on the day of Naga Panchami a bowl of rice is put out – just in case the holy man/snake turns up.

Janai Purnima On the day prior to (and on the day of) the full moon in the month of Saaun, all high-caste men (Chhetri and Brahman) must change the *janai* (sacred thread), which they wear looped over their left shoulder and tied under their right arm. The three cords of the sacred thread symbolise body, speech and mind. Young men first put on the thread in an important ritual that officially welcomes them into their religion. From that date they wear the sacred thread for the rest of their lives, changing it on this one occasion each year and any time it has been damaged or defiled.

Although only men wear the thread, anybody, including curious foreigners, can wear a *raksha* bandhan (yellow thread) around their wrist – on the right wrist for men, left for women. Wearing this thread on your wrist is said to bring good fortune and on this day priests tie the threads on all who come. You are supposed to wear it for at least a week, but preferably for three months until the Festival of Lights (during Tihar) in October–November.

Janai Purnima also brings crowds of pilgrims to the sacred Gosainkund Lake, across the mountains to the north of Kathmandu. There they garland a statue of Shiva and throw coins at the sacred lingam, which rises up from the lake. A direct channel is said to lead from the lake to the pond in the Kumbeshwar Temple in Patan and a silver lingam is installed in the pond for the occasion. The rituals at the temple attract *jhankris*, faith healers who perform in a trance while beating drums.

Ghanta Karna This festival is named after 'bell ears', a horrible demon who wore bell earrings to drown out the name of Vishnu, his sworn enemy. This festival, on the 14th day of the dark fortnight of Saaun, celebrates his destruction when a god, disguised as a frog, lured him into a deep well where the people stoned and clubbed him to death. Ghanta Karna is burnt in effigy on this night throughout Newari villages and evil is cleansed from the land for another year.

August–September

Gai Jatra This 'Cow Festival' takes place immediately after Janai Purnima on the day after the Saaun full moon, and is dedicated to those who died during the preceding year. Newars believe that after death, cows will guide them to Yama, the god of the underworld, and finding your way on this important journey will be much easier if by chance you should be holding onto a cow's tail at the moment of death. On this day cows are led through the streets of the valley's towns or, if a cow is not available, small boys dress up as cows.

The festival is celebrated with maximum energy on Bhaktapur streets.

Krishna Jayanti (Krishna's Birthday) The seventh day after the full moon in the month of Bhadra is celebrated as Krishna's birthday, sometimes also known as Krishnasthami. Krishna is an incarnation of Vishnu, and his daring exploits, good nature and general love of a good time endear him to many people. The Krishna Mandir in Patan is the centre for the celebrations and an all-night vigil is kept at the temple on the night before his birthday. Oil lamps light the temple and singing continues through the night.

Teej The Festival of Women lasts three days, from the second to the fifth day after the Bhadra new moon, and is based in Pashupatinath. Women celebrate Teej in honour of their husbands and in the hope of a long and happy married life.

The festival starts with feasting and talking, right through until midnight when women commence 24 hours of fasting. During the day of the fast, women from all over the valley converge on Pashupatinath, traditionally dressed in red and gold saris, usually the ones in which they were married. At Pashupatinath the women take ritual dips in the river and call on the gods to protect their husbands.

The following morning the women must offer their husbands small items of food which have previously been offered to the gods. The day-long fast can then be broken although some years the festival continues for an extra day (in which case this is a day of partial fasting). Another ritual bathing ceremony takes place on this day, preferably at a river confluence, such as where the Bagmati and Vishnumati Rivers meet just south of Kathmandu.

Gunla The 15 days before and after the full moon in August or early September is a full month of Buddhist ceremonies, penance and fasting. Activities are centred around Swayambhunath, west of Kathmandu. **Pancha Dan**, the Festival of Five Offerings, is a time of charity and is held in Patan during Gunla.

Indra Jatra This important festival runs from the end of the month of Bhadra into the beginning of Ashwin. Indra Jatra is a colourful and exciting festival, which manages to combine homage to Indra with an important annual appearance by Kumari (the living goddess), respects to Bhairab and commemoration of the conquest of the valley by Prithvi Narayan Shah. The festival also marks the end of the monsoon.

Indra, the ancient Aryan god of rain, was captured in the Kathmandu Valley stealing a certain flower for his mother Dagini. He was imprisoned until Dagini revealed his identity and his captors gladly released him. The festival celebrates this remarkable achievement (villagers don't capture a real god every day of the week). In return for his release Dagini promised to spread dew over the crops for the coming months and to take back with her to heaven all those who had died in the past year.

The festival honours the recently deceased and pays homage to Indra and Dagini for the coming harvests. It begins when a huge, carefully selected pole, carried via the Tundikhel, is erected outside the Hanuman Dhoka in Kathmandu. At the same time images and representations of Indra, usually as a captive, are displayed and sacrifices of goats and roosters are made; the screened doors obscuring the horrific face of White Bhairab are also opened and for the next three days his gruesome visage will stare out at the proceedings.

The day before all this activity, three golden temple chariots are assembled in Basantapur Square, outside the home of the Kumari. In the afternoon, with the Durbar Square packed with colourful and cheerful crowds, two boys emerge from the Kumari's house. They play the roles of Ganesh and Bhairab and will each ride in a chariot as an attendant to the goddess. Finally, the Kumari herself appears either walking on a rolled-out carpet or carried by attendants so that her feet do not touch the ground.

The chariots move off and the Kumari is greeted from the balcony of the old palace by the king. The procession then continues out of Durbar Square towards Hanuman Dhoka where it stops out in front of the huge Seto (White) Bhairab mask. The Kumari greets the image of Bhairab and then, with loud musical accompaniment, beer starts to pour from Bhairab's mouth! Getting a sip of this beer is guaranteed to bring good fortune, but one lucky individual will also get the small fish, which has been put to swim in the beer – this brings especially good luck.

Numerous other processions also take place around the town until the final day when the great pole is lowered and carried down to the river. It was during the Indra Jatra festival back in 1768 that Prithvi Narayan Shah conquered the valley and unified Nepal, so this important event is also commemorated in this most spectacular of Kathmandu occasions.

September–October

Pachali Bhairab Jatra The fearsome form of Bhairab, as Pachali Bhairab, is honoured on the fourth day of the bright fortnight in September or early October. The festivities for this are in line with Bhairab's bloodthirsty nature, as there are numerous sacrifices.

Dasain The pleasant post-monsoon period when the sky is clearest, the air is cleanest and the rice is ready for harvesting is also the time for Nepal's biggest annual festival. Dasain lasts for 15 days, finishing on the full-moon day of late September or early October. Although much of Dasain is a quiet family affair, there are colourful events for visitors to see both in Kathmandu and in the country. Dasain is also known as Durga Puja, as the festival celebrates the victory of the goddess Durga over the forces of evil personified by the buffalo demon Mahisasura. Since Durga is a bloodthirsty goddess, the festival is marked by wholesale blood-letting and features the biggest animal sacrifice of the year.

Before Dasain commences, Nepalis spring-clean their houses. In the country, swings and primitive hand-powered Ferris wheels are erected at the entrance to villages or in the main square. On the first day of the festival, a sacred jar of water is prepared in each house and barley seeds are planted in carefully prepared soil; getting the seeds to sprout a few centimetres during Dasain ensures a good harvest.

Although Dasain is principally a Hindu festival it has also been adopted by Buddhists and activities also take place at Buddhist shrines in Patan and Bhaktapur.

Fulpati is the first really important day of Dasain and is called the 'Seventh Day' although it may not actually fall on the seventh day. Fulpati means 'Sacred Flowers', and a jar containing flowers is carried from Gorkha to Kathmandu and presented to the king at the Tundikhel parade ground. The flowers symbolise Taleju, the goddess of the royal family, whose most important image is in the Gorkha Palace. From the parade ground, the flowers are transported on a palanquin to Hanuman Dhoka (the old Royal Palace) on Durbar Square where they are inspected again by the king and his entourage.

Maha Astami or the 'Great Eighth Day' and Kala Ratri, the 'Black Night', follow Fulpati and this is the start of the sacrifices and offerings to Durga. The hundreds of goats you may see contentedly grazing in the Tundikhel parkland prior to Maha Astami are destined to die to appease the goddess. At midnight, in a temple courtyard near Durbar

Square, eight buffaloes and 108 goats are beheaded with a single stroke of the sword or knife.

The next day is **Navami** and the Kot Square near Durbar Square, the scene of the great massacre of noblemen that led to the Rana period of Nepali history (see History in the Facts about Nepal chapter), is the scene for another great massacre. Visitors can witness the bloodshed, but you'll need to arrive early to secure a place. Sacrifices continue through the day and blood is sprinkled on the wheels of cars and other vehicles to ensure a safe year on the road. At the airport, each Royal Nepal Airlines Corporation aircraft will have a goat sacrificed to it! The average Nepali does not eat much meat, but on this day almost everybody in the country will find that goat is on the menu for dinner.

The 10th day of the festival, **Vijaya Dashami**, is again a family affair as cards and greetings are exchanged, family visits are made and parents place a *tika* (red mark) on their children's foreheads.

In the evening, the conclusion of Dasain is marked by processions and masked dances in the towns of the Kathmandu Valley. The Kharga Jatra, or sword procession, features priests dressed up as the various gods and carrying wooden swords, symbolic of the weapon with which Durga slew the buffalo demon. This day also celebrates the victory of Lord Rama over the evil, 10-headed, demon-king Ravana in the Ramayana. The barley sprouts that were planted on the first day are picked and worn as small bouquets in the hair.

Kartika Purnima, the full-moon day marking the end of the festival, is celebrated with gambling in many households, and you will see even small children avidly putting a few coins down on various local games of chance. Women fast and many of them make a pilgrimage to Pashupatinath near Kathmandu.

October–November

Tihar With its colourful Festival of Lights, Tihar (also called Diwali or Deepawali after the third day of celebrations) is the most important Hindu festival in India, and in Nepal it ranks second only to Dasain. The five days of festival activities take place in late October or early November.

The festival honours certain animals, starting with offerings of rice to the crows which are sent by Yama, the god of death, as his 'messengers of death'. On the second day, dogs are honoured with tikas and garlands of flowers. This must be a considerable surprise to most Nepali dogs, who are usually honoured with no more than the occasional kick, but the fact that in the afterworld it is dogs who guide departed souls across the river of the dead must not be forgotten. On the third day cows have their horns painted silver and gold. On the fourth day bullocks are honoured.

The third day, **Deepawali**, is the most important day of the festival when Lakshmi (Vishnu's consort and the goddess of wealth) comes to visit every home that has been suitably lit for her presence. No-one likes to turn down a visit from the goddess of wealth and so homes throughout the country are brightly lit with candles and lamps. The effect is highlighted because Deepawali falls on the new-moon day.

The fourth day is also the start of the New Year for the Newar people of the Kathmandu Valley. The fifth day is known as **Bhai Tika** and on this day brothers and sisters are supposed to meet and place tikas on each others' foreheads. Sisters offer small gifts of fruit and sweets to their brothers while the brothers give their sisters money in return. The markets and bazaars of Kathmandu are busy supplying the appropriate gifts.

Haribodhini Ekadashi An *ekadashi* falls twice in every lunar month, on the 11th day after each new and full moon, and is regarded as an auspicious day. The Haribodhini Ekadashi, falling in late October or early November (on the 11th day after the new moon) is the most important. On this day Vishnu awakens from his four-month monsoonal slumber. The best place to see the associated festivities is at Budhanilkantha, the temple of the sleeping Vishnu. Activities also take place at other Vishnu temples and many Vishnu devotees make a circuit of the important ones from Ichangu Narayan to Changu Narayan, Bishankhu Narayan and Sekh Narayan, all in the Kathmandu Valley.

Mahalakshmi Puja Lakshmi is the goddess of wealth, and to farmers wealth is rice. Therefore this harvest festival, immediately following Haribodhini Ekadashi, honours the goddess with sacrifices and colourful dances.

November–December

Mani Rimdu The Sherpa festival of Mani Rimdu takes place at the monastery of Tengboche in the Solu Khumbu region. This three-day festival features masked dances and dramas, which celebrate the victory of Buddhism over the existing Tibetan Bön religion.

Another Mani Rimdu festival takes place six months later in the lunar month of Jeth (May–June) at Thami Gompa, a day's walk west of Namche Bazaar.

Bala Chaturdashi Like Ekadashi, there are two *chaturdashis* each month; Bala Chaturdashi falls on the new-moon day in late November or early December. Pilgrims flock to Pashupatinath for this festival, burning oil lamps at night and bathing in the holy river on the following morning. A pilgrimage is then made along a traditional route through the woods overlooking Pashupatinath, and as they walk the devotees scatter sweets and seeds for their deceased relatives to enjoy in the afterlife.

The festival is at its most colourful during the first evening, and is best observed from the other side of the Bagmati River, looking down towards the temple at the lamp-lit singing and dancing pilgrims.

Sita Bibaha Panchami On the fifth day of the bright fortnight in late November or early December, pilgrims from all over Nepal and India flock to Janakpur to celebrate the marriage of Sita to Rama. It was in Janakpur that Sita was born, and she and Rama both have temples in the town. The wedding is re-enacted with a procession carrying Rama's image to Sita's temple by elephant. (Rama's birthday is celebrated in March in Janakpur and in Kathmandu.)

[Continued from page 80]

This will not only save time, but also cooking fuel, which is often firewood.

If you eat dal bhaat tarakari, most local restaurants (known as *bhojanahlaya*) and roadside stalls will be able to find you some kind of spoon (*chamchah* in Nepali), but the custom is to eat with your right hand. The number one eating rule in Nepal, as in much of Asia, is always use your right hand. The left hand, used for washing yourself after defecating, is never used to eat food and certainly should not be used to pass food (or anything at all) to someone else. Dal bhaat is often served in a metal plate called a *thali* and is an all-you-can-eat deal.

Foreign Cuisines

Although the real local food is often limited in its scope, Kathmandu's restaurants offer an amazing variety of dishes. In the days of 'Asia overlanding', when many travellers arrived in Kathmandu having made a long and often wearisome trip through Asia from Europe, Kathmandu's restaurants had a near mythical appeal.

These days, as most travellers jet straight in from abroad, the food doesn't seem quite so amazing, but Kathmandu's restaurants still give international cuisine a damn good try and they will attempt almost anything. There's a special appeal to being high in the Himalaya and being able to choose between anything from Mexican tacos to Japanese sukiyaki. Nepali interpretations of foreign dishes are sometimes a little off target but it's still a great place to try foreign cuisines, especially Tibetan and Indian dishes.

Such a variety of restaurants is particularly amazing when you consider that in 1955 Kathmandu had just one restaurant. Leave Kathmandu (and Pokhara) behind, however, and you're soon back to dal bhaat tarakari.

The culinary creativity has resulted in a number of hybrid foods that form a kind of unique Nepali 'tourist ghetto cuisine'. Chop suey, for example, comes American-style, with a sweet and sour-ish sauce over crispy noodles ('American chop suey' has a fried egg on top). 'Swiss rosti' consists of potatoes covered in cheese.

Nepal is one of the best places to try a range of Tibetan cuisine (it's certainly better than Tibet), though most dishes end up tasting remarkably similar. It's also great for Indian food. See the Nepali Menu Reader for a rundown of dishes.

Drinks

Nonalcoholic Tea is the national dink and comes in two distinct types. Tourist restaurants generally serve up the world's weakest tea, often a totally ineffectual Mechi teabag dunked into a glass of hot milk. Proper Nepali *chai* is a far more satisfying brew, where the tea leaves are boiled up together with milk, sugar and spices (sometimes called masala tea). Roadside tea stalls often make their *chai* with steamed milk from a little cappuccino-style machine.

In general *don't drink the water* (for details see the Health section earlier in this chapter). Most good restaurants do boil and filter their water (boiled water is *umaahleko pani* in Nepali), and tea is almost always safe. Lots of brands sell bottled water for about Rs 15 in the cities, though the price rises rapidly in the countryside. Kinley Water is bottled in Nepal by Coca Cola. See the Responsible Tourism section to find out what happens to all those unrecyclable plastic bottles.

Lassis – a refreshing drink of curd (yoghurt) mixed with sugar and what may be untreated water (proceed with caution) – are a highlight of travelling in the subcontinent and come in a range of sweet and salty flavours.

Alcoholic Locally produced Nepali beer is quite good, especially after a hard day's walking or bicycling around the valley. There are a number of brands that theoretically replicate the original recipes; Tuborg (Danish), Star (German), Carlsberg (Danish) and San Miguel (Filipino) are the most common, though you can also get Indian bottled Kingfisher and cans of Guinness brewed in Nepal! A 650mL bottle costs around Rs 120 in Kathmandu restaurants. Beer can usually be found in the hills as well, carried there by porters especially for thirsty trekkers, but it is unlikely to be cold.

Chang, the popular Himalayan homebrew, is a mildly alcoholic concoction made from barley, millet or rice and what may be untreated water. It's found along many trekking routes. *Tongba* is a similar brew made by pouring (and periodically re-adding) boiling water to a bamboo tube of fermented millet. It's generally drunk through a straw.

Harder spirits include *arak*, fermented from potatoes or grain, and *rakshi*, a Newari-style distilled rice wine that runs the gamut from smooth firewater to paint stripper. Kukhri Rum is probably the most famous locally bottled spirit.

Officially alcohol is not sold by retailers on the first two days and last two Saturdays of the Nepali month but this rarely affects foreigners or restaurants.

ENTERTAINMENT

Nepal is not the place to come if you're after the highlife. Nightlife is pretty much restricted to Kathmandu and to a lesser extent Pokhara; in other regional towns and cities it's very much early-to-bed territory, especially in areas that currently have an evening curfew.

Kathmandu has an increasing number of bars, mainly in the Thamel area, which stay open late, and there are a couple of low-key nightclubs. There's one cinema that shows Western films, and four casinos, all of them attached to five-star hotels.

Cultural performances are also held in Kathmandu, and as tourist entertainment at some of Chitwan's resorts. These generally involve local youths wearing a variety of dress over their jeans and performing traditional dances from Nepal's various ethnic groups, accompanied by a live band that includes a tabla, harmonium and singer.

SHOPPING

Nepal is a shopper's paradise, whether you are looking for a cheap souvenir or a real work of art. Although you can find almost anything in the tourist areas of Kathmandu, there are specialities in different parts of the Kathmandu Valley. Wherever you shop remember to bargain, although in shops that are completely tourist-oriented prices tend to be fixed.

Prices are low for foreign products in Kathmandu and Pokhara but you'll soon realise that you get what you pay for. Thamel's shops in particular are full of poor-quality Indian-printed books, Pakistani pirate CDs and locally made clothes that don't quite fit properly.

Remember that antiques cannot be taken out of the country, and baggage is inspected by Nepali customs with greater thoroughness on departure than on arrival. If you've bought something that could possibly be antique, you should get a receipt and a description of the object from the shop where you bought it. If it is (or even looks like) it could be more than 100 years old you need a permit from the Department of Archaeology to take it out of the country (see Customs earlier in this chapter).

Unless you are very sure about the reliability of the shop, do not ask the shop where you made the purchase to send it for you. See the Post section earlier for details on posting goods home.

Thangkas

Thangkas are the traditional Tibetan Buddhist paintings of religious and ceremonial subjects. The subject may be a mandala, the wheel of life, aspects of the Buddha or the various Bodhisattvas, fierce protector deities or historical figures.

Although there are genuine antique *thangkas* to be found, it's highly unlikely that anything offered to the average visitor will date from much beyond last week. Judicious use of a smoky fire can add the odd century in no time at all. *Thangkas* do vary considerably in quality but buy one because you like it, not as a valuable investment.

Thangkas are available in many locations including the Tibetan shops around Bodhnath. There are good *thangka* shops in Kathmandu's Thamel, Durbar Marg and Durbar Square areas. Like many other crafts the more you see the more you will appreciate the difference between those of average and those of superior quality. Traditionally *thangkas* are framed in silk brocade.

Paper Products

Locally produced paper (from the *lokta*, or daphne, plant) is used for the block prints of Nepali, Tibetan and Chinese deities. They are sold as pictures or are used for calendars, cards and lanterns. A print typically costs from Rs 50 to Rs 300. There's a good selection in the shops of Thamel.

Traditional Games

Nepal's national board game is *bagh chal*, which literally means 'move *(chal)* the tigers *(bagh)*'. The game is played on a lined board with 25 intersecting points. One player has four tigers, the other has 20 goats, and the aim is for the tiger player to 'eat' five goats by jumping over them before the goat player can encircle the tigers and prevent them moving. You can buy attractive brass *bagh chal* sets in Kathmandu, and in Patan where they are made.

Nepal's other popular game is carom, which looks like 'finger snooker', using discs which glide over a chalked-up board to pot other discs in the corner pockets.

Tibetan Carpets
Carpet-weaving is a major trade in Nepal. The skill was brought from Tibet by the refugees who now carry on the craft with great success in their new homes. There are carpet-weavers around the Kathmandu Valley and also in Pokhara. Some of their output is now exported to Tibet, where the Chinese have unfortunately managed to totally stamp out this archaic craft. A genuine Tibetan carpet purchased in Tibet is probably indeed made by Tibetans, but in Nepal the Tamang people also make carpets.

Jawlakhel, on the southern outskirts of Patan, is the carpet-weaving centre in the valley. You can see carpets being woven here and also in other places around the valley, including Bodhnath. The traditional size for a Tibetan carpet is 1.8m by 90cm. Small square carpets are often used to make seat cushions.

Carpet quality depends on knots per inch, and the price is worked out per square metre. A 60-knot carpet costs around Rs 1700 per sq metre, while a 100-knot carpet is Rs 4800 per sq metre.

Clothing & Embroidery
Tibetan and Nepali clothes have always been a popular buy, but Western fashions made strictly for the tourist market have also recently become a big industry. You can buy handmade shirts at outlets in Thamel.

There is still a demand for traditional styles such as the Tibetan wool jackets that are popularly known as *yakets*. Nepali coats, crossing over at the front, closed with four ties and traditionally made of purple velvet, are also a popular buy.

Embroidery has always been popular in Nepal and there are lots of little tailor shops around Kathmandu where the sewing machines rattle on late into the night adding colourful dragons and Tibetan symbols to customers' jackets and jeans. Mountaineers like to return from Nepal with jackets carrying the message that this was the Country X, Year Y expedition to Peak Z. You can also buy badges for your backpack saying that you walked to the Everest Base Camp or completed the Annapurna Circuit.

A Nepali *topi* or cap is part of Nepali formal wear for a man and they are traditionally made in Bhaktapur. There's a group of cap specialists between Indra Chowk and Asan Tole in the old part of Kathmandu. Caps typically cost from Rs 50 to Rs 300.

Pashmina
One of the latest hot souvenir items is a shawl or scarf made from fine *pashmina* (the under hair of a mountain goat). The cost of a *pashmina* depends on the percentage of *pashmina* in the mix and from which part of the goat's body that pashmina originated, starting from the cheapest back wool and rising through the belly and chest to neck hair, which is about five times more expensive than back hair.

There are literally dozens of shops in Thamel selling *pashmina* items. The cheapest shawls are a 70%/30% cotton-*pashmina* blend, and these cost around Rs 1500 for a 78cm by 2m shawl. Silk-*pashmina* blends cost around Rs 2500, while a pure *pashmina* shawl ranges from around Rs 3500 to US$275 for a *pashmina* ring shawl (named because they are fine enough to be pulled through a finger ring).

Shahtoosh is a form of *pashmina* that comes from (and results in the death of) the endangered Tibetan antelope. It is illegal in Nepal. See the Responsible Tourism section for details.

Jewellery
Kathmandu's many small jewellery manufacturers turn out a wide variety of designs with an equally wide range of standards. You can buy jewellery ready-made, ask them to create a design for you or bring in something you would like copied. There are several good shops around greater Thamel, particularly down towards Chhetrapati.

These outlets mainly cater to Western tastes but there are also many shops for the local market as Nepali women, like Indian women, traditionally wear their wealth in jewellery. Cheap ornaments can also be fun; you can buy an armful of glass bangles for a few rupees or colourful beads by the handful.

Masks & Puppets

Papier-mache masks and colourful puppets are sold at shops in Kathmandu, Patan and Bhaktapur. Thimi is the centre for manufacturing masks, which are used in the traditional masked dances in September – it's interesting to see masks being made there. Ganesh, Bhairab and the Kumari are the most popular subjects for the mask and they make good wall decorations. Prices typically range from around Rs 10 to Rs 500.

Puppets make good gifts for children and are made in Bhaktapur as well as other centres. They're often of multi-armed deities clutching little wooden weapons in each hand. The puppet heads may be made of easily broken clay or more durable papier-mache. Smaller puppets cost from around Rs 100 to Rs 400 but you can also pay from Rs 500 to Rs 1000 for a larger figure. As usual, quality does vary and the more puppets you inspect the more you will begin to appreciate the differences.

Metalwork

Patan is the valley centre for bronze casting and the best variety of metalwork is found in the shops around Patan's Durbar Square. (See Shopping under Patan in the Around the Kathmandu Valley chapter for more details.)

Other Souvenirs

A *khukuri*, the traditional knife of the Gurkhas, can cost from Rs 300 to Rs 2000. Most are made in eastern Nepal and come with a scabbard and a blade sharpener *(chakmak)*. Notice the notch *(kaudi)* in the blade which allows blood to run off before hitting the hilt. You may well have to explain the knife to customs officials (always carry it in your check-in, rather than carry-on, baggage).

Bhaktapur is the centre for woodcarving, and you can find good objects in and around Tachupal Tole.

Cassettes and CDs of Nepali, Indian and general Himalayan music are a fine souvenir of a visit to Nepal, though much of it is of the woolly New Age variety. There are lots of music shops in Kathmandu selling local music as well as pirated Western tapes and CDs (Rs 200 to Rs 250). The best-quality recordings are from Russia, though most come from Pakistan or Singapore. It's a good idea to test them out in the shop as there are a few rogues about. MP3 recordings are also available. There's a much smaller variety of tapes (Rs 90).

Tibetan crafts include a variety of religious items such as the *dorje* (thunderbolt symbol), prayer flags and the popular prayer wheels. Tibetans are keen traders, and prices at Bodhnath and Swayambhunath are often very high.

Incense *(dhoop)* is a popular buy, as are spices, ranging from single spices like cumin *(jeera)*, turmeric *(besar)* and fenugreek *(methi)* to various kinds of masala mixes.

Tea

Tea is grown in the east of Nepal, close to the border with India near Darjeeling where the finest Indian tea is grown. The Ilam, Kanyan and Mai Valley teas are the best Nepali brands, but they are not cheap. Expect to pay anything from Rs 600 (in Ilam) to Rs 1000 (in Thamel) per kilogram for good Ilam tea, which is not much cheaper than Darjeeling tea. The excellently named 'super fine tipi golden flower orange pekoe' tea is about as good as it gets. Connoisseurs choose the first or second flush, rather than substandard monsoon flush.

Getting There & Away

AIR

In the last couple of years international air connections to Nepal have been slashed. As we went to press only Thai Airways International (THAI), Qatar Airways, Gulf Air, Austrian Airlines, Indian Airlines and Biman Bangladesh Airlines were operating direct flights to Kathmandu.

Tribhuvan Airport

Kathmandu is the site of Nepal's only international airport, Tribhuvan Airport.

The international terminal is a modern building, but security measures aren't really up to scratch, as evidenced by the hijacking of an Indian Airlines plane in 1999 and frequently documented collisions between planes and birds during takeoff and landing.

Arrival & Departure When you arrive, just before immigration there is a bank that's open for flight arrivals, and which has decent exchange rates. Next door is the visa counter where you pay for your visa if you haven't got one already (see Visas in the Facts for the Visitor chapter).

There is a hotel reservations' counter as soon as you get out of customs at the airport. Most of the hotels it represents are reasonably expensive, but it has a few in the US$5 to US$10 bracket, and the staff arranges free transport. If you don't feel like tackling the touts and taxis outside the main doors, this service can be useful. Touts are excluded from the building, so everything is fairly calm until you hit the outside world.

When departing for an international flight check in at least two hours early, preferably three in the high season, as the check-in desks can be a bit of a scrum.

You need to show your ticket as you enter the departure hall, where all baggage is X-rayed and tagged. The X-ray machines that screen cargo baggage are not film-safe. Insist that the security officers physically inspect your film.

Pay your departure tax at the branch of Nabil Bank. It is possible to re-exchange Nepali rupees into US dollars here if you have the unused foreign exchange encashment receipts (the bank will keep the exchange receipt for its records). If you are

leaving for India, you can exchange between INRs 500 and INRs 2000 on presentation of your ticket.

Airlines

The notoriously unreliable Royal Nepal Airlines Corporation (RNAC) has a limited number of international services, currently to Hong Kong, Delhi, Bangkok, Osaka, Shanghai, Dubai, Bangalore and Mumbai (Bombay), but nothing to Europe. A chronic lack of aircraft means that even these skeleton services are sometimes suspended. It is worth flying with any airline other than RNAC if at all possible, as its services are frequently subject to delays and cancellations.

Austrian Airlines/Lauda Air (from Vienna) and the Dutch company Transavia (from Amsterdam) are currently the only airlines running direct flights between Europe and Nepal (Transavia was considering cutting its service at the time of writing). Two Middle Eastern airlines, Gulf Air and Qatar Airways, have connections between Europe and Nepal, with a change of plane in Dubai and Dohar respectively. Travellers arriving with other airlines from Europe or from the east coast of North America generally transfer to RNAC or Indian Airlines in New Delhi for the final short flight from New Delhi to Kathmandu.

Where to Sit

If you want to see the mountains as you fly into Kathmandu you must sit on the correct side of the aircraft. Flying in from the east – Bangkok, Kolkata (Calcutta), Hong Kong, or Yangon (Rangoon) – you want the right side. Flying in from the west – New Delhi, Varanasi or the Gulf – you want the left side

From the west coast of North America or from Australasia, Bangkok is the usual transfer point, although there are also flights to Kathmandu from Hong Kong. THAI and RNAC share the Bangkok–Kathmandu route.

Departure Tax
A departure tax of Rs 1100 is payable in Nepali rupees at the check-in counters in the departures terminal. The tax is Rs 770 if you are flying to South Asian Area Regional Cooperation (SAARC) countries (India, Pakistan, Bhutan or Bangladesh).

The UK & Europe
Two of the best budget travel agencies are STA Travel (☎ 020-7361 6262; W www.sta.co .uk) and Trailfinders (020-7938 3939; W www .trailfinders.com), but you'll find others advertised in the Sunday papers. If you're going through a smaller agency, make sure it is a member of the Association of British Travel Agents (ABTA).

London to Kathmandu costs £650 return in the high season; Gulf Air charges around £800 return. Austrian Airlines/Lauda Air charge €600 for the once-weekly return flight from Vienna to Kathmandu.

One-way air fares from Kathmandu to most European destinations cost around US$560.

The USA & Canada
Intense competition between Asian airlines on the US west coast and Vancouver has resulted in ticket discounting.

The *New York Times*, the *Chicago Tribune*, the *LA Times* and the *San Francisco Examiner* all produce weekly travel sections in which you'll find any number of travel agency ads. Student travel specialists STA Travel (☎ 800-777-0112; W www.sta.com) has offices in major US cities.

Fares to Kathmandu will often be about the same from the east coast (via Europe) or west coast (via Asia) – it's about as far away as you can get in either direction. Multiple connections can make for some mammoth trips, especially as most connections to Kathmandu involve a layover.

From New York the cheapest connection is with Aeroflot to New Delhi via Moscow and then RNAC to Kathmandu.

From the west coast most flights go to Bangkok via Tokyo, Seoul, Taipei or Singapore, staying overnight in Bangkok to catch a flight the next day with THAI.

Typical return fares are around US$1400 to US$2200.

From Kathmandu, a one-way ticket with THAI and Northwest to the US west coast and Vancouver is around US$650; to the east coast via Europe it's US$750 to US$850.

Australia & New Zealand
Both STA Travel (☎ Australia-wide 131 776; W www.statravel.com) and Flight Centre (☎ Australia-wide 131 600; W www.flight centre.com) are major dealers in cheap airfares in both Australia and New Zealand. Check the travel agency ads in the *Yellow Pages* or the travel section in the Saturday newspapers and phone around.

Fares from Australia depend on the season and typically cost around A$1500 return. Bangkok is the most popular transit point although you can also fly via Singapore or Hong Kong.

From Kathmandu to east coast Australia, a one-way ticket costs US$660 to US$700 with THAI or Singapore Airlines.

Return airfares to Kathmandu from Auckland, New Zealand start from around NZ$1980.

India
RNAC and Indian Airlines share the main routes between India and Kathmandu. Both airlines give a 25% discount to those under 30 years of age on flights between Kathmandu and India; no student card is needed.

The Nepali airline Necon Air (W www .neconair.com) also has flights that connect Kathmandu with Varanasi (US$73) and Patna (US$78).

New Delhi is the main departure point for flights between India and Kathmandu. The one-hour New Delhi to Kathmandu flight costs US$145 one way. RNAC has two flights daily, Indian Airlines has one.

Other cities in India with direct connections to Kathmandu are: Kolkata (US$99), Bangalore (US$260, US$213 discounted) and Mumbai (US$260, US$213 discounted).

Elsewhere in Asia

Other Asian destinations from Kathmandu include Bangkok (US$223), Dhaka (US$90), Karachi (US$195), Lhasa (US$273), Hong Kong (US$353), Shanghai (US$355), and Dubai (US$253). Return airfares from Osaka start at around ¥95,000.

There are also some interesting through fares; one to consider is with Biman Bangladesh Airlines, whose Kathmandu–Dhaka–Yangon–Bangkok ticket sells for US$310 one way and allows a stop in Yangon and (mandatory) Dhaka. Biman will normally put you up in a hotel for one night in Dhaka – all other costs are left to you. The Dhaka–Yangon–Bangkok leg runs once a week.

Bangkok–Kathmandu tickets are generally cheaper bought in Bangkok.

It's worth noting that THAI's Kathmandu–Bangkok flight is the most popular connection into and out of Nepal and can get booked up for weeks at a time, particularly mid-December to January. Make your booking as far in advance as possible.

LAND

Political and weather conditions permitting, there are four main entry points into Nepal by land: three from India, one from Tibet.

A steady trickle of people drive their own vehicles overland from Europe, for which an international carnet is required. If you want to abandon your transport in Nepal, you must either pay a prohibitive import duty or surrender it to customs. It is not possible to import cars more than five years old.

As this book went to print, fuel price rises had pushed train and bus fares up 20%.

India

The most popular crossing points from India are Sunauli (south of Pokhara); between Raxaul Bazaar and Birganj (south of Kathmandu); and Kakarbhitta (near Siliguri and Darjeeling in the far east). There are other less popular, but still viable, options.

All the options described in this section involve trains, buses or both.

To/From Delhi If you are travelling to or from Delhi or elsewhere in western India, the route through Sunauli and Bhairawa is the most convenient as it involves more train travel and less bus travel.

The route through Mahendranagar in the far west of Nepal allows a visit to Royal Bardia National Park on the way, but check with government travel advisories to see if there has been any Maoist activity along the Mahendra Hwy before travelling on this route.

Via Sunauli Delhi to Gorakhpur involves an overnight rail journey, from where frequent buses make the three- to four-hour run to the border at Sunauli.

Night and day buses from Sunauli to Kathmandu or Pokhara (both 10 hours) travel northeast along the beautiful Siddhartha Hwy as far as Mugling before joining the Kathmandu–Pokhara (Prithvi) Hwy.

For more information, see Sunauli & Bhairawa in The Terai & Mahabharat Range chapter.

Via Mahendranagar There are daily buses from Delhi to Banbassa, the nearest Indian village to the border (INRs 138, 10 hours). Banbassa is also connected by bus with the hill station Almora in India, as well as with Agra and Dharamsala, but train connections to the nearest broad-gauge Indian railway station at Barielly, about three hours from the border by bus, are generally more trouble than they are worth. It's a short rickshaw ride to the border, where buses take you on for the short ride to Mahendranagar bus station.

There are direct buses from Mahendranagar to Kathmandu at 2pm, but they take a gruelling 15 hours. It's much better to do the beautiful trip during daylight and to break the journey at Royal Bardia National Park (four hours from Mahendranagar) or Nepalganj (five hours from Mahendranagar) or both.

For more information on the border crossing, see Mahendranagar in The Terai & Mahabharat Range chapter.

To/From Varanasi Once again, it is the Sunauli crossing that is most convenient. There are direct buses here from Varanasi (INRs 120 to INRs 140, 10 hours). From Sunauli it's another eight to 10 hours to Kathmandu or Pokhara.

Some private Indian companies make bookings all the way through to Kathmandu and Pokhara for around INRs 400, including Spartan accommodation at Sunauli. However, if you organise things yourself as you go, it will be cheaper, and you will have more flexibility, including a choice of bus within Nepal and of accommodation in Sunauli (there are several reasonable hotels in Sunauli and nearby Bhairawa).

To/From Kolkata (Calcutta) & Patna

The entry point between Raxaul Bazaar (India) and Birganj (Nepal) is the most convenient option in the east of India.

In India, the overnight train from Kolkata to Patna takes about seven hours. It's then a six-hour journey by bus (INRs 100 to INRs 110) from Patna to Raxaul Bazaar (the Indian border town). Alternatively, take the overnight *Mithila Express* train from Kolkata to Raxaul (INRs 245/1085 2nd class/air-con two-tier). It departs at 4.30pm and arrives around 7.30am (though it's often a couple of hours late).

Raxaul Bazaar is virtually a twin town with Birganj in Nepal and it's easiest to take an autorickshaw between the two. Both towns are dirty, unattractive transit points strung along the highway and are full of heavy traffic. The border is open from 7am to 7pm every day.

Direct buses between Birganj and Kathmandu (10 hours) and Pokhara (nine hours), travel via Narayanghat and Mugling, not along the Tribhuvan Hwy via Daman. This means that all buses go through Tadi Bazaar, the jumping-off point for Sauraha and Royal Chitwan National Park.

For more information on the border crossing, see Birganj in The Terai & Mahabharat Range chapter.

To/From Darjeeling

Kakarbhitta is the entry point in the far east of Nepal, and there are good connections to West Bengal.

There are many companies that handle bookings between Darjeeling and Kathmandu (around INRs 460), although with all of them you have to change buses at Siliguri (in India) and at the border.

It's just as easy to get from Darjeeling to Kathmandu on your own, although this involves four changes – an early morning bus/jeep (INRs 50/60) from Darjeeling to Sili-

guri, a bus/jeep (INRs 12/35, one hour) from Siliguri to Panitanki on the Indian border, a rickshaw across the border to Kakarbhitta (INRs 7), and an afternoon bus on to Kathmandu. This is cheaper than the package deal, and you have a choice of buses from the border; you also have the option of travelling during the day and overnighting along the way.

There are also direct share 4WDs to the border from Kalimpong (INRs 70, three hours).

Buses from Kakarbhitta to Kathmandu (14 hours) travel via Narayanghat and Mugling. Most are night buses, which can save time and money on a hotel, but you'll miss some fine scenery and it is more dangerous; there have been cases of bandits robbing buses along the Mahendra Hwy at night, and then there's also the government night-time curfew throughout much of the region.

If you have time, it is worth considering breaking your journey at Janakpur, which is roughly halfway, and is an interesting place in its own right. This will enable you to travel during the day and get a feel for the Terai; the flood plain of the Sapt Kosi is particularly interesting. See the Kakarbhitta section in The Terai & Mahabharat Range chapter for details.

Ticket Packages Many travellers have complained about scams involving ticket packages to India. The package usually involves coordination between at least three different companies so the potential for an honest cock-up is at least as high as the potential for a deliberate rip-off.

Two long-standing and reliable Nepali companies handling through tickets are **Wayfarers Travel Service** (☎ 4266010; W www.wayfarers.com.np) in Thamel, Kathmandu; and **Yeti Travels** (☎ 4221234; e yeti@ vishnuccsl.com.np) in Durbar Marg, Kathmandu. Both require a minimum of a week to arrange tickets.

Everyone has to change buses at the border whether they book a through ticket or not and, despite claims to the contrary, there are no 'tourist' buses on either side of the border. Buses through to Varanasi cost around Rs 800, and to Darjeeling Rs 1000. Bus-and-train packages to Agra cost Rs 3350, including an air-con sleeper on the train, or Rs 1325 in a 2nd-class sleeper. Bus and train to Delhi costs Rs 3800 with air-con, Rs 1100 in a 2nd-class sleeper. These prices are significantly more expensive than buying the tickets as you go, but they do give you confirmed bookings and peace of mind. (Note that the fares given in this section are in Nepali rupees.)

It is worth considering making advance bookings on the Indian railways if you are in a hurry or are fussy over which class you want. Some trains, and especially sleeping compartments, can be heavily booked (this is apparently the case for Gorakhpur to Delhi trains). Make sure you get a receipt clearly specifying what you think you have paid for, and hang on to it.

Tibet

The bad news is that officially only organised 'groups' are allowed into Tibet. The good news is that you can temporarily join a group (of at least four other travellers) to get into Tibet and, after the 'tour', travel as a de facto independent traveller.

This is not an easy trip by any means. Altitude sickness is a real danger as the maximum altitude along the road is 5140m and budget overland tours do not allow sufficient time to safely acclimatise. Take food and drink, as there's not much available in between towns.

The road is poor and regularly closed by landslides during the monsoon. Political protests, sensitive political dates and political meetings inside Tibet or China are often followed (or preceded) by restrictions on visitors to the region.

The bottom line is that if you intend to enter or leave Nepal via Tibet you should come prepared with alternative plans in case travel along this route proves impossible.

In general, travellers face fewer restrictions entering Tibet through China and continuing on to Nepal than they do entering Tibet from Nepal.

Coming from Tibet, it's generally not possible to catch a bus direct to Kathmandu so you'll have to take one of the frequent buses to Barabise (five hours) and from there change to a Kathmandu-bound bus (two hours).

Travel Restrictions The first thing you need is a Chinese visa (see Embassies &

Consulates in the Facts for the Visitor chapter for more details). Regulations on this vary considerably, but in general you'll have more flexibility if you arrive in Nepal with a Chinese visa already in your passport.

As long as you have an individual Chinese visa, once in Tibet you can leave the tour in Lhasa and continue on your own. If this is your intention, make sure you state this when booking the tour in Kathmandu. Agencies can arrange a Chinese visa when you book your tour, but check in advance whether you will get an individual visa or get lumped onto a group visa, as splitting from a group visa in Lhasa can be a difficult and costly exercise. Agencies take about a week to get a Chinese visa in Kathmandu and costs are around US$33.

To enter Tibet you also need a Tibet Tourism Permit, which can only be arranged by a travel agent.

Tour Options A variety of options are currently available. The quickest way to get into Tibet is to buy a fly-in package to Lhasa from Kathmandu. At the time of research, agencies were offering a one-way flight (US$273) with a permit and airport transfers (US$110). At times of political tension you may have to book a return flight, though you might be able to cancel the return leg in Lhasa. China Southwest Airlines suspended its winter flights (mid-November to April) in 2002/3 so you'll have to check whether they have been reinstated if you want to travel during this time.

Several agencies advertise fixed-departure, overland trips to Tibet. The cheapest is a five-day, one-way, overland trip, currently around US$150/190, which covers transport by bus/Land Cruiser, dormitory accommodation, and permits. A seven-day, one-way package that includes Mt Everest runs to around US$300, with entry fees and hotel accommodation. Some agencies also run return trips to Mt Kailash from Kathmandu (US$1600). Rates are slightly higher in the peak season months of July, August and September.

Before handing over the cash, ascertain whether you are required to share a room, and how many people will travel in each Land Cruiser (often five, plus a driver and sometimes a guide which is a real squeeze). Note that agencies may pool customers if numbers are low. Travellers have complained that their promised Land Cruiser turned out to be a dilapidated bus (travel to the Tibet border is always in a minibus), or that the agreed bus wasn't available and that they had to pay an extra US$50 or more per person for a Land Cruiser. Buses normally only operate during the dry months of August, September and October.

The following agencies in Kathmandu operate trips to Tibet. Most agencies advertising in Thamel are agents only; they don't actually run the trips.

Adventure Silk Road (☎ 4432135, W www.silkroadgroup.com) Thamel

Arniko Travel (☎ 4439906, W www.arnikotravel.com) Baluwatar, opposite the Chinese embassy. Top-end return tours from Nepal only.

Explore Nepal Richa Tours & Travel (☎ 4423064, W www.explorenepalricha.com) PO Box 1657, Namche Bazaar Bldg, Thamel, Kathmandu

Green Hill Tours (☎ 4414968, W www.greenhilltours.com) PO Box 5072, Thamel, Kathmandu. Runs two fixed departures a week, on Saturday and Tuesday

Royal Mount Trekking (☎ 4241452, e royalmt@mos.com.np) Durbar Marg

Getting Around

Getting around Nepal can be a challenging business. The impossible terrain and extreme weather conditions, plus a high level of disorganisation, mean that trips rarely go exactly according to plan. On the other hand, Nepali ingenuity will usually get you to your destination in the end. Although travel can be frustrating, it also creates memorable moments by the score. Good humour, patience and snacks are essential prerequisites.

The whole gamut of transport options is available in Nepal, from hot-air balloons to elephants. Walking is still the most important, and the most reliable, method of getting from A to B and for moving cargo; more is carried by people and porters in Nepal than by every other form of transport combined.

One of the major considerations when using any form of public transport is to avoid travelling during festival times, especially major ones such as Dasain and Tihar (Diwali). Buses and planes are booked solid and it can be extremely difficult to get about – you will probably end up on the roof of a bus and forget flying if you haven't booked in advance. Generally, you will find it easier to get a bus seat if you catch it at it's source rather than in mid-run.

As this book went to print, rising fuel costs had pushed land transport costs up by 20%. Hopefully this price increase will be temporary!

AIR

A number of private companies operate alongside the long-running, government-owned and chronically inefficient Royal Nepal Airlines Corporation (RNAC). These airlines operate largely on the popular (ie, economically viable, tourist-oriented) routes, although government regulations require that airlines devote 40% of their capacity to non-tourist routes. The prices for the private airlines are slightly more than RNAC (by US$10 per sector), but they offer better service and are much more reliable.

Most flights operate out of Kathmandu, but there are minor air hubs at Pokhara, Nepalganj in the southwest and Biratnagar in the southeast.

RNAC operates by far the most comprehensive range of scheduled flights around the country, with flights to Bajhang, Bajura, Bhojpur, Biratnagar, Dhangadhi, Dolpo, Jomsom, Kathmandu, Lamidanda, Lukla, Mahendranagar, Manang, Nepalganj, Phaplu, Pokhara, Ramechhap, Rumjatar, Rumkum,

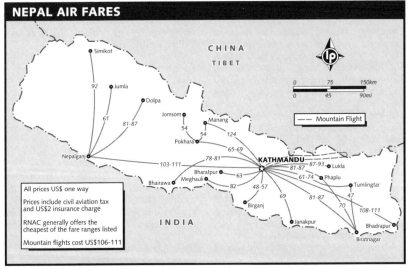

NEPAL AIR FARES

All prices US$ one way

Prices include civil aviation tax and US$2 insurance charge

RNAC generally offers the cheapest of the fare ranges listed

Mountain flights cost US$106-111

Mountain Flights

Every morning during the clear dry-season months (October to April), all the major private airlines offer mountain flights, with panoramic dawn views of the Himalaya and commentary on the passing peaks. Each passenger on six- to 30-seat turbo props is guaranteed a window seat and a visit to the cockpit.

The hour-long flight from Kathmandu costs US$111. If the weather is clear the views are stunning. Purists recommend Buddha Air as its planes are more spacious and fly you closer to Everest itself.

Sanfebagar, Simikot, Surkhat, Taplejung and Tumlingtar.

Necon Air (W *www.neconair.com*) is one of the largest private operators. It services Kathmandu, Birganj/Simara, Bhadrapur, Bhairawa, Biratnagar, Nepalganj and Pokhara.

Buddha Air (W *www.buddhaair.com*) and **Mountain Air** have fast, modern aircraft; the trip to Pokhara takes just 20 minutes, compared with up to 40 minutes with RNAC. Buddha Air has daily flights servicing Kathmandu, Biratnagar, Bhadrapur, Bhairawa, Nepalganj and Pokhara.

Cosmic Air (W *www.cosmicair.com*) services Kathmandu, Bhadrapur, Bharatpur, Jomsom, Pokhara and Tumlingtar. The Sherpa-owned **Yeti Airlines** (W *www.yeti-airlines.com*) flies to Kathmandu, Lukla, Phaplu, Lamidanda, Manang, Simara (for Birganj), Nepalganj and Dolpa, among other places.

Other airlines with websites include **Skyline Airways** (W *www.yomari.com/skyline*), **Shangri-La Air** (W *www.shangrilaair.com.np*) and **Gorkha Airlines** (W *www.gorkhaairlines.com.np*).

Some flights, such as Kathmandu to Lukla (the main airstrip in the Everest region), are used mainly by trekkers. These flights are frequent during the trekking season, but schedules can be extremely variable. Kathmandu to Jomsom flights, for example, are plagued by bad weather resulting in regular cancellations and a backlog of frustrated travellers at both ends. For flights in and out of Jomsom, Cosmic Air is the one to choose; for Lukla, Sherpa-owned Yeti Airlines.

Maoist activity temporarily closed several domestic airports in remote parts of the country in 2002, including the trekking gateways of Lukla and Jumla. Check the state of play before basing your plans around remote airports, especially in the far west.

Try to book domestic flights a week in advance and, just as for flights out of Nepal, the most important rule is to reconfirm and reconfirm again. Names can 'fall off' the passenger list, particularly when there is pressure for seats. This is much more of a problem with RNAC than private operators.

Air Fares

Residents and Nepali citizens pay approximately 35% of the tourist price for domestic air fares. Airlines will accept payment from visitors only in hard currency. See the Nepal Air Fares chart for details.

All travellers are charged an insurance surcharge (imposed in the wake of September 11) of US$2 per leg. The air fares in this book include this tax.

Domestic Airport

The domestic terminal is the old Kathmandu airport, and its age shows. It can be a chaotic spot, particularly when flights are cancelled and crowds of stressed tourists generate an atmosphere of fear and loathing. You can escape the worst of the crush in the fairly run-down restaurant on the 1st floor.

Check in an hour early for domestic flights; there is an Rs 165 airport tax payable at check-in. Don't carry pocket knives, gas cigarette lighters or matches in your carry-on luggage on any domestic flights as they will be confiscated.

It can be difficult finding a taxi into Kathmandu if you arrive late. If the worst comes to the worst, it's a 10-minute walk to the international terminal, where you are certain to find something.

See Getting Around in the Kathmandu chapter for information on transport to and from the airport.

BUS

Buses are the main form of public transport in Nepal and in relative terms they're incredibly cheap. Very often they're also incredibly uncomfortable. They run pretty much everywhere and will stop for anyone. You can jump on local buses anywhere, but for longer-distance buses it's best to book a couple of days in advance.

The government bus company, known as Sajha Yatayat, has distinctive blue-and-white buses that service all the main routes except the far east and far west. Although marginally cheaper than private buses, these buses are generally very shabby, poorly maintained and rarely run to schedule; overall they are best avoided. Each major town has a Sajha office where you can make advance reservations.

On popular tourist runs such as Kathmandu–Pokhara and Kathmandu–Nagarkot there are a number of slightly higher-grade services aimed particularly at the tourist market.

There are literally dozens of private bus companies – it seems all you need is one bus and you've got yourself a company. The condition of the buses range from reasonably comfortable minibuses to lumbering dinosaurs held together by little more than bits of wire and the combined hopes of the passengers. As with the Sajha buses, there is a booking office in each town where you can buy tickets for long-distance routes in advance.

On the longer routes there are 'express' minibuses, scheduled both by day and night. Fares are cheap, and day buses are marginally cheaper than night buses. Day travel, although slower, is generally preferable because you get to see the countryside (and there are some spectacular roads) and it's considerably safer. Express bus drivers have mastered the art of maniacal driving, and accidents are not uncommon.

Bottom of the heap are the local buses that run shorter routes, carry people, their luggage and often animals, and seem to stop more than they go. Travelling by local bus is no fun and should be kept to a minimum, although to reach many of the trekking road-heads there is little alternative.

Long-distance bus travel has slowed down recently due to the large number of tedious checkpoints set up by the Nepali military to counter potential Maoist activity. These generally involve everyone getting off the bus and walking through a checkpoint. Tourists are normally exempt and can stay on the bus. A couple of these checks can severely delay a trip, especially when buses start to back up. Hopefully this problem will ease when the political stand-off is resolved.

Air-conditioning of the Gods

Though we don't particularly recommend it, many people – locals and westerners – prefer to ride on bus roofs. While this is officially banned in the Kathmandu Valley, it is common elsewhere, particularly during Dasain when pressure for seats is greatest. The arguments in favour are that you get an exhilarating ride with great views, the opportunity to watch your bags and, sometimes, room to stretch your legs.

If you do ride on the roof, make sure you're well wedged in, so you don't catapult off when the bus swerves, brakes, or lurches. It's also best to sit facing forwards – that way you can see low-hanging wires and branches before you get swatted. Make sure you have sunscreen and appropriate clothing too as it can be surprisingly cold up there.

TRAIN

There are two train lines from Janakpur, one runs east to Jaynagar over the Indian border, and the other which runs northwest to Bijalpur, although only the former route carries passenger traffic. They're narrow-gauge trains and very slow, so they offer an interesting, if somewhat crowded, method of seeing the countryside. Note that tourists are not allowed to cross the border using the passenger train. See the Around Janakpur section in the Terai & Mahabharat Range chapter for more details.

CAR & MOTORCYCLE

There are no drive-yourself rental cars available in Nepal, but you can easily hire cars with drivers, or just a taxi. Expect to pay around US$40 a day, plus fuel, which at the time of research was set at Rs 52 per litre across the country.

It is quite popular to hire cars for return trips to both Pokhara and Royal Chitwan National Park from Kathmandu. A car to Pokhara should cost around US$30 one way, although this can rise at peak times. A car to Chitwan should cost around US$60, but could be more expensive at peak times. Remember that you'll have to pay for the driver's return trip whether or not you yourself return, as well as his food and accommodation for overnight trips.

Motorcycles can be rented in Kathmandu and Pokhara. See Getting Around in those chapters for more details about car and motorcycle rental.

If you do drive be aware that left turns are allowed without stopping, even at controlled intersections with red lights. Also, traffic entering a roundabout has priority over traffic already on the roundabout.

BICYCLE
In Kathmandu and Pokhara there are many bicycle-rental outlets and this is a cheap and convenient way of getting around. Virtually the entire Kathmandu Valley is accessible by bicycle, though if you are venturing far outside the Kathmandu and Patan area, a mountain bike is definitely worthwhile. A regular bicycle costs around Rs 50 per day to rent, and a mountain bike costs from Rs 100 to Rs 200. Children's bicycles can also be hired. See the Mountain Biking chapter for more information on cycling in Nepal.

HITCHING
Hitching is not possible in Nepal so don't bother trying. Those people waiting by the roadside are waiting for local buses.

LOCAL TRANSPORT
Taxi
Larger towns such as Kathmandu and Pokhara have taxis which, between a group of people, can be a good way to explore the Kathmandu Valley. Metered taxis have black licence plates; private cars often operate as taxis, particularly on long-distance routes or for extended periods, and have red plates.

Taxi meters are sometimes out of date (at the time of research they were OK), in which case tourists will be hard pushed to convince drivers to use them (with or without a surcharge) and will almost certainly have to negotiate the fare in advance. You will always pay more for a negotiated fare than a metered fare.

Tempo
Three-wheeled tempos are a common form of local transport throughout the country. Tempos are designed to seat about eight people; in practice they seat anything up to 15. They run on set routes, often only leave when full and can be very useful for travelling short distances; the fare is rarely more than Rs 10. Drivers pick up and drop off anywhere along the route; tap on the roof when you want to stop.

In 2000, all diesel tempos were banned in the Kathmandu Valley, and have been replaced by electric and gas powered *safa* (clean) tempos and conventional petrol minibuses. This has made a noticeable difference to the levels of air pollution in the valley; the old Vikram tempos have all been relocated and can now be seen doing their smoke-belching best to clog the air of Terai towns.

Autorickshaw & Cycle-Rickshaw
Autorickshaws, those curious and noxious three-wheeled, two-stroke-engine devices, are found in Kathmandu. They are less comfortable, but cheaper, than taxis. Like taxis, most have meters, though you may have to persuade the driver to use it.

Cycle-rickshaws are common in the old part of Kathmandu and can be a good way of making short trips through the crowded and narrow streets. They are also the most common form of short-distance public transport in towns throughout the Terai. Prices are highly negotiable.

ORGANISED TOURS
There are few organised tours available in Kathmandu or to places of interest around the valley and farther afield. It's usually a matter of organising something through a travel agent. For activities, see Organised Trekking in the Trekking chapter and Organised Tours in the Rafting & Kayaking chapter.

Kathmandu

☎ 01 • pop 700,000 • elevation 1337m

For most visitors to Nepal, Kathmandu is their arrival point and the centre of their visit. It is the capital of Nepal, the largest (and pretty much the only) city in the country and the main centre for hotels and restaurants. This amazing city seems, in places, unchanged since the Middle Ages; at other times it is just another developing-world capital rushing into a modern era of concrete and traffic pollution.

Along with the Kathmandu Valley's other two main cities – Bhaktapur and Patan – Kathmandu has an artistic and architectural tradition that rivals anything you'll find in the great cities of Europe.

Kathmandu has been attracting travellers since the 1960s and today's tourists range from well-heeled group tourists and Gore-Tex–clad climbers to the dreadlocked offspring of Nepal's original hippy trailblazers.

For many people, stepping off a plane into Kathmandu is a shock – the sights, sounds and smells can lead to sensory overload. Whether it be buzzing around the crazy polluted traffic in a taxi, trundling down the narrow winding streets of the old town in a rickshaw, marvelling at Durbar Square packed with its extraordinary temples and monuments or avoiding the tiger balm sellers and trekking touts, Kathmandu can be an intoxicating, amazing and exhausting place.

Kathmandu is the administrative and educational centre for the country and attracts hundreds of embassies, aid agencies and government offices (often converted from the grand palaces of the Rana period), as well as a heavy sprinkling of hotels, trekking agencies and tourist-related services. Despite the pressures of extreme overcrowding and poverty, the town is of a manageable size and people retain a good-humoured self-respect and integrity.

With its tourist comforts, Kathmandu is well worth a week of your time, despite the hassle and pollution, but it's all too easy to spend too much of your time stuck in touristy Thamel. Enjoy the Internet connections, the Western music and the lemon cheesecake, but make sure you also get out into the more interesting countryside, the 'real Nepal', before your time runs out.

Highlights

- Strolling around Kathmandu's medieval-like old town and soaking up its atmosphere
- Whiling away an hour or two on the steps of the Maju Deval, watching the passing parade of humanity in Durbar Square
- Dining in one of the city's superb Newari restaurants, with the accompaniment of traditional dances
- Shopping till you drop in Thamel for cut-price CDs, books, backpacks, carpets and handicrafts
- Chilling out in a rooftop garden with a good book and a slice of chocolate cake

HISTORY

The history of Kathmandu is really a history of the Newar people, the main inhabitants of the Kathmandu Valley. While the documented history of the valley goes back to the Kiratis, around the 7th century BC, the foundation of Kathmandu itself dates from the 12th century AD, during the time of the Malla dynasty.

Originally known as Kantipur, the city flourished during the Malla reign, and its superb temples, buildings and other monuments date from this time. Initially, Kathmandu was an independent city within the valley, but in the 14th century the valley was united under the rule of the Malla king of Bhaktapur. The 15th century saw the valley divided once again, this time into the three independent kingdoms of Kathmandu, Patan and Bhaktapur. Rivalry between the three city-states led to a series of wars that left each state weakened and paved the way for the 1768 invasion of the valley by Prithvi Narayan Shah of the kingdom of Gorkha.

The Shah dynasty unified Nepal and made Kathmandu the new capital – a position the city has held ever since. The Shahs also retain their position, however these days the political landscape has changed drastically.

ORIENTATION

Most of the interesting things to see in Kathmandu are clustered in the old part of town

KATHMANDU

KATHMANDU

PLACES TO STAY
4 Hacienda Apartment Hotel
16 Astoria Hotel
17 Hotel Shangri-La
21 Milarepa Guest House
25 Grand Hotel
26 Soaltee Crowne Plaza Hotel
35 Dwarika's Village Hotel; Krishnarpan Restaurant

PLACES TO EAT
29 Mike's Breakfast; Indigo Gallery
37 Bhojan Griha

OTHER
1 Balaju Swimming Pool
2 Mahendra Park
3 Kathmandu Bus Station
5 Tribhuvan University Teaching Hospital
6 Pakistan Embassy
7 Australian Embassy
8 Thai Embassy
9 Bangladesh Embassy
10 Pasang Lhamu Climbing Wall

11 Dhum Varahi Shrine
12 Chinese Embassy
13 Kathmandu Center of Healing
14 US Embassy
15 Japanese Embassy
18 Canadian Consulate
19 Mahaguthi; Sana Hastakala
20 Indian Embassy
22 Golden Amitabha Buddha
23 Natural History Museum
24 National Museum
27 Patanjali Yoga Centre
28 Banu's Total Fitness
30 Woodmaster Gallery
31 Police HQ
32 Chandra Binayak Ganesh Temple
33 Chabahil Stupa
34 Jayabageshwari Temple
36 German Embassy
38 New Zealand Honorary Consul
39 Maps of Nepal
40 International Conference Centre

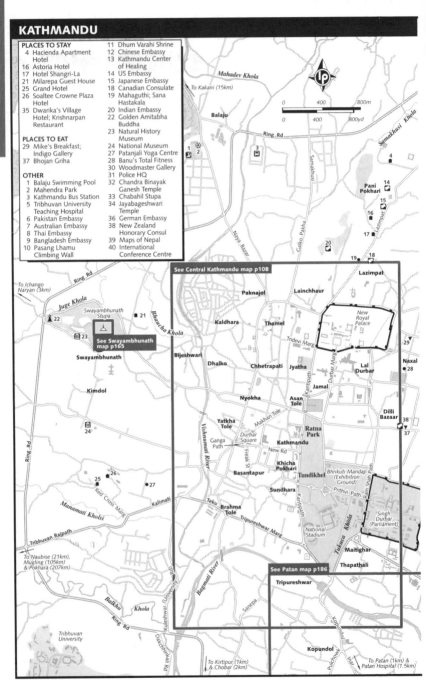

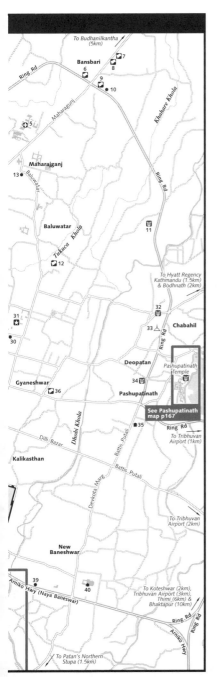

from Kantipath (the main north–south road) west towards the Vishnumati River (see the Kathmandu map). New Rd, constructed after the great earthquake of 1934, starts from the ugly ornamental gateway (where New Rd intersects with Kantipath) and goes straight into the heart of old Kathmandu, changing its name to Ganga Path before it comes to Durbar Square.

The offices of Royal Nepal Airlines (RNAC) are at the Kantipath end of New Rd, and along New Rd are banks, shops and the modern shopping area of the city. Continue farther west along New Rd to Ganga Path and you reach the large Basantapur Square, then Durbar Square and the Hanuman Dhoka (old Royal Palace). Freak St, Kathmandu's famous street from the hippie overland era, runs south off Basantapur Square.

Running northeast from Durbar Square is Makhan Tole (*tole* means street), once the main trading artery of the city and still the busiest street in old Kathmandu. This narrow road, usually thronging with people, cuts through the heart of old Kathmandu from Indra Chowk through Kel Tole to Asan Tole.

Kantipath forms the boundary between the older and newer parts of the city. South of the junction with New Rd is the main post office, easily located by the nearby Bhimsen Tower (also known as Sundhara). On the east side of Kantipath is a large, open parade ground known as Tundikhel, and on the eastern edge of this is the City bus station (also known as the 'Old' or Ratna Park bus station) for buses around the Kathmandu Valley.

At the northern end of Kantipath is the new Royal Palace compound. Beyond here Kantipath continues into the embassy and NGO district of Lazimpat and Maharajganj.

Running parallel to and east of Kantipath is Durbar Marg, a wide street flanked by travel agencies, airline offices, restaurants and expensive hotels. Its northern end is at the main entrance to the new Royal Palace. East from this intersection, Tridevi Marg enters the popular budget tourist accommodation and restaurant ghetto of Thamel (pronounced 'Ta-**mel**'). Thamel is 15 or 20 minutes' walk north from Durbar Square, the centre of Kathmandu.

The city is encircled by the Ring Rd. On this road in the north of the city is the main Kathmandu bus station and on the eastern edge is Tribhuvan Airport.

KATHMANDU

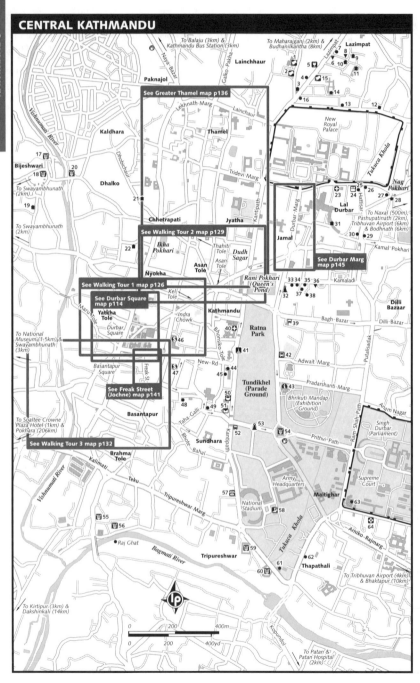

CENTRAL KATHMANDU

To Balaju (3km) &
Kathmandu Bus Station (3km)

To Maharajganj (2km) &
Budhanilkantha (8km)

Naya Bazar

Galko Patha

Lainchhaur

Lazimpat

Lazimpat

8
9
5
6 10
1
2
4
11
15
3
14
16
13
12

Paknajol

See Greater Thamel map p136

Lekhnath Marg

Lainchaur

Kaldhara

Dhobichali

Thamel

New
Royal
Palace

Takuca Khola

17
20

Bijeshwari

18

Bishnumati River

To Swayambhunath
(2km)

Dhalko

Tridevi Marg

Kantipath

19

To Swayambhunath
(2km)

21

Chhetrapati

Jyatha

See Walking Tour 2 map p129

22

Ikha
Pokhari

Thahiti
Tole

Dudh
Sagar

Asan
Tole

Asan
Tole

Nyokha

See Walking Tour 1 map p126

Kel
Tole

See Durbar Square
map p114

Yatkha
Tole

Durbar
Square

Indra
Chowk

Maru Tole

Kathmandu

46

Rani Pokhari
(Queen's
Pond)

Durbar Marg

Lal
Durbar

23
24
25
26
27
28

Jamal

31

30
29

Kamal Pokhari

Nag
Pokhari

To Naxal (500m),
Pashupatinath (2km),
Tribhuvan Airport (6km)
& Bodhnath (6km)

See Durbar Marg
map p145

Kamaladi

33 34
35 36
32
37 38

Dilli
Bazaar

Bagh Bazar

Dilli Bazar

39

Putalisadak

To National
Museum (1-5km) &
Swayambhunath
(3km)

Basantapur
Square

Freak St.

Ratna
Park

Bhotahiti Tole

New Rd

40
41
42

Adwait Marg

47
44
45

Tundikhel
(Parade
Ground)

Pradarshanti Marg

43

Aham Nagar

See Freak Street
(Jochne) map p141

48

50
49
51

Taha Galli

Basantapur

Bhrikuti Mandap
(Exhibition
Ground)

Singh
Durbar
(Parliament)

To Soaltee Crowne
Plaza Hotel (1km) &
Pokhara (206km)

See Walking Tour 3 map p132

53
52

Kantipath

Sundhara

Bhote Bahal

Prithvi Path

54

Ram Shah Path

Supreme
Court

Brahma
Tole

Kalimati

Teku

Tripureshwar Marg

Army
Headquarters

Maitighar

63

Bishnumati River

57

National
Stadium

58

64

Arniko Rajmarg

55

56

Bagmati River

Raj Ghat

Tripureshwar

59

Takuca Khola

62
61
60

Thapathali

Kupondol

To Tribhuvan Airport (4km)
& Bhaktapur (10km)

To Kirtipur (3km) &
Dakshinkali (14km)

LP

0   200   400m
0   200   400yd

To Patan &
Patan Hospital
(2km)

CENTRAL KATHMANDU

PLACES TO STAY
3   Hotel Ambassador
9   Radisson Hotel
10   Hotel Tibet
11   Hotel Manaslu
19   Hotel Vajra
21   Kathmandu Prince Hotel
22   Hotel Ganesh Himal
31   Yak & Yeti Hotel; Chimney
     Room; Sunrise Café;
     Naachgar Restaurant

PLACES TO EAT
6   Royal Hana Garden
8   Restaurant Lajana
36   Bhanchha Ghar Restaurant

OTHER
1   British Embassy
2   British Council
4   Tibetan Thangka Gallery;
     Folk Nepal
5   Jazz Upstairs
7   Bluebird Supermarket
12   Himalayan Rescue Association
13   China Southwest Airlines
14   Cultural Hall; Hotel Shankar
15   French Embassy
16   Hicola

17   Shobabaghwati Temple
18   Bijeshwari Temple
20   Indrani Temple
23   Nepal International Clinic
24   Jai Nepal Cinema
25   PIA; Gulf Air; Buddha Air
26   Mountain Air
27   Nepal Mountaineering
     Association
28   Biman Bangladesh Airlines
29   Shangri-La Air
30   Air India; Indian Airlines;
     Skyline Airways
32   Clocktower
33   Austrian Airlines; Lauda
     Airlines; Explore Nepal
34   Singapore Airlines
35   Aeroflot
37   DHL
38   Himalayan Buddhist
     Meditation Centre
39   Minibuses for Bhaktapur
40   Bir Hospital
41   Mahakala Temple
42   City Bus Station
43   Tourist Service Centre;
     Central Immigration Office
44   RNAC (International &
     Domestic Tourist Flights)

45   RNAC (Other Domestic
     Flights)
46   Standard & Chartered Bank
     (ATM only)
47   Nepal Bank
48   Goethe Institut
49   Bhimsen Tower (Sundhara)
50   Safa Tempos Stand; Tempos
     to Patan & Bodhnath
51   Main Post Office
52   Buses for Pharping &
     Dakshinkali
53   Shahid Gate (Martyrs
     Memorial)
54   Bhadrakali Temple
55   Pachali Bhairab
56   Tin Deval Temple
57   Central Telegraph Office
58   Swimming Pool
59   Tripureshwar Mahadev
     Temple
60   Kalmochan Temple
61   Bluebird Supermarket
62   Alliance Francaise
63   Dept of Archaeology
64   Babar Mahal Revisited;
     Baithak Restaurant; Chez
     Caroline

Addresses

In old Kathmandu, streets were not given names. Although some of the major roads now have names, most still don't, and smaller streets and laneways never do. Kathmandu grew as a series of interlocking squares that gradually swallowed neighbouring villages. The names of these squares, villages and other landmarks (perhaps a monastery or temple) have come to be used as addresses of sorts. For example, the address of everyone living within a 100m radius of Thahiti Tole is Thahiti Tole. Thamel is now used to describe a sprawling area with at least a dozen roads and several hundred hotels and restaurants.

Given this anarchic approach it is amazing that any mail gets delivered – it does, but slowly. Most businesses have post office boxes. If you're trying to find a particular house, shop or business, make sure you get detailed directions.

INFORMATION
Tourist Offices

The **Tourist Service Centre** (Central Kathmandu map; ☎ 4256909; Bhrikutimandap Marg; open 9am-5pm Sun-Fri), on the eastern side of Tundikhel parade ground, is a government centre that supposedly exists to provide information and service to tourists. It doesn't seem to do much of either – there is an information counter giving away a few brochures and maps, and the location of the office is a major inconvenience to travellers.

There's also a **tourist office** (☎ 4470537) in the international terminal at the airport that usually dishes out a handy free map to arriving passengers who ask for it.

There are a number of good notice boards in Thamel that are worth consulting if you are looking for information on such things as apartments, travel and trekking partners, yoga and meditation courses, language courses and cultural events. The Kathmandu Guest House has a good notice board, as do the Pumpernickel Bakery and the Fire & Ice Restaurant.

Other useful boards are at the Travellers' Information Centre, run by the **Kathmandu Environmental Education Project** (KEEP; Greater Thamel map; ☎ 4259275, 4259567; w www.keepnepal.org; open 10am-5pm Sun-Fri) in Thamel. The staff are happy to answer general queries and there's a small collection of reference books. KEEP provides a mineral-water refill service (Rs 10 per litre).

For information on offices in Kathmandu that offer trekking-related information see the Trekking chapter.

Travellers' Nepal and *Nepal Traveller* are good-quality, free monthly magazines that cover a broad range of topics and have a section of practical information.

Money

It is worth checking banks' exchange rates and commission – both vary. There are also dozens of licensed moneychangers in Thamel. Their hours are much longer than those of the banks, and rates are pretty consistent. See Money in the Facts for the Visitor chapter for information on exchange rates, commissions and transfers.

The most convenient bank for travellers staying in Thamel is the small branch of the **Himalaya Bank** *(Greater Thamel map; Tridevi Marg; open 8am-8pm Mon-Fri)*, opposite the Three Goddesses (Tridevi) Temples. You can change travellers cheques and get cash advances on a Visa card here.

There's a **Standard Chartered Bank** *(Greater Thamel map; ☎ 4228474; open 9.30am-7pm Mon-Fri, 9.30am-12.30pm Sat & Sun)* around the corner on Kantipath, with an ATM for credit-card withdrawals. It has a 1.5% charge (minimum Rs 200) for changing travellers cheques and Rs 100 per transaction for cash, but no charge for a cash advance on a credit card. There are two more Standard Chartered ATMs in Thamel – opposite the Third Eye Restaurant and in the compound of the Kathmandu Guest House – and others on New Rd, Durbar Marg and a couple of other locations around Kathmandu.

The main **Nepal Bank Ltd** *(Central Kathmandu map; ☎ 4221185; open 7am-7pm daily)*, in Dharma Path near New Rd, is handy if you're staying in Freak St, and is open long hours.

The **American Express** (AmEx) agent is **Yeti Travels** *(Durbar Marg map; ☎ 4221234, fax 226152/3; ⓔ yeti@vishnu.ccsl.com.np; open 10am-4pm Mon-Fri)*, which has its office in the forecourt of the Hotel Mayalu, just off the southern end of Durbar Marg. It provides AmEx cash advances, purchase and encashment of travellers cheques, and client mail services.

Sita World Travel *(Central Kathmandu map; ☎ 4418363; ⓔ sitaktm@sitanep.mos.com.np)*, on Tridevi Marg, is the agent for Western Union money transfers.

Post

The most convenient **post office** *(Greater Thamel map; Tridevi Marg)* to Thamel is on the east side in the basement of the Sanchaya Kosh Bhawan Shopping Centre.

Most bookshops in Thamel, including Pilgrims Book House (see Bookshops later in this chapter), sell stamps and deliver postcards to the post office, which is much easier than making a special trip to the post office yourself. Pilgrims charges a 10% commission for this service.

The **main post office** *(Central Kathmandu map; cnr Kantipath & Khichapokhari)* is close to Bhimsen Tower. Theoretically, the stamp counter is open 8am to 7pm Sunday to Friday and 11am to 3pm Saturday, but it can be a frustrating process. The **poste restante** *(open 10.15am-4pm Sun-Thur, 10.15am-2pm Fri, shorter hours Nov-Feb)* section is quite efficient. The staff sort mail into alphabetised boxes and you simply sit down and go through the appropriate box yourself. You are required to show your passport before you take anything away. The desk is inside to the left, behind the main counter.

Parcels can be sent from the **foreign post office** *(open 10am-5pm Sun-Thur, 10am-2pm Fri)*, just north of the main post office. Parcels have to be examined and sealed by a customs officer and then packed in an approved manner. It's something of a procedure, so if you're short of time you're best off using one of the many cargo agencies. **Diki Continental Exports** *(Greater Thamel map; ☎ 4417681)*, near Sam's Bar in Thamel, and **Sharmasons Movers** *(Central Kathmandu map; ☎ 4249709; ⓔ pacmov@enet.com.np)* on Kantipath are two agencies that have been recommended.

DHL *(Central Kathmandu map; ☎ 4496248 • Greater Thamel map; ☎ 4264259; closed Sat)* has a useful office in Thamel, on the 1st floor of the Arcadia Building, as well as in Kamaladi. **FedEx** *(Central Kathmandu map; ☎ 4269248, fax 4269249; open 9am-6pm Sun-Fri, 9am-1pm Sat)* has an office on Kantipath.

Telephone & Fax

International telephone calls can be made and faxes can be sent from any of the dozens of 'communication centres' in Thamel and elsewhere throughout the city. They are no more expensive, and are certainly more convenient, than the **central telegraph office** about 500m south of the post office, opposite the National Stadium. However, the central telegraph office is open 24 hours.

Many of the communication centres offer Internet phone calls, where computers are used to make phone calls to phones anywhere in the world. The cost varies from Rs 30 to Rs 40 per minute, depending on the destination. See Telephone under Post & Communications in the Facts for the Visitor chapter for more information.

Email & Internet Access
Email services are widely available in Thamel and elsewhere in Kathmandu. The best cybercafés, such as **The Cybernet Café** in the back of the supermarket on Thamel's main central junction, have scanners and printers (Rs 10 per page) plus power backup. Connection speeds are generally fast and the rates are fairly standard, and cheap – currently Rs 20 to Rs 30 per hour (Rs 1 per minute for less than 30 minutes).

Travel Agencies
Kathmandu has a great number of travel agencies, particularly along Durbar Marg, Kantipath and in Thamel. See Organised Trekking under Planning in the Trekking chapter for details of trekking agencies.

For straight-talking travel and ticketing (particularly international air tickets), try **Wayfarers Travel Service** (Greater Thamel map ☎ 42667010; W www.wayfarers.com.np) in Thamel (1st floor, Arcadia Building).

Bookshops
Kathmandu has a large number of very good bookshops. Many have a good selection of books on Nepal and particularly Tibet, including books that are not usually available outside the country. Prices for new British and US books are generally 20% to 30% cheaper than their home-market prices, and there are plenty of second-hand books for sale and trade, though these have got relatively pricey in recent years. Most dealers will buy back books for 50% of what you paid.

Pilgrims Book House (Greater Thamel map; ☎ 4424942; W www.pilgrimsbooks.com), a couple of doors north of the Kathmandu

Guest House, has an extensive collection of books on Nepal and other Himalayan regions, and is particularly strong on antiquarian travelogues, though it's pricier than the competition. There's also a branch of Pilgrims opposite the Hotel Himalaya on the road to Patan (see the Around the Kathmandu Valley chapter).

See the Greater Thamel map for the following bookstores.

Walden Book House, at Chhetrapati in greater Thamel, is another place with a good range, as is the **Barnes & Noble Bookhouse**, on the junction just south of the Kathmandu Guest House. **Tantric Book Shop** nearby has some of the best prices. **Bookworld** (Tridevi Marg) at Sanchaya Kosh Bhawan Shopping Centre is also good, and **Mandala Bookpoint** (Kantipath) has an excellent selection of books, with a good range in French and German.

Libraries & Cultural Centres
Following is a selection of the libraries and cultural centres in Kathmandu:

Alliance Francaise (Central Kathmandu map; ☎ 4224326) Thapathali, southeast of the city centre. This place has French publications and French film screenings (with a small entry charge).
British Council Library (Central Kathmandu map; ☎ 4410798, W www.britishcouncil.org.np) British Council, Lainchhaur. You'll have to become a member (Rs 700 per year, one photo required) to use this library, but nostalgic Brits can get a cheap cup of tea or lunch at the attached Tibetan café and leaf through the British newspapers or watch BBC World TV. It's open from 8.30am to 5.45pm Monday to Friday.
Goethe Institut (Central Kathmandu map; ☎ 425 0871, e gzk@wlink.com.np) Ganabahal district, near Bhimsen Tower. This place has German film screenings, occasional exhibitions and a library.
Kaiser Library (Central Kathmandu map; ☎ 4411318) Ministry of Education and Sports compound, on the corner of Kantipath and Tridevi Marg. Also known as Kesar Library, this place is worth a visit just to see the building and gardens. It has a remarkable collection of antique books and the atmospheric library boasts a stuffed tiger and a wonderful old suit of armour that you expect to spring to life at any moment. It's open 9am to 5pm Monday to Friday.

Laundry
Most hotels will do your laundry for competitive rates, or try **Wear Care Laundry Service**

KATHMANDU

(Greater Thamel map; ☎ *4265098)* in Thamel. Rates average Rs 20 for trousers or a shirt.

Photography

There are numerous places offering a same-day service for print film. (See the Greater Thamel map unless otherwise stated.) **Bandari Photo Shop** in central Thamel is a reliable source of film, as is **Color Link**, farther south, which stocks a range of Agfa film. **Advanced Photo Finisher** in the north of Thamel has a range of film and develops film in a few hours (Rs 400 for 36 6x8), as does **Nepal Colour Lab** in Chhetrapati.

Hicola *(☎ 4410200; Tridevi Marg)*, with a branch in Lazimpat, is fairly reliable and can handle colour prints and E-6 or Ektachrome slides. Mounted slide processing will cost you around Rs 300 for 36 slides; prints costs Rs 360 for 36 photos.

Ganesh Photo Lab *(Walking Tour 3 map;* ☎ *4216898)*, in an alley southwest of Durbar Square, is an unlikely-looking but reputedly good place for black-and-white processing.

A few photo shops in Thamel hire out cameras, starting at Rs 150 per day, depending on the type of camera. You'll need to give a hefty deposit.

Immigration Office

To get a visa extension in Kathmandu, go to the **Central Immigration Office** *(Central Kathmandu map;* ☎ *4223681, 4223590;* e *dept imi@ntc.net.np; Bhrikutimandap Marg; open 9am-4pm Mon-Fri)* next to the Tourist Service Centre. If you apply before 2pm you should get your passport back the same day at 3.30pm. It's wise to start the process early, as renewing a visa can be time-consuming. See Visas in the Facts for the Visitor chapter for more details.

Medical Services

The best bet in the Kathmandu Valley is the **Patan Hospital** *(Patan map;* ☎ *4521034)*, which is partly staffed by Western missionaries and is in the Lagankhel district of Patan, near the last stop of the Lagankhel bus. It also has an **ambulance service** *(☎ 4521048)*.

Reasonably well equipped (and carrying a ventilator) is the **Tribhuvan University Teaching Hospital** *(Kathmandu map;* ☎ *4412363)* northeast of the centre in Maharajganj. The centrally located, government-operated **Bir Hospital** *(☎ 4221119)* is not recommended.

The **CIWEC Clinic Travel Medicine Center** *(Durbar Marg map;* ☎ *4228531;* w *www.ciwec-clinic.com; open 9am-4pm Mon-Fri)*, just off Durbar Marg near the Yak & Yeti Hotel, is used by many foreign residents. It has operated since 1982 and has developed an international reputation for research into travellers' medical problems. The clinic is staffed mostly by foreigners and there a doctor is on call around the clock. A consultation costs around US$45.

The **Nepal International Clinic** *(Central Kathmandu map;* ☎ *4434642, 435357;* w *www.nepalinternationalclinic.com; open 9am-5pm daily)* is just south of the new Royal Palace, east of Thamel. It has an excellent reputation and is slightly cheaper than the CIWEC clinic. A consultation costs about US$35 (US$50 at weekends).

Emergency

Fire Brigade	☎ 101, 4221177
Police, Durbar Square	☎ 100, 4223011
Tourist Police	☎ 4247041
Red Cross Ambulance	☎ 4228094

THREE GODDESSES TEMPLES

Next to the modern Sanchaya Kosh Bhawan Shopping Centre in Thamel are the Three Goddesses Temples. The street on which the temples are located is named Tridevi Marg – *tri* means 'three' and *devi* means 'goddesses'. The goddesses are Dakshinkali, Mankamna and Jawalamai, and the roof struts have some interesting erotic carvings illustrating some creative positions.

MAHAKALA TEMPLE

On the eastern side of Kantipath, just north of New Rd, Mahakala Temple (see the Central Kathmandu map) was very badly damaged in the 1934 earthquake and is now of little architectural merit. If you can see inside the darkened shrine you may be able to make out the 1.5m-high figure of Mahakala, the 'Great Black One', a particularly ferocious form of Shiva. *Kal* means 'death' as well as 'black' in Nepali so it can also be described as the Temple of Great Death. The Tantric god has Buddhist as well as Hindu followers.

You can climb to the top of one of the buildings around the courtyard to look over the Tundikhel parade ground.

[Continued on page 123]

Kathmandu

Phere, Kanchenjunga Trek

Pashupatinath, Kathmandu Valley

Gadi Baithak, Durbar Square, Kathmandu

Narrow side street, Patan

DURBAR SQUARE (KATHMANDU)

Kathmandu's Durbar Square (*durbar* means 'palace') was where the city's kings were once crowned and legitimised, and from where they ruled. Rebuilt over the generations, most of the square dates from the 17th and 18th centuries. The king no longer lives in the Hanuman Dhoka (old Royal Palace) in Kathmandu – the palace was moved north to Narayanhiti about a century ago – but the square remains the traditional heart of the old town and a spectacular legacy of traditional architecture.

It's easy to spend hours wandering around the often crowded Durbar Square and the adjoining Basantapur Square. This is very much the centre of old Kathmandu and watching the world go by from the terraced platforms of the towering Maju Deval is a wonderful way to get a feel for the city. Although many of the buildings around the square are very old, a great deal of damage was caused by the great earthquake of 1934 and many were rebuilt, not always in their original form. The entire square was designated a World Heritage Monument in 1979.

The Durbar Square area is actually made up of three loosely linked squares. To the south is the open Basantapur Square area, off which runs Freak St. The main Durbar Square area, with its popular watch-the-world-go-by temples, is to the west. Running northeast is a second part of Durbar Square, which contains the entrance to the Hanuman Dhoka and an assortment of temples. From this open area Makhan Tole, at one time the main road in Kathmandu and still the most interesting street to walk down, continues northeast.

A good place to start an exploration of the square is with what may well be the oldest building in the valley, the unprepossessing Kasthamandap. Note that the numbers in the following section correspond to item numbers on the key for the Durbar Square (Kathmandu) map.

Tickets Entry to Durbar Square (no opening hours) is Rs 200 and the ticket is dated and valid for one week. If you want a longer duration you need to go to the 'site office' on the south side of Basantapur Square to get a free visitor pass, which allows you access for as long as the validity of your visa. You will need your passport and one photo and the process takes about two minutes. You generally need to show your ticket even if you are just transiting the square to New Rd or Freak St.

Kasthamandap (37) In the southwestern corner of the square, the Kasthamandap (House of Wood) is the

Kasthamandap

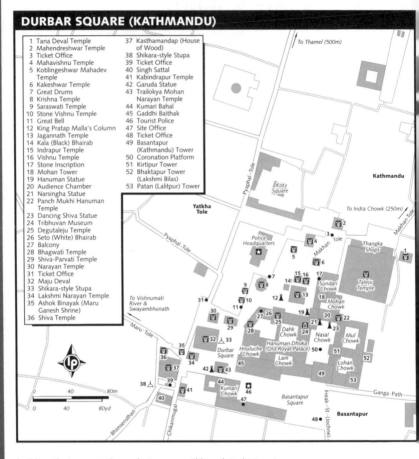

DURBAR SQUARE (KATHMANDU)

1 Tana Deval Temple
2 Mahendreshwar Temple
3 Ticket Office
4 Mahavishnu Temple
5 Kotilingeshwar Mahadev Temple
6 Kakeshwar Temple
7 Great Drums
8 Krishna Temple
9 Saraswati Temple
10 Stone Vishnu Temple
11 Great Bell
12 King Pratap Malla's Column
13 Jagannath Temple
14 Kala (Black) Bhairab
15 Indrapur Temple
16 Vishnu Temple
17 Stone Inscription
18 Mohan Tower
19 Hanuman Statue
20 Audience Chamber
21 Narsingha Statue
22 Panch Mukhi Hanuman Temple
23 Dancing Shiva Statue
24 Tribhuvan Museum
25 Degutaleju Temple
26 Seto (White) Bhairab
27 Balcony
28 Bhagwati Temple
29 Shiva-Parvati Temple
30 Narayan Temple
31 Ticket Office
32 Maju Deval
33 Shikara-style Stupa
34 Lakshmi Narayan Temple
35 Ashok Binayak (Maru Ganesh Shrine)
36 Shiva Temple
37 Kasthamandap (House of Wood)
38 Shikara-style Stupa
39 Ticket Office
40 Singh Sattal
41 Kabindrapur Temple
42 Garuda Statue
43 Trailokya Mohan Narayan Temple
44 Kumari Bahal
45 Gaddhi Baithak
46 Tourist Police
47 Site Office
48 Ticket Office
49 Basantapur (Kathmandu) Tower
50 Coronation Platform
51 Kirtipur Tower
52 Bhaktapur Tower (Lakshmi Bilas)
53 Patan (Lalitpur) Tower

building that gave Kathmandu its name. Although its history is uncertain, it was possibly constructed around the 12th century. A legend relates that the whole building was constructed with the wood from a single sal tree. At first it was a community centre where visitors gathered before major ceremonies, but later it was converted to a temple dedicated to Gorakhnath.

A central wooden enclosure houses the image of the god. In the corners of the building are images of Ganesh. There are also shrines to a number of other gods. Bronze lions guard the entrance and Hindu epics are illustrated around the corner platforms of the three-storey building.

The squat, medieval-looking building is busy in the early morning hours when porters sit here waiting for customers.

Ashok Binayak (35) On the northern side of the Kasthamandap, at the top of Maru Tole (the laneway down to the river), stands the tiny Ashok Binayak, or Maru Ganesh Shrine. The small size of this shrine belies its importance, as this is one of the four most important Ganesh shrines in the valley. Ganesh is a much-loved god and there is a constant stream of visitors here. A visit to this shrine is highly recommended by Hindus to ensure safety on a forthcoming journey. Pilgrims receive a *tika* (red mark) and walk around the shrine, ringing the bells at the back. It's uncertain how old the temple is, although its gilded roof was added in the 19th century.

Maru Tole This *tole* (street) leads you away from Durbar Square and down to the Vishnumati River where a footbridge meets the pathway to Swayambhunath on the other side. This was a busy street in the days of hippies and flower power, but today there's little sign of why it should have been called either Pie or Pig Alley – not only are the pie shops gone but it's also much cleaner than it once was. One thing Maru Tole does have is Maru Hiti, one of the finest sunken water conduits in the city.

Maju Deval (32) A pleasant hour can easily be spent sitting on the platform steps of the Shiva temple known as the Maju Deval. From here you can watch the constant activity of fruit-and-vegetable hawkers, the comings and goings of taxis and rickshaws, and the flute and other souvenir sellers importuning tourists. The nine-stage ochre platform of the Maju Deval is probably the most popular meeting place in the city. The large, triple-roofed temple has erotic carvings on its roof struts and offers great views over the square and across the roofs of the city. Marigold sellers set up shop on the ground level.

The temple dates from 1690 and was built by the mother of Bhaktapur's King Bhupatindra Malla. Although the temple has a well-known Shiva lingam (phallic symbol) inside, the roof is topped by a pinnacle shaped like a Buddhist stupa. At the bottom of the temple stairway on the east side is a small temple to Kam Dev, a 'companion' of Shiva. It was built in the Indian *shikhara* style, with a tall corncob-like spire.

Trailokya Mohan Narayan Temple (43) The other temple standing in the open area of the square is the smaller Trailokya Mohan Narayan. This temple has five tiers and was built by Prithvibendra Malla in 1680. It is easily identified as a temple to Narayan, or Vishnu, by the fine Garuda kneeling before it. The **Garuda figure (42)** was a later addition, erected by the king's widow soon after his death. Look for the Vaishnavite images on the carved roof struts and the window screens with their decoratively carved side medallions. Dances depicting the 10 incarnations of Vishnu are performed on the platform to the east of the temple during the Indra Jatra festival.

Maju Deval

Shiva-Parvati Temple (29) From the steps of the Maju Deval you can look across the square to the Shiva-Parvati Temple, where images of Shiva and his consort look out from the upstairs window on the comings and goings below them. The temple was built in the late 1700s by Bahadur Shah, the son of Prithvi Narayan Shah. Although the temple is not very old by Kathmandu standards, it stands on a two-stage platform, which may have been an open dancing stage hundreds of years earlier. A Narayan (Vishnu) temple stands to the west side.

Kumari Bahal (44) At the junction of Durbar and Basantapur Squares is a white, three-storey building with intricately carved windows. The Kumari Bahal (House of the Living Goddess) faces Durbar Square, its door guarded by stone lions. The building, in the style of the courtyarded Buddhist *viharas* (abodes) of the valley, was built in 1757 by Jaya Prakash Malla. Inside lives the young girl (the Kumari), who is selected to be the town's living goddess until she reaches puberty and reverts to being a normal mortal! (See the boxed text 'Kumari Devi' in the Kathmandu chapter.)

Inside the building the three-storey courtyard, or Kumari Chowk, is enclosed by magnificently carved wooden balconies and windows. Photographing the goddess is forbidden, but you are quite free to photograph the courtyard when she is not present. The courtyard contains a miniature stupa carrying the symbols of Saraswati, the goddess of learning. Non-Hindus are not allowed to go beyond the courtyard.

The big gate to the right of the Kumari Bahal serves to conceal the huge chariot that takes the Kumari around the city of Kathmandu once a year, an annual festival that was begun during the rule of Jaya Prakash Malla. In front of the Kumari Bahal are the huge wooden runners that are used to transport the chariot. The wood is considered sacred and so cannot be used for firewood or other purposes.

Gaddhi Baithak (45) The eastern side of Durbar Square is closed off by this white neoclassical building. The Gaddhi Baithak, with its imported European style, was built as part of the palace in 1908 during the Rana period and it makes a strange contrast to the traditional Nepali architecture that dominates the square.

Bhagwati Temple (28) Next to the Gaddhi Baithak, this triple-storey, triple-roofed temple is easily missed since it surmounts the building below it, which has *thangka* (religious Tibetan painting on cloth) shops along its front. The best view of the temple with its golden roofs is probably from the Maju Deval, across the square. The temple was built by Jagat Jaya Malla and originally had an image of Narayan. This image was stolen in 1766, so when Prithvi Narayan Shah conquered the valley two years later he simply substituted it with an image of the goddess

Bhagwati Temple

Bhagwati, which he just happened to be toting around with him. In April each year the image of the goddess is conveyed to the village of Nuwakot, 65km to the north, then returned a few days later.

Great Bell (11) On your left as you leave the main square along Makhan Tole is the Great Bell, elevated atop a white building erected by Rana Bahadur Shah (son of Prithvi Narayan Shah) in 1797. During the Malla era a novel addition to one of the valley's *durbar* squares would almost immediately be imitated in another. Curiously, Patan and Bhaktapur got their bells in 1736, while the Kathmandu version did not follow until long after the fall of the Mallas. The bell's ring will drive off evil spirits, but it is only rung during *puja* (worship) at the **Degutale-ju Temple (25)**.

Across from the great bell is a very ornate **balcony (27)**, decorated in gorgeous copper and ivory, from where members of the royal court could view the festival action taking place in Durbar Square.

Krishna Temple (8) The history of the octagonal Krishna Temple is well documented. It was built in 1648 by Pratap Malla, perhaps as a response to Siddhinarsingh's magnificent Krishna Temple in Patan. Inside there are images of Krishna and two goddesses, which, according to a Sanskrit inscription, are modelled on the king and his two wives. The temple also has a Newari inscription, but this neglects to mention the king's little act of vanity. The temple is a favourite of sadhus (wandering holy men) who pose (and expect to be paid) for photos here.

Great Drums (7) & Kot Square Just beyond the temple are the Great Drums, to which a goat and a buffalo must be sacrificed twice a year. In front of these is the police headquarters building (currently sandbagged against possible Maoist attacks). Beyond here is Kot Square, where Jung Bahadur Rana perpetrated the famous 1846 massacre that led to a hundred years of Rana rule (see History in the Facts about Nepal chapter). *Kot* means 'armoury' or 'fort'. During the Dasain festival each year, blood again flows in Kot Square as hundreds of buffaloes and goats are sacrificed. Young soldiers are supposed to lop off each head with a single blow. The square is closed off to the public.

King Pratap Malla's Column (12) Across from the Krishna Temple is a host of smaller temples and other structures, all standing on a raised platform in front of the Hanuman Dhoka and the towering Taleju Temple behind. The square stone pillar, known as the Pratap Dhvaja, is topped by a statue of the famous King Pratap Malla (1641–74), seated with folded hands

Krishna Temple

and surrounded by his two wives and his five (including an infant) sons. He looks towards his private prayer room on the 3rd floor of the **Degutaleju Temple (25)**. The column was erected in 1670 by Pratap Malla and preceded the similar columns in Patan and Bhaktapur.

This area and its monuments are usually covered in hundreds if not thousands of pigeons, and you can buy packets of grain to feed them. This is Kathmandu's answer to Trafalgar Square.

Seto (White) Bhairab (26) Seto (White) Bhairab's horrible face is hidden away behind a grille opposite King Pratap Malla's column. The huge mask dates from 1794, during the reign of Rana Bahadur Shah, the third Shah dynasty king. Each September during the Indra Jatra festival the gates are swung back to reveal the mask for a few days. At that time the face is covered in flowers and rice and at the start of the festivities beer is poured through the horrific mouth. Crowds of men fight to get a drink of this blessed beer! At other times of year you can peek through the lattice to see the mask, which is used as the symbol of Royal Nepal Airlines.

Jagannath Temple (13) This temple, noted for the erotic carvings on its roof struts, is the oldest structure in this part of the square. Pratap Malla claimed to have constructed the temple during his reign, but it may actually date back to 1563, during the rule of Mahendra Malla. The temple has a three-tiered platform and two storeys. There are three doors on each side of the temple, but only the centre door opens.

Degutaleju Temple (25) This triple-roofed temple is actually part of the Hanuman Dhoka (old Royal Palace), but is most easily seen from outside the palace walls. Degutaleju is another manifestation of the Malla's personal goddess Taleju. This temple was built by Shiva Singh Malla and is integrated into the palace structure itself. The temple actually starts from above the common buildings it surmounts.

Kala (Black) Bhairab (14) Behind the Jagannath Temple is the large figure of Kala (Black) Bhairab. Bhairab is Shiva in his most fearsome aspect, and this huge stone image of the terrifying Kala Bhairab has six arms, wears a garland of skulls and tramples a corpse, which is symbolic of human ignorance. The figure is said to have been brought here by Pratap Malla, having been found in a field to the north of the city. The image was originally cut from a single stone, but the upper left-hand side has been repaired with another stone. It is said that telling a lie while standing before Kala Bhairab will bring instant death and it was once used as a form of trial by ordeal.

Indrapur Temple (15) Immediately to the east of horrific Bhairab stands the mysterious Indrapur Temple. This curious temple may be of great antiquity but has been renovated recently and little is known of its history. Even the god to which it is dedicated is controversial – inside there is a lingam indicating that it is a Shiva temple. However, half-buried on the southern side of the temple is a Garuda image, indicating that the temple is dedicated to Vishnu. To compound the puzzle, however, the temple's name clearly indicates it is dedicated to Indra! The temple's unadorned design and plain roof struts together with the lack of an identifying *torana* (pediment above the temple doors indicating the deity to which it is dedicated) give no further clues.

Vishnu Temple (16) Little is known about the adjoining Vishnu Temple. This triple-roofed temple stands on a four-level base. The roof-strut carvings and the golden image of Vishnu inside show that it is a Vishnu temple, but it is not known how old the temple is, although it was in existence during Pratap Malla's reign.

Kakeshwar Temple (6) This temple was originally built in 1681 but rebuilt after it was badly damaged in the 1934 earthquake. It may have been considerably altered at that time as the temple is a strange combination of styles. It starts with a two-level base that rises from a lower floor (in typical Nepali style). Above the 1st floor, however, the temple is in the Indian *shikhara* style, topped by a spire shaped like a *kalasa* (water vase), indicative of a female deity.

Stone Inscription (17) On the outside of the palace wall, opposite the **Vishnu Temple** (16), is a long, low stone inscription to the goddess Kalika written in 15 languages, including one word of French. King Pratap Malla, renowned for his scholastic abilities, set up this inscription in 1664 and a Nepali legend relates that milk will flow from the spout in the middle if somebody is able to read all 15 languages!

Kotilingeshwar Mahadev Temple (5) This early Malla temple dates from the reign of Mahendra Malla in the 16th century. The three-stage plinth is topped by a temple in the *gumbhaj* style, which basically means a square structure topped by a bell-shaped dome. The bull facing the temple on the west side indicates that it is a Shiva temple.

Mahavishnu Temple (4) Built by Jagat Jaya Malla, this double-roofed temple on a four-level plinth was badly damaged in the 1934 earthquake and was badly restored. Only the golden spire, topped by a golden umbrella, hints at its prior appearance.

Mahendreshwar Temple (1) At the extreme northern end of the square, this busy temple dates from 1561, during Mahendra Malla's reign. The temple was restored in 1963 and is dedicated to Shiva. A small image of Shiva's bull Nandi fronts the temple and at the northeastern corner there is an image of Kam Dev. The temple has a wide, two-level plinth and a spire topped by a golden umbrella.

Kakeshwar Temple

Taleju Temple The square's most magnificent temple stands at its northeastern extremity but it is not open to the public. Even for Nepalis entry is restricted; they only visit the temple during the annual Dasain festival.

The Taleju Temple was built in 1564 by Mahendra Malla. Taleju Bhawani was originally a goddess from the south of India, but she became the titular deity or royal goddess of the Malla kings in the 14th century. Taleju temples were erected in her honour in Patan and Bhaktapur as well as in Kathmandu.

The temple stands on a 12-stage plinth and reaches over 35m high, not surprisingly dominating the Durbar Square area. The eighth stage of the plinth has a wall around the temple, in front of which are 12 miniature temples; four more miniature temples stand inside the wall, which has four beautifully carved wide gates. If entry to the temple were permitted it could be reached from within the Hanuman Dhoka or from the Singh Dhoka (Lion Gate) from the square.

From here you can either head south to visit the Hanuman Dhoka or continue northeast along Makhan Tole (see the Walking Tour 1 map).

Hanuman Dhoka This **palace complex** *(entry Rs 250, no cameras allowed; open 9.30am-4pm Tues-Sat Feb-Oct, 9.30am-3pm Nov-Jan)* was originally founded during the Licchavi period, but as it stands today most of it was constructed by King Pratap Malla in the 17th century. The palace was renovated many times in later years. The oldest parts are the smaller Sundari Chowk and Mohan Chowk at the northern part of the palace (both closed). From here construction moved south and in all there are 10 *chowks* (courtyards) in the palace.

Hanuman's very brave assistance to the noble Rama during the exciting events of the Ramayana has led to the monkey god's appearance guarding many important entrances. Here, cloaked in red and sheltered by an umbrella, a **Hanuman statue (19)** marks the *dhoka* (entrance) to the Hanuman Dhoka and has even given the palace its name. The statue dates from 1672, but the god's face has disappeared under a coating of red paste applied by faithful visitors.

Standards bearing the double-triangle flag of Nepal flank the statue, while on each side of the palace gate are stone lions, one ridden by Shiva, the other by his wife Parvati. Above the gate a brightly painted niche is illustrated with a figure of a ferocious Tantric version of Krishna in the centre. On the left side is the gentler Hindu Krishna in his traditional blue colour accompanied by two of his comely *gopis* (milkmaids). On the other side are King Pratap Malla and his queen.

Talejui Temple

Nasal Chowk From the entrance gate of the Hanuman Dhoka you immediately enter the most famous *chowk*. Although the courtyard was constructed in the Malla period, many of the buildings around the square are Rana constructions. During that time Nasal Chowk became the square used for coronations, a practice that continues to this day. The slain King Birendra was crowned in the 1975 ceremony on the **coronation platform (50)** in the centre of the courtyard. The nine-storey **Basantapur (Kathmandu) Tower (49)** looms over the southern end of the courtyard.

The rectangular courtyard is aligned north-south and the entrance is at the northwestern corner. Near the entrance there is a surprisingly small and beautifully carved doorway, which once led to the Malla kings' private quarters. The panels feature images of four gods.

Beyond the door is the large **Narsingha Statue (21)**, Vishnu in his man-lion incarnation, in the act of killing a demon. The stone image was erected by Pratap Malla in 1673 and the inscription on the pedestal explains that he placed it here in fear that he had offended Vishnu by dancing in a Narsingha costume. The **Kabindrapur Temple (41)** in Durbar Square was built for the same reason.

Next there is the **Audience Chamber (20)** of the Malla kings. The open verandah houses the Malla throne and portraits of the Shah kings. Images of the present king and queen dominate the eastern wall.

Panch Mukhi Hanuman Temple (22) At the northeastern corner of the Nasal Chowk stands the Panch Mukhi Hanuman with its five circular roofs. Each of the valley towns has a five-storey temple, although it is the great Nyatapola Temple of Bhaktapur that is by far the best known. Hanuman is worshipped in the temple in Kathmandu, but only the priests of the temple may enter it.

Dancing Shiva Statue (23) In Nepali *nasal* means 'dancing one', and Nasal Chowk takes its name from this Shiva statue inside the whitewashed chamber on the eastern side of the square.

Tribhuvan Museum (24) The part of the palace west of Nasal Chowk, overlooking the main Durbar Square area, was constructed by the Ranas in the middle to late part of the 19th century. Ironically, it is now home to a museum that celebrates King Tribhuvan (ruled 1911–55) and his successful revolt against their regime, along with memorials to kings Mahendra (1955–72) and Birendra (ruled 1972–2001).

Exhibits with names such as 'the Royal Babyhood' include some fascinating re-creations of the foppish king's bedroom and study, with genuine personal effects that give quite an eerie insight into his life. Some of the exhibits, like the king's favourite stuffed bird and his boxing gloves, add some surreal moments. There are several magnificent thrones, some superb stone carvings and the requisite coin collection.

Halfway through the museum you descend before ascending the steep stairways of the nine-storey **Basantapur Tower (49)**, which was extensively restored prior to King Birendra's coronation. There are superb views over the palace and the city from the top. The struts along the facade of the Basantapur Tower, particularly those facing out to Basantapur Square, are decorated with erotic carvings.

It's hard not to rush through the second half of the museum, full of dull press clippings and gifts from foreign governments. The displays end glossing over the massacre of King Birendra by his son in 2001 (see the boxed text 'The Royal Massacre – for the Love of a Woman?' in the Facts about Nepal chapter). The museum exits into Lohan Chowk.

Lohan Chowk King Prithvi Narayan Shah was involved in the construction of the four red-coloured towers around the Lohan Chowk. The towers represent the four ancient cities of the valley, the towers include the **Kathmandu or Basantapur Tower (49)**, the **Kirtipur Tower (51)**, the **Bhaktapur Tower** or **Lakshmi Bilas (52)** and the **Patan** or **Lalitpur Tower (53)**.

Other Chowks The palace's other courtyards are currently closed to visitors, but you can get glimpses of them from the Tribhuvan Museum and they might reopen at a future date.

North of Lohan Chowk, **Mul Chowk** was completely dedicated to religious functions within the palace and is configured like a *vihara* (a dwelling place for Buddhist monks), with a two-storey building surrounding the courtyard. Mul Chowk is dedicated to Taleju Bhawani, the royal goddess of the Mallas, and sacrifices are made to her in the centre of the courtyard during the Dasain festival. A smaller Taleju temple stands in the southern wing of the square and the image of the goddess is moved here from the main temple during the Dasain festival. Images of the river goddesses, Ganga and Jamuna, guard the golden temple doorway, which is topped by a golden *torana*.

North of the Nasal Chowk is **Mohan Chowk**, the residential courtyard of the Malla kings. It dates from 1649 and at one time a Malla king had to be born here to be eligible to wear the crown. (The last Malla king, Jaya Prakash Malla, had great difficulties during his reign, even though he was the legitimate heir, because he was born elsewhere.) The golden waterspout, known as Sun Dhara, in the centre of the courtyard delivers water from Budhanilkantha in the north of the valley. The Malla kings would ritually bathe here each morning.

[Continued from page 112]

BHIMSEN TOWER

Towering like a lighthouse over the old town, this white, minaret-like watchtower (also known as Sundhara) is a useful landmark near the main post office (see the Central Kathmandu map). It was originally built by a Rana prime minister as part of the city's first European-style palace. It was rebuilt after being severely damaged in the 1934 earthquake.

PACHALI BHAIRAB & THE SOUTHERN GHATS

Between Tripureshwar Marg and the Bagmati River is a huge, ancient pipal tree (see the Central Kathmandu map). The tree forms a sanctuary the Pachali image, surrounded by tridents. Nearby lies what some believe to be the brass body of Baital, one of Shiva's manifestations. Others believe it is Surya, the sun god. Worshippers gather here on Tuesday and Saturday. It is particularly busy here during the festival of Pachali Bhairab Jatra (see the special section 'Festivals of Nepal' in the Facts for the Visitor chapter).

From the temple you could explore the temples and ghats that line the holy Bagmati river. Just south of Pachal Bhairab is the interesting **Tin Deval Temple**, easily recognisable by its three spires. From here you can continue east past some of Kathmandu's poorest communities to the huge triple-roofed **Tripureshwar Mahadev Temple**. Farther east is the Mughal-style **Kalmochan Temple** (built 1873).

ACTIVITIES

See the Around the Kathmandu Valley chapter for rafting, canyoning and bungy-jumping at the Last Resort and Borderlands.

Adventure Centre Asia *(Greater Thamel map;* ☎ *4425894;* Ⓦ *www.adventurecentre asia.com)*, next to Northfields Café in Thamel, houses Borderlands, Ultimate Descents Nepal and Himalayan Mountain Bikes. See the Rafting & Kayaking and Mountain Biking chapters for details of these and other adventure companies that offer those activities.

Pools & Fitness Centres

Generally, pools in the major hotels can be used by friends of hotel guests, or at some hotels (such as Hotel de l'Annapurna) by outsiders, for a US$2 to US$3 charge. The Yak & Yeti Hotel charges Rs 500 for a one-time use of its two pools, plus another Rs 500 for its health club.

There are public pools at **Balaju** *(Kathmandu map; Rs 40; open 9am-4pm Mar-Sept)*, northwest of Thamel, and at the **National Stadium** *(Central Kathmandu map;*

Erotic Art

The most interesting woodcarving on Nepali temples is on the roof struts, or *tunala*, and on many temples these carvings include erotic scenes. These scenes are rarely the central carving on the strut, they're usually the smaller carving at the bottom of the strut, like a footnote to the larger image. Nor are the carvings sensuous and finely sculptured like those at Khajuraho and Konark in India. In Nepal the figures are often smaller and cruder, even quite cartoon-like.

The themes have a Tantric element, a clear connection to the intermingling of Tibetan Buddhist and Hindu beliefs in Nepal, but their real purpose is unclear. Are they simply a celebration of an important part of the life cycle? Are they a more explicit reference to Shiva's and Parvati's creative roles than the enigmatic lingams and yonis scattered around so many temples? Or are they supposed to play some sort of protective role for the temple? It's popularly rumoured that the goddess of lightning is a shy virgin who wouldn't dream of striking a temple with such goings-on, although that's probably more a tourist-guide tale than anything else.

Whatever the reason for their existence, the Tantric elements can be found on temples throughout the valley. Some temples may reveal just the odd depiction while on others something will be depicted on every roof strut. The activities range from straightforward exhibitionism to scenes of couples engaged in often quite athletic acts of intercourse. More exotic carvings include *ménages à trois* scenes of oral or anal intercourse or couplings with demons or animals. The towns in the Kathmandu Valley with some of the more interesting erotic carvings include Kathmandu, Patan, Bhaktapur, Chobar and Gokarna.

Kumari Devi

Not only does Nepal have countless gods, goddesses, deities, Bodhisattvas (near Buddhas), avatars (incarnations of deities) and manifestations – which are worshipped and revered as statues, images, paintings and symbols – but it also has a real living goddess. The Kumari Devi is a young girl who lives in the building known as the Kumari Bahal, right beside Kathmandu's Durbar Square.

The practice of having a living goddess probably came about during the reign of Jaya Prakash Malla, the last of the Malla kings of Kathmandu, whose reign abruptly ended with the conquest of the valley by Prithvi Narayan Shah in 1768. As usual in Nepal, where there is never one simple answer to any question, there are a number of legends about the Kumari.

One such legend relates that a paedophile Malla king had intercourse with a pre-pubescent girl. She died as a result of this and in penance he started the practice of venerating a young girl as a living goddess. Another tells of a Malla king who regularly played dice with the goddess Taleju, the protective deity of the valley. When he made an unseemly advance she threatened to withdraw her protection, but relented and promised to return in the form of a young girl. Yet another tells of a young girl who was possessed by the goddess Durga and banished from the kingdom. When the furious queen heard of this she ordered her husband to bring the young girl back and keep her as a real goddess.

Whatever the background, in reality there are a number of living goddesses around the Kathmandu Valley, although the Kumari Devi, or Royal Kumari, is the most important. The Kumari is selected from a particular caste of Newari gold and silversmiths. Customarily, she is somewhere between four years old and puberty and must meet 32 strict physical requirements ranging from the colour of her eyes and shape of her teeth to the sound of her voice. Her horoscope must also be appropriate, of course.

Once suitable candidates have been found they are gathered together in a darkened room where terrifying noises are made, while men dance by in horrific masks and gruesome buffalo heads are on display. Naturally these goings-on are unlikely to frighten a real goddess, particularly one who is an incarnation of Durga, so the young girl who remains calm and collected throughout this ordeal is clearly the new Kumari. In a process similar to the selection of the Dalai Lama, the Kumari then chooses items of clothing and decoration worn by her predecessor as a final test.

Once chosen as the Kumari, the young girl moves into the Kumari Bahal with her family and makes only a half-dozen ceremonial forays into the outside world each year. The most spectacular of these occasions is the September Indra Jatra festival, when she travels through the city on a huge temple chariot over a three-day period. During this festival the Kumari customarily blesses the king of Nepal.

The Kumari's reign ends with her first period, or any serious accidental loss of blood. Once this first sign of puberty is reached she reverts to the status of a normal mortal, and the search must start for a new Kumari. During her time as a goddess the Kumari is supported by the temple income and on retirement she is paid a handsome dowry. It is said that marrying an ex-Kumari is unlucky, but it's more likely believed that taking on a spoilt ex-goddess is likely to be too much hard work!

---

entry Rs 15; open 10am-5pm daily, closed Oct-Feb), in the south of Kathmandu. Monday is reserved for women at the National Stadium. The Balaju pool is accessed from Mahendra Park (see Balaju in the Around the Kathmandu Valley chapter) and can get very crowded.

A recommended health club for aerobic classes is **Banu's Total Fitness** *(Kathmandu map;* ☎ 4434024; e *banu94@yahoo.com; open 6am-9pm Sun-Fri)* hidden down an alleyway southeast of the new Royal Palace. There are aerobic classes at 7am and 5.30pm. A visit costs Rs 150 for nonmembers, though officially you have to be a guest of a member. A

number of the five-star hotels have fitness centres, such as the Clark Hatch gym at the Radisson, north of the new Royal Palace.

Hot-Air Ballooning

On a clear day hot-air ballooning is a breathtaking way to view the vast expanse of the Himalaya – from over 2000m up – and it's a chance to get some clean air!

Flights take place daily during the main tourist season (October to November) and, depending on the wind, fly either east to west or vice versa over the city. It's an amazing

[Continued on page 135]

WALKING TOURS

A stroll around Kathmandu will lead the casual wanderer to many intriguing sights, especially in the crowded maze of streets, courtyards and alleys in the market area north of Durbar Square. There are temples, shrines and many individual statues and sculptures hidden away in the most unlikely places. You can really appreciate Kathmandu's museum-like quality when you stumble upon a 1000-year-old statue – something that would be a prized possession in many Western museums – here being used as a children's plaything or a washing line. The walks described in this section can be done whenever you have an hour or two to spare. Walking Tours 1 and 2 can be used as routes from the accommodation centre of Thamel to the central Durbar Square area.

Each of the three walks will take you to a number of markets, temples and *chowks* (courtyard or marketplace), which remain the focus of Nepali life. A number of *chowks* are surrounded by *bahils* or *bahals* (dwellings for monastic Buddhist communities), although none are used for that purpose today – they have been taken over by families and sometimes by schools. The courtyards may be large and open, dotted with *chaityas* (small stupas, or hemispherical Buddhist religious structures) and shrines, or they may be enclosed within a single building. A *bahil* is distinguished from a *bahal* because it includes accommodation for non-monastic visitors, it's generally simpler than a *bahal*, and the main shrine is not necessarily in the centre of the courtyard.

The walks can be made as individual strolls or linked together into one longer walk. Walking Tour 1 gives you a taste of the crowded and fascinating shopping streets in the oldest part of Kathmandu and takes you to some of the city's most important temples. Walking Tour 2 visits some very old *bahals* and an important Buddhist stupa, and it passes by a number of ancient and important stone icons and introduces you to a toothache god. Walking Tour 3 takes you to a lesser-known section of Kathmandu, without spectacular attractions but where the everyday life of city dwellers goes on and tourists are fairly rare.

Walking Tour 1 – North from Durbar Square

Walking
Tour 1

Duration: 1-1½ hours

Makhan Tole, the road angling across the city from Durbar Square to the Rani Pokhari pool (see the Walking Tour 2 map), is the most interesting street in old Kathmandu. Modern roads such as Durbar Marg are no match for this narrow artery's varied and colourful shops, temples and people. The road was at one time the main street in Kathmandu, and it was the start of the route to Tibet. It was not replaced as Kathmandu's most important street until the construction of New Rd after the great earthquake of 1934, and it was not paved until the 1960s.

Makhan Tole This crowded street (*makhan* is the Nepali word for butter, *tole* means street) starts from the northeastern corner of Durbar Square and then runs towards the busy marketplace of Indra Chowk. Many worthwhile shops along this stretch sell brightly-coloured Tibetan *thangkas* (religious paintings).

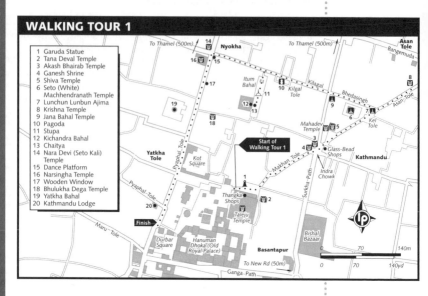

WALKING TOUR 1

1 Garuda Statue
2 Tana Deval Temple
3 Akash Bhairab Temple
4 Ganesh Shrine
5 Shiva Temple
6 Seto (White)
  Machhendranath Temple
7 Lunchun Lunbun Ajima
8 Krishna Temple
9 Jana Bahal Temple
10 Pagoda
11 Stupa
12 Kichandra Bahal
13 Chaitya
14 Nara Devi (Seto Kali)
   Temple
15 Dance Platform
16 Narsingha Temple
17 Wooden Window
18 Bhulukha Dega Temple
19 Yatkha Bahal
20 Kathmandu Lodge

Directly across from the Taleju Temple (see the Durbar Square special section in this chapter) is a 10th-century kneeling **Garuda statue (1)**. It faces a small Vishnu Temple. To your right, in a walled courtyard just past the long row of stalls, is the **Tana Deval Temple (2)**, with three carved doorways and multiple struts, the latter of which show the multi-armed Ashta Matrikas (Mother Goddesses). It's possible to enter the temple.

Indra Chowk The busy shopping street of Makhan Tole spills into Indra Chowk, the courtyard named after the ancient Vedic deity, Indra. On the left of the square is the **Akash Bhairab Temple (3)**, or Bhairab of the Sky Temple. From the balcony four metal lions rear out over the street. The temple's entrance is at the right-hand side of the building, guarded by two more metal lions, but non-Hindus cannot enter. The silver image inside is visible through the open windows from out in the street, and during important festivals, particularly Indra Jatra (September), the image is displayed in the square. A large lingam (phallic symbol) is also erected in the centre of the square at that time.

In a small niche just near the Akash Bhairab Temple is a very small but much-visited brass **Ganesh shrine (4)**.

Indra Chowk is traditionally a centre for the sale of blankets and cloth, and there are often many merchants on the platforms of the Mahadev Temple. Shawls and woollen rugs are sold on the platform of the **Shiva Temple (5)**, which is a smaller and simplified version of Patan's Krishna Temple.

From the south of the square Surkha Path leads to New Rd; the shops along this road sell consumer goods imported from Hong Kong and Singapore, and many of them end up in India. The road heading north from Indra Chowk leads to Thamel.

• Garuda Statue

• Tana Deval Temple

• Akash Bhairab Temple

• Ganesh Shrine

• Shiva Temple

Before you leave Indra Chowk, look for the narrow alley to the right, crowded with stalls selling the glass bangles and beads that are so popular with Nepali women.

Kel Tole It's only a short stroll from Indra Chowk to the next square, Kel Tole, where you'll find one of the most important and ornate temples in Kathmandu, **Seto (White) Machhendranath Temple (6)**. The arched entrance to the temple is guarded by a small Buddha figure on a high stone pillar in front of two metal lions. The temple attracts both Buddhists and Hindus – Buddhists consider Seto Machhendranath to be a form of Avalokiteshvara, while to Hindus he is a rain-bringing incarnation of Shiva. Although the temple's age is not known, it was restored during the 17th century.

In the courtyard there are numerous small shrines, *chaityas* and statues, including a mysteriously European-looking female figure facing the temple. It may well have been an import from Europe that has simply been accepted into the pantheon of gods. Facing the other way, just in front of the temple, are two graceful bronze figures of the Taras seated on top of tall pillars.

Inside the temple you can see the white-faced image of the god covered in flowers. The image is taken out of the temple during the Seto Machhendranath festival in March/April each year and paraded around the city in a chariot. The procession ends at the Machhendranath Temple in the south of the city (visited on Walking Tour 3).

In this area you may see many men standing around holding what looks like a bizarre string instrument. This tool is used to separate and fluff up the down-like cotton padding that is sold in bulk nearby. The string is plucked by a wooden double-headed implement that looks like a cross between a dumbbell and a rolling pin.

As you leave the temple, to the left is the small, triple-roofed **Lunchun Lunbun Ajima (7)**, a Tantric temple that's red-tiled around the lower level and has some erotic carvings at the base of the struts at the back.

The diagonal street continues to Asan Tole, the busiest of the junctions along the old street (covered in Walking Tour 2). Walk partway towards Asan Tole. On the left, the polygonal **Krishna Temple (8)** is jammed between other buildings, with the ground floor occupied by shops. It looks like it's falling apart, but the woodcarvings on this temple are very elaborate, depicting beaked monsters and the Tibetan protector holding a tiger on a chain like he's taking the dog for a walk.

Return to Kel Tole and turn right (west). The shops along this stretch specialise in *topis* (Nepali caps). At the next junction the large **Jana Bahal Temple (9)** is on your left but is of little interest.

Kilgal Tole to Itum Bahal Continue across the junction and on the left you pass the small Kilgal Tole beside the road. It's a grubby little square with a **pagoda (10)**, a popular water source and, in the middle, a fine *chaitya* with faces on each side.

About 20m past here, an opening on the left leads into the long, rectangular courtyard of **Itum Bahal**. A small, white-painted **stupa (11)** stands in the centre of the courtyard. On the western side of the courtyard is the **Kichandra Bahal (12)**, one of the oldest *bahals* in

Seto (White)
Machhednranath
Temple

Lunchun
Lunbun Ajima

Krishna Temple

Bahal Temple

Pagoda

Itum Bajal
Stupa

Kichandra Bahal

the city, dating from 1381. A **chaitya (13)** in front of the entrance is completely shattered by a bodhi tree, which has grown right up through its centre. The square is a peaceful haven of rural life, with piles of corn left to dry in ornate patterns.

Inside the Kichandra Bahal is a central pagoda-like sanctuary, and to the south is a small *chaitya* decorated with graceful Bodhisattvas in a standing, rather than the usual sitting, position. On the northern side of the courtyard are four brass plaques mounted on the upper-storey wall. The one on the extreme left shows a demon known as Guru Mapa taking a misbehaving child from a woman and stuffing it greedily into his mouth. Eventually the demon was bought off with the promise of an annual feast of buffalo meat, and the plaque to the right shows him sitting down and dipping into a pot of food.

To this day Guru Mapa is said to live in a tree in the Tundikhel parade ground in central Kathmandu; a buffalo is sacrificed to him annually. With such a clear message on juvenile misbehaviour it is fitting that the courtyard houses a primary school – right under the Guru Mapa plaques!

Nara Devi Temple From Kichandra Bahal go back into the large courtyard, exit at the north and turn left (west). On your right at the next junction is the **Nara Devi Temple (14)**. The temple is dedicated to Kali, Shiva's consort in her destructive incarnation, and is also known as the Seto Kali (White Kali) Temple.

Although the temple, with its three tiers, golden roof and red and white guardian lions, is quite old, some of the decorations are clearly more recent additions. It is said that Kali's powers protected the temple from the 1934 earthquake, which destroyed so many other temples in the valley. A Malla king once stipulated that a dancing ceremony should be held for the goddess every 12 years, and dances are still performed on the small **dance platform (15)** that is across the road from the temple. Also across the road is a three-roofed **Narsingha temple (16)** to Vishnu as the demon-destroying man-lion, but it's hard to find through a maze of small courtyards.

Postage-Stamp Window At the Nara Devi corner, turn left (south) and you soon come to a photocopy shop by a nondescript modern building on your left with an utterly magnificent **wooden window (17)**. It has been called *deshay madu* in Nepali, which means 'there is not another one like it'. A postage stamp worth Rs 0.50 was issued in 1978, which showed the window. Next to the building is the recently restored triple-roofed **Bhulukha Dega Temple (18)**, dedicated to Shiva.

A little farther south and on your right is the entrance to the **Yatkha Bahal (19)**, a huge open courtyard with an unremarkable stupa in the centre. Directly behind it is an old building, whose projecting upper storey is supported by four superb carved-wood struts. Dating from the 14th century, they are carved in the form of *yakshas* (attendant deities or nymphs), one of them gracefully balancing a baby on her hip. The struts are being restored by the Department of Architecture, Unesco and the Kathmandu Valley Preservation Trust.

Back on the road and heading south you soon see Durbar Square ahead.

● Chaitya

● Nara Devi Temple

● Dance Platform
● Narsingha Temple

● Wooden Window

● Bhulukha Dega Temple
● Yatkha Bahal

Finish

Walking Tour 2 – South of Thamel

Duration: 1-1¼ hours

This walk can be started from the southern end of Thamel or it can easily be linked to Walking Tour 1 to make a 'figure eight' starting from either Thamel or Durbar Square. This walk can also be started from the bustling Thahiti Tole or, if that's hard to find, from the Hotel Gautam on Kantipath. To get to Thahiti Tole walk south from Thamel on the road from the main Thamel Chowk; the first open square you will come to is Thahiti.

Thahiti Tole In the **stupa (1)** in the centre of the square is a stone inscription indicating it was constructed in the 15th century. Legends relate that it was built over a pond plated with gold and that the stupa served to keep thieves at bay. Or perhaps the pond was full of dangerous snakes and the stupa kept the snakes in their place – the legends vary!

Nateshwar Temple (2), on the northern side of the square, is dedicated to Shiva; the metal plates that surround the doors show creatures busily playing a variety of musical instruments. Above the door are somewhat crudely painted pictures of Shiva's *ganas* (companions), in this case a skeleton-like creature and what looks like a yeti.

Two Ancient Bahals Leave the northeastern corner of the square taking the narrow road running east. You soon come to the entrance of the **Musya Bahal (3)** on your right, with a modern facade and guarded by stone lions. The road continues east and then takes a right then left bend, at the corner of which is a second old monastery, the recently restored 330-year-old **Chusya Bahal (4)**.

This stretch of street is popular with potters, and you often see them working on the roadside outside the *bahals* or see their products piled

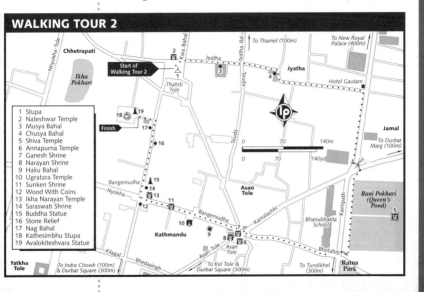

WALKING TOUR 2

1 Stupa
2 Nateshwar Temple
3 Musya Bahal
4 Chusya Bahal
5 Shiva Temple
6 Annapurna Temple
7 Ganesh Shrine
8 Narayan Shrine
9 Haku Bahal
10 Ugratara Temple
11 Sunken Shrine
12 Wood With Coins
13 Ikha Narayan Temple
14 Saraswati Shrine
15 Buddha Statue
16 Stone Relief
17 Nag Bahal
18 Kathesimbhu Stupa
19 Avalokiteshvara Statue

up inside. Often these are just the simple little disposable cups used by *chai* (milk tea) sellers.

Beyond the second *bahal* there is a string of hotels, and just before the road joins the busy Kantipath is the Hotel Gautam. Turn right (south) and then cross the road via the footbridge to Rani Pokhari (Queen's Pond). Hawkers crouch at the base of the bridge selling whatever snacks are in season, from coconut to gooseberries. The bridge itself offers a decent view over Rani Pokhari, although photos will be somewhat obscured by the tangle of electric wires. The *chowk* has rather optimistically been declared a no horn zone!

Rani Pokhari This large fenced tank (or small lake) was built by King Pratap Malla in 1667 to console his queen over the death of their son. Various legends and tales are connected with the tank and it's believed that it may have been built by Pratap Malla at an earlier date and renamed for his queen only after their son died (according to records the son was trampled by an elephant).

Unfortunately, the gate to the tank is unlocked only one day each year, during the festival of Tihar, so you will have to be content with peering through the fence. A causeway leads across the tank to a small and undistinguished **Shiva Temple (5)**.

● Shiva Temple

Across Kantipath from the tank is a long building originally known as the Durbar School, which was the first school in Nepal (1854). It has since been renamed the **Bhanubhakta School**, after the Nepali poet of that name. Walk south along Kantipath to the footbridge at the southern end of Rani Pokhari, and cross Kantipath. This footbridge affords the best views of Rani Pokhari. From here head straight into the old part of the city to Asan Tole.

● Bhanubhakta School

Asan Tole From dawn until late at night Asan Tole is jammed with buyers, sellers and passers-by. The six roads meeting at this junction make it the busiest in Kathmandu. Cat Stevens wrote his hippie-era song 'Kathmandu' in a smoky teahouse in Asan Tole. Every day produce is carried to this popular marketplace from all over the valley so it is fitting that the three-storey **Annapurna Temple (6)** is dedicated to the goddess of abundance, Annapurna. The smaller two-storey **Ganesh shrine (7)** is coated in bathroom tiles. On the western side of the square are shops, which sell spices and dried fruit. Near the centre of the square is a small **Narayan shrine (8)** (Narayan is a form of Vishnu).

● Annapurna Temple
● Ganesh Shrine

● Narayan Shrine

West of Asan Tole Take the road leading west out of Asan Tole and, after a short distance, on your left you will find an anonymous entrance that leads into **Haku Bahal (9)**. Look for the sign that advertises 'The Spects Shop'. This tiny *bahal* has a finely carved wooden window overlooking the courtyard.

● Haku Bahal

About 20m farther west you'll come to the triple-roofed **Ugratara Temple (10)** at a small square known as Nhhakantalla. Come here if your eyes are sore; a prayer at the shrine is said to work wonders for the eyes, which is perhaps why the shrine is covered in mirrors. A little farther along is a small, **sunken shrine (11)** on the left and a Ganesh shrine set into the wall on the right. Soon after you'll arrive at a crossroads with an

● Ugratara Temple

● Sunken Shrine

open square to the north. Turn left (south) and on your left you will see a lump of **wood with coins (12)** into which thousands of coins have been nailed. A coin and nail embedded in the wood is supposed to cure toothache, and the deity who looks after this ailment is represented by a tiny image in the ugly lump of wood. The square at the junction is known as Bangemudha, which means 'Twisted Wood'.

Ancient Buddha Turn north into the open square and you'll see a small, double-roofed **Ikha Narayan temple (13)**, easily identified by the kneeling Garuda figure facing it. The temple houses a beautiful 10th- or 11th-century four-armed Vishnu figure that sadly isn't generally on display. The square also has a fine image of the goddess Saraswati playing her lute at the **Saraswati Shrine (14)**, with Shiva to the left.

The northern side of the square is closed off by a modern building with shops on the ground floor. In the middle of this nondescript frontage, directly beneath the 'Raj Dentral [sic] Clinic' sign, is a standing **Buddha statue (15)** framed by modern blue and white tilework. The image is only about 60cm high but dates from the 5th or 6th century. A very similar Buddha figure stands on the riverbank near the temple of Pashupatinath.

If the toothache god hasn't done his duty, as you take the road north from the square you'll pass a string of dentists shops – proclaimed by the standard signs showing a smiling mouthful of teeth. On the right is a small open area surrounded by concrete with an orange-coloured Ganesh head and a small but intricate central **stone relief (16)** dating from the 9th century. It shows Shiva sitting with Parvati on Mt Kailash, her hand resting proprietarily on his knee in the pose known as Uma Maheshwar. Various deities and creatures, including Shiva's bull Nandi, stand around them.

There's an impressive wooden balcony across the road, which is said to have had the first glass windows in Kathmandu. A little farther on your left, a single broken stone lion (his partner has disappeared) guards a passageway, above which hangs a carved wooden *torana* (pediment above temple doors that can indicate the god to whom the temple is dedicated). Inside is the small enclosed courtyard of **Nag Bahal (17)**, with painted murals above the shrine, which is flanked by banners with double-triangle flags.

Kathesimbhu Stupa Just a couple of steps beyond the Nag Bahal entrance is the entrance to the **Kathesimbhu Stupa (18)**, just southwest of Thahiti Tole. The entrance is flanked by metal lions atop red ochre concrete pillars.

In the courtyard is a small copy (dating from around 1650) of the great Swayambhunath complex outside Kathmandu, making this the most popular Tibetan pilgrimage site in Kathmandu's old town. Just as at Swayambhunath, there is a two-storey pagoda to Harti, the goddess of smallpox, right behind the main stupa.

Various statues and smaller *chaityas* stand around the temple, including a fine standing **Avalokiteshvara statue (19)** enclosed in a glass case and protective metal cage. Avalokiteshvara carries a lotus flower in his left hand, and the Dhyani Buddha Amitabha is seen in the centre of his crown.

Wood with Coins
Ikha Narayan Temple
Saraswati Shrine
Buddha Statue
Stone Relief
Nag Bahal
Kathesimbhu Stupa
Avalokiteshvara Statue
Finish

There are lots of *malla* (prayer beads) stalls in the square, as well as a little teahouse on the corner if energies are flagging. From Kathesimbhu Stupa it's only a short walk north to Thahiti Tole, the starting point of the walking tour.

Walking Tour 3 – South from Durbar Square

Duration: 45 minutes-1 hour

Starting from the Kasthamandap in Durbar Square a circular walk can be made to the older parts in the south of the city. This area is not as packed with historical interest as the walks north of Durbar Square, but the streets are less crowded and you are far less likely to run into other tourists.

Walking Tour 3

Bhimsen Temple Starting from the **Kasthamandap (1)** in the southwestern corner of Durbar Square, the road out of the square forks almost immediately around the **Singh Sattal (2)**, built with wood left over from the Kasthamandap Temple. The squat building has small shop stalls around the ground floor and golden-winged lions guarding each corner of the upper floor and is a popular place for devotional music *(bhajan)* in the mornings and evenings. Take the road running to the right of this building and you soon come to a square tank-like **hiti (3)**, or water conduit, where people will usually be washing clothes.

● Kasthamandap

● Singh Sattal

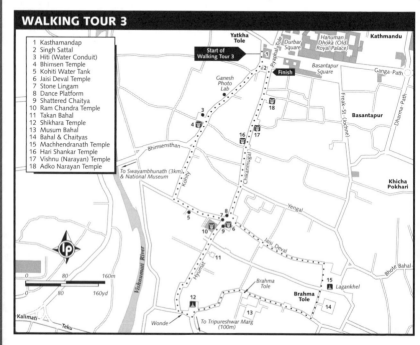

WALKING TOUR 3

1 Kasthamandap
2 Singh Sattal
3 Hiti (Water Conduit)
4 Bhimsen Temple
5 Kohiti Water Tank
6 Jaisi Deval Temple
7 Stone Lingam
8 Dance Platform
9 Shattered Chaitya
10 Ram Chandra Temple
11 Takan Bahal
12 Shikhara Temple
13 Musum Bahal
14 Bahal & Chaityas
15 Machhendranath Temple
16 Hari Shankar Temple
17 Vishnu (Narayan) Temple
18 Adko Narayan Temple

Immediately beyond is the highly decorated **Bhimsen Temple (4)**, which is fronted by a brass lion ducking under the electric wires and has white-painted lions guarding the two front corners. Bhimsen is supposed to watch over traders and artisans so it's quite appropriate that the ground floor of this well-kept temple should be devoted to shop stalls. An image of Bhimsen used to be carried to Lhasa in Tibet every 12 years to protect those vital trade routes, until the route was closed by Chinese control and the flight of the Dalai Lama in 1959. There are some lovely *chaityas* here.

Jaisi Deval Temple Continue south beyond the Bhimsen Temple then turn sharp left (uphill) where the road ends, passing the ornate **Kohiti water tank (5)** en route. At the top of the hill you'll come out by the tall, triple-roofed, 17th-century **Jaisi Deval Temple (6)**, which stands on a seven-level base. This is a Shiva temple, as indicated by the bull on the first few steps and the mildly erotic carvings on some of the temple struts. Right across the road from the temple is a **stone lingam (7)** rising a good 2m from a yoni (female equivalent of a phallic symbol). This is definitely a god-sized phallic symbol and a prayer here is said to aid fertility.

In its procession around the town during the Indra Jatra festival, the Kumari Devi's chariot pauses here. During its stop, dances are held on the small **dance platform (8)** across the road from the temple. This area of Kathmandu was the heart of the ancient city in the Licchavi period (4th to 9th centuries).

Southwest of the temple, in front of a **shattered chaitya (9)**, enter the courtyard of the **Ram Chandra Temple (10)**, named after Ram, incarnation of Vishnu and the hero of the Hindu epic Ramayana. This small temple is notable for the tiny erotic scenes on its roof struts. This is straightforward sex and no funny business; it looks as if the carver set out to illustrate 16 different positions, starting with the missionary position, and just about made it before running out of ideas. The north side of the courtyard is used as a cow stable, highlighting the wonderful mix of the sacred and profane in Nepal.

Machhendranath Temple There is a series of *bahals* on the next stretch of the walk, but most are of little interest apart from the small and very much lived-in courtyard of the **Takan Bahal (11)**. The surprisingly large 14th-century stupa in the centre has recently been restored and is now in fine condition.

The road continues with a few slight bends then turns sharply left (east) at Wonde junction, which is marked by several temples, including a taller **shikhara temple (12)**. If you take the downhill road leading from this junction (and off the Walking Tour 3 map) you emerge onto Tripureshwar Marg, from where you can continue to the Pachali Bhairab Temple (see the Kathmandu chapter for details). Our walk continues past Brahma Tole to the **Musum Bahal (13)**, with its phallic-shaped Licchavi (5th century) *chaityas* and an enclosed well. Turn sharp left (north) at the next main junction and look out for a large, open **bahal** and many **chaityas (14)**.

The road opens into Lagankhel, an open square featuring the 5m-high **Machhendranath Temple (15)**, as well as neighbourhood

Kohiti Water Tank

Jaisi Deval Temple

Stone Lingam

Dance Platform

Shattered Chaitya
Ram Chandra
Temple

Takan Bahal

Shikhara Temple

Musum Bahal

Bahal & Chaityas

Machhendranath
Temple

cricket matches, snack stalls and playing kids. During the annual Seto Machhendranath festival, the image of the god is transported here from the Seto Machhendranath Temple in Kel Tole (see the Walking Tour 1 map). The final stage of the procession is to pull the god's chariot three times around the temple, after which the image is taken back to its starting point on a palanquin while the chariot is dismantled here.

Turn left out of Lagankhel and walk back to the tall **Jaisi Deval Temple (6)**, then turn right (northeast) back towards Durbar Square.

● Jaisi Deval Temple

Shiva & Vishnu Temples
At the next crossroads the small, slender **Hari Shankar Temple (16)** stands to the left of the road.

● Hari Shankar Temple

Continue north past a **Vishnu (Narayan) temple (17)** to a second Vishnu temple, the **Adko Narayan Temple (18)**. Although this may not look impressive, it is said to be one of the four most important Vishnu temples in Kathmandu. Twin feathered Garuda figures front the temple, while lions guard each corner.

● Vishnu (Narayan) Temple

● Adko Narayan Temple

Beyond the temple you pass the Singh Sattal building once again and arrive back at the starting point. Alternatively head east through the backstreets for a reviving chocolate cake and tea at Freak Street's Snowman Restaurant.

Finish

[Continued from page 124]

experience, although crossing right over the international airport is a little unnerving. The rice field landings usually attract a huge, excited and curious crowd of local villagers.

The cost of a one-hour flight is US$195 per person, which includes transport to and from your hotel and a buffet breakfast at a Thamel restaurant. For bookings contact a travel agent or **Balloon Sunrise Nepal** (☎ 4424131; W www .balloon-sunrise-nepal.com.np).

Golf

At Gokarna, east of Bodhnath (Boudha), the 18-hole **Gokarna Forest Golf Resort** (*Kathmandu Valley map;* ☎ 4224399; e go karna@mos.com.np) has a beautiful setting in one of the valley's few remaining forested areas. Accommodation is offered at the resort courtesy of **Le Meridien** (W www.gokarna .com/html/the_hotel.html; singles/doubles US$160/180). The course is aimed at high-rolling expats. Currently a three-day package with accommodation, golf, meals and drinks costs US$360/450 for a single/double.

Climbing

If you need to polish up or learn some climbing skills before heading off into the mountains, the **Pasang Lhamu Climbing Wall** (*Kathmandu map;* ☎ 4370742; W www.pasang lhamu.org; open 6am-9pm daily) is Nepal's first, out on the northeast edge of the city. A day's membership costs Rs 350 and equipment is available for rent. You are allowed one free climb to try out the 14m-high wall; after that you need to complete a short orientation and safety class. Various week-long climbing courses are available.

The wall is on the Ring Rd, near the Bangladesh embassy, and is part of the Pasang Lhamu Mountaineering Federation, named after the first Nepali woman to summit Everest.

PLACES TO STAY

Kathmandu has an excellent range of places to stay, from expensive international-style hotels to cheap and comfortable lodges, and almost all offer competitive prices. Most of Kathmandu's accommodation offers some form of discount (see the boxed text 'A Note on Hotel Prices' in the Facts for the Visitor chapter).

It's difficult to recommend hotels, especially in the budget and middle brackets, because rooms in each hotel can vary widely. Many of these hotels have additions to additions, and while some rooms may be very gloomy and run-down, others might be bright and pleasant. A friendly crowd of fellow travellers can also make all the difference. Quite a few hotels bridge the budget and mid-range categories by having a range of room standards – these places have been grouped according to their lowest price.

Normal high-season rates are given here, followed where relevant by the amount of discount being offered on this rate at the time of research.

For budget and mid-range places the Thamel area is the main locale, and it is something of a tourist ghetto. The name Thamel describes a sprawling area with several hundred hotels, restaurants, Internet cafés, travel agencies and shops, and a bustling cosmopolitan atmosphere. It's a convenient and enjoyable area to stay for a short time, especially to meet fellow travellers or for a budget-priced apple crumble and a hot shower, but you are likely to tire of the place in a couple of days.

In an attempt to establish some order, we have somewhat arbitrarily divided the greater Thamel area (see the Greater Thamel map) into: Thamel, around the two main intersections; Paknajol, to the north; Bhagwan Bahal, to the northeast; Jyatha, to the southeast; and Chhetrapati, to the southwest.

There is still a scattering of really rock-bottom places along Freak St (see the Freak Street map), close to Durbar Square, and these offer the impecunious an escape from the Thamel crowds.

Mid-range places are widely scattered, with a majority in and around Thamel. Kathmandu's limited number of international-standard hotels are also widely spread, some of them quite a distance from the city centre.

Some travellers are base themselves farther afield, outside Kathmandu in Patan or Bodhnath, to escape the worst of the traffic, pollution and commercialism of Thamel (see the Around the Kathmandu Valley chapter for details). For something quieter still, there is an increasing number of mostly top-end resorts around the Kathmandu Valley, which offer a peaceful rural atmosphere less than an hour from the centre of Kathmandu.

KATHMANDU

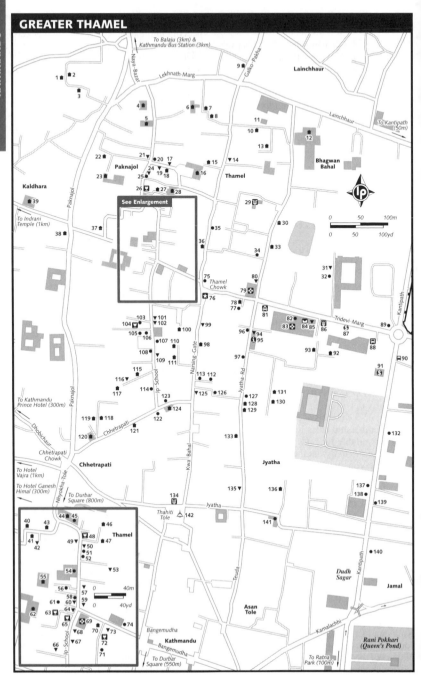

GREATER THAMEL

PLACES TO STAY
1 Kathmandu Garden House
2 Kathmandu Peace Guest House
3 Tibet Peace Guest House
4 Hotel Manang
5 Hotel Marshyangdi
6 Hotel Gauri Shankar
7 Hotel Greeting Palace
8 Pilgrims Guest House
9 Hotel Encounter Nepal
10 Hotel Crown
12 Malla Hotel; Druk Air
13 Hotel Norbu Linka
15 Hotel Thamel
16 Hotel Vaishali
18 Hotel Shree Tibet
22 Hotel New Florid
23 Courtyard Hotel
27 Mustang Guest House
28 Hotel Tashi Dhargey
30 Panda Hotel
33 Hotel Earth House
36 Hotel Centre Point
37 Hotel Tradition
38 Hotel Metropolitan Kantipur
39 International Guest House
40 Hotel Down Town
41 Prince Guest House
43 Holy Lodge
44 Hotel Garuda
46 Acme Guest House
47 Hotel Red Planet
55 Kathmandu Guest House; Las
   Kus Restaurant; Dawn Till
   Dusk; Himalayan Encounters;
   Standard Chartered Bank
   (ATM only)
62 Pheasant Guest House
71 Hotel Potala; Botega
79 Marco Polo Guest House;
   Student Guest House
93 Mustang Holiday Inn
94 Imperial Guest House
99 Hotel Puska
101 Hotel Pacifist
110 Hotel Tashi Dhelek
111 Thorong Peak Guest House
116 Hotel California
118 Hotel Horizon
119 Hotel Hama
120 Nirvana Garden Hotel
121 Tibet Guest House
122 Khangsar Guest House
125 Potala Guest House
129 Hotel Norling
130 Hotel Utse; Utse Restaurant
131 Fuji Guest House
132 Hotel Dynasty
134 Sidhartha Garden Hotel
137 Kantipur Temple House

PLACES TO EAT
14 Thamel House Restaurant
17 Rum Doodle Restaurant & Bar
19 BK's Place
21 Thakali Kitchen
24 Krua Thai Restaurant
31 Dechenling Beer House
42 Delima Garden Cafe
49 Northfield Café; Adventure
   Centre Asia; Borderlands
50 Nargila Restaurant;
   Tom & Jerry Pub
53 New Orleans Café
57 Brezel Bakery
59 La Dolce Vita;
   Tashi Delek Rest
60 Le Bistro Restaurant
64 Hot Bread Outlet
66 Yin Yang Restaurant;
   Third Eye Restaurant
68 K-Too Beer & Steakhouse
69 Café Jalapeno;
   Alice's Restaurant
74 Pumpernickle Bakery
81 Dahua Restaurant
86 Fire & Ice; Dechenling
   Restaurant
95 Kilroy's of Kathmandu;
   Dawn Till Dusk Workshop
100 Sandwich Point
102 Weizen Bakery
103 Helena's
109 Koto Restaurant
112 Himalatte Café
117 Chang Cheng Restaurant
126 Café Mitra
136 Dolma Momo Center

OTHER
11 Thamel Gaa Hiti (water tank)
20 Advanced Photo Finisher
25 Diki Continental Exports
26 Sam's Bar
29 Bhagwan Bahal
32 Sita World Travel;
   Western Union; ITC
34 Gandharba Organisation
35 Porters' Progress
45 Equator Expeditions
48 Jump Club
51 Bandari Photo Shop;
   Himalayan Wonders
52 Thamel Nepali Language
   Institute
54 Pilgrims Book House;
   Pilgrims Feed N Read
56 Ultimate Rivers; Green Hill
   Tours; The Last Resort
58 Tantric Book Store
61 Massif Mountain Bikes

63 Pub Maya
65 Paddy Foley's Irish Bar;
   Barnes & Noble Bookhouse
67 Arcadia Building; Roadhouse
   Café; Arcadia Apartments;
   DHL; Wayfarers Travel
   Service; Standard Chartered
   Bank (ATM only)
70 Supermarket; Bakery;
   The Cybernet Café
72 Adventure Silk Road
73 Maya Cocktail Bar
75 Raging River Runners
76 Bicycle & Motorcycle Hire;
   Souvenir Stalls
77 Police Booth
78 Tea World
80 Best Shopping Centre
82 Taxi & Autorickshaw Stand
83 Hicola; Cottage Crafts
84 Sanchaya Kosh Bhawan
   Shopping Centre
85 Post Office; Bookworld;
   ACAP
87 Three Goddesses Temple
88 Himalaya Bank
89 Greenline
90 Kaiser Library
91 Bus Stop for Pokhara
   Tourist Buses
92 Standard Chartered Bank
96 KEEP; Travellers Information
   Centre; Himalayan
   Explorers Club
97 Gift for Aid
98 Shona's Alpine Rental
104 Wear Care Laundry
105 Jatra
106 United Books
107 Color Link
108 Ladybird Gift Shop
113 Bike Hire
114 Maheela
115 Amrita Craft Collection
123 Walden Book House
124 Nepal Colour Lab
127 Phapa Chengreshi Thanka
   Painting School
128 Kathmandu Institute of
   Nepali Language
133 Sharmasons Movers
135 Nateshwar Temple
138 Jyoti Bhawan; Nepal
   Vipassana Center Office
139 Qatar Airlines;
   Gorkha Airlines
140 FedEx
141 Mandala Bookpoint
142 Chusya Bahal
143 Stupa

PLACES TO STAY – BUDGET

Intense competition between Kathmandu's enormous number of low-priced hostels means that you can find hot showers in even the cheapest places, although they are sometimes solar-heated and are only hot in the late afternoon.

Hotels in this category do not have heating, and Kathmandu in winter is a rather chilly place. In winter you'll appreciate places with a garden as it's always pleasant to sit outside during the cool, but invariably sunny, autumn and winter days. A south-facing room will mean you get some sunlight in your room. In general, the top-floor rooms are the best, as you stand a chance of getting a view and have easy access to the roof (often a nice place to relax).

Thamel

Kathmandu Guest House (☎ 4413632; **W** www.ktmgh.com; singles from US$2-12, doubles US$4-14, singles/doubles with private bathroom US$17/20, with garden view US$25/30, air-con standard US$35/45, air-con deluxe US$50/60) was the first hotel to open in the area and it's still one of the most popular. It also serves as the central landmark – everything is 'near the Kathmandu Guest House'. In strictly dollar terms you can get better rooms elsewhere, but most people enjoy the bustling atmosphere and it's usually booked out weeks in advance during the high season. There's parking, BBC TV in the lobby, a front courtyard and very pleasant rear garden, a storage facility for luggage and valuables, a travel desk and even a sauna (Rs 300 per person) – this is budget travel in the deluxe category!

The cheapest rooms without bathroom form part of the original 13-room guesthouse and really aren't up to much – you'll certainly get better-value rooms elsewhere – but at least the common showers are clean and hot. In the newer wing, the best-value rooms are probably the garden-facing rooms. At the top of the scale are large, modern rooms with air-con, though these vary quite a lot. There's a 12% tax on top of all these prices.

If this is too extravagant for your budget you don't have to go far for something cheaper – there are a dozen or more places within a stone's throw. Turning south from the Kathmandu Guest House there's a cluster of hotels.

Pheasant Guest House (☎ 4417415; singles/doubles with shared bathroom Rs 100/150) is tucked farther around the laneway, so it's quiet despite the central location. There's a courtyard, and the rooms are very cheap. The main downside is the grotty toilets.

Hotel Horizon (☎ 4220904; **W** www.hotelhorizon.com; rooms with private bathroom US$3.50-6, deluxe singles/doubles US$8/10) is a good choice off the main street, making it a quiet option. It has a range of rooms at reasonable prices, all with bathroom, most of which are bright and spacious.

Hotel California (☎ 4242076; dorm beds Rs 75, rooms with shared bathroom Rs 125-250, with bathroom Rs 250-350), in the same lane as Hotel Horizon, is very cheap and offers spartan but clean-enough rooms; the better ones have a balcony. Unusually for Thamel, there is also a five-bed dorm on the roof. It's a decent, friendly place.

Hotel Potala (☎ 4419159; singles/doubles with shared bathroom Rs 125/250), down an alleyway near Botega, is also close to the heart of Thamel. This small Tibetan-run place is cheap and cheerful, though the rooms are dark and the hot water iffy.

Hotel Pacifist (☎ 4258320; singles/doubles/triples Rs 165/220/250), tucked away down an alley, is a bit gloomy but has good-sized rooms, all with a slightly crummy bathroom, and some with balcony.

Hotel Puska (☎ 4228997; singles/doubles with shared bathroom from Rs 100/150, with private bathroom Rs 300/400), just south of Thamel Chowk, isn't great but it is decent value and there's a wide range of rooms in various blocks (including some real stinkers, so have a look at a few rooms).

Marco Polo Guest House (☎ 4251914; **e** marcopolo@wlink.com.np; doubles with shared bathroom US$2-3, with private bathroom US$6-8) is a popular place on the eastern edge of Thamel, on the traffic-choked extension of Tridevi Marg. The rooms at the back are surprisingly quiet, with some pleasant rooftop patios, though the management is a bit morose.

Student Guest House (☎ 4251551; **e** krishna@student.wlink.com.np; singles/doubles with private bathroom Rs 350/550) is right next door to Marco Polo; it's quiet and clean but the nearby buildings are so crammed in that there's little natural light and no views, making it a little charmless.

Hotel Red Planet (☎ 4432879; e telstar@ wlink.com.np; singles/doubles from US$5/7) tucked away just north of Kathmandu Guest House and is a good Thamel cheapie, and far enough off the main strip not to be noisy. Rooms are clean and good value with decent bathrooms; try to get a garden-side room with a balcony.

Acme Guest House (☎ 4414811; e acme@ mos.com.np; singles/doubles from Rs 200/250, with private bathroom US$6/8, garden-facing with balcony US$8/10) is next to Hotel Red Planet. The rooms are quite large and there is an open lawn area, which is something of a rarity in crowded Thamel. The rooms with balcony overlooking the lawn are the best value; those at the back can be dark.

Paknajol
This area lies to the north of Thamel (see the Greater Thamel map) and can be reached by continuing north from the Kathmandu Guest House, or by approaching on Lekhnath Marg.

Mustang Guest House (☎ 4426053; e chit aure@mos.com.np; singles/doubles with shared bathroom Rs 130/180, with private bathroom Rs 200/250), tucked away down an inconspicuous laneway, is good value, with decent, quiet rooms but a dearth of natural light.

New Hotel Florid (☎ 4416155; e florid@ wlink.com.np; singles/doubles with shared bathroom US$5/7, with private bathroom US$8/10) is down a lane west of Advanced Photo Finisher. There is a small garden at the rear and no buildings behind so there's a feeling of space that is often lacking in Thamel. The top-floor rooms are bright, spacey and best; lower rooms are smaller and cheaper.

Not far from the steep Paknajol intersection with Lekhnath Marg (northwest of Thamel) there are a few pleasant guesthouses. They're away from traffic, a short walk from Thamel (but it could be a million miles), and they have beautiful views across the valley towards Balaju and Swayambhunath.

Tibet Peace Guest House (☎ 4415026; e tpghouse@wlink.com.np; rooms Rs 250-500) is friendly, small and family-run, with a lovely garden and small restaurant. This place offers well-equipped rooms with lockers, bathrooms and phones, but the rooms vary a lot so look at a few.

Kathmandu Peace Guest House (☎ 443 9369; e ktmpeacegh@visitnepal.com; singles/ doubles US$6/8, doubles with bathtub US$12), farther along the road, is a little more upmarket, offering phones and satellite TV in the comfortable rooms. There are superb views from the rooftop.

Kathmandu Garden House (☎ 4415239; e ktmghouse@wlink.com.np; doubles with shared bathroom Rs 200, with private bathroom Rs 400), opposite Peace Guest House, is deservedly popular and offers excellent-value doubles with hot-water shower. The views are excellent and the sitting area and lovely garden is good for relaxing.

Back in Paknajol, head southwest from the Hotel Garuda to find several reasonable cheapies.

Holy Lodge (☎ 4416265; e holylodge@ wlink.com.np; singles/doubles from Rs 200/ 300, with private bathroom up to Rs 500/700) offers neat, clean rooms but there's a sad lack of garden, sitting areas or views, especially in the warren-like back building.

Hotel Down Town (☎ 4430471; rooms with shared bathroom from Rs 250, with private bathroom Rs 350-500), one door down from Holy Lodge, is a fairly standard Thamel hotel, with a cybercafé and a wide range of rooms, the best of which are on the rooftop.

Prince Guest House (☎ 4414456; singles/ doubles Rs 300/450), across the road from Down Town, is a very decent budget place, with pleasant rooftop and rear gardens. Rooms have bathroom and phone.

Hotel Metropolitan Kantipur (☎ 4251 558; w www.mkantipur.net; singles/doubles US$8/10), just west of the Thamel action, is an excellent find, with a nice garden and friendly staff. Rooms are spacious and clean and come with TV, bathroom and hot water.

There's a small group of hotels built around a cul de sac south off Lekhnath Marg.

Pilgrims Guest House (☎ 4440565; e pilgrimsguesthouse@yahoo.com; singles with shared bathroom $5, singles with bathroom $6-10, doubles with private bathroom $8-15) has a good range of rooms, from the top-floor rooms with a sofa and balcony, to the cheapest singles, which are little more than a box. The place is well managed and friendly. There's an email centre and nice outdoor garden restaurant – it's just a niggling shame the drinks are overpriced.

Hotel Greeting Palace (☎ 4417212; e gpal ace@wlink.com.np; singles/doubles US$8/10) is a popular hotel just behind Pilgrims

Guest House, and offers good-sized carpeted rooms, some with a balcony, and a good-value restaurant. The rooftop rooms are generally best and have good views. There are some cheaper rooms with shared bathroom and balcony.

Hotel Gauri Shankar (☎ 4417181; e *hg shankar@wlink.com.np; singles/doubles US$6/ 10, deluxe US$10/15*) is a modern place with smallish but OK rooms and a slightly inconvenient location. Not much separates the ordinary and deluxe rooms, except the price.

Hotel Encounter Nepal (☎ 4440534; W *www.encounternepal.com; singles/doubles US$8/12, deluxe $20/30, 50% discount*) is a good-value place to the north, in a more lived-in part of Kathmandu. The hotel consists of an old and new block separated by garden. The old block is sunny, spacious and good value, and the spiffier new block has nice corner rooms with views over the valley, some with balcony. The only downer is that you take your life in your hands crossing diabolical Lekhnath Marg to get here.

Hotel Shree Tibet (☎ 4419902; e *sritibet@ ccsl.com.np; singles/doubles US$10/15, 50% discount*), north from the Kathmandu Guest House, is Tibetan-run and at the upper budget end. It's a clean and quiet (often deserted) place with cosy rooms decorated with Tibetan prayer flags, although many are dark and smallish due to the buildings being very close together. The small restaurant serves decent Tibetan food.

Hotel Tashi Dhargey (☎ 4417030, fax 4423543; W *www.hoteltashidhargey.com; singles/doubles Rs 350/500, with air-con/ heating Rs 800/1000*) is a pretty good choice down a back alley with entrances on two different roads. It has a wide range of slightly old-fashioned but spacious rooms, the best of which are on the upper floors.

Bhagwan Bahal

This area to the northeast of Thamel (see the greater Thamel map) takes its name from a Buddhist monastery. Some travellers like the area because it is much quieter than Thamel proper, and has not yet been completely taken over by restaurants, souvenir shops and travel agencies.

Hotel Earth House (☎ 4418197; *singles/ doubles with shared bathroom Rs 150/200, rooms with private bathroom Rs 200-700*) is a

good budget hotel, though the caged stairwells feel a little institutional. However, it does have friendly staff, a nice rooftop garden and a variety of clean and decent rooms. The rooms at the back are best as they are quieter and brighter.

Panda Hotel (☎ 4424683; *rooms with shared bathroom Rs 150, with private bathroom Rs 200-400*) is a little beyond the Earth House. The rooms with balconies are good value, particularly at the back; others can be dark.

Hotel Crown (☎ 4416285; W *www.hotel crown-np.com; rooms US$4-6*), farther north near the Hotel Norbu Linka, is down a somewhat scruffy side alley. The rooms are smallish but clean and comfortable and most come with private bathroom. With discounts it's excellent value.

Chhetrapati

This area is named after the important five-way intersection (notable by its distinctive bandstand) to the southwest of Thamel (see the Greater Thamel map). The farther you get from Thamel, the more traditional the surroundings become.

Khangsar Guest House (☎ 4260788; *rooms $4-5*) is friendly, central and good value, making it one of the best of the cheapies. Rooms come with a thin but clean bathroom with (generally) hot water, plus there's a Korean restaurant and a rooftop bar .

Hotel Hama (☎ 4251009; e *hama@info .com.np; rooms US$7-9*) is a quiet place right opposite the Tibet Guest House. The draws here are the bright corner rooms and the sunny balconies, and there's a small garden in front of the hotel.

Freak Street (Jochne) & Durbar Square

Although Freak St's glory days have passed, a few determined restaurants and lodges have hung on. Staying here offers two big pluses – you won't find anything cheaper and you're right in the heart of the old city. On the downside, the pickings are slimmer and the lodges generally grungier than in Thamel. All the places below can be found on the Freak St (Jochne) map.

Hotel Sugat (☎ 4245824; e *maryman@ smos.com.np; singles/doubles with shared bathroom from Rs 110/300, with private bathroom Rs 300/400*), overlooking the square, is one of the better options. The cheaper rooms

FREAK STREET (JOCHNE)

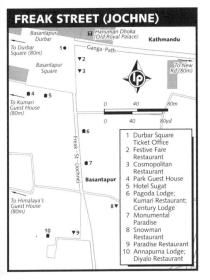

1	Durbar Square Ticket Office
2	Festive Fare Restaurant
3	Cosmopolitan Restaurant
4	Park Guest House
5	Hotel Sugat
6	Pagoda Lodge; Kumari Restaurant; Century Lodge
7	Monumental Paradise
8	Snowman Restaurant
9	Paradise Restaurant
10	Annapurna Lodge; Diyalo Restaurant

tend to be dark and creaky, with mildewy bathrooms but the more expensive rooms are large and decent. You are really paying for the location more than the quality of the rooms. There's a fine rooftop area.

Park Guest House (*☎ 4247487; singles/doubles with shared bathroom Rs 250/400, with private bathroom Rs 400/500*), almost next door to Hotel Sugat, has small rooms with fan and TV, some of which overlook Basantapur Square. It's modern and consequently a bit more expensive than some places in this area.

Annapurna Lodge (*☎ 4247684; singles/doubles with shared bathroom Rs 125/175,* with private bathroom Rs 250/250), just off Freak St proper, is well kept, cheerful and cosy. The attached Diyalo Restaurant (see Places to Eat later in this chapter) is a good place to eat and there are evening movies.

Century Lodge (*☎ 4247641; singles/doubles with shared bathroom Rs 150/200, with private bathroom Rs 200/250*) is one of Freak St's long-term survivors. It treads a fine line somewhere between atmospheric and dingy but remains popular. The new top-floor rooms are the cleanest. There's a small library for book rental.

Pagoda Lodge (*☎ 4247629; singles/doubles with shared bathroom Rs 100/180*) is reached from the same courtyard as Century Lodge in the heart of Freak St. It's as basic as they get, and even this price is negotiable.

Himalaya's Guest House (*☎ 4246555; singles/doubles with shared bathroom from Rs 150/250, doubles with private bathroom Rs 400*), a couple of short blocks west of Freak St, occupies the top floors of a family house. Rooms are clean and comfortable and top-floor rooms are particularly bright and sunny, but rooms are a little overpriced.

Monumental Paradise (*☎ 4240876; singles Rs 250-300, doubles Rs 300-400*) is a new place that's a lot more modern than the rest of Freak St. Rooms are clean and fresh and the back rooms come with a private balcony. There's a rooftop bar and restaurant and one suite (Rs 500) in the crow's nest with its own balcony, hammock and excellent views.

PLACES TO STAY – MID-RANGE

Mid-range prices in Kathmandu means from around US$10 to US$50 for a double. The

Freak Street – the End of the Road

Running south from Basantapur Square, Freak St dates from the overland days of the late 1960s and early 1970s, when it was one of the great gathering places on 'the road east'. In its hippy prime this was the place for cheap hotels (Rs 3 a room!), colourful restaurants, hash shops, the sounds of Jimmy and Janis blasting from eight-track players and, of course, the weird and wonderful foreign 'freaks' who gave the street its name. Along with Bodhnath and Swayambhunath, Freak St was a magnet for those in search of spiritual enlightenment, freedom and cheap dope.

Times change and Freak St (better known these days by its real name, Jochne) is today only a pale shadow of its former funky self. While there are still cheap hotels and restaurants, it's the Thamel area in the north of the city that is the main gathering place for travellers. However, for those people who find Thamel altogether too much of a scene, Freak St offers a quiet and interesting alternative. It retains a faint echo of mellower days and it is right in the heart of old Kathmandu where real local life continues.

borderlines are fuzzy and many of the mid-range hotels slip into the budget range with discounts. These places are on the Greater Thamel map unless otherwise stated.

Thamel

Thorong Peak Guest House (☎ 4253458, fax 4251008; singles/doubles with shared bathroom US$8/12, with private bathroom US$14/18, 50% discount) is in the centre of things but is off the main street in a small cul de sac. Most rooms are large and airy and there are nice communal balconies and a rooftop terrace but rates are still a little overpriced.

Hotel Tashi Dhelek (☎ 4251720; singles/doubles US$12/20, with TV US$15/25, 30-50% discount), next door and similar to the Thorong Peak Guest House, is comfortable and spacious but rooms vary considerably. Neither hotel gets much sunlight in winter.

Hotel Garuda (☎ 4416340; e garuda@ mos.com.np; singles US$10-35, doubles US$15-40, 20-40% discount) is in a busy area of Thamel, about 100m north of the Kathmandu Guest House. It is well run and clean but some rooms are dark. Budget rooms don't have the deluxe room's TV or balcony, but are quieter and better value. There's a great view over Thamel from the rooftop.

Hotel Centre Point (☎ 4424522; e centpoint@wlink.com.np; singles/doubles US$55/65, discounted to US$20/25), just north of Thamel Chowk, is a fairly charmless modern block. It is set back slightly from the street, but has no garden or views. The rooms are comfortable and a decent size but fairly gloomy.

Paknajol

See the Greater Thamel map.

The stylish new **Courtyard Hotel** (☎ 442 5648; e hotel@courtyard.wlink.com.np; singles/doubles US$15/20, suites US$35) was built in traditional style with oil bricks and Newari-style carved wooden lintels. It's very insulated from the Thamel madness and there are nice sitting areas and parking. Rooms are spacious and have fridge and satellite TV. The discounted rates are a steal.

Follow the double bend north of Kathmandu Guest House and turn left towards the Holy Lodge, continuing through several more sharp bends (known as Satghumti, or 'Seven Bends'), and you'll find one of a new breed of Thamel hotels.

At seven storeys the **Hotel Tradition** (☎ 4428217; w www.hoteltradition.com; standard singles/doubles US$30/40, deluxe US$55/65, 50% discount) is probably the tallest in the area and a good choice. The rooms are comfortable and well furnished, though some are a bit small. The views from the top-floor terrace restaurant are sensational and food prices are very reasonable.

International Guest House (☎ 4252299; e igh@wlink.com.np; singles/doubles with private bathroom from US$16/20, deluxe rooms US$20/25, 20% discount), farther west along the same road as Hotel Tradition in an area known as Kaldhara, is nicely decorated and furnished, with lots of plants, natural wood and sitting areas, plus one of the best rooftop views in the city. The deluxe rooms are probably the best value; standard rooms vary and can be small and dark. This area is quieter and less of a scene than Thamel, but not too far away from the restaurants.

Hotel Thamel (☎ 4417643; e hoteltham el@visitnepal.com; singles/doubles US$30/40, deluxe with air-con from US$45/55, 50% discount), down a lane almost opposite the Thamel House Restaurant, is one of the modern breed of comfortable, concrete monstrosities, with deluxe air-con rooms, and rooms with private sunny balconies looking back to the city (all with TV and phone). It's quiet and central but nothing special.

Bhagwan Bahal

Hotel Norbu Linka (Greater Thamel map; ☎ 4414799; e lama@lamaart.com; singles/doubles US$20/30, discounted to US$12/15, deluxe room US$50, discounted to US$25) is a modern, secluded place, down an alley opposite the interesting Thamel Gaa Hiti (water tank). The spacious rooms have Tibetan decor, TV and en suites, and are good value at the discounted price, plus there's a nice rooftop garden area. The brochure even boasts 'baby sisters on request'!

Jyatha

The neighbourhood southeast of Thamel is traditionally known as Jyatha, but the word is also used to describe the main north–south road that runs into the western end of Tridevi Marg. See the Greater Thamel map.

Sidhartha Garden Hotel (☎/fax 4222253; w www.sidhartagardenhotel.com; singles US$10-15, doubles US$12-17, deluxe rooms

US$20-25) is a well-run and very stylish place with nicely decorated rooms, a small garden with fruit trees and oodles of French charm – perfect for couples who can afford a little more than budget travel. The more expensive rooms face the street and can be noisy. It's just south of the Hotel Utse and reservations are recommended. Small discounts are offered off-season only (September to November, and March to mid-May).

Hotel Utse *(☎ 4228952; e utse@wlink .com.np; standard singles/doubles US$15/21, deluxe US$19/25, super deluxe US$24/30, 20% discount)* is a comfortable Tibetan hotel owned by Ugen Tsering, one of the original Thamel pioneers with his long-running and popular Utse Restaurant. It's a well-run hotel, with a good rooftop area and nice lobby area, but the bathrooms in particular are looking a bit tired now. Deluxe rooms have Tibetan decor but the standard rooms probably offer best value. Try not to get a room roadside.

Hotel Norling *(☎ 4240734, fax 4226735; standard singles/doubles US$10/16, deluxe doubles US$19-25)* is a thin slice of a hotel next door to the Hotel Utse. Also Tibetan-run, it has small but neat rooms and a lush rooftop garden. You should get discounts on these prices.

Turn south off Tridevi Marg, walk only a short distance down the Jyatha Rd, and a couple of twists and turns will bring you to a neat little cluster of modern guesthouses, directly behind the Sanchaya Kosh Bhawan Shopping Centre. This is a central but quiet location that feels a million miles from Thamel's hustle.

Mustang Holiday Inn *(☎ 4249041, fax 4249016; w www.mustangholidayinn.com .np; singles/doubles with private bathroom US$8/10, singles/doubles US$15/20, deluxe US$22/30, 50% discount)* has pleasant rooms decorated in Tibetan style and is well run. Rooms are clean, spacious and comfortable and offer great value with discounts.

Imperial Guest House *(☎ 4249339, fax 4249733; singles/doubles US$12/15, 40% discount)*, also in this quiet little enclave, is another good choice. The pleasant rooftop sitting area overlooks a small shrine.

Hotel Dynasty *(☎ 4263172; e hoteldyn@ wlink.com.np; singles/doubles without air-con US$40/50, deluxe rooms with air-con US$50/ 60, super deluxe US$60/70, 50% discount)*,

tucked away in a lane behind the Utse, is a good mid-range find frequented by small tour groups. It's a modern, upmarket place that even has a lift. The rooms are a good size and have air-con, TV, phone and some have balconies. The deluxe rooms are the best value.

Fuji Guest House *(☎ 4250435; e fujig house@wlink.com.np; singles/doubles with shared bathroom US$6/10, with private bathroom US$10/15, with balcony US$15/20, 20% discount)* is a well-run place in the same lane as Hotel Dynasty. It's popular with Japanese travellers and is a little overpriced, but rooms are neat, quiet and spotlessly clean, and the more expensive rooms have balconies, towels and bathtubs. The rooms with shared bathroom are a good deal.

Chhetrapati
See the Greater Thamel map unless otherwise stated.

Potala Guest House *(☎ 4220467; w www .potalaguesthouse.com; singles US$10-50, doubles US$15-60, 40% discount)* is popular. There's hot water and a small, quiet garden, though the rooms themselves are ordinary.

Tibet Guest House *(☎ 4254888; w www .tibetguesthouse.com; singles/doubles US$16/ 19, main block rooms US$24/27, deluxe US$40/44, 40% discount)* has good-sized and well-maintained rooms with bathroom; main-block superior rooms have a fridge and TV. It has a restaurant, parking and offers good views from the rooftop garden.

Nirvana Garden Hotel *(☎ 4256200; e nir vana@wlink.com.np; singles/doubles US$20/ 27)* has pleasant, fresh rooms, each with balcony, TV, phone and private bathroom. There's a relaxing garden, parking and at the discounted rate of US$15/20 it is good value.

Kathmandu Prince Hotel *(Central Kathmandu map; ☎ 4255961; e ktphotel@wlink .com.np, singles/doubles US$26/30, deluxe US$30/40, 50% discount)* is a concrete block with a hint of tour group about it, but rooms are comfortable and the bathrooms clean and modern. Balcony rooms are most spacious and get a lot of sun. It's just east of Chhetrapati Chowk.

Hotel Ganesh Himal *(Central Kathmandu map; ☎ 4263598; e htlganesh@wlink.com.np; standard singles/doubles US$14/18, deluxe US$20/25, up to 50% discount)* is a well-run and friendly place five to 10 minutes southwest of Thamel. The rooms are among the best value in Kathmandu, with endless hot water, satellite TV and lots of balcony and garden seating. Deluxe rooms are more spacious, a little quieter and come with a bath tub.

Lazimpat

North of Thamel is the Lazimpat embassy area. There are a few options in this area, and it's much less frenetic than Thamel.

Hotel Ambassador *(Central Kathmandu map; ☎ 4410432; e ambassador@ambassador .com.np; singles/doubles from US$20/25, 25% discount)* is run by the same people as Kathmandu Guest House. There's a good restaurant and a small garden, but it is on a rather noisy intersection. Rooms are a bit old-fashioned and can be dim. It's within walking distance of Thamel and Durbar Marg.

Hotel Tibet *(Central Kathmandu map; ☎ 4429085; e hotel@tibet.mos.com.np; singles/ doubles US$70/80, discounted to US$35/40)*, just in front of the Radisson Hotel, is a good mid-range choice, especially for Tibetophiles. The hotel is run by a friendly Tibetan family and rooms come with TV, air-con and private bathroom. There's also a nice rooftop terrace and meditation chapel.

Hotel Manaslu *(Central Kathmandu map; ☎ 4410071; e hmanaslu@mos.com.np; standard singles/doubles US$28/32, deluxe US$40/ 45, 20-30% discount)*, just beyond Hotel Tibet, is a very nice modern hotel with a pleasant garden area and pool, though it's not as cosy as some hotels. Standard rooms are brighter and have better views than the deluxe rooms. The slightly inconvenient location explains the cheap price.

Astoria Hotel *(Kathmandu map; ☎ 4428 810; e nepcraft@mos.com.np; singles/doubles US$28/35, deluxe US$50/60)*, a little farther north of Hotel Tibet, signposted to the side of Hotel Shangri-La, is excellent. This hotel is tucked away in a quiet area and it has pleasant gardens, including a vegetable garden, which supplies the small restaurant with fresh produce. The light and airy rooms are spotlessly clean, and have TV, carpet and private bathroom. Standard rooms vary in size; deluxe rooms are slightly bigger and have air-con and a minibar.

Elsewhere

There are two choices west of Thamel, en route to Swayambhunath.

Hotel Vajra *(Central Kathmandu map; ☎ 4271545; w www.hotelvajra.com; singles/ doubles with shared bathroom US$14/16, with private bathroom from US$33/38, new wing rooms from US$53/61, 50% discount)*, across the Vishnumati River in the Bijeshwari area, is one of Kathmandu's most interesting hotels in any price category. The complex feels more like a retreat than a hotel, with an art gallery, a library of books on Tibet and Buddhism, a rooftop bar and an Ayurvedic massage room. The cheapest rooms have shared bathrooms and mattresses that might be too narrow for some couples. The new-wing rooms are much swankier but can be booked out by groups so make a reservation. The one catch to staying at Hotel Vajra is its location, which, though scenic, makes it terrible for getting a taxi.

Milarepa Guest House *(Kathmandu map; ☎ 4275544; e nya@phel.wlink.com.np; standard/deluxe doubles with private bathroom US$10/15, 20% discount)* is not far from the eastern steps of Swayambhunath and is owned by the Nyanang Phelgyeling Monastery next door, so is a great place for those interested in Tibetan Buddhism (there's a top-floor meditation hall). The hotel itself is a large, modern place with clean and comfortable rooms but limited hot water. Many of the rooms have views of Swayambhunath, which is only 200m away.

PLACES TO STAY – TOP END

Top-end hotels in Kathmandu start at US$50 for a double room. Only a handful of these hotels are centrally located, although the less conveniently positioned hotels usually offer a free bus service into town. All accept credit cards.

Thamel Area

Hotel Manang *(☎ 4410993; w www.hotel manang.com; singles/doubles US$55/65, deluxe US$80/90, 25% discount)* in Paknajol is a modern three-star hotel with everything you could possibly need. Many of the rooms have magnificent views, some with private balcony, and all have TV, air-con, phone and minibar. Facilities include a restaurant, room service and a parking area.

Hotel Marshyangdi *(☎ 4414105; e htl gold@mos.com.np; standard singles/doubles US$60/70, deluxe US$75/80, 40% discount)*, next door to Hotel Manang, has been established longer and offers a similarly high standard. The rooms are well furnished, with writing desks and chairs, though the corner deluxe rooms offer the best value. There's also a nice garden and restaurant with good Nepali set meals.

Hotel Vaishali (☎ 4413968; W www.vaishali hotel.com; singles/doubles US$90/110) is well located and has pleasantly furnished but small rooms with air-con, TV and minibar. Rooms seem to be on offer at a more realistic US$40/60 much of the time, but even that is a little overpriced. A bonus here in summer is the small outdoor swimming pool.

Malla Hotel (☎ 4418385; e malla@htgrp .mos.com.np; singles/doubles US$130/156, deluxe US$150/182, 20-30% discount) is on the northeastern edge of Thamel, west of the new Royal Palace in Bhagwan Bahal, but is still only a five-minute walk to all the Thamel restaurants. Rooms have air-con, TV, phone and minibar and either pool or garden views. There are several restaurants, a teahouse, a good swimming pool and a superb garden, complete with a mini-*stupa*. It's one of the nicest top-end places. There are special deals for month-long apartment stays.

Kantipur Temple House (☎ 4250131; e kantipur@tmplhouse.wlink.com.np; singles/ doubles US$50/60, deluxe US$70/90, up to 20% discount), along an alley at the southern end of Jyatha, is one of the more interesting top-end places. It's a new hotel that has been built in old Newari temple style, and has been done very well. A new block will soon encircle a traditional courtyard. The rooms are tastefully decorated, with carved wood and *dhaka* (hand-woven) cloth bedspreads commissioned from local fair trade shops. This place is doing its best to be eco-friendly – guests are given cloth bags to use when shopping and bulk mineral water is available free of charge, so you don't need to buy plastic bottles. In fact there's no plastic anywhere in the hotel. The old town location is close to almost anywhere in town, but taxi drivers might have a hard time finding it.

Durbar Marg

Yak & Yeti Hotel (Central Kathmandu map; ☎ 4248999; W www.yakandyeti.com; standard doubles US$185-205 with tax & breakfast, discounted to US$100-120), entered from Durbar Marg, but set well back from the road, boasts probably the best-known hotel in

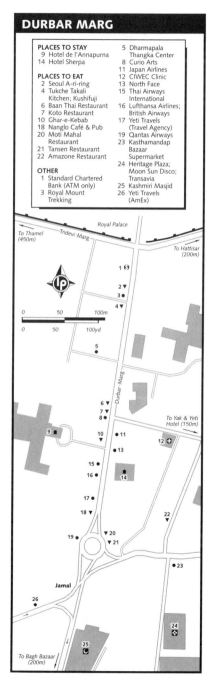

DURBAR MARG

PLACES TO STAY		5	Dharmapala
9	Hotel de l'Annapurna		Thangka Center
14	Hotel Sherpa	8	Curio Arts
		11	Japan Airlines
PLACES TO EAT		12	CIWEC Clinic
2	Seoul A-ri-ring	13	North Face
4	Tukche Takali	15	Thai Airways
	Kitchen; Kushifuji		International
6	Baan Thai Restaurant	16	Lufthansa Airlines;
7	Koto Restaurant		British Airways
10	Ghar-e-Kebab	17	Yeti Travels
18	Nanglo Café & Pub		(Travel Agency)
20	Moti Mahal	19	Qantas Airways
	Restaurant	23	Kasthamandap
21	Tansen Restaurant		Bazaar
22	Amazone Restaurant		Supermarket
		24	Heritage Plaza;
OTHER			Moon Sun Disco;
1	Standard Chartered		Transavia
	Bank (ATM only)	25	Kashmiri Masjid
3	Royal Mount	26	Yeti Travels
	Trekking		(AmEx)

Nepal, due to its connections with the legendary Boris Lissanevitch, its original owner. The oldest section of the hotel is part of the Lal Durbar, a Rana palace, and it houses the hotel's restaurants and casino; these retain an overblown but spectacular Rana-baroque decor. The rooms are in two modern wings; the Newari Wing is the older of the two and the rooms incorporate elements of carved wood and local textiles without being kitsch. Businesspeople will find an executive floor and a well-equipped business centre with secretarial, translation and interpretation facilities. There's also a beautiful garden, two swimming pools (Rs 500 for nonguests), tennis courts, a fitness centre and a 24-hour casino.

Hotel de l'Annapurna (Durbar Marg map; ☎ 4221711; W www.taj-annapurna.com.np; standard singles/doubles US$120/130, deluxe US$160/170), just off Durbar Marg, is one of Kathmandu's longest-established hotels that is starting to show its age. Its central location on Durbar Marg is convenient, and apart from the usual five-star facilities, including bars and restaurants, it has a casino and nightly dance shows, plus the largest hotel swimming pool in Kathmandu (about 25m). If business is lax you should get a plush deluxe room for the price of a standard room.

Hotel Sherpa (Durbar Marg map; ☎ 422 7000; W www.hotel-sherpa.com; singles/doubles US$105/115, up to 40% discount), opposite Hotel de l'Annapurna, is cheaper and rates four stars, although it is a bit gloomy. It has a pleasant rooftop plunge pool and garden, but it can be noisy as it's right next to the road. The rooms are well equipped and quite pleasant; discounts can make this place a bargain.

Lazimpat
Radisson Hotel (Central Kathmandu map; ☎ 4423888; e radisson@radkat.com.np; standard/deluxe rooms US$175/185, discounted to US$120/130) is north of the city in the Lazimpat embassy area. It's a very modern, well-maintained and pleasantly decorated hotel with excellent facilities, including a 5th-floor pool with great views and a good gym operated by Clark Hatch. Rooms come with nice touches such as coffeemakers and data ports for laptop computers.

Hotel Shangri-La (Kathmandu map; ☎ 441 2999; W www.nepalshangrila.com; doubles US$130, 20% discount), farther north again of the Radisson, is one of Kathmandu's best hotels. The decor is tasteful, the service is swift and professional, and there are several restaurants and a jazz bar. Best of all, there's a beautiful garden with an adjoining restaurant and a swimming pool. This is good value in this range.

Elsewhere
Soaltee Crowne Plaza Hotel (Kathmandu map; ☎ 4273999; e crowneplaza@shicp.com .np; singles/doubles US$180/190, deluxe US$200/210 plus 12% tax) is on the western edge of town, but it operates a bus service into town for its guests. It's one of the largest hotels in Nepal and apart from good restaurants, spacious grounds, bars, a health club, swimming pool it also has a casino.

Grand Hotel (Kathmandu map; ☎ 4282482; W www.grandhotelnepal.com; singles/doubles US$95/105, discounted to US$35/45), a new, large multistorey hotel very close to Soaltee Crowne Plaza Hotel, has decent facilities and is excellent value but lacks any real atmosphere.

Dwarika's Village Hotel (Kathmandu map; ☎ 4470770; W www.dwarikas.com; singles/doubles US$135/155, deluxe US$175/195, 20% discount) is an outstanding and unusual hotel, built in traditional style and featuring superb examples of antique woodwork. The owners have rescued thousands of carvings from around the valley (from buildings facing demolition or collapse) and many have been incorporated into the complex, which consists of a small cluster of buildings (including a library and pool) separated by pleasant brick-paved courtyards. The end result is a beautiful hybrid – a cross between a museum and a boutique hotel, with a lush romantic feel. Its only disadvantage is its poor location – on a busy street and a bit of a distance to the restaurants of Thamel and Durbar Marg – but finding a taxi is never a problem. The rooms are spacious, comfortable and all unique, but do not have air-con or TV (the latter is available on request).

Hyatt Regency Kathmandu (off Kathmandu map; ☎ 4491234; e info@hyatt.com.np; doubles from US$210, up to 60% discount), in between Kathmandu centre and Bodhnath, is superb. No expense has been spared on this place, and the architecture is very much in keeping with the older buildings in the valley. It's worth coming here en route to Bodhnath just to admire the sculptures in the lobby (there's a lamp-lighting ceremony at dusk). As you'd expect, the rooms are tastefully furnished and many have views over Bodhnath *stupa*. If you like this level of comfort you won't find any better place in the valley. There's also a large swimming pool, tennis courts, fitness centre, business centre, a café, restaurant and bar with DJs.

Long-Stay Accommodation

If you are in and around the valley for some time, it's worth looking into something other than a regular hotel, although most hotels will negotiate pretty good long-term rates.

Arcadia Apartments *(Greater Thamel map; ☎ 4260187; e arcadia@mos.com.np; apartments per day/month US$25/450)*, a new place right in the heart of Thamel, is on the top floor of the brash Arcadia Building. The apartments have basic cooking facilities, fridge, TV, sofa, separate bedroom and a balcony. There are only six apartments and a couple are normally rented long-term so make a reservation ahead of time.

Hacienda Apartment Hotel *(Kathmandu map; ☎ 4410216; w www.hacienda.com.np; 1-bedroom/2-bedroom apartments US$65/95, 40% discount)* in the embassy district of Lazimpat is very comfortable. This place is peaceful luxury, offering beautifully furnished apartments in a tasteful old building. The apartments all have cooking facilities, air-con, TV, desk, balcony, modem hook-ups and fridge. Staff will even do your grocery shopping for a 15% fee. Monthly rates are discounted further to US$700/1200.

PLACES TO EAT

Kathmandu has an astounding array of restaurants. Indeed, there are few places in south Asia where you can eat Indian, Chinese, Japanese, Mexican, Korean, Italian or Irish, all within a five-minute walk. And there are even some Nepali restaurants... After long months on the road in India or long weeks trekking in Nepal most travellers find Kathmandu a culinary paradise.

Thamel's restaurant scene has been sliding upmarket for a few years now, with a slew of places now costing US$4 to US$5 per meal – still a great bargain but unthinkable a few years ago. Still, if you stay away from beer, you can eat until you burst for

less than Rs 200. A bottle of beer can cost anything from Rs 90 to Rs 150 and nearly double your bill in a budget restaurant.

Kathmandu's big hotels have some interesting restaurant options and there's an ever-growing number of high-class restaurants dotted around the city.

Tipping is accepted (and appreciated) in Nepal, but your loose change (or 5%) is fine in cheaper places; a bit more will be expected in the expensive restaurants.

Thamel

Thamel restaurants spill into Paknajol, Jyatha and Chhetrapati, just like the hotels. The junction outside the Kathmandu Guest House is the epicentre of Thamel dining and you can find numerous budget-priced restaurants within a minute's walk in either direction.

While there are literally dozens of budget restaurants here, there is often little between them in what they offer. A standard menu has pretty well everything on it, and the food tends to be remarkably similar and often very bland. What marks the difference between these places is the atmosphere, music, service and who happens to be there on the night.

Pumpernickel Bakery, on the same stretch of Thamel's restaurant centre as Maya Cocktail Bar, is a place for freshly baked bread. In the morning, tourists crowd in for fresh croissants, rolls, pastries and filter coffee in the pleasant garden area at the back.

Café Jalapeno *(mains Rs 90-150)*, on the 1st floor of the Namche Bazaar building on the intersection near Kathmandu Guest House, is most popular for its window seats, which offer a great view of the passing parade. The food itself is nothing remarkable, but the pleasant decor, top location and attentive service make it worth a visit. Oh, and it has about the cheapest beer in Thamel.

Alice's Restaurant *(mains Rs 90-150)*, on the floor above Café Jalapeno, is a popular, decent place and a cut above the cheapies, but still very reasonable and it has great views. There are some good Indian dishes.

Opposite Alice's is a **Hot Bread** outlet, which does a roaring trade in sandwiches, bread rolls, pizza slices and pastries. These are very popular at lunch time, and the ham and cheese rolls (Rs 65) make a great lunch on the run. Bakery items are 50% off after 9.30pm. There's a similar bakery across the road.

Yin Yang Restaurant (☎ 4425510; *Thai curries Rs 250*), just south of the intersection, is one of Thamel's most highly regarded restaurants. It serves authentic Thai food cooked by a Thai chef. It's not particularly cheap, but the food is a definite cut above the imitation Thai food found elsewhere.

Third Eye Restaurant (*mains Rs 200-230*), next door to Yin Yang, is a long-running favourite that retains something of the old Kathmandu atmosphere. There's a sit-down section at the front, and a more informal section with low tables and cushions at the back and a rooftop terrace. Indian food is the speciality, but there are also a small number of continental offerings. The tandoori dishes here are especially good.

Roadhouse Café (*pizzas Rs 200-300, mains Rs 220*) is in the Arcadia Building. The big attraction here is the pizzas from the wood-fired oven (we have been assured the wood is offcuts from a Terai timbermill). The pizzas are pretty darn good, and the decor, especially the courtyard out back, is warm and intimate. Credit cards are accepted.

K-Too Beer & Steakhouse (*mains Rs 160-400*), run by the same people who run Kilroy's (see the Jyatha entry later), is in the same congested area as the Roadhouse Café. The decor and furnishings are deliberately rough and ready pub-style, and the atmosphere and food are good. Dishes range from Irish stew to sizzling fajitas, and the excellent pepper steak (Rs 260) is already a post-trekking classic. Live European and British football is shown on the TV.

Weizen Bakery, down the road from Yin Yang, serves good vegetarian food. It has a pleasant garden and is a nice quiet place for breakfast, with newspapers to read and music playing in the background. This is another place with decent cakes, breads (particularly the pretzels!) and pastries, discounted 50% after 7pm.

Helena's, next door, is popular for its set breakfasts (Rs 65), one of the highest rooftops in Thamel and good service, with a wide range of coffee, cakes, tandoori dishes and steaks. It's warm and cosy in winter.

La Dolce Vita (*pasta Rs 175-195, pizzas Rs 185-240*) makes the best attempt at true Italian cuisine and the menu is a bit more imaginative than the standard Thamel offerings, with delights such as *tiramisu* (Rs 110) and hard-to-find extras like baked potatoes and

wine by the glass (Rs 175). There are both indoor and open-air sections, and the atmosphere and food are generally excellent. Prices are a little higher than the rock-bottom Thamel average but then so is the quality. It's right on the corner opposite Kathmandu Guest House.

Chang Cheng Restaurant (*vegetarian dishes Rs 80-120, meat Rs 130-200*) is the real deal for Chinese food, and is frequented by visiting Chinese businessmen and Chinese Tibetans who smoke and slurp their way through large portions of spicy Sichuan food.

Dahua Restaurant (*dishes from Rs 80*) at the eastern edge of greater Thamel is a less authentic version, full of sticky sweet-and-sours and fried rice but still tasty and with a cosy atmosphere.

Koto Restaurant (☎ 4256449; *set meals Rs 130-270*) is a budget branch of the acclaimed Durbar Marg restaurant. The Japanese flavours are subtle and complex – great if you need a break from Thamel backpacker food – and the decor is characteristically elegant. The sukiyaki 'young person' set meal is a good deal, with all kinds of trimmings, miso soup and unlimited rice, but the menu spreads to udon noodles and even sushi.

Tashi Delek Rest (*mains Rs 50-100*) feels like a trekking lodge that's been transplanted from the Annapurna Circuit into a Thamel time warp. Prices are cheap and the enchilada spinach mushroom (Rs 85) is pretty good.

Pilgrims Feed 'N Read is a relaxed place, with indoor and outdoor areas. It's accessible from the rear of Pilgrims Book House or the Borderlands office compound. The focus is on herbal teas (Rs 70 per pot) and Indian food (Rs 150 to Rs 200), and *tungba* (Tibetan millet beer) is available (Rs 80).

Northfield Café (*breakfasts around Rs 100, mains Rs 180-270*), next door to Pilgrims, is an open-air spot. This is the place for serious breakfast devotees (huevos rancheros included) and you can get a bottomless ground coffee for Rs 45. The Mexican lunch dishes are also good, although prices are a bit higher than elsewhere.

Las Kus Restaurant, at the Kathmandu Guest House, serves straightforward, well-prepared food; the outdoor breakfast buffet (Rs 250) is also popular. The Newari special buffet (Rs 300) is a good place to try traditional Newari dishes such as *choyla* (marinated roast buffalo) and *chatamari* (small rice-flour pancakes). The courtyard also has an outlet of **New York Pizza** and **Himalayan Java**, which turn out pretty decent pizzas and ice coffee respectively.

Brezel Bakery, directly across the road from the Kathmandu Guest House and upstairs, is a pleasant rooftop spot overlooking the Thamel activity below. This is another decent breakfast place, though the fresh brown breads are better than the pastries.

New Orleans Café *(mains Rs 150-270)* is near Brezel Bakery and tucked away off the street. It's a good, popular spot for a meal or a drink; there's live music on weekends. The menu ranges far and wide, from Thai curries to Cajun chicken and Creole jambalaya – a New Orleans chicken and rice dish (Rs 220). It's also a popular spot for breakfast.

Nargila Restaurant *(mains Rs 60-110)*, a few doors along from New Orleans Café on the 1st floor, is one of the very few places to offer good Middle Eastern food and is a fine place to just take a break from the bustle outside. Felafel or shwarma (grilled meat) and pitta is Rs 105, couscous is Rs 75 and dips such as baba ghanoush or hummus served with pitta cost Rs 55 to Rs 60.

Delima Garden Café *(mains Rs 90-120)* has cheap and tasty Indian dishes plus all your trusty Thamel standards in a secluded garden courtyard well away from the traffic in Paknajol.

Rum Doodle Restaurant & Bar *(☎ 4443208; mains Rs 220-270, pint of beer Rs 105)* was named after the world's highest mountain, the 40,000½ft Mt Rum Doodle (see Books in the Facts for the Visitor chapter). The restaurant has moved to trendier digs but still specialises in steak and pasta. It's a favourite meeting place for mountaineering expeditions – Edmund Hillary, Reinhold Messner and Rob Hall have left their mark on the walls of the 40,000½ Foot Bar. You can eat here free for life – the only catch is that you have to conquer Everest first!

Krua Thai Restaurant *(soups Rs 180-210, mains Rs 210-440)*, north of Sam's Bar, is another good open-air Thai place. The food is reasonably authentic (ie, spicy) although not that cheap.

BK's Place *(chips Rs 50-100)* has a growing reputation for good old-fashioned chips (french fries), with a variety of sauces. It's a diminutive place, just west of Rum Doodle and down a side street.

Sandwich Point *(open 24 hr)*, a tiny place back at the main Thamel Chowk, is a good little spot with small (from Rs 50) and large (from Rs 70) rolls, which they stuff full with a variety of fillings. It's just the place for late-night munchies.

Botega *(mains Rs 220-240)*, close to the Thamel Chowk, is a good Mexican place that does everything from chimichangas to enchiladas, and even authentic *mole* (chocolate-based) sauce. It also has good music and a bar with a fine repertoire of tequila cocktails (Rs 160). The entrance is just down an alley and is shared by the Potala Guest House.

Himalatte Café *(mains Rs 180-210, set meals Rs 300-350)*, south from Thamel Chowk, has an American coffeehouse feel, right down to the comfy sofas and magazines. There's an impressive array of coffees and teas (Rs 40 to Rs 70), plus decent food (good cheeseburgers Rs 180) and daily set meal specials.

Café Mitra *(☎ 4259015; mains Rs 220-400)*, farther down the street, is an upmarket restaurant that seems somewhat out of place in the heart of budget Thamel. Continental dishes include Japanese mackerel with soy sauce and ginger (Rs 390) and rilletes of duck (Rs 190), topped off with desserts like banofee cheesecake (Rs 140). The tiny place is chic and intimate so expect your conversation to be heard at the next table.

In the modern Sanchaya Kosh Bhawan Shopping Centre on Tridevi Marg there are a couple of places worth detouring for. **Fire & Ice Restaurant** *(pizzas Rs 210-320, glass of wine Rs 190)* is an excellent open-air Italian place serving some of the best pizzas in Kathmandu, imported Italian soft-serve ice cream, seriously good coffee and rousing opera – Italian, of course. It's deservedly popular and you'll need a reservation in the high season, or be prepared to eat early.

Next door is the **Dechenling Restaurant**, a good, reasonably priced Tibetan place with some interesting Bhutanese dishes (Rs 150) like *khewa datsi* (potatoes and cheese), though portions are small and 12% tax is added. The *thentuk* (Rs 85) is the best in Thamel. The **Dechenling Beer House** around the corner, has a more spacious and attractive garden. The menu is similar but with a few more Indian dishes.

Jyatha

The following places are on the Greater Thamel map unless otherwise stated.

Kilroy's of Kathmandu (☎ 4250441), named after the Irish owner and head chef, is where Ireland meets Nepal. You can sit inside, or outside in the shady garden, complete with waterfall. The prices are definitely a cut above the average Thamel restaurant, but then again, so is the food. The menu ranges from a Royal dal bhaat (Rs 280) to beef and Guinness hotpot (Rs 355). It's the only place in town to offer such interesting hybrids as Balti chicken (Rs 300) and seafood thugpa (Tibetan soup) with lemongrass. The bread and butter pudding (Rs 145) is excellent. There's always some kind of special going on, from Friday specials to champagne brunches.

Utse Restaurant (Tibetan dishes Rs 60-80), in the hotel of the same name, is one of the longest-running restaurants in Thamel and it turns out excellent Tibetan dishes, such as momos (meat/veg-filled pasta), kothey (fried pasta stuffed with meat/vegetables) and talumein (egg noodle soup). Gacok (also spelt gyakok) is a meal named after the brass tureen that is heated at the table and from which various meats and vegetables are served (Rs 675 for two).

Dolma Momo Center, a bit farther south from the Utse, is typical of the Tibetan eateries dotted around town – it's just a hole in the wall, and momos and a few stains are the only things on the menu. But the momos are excellent, and at Rs 10 to Rs 15 for a plate and Rs 5 for milk tea, they're top value.

Freak Street (Jochne)

Freak St has a number of restaurants where you can find good food at lower prices than Thamel. Even if you're staying in other areas of the city it's nice to know there are some good places for lunch if you're sightseeing around Durbar Square.

Diyalo Restaurant, at the Annapurna Lodge, is a good, popular little place with a large menu, which includes crepes, burgers and a few Chinese and Indian dishes, all for less than Rs 90.

Kumari Restaurant (mains Rs 70-90, set Nepali meals Rs 60-80), down a side alley near the Century Lodge, is a friendly hangout that seems to have hung onto some of the mellowness of times past. Time just seems to slip away as you take your seat. All the travellers' favourites are here and the prices are some of the best in town.

Paradise Restaurant (mains Rs 70-80) is a slightly gloomy but good vegetarian place, with generous dishes such as lasagne and vegetarian schnitzel burgers.

Snowman Restaurant (cakes Rs 30-40), a long-running and mellow place, is one of those rare Kathmandu hang-outs that attracts both locals and backpackers, drawn to some of the best cakes in town. The to-die-for chocolate cake has been drawing travellers for 25 years.

Cosmopolitan Restaurant (mains Rs 90-150), at the Basantapur Square end of Freak St, is a quiet, old-fashioned place with friendly staff and a menu that ranges from moussaka to crepes.

Festive Fare Restaurant overlooking the square has unsurpassed views from its top-floor terrace and attracts more of a tour-group crowd. Prices are about double those of the Freak St cheapies.

Central Kathmandu

The restaurants in the Kantipath and Durbar Marg areas are generally more expensive than around Thamel, although there are a few exceptions. See the last few listings here and the boxed text 'Nepali Restaurants' for some of Kathmandu's worthwhile splurges.

Dudh Sagar (Central Kathmandu map; dishes Rs 35-60) on Kantipath specialises in cheap and authentic South Indian food. This is the place to reacquaint yourself with dosas (crepes filled with potato curry) and idly (pounded rice cakes), topped off with Indian sweets like barfi (fudge) and gulab jamun (deep-fried milk balls in rose-flavoured syrup).

The following places are on the Durbar Marg map unless otherwise indicated.

Amazone Restaurant (☎ 4230504; dishes Rs 40-75) is the cheapest option in the Durbar Marg area. It has all the backpacker specials (even though the clientele is predominantly Nepali) and there's a range of Indian dishes, plus a set Nepali meal at Rs 80/100 for veg/nonveg.

Nanglo Café & Pub (mains Rs 90-120, pizza Rs 200) has a popular open-air terrace dining area and an international menu. There's a huge banyan tree in the middle of the restaurant and quite a lively atmosphere.

Food ranges from burgers and pasta to the Nepali set lunch with rice, dal, meat, vegetable curry, pickle and green salad (Rs 185).

Koto Restaurant (dishes Rs 250-300, set menu Rs 500), which some say prepares the best Japanese food in town, is among other Durbar Marg options. It offers a wide range of dishes, from cold soba noodles to sukiyaki and even fresh mackerel, plus several set menus. It's up a dingy little stairwell but the decor is cosy and intimate. There's a less expensive branch in Thamel.

Baan Thai Restaurant serves excellent Thai food, and the service is very attentive. Expect to pay around Rs 450, plus service and drinks.

Kushifuji (☎ 4220545; set meals Rs 450-680, mains Rs 280-350), close to Tukche Thakali Kitchen, is a Japanese place with both traditional and table seating. You can order à la carte from the extensive menu, or there is a variety of set meals, all with miso soup.

Seoul A-ri-ring (set menus Rs 350-500), at the northern end of Durbar Marg, has a pleasant rooftop area and serves dishes barbecued at your table, as well as Korean classics such as bulgogi (beef and ginger) and bibimbap (rice with beef, vegetables and hot sauce; Rs 200). The owner is Korean but the chefs are Nepali.

Ghar-e-Kebab (dishes Rs 350-500), outside Hotel de l'Annapurna, has some of the best North Indian and tandoori food in the city. Indian miniatures hang on the walls and in the evenings classical Indian music is played and traditional Urdu ghazals (love songs) are sung. A complete meal for two, including drinks, costs about Rs 2000, though you get stung for bread and rice at Rs 100 each. Try one of the traditional sherbets for dessert.

Moti Mahal Restaurant (☎ 4225647; veg dishes Rs 80-120, nonveg Rs 160-170), at the south end of Durbar Marg on the other side of the road, serves pretty decent Indian food, including a good lunch-time thali (Rs 160 to Rs 190) and some South Indian dishes.

Chimney Room (Central Kathmandu map; ☎ 4248999; mains Rs 600-1100, dinner only), at the Yak & Yeti Hotel northwest of the centre, is one of Kathmandu's most famous restaurants and the central, open fireplace gives it plenty of atmosphere. It now serves mostly continental cuisine, with the excellent borsch (beetroot soup; Rs 160) one of

its last links with its Russian roots. The hotel's **Sunrise Café** also serves good lunch and dinner continental buffets (Rs 700).

Naachghar Restaurant (Central Kathmandu map; ☎ 4248999; veg dishes Rs 170-360, nonveg Rs 370-450) is also in the Yak & Yeti. It's a grand, baroque room with high ceilings, gilt mirrors, marble features and ornate plasterwork. Performances of Nepali music and dance are given; ring ahead to check which nights. The menu is strong on both Indian and Nepali dishes – those from the tandoor oven are said to be good – but there are also some continental options.

Elsewhere

You can start the day at one of the best and most popular breakfast places in the city.

Mike's Breakfast (Kathmandu map; mains Rs 160-250; open 7am-9pm daily), as the name suggests, specialises in breakfasts, and it does them well. The restaurant is in the suburb of Naxal, about a 15-minute walk from the top end of Durbar Marg, and Mike presides over the whole operation. Meals are served in the attractive, leafy garden of an old Rana house. It's not cheap, but is certainly a laid-back way to start the day. The breakfast menu includes excellent waffles with yoghurt, fruit and syrup (Rs 190) and great eggs Florentine (Rs 250). Lunch is also good, with dishes such as quiche and salad. While you're here take a look at the excellent Indigo Gallery (see Shopping later).

Royal Hana Garden (Central Kathmandu map; ☎ 4416200; mains Rs 200-300; open 10am-10pm daily), in Lazimpat, is just north along the main road from the Hotel Ambassador. This place is a bit of a find – there are two outdoor hot-spring **baths** (entry Rs 250; open 2pm-8.30pm daily) where you can luxuriate for as long as you like before heading inside for a Japanese meal. At the baths, towels and bathing wear are provided. The restaurant serves very reasonably priced Japanese food. It is worth ringing ahead to book a soak.

Chez Caroline (Central Kathmandu map; mains Rs 220-300), in the Babar Mahal Revisited (see Shopping), is a swanky (pretentious even?) outdoor restaurant popular with many expats. It offers French-influenced main courses such as quiche and crepes, plus a wide range of patisseries and wines.

Nepali Restaurants

There is a growing number of restaurants around town that specialise in Nepali (mostly Newari) food (see Food & Drinks in the Facts for the Visitor chapter for a discussion of the cuisine). These run the gamut from unobtrusive little places in Thamel to fancy converted palaces with cultural shows and 15-course banquets. Most places offer a set meal, either veg or nonveg, and you dine on cushions at low tables. The 'cultural shows' consist of musicians and dancers performing 'traditional' items. The whole thing is generally pretty touristy, but popular nonetheless. At most places it's a good idea to make a reservation during the high season.

In Paknajol, in greater Thamel, the **Thamel House Restaurant** (☎ 4410388; dishes Rs 70-180) is set in a traditional old Newari building and has bags of atmosphere. The food is traditional Nepali, although they may try to lumber you with the set menu at Rs 550. Ask for the à la carte menu and choose individual dishes; there are a few unusual ones, such as wild boar. It's a good night out, although the service can be patchy. It's also open for lunch, and the Rs 250 set menu is not bad value.

Also in Thamel is the **Thakali Kitchen**, a modern budget place popular with local people working in Thamel. A simple set meal here is around Rs 100.

On Durbar Marg there's the small and cosy **Tukche Thakali Kitchen** (☎ 4225890; dishes Rs 110-150), which also serves Tibetan dishes. The interior is authentically gloomy but the food is good and reasonably priced at Rs 150 for a veg set lunch and Rs 195 with meat. In the evenings it's Rs 450 for a fixed menu of around 10 dishes.

Near the entrance to the Radisson Hotel in Lazimpat (see the Central Kathmandu map) is the **Restaurant Lajana** (☎ 4413874; Rs 700 set dinner). The building is done in traditional Newari style, the food is the usual multi-course set meal and the price includes a dance show (no live music) at 7pm.

Bhanchha Ghar (☎ 4225172; Rs 1000 per person, plus 12% tax, beer Rs 210; open 11am-10.30pm daily) is in a traditional three-storey Newari house in Kamaladi, just east of Durbar Marg from the turn-off by the clock tower (see the Central Kathmandu map). There is an upstairs loft where you can stretch out on handmade carpets and cushions for a drink, snacks and a brief 'cultural show' featuring the various ethnic costumes of Nepal (try to arrive before 7.30pm). You can then move downstairs to take advantage of an excellent menu of traditional Nepali dishes and delicacies. Musicians stroll between the tables playing traditional Nepali folk songs. It's not all that cheap but the food is very good.

See the Kathmandu map for the locations of the following restaurants.

In the same vein as Bhanchha Ghar, but perhaps more ambitious, is **Bhojan Griha** (☎ 4416423) in a recently restored 150-year-old mansion in Dilli Bazaar, just east of the city centre. It's worth eating here just to see the imaginative renovation of this beautiful old building, once the residence of the caste of royal priests. Again, dancers and musicians stroll through the various rooms throughout the evening, depicting Nepal's major ethnic groups. Most of the seating is traditional (ie, on cushions on the floor, although these are actually legless chairs, which saves your back and knees), but there are a couple of rooms with conventional tables for those who prefer them. The set menu is Rs 997, plus tax and drinks and it's a worthwhile night out. In an effort to reduce waste, plastic is not used in the restaurant and mineral water is bought in bulk and sold by the glass.

One of the best places for Nepali food is the **Krishnarpan Restaurant** (☎ 4470770) at Dwarika's Village Hotel, east of the centre near the Ring Rd. The atmosphere is superb and the food gets consistent praise from diners. Prices range from US$19 for a six-course meal up to US$28 for a full 16-course extravaganza. Bookings are advisable. Arrive in time for the 6pm dance show in the hotel courtyard.

At Babar Mahal Revisited, southeast of the centre (see Shopping later in this chapter), **Baithak Restaurant** (Central Kathmandu map; ☎ 4267346; 12-course set menu Rs 945) has a dramatic and regal, almost Victorian, setting where diners are watched over by huge portraits of various Ranas. The menu features 'Rana cuisine', a courtly cuisine created by Nepali Brahmin chefs and heavily influenced by North Indian Mughal cuisine. The setting is probably the most memorable part of the restaurant. Vegetarians will find plenty to eat here.

Dwarika's Village Hotel (see Places to Stay – Top end earlier) has a good-value Friday night poolside barbecue (Rs 625) that makes for a good splurge. See the boxed text 'Nepali Restaurants' for details of the hotel's Krishnarpan Restaurant.

Self-Catering
In Thamel, for trekking food such as noodles, nuts, dried fruit and cheese, there are a number of small supermarkets such as the Best Shopping Centre at the end of Tridevi Marg, where the road narrows and enters Thamel proper. There are a couple of supermarkets opposite Barnes & Noble Bookhouse, though prices are higher here than elsewhere.

The Bluebird supermarkets have a wide variety of goods. There's a branch by the main bridge across the Bagmati River to Patan, and another branch in Lazimpat, near the French embassy (both are on the Central Kathmandu map). The Kasthamandap Bazaar Supermarket, just off Durbar Marg, also has a good selection.

ENTERTAINMENT
Nepal is an early-to-bed country and even in Kathmandu you'll find few people on the streets after 10pm. Thamel has long been the exception to this, which is not surprising as Thamel isn't really Nepal, but in the last year or so an unofficial curfew in Kathmandu has meant that even here most bars close their doors by 11pm (though a few keep serving those inside).

Bands play at various restaurants in Thamel in the high season – just follow your ears. Kathmandu also has a couple of discos, and there are cultural shows and four of west Asia's very few casinos.

Bars
There are a few bars scattered around Thamel, (see the Greater Thamel map) all within a short walk of each other. Each has quite a distinctive atmosphere, so it's worth poking your nose in to see which has the crowd and style that appeals to you. Most places have a happy hour between 5pm and 8pm, with two cocktails for the price of one or a small discount on a bottle of beer. .

Pub Maya, near Kathmandu Guest House, is a long-running favourite that remains popular, as is the associated Maya

Cocktail Bar. The two-for-one cocktails between 5pm and 8pm (with free popcorn) are a guaranteed jumpstart to a good evening.

Tom & Jerry Pub, close to Nargila Restaurant, is a long-running, rowdy upstairs place with pool tables.

New Orleans Café, near Tom & Jerry Pub, is popular and often has live blues. It has a great atmosphere. See Places to Eat earlier in this chapter for food options here.

Sam's Bar (open after 5pm), farther north, is a very cosy little place with good music.

Jatra (☎ 4211010; mains Rs 160-220) is an intimate and pretty cool venue for a beer or dinner, with indoor and outdoor seating. Friday nights bring live music jams.

Rum Doodle Restaurant & Bar (see Places to Eat earlier in this chapter), one of the most well-known bars, attracts an interesting crowd of adventurers and often has live music on Friday nights.

Paddy Foley's Irish Bar is on the top floor of the new building between the Kathmandu Guest House and the Yin Yang Restaurant. This place has an outdoor terrace and often has live music.

Discos
Kathmandu has a couple of discos, such as the Moon Sun Disco (Durbar Marg map; open until late daily) at the Heritage Plaza in Kamaladi, but these are much more popular with well-to-do Nepalis than tourists.

Perhaps a better bet is one of Thamel's bars, such as the Jump Club, in the same area as New Orleans Café, which has a DJ and small dance floor.

Casinos
Kathmandu's casinos are all attached to upmarket hotels and open 24 hours. Polish up your best James Bond impersonation and head for the Casino Royale at the Yak & Yeti Hotel (see the Central Kathmandu map). Other casinos are at the Soaltee Crowne Plaza Hotel (see the Kathmandu map) and Hotel de l'Annapurna (see the Durbar Marg map).

If you turn up at any of them within a week of arrival with your onward airline ticket and passport you can get Indian Rs (INRs) 200 of free coupons. You can play in either INRs (almost a hard currency in Nepali terms) or US dollars, and winnings (in the same currency) can be taken out of the country when you leave. The casinos will ply you with free beer and food if you're actually playing at the tables. The main games offered are roulette and blackjack, and the main clients are Indians. Nepalis are officially forbidden from entering.

Music & Dance
There are regular performances of Nepali music and dancing in Kathmandu. Most take place in the restaurants of the top-end hotels, usually around 7pm.

The Himalchuli Cultural Group is a dance troupe that performs nightly at the **Cultural Hall** attached to the Hotel Shankar in Lazimpat, north of the new Royal Palace (see the Central Kathmandu map). The hour-long show costs Rs 350 and starts at 7pm in summer (October to April) and 6.30pm in winter (May to September).

Nepali dances (and occasional theatre) are performed at the **Kalamandapa Institute of Classical Nepalese Performing Arts** (☎ 4271545; entry Rs 400 with tea) at the Hotel Vajra (see the Central Kathmandu map) most Tuesdays at 7pm. Phone ahead to check schedules.

The **Gandharba Association** is an organisation for the city's musician caste. It often has music jams around 5.30pm in a back room behind Equator Expeditions but also plays the occasional concert in restaurants like the Northfield Café. For details and locations call in at the office in Bhagwan Bahal in the east of Greater Thamel.

There are classical **sitar concerts** (entry Rs 300) three times a week at 7pm at Pilgrim's Book House in Thamel.

Jazz Upstairs in Lazimpat (see the Central Kathmandu map) has live jazz in its tiny bar every Wednesday and Saturday that is patronised by a interesting mix of locals and expats.

See Bars earlier for a list of places that feature live local bands.

Cinemas
As made famous by the title of Pico Iyer's book *Video Night in Kathmandu* (see Books in the Facts for the Visitor chapter), a number of Thamel restaurants show Western movies almost as soon as they hit the cinemas in the West. There's no charge to watch the films as long as you order dinner but the food is average at best and the film sound quality is often atrocious, since the films are pirate copies (it's not uncommon to see someone's head walking past the camera on screen!) You'll see the movies chalked up on pavement blackboards.

The Kathmandu Guest House shows films in its better-quality **mini-theatre** (Rs 200).

The **Jai Nepal Cinema** (Central Kathmandu map; stalls Rs 100-135, balcony Rs 170), on the south side of the new Royal Palace, shows foreign films in English and is the best in town.

Elsewhere, Indian films, mostly without subtitles, are the usual cinematic fare. Entry charges are minimal (around Rs 30) and catching a Hindi movie is well worthwhile since understanding the language is only a minor hindrance to enjoying these comedy-musical spectaculars. Indians call them 'masala movies' as they have a little bit of everything in them.

SHOPPING
Everything that is turned out in the various centres around the valley can be found in Kathmandu, although you can often find a better choice, or more unusual items, in the centres that produce the items – for example, Jawlakhel (south of Patan) for Tibetan carpets; Patan for cast metal statues and other craftwork; Bhaktapur for the finest woodcarvings and pottery; and Thimi for more pottery and masks. See Shopping in the Patan and Bhaktapur sections of the Around the Kathmandu Valley chapter for more details.

Thamel in particular can be a stressful place to shop, what with all the tiger balm sellers, rickshaw drivers and seemingly suicidal motorbikers. Dive into a side street or garden haven when stress levels start to rise.

One place you could start is the **Amrita Craft Collection** (Greater Thamel map; ☎ 424 0757; W www.amrita.com.np), south of the Kathmandu Guest House in Chhetrapati. It has quite a broad collection of crafts and clothing. Subtract 20% from its prices and you get a good benchmark for what you should pay on the street if you are an excellent bargainer.

Another is the upmarket shopping complex at **Babar Mahal Revisited** (Central Kathmandu map) in the southeast of the city near the Singh Durbar government offices. The unique complex consists of old Rana palace outbuildings that have been redeveloped to house a warren of antique shops, designer galleries, clothes stores and the obligatory carpet shop, as well as a couple of top-end restaurants (see Places to Eat earlier in this chapter). It's aimed at local expats, wealthy locals and tour groups, but it's worth a visit if you are looking for top-quality merchandise.

Bronze Statues
The best place to start is on Durbar Marg. This is one area where research is vitally important, as quality and prices do not necessarily correlate. **Curio Arts** is a good place to start.

Curios
An endless supply of curios, art pieces and plain junk is turned out for tourists. Most does not come from Tibet but from the local Tamang community and doesn't date back much further than, well, last month, but that doesn't put most people off. Basantapur Square is the headquarters for this trade, but before you lock wits with these operators, visit the **Amrita Craft Collection** (Greater Thamel map; ☎ 4240757).

Thangkas
The main centre for *thangkas* is just off Durbar Square, and this is where you'll find the best salespeople (not necessarily the best *thangkas*). For modern work there are plenty of places in Thamel. You can see *thangkas* being painted on the spot at **Phapa Chengreshi Thangka Painting School** in Thamel.
    Dharmapala Thangka Center (Durbar Marg; ☎ 4223715; W www.thangka.de), down the Shakya Arcade, is a showroom for a local school of *thangka* painting.
    Tibetan Thangka Gallery (Central Kathmandu map; ☎ 4428863), just past the Hotel Ambassador, is another good little place. *Thangkas* are painted on the spot (you can watch the artists at work) and many pieces from here end up in the Durbar Square shops with higher price tags.
    Indigo Gallery (Kathmandu map), at Mike's Breakfast in Naxal, has some excellent pieces.

Clothing
Kathmandu is the best place in the valley for clothes and many places have good-quality ready-to-wear Western fashions, particularly shirts. Amusing embroidered T-shirts are a popular speciality. There are lots of good tailors around Thamel and, apart from embroidered T-shirts, they'll also embroider just about anything you want on your own jacket or jeans. A few tailors stock Chinese silks and can make pretty much anything that you can explain.
    Maheela, down a side street off Jyatha, is an NGO that makes clothes, cushions, bags and Lao-like ornamental weavings from *dhaka* cloth, as well as natural beeswax products. The organisation is part of the Women's Foundation (see the special section 'Responsible Tourism') and 50% of monies earned goes to the producers, while 25% is donated to women's shelters, educational programmes and legal assistance programmes.

Handicrafts
For general handicrafts such as handmade paper, ceramics and woodwork – much of it made by disadvantaged or minority groups – the best places are the showrooms of the nonprofit development organisations that are based in the Kupandol district of Patan. Two of these shops, **Mahaguthi** (☎ 4438760) and **Sana Hastakala** (☎ 4436631), have outlets in Lazimpat (see the Kathmandu map). See the Patan section in the Around the Kathmandu Valley chapter for details.
    Ladybird Gift Shop, in Thamel, is a craft shop whose profits go to support orphan girls.
    Woodmaster Gallery (Kathmandu map), in Naxal opposite the police headquarters, displays beautiful pieces made by Newar woodcarvers of the valley. Prices are generally high, but so is the quality. You can also arrange a visit to the workshop in Jawlakhel.

Gems & Jewellery
Buying gems is always a risky business unless you know what you're doing – see Dangers & Annoyances in the Facts for the Visitor chapter for a warning on gem scams. Be immediately suspicious of anyone who tells you that you will be able to make an enormous profit – if this was possible and legal they would do it themselves.
    There are dozens of jewellery shops in Kathmandu – including in Thamel, on New Rd and Durbar Marg. The merchandise is

produced both in India and locally. When walking between Thamel and Durbar Square you'll often come across small shops with a few craftspeople working with silver.

The prices for silver jewellery are very low compared with what you'd pay at home, and many people have jewellery made to order. You buy the stones or draw the design and they'll make it up, usually in just a day or two. The quality is usually excellent, but be sure to agree on a price before giving the go-ahead to have anything made.

Tibetan Antiques

Kathmandu seems to be the world clearing house for a continual stream of antiques from Tibet, including *thangkas*, carpets, jewellery, storage chests, carvings, religious objects, saddles and clothing. Since the Chinese have done their utmost to destroy Tibetan culture, removing some of what remains to safety is perhaps more morally acceptable than some other 'collecting' that goes on in Nepal. There are a number of good shops on Durbar Marg, but don't go without a very healthy wallet.

Indian Goods

Since the war in Kashmir killed the tourist trade there, many Kashmiris have migrated to Nepal to sell traditional crafts such as carpets, cushions, tapestry, woollen shawls and papier-mache. These guys are excellent salespeople, so buy with caution.

Cottage Crafts on the ground floor of the Sanchaya Kosh Bhawan Shopping Centre in Jyatha (see the Greater Thamel map) has a good selection and reliable prices, but there are many others.

You'll also find a fair amount of embroidered clothing, cushions and bed linen from Gujarat and Rajasthan. Prices are higher than if you buy in India, but considerably less than if you buy in the West. Tridevi Marg is lined with colourful Indian bedspreads.

Other Goods

An excellent place to buy tea is **Tea World**, down a long corridor beside the Student Guest House in Thamel. The manager offers free tasting and will tell you a lot about the teas on offer. See Shopping in the Facts for the Visitor chapter for more on Nepali tea.

Thamel has some excellent trekking gear for sale – see What to Bring under Planning in the Trekking chapter for details.

GETTING THERE & AWAY

See the Getting There & Away chapter for details of getting to Kathmandu both by air and by land.

Air

Kathmandu is the only international arrival point for flights to Nepal and is also the main centre for domestic flights.

International Airlines The following airline offices appear on the Central Kathmandu map unless indicated otherwise. Most don't have flights from Kathmandu but have codeshares with airlines that do. Most airline offices are closed weekends and between 1pm and 2pm (though THAI is open Sunday):

Aeroflot (☎ 4227399) Kamaladi
Air India (☎ 4415637) Hattisar
Austrian Airlines/Lauda Airlines (☎ 4241506) Kamaladi
Bangladesh Biman (☎ 4434525) Naxal
British Airways (☎ 4222266) Durbar Marg
China Southwest Airlines (☎ 4440650) Lazimpat
Druk Air (☎ 4410089, e drukair@mallatraks .com) Malla Treks, Lekhnath Marg
Gulf Air (☎ 4434464) Hattisar
Indian Airlines (☎ 4410906) Hattisar
Japan Airlines (Durbar Marg map; ☎ 4224854) Durbar Marg
Lufthansa (Durbar Marg map; ☎ 4223052) Durbar Marg
Necon Air (☎ 4473860) Sina Mangal; (☎ 425 8664, e reservation@necon.mos.com.np) Tridevi Marg, Thamel
Pakistan International Airlines (PIA; ☎ 4439234) Hattisar
Qantas Airways (Durbar Marg map; ☎ 4224956) Durbar Marg
Qatar Airlines (Greater Thamel map; ☎ 4256579) Kantipath
Royal Nepal Airlines (RNAC; ☎ 4220757) Kantipath
Singapore Airlines (☎ 4220759) Kamaladi
Thai International Airlines (THAI; Durbar Marg map; ☎ 4223565, 4224917) Durbar Marg
Transavia (Durbar Marg map; ☎ 4247215) Heritage Plaza, Kamaladi

There are three important rules with flights out of Kathmandu: reconfirm, reconfirm and reconfirm! This particularly applies to Royal Nepal Airlines; at peak times when flights are heavily booked you should reconfirm when you first arrive in Nepal and reconfirm again towards the end of your stay. Even this may not guarantee you a seat – make sure you get to the airport very early as people at the end of the queue can still be left behind. Thai doesn't require reconfirmation.

Domestic Airlines The various domestic airlines have offices around the city. However, these companies, their offices and their phone numbers seem to change with the weather. It's far less hassle to buy tickets through a travel agency or your hotel; you might even get a better deal this way.

Domestic airlines with offices in Kathmandu include:

Buddha Air (Central Kathmandu map; ☎ 443 7025, ⒺⓁ buddhaair@buddhaair.com) Hattisar
Cosmic Air (☎ 4427150, ⒺⓁ soi@wlink.com.np) Maharajganj
Gorkha Airlines (Greater Thamel map; ☎ 443 5121, ⒺⓁ gorkha@mos.com.np) Hattisar
Mountain Air (Durbar Marg map; ☎ 4489065, ⒺⓁ mountainair@sbbs.wlink.com.np) Hattisar
Necon Air (☎ 4258664, ⒺⓁ reservation@ necon.com.np) Tridevi Marg, Thamel
Royal Nepal Airlines (RNAC; Central Kathmandu map; ☎ 4225347, fax 4225348) Kantipath
Shangri-La Air (Central Kathmandu map; ☎ 4439693) Hattisar
Skyline Airways (Central Kathmandu map; ☎ 4488657, ⒺⓁ res@skyair.com.np) Hattisar
Yeti Airlines (☎ 4421215) Lazimpat

RNAC has computerised booking only on five routes: Pokhara, Jomsom, Lukla, Bharatpur and mountain flights. These can be booked at the main **RNAC office** (open 9am-1pm & 2pm-5pm daily) on Kantipath and the corner of New Rd.

All other domestic flights are booked in a haphazard manner at a small **domestic office** (☎ 4224497; open 9am-4pm daily) just around the corner. Here it seems the booking clerk keeps issuing tickets as long as people keep fronting up with money. With no apparent reservation charts to speak of, the potential for overbooking is high. Confirm more than once, and get to the airport early. The other domestic carriers seem to be well organised.

Bus

The **main bus station** (Kathmandu map; Ring Rd, Balaju) is north of the city centre. It is officially called the Gongbu Bus Park, but is generally known as the Kathmandu Bus Terminal, or simply 'bus park'. This bus station is basically for all long-distance buses, including to Pokhara and destinations in the Terai. It's a huge and busy place, there are no signs in English, and unless you read Nepali it can be thoroughly confusing, but most of the ticket sellers are very helpful. There's often more than one reservation counter for each destination and bookings for long trips should be made a day in advance.

Bus No 23 (Rs 5) runs to the bus station from Lekhnath Marg on the northern edge of Greater Thamel.

See the table 'Buses from Kathmandu Bus Station' for a list of destinations served from Kathmandu.

Buses for destinations within the Kathmandu Valley, and for those on or accessed from the Arniko Hwy (Jiri, Barabise, and Kodari on the Tibetan border) operate from the old (Ratna Park) bus station, also known as the City bus station, in the centre of the city on the eastern edge of Tundikhel parade ground (see the Central Kathmandu map). The station is a bit of a horror; drenched in diesel fumes, with no English signs and not much English spoken.

The exceptions to this are the more expensive tourist buses to Pokhara (Rs 250) – heavily promoted in Thamel – that depart from the Thamel end of Kantipath (see the Greater Thamel map). For more details see Getting There & Away entries in the Pokhara chapter and the Royal Chitwan National Park section in the Terai & Mahabharat Range chapter.

Greenline (Greater Thamel map; ☎ 4257544, 4253885, Ⓦ www.catmando.com/greenline; Tridevi Marg) offers air-con deluxe services that are considerably more expensive than the tourist minibuses. Buses to Pokhara leave daily at 8am (US$10) with a break in Kurintar, where you can catch other Greenline buses to Chitwan (US$8). The Lumbini service (US$15) is currently on hold but could be reinstated. Book in advance.

GETTING AROUND

The best way to see Kathmandu and the valley is to walk or ride a bicycle (see the Mountain Biking chapter for a detailed discussion). Most of the sights in Kathmandu itself can easily be covered on foot, and this

Buses from Kathmandu Bus Station

destination	km	duration (hrs)	cost (Rs) night/day	ticket window
Besisahar	150	6	175 minibus	25 & 26
Bhairawa/Sunauli	282	8-10	207/170 (Rs 227 minibus)	24
Biratnagar	541	14	345/-	14
Birganj	298	10	175/160	15 & 17
Butwal	237	7-9	190/155	22 & 23
Dharan Bazaar	539	14	369/353	11
Dhunche	119	7-8	-/110	28
Gorkha	141	5	92/82 (105 minibus)	17 & 18
Hile	635	14	405/-	10
Ilam	697	20	500/-	3
Janakpur	375	11	242/200	13 & 17 (day bus)
Kakarbhitta	610	15	450/-	1 & 2
Mahendranagar	695	8-9	513/480	6
Narayanghat	146	3	110/90	17
Nepalganj	531	13	391/324 (375 minibus)	19
Pokhara	202	8	155/135 (210 minibus)	20 & 25 (minibus)
Tansen (Palpa)	302	12	227/174 (240 minibus)	17 & 24
Trisuli Bazaar	68	4	53	28

is by far the best way to appreciate the city. If and when you run out of steam, there are plenty of reasonably priced taxis and auto-rickshaws available.

To/From the Airport

Kathmandu's international airport is named Tribhuvan Airport after the late king; the area's former name Gaucher (literally 'cow pasture') says a lot about Kathmandu's rapid urban expansion.

Getting into town is quite straightforward. There is an organised taxi service on the ground-floor foyer immediately after you leave the baggage collection and customs section. The taxis have a fixed fare of Rs 250 to Thamel or Rs 200 to Durbar Marg.

If you don't want to take one of these, once outside the international terminal you will be confronted by hordes of hotel touts, who are often taxi drivers making commission on taking you to a particular hotel. Many hold up a signboard of the particular hotel they are connected with, and if the one you want is there, you can get a free lift. The only drawback is that the hotel is then much less likely to offer you a discount, as it will be paying a hefty commission (up to 50% of the room) to the taxi driver.

If you don't want to be taken to a hotel of their choice, a ride to Thamel or the city centre should cost no more than Rs 200, although in the opposite direction you should be able to get a taxi for Rs 100 during daylight hours.

Public buses leave from the main road – about 300m from the terminal – but they're only really useable if you have very little luggage and know exactly how to get to where you want to go.

Bus

While bus travel is very cheap, it is often unbelievably crowded. The primary disadvantage, apart from severe discomfort, is that you cannot see the views or stop when you want. Still, if you're short of cash and want to get from point A to B *reasonably* quickly, the buses will do the trick. Over a short distance – say from Thamel to Bodhnath – you'll probably be just as quick on a bicycle. The smaller minibuses are generally quicker than the buses and are slightly more expensive.

Nearly all buses to points around the valley operate from the City bus station. As with anything in Nepal, however, there are exceptions to the rule.

Buses to Pharping (Dakshinkali) leave from Shahid Gate (Martyrs' Memorial) at the southern end of the Tundikhel parade ground.

Buses to Bungamati, Godavari and Chapagaon leave from Patan. See the Patan section in the Around the Kathmandu Valley chapter for more details.

Safa Tempos

These electric three-wheeled vans serve various routes around town from a confusing collection of stands alongside the main post office. They offer an admirably ecofriendly form of transport (*safa* means clean) but unfortunately few of the tempos carry any English signs, few drivers speak English and the routes can be fiendishly complicated. A few routes are highlighted throughout the Around the Kathmandu Valley chapter. Blue signs marked with the white outline of a tempo indicate a stop.

Taxi

Taxis are quite reasonably priced. The charge for a metered taxi is Rs 7 flagfall and Rs 2.40 for every 200m; drivers don't usually take too much convincing to use the meter for short trips, although in the evenings you may have to negotiate. Shorter rides around town rarely come to more than Rs 50. Taxis can be booked in advance on ☎ 4420987; at night call ☎ 4224374.

Between several people, longer taxi trips around the valley, or even outside it, are affordable. A half-day sightseeing trip within the valley should cost around Rs 800, and a full-day trip, Rs 1500. For longer journeys outside the valley count on about Rs 2500 per day plus fuel.

Other approximate taxi fares (from Thamel) include:

destination	fare (Rs)
Pashupatinath	80
Bodhnath	100
Patan	80-100
Bhaktapur	250
Changu Narayan	600
Dhulikhel/Nagarko	800

Car

Although you cannot rent cars on a drive-yourself basis they can be readily rented with a driver from a number of operators. Try **Gorkha Travels** (☎ 4224896) or **Yeti Travels** (☎ 4221234) off Durbar Marg, or one of the many travel agencies in Thamel.

The rental cost is high, both in terms of the initial hiring charge and fuel. Charges are as high as Rs 3000 a day, although they can be lower, especially if you are not covering a huge distance. All in all, you are probably better off hiring a taxi for the day.

Motorcycle

There are a number of motorcycle rental operators around Thamel. Officially, you need an international driving licence, but no-one ever checks. You are required to leave a substantial deposit or your passport. For Rs 400 per day you'll get a 100cc Indian-made Honda road bike, and will basically be restricted to the Kathmandu Valley (but also including places just outside such as Daman, Kakani, Nagarkot and Dhulikhel). A 250cc trail bike costs around Rs 1000 per day.

Try Pheasant Guest House, the Singh Motorbike Reconditioning Centre or the rather disreputable-looking collection of bikes and motorbikes at Thamel Chowk, which are cheapest at Rs 300 per day. Fuel currently costs Rs 53 per litre and you'll only need a couple of litres for a day trip.

Motorcycles can be great fun outside the town, once you master the traffic. The main problem is getting out of Kathmandu, which can be a stressful, choking and highly dangerous experience. You will need a pair of goggles and some kind of face mask (available in most pharmacies) to deal with the horrific pollution.

Think carefully before you do hire a motorcycle, as you will be encouraging the proliferation of noisy, polluting machines – part of the problem, instead of part of the solution. Most reasonably fit people will find that a mountain bike is a better option, especially as you can get to more places.

Autorickshaw & Cycle-Rickshaw

Three-wheeled metered autorickshaws are quite common in Kathmandu and cost as little as half of what you would pay for a cab. Flagfall is Rs 2, plus Rs 6 per kilometre. They're still a bit of a lottery – most will blankly refuse to use the meter, and if this is the case make sure you establish a price. Most rides around town should cost less than Rs 40.

Cycle-rickshaws cost Rs 30 to Rs 50 for most rides around town – they can be more expensive than going by autorickshaw or taxi. The tourist rate from Thamel to Durbar Square is Rs 40, or from Thamel to the Hotel de l'Annapurna it's Rs 25. You must agree on a price before you start.

Bicycle

Once you get away from the crowded streets of central Kathmandu, cycling is a pleasure, and if you're in reasonable shape this is the ideal way to explore the valley. See the Mountain Biking chapter for general information on biking.

Mountain bikes start at around Rs 150 to Rs 200 per day for poor-quality Chinese- or Indian-made bicycles, which should be fine for light use around the valley. Check the brakes before taking it out and be certain to lock it whenever you leave it. Imported bicycles are available for hire for Rs 400 and up, and this is generally money well spent. It's a real pleasure to surge up the long hill into Patan, sweeping by all the riders of regular bicycles who have to get off and push.

In Thamel, the **bike hire shop** (☎ 4268980), down the side alley by the Maheela shop, hires out basic bikes from Rs 150 to Rs 250 (21 gears but no suspension).

For high-quality equipment, **Dawn Till Dusk** in the Kathmandu Guest House compound hires out bikes with no suspension for Rs 300 or with full suspension for Rs 750. **Massif Mountain Bikes** in the centre of Thamel offers bikes with/without front suspension for Rs 350/550 per day. If you want an early start, get the bike the evening before.

Around the Kathmandu Valley

The small, mountain-sheltered Kathmandu Valley is the historical centre of Nepal, the place where kingdoms rose and fell, palaces and temples were built, destroyed and re-built, and Nepali art and culture were developed and refined.

The ancient Buddhist stupa of Swayambhunath (commonly known as the 'Monkey Temple'), a dramatic spot within walking distance of central Kathmandu, is one of the best-known sites in Nepal; it attracts a constant stream of worshippers. The hilltop site offers a fine view over the valley that is helpful for orienting yourself if you've just arrived.

The most important Hindu temple is Pashupatinath, on the eastern side of Kathmandu near Tribhuvan Airport. It's a centre for pilgrims and *sadhus* (holy men) from all over the subcontinent. A visit here can be combined with Bodhnath (Boudha), another huge Buddhist stupa and the centre for a thriving Tibetan community.

The valley's second city, Patan, a short taxi ride from Kathmandu, is famed for its Durbar Square that's packed with a superb variety of temples, as well as many *bahals* (Buddhist monasteries).

Bhaktapur, the third largest town in the valley, is towards the eastern end of the valley and its relative isolation is reflected in its slower pace and more distinctly medieval atmosphere. All the above sites are easily visited as day trips from the capital.

You can find good hikes in the valley, ranging from downhill strolls to more ambitious overnight hikes. If you don't have the opportunity to trek elsewhere in Nepal, it's worth visiting one of the famous viewpoints on the rim of the valley, such as Nagarkot or Dhulikhel, from where you can feast your eyes on an unbroken line of frozen Himalayan peaks.

If you have more time, there are lesser-known, although important, temples such as Changu Narayan, north of Bhaktapur and a treasure house of Nepali art; Dakshinkali, in the southwestern corner of the valley and the site for animal sacrifices to Kali; and Budhanilkantha, north of Kathmandu, with a huge 1400-year-old statue of Vishnu.

The valley beyond the cities has certainly changed over the years. Fortunately, how-

Highlights

- Viewing the stunning Newari architecture and superb museum in Patan's Durbar Square
- Admiring the famous Golden Gate and peacock window and exploring the fascinating backstreets of Bhaktapur
- Visiting the ancient Buddhist stupa of Swayambhunath, with its colourful Tibetan pilgrims and excellent views of Kathmandu
- Joining Tibetan pilgrims on a pilgrimage around Bodhnath stupa, the largest in Nepal
- Exploring the corners and traditional Newari villages of the Kathmandu Valley by foot, mountain bike or motorbike
- Learning about Tibetan Buddhism at the popular Kopan Monastery

AROUND THE KATHMANDU VALLEY

ever, aspects of traditional life are maintained as the people of the valley coax their livelihood from the land, and temples continue to provide a focal point for their lives. The seasons roll on, and the timeless demands of the fields, the family and the gods remain fundamental priorities.

HISTORY

The Kathmandu Valley has long been a cultural and racial melting pot, with people coming from both east and west. This fusion has resulted in the unique Newari culture that is responsible for the valley's superb art and architecture. For more information on Newari culture see the Society and Religion sections in the Facts about Nepal chapter.

The Newari golden age peaked in the 17th century when the valley conssisted of small city-states, and Nepal was a vitally important trading link between Tibet and the north Indian plains. It was during the reign of the Malla kings (see History in the Facts about Nepal chapter), particularly in the 17th and 18th centuries, that many of the valley's finest temples and palaces were built.

Sorting out who built what (and when) is considerably complicated by the fact that at any one time there was not just one Malla

KATHMANDU VALLEY

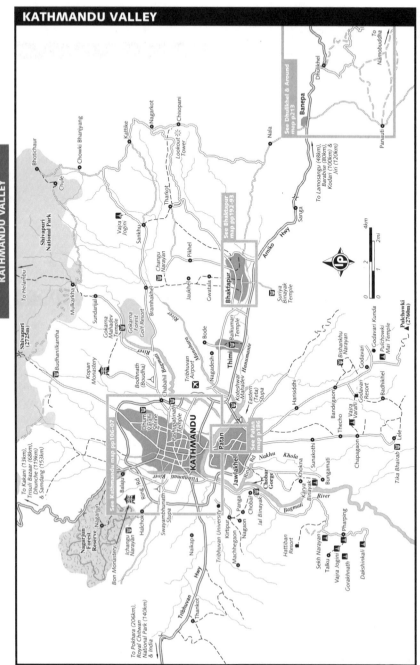

Newari Towns

The Newars have over the centuries created an urban culture unequalled in the Himalaya. The cities and towns of the Kathmandu Valley are a compact network of interlocking squares, courtyards, twisting alleyways, ponds and temples, often centred on a main square. Though modern building methods have affected aesthetics and village structure, much of the traditional structure remains. Decorated with carved windows and doorways, statues and shrines, and humming with gregarious people, a Newari town is a remarkable synthesis of art and everyday life.

The family house was the starting point for urban development. Rich Newars built handsomely proportioned brick houses that were up to five storeys high with tiled roofs. Symbolically a Newari house becomes ritually purer as you ascend floors. The *chhyali* (ground floor) is used for commerce or the stabling of animals, or both. The *mattan* (first floor) consists of a bedroom and a room for visitors. Windows are small and latticed for both privacy and security. The *chota* (second floor) is the most active floor in the house and holds the living room, bedrooms and workroom for weaving and the like. It also houses a *dhukuti* (storeroom). Windows on this floor are larger and have outward-opening shutters. The *baiga* (attic floor) has the kitchen and dining room, a *pujakuthi* (shrine room) and a roof terrace.

Newari community life developed when a series of houses was built in a rectangle around a *chowk* (courtyard or square), often by a single clan or extended family. The chowk, with its water supply and a temple or shrine, became the centre of day-to-day life, as it is today to a large extent. Elaborately decorated *hitis* (water tanks) provide a communal washing area and running water. Shrines, temples and *pathi* (platforms used by the community and travellers) were erected over time by philanthropists.

In larger towns like Patan, monastery complexes were built and run by a unique cooperative religious and social institution known as a *guthi*. Today many of the *bahals* (monastery courtyards) formerly run by the guthis have been converted into courtyard communal living spaces (Patan alone has over 260 bahals). Here, the markets buzz, children play, women chat and work (weaving, washing, drying grain), old people doze in the sun, men talk over the community's business and religious ceremonies take place, as they have for centuries.

king. Each of the three city-states in the valley – Kathmandu, Patan and Bhaktapur – had its own.

The unification of Nepal in 1768 by Gorkha's King Prithvi Narayan Shah signalled the end of the Kathmandu Valley's fragmentation. Nepali, an Indo-European language spoken by the Khas of western Nepal, replaced Newari as the country's language of administration.

GETTING AROUND
Bicycle, Bus & Motorcycle
Swayambhunath and Pashupatinath can be reached on foot from Kathmandu, but by far the easiest and most economical way of getting around the valley is by bicycle. Bicycle speed allows you to appreciate your surroundings and stop whenever you like. If you are aiming for somewhere on the rim of the valley, make sure you have a multigeared mountain bike (see the Kathmandu chapter for places to hire bikes). A reasonably fit person can cycle anywhere in the valley and

return to Kathmandu within daylight hours. Also see the Mountain Biking chapter for recommended routes through the Kathmandu Valley and for general information on biking.

If you intend to do any biking, hiking or just plain exploring it's worth getting Nepa Maps' 1:50,000 *Around the Kathmandu Valley* (Rs 400).

Buses and minibuses service all of the roads, but although cheap, they are uncomfortable and limiting. If you are part of a group or if the budget allows, you could consider hiring a car or taxi (about Rs 800 per half day, or Rs 1500 per full day). Motorcycles also offer a way of accessing most parts of the valley.

Organised Tours
Wayfarers Travel Service (☎ 4266010, fax 4264245; W www.wayfarers.com.np) offers twice-weekly, one-day guided walks of the settlements of the southern valley rim: Kirtipur, Khokna, Bungamati and Chapagaon. It also offers three-day guided hikes, which

take in Sankhu, Namobuddha, Dhulikhel and Nagarkot. Day hikes cost US$30 with guide, transport, lunch and breakfast, or US$20 if you travel by bus. Three-day hikes cost US$115, including lunch, breakfast and a porter.

Valley Walks

There are many interesting walks around the valley, which can take you between traditional villages and temples, and along ridge tops to mountain viewpoints; many of them make pleasant alternatives to travelling by vehicle or bicycle. You can, for example, follow a trail from Kirtipur to Chobar, from the Gokarna Mahadev Temple to Bodhnath, or from Dhulikhel to Panauti via the pilgrimage site of Namobuddha. There are several (downhill) hikes from Nagarkot. These walks, among others, are detailed throughout this chapter.

It's possible to link up a series of day hikes to form a multiday trek of anything from two days to a week, taking in a combination of Panauti, Namobuddha, Dhulikhel, Banepa, Nagarkot, Chisopani and Sundarijal.

Around Kathmandu

The sights in this section can all be visited as easy day trips from the capital.

SWAYAMBHUNATH

The Buddhist temple of Swayambhunath (entry Rs 50), on the top of a hill west of Kathmandu, is one of the most popular and instantly recognisable symbols of Nepal. The temple is colloquially known as the 'Monkey Temple', after the large tribe of handsome monkeys that guards the hill and amuses visitors and devotees with tricks (including sliding gracefully down the double banisters of the main stairway to the temple). The roving monkeys quickly snatch up any offerings of food made by devotees and will just as quickly grab anything you may be carrying.

Geologists believe that the Kathmandu Valley was once a lake, and legends relate that the hill on which Swayambhunath stands was an island in that lake (see the boxed text 'Legend of the Chobar Gorge' later in this chapter). It is said that Emperor Ashoka paid a visit to the site over 2000

years ago. An inscription indicates that King Manadeva ordered work done here in 460 AD. By the 13th century it was an important Buddhist centre. In 1346 Mughal invaders from Bengal broke open the stupa to search for gold. The Mallas made improvements, and the stairway to the stupa was constructed by King Pratap Malla in the 17th century.

From its hilltop setting, Swayambhunath offers fine views over Kathmandu and the valley. It's particularly striking in the early evening when the city is illuminated, and the site is also very attractive under the soft glow of moonlight. There are several curio shops around the stupa, as well as a couple of reviving cafés.

Eastern Stairway

Although you can get to the temple by vehicle, the long climb up the eastern stairway is by far the best way of approaching Swayambhunath. Look for the yellow-and-red stone seated figures of the Buddha at the base of the hill. The bottom end of the steps is guarded by figures of Ganesh and Kumar on their vehicles. Near the start of the steps is a huge 'footprint' on a stone, said to be either that of the Buddha or the Bodhisattva Manjushri. Halfway up the steps there is another small collection of stonework, including a scene showing the birth of the Buddha, his mother holding a tree branch and the Buddha taking seven miraculous steps immediately after his birth. You'll see Tibetan astrologers plying their trade around here.

As you climb the final (steepest) stretch, look for the pairs of animals – Garudas, lions, elephants, horses and peacocks – the 'vehicles' of the Dhyani Buddhas. When you reach the top, remember to walk around the stupa in a clockwise direction.

Great Thunderbolt

As well as building the great stairway, Pratap Malla added a pair of *shikharas* and the stone lions and *dorje*, which visitors see immediately upon reaching the top of the stairs. 'Dorje' is the Tibetan word for this thunderbolt symbol; in Sanskrit it is called a *vajra*. *Dorjes* are often accompanied by a bell, or *drilbu*; the thunderbolt symbolises male force and the bell symbolises female wisdom. Around the pedestal supporting Swayambhunath's mighty *dorje* are the animals of the Tibetan calendar.

SWAYAMBHUNATH

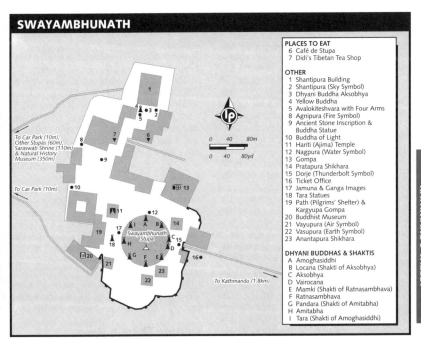

PLACES TO EAT
6 Café de Stupa
7 Didi's Tibetan Tea Shop

OTHER
1 Shantipura Building
2 Shantipura (Sky Symbol)
3 Dhyani Buddha Aksobhya
4 Yellow Buddha
5 Avalokiteshvara with Four Arms
8 Agnipura (Fire Symbol)
9 Ancient Stone Inscription & Buddha Statue
10 Buddha of Light
11 Hariti (Ajima) Temple
12 Nagpura (Water Symbol)
13 Gompa
14 Pratapura Shikhara
15 Dorje (Thunderbolt Symbol)
16 Ticket Office
17 Jamuna & Ganga Images
18 Tara Statues
19 Path (Pilgrims' Shelter) & Kargyupa Gompa
20 Buddhist Museum
21 Vayupura (Air Symbol)
22 Vasupura (Earth Symbol)
23 Anantapura Shikhara

DHYANI BUDDHAS & SHAKTIS
A Amoghasiddhi
B Locana (Shakti of Aksobhya)
C Aksobhya
D Vairocana
E Mamki (Shakti of Ratnasambhava)
F Ratnasambhava
G Pandara (Shakti of Amitabha)
H Amitabha
I Tara (Shakti of Amoghasiddhi)

To Car Park (10m),
Other Stupas (60m),
Saraswati Shrine (110m)
& Natural History
Museum (350m)

To Car Park (10m)

Swayambhunath Stupa

To Kathmandu (1.8km)

Stupa

From the flattened top of the hill, a gold-coloured square block tops the soaring swell of the central stupa and the watchful eyes of the Buddha gaze out across the valley in each direction. The question mark-like 'nose' is actually the Nepali number *ek* (one) and is a symbol of unity. Between and above the two eyes is a third eye, which symbolises Buddha's perception.

Set around the base of the central stupa is a continuous series of prayer wheels, which pilgrims, circumambulating the stupa, spin as they pass by. Each prayer wheel carries the sacred mantra *om mani padme hum* (hail to the jewel in the lotus). The prayer flags fluttering from the lines leading to the stupa's spire also carry Tibetan mantras. The stupa's white-painted base represents the four elements – earth, fire, air and water – while the 13 concentric rings on the spire symbolise the 13 degrees of knowledge and the 13 steps that must be taken to reach nirvana (final escape from the continuous cycles of existence), which in turn is represented by the umbrella on the top of the stupa.

Stupa Platform

The great stupa is only one of many points of interest at Swayambhunath. Two white temples in the Indian *shikhara* style, both dating from 1646, flank the dorje at the top of the stairs. The one to the right, in front of the *gompa* (Tibetan Buddhist monastery), is the **Pratapura shikhara**, while to the left is the identical **Anantapura shikhara**.

Behind the stupa, adjacent to a small museum, is a **path** (pilgrims' shelter) with an open ground floor and a Kargyupa-school *gompa* above it.

North of the pilgrim shelter is the pagoda-style **Hariti (Ajima) Temple**, with a beautiful image of Hariti, the goddess of smallpox. This Hindu goddess (to the Newars she is known as Ajima), who is also responsible for fertility, illustrates the constant interweaving of Hindu and Buddhist beliefs in Nepal.

Near the Hariti Temple are pillars on which figures of various gods and goddesses are seated. Look for the figure of Tara making the gesture of charity. Actually, there are two Taras, Green Tara and White Tara, who are sometimes believed to be the two wives of King Songtsen Gampo, the first royal patron of Buddhism in Tibet. The Taras are two of the female consorts to the Dhyani Buddhas, which sit at the cardinal points of the stupa. Nearby bronze images of the river goddesses **Jamuna** and **Ganga** guard an eternal flame in a cage.

Back at the northeast corner of the complex is another **gompa** where, with a great deal of crashing, chanting and trumpeting, a service takes place every day at around 4pm. Inside the *gompa* there's a 6m-high figure of Avalokiteshvara.

The symbols of the four elements – earth, air, water and fire – can be found around the hilltop. Behind the Anantapura *shikhara* are **Vasupura**, the earth symbol, and **Vayupura**, the symbol for air. **Nagpura**, the symbol for water, is just north of the stupa, while **Agnipura**, the symbol for fire, is at the northwestern corner of the platform. **Shantipura**, which is the symbol for the sky, is at the extreme north of the platform, in front of the Shantipura building.

In this same northern area of the platform you will find an ancient stone inscription, dating from 1372, and a large image of the Buddha, next to the Agnipura symbol.

Around the Stupa

A smaller stupa stands on the hillock just west of the main stupa, with an adjacent *gompa* and an important **shrine** to Saraswati, the goddess of learning. At exam time, many scholars come here to improve their chances and schoolchildren come here during Basant Panchami, the Festival of Knowledge.

The **Natural History Museum** *(entry Rs 30; open 10am-5pm Sun-Fri, closed government holidays)*, below Swayambhunath by the road that climbs to the west entrance, has a large collection of butterflies, fish, reptiles, birds and animals.

There are various Tibetan settlements, shrines and monasteries scattered around the base of the Swayambhunath hill. It's worth investing an hour or so to join the occasional Tibetan pilgrim in a clockwise *kora* (pilgrim circuit) of the entire hill, past lines of prayer wheels, chapels, giant prayer wheels and stone carvings. The route passes a huge golden Amitabha Buddha statue on the west side and returns to the eastern entrance via the north side of the hill.

Around 800m south of Swayambhunath, the **National Museum** *(entry Rs 50; open*

9.30am-4.30pm Tues-Sat May-Sept, 9.30am-3pm Tues-Sat Oct-Apr) is a bit hit-and-miss, but has a fine collection of religious art and is worth a visit. A visit can easily be combined with a trip to Swayambhunath.

The history museum has a rather eclectic collection that includes some moon rock and whale bones, a number of moth-eaten, stuffed animals, a vast number of uniforms, swords and guns, an extremely dull coin collection and a fine portrait gallery. The most interesting museum exhibit is a leather Tibetan cannon; the most eccentric is an electrical contraption that fires a normal rifle.

The art gallery displays a superb collection of statues and carvings (stone, wood, bronze and terracotta) – some pieces date to the 1st century BC. Also worth a look is the new **gallery of Buddhist art**, which offers an excellent overview of Buddhist art and iconography, with separate sections on Terai and Kathmandu art.

Note that ticket sales stop an hour before closing time and it costs Rs 50 to bring in a camera. Bags must be deposited at the gate.

Getting There & Away

You can approach Swayambhunath by taxi or under your own power – either on foot or by bicycle. The easy stroll from Kathmandu is quite pleasant (see Walking & Cycling below). See the Kathmandu map in the Kathmandu chapter for an overview of the area.

Unless you ask to be taken to the eastern stairway, taxis will take you on the road via the National Museum and deposit you at the car park on the western side, from where it's an easy stroll to the stupa. The eastern stairway entails a steep climb but this is a far more interesting way to approach Swayambhunath. From Thamel, taxis to the car park cost around Rs 80, and Rs 60 to the bottom of the stairway.

Safa tempo No 20 shuttles between Swayambhunath's eastern stairway and Kathmandu's main post office and costs Rs 7.

Walking & Cycling There are two popular walking or bicycle routes to Swayambhunath – using both makes the trip into a pleasant circuit, either in the direction described or in reverse.

Starting at the Chhetrapati Tole junction near Thamel, the road descends to the Vishnumati River (with the Swayambhunath stupa clearly visible in the distance), and passes three interesting temples (see the Central Kathmandu map in the Kathmandu chapter). The **Indrani Temple**, just beside the river on the Kathmandu side, is chiefly notable for the brightly coloured erotic scenes on its roof struts. There are cremation ghats (riverside steps) beside the river; in 1989 the bridge here collapsed during a heavy monsoon. Across the river and just upstream is the **Shobabaghwati Temple**. A footpath runs from here up the steep hill to the **Bijeshwari Temple**, from where the road continues to the Swayambhunath hill. This final section passes a couple of tea houses and lots of shops selling rosary beads.

The alternative route starts at Durbar Square, and follows Maru Tole (Pie Alley) down to the Vishnumati River, where a footbridge crosses to the western side by some stone cremation ghats. From here, the path heads west, then north through a Tibetan area, where you'll probably see people working in gardens and preparing wool for Tibetan carpets. This route also passes the National Museum (see the 'Around the Stupa' section earlier), which is worth popping into en route to or from Swayambhunath.

AROUND SWAYAMBHUNATH
Ichangu Narayan
At the edge of the valley floor, and about 3km northwest of Swayambhunath, the shrine of Ichangu Narayan (not to be confused with Changu Narayan east of Kathmandu) is one of the Kathmandu Valley's important Vishnu shrines. This two-storey, 18th-century temple is fronted by two square stone pillars bearing Vishnu's sankha and chakra symbols atop a tortoise. The site was actually consecrated in 1200 and an earlier temple was built here after a famine in 1512. The walk or bike ride here is probably of more interest than the temple itself.

The 3km road to Ichangu Narayan starts beyond Kathmandu's Ring Rd, near the golden statue of the Buddha, on the western side of the Swayambhunath hill. It quickly changes from a road to a track as it climbs a steep hill to Halchok village (look back for the views over the valley). From the top of the hill, marked by a small temple, the trail continues past three Mughal-style Shiva shrines and a bamboo swing (erected anew each year during the Dasain festival) to the

temple compound. Going back to Kathmandu by bicycle is one long downhill breeze, but you'll certainly work up a sweat getting to the temple.

Another route to Ichangu Narayan is a day walk from the Nagarjun Forest Reserve to the northwest of Kathmandu (see Nagarjun Forest Reserve later in this section).

PASHUPATINATH
Nepal's most important Hindu temple stands on the banks of the Bagmati River, between Kathmandu and the Tribhuvan Airport and slightly southwest of Bodhnath. You can visit Pashupatinath en route to Bodhnath, as the two sites are an interesting short walk apart. There is an entry charge of Rs 250 to the Pashupatinath area.

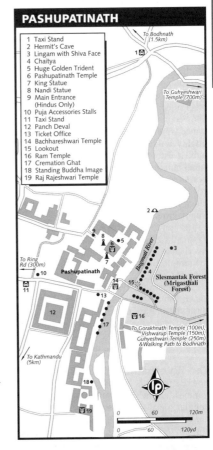

PASHUPATINATH

1 Taxi Stand
2 Hermit's Cave
3 Lingam with Shiva Face
4 Chaitya
5 Huge Golden Trident
6 Pashupatinath Temple
7 King Statue
8 Nandi Statue
9 Main Entrance
   (Hindus Only)
10 Puja Accessories Stalls
11 Taxi Stand
12 Panch Deval
13 Ticket Office
14 Bachhareshwari Temple
15 Lookout
16 Ram Temple
17 Cremation Ghat
18 Standing Buddha Image
19 Raj Rajeshwari Temple

Pashupatinath Temple

Not only is Pashupatinath the most important Hindu temple in Nepal, it's one of the most important Shiva temples on the subcontinent and draws devotees from all over India, including many colourful sadhus, those wandering ascetic Hindu holy men.

Shiva is the destroyer and creator of the Hindu pantheon and appears in many forms. His 'terrible' forms are probably best known, particularly his appearances in Nepal as the cruel and destructive Bhairab, but he also has peaceful incarnations including those of Mahadev and Pashupati, the lord of the beasts. As the shepherd of both animals and humans, Shiva as Pashupati shows his most pleasant and creative side.

Pashupati is considered to have a special concern for Nepal and, accordingly, he features in any official message from the king. Before commencing an important journey, the king will always pay a visit to Pashupatinath to seek the god's blessing.

Most people are dropped off at a taxi stand southwest of the main temple. An alley to the main temple entrance north of here is lined with vendors selling marigolds, incense and other offerings. Although non-Hindus are not allowed inside the temple, from the main entrance you may catch a glimpse inside of the mighty golden backside of Nandi, Shiva's bull. It dates from the 19th century but the small bull in front of the temple is about 300 years old. The black, four-headed image of Pashupati inside the temple is said to be even older; an earlier image was destroyed by Mughal invaders in the 14th century.

For non-Hindus there is more to be seen by heading east of the taxi stand to the riverbanks, where you can look down into the temple from the terraced hillside on the opposite bank.

En route to the riverbanks you'll pass the **Panch Deval** (Five Temples), a former five-shrined complex that now acts as a social welfare centre for a heartbreaking collection of destitute local elderly. A donation box offers a way for visitors to directly contribute.

The Riverbanks of the Bagmati

The Bagmati is a holy river and, as at Varanasi on the Ganges, Pashupatinath is a popular place to be cremated. The burning ghats immediately in front of the temple, north of the footbridges, are reserved for the

cremation of royalty, although you will often see ritual bathing taking place in the river here.

Just north of the main bridge across the Bagmati, but still on the western bank of the river, is the ancient 6th-century **Bachhareshwari Temple**, with Tantric figures, painted skeletons and erotic scenes. It is said that at one time Maha Shivaratri festival activities included human sacrifices at this temple. Right at the end of the western embankment, is a half-buried, but still quite beautiful, 7th-century **standing Buddha image**.

The six square **cremation ghats** just south of the bridges are for the common people and there is almost always a cremation going on here. The log fires are laid, the shrouded body lifted on top and the fire lit with remarkably little ceremony. It's a powerful place to contemplate notions of death and mortality.

Two footbridges cross the Bagmati River, and facing the temple from across the river are 11 stone *chaityas* (small stupas) each containing a *lingam* (a phallic symbol of Shiva's creative powers). From here you can watch the activities on the other bank, in front of the temple. Offerings and flowers are on sale, devotees dip in the river and there's a constant coming and going. From the northern end of the embankment you can see the **cave-like shelters**, once used by hermits and sadhus. These days the *yogis* (yoga masters) and sadhus head for the **Ram Temple**, next to the main bridge, especially during the festival of Maha Shivaratri.

The Terraces

Climb up the steps from the eastern riverbank to the terrace, where you can look down into the Pashupatinath Temple from several convenient benches. The central two-tiered pagoda dates from 1696. Look for the enormous **golden trident** rising up on the right (northern) side of the temple and the golden figure of the king kneeling in prayer under a protective hood of *nagas* (snake spirits) on the left side. Behind the temple, you can see a brightly coloured illustration of Shiva and his *shakti* looking out over the temple.

At the northern end of this terrace is a **Shiva lingam** on a circular pedestal. A finely featured face of the god has been sculptured on one side of the lingam. It is an indication of the richness of Nepal's artistic heritage that this piece of sculpture, so casually standing on the grassy terrace, is actually a masterpiece dating from the 5th or 6th century!

Gorakhnath & Vishwarup Temples

The steps continue up the hill from the terraces to the Gorakhnath Temple complex at the top of the hill. A *shikhara* fronted by a towering Shiva trident is the main structure, but there's a positive jungle of temples, images, sculptures and *chaityas* with Shiva imagery everywhere. Images of the bull Nandi stand guard, tridents are dotted around, lingams rise up on every side and monkeys play in the treetops, creating a peaceful and evocative atmosphere.

Non-Hindus can't enter the Vishwarup Temple, so continue instead beyond the Gorakhnath Temple where the pathway turns steeply downhill to the river. You'll soon get views of the Bodhnath stupa rising up in the distance.

Guhyeshwari Temple

The Guhyeshwari Temple is dedicated to Shiva's shakti in her terrible manifestation as Kali. Like the Pashupatinath Temple, entry is banned to all but Hindus, and the high wall around the temple prevents you from seeing anything except the four huge gilded snakes arching up to support the roof finial. Guhyeshwari was built by King Pratap Malla in the 17th century and the temple stands in a paved courtyard surrounded by *dharamsalas* (pilgrims' resthouses). The temple's main entrance gate by the river is an imposing and colourful affair. To the west of the main temple building is a series of white, stupa-like temples.

The temple's curious name comes from *guhya* (vagina) and *ishwari* (goddess) – it's the temple of the goddess' vagina! Legend has it that when Shiva was insulted by his father-in-law, Parvati was so incensed that she burst into flames and it was this act of self-immolation that gave rise to the practice of *sati* (or *suttee),* where a widow was consigned to the same funeral pyre as her deceased husband. The grieving Shiva carried off his shakti's corpse but as he wandered aimlessly, the body disintegrated and this is where her *yoni* (genitals) fell.

Special Events

Activities take place at Pashupatinath almost all the time, but it is generally busiest (with genuine pilgrims, not tourists) from 6am to 10am and again from 6pm to 7.30pm. The best time to visit the temple is on Haribodhini Ekadashi – 11 days after the full and new moon each month. On those days there will be many pilgrims and in the evening the ringing of bells will indicate that the *arati* (light) ceremony is to take place.

In February/March each year, the festival of Maha Shivaratri celebrates Shiva's birthday with a great fair at the temple. Pilgrims come from all over Nepal and India for this festival, and if you're in Kathmandu at the time don't miss it. The Bala Chaturdashi fair takes place in November/December. See the Festivals of Nepal special section for more details.

Getting There & Away

By far the most convenient way to Pashupatinath is by taxi, which costs around Rs 80 from Thamel.

Buses to Bodhnath go via Pashupatinath from Kathmandu's City bus station; the stop for Pashupatinath is called Gosala.

Pashupatinath is an easy bicycle ride from Kathmandu via the Naxal district, though the various one-way systems complicate things somewhat and traffic can be heavy.

It is a pleasant and short (20 minutes) walk through villages and farmland between Pashupatinath and Bodhnath, accompanied by strings of prayer flags and dhobi washing and the sounds of Hindi music. Take the footbridge across the river right in front of Guhyeshwari and head north for five minutes, then turn right at the signposted junction, by a tree temple. At the next junction take the middle (straight) path. You eventually come out on the main road, right across from the main Bodhnath stupa.

CHABAHIL

The Chabahil Stupa is like a small replica of Bodhnath, about 1.5km west of Bodhnath, back towards Kathmandu. The small village of Chabahil has been virtually swallowed up by the expansion of Kathmandu, but the site is very old and the original stupa was said to have been built by Ashoka's daughter, Charumati. It certainly predates Bodhnath and around the main stupa are a number of small *chaityas* from the Licchavi period, dating back to some time between the 5th and 8th centuries. The site includes a 1m-high, 9th-century statue of a Bodhisattva, which is claimed to be one of the finest pieces of sculpture in the valley.

Nearby is the small **Chandra Binayak Ganesh Temple**, with a double roof in brass. Ganesh's shrew stands on a pillar in front of the shrine, waiting for the tiny image of the god inside. A short distance south, but still on the Kathmandu side of the main road, is the well-designed **Jayabageshwari Temple**, dating from the late 17th century.

BODHNATH (BOUDHA)

On the eastern side of Kathmandu, just north of the airport and around 6km from Thamel, is the huge stupa of Bodhnath (also known as Boudha – pronounced **boe**-da), the largest stupa in Nepal and one of the largest in the world. It is the religious centre for Nepal's considerable population of Tibetans and there are a number of thriving monasteries and many small shops selling Tibetan artefacts (prices are high and bargaining is essential). This is one of the few places in the world where Tibetan culture is accessible, vibrant and unfettered.

Many of these Tibetans are refugees who fled their country following the unsuccessful uprising against the Chinese Communists in 1959. They have been both energetic and successful in the intervening years, as the large houses surrounding Bodhnath testify. Apart from the local Tibetans and Nepalis

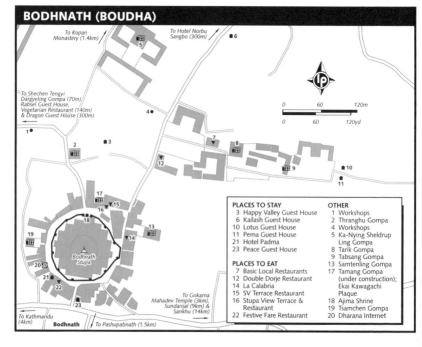

BODHNATH (BOUDHA)

To Kopan Monastery (1.4km)

To Hotel Norbu Sangbo (300m)

To Shechen Tengyi Dargyeling Gompa (70m), Rabsel Guest House, Vegetarian Restaurant (140m) & Dragon Guest House (300m)

Bodhnath Stupa

To Gokarna Mahadev Temple (3km), Sundarijal (9km) & Sankhu (14km)

To Kathmandu (4km)

Bodhnath

To Pashupatinath (1.5km)

PLACES TO STAY
3 Happy Valley Guest House
6 Kailash Guest House
10 Lotus Guest House
11 Pema Guest House
21 Hotel Padma
23 Peace Guest House

PLACES TO EAT
7 Basic Local Restaurants
12 Double Dorje Restaurant
14 La Calabria
15 SV Terrace Restaurant
16 Stupa View Terrace & Restaurant
22 Festive Fare Restaurant

OTHER
1 Workshops
2 Thranghu Gompa
4 Workshops
5 Ka-Nying Sheldrup Ling Gompa
8 Tarik Gompa
9 Tabsang Gompa
13 Samtenling Gompa
17 Tamang Gompa (under construction); Ekai Kawagachi Plaque
18 Ajima Shrine
19 Tsamchen Gompa
20 Dharana Internet

Visiting Tibetan Monasteries

The crash of cymbals, thump of Tantric drums and murmuring of Tibetan chats make a visit to a *gompa* (Tibetan monastery) a dramatic and often moving experience. What you'll soon notice beyond this is that monasteries share a remarkable continuity of design, decoration and symbolism.

All *gompas* are decorated with impressive mural paintings and *thangkas* (paintings on cotton, framed in brocade and hung). The subjects are usually either meditational deities, great past lamas or ritual *mandalas* (diagrams that represent the forces of the universe and aid meditation). As you enter a monastery you will commonly see murals of four guardian protectors and the Wheel of Life, a highly complex symbolic diagram representing the Buddha's insights into the way humans are chained by desire to the endless cycle of birth, death and rebirth. Rigid rules govern these traditional arts, stressing spirituality, order and symmetry over originality, flair and personal expression.

Symbolism extends throughout the monastery: prayer wheels are filled with thousands of Buddhist prayers which are 'activated' with each turning of the wheel; prayer flags work on a similar precept and are printed in the five elemental colours. On the monastery roof you'll see the statue of two deer on either side of the Wheel of Law, symbolising the Buddha's first sermon at the deer park of Sarnath.

Past the rows of monks' cushions, the main monastic prayer hall is headed by an altar adorned with seven bowls of water, butter lamps, and offerings of grain and fruit. Here you'll find the main statues, often of the Past, Present and Future Buddhas, along with pictures of the Dalai Lama and other lamas related to the monastery's particular school of Tibetan Buddhism. Fierce protector deities often occupy side chapels and Tibetan manuscripts line the side walls.

Cultural Considerations

Visitors are welcome in most monasteries and to keep the good faith please bear in mind the following guidelines, particularly if prayers are in progress.

- Remove your shoes and hat before you enter a *gompa*.
- Ask before taking photos and avoid taking photos during a service.
- Smoking is not permitted anywhere in the main compounds.
- Do not step over or sit on the monks' cushions, even if no-one is sitting on them.z
- During ceremonies, enter quietly and stand by the wall near the main entrance; do not walk around in front of the altar, or between the monks, or cross the central area of the temple.
- It is appropriate to make an offering, especially if you do take photographs. A *khata* (white scarf) is traditional, but these days rupees are also appreciated; monasteries depend for their existence on the donations of the faithful.

there's a sizeable community of foreign Buddhist students, which contributes to occasional factional tensions between the various different schools.

Late afternoon is a good time to visit Bodhnath, when the group tours depart and the place once again becomes a Tibetan town. Prayer services are held in the surrounding *gompas* and, as the sun sets, the community turns out to circumambulate the stupa – a ritual that combines religious observance with a social event. Remember to walk around the stupa in a clockwise direction.

Bodhnath has always been associated with Lhasa and Tibetan Buddhism. One of the major trade routes coming from Lhasa went through Sankhu, and Bodhnath therefore lies at the Tibetan traders' entry to Kathmandu. One can easily imagine the traders giving thanks for their successful journey across the Himalaya, or praying for a safe return. People still come here to pray before undertaking a journey in the Himalaya.

Information

There are a couple of Internet cafés, such as **Dharana Internet** *(Rs 30 per hour)* on the west side of the stupa.

The Bodhnath Stupa

There doesn't seem to be much agreement on how old the Bodhnath site is, but it is likely that the first stupa was built some time after AD 600, after the Tibetan king,

Songtsen Gampo, was converted to Buddhism by his two wives: the Nepali princess Bhrikuti and Wencheng Konjo from China. The current stupa structure was probably built after the depredation of the Mughal invaders in the 14th century.

Stupas were originally built to house holy relics. It is not certain if there is anything interred at Bodhnath, but some believe that there is a piece of bone that once belonged to Gautama Buddha.

Around the base of the stupa's circular mound are 108 small images of the Dhyani Buddha Amitabha. A brick wall around the stupa has 147 niches, each with four or five prayer wheels bearing that immortal mantra 'om mani padme hum'. Access to the stupa is gained through the northern entrance, where there is a small **shrine** dedicated to Ajima, the goddess of smallpox. It's possible to walk up onto the upper layers of the stupa. Pilgrims often find a private space in the inner lower enclosure and perform prostrations. It's a powerful, evocative place that's brought alive by the Tibetan pilgrims who circumambulate the stupa, twirling their prayer wheels, chatting and murmuring prayers.

For more on the symbolic structure of stupas, see the boxed text 'Temple Architecture' in the Facts about Nepal chapter.

The Gompas

A number of monasteries have been rebuilt since the 1960s but none compares with the great monasteries of Tibet, Ladakh or Bhutan. Most are closed in the middle of the day. See the boxed text 'Visiting Tibetan Monasteries' for some guidelines on visiting the *gompas*.

Tsamchen Gompa is the only *gompa* that opens directly onto the stupa (on the western side). There are some fine paintings and a magnificent Tara covered in beautiful embroideries. Don't miss the massive enclosed prayer wheel on the left of the entrance.

Thrangu Gompa is on the right of the path that leaves to the north of the stupa and belongs to the Kagyud school.

To the right of the lane that runs east from the stupa, the Gelugpa **Samtenling Gompa** is the oldest monastery in Bodhnath, and still attracts large crowds of worshippers and has many young monks.

Northwest of the stupa, **Shechen Tengyi Dargyeling Gompa** is one of the most

recently completed (1984) and impressive *gompas*, established by the famous Nyingmapa lama Dilgo Khyentse Rinpoche to act as an exiled version of Shechen Gompa in eastern Tibet. It has a large and thriving community of over 180 monks and is a popular destination for Tibetan pilgrims. The fine interior decorations are the work of artists from Bhutan. To the right of the main building is the Tsering Art School, whose shop sells incense, CDs and a few Buddhist books.

The Sakyapa sect **Tarik Gompa** to the northeast of the stupa does not have the imposing architectural unity of the others – it has obviously been built in stages over a number of years – but it is no less interesting. There are some high-quality frescoes (inside the vestibule) and the main room is richly gilded and atmospheric. Just east of here is **Tabsang Gompa**, a Kargyud monastery.

North of here, down a side alley, is the large 'white *gompa*' of **Ka-Nying Sheldrup Ling Gompa**, one of the largest monasteries in Bodhnath and has a richly decorated interior with some fine paintings and *thangkas*. The *gompa* hosts an annual seminar on Vajrayana training, usually for two weeks in October (see Courses in the Facts for the Visitor chapter). You'll hear the tap-tap-tapping of handicraft workshops in the street leading up to the monastery.

The new **Tamang Gompa** is currently being built on the north side of the stupa enclosure. A small plaque here honours Ekai Kawaguchi (1866–1945), the first Japanese to make it to Tibet and Bodhnath. For an excellent account of his remarkable travels see Scott Berry's book *A Stranger in Tibet*, available in Thamel bookshops.

Special Events

The Losar (Tibetan New Year) in February or early March is celebrated by large crowds of Tibetan pilgrims. Long copper horns are blown, a portrait of the Dalai Lama is paraded around, and masked dances are performed.

Places to Stay

There are a number of guesthouses in the tangle of lanes north and east of the stupa, which offer an interesting alternative to basing yourself in Kathmandu. Prices are marginally higher than in Thamel.

Kailash Guest House (☎ 4480741; singles/ doubles with shared bathroom Rs 200/250, with private bathroom Rs 250/300) is above a clinic on the road leading north from the Double Dorje Restaurant. It's quite basic, with solar heated water only, but the management is friendly, and the rooms not bad.

Lotus Guest House (☎ 4472320; singles/ doubles with shared bathroom Rs 250/350, with private bathroom Rs 290/390, deluxe rooms Rs 490-750) is a very pleasant option if you want to escape the madness of Kathmandu for some peace and quiet. Rooms are spotlessly clean and spacious, and there is a nice garden and sitting area. The hotel is run by the Tabsang Gompa.

Pema Guest House (☎ 4495662; rooms with shared/private bathroom Rs 350/500, deluxe rooms Rs 850), is a multistorey place right across the lane from Lotus Guest House and has comfortable rooms, clean bathrooms and lots of sun in winter.

Rabsel Guest House (☎ 4479009; w www .rabselguesthouse.com; singles/doubles Rs 620/840, 15% discount May-Aug) is a well-run guest house attached to Shechen Gompa. There's a relaxing garden and an excellent vegetarian restaurant. It's a good choice if you are interested in Tibetan Buddhism.

Dragon Guest House (☎ 4479562; e drag on@ntc.net.np; singles Rs 250, doubles Rs 360-450) is popular for its friendly staff and small garden. It's in the backstreets and hard to find; the easiest way is to head north out of the main gates of Rabsel Guest House. Rooms vary; the sunny side rooms are by far the best.

Happy Valley Guest House (☎ 4471241; e happy@mos.com.np; singles/doubles US$20/ 25, deluxe singles/doubles US$25/30, suites US$50, 25% discount), a modern mid-range hotel north of the main stupa, is also good and is popular with visiting western Buddhists and tour groups. It has excellent rooftop views out over the stupa, but only the deluxe rooms have views from the rooms.

Hotel Padma (☎ 4479052; e hotelpadma@ wlink.com.np; singles/doubles US$18/25, 20% discounts), is a modern place right on the square, but doesn't take advantage of this excellent position as all rooms are inside with no views.

Hotel Norbu Sangpo (☎ 4477301; singles/ doubles US$30/40, 50% discount) is an excellent modern mid-range place in the north of the town, with bright, comfortable and spacious rooms. Corner rooms are generally the best. Suites with kitchen and living room are available for US$300 per month.

Places to Eat

There are a number of restaurants around the stupa itself. Unfortunately, the views are often more inspiring than the food.

An exception is the German-run **Stupa View Terrace & Restaurant** (mains Rs 140-250), which does have a stupendous view. Main meals include an range of vegetarian and Italian dishes, plus some unusual dishes such as zaziki (Rs 140), baked lentil curry with coconut, walnut and spices, and full moon specials. Right next door is the **SV Terrace Restaurant** (mains Rs 70-120), where the food is cheaper but less imaginative.

La Calabria (pasta & pizza Rs 100-150, Sherpa dishes Rs 50), on the eastern edge of the enclosure, is a good-value Italian restaurant run by Maria Sherpa, a resident Italian. The food is surprisingly authentic (foccacia bread!), and there are some cheaper Sherpa dishes. It also has good rooftop views.

Festive Fare Restaurant (Nepali dishes Rs 160-250, Continental dishes Rs 280-315), on the southwest side of the stupa, has rooftop tables with good views and tourist group prices.

Double Dorje Restaurant (☎ 4488947; dishes Rs 50-70) is a cosy Tibetan-run place that's popular with backpackers and the local Dharma crowd, both attracted to comfortable sofa seating and low prices. There's plenty of western food, plus Tibetan specials, but don't be in a hurry as service can be slow. This is a good place to try Tibetan butter tea (Rs 10 a glass) and tsampa (Rs 50; on the menu as 'champa') – roasted barley meal that tastes a bit like porridge.

Rabsel Guest House Vegetarian Restaurant (Rs 70-110) is an oasis of garden calm attached to the Shechen Gompa (see Places to Stay earlier). There are daily specials such as lasagne and quiche, plus soup and homemade bread, and even mulled wine.

For those on a shoestring budget, there are plenty of small Tibetan eating houses in the streets behind the stupa that serve up authentic Tibetan thugpa (noodle soup) – any place with a curtain across an open door is probably one.

For a quick rundown of Tibetan dishes see Food & Drinks in the Facts for the Visitor chapter.

Getting There & Away

Buses to Bodhnath run regularly from Kathmandu's City bus station (Rs 5, 30 minutes). The tempos that leave from Kantipath in Kathmandu (routes 2 and 28) are slightly quicker and more expensive. A taxi is the easiest option at around Rs 100. The road to Bodhnath is very busy and a bit of a nightmare for bicycles. There's also an interesting short walk between Bodhnath and Pashupatinath (see Getting There & Away under Pashupatinath earlier in this section).

AROUND BODHNATH
Kopan Monastery

The Kopan Monastery (☎ 4481268; ⓦ www .kopan-monastery.com), a popular centre for courses on Buddhism and other Tibetan-related subjects, stands on a hilltop to the north of Bodhnath. You can visit Kopan on a walk between Bodhnath and the Gokarna Mahadev Temple.

The centre has short courses on Tibetan medicine, *thangka* painting and other subjects, but the major attraction for Westerners are the 10-day residential courses introducing Buddhist psychology and philosophy. See Courses in the Facts for the Visitor chapter for more details.

When Kopan's founder, Lama Thubten Yeshe, died in 1984 a young Spanish boy, Osel Torres, was declared his reincarnation. The young reincarnation, who was partly the inspiration for Bernardo Bertolucci's film *Little Buddha*, no longer resides at Kopan.

Gokarna Mahadev Temple

Only a short distance northeast of Bodhnath, the Sundarijal road branches north off the Sankhu road and after a couple of kilometres of twists and turns takes you to the old Newari village of Gokarna, 10km from Kathmandu. The village is notable for its fine riverside Shiva temple.

Built in 1582, the triple-roofed Mahadev (Great God) or Gokarneshwar (Lord of Gokarna) Temple stands on the banks of the Bagmati River; its inner sanctum enshrines a particularly revered Shiva lingam. Over the temple entrance is a golden *torana* (a portico that can indicate the god to whom the temple is dedicated), with Shiva and Parvati making an appearance in the centre in the Uma Maheshwar position (where Parvati sits on

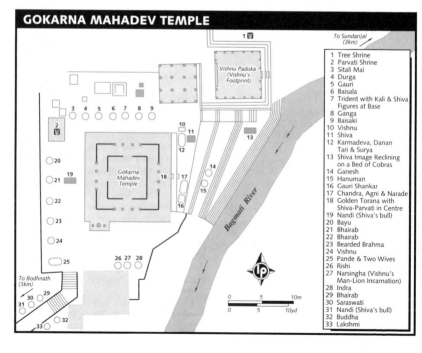

GOKARNA MAHADEV TEMPLE

Vishnu Paduka (Vishnu's Footprint)

Gokarna Mahadev Temple

Bagmati River

To Sundarijal (3km)

To Bodhnath (3km)

1 Tree Shrine
2 Parvati Shrine
3 Sitali Mai
4 Durga
5 Gauri
6 Baisala
7 Trident with Kali & Shiva Figures at Base
8 Ganga
9 Baisaki
10 Vishnu
11 Shiva
12 Karmadeva, Danan Tari & Surya
13 Shiva Image Reclining on a Bed of Cobras
14 Ganesh
15 Hanuman
16 Gauri Shankar
17 Chandra, Agni & Narade
18 Golden Torana with Shiva-Parvati in Centre
19 Nandi (Shiva's bull)
20 Bayu
21 Bhairab
22 Bhairab
23 Bearded Brahma
24 Vishnu
25 Pande & Two Wives
26 Rishi
27 Narsingha (Vishnu's Man-Lion Incarnation)
28 Indra
29 Bhairab
30 Saraswati
31 Nandi (Shiva's bull)
32 Buddha
33 Lakshmi

Shiva's thigh and leans against him) and a figure of the Garuda above them.

The temple's great interest is the surprisingly varied collection of sculptures and reliefs all around the site, some dating back more than a thousand years. They even line the pathway down from the road to the temple courtyard.

The sculptures illustrate an A to Z of Hindu mythology, including early Vedic gods such as Aditya (Sun God), Chandra (Moon God), Indra (on an elephant) and Ganga (with four arms and a pot on her head). Shiva appears in several forms, including as Kamadeva, the God of Love, and Vishnu appears as Narsingha, making a particularly thorough job of disembowelling a nasty demon (see the boxed text 'Narsingha'). The god Gauri Shankar is interesting since it contains elements of both Shiva and Parvati.

The finest of the Gokarna statuary is in the small shrine house, which is in the northwestern corner of the courtyard. This 8th-century sculpture of the beautiful goddess Parvati shows her at her radiant best.

To one side of the main temple, just above the river, is the small, open, single-storey **Vishnu Paduka**. This relatively recent addition shelters a metal plate bearing Vishnu's footprint. Outside, set into the steps above the river, is an image of Shiva reclining on a bed of cobras, just like the reclining Vishnu images at Budhanilkantha and Balaju. To the north, behind the pavilion, is a remarkable shrine that has been almost entirely taken over by a tree that must have started as a seed on its roof.

Those who have recently lost a father often visit the temple, particularly during Gokarna Aunsi, the Nepali equivalent of Father's Day.

The temple guardians here can be touchy about photos being taken, so ask permission before firing away. There's no entry fee.

Getting There & Away

You can walk, cycle, take a minibus (easiest from Bodhnath) or hire a taxi to Gokarna. Expect to pay a Rs 500 return fare from Kathmandu or Rs 150 one way to Bodhnath.

Gokarna–Kopan–Bodhnath Walk

There's also an interesting walking route between Gokarna and Bodhnath via the monastery at Kopan. The clear trail starts from just opposite the Gokarna Mahadev temple, to the right of a roadside statue, and quickly branches left at the Sahayogi Higher Secondary School. After five minutes, branch right onto a new dirt road as it follows the side of a pine-clad hill. You can see the yellow walls of Kopan Monastery ahead atop a hill and the Bodhnath stupa down below in the valley.

After another five to 10 minutes, branch left when you meet a junction with a paved road. The track soon becomes a footpath (OK for mountain bikes). After another five minutes, branch left, passing below a new monastery and follow the hillside to a saddle on the ridge. A couple of minutes later take a path heading uphill to the right – this takes you up the side of another monastery to the entrance of Kopan (45 minutes).

From Kopan, just follow the main road south for 40 minutes to Bodhnath, or jump on one of the frequent minibuses. Before you hit the built-up area of Bodhnath you want to branch left into the village, otherwise you'll end up west of Bodhnath, close to the Hyatt Regency Hotel.

SUNDARIJAL

At the northeastern edge of the valley, around 15km from Kathmandu, the streams

---

Narsingha

The image of Vishnu as Narsingha (or Narsimha) is a common one throughout the valley. In his man-lion incarnation the god is traditionally seen with a demon stretched across his legs, in the act of killing the creature by disembowelling it. You can find Narsingha at work at Changu Narayan, in front of the palace in Patan, just inside the Hanuman Dhoka entrance in Kathmandu and at the Gokarna Mahadev Temple.

The demon was supposedly undefeatable as it could not be killed by man or beast, by day or night or by any weapon. Vishnu's appearance as Narsingha neatly overcame the first obstacle, for a man-lion is neither a man nor a beast. He then waited until dusk to attack the demon, for dusk is neither day nor night. And instead of a weapon Narsingha used his own nails to tear the demon apart.

that eventually join the Bagmati River flow over the waterfalls at Sundarijal into a century-old reservoir. This place is also the starting point for the popular trek to Helambu (see the Trekking chapter for details). The main reservoir that supplies drinking water to the valley is about a two-hour walk uphill from here. A smaller trail forks off before the reservoir to a small rock cave, where a 13th-century image of Mahadevi can be found.

See Hikes from Nagarkot in the Eastern Valley section later in this chapter for details of the long valley-rim walk to Sundarijal from Nagarkot. Buses leave from Kathmandu's City bus station (Rs 20). Otherwise, it's a pleasant bicycle ride along the quiet roads past Gokarna.

BALAJU
The industrial centre of Balaju is less than 2km north of Thamel, just beyond Kathmandu's Ring Rd, and the expansion of the capital has virtually swallowed up this nearby suburb. The only reasons to come here are to see the sleeping Vishnu image in Mahendra Park or hike in the nearby Nagarjun Forest Reserve.

Mahendra Park
The gardens at Balaju were originally constructed in the 18th century and are now known as Mahendra Park (*entry Rs 5; open 7am-7.30pm daily*). They are somewhat of a disappointing – there's a lot of concrete and litter. Most interesting are the statues in the right-hand corner as you enter the park.

The Balaju Vishnu image is said to be a copy of the older image at Budhanilkantha, but there is no positive proof of which one is actually older. Although the king of Nepal cannot visit Budhanilkantha (since he is an incarnation of Vishnu and to gaze on his own image could be disastrous), no such injunction applies to Balaju.

Apart from the Vishnu image, there are a couple of small temples, an interesting group of *chortens* (Tibetan Buddhist stupas) and lingams. The 19th-century Shitala Mai Temple stands in front of the Vishnu image. The 22 painted waterspouts from which the park takes its local name, Bais Dhara Balaju, are in the centre of the park. Entry costs another Rs 2 if you take in a camera.

The **swimming pool** (*entry Rs 40; open 9am-4pm Mar-Sept*) at the back of the park can be very crowded.

Getting There & Away
Tempos, buses and minibuses go to Balaju from Lekhnath Marg, on the northern edge of Thamel.

NAGARJUN FOREST RESERVE
On the hill behind Balaju is the walled Nagarjun Forest Reserve (*entry per person Rs 10, per car/motorcycle Rs 100/30; open 7am-10pm daily*), which is home to pheasants, deer, monkeys and a couple of military posts. This, along with the former Gokarna Park and Pulchowki, is one of the last significant areas of untouched forest in the valley.

A 30km unpaved road and a much more direct footpath lead to the summit, which is a popular Buddhist pilgrimage site. There's a small shrine to Padmasambhava (Guru Rinpoche in Tibetan) and prayer flags stretch across the hilltop. A viewing tower offers one of the valley's widest mountain panoramas, stretching on a clear day all the way from the Annapurnas to Langtang Lirung, via Machhapuchhare, Manaslu and Ganesh himal (a plaque at the bottom of the tower identifies all the peaks). There are also grand views of Kathmandu and its valley laid at your feet to the south.

For details of the enjoyable cardio-hike up to the summit see the boxed text 'The Nagarjun to Ichangu Naryan Hike' later.

Getting There & Away
The main entrance to the reserve, Phulbari gate, is about 2km north of Balaju (a 5km bicycle ride from Thamel). It's not a pleasant walk along the busy main road from Balaju so it makes sense to take a taxi to the gate.

DHUM VARAHI SHRINE
Lying in an unprepossessing schoolyard just inside Kathmandu's Ring Rd to the northeast of Kathmandu city proper, a huge pipal tree encloses a small shrine and a dramatic 5th-century sculpture of Vishnu. Vishnu is shown reincarnated as a wild boar with a stocky human body, holding Prithvi, the earth goddess, on his left elbow.

From a historical point of view, the statue is interesting because it is an original depiction of an animal-human, created before

Statue of the Buddha, Svayambhu Hill, Kathmandu Valley

Group of women, Patan

Prayer beads in the hand of a monk

RYAN FOX

Shrine, Bagmati River bank

RICHARD I'ANSON

Prayer wheels, Minanath temple, Patan

PAUL DYMOND

Shiva lingam, Pashupatinath

BILL WASSMAN

iconographic rules were established, which perhaps contributes to the unusual sense of movement and vitality that the statue possesses. The statue shows Vishnu rescuing Prithvi from the clutches of a demon.

Getting There & Away

A visit to Dhum Varahi is best combined with a visit to Budhanilkantha or Pashupatinath. If you are headed along the Ring Road from Pashupatinath, take a left at the sign for the 'Tiger Overseas Employment Services/ Sherpa Technical Consultant Institute', about 200m north of the bridge over Dhobi River. The statue lies 100m down the dirt track under a huge pipal tree in the grounds of the Shridhumrabarah Primary School.

BUDHANILKANTHA

Vishnu has many incarnations and in Nepal he often appears as Narayan, the creator of all life, the god who reclines on the cosmic sea. From his navel grew a lotus and from the lotus came Brahma, who in turn created the world. Ultimately everything comes from Vishnu, and at Budhanilkantha the legend is set in stone.

The 5m-long image of Vishnu as Narayan was probably created in the 7th or 8th century and is the most impressive, if not the most important, Vishnu shrine in the country. It was sculpted during the Licchavi period, probably somewhere outside the valley and laboriously dragged here.

Narayan lies back peacefully on a most unusual bed: the coils of the multiheaded snake, Ananta. The snake's 11 hooded heads rise protectively around Narayan's head. Narayan's four hands hold the four symbols of Vishnu: a chakra (representing the mind), a mace (primeval knowledge), a conch shell (the four elements) and a lotus seed (the moving universe).

During the early Malla period, Vishnu-ism went into decline as Shiva became the dominant deity. King Jayasthiti Malla is credited with reviving the popularity of Vishnu, he did this in part by claiming to be an incarnation of the multi-incarnated god. To this day, the kings of Nepal make the same claim and because of this they are forbidden, on pain of death, from seeing the image at Budhanilkantha.

The sleeping Vishnu image, which lies in a small sunken pond enclosure, attracts a constant stream of pilgrims, and prayers take place at 9am every morning (the best time for photographs due to the angle of the sun).

The Nagarjun to Ichangu Naryan Hike

The two-hour hike up to the summit of Nagarjun is a great way to temporarily escape the pollution and noise of Kathmandu, without getting too far from the city.

The clear walking trail to the summit of Nagarjun branches off to the right just past the Phulbari gate. It's a steep climb – imagine 90 minutes on a Stairmaster – but it's a great workout and a couple of flat patches allow you to catch your breath. A break in the forest halfway up offers you your first view of hazy Kathmandu below. Take plenty of water and some snacks, as you won't find any en route.

The most direct route down from the summit is to simply return the way you came (or try catching a ride on a tourist or pilgrim bus from the summit, especially at weekends). Don't take the road if you're on foot – it's 30km long.

A more interesting option is to walk back to Kathmandu via Ichangu Naryan, making for a total hike of around five hours. The most direct route in this case is to take the steep and slippery trail (don't try it after rainfall) that drops down the hillside from a couple of concrete picnic areas draped in prayer flags southeast of the summit. Take care not to sprain an ankle as you won't find any fellow hikers up here. The faint trail is hard on the knees and toes for the first 20 minutes, but then dips into a rivulet and follows a ridge east. Around 45 minutes from the summit you'll hit the road that runs between Phulbari gate and the summit.

Turn right at the road and walk for 30m and you'll see a trail dropping to the south. Take this trail and after 10 minutes or so you'll reach the first house on the valley side. A path passes in front of this house and then drops down to a path, which becomes a track and joins the main dirt road by a local store after about 30 minutes. From here you can head right to Ichangu Naryan (20 minutes) or left to Swayambhunath (30 minutes).

Vishnu is supposed to sleep through the four monsoon months, waking at the end of the monsoon. A great festival takes place at Budhanilkantha each November, on the day Vishnu is supposed to awaken from his long annual slumber (for dates see the Festivals of Nepal special section).

Non-Hindus cannot enter the enclosure, but there are some unobstructed views from outside the fence surrounding it. There's no entry fee but there is a Rs 5 parking fee, which is money well spent.

Places to Stay

Park Village Hotel (☎ 4375289; e pvh@ nepalhotel.com; rooms US$60-90, up to 50% discount) is a peaceful mid-range retreat just downhill from the Vishnu image. Rooms are all south facing, away from the hills but towards the winter sun, and are set in a two-hectare garden, with lots of sitting areas and even a meditation room. There are plans for a health club and a pool. Rooms are spacious and most come with some sort of balcony area (the deluxe rooms are as comfortable as the suites and a lot cheaper).

The hotel is run by the people who own the Kathmandu Guest House and you'll often get the best discount by booking at the travel desk there. Ask about a lift on the free shuttle bus when booking.

Getting There & Away

Buses to Budhanilkantha (Rs 6) as well as minibuses and tempos (Rs 8, route 5) leave from the Kathmandu City bus station (one hour). The shrine is about 100m uphill from the bus and tempo terminus. From Thamel a taxi costs around Rs 200.

By bicycle it's a gradual, uphill haul of 15km – hard, sweaty work rewarded with a very pleasant return trip. You could pause at Dhum Varahi Shrine on the way back.

Patan

☎ 01 • pop 160,000

Patan (**pa**-tan) is separated from Kathmandu by the Bagmati River and is the second-largest town in the valley. It has historically been known by the names Yala and Lalitpur, the latter of which means 'City of Beauty'. Patan has a long Buddhist history and the four corners of the city are marked by stupas

said to have been erected by the great Buddhist emperor Ashoka around 250 BC. Later inscriptions refer to palaces in the city in the 5th century AD, although Patan's great building boom took place under the Mallas in the 16th, 17th and 18th centuries.

Patan's central Durbar Square is packed with temples, with a far greater concentration of architecture per square metre than in Kathmandu or Bhaktapur. Numerous other temples of widely diverse style, as well as many *bahals* (Buddhist monasteries), are scattered around the fascinating old town.

Patan makes a great day trip from Kathmandu. It is possible to stay the night here, although it's so close to Kathmandu that it's not really necessary. The choice of accommodation and restaurants is far more limited, but on the bright side the old town is quieter and less polluted than Kathmandu and you'll likely have the town largely to yourself at the beginning and end of the day.

ORIENTATION & INFORMATION

Durbar Square forms the heart of Patan. From here, four main roads lead to the four Ashoka stupas (see the 'Ashoka Stupas' boxed text later in this section). Jawlakhel, to the southwest of the city, has a major Tibetan population and is the centre for carpet-weaving in the valley. South of Jawlakhel is the Kathmandu ring road.

Buses from Kathmandu drop you at Patan Dhoka, the original entrance to the city, about a 15-minute walk from Durbar Square. Taxis might drop you here, but will probably continue to the south side of Durbar Square. The Lagankhel bus station, 10 minutes' walk south of Durbar Square, near the Southern (Lagan) Stupa, has a few bus services to the southern Kathmandu Valley.

Patan Hospital (☎ 5521034), in the Lagankhel district, is the best in the Kathmandu Valley (see Information in the Kathmandu chapter for details).

NORTH OF DURBAR SQUARE

The following sights are north of Durbar Square (see the Patan map) and can be visited as part of the Patan Walking Tour (see the boxed text 'Patan Walking Tour').

Golden Temple

Also sometimes known as the Kwa Bahal or the Suwarna Mahavihara (Golden Temple), this unique Buddhist monastery *(entry Rs 25, open dawn-dusk daily)* is just north of Durbar Square. Legends relate that the monastery was founded in the 12th century, although the earliest record of its existence is 1409. From the street, a sign points to the monastery, entered through a doorway flanked by painted guardian lion figures, giving no hint of the magnificent structure within.

The large rectangular building has three roofs and a copper-gilded facade. Inside the shrine are images of the Buddha and Avalo kiteshvara; a stairway leads up to the 1st floor, where monks will show you the various Tibetan-style frescoes that illustrate the walls. The life of the Buddha is illustrated in a frieze that you'll see in front of the main shrine.

The inner courtyard has a railed walkway around three sides. Shoes and other leather articles must be removed if you leave the walkway and enter the inner courtyard. In the centre of the courtyard is a small, richly decorated temple with a golden roof that has an extremely ornate *gajur* (bell-shaped top). Look for the sacred tortoises pottering around in the courtyard – they are temple guardians.

Kumbeshwar Temple

Directly north of Durbar Square is Kumbeshwar Temple, one of the valley's three five-storey temples. The temple dominates the surrounding streets and is said to date from 1392, making it the oldest temple in Patan. The temple is noted for its graceful proportions and fine woodcarvings.

The statues and sculptures around the courtyard date from a number of Nepali dynasties, from the Licchavis to the Mallas, and includes a particularly fine Ganesh figure. The temple is, however, dedicated to Shiva, as indicated by the large Nandi, or bull, facing the temple.

The temple platform has two ponds whose water is said to come straight from the holy lake at Gosainkund, a long trek north of the valley (see Via Gosainkund under Langtang Trek in the Trekking chapter). An annual ritual bath in the Kumbeshwar Temple's tank is claimed to be as meritorious as making the arduous walk to Gosainkund.

On the southeastern edge of the courtyard, behind a black lacquered grill, is an important **Bhairab Temple**, with a life-size wooden image of the god. Next door is the single-storey **Baglamukhi Temple**. On the western side of the Kumbeshwar Temple courtyard is the large **Konti Hiti**, a popular gathering place for local women. On the northern side is the Kumbeshwar Technical School (see Shopping later in this section).

Thousands of pilgrims visit the temple during the Janai Purnima festival in July or August each year to worship the silver and gold lingam that is set up in the tank. It's a colourful occasion: bathers immerse themselves in the tank while members of the Brahmin and Chhetri castes replace the sacred thread they wear looped over their left shoulder. *Jhankris* (faith healers) beating drums and wearing colourful headdresses and skirts dance around the temple to complete the dramatic scene.

Uma Maheshwar Temple

En route from Kumbeshwar Temple to Durbar Square, the small and inconspicuous double-roofed Uma Maheshwar Temple is set back from the road on its eastern side. Peer inside the temple (a light will help) to see a very beautiful black-stone relief of Shiva and Parvati in the pose known as Uma Maheshwar – the god sitting cross-legged with his *shakti* (consort) leaning against him rather seductively. A similarly named temple near the Golden Temple has a similar statue.

SOUTH OF DURBAR SQUARE

The following sights are south of Durbar Square in the backstreets of the bustling Haugal district (see the Patan map).

Bishwakarma Temple

Walk south from Durbar Square, past several brassware shops and workshops. There is a small *bahal* almost immediately on your right (west) and then a laneway also leading west. A short distance down this lane is the brick Bishwakarma Temple, with its entire facade covered in sheets of embossed copper. Directly above the doorway is what looks like a Star of David. The temple is dedicated to carpenters and craftspeople and, as if in proof, you can often hear the steady clump and clang of metalworkers' hammers from nearby workshops.

[Continued on page 185]

AROUND THE KATHMANDU VALLEY

DURBAR SQUARE (PATAN)

As in Kathmandu, the ancient Royal Palace of Patan faces on to a durbar (royal square) and this concentrated mass of temples is undoubtedly the most visually stunning display of Newari architecture to be seen in Nepal. The rectangular square has its longer axis running approximately north–south and the palace forms the eastern side of the square. A continuous row of temples in widely diverse styles faces the palace on the western side.

The square rose to its full glory during the Malla period (14th to 18th centuries), and particularly during the reign of King Siddhinarsingh Malla (1619–60). Patan's major commercial district, the Mangal Bazaar, runs to the southern edge of the square.

An entry fee of Rs 200 is payable at the southern end of Durbar Square. For repeated visits to Durbar Square ensure that your visa validity date is written on the back of your ticket.

Bhimsen Temple (8) At the northern end of Durbar Square, the Bhimsen Temple is dedicated to the god of trade and business, which possibly explains its well-kept and prosperous look. Bhimsen, a hero of the *Mahabharata*, was said to be extraordinarily strong. Look out for the place settings with bowls, spoons and cups nailed up on the roof struts as offerings.

The three-storey temple has had a chequered history. Although it is not known when it was first built, an inscription records that it was rebuilt in 1682 after a fire. Restorations also took place after the great 1934 earthquake, and again in 1967. A lion tops a pillar in front of the temple, while the brick building has an artificial marble facade and a gilded facade on the 1st floor.

Manga Hiti (6) Immediately north of the palace is the sunken Manga Hiti, one of the water conduits with which Patan, and even more so Bhaktapur are so liberally endowed. This one has a lotus-shaped pool and three wonderfully carved stone *maksara* (mythological crocodiles) head waterspouts. Next to it is the **Mani Mandap (7)**, a pavilion built in 1700 and used for royal coronations.

Vishwanath Temple (9) South of the Bhimsen Temple stands the Vishwanath (Shiva) Temple. This elaborately decorated two-storey temple was built in 1627 and has two large stone elephants guarding the front entrance. The pillars are particularly ornate. Shiva's vehicle, the bull, is on the other side of the temple, while inside is a large *lingam* (phallic symbol). The temple has been restored in recent years.

Krishna Mandir (11) Continuing into the square, the third temple you reach is the Krishna Mandir, which is dedicated to Krishna and was built by King Siddhinarsingh Malla. Records indicate that the temple was completed with the installation of the image on the 1st floor in 1637. With its strong Mughal influences, this stone temple is clearly of Indian design, unlike the nearby brick-and-timber, multiroofed Newari temples. The 1st and 2nd floors

Krishna Mandir

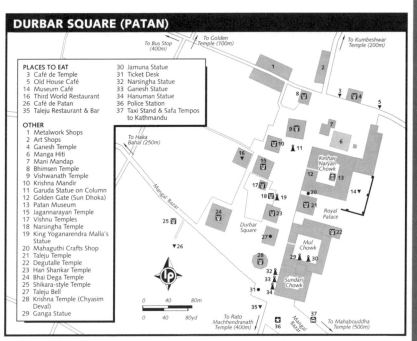

DURBAR SQUARE (PATAN)

To Bus Stop (400m)
To Golden Temple (100m)
To Kumbeshwar Temple (200m)

PLACES TO EAT
3 Café de Temple
5 Old House Café
14 Museum Café
16 Third World Restaurant
26 Café de Patan
35 Taleju Restaurant & Bar

OTHER
1 Metalwork Shops
2 Art Shops
4 Ganesh Temple
6 Manga Hiti
7 Mani Mandap
8 Bhimsen Temple
9 Vishwanath Temple
10 Krishna Mandir
11 Garuda Statue on Column
12 Golden Gate (Sun Dhoka)
13 Patan Museum
15 Jagannarayan Temple
17 Vishnu Temples
18 Narsingha Temple
19 King Yoganarendra Malla's Statue
20 Mahaguthi Crafts Shop
21 Taleju Temple
22 Degutalle Temple
23 Hari Shankar Temple
24 Bhai Dega Temple
25 Shikara-style Temple
27 Taleju Bell
28 Krishna Temple (Chyasim Deval)
29 Ganga Statue

30 Jamuna Statue
31 Ticket Desk
32 Narsingha Statue
33 Ganesh Statue
34 Hanuman Statue
36 Police Station
37 Taxi Stand & Safa Tempos to Kathmandu

To Haka Bahal (250m)

Mangal Bazar

Keshav Narayan Chowk

Royal Palace

Durbar Square

Mul Chowk

Sundari Chowk

To Rato Machhendranath Temple (400m)

Mangal Bazar

To Mahabouddha Temple (500m)

0   40   80m
0   40   80yd

of this temple are made up of a line of pavilions, from the top of which rises a shikhara-style (corncob-like) spire. Musicians can often be heard playing upstairs.

Krishna is an incarnation of Vishnu, so the god's vehicle, the man-bird Garuda, kneels with folded arms on top of a **column (11)** facing the temple. The stone carvings along the beam above the 1st-floor pillars recount events of the Mahabharata, while on the 2nd floor there are scenes from the Ramayana (see the boxed text 'The Romance of Rama' in The Terai & Mahabharat Range chapter for more). These fine friezes are accompanied by explanations in Newari of the narrative scenes. Non-Hindus are not allowed inside.

A major festival is held here in August/September (Bhadra) for Krishna's birthday, Krishnasthami.

Jagannarayan Temple (15) The two-storey brick Jagannarayan (or Charnarayan) Temple is dedicated to Narayan, one of Vishnu's incarnations. Dating from 1565, it is reputed to be the oldest temple in the square, although an alternative date in the late 1600s has also been suggested. The temple stands on a brick plinth with large stone lions, above which are two guardian figures. The roof struts are carved with explicit erotic figures.

King Yoganarendra Malla's Statue (19) Immediately north of the Hari Shankar Temple (see following) is a tall column topped by a figure of King Yoganarendra Malla. The golden figure of the kneeling king, atop a lotus bud and protected by the hood of a cobra, has been facing towards his palace since the year 1700. On top of the cobra's head is the figure of a bird; legend has it that as long as the bird remains there the king may still return to his palace. Accordingly, a door and window of the palace are always kept open and a *hookah* (a water pipe used for smoking) is kept ready for the king should he return. A rider to the legend adds that when the bird flies off, the elephants in front of the Vishwanath Temple will stroll over to the Manga Hiti for a drink!

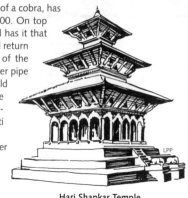

Behind the statue of the king are three smaller Vishnu temples. The small, plastered *shikhara*-style temple was built in 1590 and is dedicated to Narsingha, Vishnu's man-lion incarnation.

Hari Shankar Temple

Hari Shankar Temple (23) This three-storey temple to Hari Shankar, the half-Vishnu, half-Shiva deity, has roof struts carved with scenes of the tortures of the damned – a strange contrast to the erotic scenes on the Jagannarayan. It was built in 1704–5 by the daughter of King Yoganarendra Malla.

Taleju Bell (27) Diagonally opposite Taleju Temple in the palace complex, the large bell, hanging between two stout pillars, was erected by King Vishnu Malla in 1736. An earlier bell, erected in 1703, was then moved to the Rato Machhendranath Temple. Petitioners could ring the bell to alert the king to their grievances. Shop stalls are in the building under the bell platform, and behind it is a lotus-shaped pool with a bridge over it.

Krishna Temple (28) This attractive, octagonal stone temple, also known as the Chyasim Deval, completes the 'front line' of temples in the square. The stairway to the temple, which faces the palace's Sundari Chowk, is guarded by two stone lions. The temple was built in 1723 and, like the square's Krishna Mandir (see earlier), is a stark contrast to the usual Newari pagoda temple designs.

Bhai Dega Temple (24) Behind the Krishna Temple stands the squat Bhai Dega, or Biseshvar, dedicated to Shiva. It's a singularly unattractive temple, although it is said to contain an impressive lingam. A few steps back from the square is another stone ***shikhara*-style temple (25)**, clearly owing inspiration to the important Krishna Mandir of the square. This same design pops up in several other temples around Patan.

Royal Palace Forming the whole eastern side of the Durbar Square is the Royal Palace of Patan. Parts of the palace were built in the 14th century, but the main construction was during the 17th and 18th centuries by Siddhinarsingh Malla, Srinivasa Malla and Vishnu Malla. The Patan palace predates the palaces of Kathmandu and Bhaktapur. It was severely damaged during the conquest of the valley by Prithvi Narayan Shah in 1768 and also by the great earthquake of 1934, but it remains one of the architectural highlights of the valley, with a series of connecting courtyards and three temples dedicated to the valley's main deity, the goddess Taleju.

Keshav Naryan Chowk The northern courtyard of the Royal Palace and museum are entered from the square by the **Golden Gate (12)**, or Sun Dhoka. Completed in 1734, this is the newest part of the palace. The courtyard is entered through a magnificent gilded door topped by a golden *torana* (portico above the door indicating to whom the temple is dedicated) showing Shiva, Parvati, Ganesh and Kumar. Directly above the golden door is a golden window, at which the king would make public appearances.

Patan Museum (13) This part of the palace around Keshav Naryan Chowk has been superbly renovated and houses one of the subcontinent's finest museums (☎ *521492; entry Rs 250, SAARC countries Rs 50; open 10.30am-5.30pm daily)*. There have been some modern elements added to the building as part of the renovations, and the result is a beautiful synthesis of old and new.

The main feature of the museum is an outstanding collection of cast-bronze and gilt-copper work, mostly of Hindu and Buddhist deities. One gallery shows the stages involved in the production of hammered sheet-metal relief designs (known as *repoussé*) and the 'lost-wax' (*thajya* in Nepali) method of casting. In another there are also some fascinating photos of Patan at the turn of the 19th and 20th centuries. The text gives an excellent introduction to Nepal's Buddhist and Hindu iconography, religion and art.

You need at least an hour, and preferably two, to do this place justice. There's so much to take in that it's worth taking a break at the excellent Museum Café (see Places to Eat in the Patan section of the Around the Kathmandu Valley chapter) before diving in for another round. The café is in a rear courtyard, which was used for dance and drama performances during the Malla period. The museum also has a shop and toilets.

For a sneak preview of the museum's highlights and the story of its renovation check out its website at ⓦ www.patanmuseum.gov.np.

Taleju Temple

Mul Chowk The central courtyard is the largest and oldest of the palace's three main *chowks* (squares). Two stone lions guard the entrance to the courtyard, which was built by Siddhinarsingh Malla, destroyed in a fire in 1662 and rebuilt by Srinivasa Malla in 1665-6. At the centre of the courtyard stands a small, gilded Bidya Temple.

The palace's three Taleju temples stand around the courtyard. The doorway to the Shrine of Taleju or Taleju Bhawani, on the southern side of the courtyard, is flanked by the statues of two river goddesses **Ganga (29)** on one side on a tortoise, and **Jamuna (30)** on the other on a nice mythical (crocodile).

The five-storey **Degutalle Temple (22)**, topped by its octagonal triple-roofed tower, is on the northeastern corner of the square. The larger, square, triple-roofed **Taleju Temple (21)** is directly north, looking out over Durbar Square. It was built by Siddhinarsingh Malla in 1640, rebuilt after a fire and rebuilt after the 1934 earthquake, which completely demolished it. The goddess Taleju was the personal deity of the Malla kings from the 14th century, and Tantric rites were performed to her in this temple.

Sundari Chowk South of Mul Chowk is the smaller Sundari Chowk, with its superbly carved sunken water tank known as the Tusha Hiti. The courtyard is currently closed, though guardians of Mul Chowk slyly offer to show people around for a *baksheesh* (tip) of Rs 100 to Rs 200. Don't encourage them. Behind Sundari Chowk, and also not open to the public, is the Royal Garden and Kamal Pokhari water tank.

Back in main Durbar Square the blocked-off entrance to Sundari Chowk is guarded by stone statues of **Hanuman (34)**, **Ganesh (33)** and Vishnu as **Narsingha (32)**, the man-lion. The gilded metal window over the entrance from the square is flanked by windows of carved ivory.

[Continued from page 179]

Minanath Temple

Further south is a two-storey temple dedicated to a Buddhist Bodhisattva who is considered to be the brother of Rato Machhendranath (see following). The Minanath image is towed around town during the Rato Machhendranath festival, but in a much smaller chariot. The quiet temple dates from the Licchavi period (3rd to 9th centuries), but has undergone several recent restorations and has roof struts carved with figures of multi-armed goddesses, all brightly painted. A large prayer wheel stands in a cage beside the temple and there's a large *hiti* in front.

Rato Machhendranath Temple

South of Durbar Square, on the western side of the road, is the Rato (Red) Machhendranath Temple. Rato Machhendranath, the god of rain and plenty, comes in a variety of incarnations. To Buddhists he is the Tantric edition of Avalokiteshvara, while to Hindus he is another version of Shiva.

Standing in a large courtyard, the three-storey temple dates from 1673, although an

Patan Walking Tour

The Patan Tourist Development Organisation has developed a fascinating walk that winds its way through the complex interlinked courtyards and laneways of the old town. It's great fun to dive through the tunnelled passageways into hidden courtyards. Moreover, the route gives an insight into the communal lifestyle and traditional structure of Newari villages.

The walk is marked on the Patan map and outlined briefly here, but is described in more detail in a recommended small booklet entitled *Patan Walkabout* (Rs 100), which is available from the bookshop at Pathan Dhoka. The walk starts at the Pathan Dhoka, ends at Durbar Square and takes about an hour.

The Route

Walk through Pathan Dhoka to the nearby **Ganesh shrine** and its popular water well, then turn right into **Sulima Square**, with its central 17th-century Shiva shrine. On the east side of the square is the semi-destroyed house of a famous 16th-century Tantric master; on the south side is a shrine with a fine wooden balustrade.

Continue south to the **Pim Bahal Pokhari** pond and go round it anticlockwise, past the Chandeshwari Temple to a large 600-year old whitewashed stupa that was damaged by the Muslim invader Shams-ud-din in the 14th century.

At the road junction take the angled road northeast past some fine wooden windows to an open courtyard. On the south side is the **Lokakirti Mahavihar**, once a monastery and now a school. As you enter the monastery compound you will step over the wooden frame of the chariot used to transport Rato Machhendranath during his festival (see the Festivals of Nepal special section for details). Masked dances are performed at festival time on the *dabali* (platform) in front of the monastery.

Look for the alley leading north off the square, signposted 'Bhaskar Varna Mahabihar', to the **Nyakachuka Courtyard**. There's always something going on in this interesting courtyard. Look for the central stupas and the deities painted over the lintels on the right (east) side of the square. Head to the eastern wall, to the end of a row of four stupas, and go through the covered alley into another courtyard, the **Naga Bahal**. Walk past the statue of a bull to a **hiti** (water tank) and look for the painting of a naga on the wall, repainted every five years during the Samyak festival.

Go through the eastern passageway to a further **courtyard** with the Harayana library in the corner. Follow a diagonal path to a stupa with prayer wheels in its four corners. Behind is an excellent carved wooden monastery shrine room. Pass through the nearby wooden torana into the back courtyard of the **Golden Temple** (see the main text). After visiting the temple, exit east onto the main street, turn left and after 10m you'll see a sign for yet another courtyard, the **Manjushri Temple**. From here continue north past a group of ancient megaliths, possibly the oldest objects of worship in the entire Kathmandu Valley, down to the Kumbeshwar Temple (see the main text). From here head east and then south back to Durbar Square via the **Uma Maheshwar Temple** (see the main text) and **Rada Krishna Temple**.

PATAN

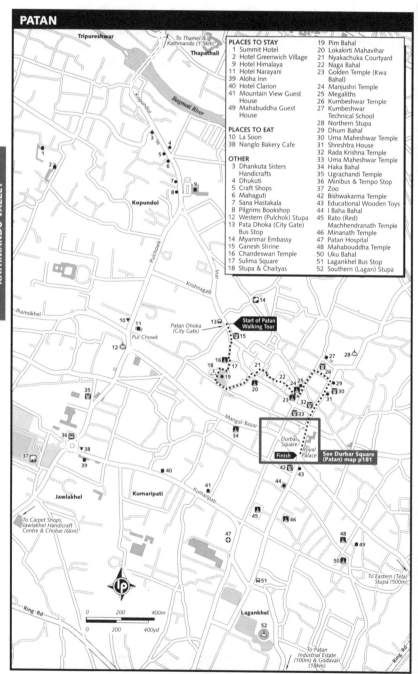

PLACES TO STAY
1 Summit Hotel
2 Hotel Greenwich Village
9 Hotel Himalaya
11 Hotel Narayani
39 Aloha Inn
40 Hotel Clarion
41 Mountain View Guest House
49 Mahabuddha Guest House

PLACES TO EAT
10 La Soon
38 Nanglo Bakery Cafe

OTHER
3 Dhankuta Sisters Handicrafts
4 Dhukuti
5 Craft Shops
6 Mahaguti
7 Sana Hastakala
8 Pilgrims Bookshop
12 Western (Pulchok) Stupa
13 Pata Dhoka (City Gate) Bus Stop
14 Myanmar Embassy
15 Ganesh Shrine
16 Chandeswari Temple
17 Sulima Square
18 Stupa & Chaityas
19 Pim Bahal
20 Lokakirti Mahavihar
21 Nyakachuka Courtyard
22 Naga Bahal
23 Golden Temple (Kwa Bahal)
24 Manjushri Temple
25 Megaliths
26 Kumbeshwar Temple
27 Kumbeshwar Technical School
28 Northern Stupa
29 Dhum Bahal
30 Uma Maheshwar Temple
31 Shreshtra House
32 Rada Krishna Temple
33 Uma Maheshwar Temple
34 Haka Bahal
35 Ugrachandi Temple
36 Minibus & Tempo Stop
37 Zoo
42 Bishwakarma Temple
43 Educational Wooden Toys
44 I Baha Bahal
45 Rato (Red) Machhendranath Temple
46 Minanath Temple
47 Patan Hospital
48 Mahabouddha Temple
50 Uku Bahal
51 Lagankhel Bus Stop
52 Southern (Lagan) Stupa

earlier temple may have existed on the site since 1408. The temple's four carved doorways are each guarded by lion figures and at ground level on the four corners of the temple plinth are reliefs of a curious yeti-like demon known as a *kyah*. A diverse collection of animals (including peacocks, horses, bulls, lions, elephants and fish) tops the pillars facing the northern side of the temple. The metal roof is supported by struts, each showing Avalokiteshvara standing above figures being tortured in hell. Prayer wheels are set into the base of the temple.

The Machhendranath image is a crudely carved piece of red-painted wood, but each year during the Rato Machhendranath celebrations it's paraded around the town on a temple chariot. The celebration moves the image from place to place over several weeks in the month of Baisakh (April/May), ending at Jawlakhel, where the chariot is dismantled.

Occurring on a 12-year cycle (most recently in 2003), the procession continues out of Patan to the village of Bungamati, 5km to the south. Dragging the heavy chariot along this bumpy and often uphill track is no easy feat. In the village the god has another temple where, since 1593, it has been the custom for the image to spend six months of each year. See the Festivals of Nepal special section for more details.

Mahabouddha Temple

Despite its height, the Mahabouddha Temple (Temple of a Thousand Buddhas) is obscured because it's surrounded by other buildings. It's a *shikhara* (Indian-style) temple, modelled on the Mahabouddha Temple at Bodhgaya in India, where the Buddha gained enlightenment. The temple takes its name from the terracotta tiles with which it is covered, each bearing an image of the Buddha. The building probably dates from 1585, but suffered severe damage in the 1934 earthquake and was totally rebuilt. Unfortunately, without plans to work from, the builders ended up with a different-looking temple and there were enough bricks left over to construct a *shikhara*-style shrine to Maya Devi, the Buddha's mother, which stands to the southwest of the Mahabouddha.

The Mahabouddha Temple is about 10 minutes' walk southeast of Durbar Square. A signpost points down a lane full of curio shops leading to the temple; if you have trouble finding it, simply ask directions. The roof terrace of the shops at the back of the courtyard has a good view of the temple.

Uku Bahal (Rudra Varna Mahavihar)

This Buddhist monastery near the Mahabouddha Temple is one of the best known in Patan. A large rectangular structure with two-storey gilded roofs encloses a courtyard absolutely packed with interesting bits and pieces. There are *dorjes* (thunderbolt symbols of Buddhist power), bells, peacocks, elephants, Garudas, rampant goats, kneeling devotees and a regal-looking statue of a Rana general. The lions are curious, seated on pillars with one paw raised in salute, looking as if they should be guarding a statue of Queen Victoria in her 'not-amused' incarnation, rather than a colourful Nepali monastery.

As you enter the courtyard from the north look for the finely carved wooden struts straight ahead. They are said to be among the oldest of this type in the valley and prior to restoration they were actually behind the monastery, but were moved to this safer location inside the courtyard. The monastery in its present form probably dates from the

Ashoka Stupas

The four stupas marking the boundaries of Patan are said to have been built when the great Buddhist emperor Ashoka visited the valley 2500 years ago, and are the Kathmandu Valley's oldest Buddhist monuments. Although remains of all four can still be seen today, they probably bear little similarity to the original stupas.

The northern stupa is just beyond the Kumbeshwar Temple, not far from Durbar Square. It's well preserved and whitewashed. The other three are all grassed over. The Southern, or Lagan, Stupa is just south of the Lagankhel bus stop and is the largest of the four. The smaller western, or Pulchok Stupa is beside the main road from Kathmandu that runs through to Jawlakhel and across from the Hotel Narayani. Finally, the small Eastern, or Teta, Stupa is well to the east of centre, across Kathmandu's Ring Rd and just beyond a small river.

19th century, but certain features and the actual site are much older.

HAKA BAHAL

Take the road west from the southern end of Durbar Square, past Café de Patan, and you come to the Haka Bahal, a rectangular building with an internal courtyard (see the Patan map). Traditionally, Patan's Kumari (living goddess) is a daughter of one of the priests of this monastery.

ZOO

Nepal's only zoo (Patan map; adult/child Rs 100/50, camera Rs 10; open 10am-6pm Tues-Sun, last entry 5pm) is in the southwestern part of Patan, just north of Jawlakhel. It includes a reasonably extensive collection of Nepali wildlife, including rhinos, tigers, leopards, monkeys and birds. While it is yet another depressing animal prison, it is a quiet, shady place and you can hire pedal boats for a paddle around the lake. There's also a small aquarium here. Keen naturalists, students of the grotesque and young kids may still enjoy a visit.

PLACES TO STAY

There's a small but decent spread of accommodation for all budgets in Patan and a few tourists base themselves here.

Places to Stay – Budget

The **Mahabuddha Guest House** (Patan map; ☎ 5540575; e nfosterm@wlink.com.np; singles/doubles Rs 180/300, dorm beds Rs 80), near Mahabouddha Temple southeast of Durbar Square, is comfortable and in an atmospheric location. Rooms in the old block are with shared bathroom; new block rooms have attached bathroom, which the management says will cost the same. The singles are much smaller than doubles, and the four-bed dorms have bathrooms. Prices for laundry and breakfast are good value.

Mountain View Guest House (Patan map; ☎ 5538168; singles/doubles with shared bathroom Rs 180/280, with private bathroom Rs 250/350) is between Jawlakhel and Durbar Square, down a side street off the main road. It's not great, with small rooms, sullen staff and noise from the neighbouring motorbike repair workshop, but it is a cheap option.

Café de Patan (Durbar Square map; ☎ 5537599; e pcafe@ntc.net.np; singles/ doubles with shared bathroom Rs 300/400, with private bathroom Rs 500/600) has a handful of good-value rooms around and above its pleasant café courtyard (see Places to Eat later). Rooms are bright, clean and of a good size, though for any kind of view you'll have to head up to the rooftop. There are only two rooms with attached bathrooms. There's a worrying karaoke machine in the main bar/lounge.

Places to Stay – Mid-Range & Top End

All of these places appear on the Patan map unless otherwise stated.

Aloha Inn (☎ 5522796; e info@alohainn .com; singles/doubles US$30/40, deluxe singles/doubles US$35/45, up to 30% discount) is located in the Jawlakhel area, a bit far to walk from the old city. It's a friendly place that's clean, quiet, a little plain and a little overpriced. Bigger deluxe rooms come with a desk and fridge.

Hotel Clarion (☎ 5524512; e clarion@ wlink.com.np; singles/doubles US$50/60, 50% discount), near the Aloha Inn on the main drag, is set in a pleasant garden but is still close to the noisy road – ask for a room at the back. The comfortable, well-kept rooms have TV, phone and private bathroom, and are popular with aid consultants.

Patan also has a number of top-end hotels, although none of them are close enough to the interesting centre of the old city to be particularly convenient.

Summit Hotel (Kathmandu map; ☎ 552 1810; w www.summit-nepal.com; budget singles/doubles US$25/35, better rooms from US$65/75, 20% discount Oct-Apr, 35% discount May-Sept) tops a hillock in the Kopundol area and has great views across the river to Kathmandu and the distant mountains. It's a relaxed, stylish Dutch-run resort with a very beautiful garden, a swimming pool in summer and open fires in the winter. The garden wing rooms are a little small but all have modern bathrooms and lovely sitting areas. The spacious budget rooms are in a separate block with clean, shared bathrooms and a sitting area but no views. These rooms are the only ones not discounted in the high season (but there are 30% discounts in the summer). There's a pleasant bar and the garden restaurant turns out superb food.

Hotel Greenwich Village (Kathmandu map; ☎ 5521780; W www.godavariresort.com.np; singles/doubles US$60/70, deluxe rooms US$80, 50% discount), also topping the Kopundol hill near Summit Hotel, is very peaceful (unless a tour group is in residence), with a lovely poolside terrace and café. Rooms are a little old-fashioned but decent.

Hotel Narayani (☎ 5525015; W www .go-nepal.com; singles/doubles US$70/85, 25% discount) has a garden and a swimming pool. It's professionally run but rooms are a little old-fashioned.

Hotel Himalaya (Kathmandu map; ☎ 552 3900; singles/doubles US$110/120, 40% discount), modern and marbly, has terrific views, a swimming pool, tennis and badminton courts, folk dancing in the restaurant twice a week and comfortable rooms (but little intimacy). The hotel has five shuttle buses a day to the Kathmandu city centre.

PLACES TO EAT
Most of Patan's restaurants overlook Durbar Square and are aimed at day-tripping tour groups. Prices are inflated but not outrageously so and the views are superb. See the Durbar map unless otherwise stated.

Café de Patan (dishes Rs 60-150), just a few steps from the southwestern corner of Durbar Square, is a small, long-running favourite, with a pleasant open-air courtyard and a rooftop garden (with one table right at the very top of the building). It's a good place for a drink, snack or even a meal. It turns out a superb lassi and a number of good-value dishes, such as pizza and chicken.

Third World Restaurant (meals Rs 150-250), on the quiet western side of the square, has a brilliant rooftop area with views over Patan and, on a clear day, pagodas with a Himalayan backdrop.

Café de Temple (mains Rs 125-215, set meal Rs 200-300) on the northern edge of the square, has excellent rooftop views, and an ambitious menu, with snacks and main meals (continental, Indian and Chinese).

Old House Café (mains Rs 150-250, set Nepali meal Rs 250-290), true to its name, is set in an old Newari house. It's in the northeastern corner of the square, but is tucked into the least interesting corner and doesn't have views of the square. Prices are more reasonable here than elsewhere.

Museum Café (light meals Rs 110-240, coffee Rs 60), in the rear courtyard of the Patan Museum, is an excellent open-air place operated by the Summit Hotel. Prices are a little higher than elsewhere, but the gorgeous setting more than compensates.

Taleju Restaurant & Bar (mains Rs 75-110) is at the southern end of the square. Head for the 5th-floor terrace, as the views from here are outstanding, especially on a clear day when you have the snow-capped Ganesh himal as a great backdrop. The prices are the most reasonable in the square, making this the best budget bet with a view.

Near the zoo roundabout at Jawlakhel is the **Nanglo Bakery Café** (Patan map). It's a good place to drop in for a snack.

La Soon (Patan map; ☎ 5535290; light lunches Rs 120-170, dinners Rs 220; open 10.30am-10pm Mon-Sat) is a bright restaurant popular at lunch with local aid workers. The food is international with good quality pasta, feta wraps and peanut soup.

SHOPPING
Patan has many small handicraft shops; it is the best place in the valley for certain crafts. The Tibetan Jawlakhel area in Patan's southwest is great for Tibetan crafts and carpets.

The **Patan Industrial Estate**, in the south of Patan, doesn't sound like a very promising place to shop for handicrafts. It is, however, more like a large compound, containing a number of handicraft factory-cum-showrooms. While these places are definitely aimed at the group tourist, there is nothing to stop individuals having a wander around. Generally there is no pressure to buy and you can often see craftspeople at work. The crafts include carpets, woodwork and metalwork.

Fair Trade Shops
Those interested in crafts should definitely visit the string of interesting shops at Kopundol, just south and uphill from the main Patan bridge (see the Patan map). A number are run as nonprofit development organisations, so their prices are fair, and the money actually goes to the craftspeople, and some goes into training and product development.

One of the best of these organisations is **Mahaguthi** (☎ 5521607), which was established with the help of Oxfam. It has three shops and sells a wide range of crafts produced by thousands of people. Among other things, it sells beautiful hand-woven *dhaka* weavings, rice paper, pottery, block prints, woven bamboo, woodcrafts, jewellery, knitwear, embroidery and Mithila paintings (see the boxed text 'Mithila Painting' in The Terai & Mahabharat Range chapter). The Kopundol branch is on the right as you go up the hill (the main street) approaching from Kathmandu, but there are also shops on Durbar Square (see the Durbar Square (Patan) map), and in Kathmandu's Lazimpat district.

Other shops worth looking at nearby (see the Patan map) include **Dhukuti** for a wide range cloth, batiks, bags and even Christmas decorations; **Sana Hastakala** (☎ 5522628) for paper and batiks; and **Dhankuta Sisters** (☎ 5543209; closed weekends) for woven *dhaka* cloth from eastern Nepal. The other craft shops in this area are commercially run and mostly stock larger home design items aimed at local expats.

Near the Kumbeshwar Temple, the **Kumbeshwar Technical School** (☎ 5537484; ⓦ www.geocities.com/kumbeshwar2000) provides the untouchable community of Patan with skills; they produce locally made carpets, jumpers and woodwork direct to the consumer. The small showroom is on the ground floor of the school, down a short alley to the right of the school entrance.

Metalwork

Patan is the centre for bronze-casting and other metalwork. The statues you see on sale in Kathmandu were probably made in Patan and there are a number of excellent metalwork shops just to the north of Durbar Square. Good-quality gold-plated and painted bronze figures will cost Rs 2000 to Rs 5000 for smaller ones, up to more than Rs 10,000 for large images.

Paintings

North of Durbar Square, just beyond the Bhimsen Temple, are a number of interesting art shops. Some sell colourful Sherpa-style paintings. It's clearly something developed for the tourist trade, but never mind – they're nicely done and you can have all of the Kathmandu Valley, or even all of Nepal, in one painting. Prices start at Rs 2000.

Carpets

Those interested in carpets must visit Jawlakhel, the former Tibetan refugee camp,

where Nepal's enormous carpet industry of today was born. Tibetan carpet shops proliferate the approach road past the zoo.

The **Jawlakhel Handicraft Centre**, established in 1960, is a large cooperative workshop where you can watch the carpet-making process, as well as check out the centre's showrooms (with marked prices). It's opposite a Tibetan monastery.

The carpets at the Kumbeshwar Technical School (see earlier) are fairly priced, and this is possibly the only place where you can buy carpets made from 100% pure Tibetan wool. Carpets here cost around US$100 for a 1m x 1.5m size or US$150 for 1.75m x 1.2m. For more information see the boxed text 'Tibetan Carpets' in Facts about Nepal chapter.

Toys

Just south of Durbar Square is **Educational Wooden Toys** (Durbar Square map) which sells wonderful wooden toys including models of Swayambhunath and authentic Nepali trucks, autorickshaws and rickshaws (Rs 300 to Rs 600). You can find these toys for sale in Kathmandu, but they're cheaper here where they're made. The factory is only a stone's throw from the shop and it's fascinating to see the parts being cut out with pedal-operated jigsaws.

GETTING THERE & AWAY

You can get to Patan from Kathmandu easily, whether by bicycle, taxi, bus or *tempo* (three-wheeled minivan). It's an easy but choking 5km bike ride from Thamel to Patan's Durbar Square. The same trip costs around Rs 100 by taxi.

Buses (Rs 3) leave regularly from Kathmandu's City bus station and drop you at the Patan Dhoka city gate bus stop, a short walk from Durbar Square. Safa (electric) tempos (Rs 6, route 14A) also leave from the Kathmandu main post office as soon as they have 10 passengers. Double-check the destination when getting in a tempo. Some run to Durbar Square, others to Lagankhel bus station: when returning, some tempos branch right to Koteshwar instead of continuing to Kathmandu centre.

Buses to the southern valley towns leave from Patan's Lagankhel bus stop, including to Godavari, Bungamati and Chapagaon.

If you come to Patan by bicycle, an interesting route from Kathmandu is to take the track down to the river from opposite the big convention centre on the Bhaktapur road. A footbridge crosses the river here and you enter Patan by the Northern Stupa near the Kumbeshwar Temple.

Bhaktapur

☎ 01 ● pop 65,000

Bhaktapur, also known as Bhadgaon (pronounced **bud**-gown) in Nepali, or Khwopa (City of Devotees) in Newari, is the third major town of the valley. Traffic-free, the traditionally intact town is also in many ways the most timeless. The cobblestone streets link a string of temples, monastery courtyards and monumental squares, and the side streets are peppered with shrines, wells and water tanks at every turn.

The lack of traffic makes walking through Bhaktapur a particular pleasure. The town's cultural life is also vibrant, with strong communities of potters, woodcarvers and weavers. Look for grain laid out to dry in the sun, people collecting water or washing under the communal taps, dyed yarns hung out to dry, children's games, fascinating shops and women pounding grain – there's plenty to see. Perhaps most entrancing of all is Bhaktapur's effortless blending of the modern and medieval.

The oldest part of the town is around Tachupal Tole, to the east. Bhaktapur was the capital of the valley during the 14th to 16th centuries. During that time the focus of the town shifted west, to the Durbar Square area. Much of the town's great architecture dates from the end of the 17th century, during the rule of King Bhupatindra Malla. It's continued charm is due largely to the German-funded Bhaktapur Development Project, which restored buildings, paved dirt streets and established sewerage and waste water management facilities in the 1970s.

The description of sights in this section will lead you on a walk from west to east through the old town. To dive into the backstreets follow the Backstreets Walking Tour, which is marked on the Bhaktapur map.

ORIENTATION

Bhaktapur rises up on the northern bank of the Hanumante River. It's basically a pedestrian's city, and much better for it. Public buses, minibuses and taxis stop at Navpokhu Pokhari on the western edge of town and tour buses stop at the tourist bus and taxi park on the northern edge of Bhaktapur; both are a short walk from the heart of the city.

For the visitor, Bhaktapur is really a town of one curving road, which links several squares. From the bus stop at Navpokhu Pokhari you come first to Durbar Square, then Taumadhi Tole with the famous five-storey Nyatapola Temple, then to Tachupal Tole.

INFORMATION

Foreigners visiting the town are charged a hefty fee of Rs 750 (US$10). This is collected at over a dozen entrances to the city. On the larger streets there are ticket booths; smaller streets have roaming ticket collectors who pop up out of the woodwork when someone tries to enter by this way. If you are staying in Bhaktapur for up to a week, you need only pay the entrance fee once, but you must state this at the time of buying the ticket.

For longer stays (up to one year), a Bhaktapur Visitor Pass is available within a week of purchasing your entry ticket. Passes are issued by the Bhaktapur Municipality (at the ticket booth on the western end of Durbar Square) and require you to supply two photos and a photocopy of your visa and passport details.

There are moneychangers in Taumadhi Tole and Tachupal Tole and a couple of Internet cafés, including **Surfer's Edge** *(Rs 30 per hour; open until 8pm)* just north of Potters' Square.

THE WESTERN GATES TO TACHUPAL TOLE

The main road heading through Bhaktapur starts at Siddha Pokhari. The southern road in this fork is much more interesting as it is the main road through Bhaktapur, connecting Taumadhi Tole and Tachupal Tole. The descriptions below connect to form a guided walk along this road through the heart of the city from west to east. For a rundown of the sights when you get to Durbar Square or Taumadhi Tole see the Durbar Square (Patan) and Bhaktapur Squares special sections.

To get onto this west–east road from Navpokhu Pokhari turn south from the

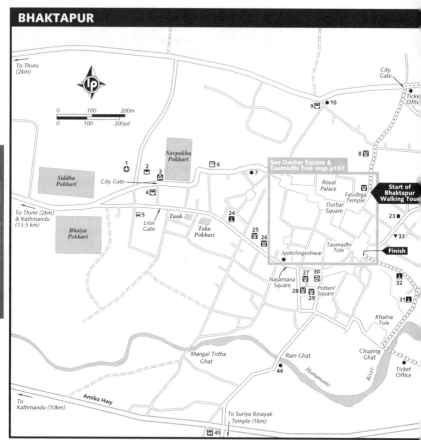

BHAKTAPUR

corner of the *pokhari* (large water tank) and then left on the road, passing a ticket office by the town's Lion Gate.

Lion's Gate to Potters' Square

Heading east from Lion's Gate you pass a small tank on your right and then the much larger **Teka Pokhari**. Just before the next major junction, to your left, is the constricted, tunnel-like entrance to the tiny **Ni Bahal** (signposted as 'Jet Barna Maha Bihar'), dedicated to Maitreya Buddha, the Buddha yet to come.

Cross the junction, where the road runs downhill to the Mangal Tirtha Ghat, and you will see on your left the red-brick **Jaya Varahi Temple**. There are elaborately carved wooden *toranas* over the central door and

the window above it. At the eastern end of the temple is the entrance to the upper floor, flanked by stone lions and banners. The two ornate windows, on either side of the upper *torana,* have recently been repainted their original gold.

A few more steps bring you to a small **Ganesh shrine** jutting out into the street. Continue to **Nasamana Square**, which is somewhat decrepit but has a Garuda statue without a temple. Almost immediately after this is a second square with the **Jyotirlingeshwar**, a *shikhara*-style temple that houses an important lingam. Behind the shrine is an attractive *hiti,* one of Bhaktapur's many sunken water conduits. Continue straight and you will arrive at the turn-off to Potters' Square. Walk a little farther on and

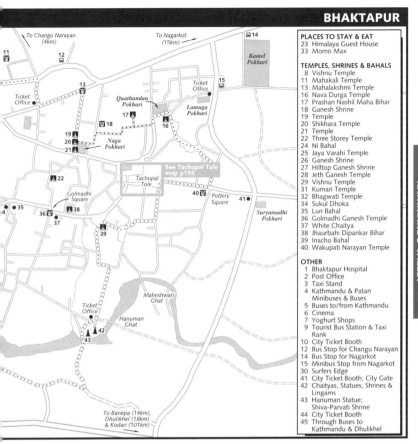

BHAKTAPUR

PLACES TO STAY & EAT
23 Himalaya Guest House
33 Momo Max

TEMPLES, SHRINES & BAHALS
8 Vishnu Temple
11 Mahakali Temple
13 Mahalakshmi Temple
16 Nava Durga Temple
17 Prashan Nashil Maha Bihar
18 Ganesh Shrine
19 Temple
20 Shikhara Temple
21 Temple
22 Three Storey Temple
24 Ni Bahal
25 Jaya Varahi Temple
26 Ganesh Shrine
27 Hilltop Ganesh Shrine
28 Jeth Ganesh Temple
29 Vishnu Temple
31 Kumari Temple
32 Bhagwati Temple
34 Sukul Dhoka
35 Lun Bahal
36 Golmadhi Ganesh Temple
37 White Chaitya
38 Jhaurbahi Dipankar Bihar
39 Inacho Bahal
40 Wakupati Narayan Temple

OTHER
1 Bhaktapur Hospital
2 Post Office
3 Taxi Stand
4 Kathmandu & Patan Minibuses & Buses
5 Buses to/from Kathmandu
6 Cinema
7 Yoghurt Shops
9 Tourist Bus Station & Taxi Rank
10 City Ticket Booth
12 Bus Stop for Changu Narayan
14 Bus Stop for Nagarkot
15 Minibus Stop from Nagarkot
30 Surfers Edge
41 City Ticket Booth; City Gate
42 Chaityas, Statues, Shrines & Lingams
43 Hanuman Statue; Shiva-Parvati Shrine
44 City Ticket Booth
45 Through Buses to Kathmandu & Dhulikhel

you will come to Taumadhi Tole (see the special section 'Bhaktapur Squares' for details).

Potters' Square

Potters' Square can be approached from Durbar Square, Taumadhi Tole or along the western road into town from Siddha Pokhari.

On the northern side of the square a small hillock is topped by a **Ganesh shrine** and a shady pipal tree. There are fine views over the river to the hills south of Bhaktapur. The square itself has two small temples: a solid-brick **Vishnu Temple** and the double-roofed **Jeth Ganesh Temple**. The latter is an indicator of how long the activity all around the square has been going on – a wealthy potter donated the temple in 1646 and to this day its priest is chosen from the potter caste.

Pottery is very clearly what this square is all about. Under the shady, open verandas and tin-roofed sheds located all around the square, the potters' wheels spin and clay is thrown. In the square itself (and elsewhere around town – particularly in the east), hundreds of finished pots sit out in the sun to dry, and are sold in the stalls around the square and also between the square and Taumadhi Tole. Large stores of clay are deposited on the eastern edge of the square.

Taumadhi Tole to Tachupal Tole

The curving main road through Bhaktapur runs from beside the Bhairabnath Temple in Taumadhi Tole to Tachupal Tole, the old centre of town. The first stretch of the street is a busy shopping thoroughfare with a constant hum of activity – everything is on sale, from porters' *tumplines* (the leather or cloth strips across the forehead or chest used to support a load carried on the back) to video cassettes.

At the first bend there are two interesting old buildings on the right-hand (southern) side. The **Sukul Dhoka** is a *math* (Hindu priest's house), with superb woodcarving both on its facade and inside in the courtyard. Almost next door is the **Lun Bahal**, originally a 16th-century Buddhist monastery that was converted into a Hindu shrine with the addition of a stone statue of Bhimsen. If you look into the sanctum, in the inner courtyard, you can see the statue, dating from 1592, complete with a ferocious-looking brass mask.

A little farther along, the road joins **Golmadhi Square** with a deep *hiti*, the small, triple-roofed **Golmadhi Ganesh Temple** and adjacent to it a **white chaitya**. A farther 100m brings you to another small open area with a *path* (pilgrim's shelter) on your right. Behind it is a tank and, set behind a gateway, the **Inacho Bahal** (see the Backstreets Walking Tour later in this section). A few more steps bring you to Tachupal Tole.

TACHUPAL TOLE

Tachupal Tole was probably the original central square of Bhaktapur, so this is most likely the oldest part of the town. South from this square a maze of narrow laneways, passageways and courtyards runs down to the ghats on the river.

The tall, square **Dattatraya Temple** was originally built in 1427, but alterations were made in 1458. Like some other important structures in the valley it is said to have been built using the timber from a single tree. The temple is dedicated to Dattatraya, although the Garuda-topped pillar and the traditional weapons of Vishnu (conch and a disc) on their pillars indicate that Dattatraya is actually another of Vishnu's many incarnations. He is also said to have been Shiva's teacher and is even claimed to have been a cousin of the Buddha, so the temple is important to Shaivites, Vaishnavites and Buddhists.

The three-storey temple is raised well above the ground on its base, whose sides are carved with some erotic scenes. The front section, which was a later addition to the temple, stands almost separate and the temple entrance is guarded by the same two

Malla wrestlers who watch over the first plinth of the Nyatapola Temple.

At the other end of the square is the two-storey **Bhimsen Temple**, variously dated to 1605, 1645 or 1655. The temple is squat, rectangular and open on the ground floor. It's fronted by a platform with a small double-roofed Vishnu Temple (with more erotic carvings) and a pillar topped by a brass lion. Steps lead down behind it to the deeply sunken Bhimsen Pokhari.

There are 10 buildings around the square that were originally used as *maths*. The best known was the **Pujari Math**. It was originally constructed in the 15th century during the reign of King Yaksha Malla, but was restored in 1763. Until the 20th century, an annual caravan brought tributes to the monastery from Tibet.

The Pujari Math is principally famed for the superb **peacock window** down a small alley on its left-hand side if you face it from the square. It is reputed to be the finest carved window in the valley and is the subject of countless postcards and photographs. There are some extraordinarily rich woodcarvings inside the building's courtyard.

The building now houses a **Woodcarving Museum** (entry Rs 20; open 9am-4pm Tues-Fri), which has some fine examples of the woodcarving for which Bhaktapur has long been famous. It costs an additional Rs 20 to take photos; but there's not really enough light to make that worthwhile; bring a torch (flashlight). The ticket also covers entry to the Brass & Bronze Museum (see following) and the National Art Gallery (see the Bhaktapur Squares special section).

Directly across the square from the Pujari Math is the **Brass & Bronze Museum** (entry Rs 20; open 9am-4pm Tues-Fri), with poorly lit examples of metalwork and ceremonial vessels from around the valley.

On the north side of Tachupal Tole is another open area, with the small **Salan Ganesh Temple**, dating from 1654. The open temple is ornately decorated, but the image is just a rock with only the vaguest elephant-head shape. To one side of the temple is the Ganesh Pokhari, a large tank.

BACKSTREETS WALKING TOUR

See the Bhaktapur map earlier for the route of this circular walking tour, which takes about two hours.

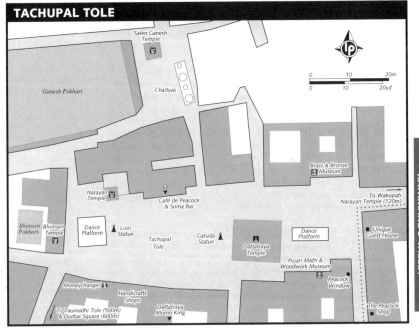

TACHUPAL TOLE

North of Durbar Square

Starting from the northeastern corner of Durbar Square, walk to the east of the high Fasidega Temple, and continue a little farther up the road past a **walled-in shrine** to a school that was formerly a **Vishnu Temple (8)**. Cross the junction and walk downhill past a large water tank and out of the newly built city gate. Turn right (east) on the road towards Nagarkot and you soon come to the modern **Mahakali Temple (11)**, where the shrine tops a small hill and is reached by a steep flight of steps.

Just beyond this temple, turn right, walk uphill and then turn left just before a small pool. Continue walking until you reach the tiny, open, yellow-roofed **Mahalakshmi Temple (13)**. Turn right (south) here and continue down to another large tank, the Naga Pokhari. Here the typically green water contrasts nicely with the dyed yarns hung out to dry alongside the tank. On the western side of the tank, **two temples (19 & 21)** flank a central white **shikhara (20)**, while a cobra rears up from the centre of the tank.

Pass along the north side of the tank, swing north and then, 10m before a roofed

Ganesh shrine **(18)**, pop into a low doorway on the right (marked by three steps) into a tiny courtyard with lovely woodcarvings and a central *chaitya*. Continue out the far end, follow the alley past another courtyard and then on the left you'll see the white-pillared entrance of the **Prashan Nashil Maha Bihar (17)**. This Buddhist temple has some nice stone carvings and occasional devotional music.

Continue east to the road junction, marked by a lotus-roofed shrine, and take a left to the large pool known as the Quathandau Pokhari. Head right along the tank to its southeast corner and the **Nava Durga Temple (16)**, a Tantric temple said to be the site for strange sacrificial rites. The golden door is surmounted by a golden window and is guarded by metal lions. It all contrasts nicely with the red-painted brick frontage.

Continue southeast past some wonderfully carved balconies to the main east–west road, which runs through Tachupal Tole and Taumadhi Tole. Around this area there are

[Continued on page 201]

BHAKTAPUR SQUARES

Durbar Square and Taumadhi Tole sit side by side in the west of Bhaktapur and are the first areas to explore when you arrive from Kathmandu.

Durbar Square

Bhaktapur's Durbar Square is much larger than Kathmandu's, much less crowded with temples than Patan's and less vibrant than either. It wasn't planned that way: Victorian illustrations show the square packed with temples and buildings, but the disastrous earthquake of 1934 destroyed many of them and today empty plinths show where some once stood.

Erotic Elephants Temple (3) Just before you enter the square, coming from the minibus and bus stop, pause for a little bit of Newari humour. On your right, not far from the Taleju Guest House, perhaps 70m before the main Durbar Square entrance gate, is a tiny double-roofed Shiva Parvati temple with some erotic carvings on its temple struts. There are copulating annimals, including elephants in the missionary position! It's a *hathi* (elephant) Kamasutra.

Ugrachandi & Bhairab Statues (10) When entering Durbar Square from the west you will pass by an entry gate (to a school) with two large stone lions built by King Bhupatindra Malla. On the northern wall are statues of the terrible Bhairab (right) and the equally terrible Ugrachandi, or Durga (left), the fearsome manifestation of Shiva's consort Parvati. The statues date from 1701 and it's said that the unfortunate sculptor had his hands cut off afterwards, to prevent him from duplicating his masterpieces.

Ugrachandi has 18 arms holding various Tantric weapons and symbols (symbolising the multiple aspects of her character) and she is in the act of casually killing a demon with a trident (symbolising the victory of wisdom over ignorance). Bhairab has to make do with just 12 arms. Both god and goddess are garlanded with necklaces of human heads. The gates and courtyard that these powerful figures guard are not of any particular importance.

Western End Temples A number of less significant temples crowd the western end of Durbar Square. They include the **Rameshwar Temple (11)** dedicated to Shiva and the **Bhadri Temple (12)** dedicated to Vishnu as Narayan. In front of them is an impressive, larger **Krishna Temple (13)** and just beyond that is a brick shikhara-style **Shiva Temple (15)** erected by King Jitamitra Malla in 1674.

King Bhupatindra Malla's Column (26) King Bhupatindra Malla was the best known of the Malla kings of Bhaktapur and had a great influence on the art and architecture of the town. Like the similar column in Patan's Durbar Square, this one was a copy of the original in Kathmandu. The king sits with folded arms, studying the magnificent golden gate to his palace.

Vatsala Durga Temple (27) & Taleju Bell (25)
Beside the king's statue and directly in front of the

Vatsala Durga Temple

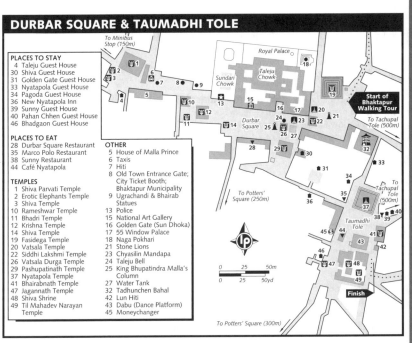

DURBAR SQUARE & TAUMADHI TOLE

To Minibus
Stop (150m)

Royal Palace

Taleju
Chowk

Sundari
Chowk

Start of
Bhaktapur
Walking Tour

To Tachupal
Tole (500m)

Durbar
Square

To Potters'
Square (250m)

To
Tachupal
Tole
(500m)

Taumadhi
Tole

Finish

To Potters' Square (300m)

PLACES TO STAY
4 Taleju Guest House
30 Shiva Guest House
31 Golden Gate Guest House
33 Nyatapola Guest House
34 Pagoda Guest House
36 New Nyatapola Inn
39 Sunny Guest House
40 Pahan Chhen Guest House
46 Bhadgaon Guest House

PLACES TO EAT
28 Durbar Square Restaurant
35 Marco Polo Restaurant
38 Sunny Restaurant
44 Café Nyatapola

TEMPLES
1 Shiva Parvati Temple
2 Erotic Elephants Temple
3 Shiva Temple
10 Rameshwar Temple
11 Bhadri Temple
12 Krishna Temple
14 Shiva Temple
19 Fasidega Temple
20 Vatsala Temple
22 Siddhi Lakshmi Temple
26 Vatsala Durga Temple
29 Pashupatinath Temple
37 Nyatapola Temple
41 Bhairabnath Temple
42 Jagannath Temple
48 Shiva Shrine
49 Til Mahadev Narayan
   Temple

OTHER
5 House of Malla Prince
6 Taxis
7 Hiti
8 Old Town Entrance Gate;
   City Ticket Booth;
   Bhaktapur Municipality
9 Ugrachandi & Bhairab
   Statues
13 Police
15 National Art Gallery
16 Golden Gate (Sun Dhoka)
17 55 Window Palace
18 Naga Pokhari
21 Stone Lions
23 Chyasilin Mandapa
24 Taleju Bell
25 King Bhupatindra Malla's
   Column
27 Water Tank
32 Tadhunchen Bahal
42 Lun Hiti
43 Dabu (Dance Platform)
45 Moneychanger

0   25   50m
0   25   50yd

Royal Palace is the stone Vatsala Durga Temple, which was built by King Jagat Prakash Malla in 1672. The shikhara-style temple has some similarities to the Krishna Mandir in Patan. In front of the temple is the large **Taleju Bell**, which was erected by King Jaya Ranjit Malla in 1737 to call the faithful to prayer at the Taleju Temple.

A second, smaller bell stands on the temple's plinth and is popularly known as 'the barking bell'. It was erected by King Bhupatindra Malla in 1721, supposedly to counteract a vision he had in a dream, and to this day dogs are said to bark and whine if the bell is rung.

Royal Palace Bhaktapur's Royal Palace was founded by Yaksha Malla and was added to by successive kings, particularly Bhupatindra Malla. As with the old palaces of Kathmandu and Patan, visitors are restricted to certain areas, but only seven courtyards remain of the 99 the palace was once claimed to have. Unfortunately, the palace suffered great damage in the terrible 1934 earthquake and its subsequent reconstruction did not match its original artistry.

National Art Gallery (16) The western end of the palace has been made into an art gallery (entry Rs 20; open 9.30am-3.30pm, Tues-Sat). The entrance to the gallery is flanked by figures of Hanuman the monkey god and Vishnu as Narsingha, his man-lion incarnation. These guardian figures date from 1698 and Hanuman appears in Tantric form as the four-armed Hanuman-Bhairab. This part of the palace was once known as the Malati Chowk.

The gallery has a fine collection of Hindu and Buddhist paintings, palm-leaf manuscripts, *thangkas* (paintings on cloth) and metal, stone and woodcrafts; it's the best of the town's three museums.

Once paid, your entry ticket is valid for both the Woodcarving and Brass & Bronze Museums in Tachupal Tole.

Golden Gate (17) & 55 Window Palace (18)

Adjoining the gallery, the magnificent Golden Gate, or Sun Dhoka, is the entrance to the 55 Window Palace. The Golden Gate is generally agreed to be the single most important piece of art in the whole valley. The gate and palace were built by King Bhupatindra Malla, but were not completed until 1754 during the reign of Jaya Ranjit Malla.

A Garuda, the vehicle of Vishnu, tops the *torana* (portico above the door indicating to whom the temple is dedicated) and is shown here disposing of a number of serpents, which are the Garuda's sworn enemies. The four-headed and 10-armed figure of the goddess Taleju Bhawani is featured directly over the door. Taleju Bhawani is the family deity of the Malla dynasty and there are temples to her in the royal palaces in Kathmandu and Patan as well as Bhaktapur.

The Golden Gate opens to the inner courtyards of the palace, but you cannot proceed further than the ornate entrance to colourful Taleju Chowk, featuring the multi-armed Tantric goddess Taleju and a host of others. Non-Hindus can check out the nearby **Naga Pokhari**, a water tank encircled by a writhing stone snake, or *naga*. The nagas rise up on scaled pillars and water pours from a goat's head that protrudes from the mouth of a *maksara* (crocodile demon).

Chyasilin Mandapa (24)

Beside Vatsala Durga Temple is an attractive **water tank (28)** and in front of that is the Chyasilin Mandapa. This octagonal temple was one of the finest in the square until it was destroyed by the 1934 earthquake. Using some of the temple's original components, it has been totally rebuilt. There's a good view over the square from inside; note the metal construction inside this outwardly authentic building.

Pashupatinath Temple (30)

Behind the Vatsala Durga Temple, this temple is dedicated to Shiva as Pashupati. It dates from the 17th century and is a replica of the main shrine at Pashupatinath. It's notable for the erotic carvings on the roof struts, which show some exhausting-looking positions.

Siddhi Lakshmi Temple (23)

By the southeastern corner of the palace stands the stone Siddhi Lakshmi Temple. The steps up to the temple are flanked by male and female attendants, each leading a rather reluctant child and a rather eager-looking dog. On successive levels the stairs are flanked by horses, rhinos, man-lions and camels.

The 17th-century temple marks the dividing line between the main Durbar Square and its secondary part, at the eastern end of the Royal Palace. Behind

Pashupatinath Temple

the temple is another **Vatsala Temple (21)**, while to one side of it are two rather lost-looking large **stone lions (22)**, standing by themselves out in the middle of the square.

Fasidega Temple (20) The large, white, rather ugly Fasidega Temple is dedicated to Shiva and stands in the centre of the secondary part of Durbar Square. There are various viewpoints around the valley – the Changu Narayan Temple is one of them – from where you can study Bhaktapur at a distance. In each case the white bulk of the Fasidega is always an easy landmark to pick out. The temple sits on a six-level plinth with elephant guardians at the bottom of the steps, and with lions and cows above them.

Tadhunchen Bahal (33) The southern and eastern side of the secondary part of the square is made up of double-storey *dharamsalas* (rest houses for pilgrims), now used as shops. As you enter the street leading east from the square, the Tadhunchen Bahal, or Chatur Varna Mahavihara, is an ancient-looking monastery on the southern side. In the inner courtyard the roof struts on the eastern side have some highly unusual carvings showing the tortures of the damned. In one a snake is wrapped around a man, another shows two rams butting an unfortunate's head from opposite sides, while a third strut shows a nasty tooth extraction being performed with a large pair of pliers! The monastery dates from the 15th century.

Taumadhi Tole

A short street lined with tourist shops leads downhill from behind the Pashupatinath Temple in Durbar Square to the second great square of Bhaktapur, the Taumadhi Tole. Here you'll find Nyatapola Temple, the highest temple in the valley and also the Café Nyatapola, whose balconies provide a great view over the square. The building was renovated for its new purpose in 1977 and it has some finely carved roof struts.

Nyatapola Temple (38) The five-storey, 30m-high Nyatapola Temple is not only the highest temple in the whole Kathmandu Valley, but also one of the best examples of traditional Newari temple architecture. The towering temple is visible from Durbar Square, but some of the finest views of the temple are from farther away. If you take the road running out of the valley east to Banepa and Dhulikhel or walk up towards the Suriya Binayak Temple south of Bhaktapur, you can see the temple soaring up above the other buildings, with the hills at the edge of the valley as a backdrop.

The elegant temple was built during the reign of King Bhupatindra Malla in 1702, and its design and construction were so solid that the 1934 earthquake caused only minor damage. The stairway leading up to the temple is flanked by guardian figures at each plinth level. The bottom plinth has the legendary wrestlers Jayamel and Phattu, said to have the strength of 10 men. On the plinths above are two elephants, then two lions, then two griffins and finally two goddesses – Baghini in the form of a tiger and Singhini in the form of a lion. Each figure is said to be 10 times as strong as the figure on the level below; presiding over all of them, but hidden away inside the temple, is the mysterious Tantric goddess Siddhi Lakshmi, to whom the temple is dedicated.

Only the temple's priests are allowed to see the image of the goddess, but the temple's 108 carved and painted roof struts depict her in her various forms. Various legends and tales relate to the temple and its enigmatic inhabitant. One is that she maintains a balance with the powers of the terrifying Bhairab, comfortably ensconced in his own temple just across the square.

Bhairabnath Temple (42) The recently restored, triple-roofed Bhairabnath Temple (also known as the Kasi Vishwanath or Akash Bhairab) has an unusual rectangular plan and has had a somewhat chequered history. It was originally built as a one-storey temple in the early 17th century, but was rebuilt with two storeys by King Bhupatindra Malla in 1717. The 1934 earthquake caused great damage to the temple and it was completely rebuilt and a 3rd floor added.

Casually stacked beside the temple are the enormous wheels and other parts of the temple chariot on which the image of Bhairab is conveyed around town during the Bisket festival in mid-April (see the boxed text 'Bisket Jatra at Khalna Tole' in the Around the Kathmandu Valley chapter). Curiously, despite Bhairab's fearsome powers and his massive temple, his image is only about 30cm high! A small hole in the central door (below a row of carved boar snouts) is used to push offerings into the temple's interior, but the actual entrance to the Bhairabnath Temple is through the small Betal Temple, behind the main temple.

The temple's facade is guarded by two brass lions and includes an image of Bhairab on rattan with real dried intestines draped across it! Head here at dusk to catch the nightly devotional music.

Til Mahadev Narayan Temple (50) It's easy to miss the square's third interesting temple, as it is hidden away behind the buildings on the southern side of the square. You can enter the temple's courtyard through a narrow entrance through those buildings, or through an arched entrance facing west, just to the south of the square.

This double-roofed Vishnu Temple has a Garuda kneeling on a high pillar in front, flanked by pillars bearing Vishnu's *sankha* (conch shell) and *chakra* (disc-shaped weapon) symbols. Some of the temple's struts also have Garudas. A *lingam* (phallic symbol) in a *yoni* (female equivalent of the phallic symbol) stands inside a wooden cage in front and to one side of the temple. A plaque to the lower right of the door depicts the goddess Vajra Jogini in characteristic pose with her left leg high in the air.

Despite the temple's neglected setting it is actually an important place of pilgrimage as well as one of the oldest temple sites in the town: An inscription indicates that the site has been in use since 1080. Another inscription states that the image of Til Mahadev installed inside the temple dates from 1170.

Til Mahadev Narayan Temple

[Continued from page 195]

more potters at work. Turn right and immediately on your left is the entrance to the **Wakupati Narayan Temple (40)**. The ornate, golden temple is double-roofed and is fronted by a line-up of no less than five Garudas on the backs of turtles. You can often find woodcarvers or spinners in this courtyard. Continue from here to Tachupal Tole (see that entry earlier in this section if you want to check out the tole at this point).

South of Tachupal Tole

From Tachupal Tole turn left down the side of the Pujari Math; directions to its famous peacock window are well signposted. Jog right, left, right at a small square and left again, then immediately on your left is the unassuming gateway to the ornate little **Inacho Bahal (39)** with prayer wheels, figures of the Buddha and a strange miniature pagoda roof rising up above the courtyard.

From here the road drops down to the Hanumante River, and enters rural surroundings. At the bottom of the hill is a Ram Temple and a curious collection of **chaityas, statues, shrines** and **lingams (42)**, including a bas-relief of a nude Shiva (obviously pleased to see you) and an octagonal Shiva lingam. Head down to the sacred river confluence for a collection of shrines and statues including one of **Hanuman (43)**, the faithful ally of Rama and Sita. On the nearby building are four paintings, partly obscured by a photogenic tree, including one on the far right showing Hanuman returning to Rama from his Himalayan medicinal herb foray, clutching a whole mountain in his hand.

Cross the bridge and then take a hairpin turn back from the road onto a small footpath. This rural stroll ends with another temple complex, where you cross the river by the **Chuping Ghat**, where there are areas for ritual bathing and cremations.

Above the river is **Khalna Tole**, the centre for the spectacular activities during the annual mid-April Bisket Jatra (see the boxed text 'Bisket Jatra at Khalna Tole'). Just south is the pretty temple complex that now serves as Tribhuvan University's Department of Music (generally closed to the public).

The circular walk ends with a gentle climb back into the town, past a couple of temples, emerging at a small livestock market on the southern side of Taumadhi Tole.

SURIYA BINAYAK TEMPLE

About 1km south of town, this 17th-century Ganesh Temple is said to be a good place to visit if you're worried about your children being late developers! It's also popular with Nepali marriage parties. To get there, take the road down past Potters' Square to Ram

Bisket Jatra at Khalna Tole

Bisket Jatra heralds the start of the Nepali New Year and is one of the most exciting annual events in the valley. In preparation, Bhairab's huge triple-roofed chariot is assembled from the parts scattered beside the Bhairabnath Temple and behind the Nyatapola Temple in Taumadhi Tole. The huge and ponderous chariot is hauled by dozens of villagers to Khalna Tole with Betal, Bhairab's sidekick from the tiny temple behind the Bhairabnath Temple, riding out front like a ship's figurehead, while Bhadrakali, his consort, accompanies them in her own chariot.

The creaking and swaying chariots lumber around the town, pausing for a huge tug of war between the eastern and western sides of town. The winning side is charged with looking after the images of the gods during their week-long riverside sojourn in Khalna Tole's octagonal *path* (pilgrims' shelter). After the battle the chariots slither down the steep road leading to Khalna Tole, where a huge 25m-high *lingam* (phallic symbol) is erected in the stone *yoni* (female genital symbol) base.

In the evening of the following day (New Year's day), the pole is pulled down, again in an often violent tug of war. As the pole crashes to the ground, the New Year officially commences. Bhairab and Betal return to Taumadhi Tole, while Bhadrakali goes back to her shrine by the river.

Other events take place around Bhaktapur for a week preceding New Year and then for days after, with locals often dressed in the town's traditional red, white and black striped cloth. Members of the potters' caste will put up and haul down their own lingam, and processions also carry images of Ganesh, Lakshmi and Mahakali around town.

Ghat (where there are areas for ritual bathing and cremations), cross the river and continue to the main road. The road continues across the other side has some fine views back over the rice paddies to Bhaktapur. It's about a 45-minute walk from central Bhaktapur.

Where the road turns sharp right, a steep stairway climbs up to the temple on a forested hilltop. As you step inside the temple enclosure, the very realistic-looking rat, on top of a tall pillar, indicates that this temple belongs to Ganesh. The image of the god sits in an enclosure, awash in red paste, marigolds, rice offerings and melted candles. Statues of kneeling devotees in a range of traditional headdresses face the image and the *shikhara* is flanked by large bells.

There are twice-weekly *puja* ceremonies on Tuesday and Saturday mornings; get here early and grab a tea and omelette breakfast at the pilgrim stalls. If you are feeling energetic, steps lead up the hillside to the right of the temple for the best valley views.

PLACES TO STAY

A growing number of visitors to Bhaktapur are staying overnight. There's plenty to see, no screaming motorbikes or air pollution and once evening falls all the Kathmandu day-trippers disappear and they don't return until after breakfast the next day.

Most guesthouses have only a handful of (generally small) rooms so you may have to hunt around the first night. In general you pay more for the location and views than the quality of the room and your rupees won't go as far in Bhaktapur as they do in Kathmandu. Single rooms are in short supply.

PLACES TO STAY – BUDGET

All the places below appear on the Durbar Square & Taumadhi Tole map unless indicated otherwise.

Shiva Guest House (☎ 6613912; e bisket@ wlink.com.np; *singles/doubles with shared bathroom US$6/8, with private bathroom US$15/20*) is entered from behind the Pashupatinath Temple on Durbar Square. The corner rooms have fantastic views over Durbar Square, but even this hardly justifies the price. There's a good restaurant on the ground floor (mains Rs 150 to Rs 180).

Golden Gate Guest House (☎ 6610534; w www.goldengateguesthouse.com; *singles/ doubles with shared bathroom Rs 200/350,*

with private bathroom Rs 400/500, deluxe US$8/12) is a friendly place entered through a passageway from Durbar Square or from the laneway between Durbar Square and Taumadhi Tole. Rooms vary but are generally clean and some have balconies. The top-floor deluxe rooms are best. There are fine rooftop views and there's also a good restaurant downstairs (try the crepes), featuring a stunning 400-year-old carved window.

New Nyatapola Inn (☎ 6611852; *singles/ doubles with private bathroom Rs 350/400*) is off the same laneway as Golden Gate Guest House and is not bad value, though the single rooms in particular are small and spartan.

Pagoda Guest House (☎ 6613248; w ghpagoda.tripod.com; *singles/doubles with shared bathroom Rs 300/400, with private bathroom Rs 700/900*), just off the northwestern edge of Taumadhi Tole, is friendly and family-run. There are only six rooms, all different, good value and neat as a button. The cheaper rooms come with towels and a heater; the pricier rooms have clean bathroom and TV. There's also a decent rooftop restaurant but the views are limited.

Nyatapola Guest House (☎ 6612415; *doubles with shared bathroom Rs 200*), north of the Nyatapola Temple off Taumadhi Tole, has basic barracks-style rooms for twice what you'd pay in Thamel. This is about as cheap as you'll get, but it's really worth spending more elsewhere.

Himalaya Guest House (Bhaktapur map; ☎ 6613945, fax 6258222; *singles/doubles with private bathroom Rs 300/400*), on the road that connects Taumadhi and Tachupal Toles, is run by the same people as the hotel of the same name in Kathmandu's Freak St. The rooms vary but are generally decent value, plus there are backpacker perks like cheap food and a laundry service.

Taleju Guest House (☎ 6611078; e taleju_ghr@hotmail.com; *doubles with shared /private bathroom Rs 500/800*) has a useful location just east of the main entrance to Durbar Square. It's a modern, multistorey building, with one of the tallest rooftop views around. The price is a bit steep, but rooms are clean, bright and spotless.

PLACES TO STAY – MID-RANGE

Bhadgaon Guest House (☎ 6610488; e bhadgaon@mos.com.np; *singles US$10-20, doubles US$15-25*) near the southwestern corner of

Taumadhi Tole, has excellent rooftop views, and pleasant sitting areas. The rooms, all with private bathroom, are clean and comfortable but a little small; those at the back are bigger. The deluxe rooftop room has superb views from its private balcony. The rooftop restaurant is popular and reasonably priced (mains Rs 120 to Rs 200).

Pahan Chhen Guest House *(☎ 6612887; e srp@mos.com.np; singles with private bathroom US$12, doubles with bathroom US$20-25, 40% discount)*, on the northeastern corner of Taumadhi Tole, has very comfortable rooms, although they are a bit on the small side (the singles are tiny). The views from the roof are as good as you'll get.

Sunny Guest House *(☎ 6612004; rooms US$7-20)* is a new hotel right next door. It has small but quite chic rooms with nice lighting, carpet and carved window lattices but tiny bathrooms. There's a nice balcony restaurant (see Places to Eat).

Unique Guest House *(Tachupal Tole map; ☎ 6611575; e unique@col.com.np; singles/doubles US$10/15)* is a tiny place with only four rooms in a low-ceilinged, creaky and slightly claustrophobic old building on Tachupal Tole. It's the only hotel in this part of the town, which helps create a powerful atmosphere once the crowds disappear. It's probably no good if you are much over six feet tall, though.

PLACES TO EAT

Bhaktapur is certainly no competition for Kathmandu when it comes to restaurants, but don't worry, you won't starve. Don't forget to try Bhaktapur's famous speciality: *jujudhau*, 'the king of curds' (yoghurt) while you are here. You can have it in the town's tourist restaurants for Rs 50 to Rs 60, but there are also several hole-in-the-walls between Durbar Square and Navpokhu Pokhari (look for the pictures of curd outside), where you can get a small cup for Rs 7 or a giant family-sized bowl for Rs 60.

All the places below appear on the Durbar Square & Taumadhi Tole map unless indicated otherwise.

Café Nyatapola *(snacks Rs 150, mains Rs 200-250, pot of tea Rs 55; lunch & breakfast only)*, right in Taumadhi Tole, is in a building that was once a traditional pagoda temple – it even has erotic carvings on some of the roof struts. From upstairs there are good

views over the square, but it is very cramped and often dominated by large groups of tourists. Prices are comparatively high.

Durbar Square Restaurant *(☎ 6614812)* is an equally atmospheric restaurant with an identical menu to the Café Nyatapola and the same owners, but this time with views of Durbar Square.

Marco Polo Restaurant *(dishes around Rs 110)*, on the corner of the square and beside the Nyatapola Temple, is a cheaper bet if you want a substantial meal. There's a small balcony with limited views over Taumadhi Tole.

Sunny Restaurant *(mains Rs 140-160)* consists of two places; one atop the guesthouse of the same name and the other next door. Both offer a terrace and great views over the square, though the hotel restaurant is 10% more expensive.

Café de Peacock & Soma Bar *(Tachupal Tole map; open 9am-9pm daily; mains Rs 220-320, veg/nonveg set Nepali meal Rs 275/375)*, opposite the Dattatraya Temple, is one of the best spots in the valley to while away an afternoon. The food is good and the views of the beautiful square mesmerising. Tour groups often reserve the best tables at lunchtime. The menu covers most bases, with a pot of tea weighing in at Rs 50.

If you are on a tight budget, there are several basic snack bars such as **Momo Max** *(Bhaktapur map)* or **Dattatraya Momo King** *(Tachupal Tole map)* a friendly place hidden in a courtyard off Tachupal Tole, where you can get a bowl of momos, chow mien or Newari beer snacks for less than Rs 25. The food is definitely low grade but you can fill up for pennies.

SHOPPING

As in Patan, there are a number of crafts for which Bhaktapur is the centre. Shops and stalls catering to visitors are concentrated around Tachupal Tole.

Pottery

Bhaktapur is the pottery centre of the valley and a visit to Potters' Square is a must (see earlier in this section). There are many stalls around the square and just below Taumadhi Tole selling pottery. Much of the work is traditional pots for use in Nepali households (nice but not very transportable), but there are also items catering to tourist tastes, such as attractive elephant and dragon planters.

Woodcarving & Puppets

Bhaktapur is renowned for its woodcarving and you'll see good examples in stalls around Tachupal Tole and the alley beside the Pujari Math, right under the Peacock Window in fact. Popular pieces include copies of the peacock window or masks depicting the god Bhairab.

If you buy anything that looks like it might be old, make sure you get a descriptive receipt for it, as it's likely to be checked on departure from Kathmandu. If it really is very old you will not be allowed to take it out of the country (see Customs in the Facts for the Visitor chapter).

Some of the best puppets, which are on sale in their thousands in all the valley towns, come from Bhaktapur and nearby Thimi.

Paper

Hand-made writing paper, cards, albums and other paper products are available throughout town. One good place to check out is **The Peacock Shop** (Tachupal Tole map; ☎ 6610820), near the Peacock Window down the side of Pujari Math. You can visit the workshop out back and observe the pressing, drying, smoothing, cutting and printing processes involved in making the paper. You can also see the raw *lokta* (daphne bush) plant material from which the paper is made.

GETTING THERE & AWAY
Bus, Minibus & Taxi

Minibuses from Kathmandu (Rs 6, one hour) drop off and depart from a stand just south-west of Bhaktapur's Navpokhu Pokhari pool in the west of the town, a short walk from Durbar Square. The last minibus back to Kathmandu leaves at about 6pm.

Taxis from Kathmandu cost around Rs 250 one way.

Buses for Nagarkot (Rs 10, one hour) leave regularly from the northeastern corner of the city. Buses to Changu Narayan (Rs 6, 30 minutes) leave every 30 minutes or so from the northern junction with the Changu Narayan road.

For Dhulikhel you'll have to walk 10 minutes down to the Arniko Highway (via Potters' Square and Ram Ghat) and catch a (probably packed) through bus from Kathmandu.

Bicycle

The main Arniko Highway to Bhaktapur carries a lot of bellowing, belching buses and trucks so it's better to turn off the highway at Thimi and follow the parallel road to Bhaktapur from the north end of Thimi. Avoid peak hours.

AROUND BHAKTAPUR
Thimi

Thimi (known historically as Madhyapur) is the fourth-largest town in the valley, outranked only by Kathmandu, Patan and Bhaktapur. It's a typical Newari town and its 'capable people' (the name of the town is derived from this Newari expression) operate thriving cottage industries producing pottery and papier-mache masks. You'll pass a string of mask shops if you head west from Thimi along the northern road to Bhaktapur. There's not much to see in Thimi itself, but the lack of traffic or tourists and the mellow vibe make it a pleasant stop-off en route to Bhaktapur.

The town's main road runs north–south between the old and new (Arniko Highway) Bhaktapur roads, which form the northern and southern boundaries of the town. From the southern gate on the main highway there's a short but stiff walk up to the main southern square and the 16th-century **Balkumari Temple**. Balkumari is one of Bhairab's shaktis and the temple's entrance is plastered in chicken feathers from previous sacrifices. A statue of Balkumari's vehicle, a peacock, stands in front of the temple. Further north, past a *shikhara*-style temple, is a 16th-century **Narayan Temple** and a well-crafted **Bhairab Temple**, with erotic carvings on the struts and a small brass plaque of Bhairab on the south side.

At the north end of Thimi is the crossroads with the old road to Bhaktapur; turn left here, and head downhill past a small shrine and water tank. Take a detour right off the main road for a couple of minutes to see the village of **Nagadesh** and the impressive Ganesh Dyochen (a *dyochen* is a Tantric temple). Through the gateway and to the right is the triple-roofed **Ganesh Temple**, whose facade is often smeared with sacrificial blood.

Back at the northern crossroads, a 10-minute walk north will bring you to the satellite village of **Bode**. From a crossroads marked by a couple of corner stores take a left for five minutes into the brick alleys of the village and then take a right at a pool and a *shikhara*-style temple. Just ahead, by a school, is the 17th-century **Mahalakshmi Temple**. There's an interesting belt-driven contraption nearby that villagers use to roast corn.

Special Events During Bisket Jatra (Nepali new year's day) festivities, 32 deities are carried to the Balkumari Temple in palanquins during the colourful Balkumari Jatra. A similar but smaller ceremony also takes place at the Mahalakshmi Temple in Bode.

Getting There & Away Any Bhaktapur-bound minibus will be able to drop you at Thimi, probably at the southern entrance but possibly the northern entrance, and you catch another minibus on to Bhaktapur from either junction. A taxi from Kathmandu to the southern entrance will cost you around Rs 150.

If you are continuing by bike to Bhaktapur, the northern (old) road offers a far more pleasant ride.

Changu Narayan Temple

The beautiful and historic temple of Changu Narayan *(entry Rs 60)* stands on a hilltop at the eastern end of the valley, about 4km north of Bhaktapur and 22km from Kathmandu. Although the temple dates from 1702, when it was rebuilt after a fire, its origins go right back to the 4th century and there are many important stone images as well as sculptures dating from the Licchavi period.

Despite the temple's beauty and interest it attracts relatively few visitors, although these days you can drive or catch a bus from Bhaktapur right to the temple. Alternatively, it makes a pleasant walk from that town or an interesting destination on the walk down from Nagarkot.

The double-roofed temple is dedicated to Vishnu in his incarnation as Narayan and is exceptionally beautiful, with quite amazingly intricate roof struts depicting multi-armed Tantric deities. It is fronted by a kneeling figure of Garuda said to date from the 5th century. The man-bird mount of Vishnu has a snake around his neck and kneels with hands in the 'namaste' position

AROUND THE KATHMANDU VALLEY

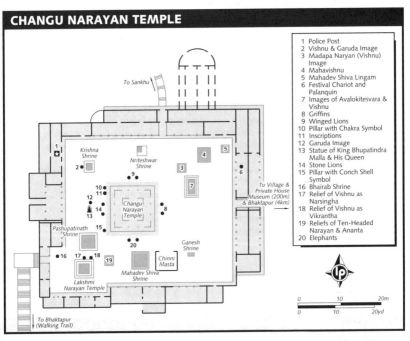

CHANGU NARAYAN TEMPLE

To Sankhu

Krishna Shrine

Nriteshwar Shrine

1
2

10
11
12
13
14
15

Changu Narayan Temple

9

4

5

3

7

6

8

To Village & Private House Museum (200m) & Bhaktapur (4km)

Pashupatinath Shrine

16   17   18
19

Lakshmi Narayan Temple

20

Chinni Masta

Mahadev Shiva Shrine

Ganesh Shrine

To Bhaktapur (Walking Trail)

1 Police Post
2 Vishnu & Garuda Image
3 Madapa Naryan (Vishnu) Image
4 Mahavishnu
5 Mahadev Shiva Lingam
6 Festival Chariot and Palanquin
7 Images of Avalokitesvara & Vishnu
8 Griffins
9 Winged Lions
10 Pillar with Chakra Symbol
11 Inscriptions
12 Garuda Image
13 Statue of King Bhupatindra Malla & His Queen
14 Stone Lions
15 Pillar with Conch Shell Symbol
16 Bhairab Shrine
17 Relief of Vishnu as Narsingha
18 Relief of Vishnu as Vikrantha
19 Reliefs of Ten-Headed Narayan & Ananta
20 Elephants

0   10   20m
0   10   20yd

LP

facing the temple. Stone lions guard the wonderfully gilded door, which is flanked by equally detailed gilded windows. Two pillars at the front corners carry the four traditional symbols of Vishnu. Non-Hindus are not allowed inside the temple itself.

In Nepali terms, the temple is relatively new. The much older images found in the temple courtyard are of equal interest. There are various images of Vishnu carrying the symbols associated with the god in his four hands.

In the southwest corner are several notable images, including one of Vishnu as Narsingha, his man-lion incarnation, in the act of disembowelling a demon. Another shows him as Vikrantha, the six-armed dwarf who transformed into a giant capable of crossing the universe in three gigantic steps. He is in a characteristic 'action pose', with his leg raised high. To the side of these two images is a small black slab showing a 10-headed and 10-armed Vishnu in the centre, with Ananta reclining on a serpent below. The scenes are divided into three sections – the underworld, the world of man and the heavens. The beautifully carved image is around 1500 years old.

In the northwestern corner there is an image of Vishnu astride the Garuda, which is illustrated on the Rs 10 banknote. Beside the Garuda figure that faces the front of the temple is one of the oldest Licchavi stone inscriptions in the valley (5th century).

Also interesting are the statues of King Bhupatindra Malla and his queen, kneeling in a gilded cage in front of the temple. In the centre of the courtyard, triangular bricks are used, while out towards the edge there are older, rounded-corner bricks.

Back in the village is a **Private House Museum** *(entry Rs 50; open daylight hours)*,

Short Hikes from Changu Narayan

A couple of hours' walk from Changu Narayan will take you through some lovely scenery to Sankhu, Nagarkot or Bhaktapur, allowing you to link up different parts of the valley and avoid backtracking by hitting some village trails. If you are hiking to Changu Narayan you can recognise the temple by its golden roof atop the final bump of a lengthy spur running down from the eastern edge of the valley.

To/From Bhaktapur

It takes about two hours on foot or about an hour on a mountain bike to get to Changu Narayan from Bhaktapur. By bike it's a wonderful downhill run on the way back (30 minutes), but quite a steep climb on the way there. Perhaps the best option is to take a bus or taxi to Changu Naryan and then walk back. A network of walking trails lead back to Bhaktapur; just keep asking the way.

To/From Sankhu

From the northern and western entrances of the Changu Narayan Temple a short and steep path descends to the Manohara River, which is crossed easily by wading or by a temporary bridge during the dry season (impossible in the monsoon). This brings you out to the Sankhu road at Bramhakhel, which is about 3.5km southeast of Gokarna. From here you can continue east to Sankhu or west to Gokarna or Bodhnath.

Coming from the other direction, you'll see a small sign for Changu Narayan on a building wall on the south side at the entry to Bramhakhel. It's a five-minute walk across the fields to the river and the temporary bridge. It's quite a steep and difficult scramble up the hill that will take at least 45 minutes (especially if you're carrying a bicycle). You might like to go slower, as there are a couple of small Newari hamlets along the way, and great views. There's quite a labyrinth of paths up the hill and it's not a bad idea to have a guide (and bicycle carrier). You will probably find small boys offering their carrying services – establish a price in advance.

To/From Nagarkot

A third way of reaching Changu Narayan is by the pleasant downhill stroll from Nagarkot (see Hikes from Nagarkot in the following Eastern Valley section). You can do the stroll in the opposite direction and then catch a bus for the final uphill stretch to Nagarkot.

which gives a funky introduction to trad itional life in the valley, exhibited in a 160-year-old house. Entry includes a guided tour. Look out for the rhino-skin shield, the 2nd-century leather coins, Tantric astrology books and 220-year-old rice! It's worth a visit.

Places to Stay & Eat

Changhu Guest House (☎ 6613242; lower/ upper floor rooms US$5/7, 50% discount), just before the temple, has four clean and pleasant double rooms and two shared bathrooms. The upper floor rooms are a little more expensive but worth it as they come with a balcony and views over Bhaktapur. The accommodation is better value than the attached restaurant. The owners can hook you up with a local guide for visits to local villages, including local Tamang village distilleries.

Changu Narayan Hill Resort (rooms Rs 200), 1km east of the village, along the track to Nagarkot, could be really nice, with great views and a homely atmosphere, but the dirty cold-water bathrooms detract a little.

Binayak Restaurant and **Valley View Restaurant** are both by the car park at the entrance to Changu village and offer decent food.

Getting There & Away

Bus & Taxi Public buses run regularly between Changu Narayan and Bhaktapur (Rs 6, 30 minutes), with the last bus around dusk. A taxi from Kathmandu costs around Rs 600 return, and from Bhaktapur around Rs 200.

The Eastern Valley

Beyond Bhaktapur the Kathmandu Valley walls start to rise, revealing views beyond the valley bowl. Dhulikhel and the destinations around it actually lie beyond the valley, but are easily visited from Kathmandu and from other destinations in the valley. See Touring Routes in the Mountain Biking chapter for ideas on a bike ride through the eastern valley.

SANKHU

Sankhu was once an important post on the trading route between Kathmandu and Lhasa (Tibet), and although the town's flower has faded somewhat, you can still see many signs of its former prosperity. The

town was first settled in the Licchavi era and there are many homes decorated with old woodcarvings. Although many traditional aspects of Newari life continue here, the most persuasive reason to visit is the beautiful Vajra Jogini Temple complex, an easy 45-minute walk or bicycle ride about 2km northeast of town.

Getting There & Away

Buses to Sankhu leave from Kathmandu's City bus station (Rs 10, two hours) and pass a major checkpoint; the last bus back to Kathmandu leaves Sankhu around 6pm.

It's easy to reach Sankhu by bicycle from Kathmandu (20km). The road is sealed and flat (with a few minor exceptions), and it's an attractive and interesting ride, taking about 1½ hours beyond Bodhnath.

For a loop trip it's possible (in the dry season at least) to cross the Manohara River and climb to the fascinating Changu Narayan Temple (see the boxed text 'Short Hikes from Changu Narayan' earlier in this chapter). For a longer loop you could cycle or bus to Nagarkot and then cycle or walk down from there (see Hikes from Nagarkot later in this section for details).

AROUND SANKHU
Vajra Jogini Temple

Perched high above the valley, in a grove of huge, ancient trees, this complex of temples is worth a visit. The main temple was built in 1655 by Pratap Malla of Kathmandu, but it seems likely the site has been used for much longer than that. It's a sublimely peaceful site, the silence broken only by the chatter of wild monkeys drinking from the many water spouts.

The climb up the stone steps to the temples is steep and hot. About halfway up there is a shelter and some carvings of Kali and Ganesh. A natural stone here represents Than Bhairab and sacrifices are made at its foot.

As you enter the main temple compound you will see a large bell (the Tantric female equivalent to the *vajra* or thunderbolt) on your right. There are two temples and the one nearest to the entrance is the Vajra Jogini Temple, a pagoda with a three-tiered roof of sheet copper. There is some beautiful repoussé work on the southern facade, though the actual image of the goddess can only be seen when the priest opens the door for *puja* (religious ritual).

The two-tiered temple farthest from the entrance enshrines a *chaitya* and commemorates Ugra Tara, or Blue (Nilo) Tara, a Tantric Buddhist goddess. The woodcarving around the doors is particularly fine. The rock between the two temples represents the naga god, as indicated by the encircling stone snake. In the northwestern corner of the courtyard (the far left when you enter) are a couple of caves used for Tantric practices. Behind the temples and up some stairs are buildings that were once used as pilgrim resthouses and priests' houses.

Getting There & Away At Sankhu, turn left at the bus stop and walk north through the village (where there is some beautiful woodcarving). Just after the road turns to the right, take the road on the left, which runs out of the village (under an ugly concrete archway). There are some fine stone carvings of Vishnu and Ganesh after the arch. The road then forks: The left fork is the traditional approach for pedestrians and descends down to the small river; the right fork is drivable (though rough) and is OK for bicycles.

NAGARKOT

There are various places around the edge of the Kathmandu Valley that offer great mountain views, but the resort village of Nagarkot, 30km from Kathmandu, is generally held to be the best. Mountain watchers make their way up to the village, stay overnight in one of Nagarkot's lodges, then rise at dawn to see the sun appear over the Himalaya.

Between October and March a trip to Nagarkot will nearly always be rewarded with a view, but you will be very lucky to catch more than a glimpse through the clouds of some snow-capped mountains in the June to September monsoon period. It can get very cold at Nagarkot in autumn and winter, so if you're staying overnight come prepared with warm clothing. A torch (flashlight) is useful to help get you to those dawn views. There's not much to do in the evenings, so bring a book.

Nagarkot originally owed its existence to the local army camp, but now it relies on tourism. It was never a traditional village, so while the views can be stunning, and the surrounding countryside is great for walk-

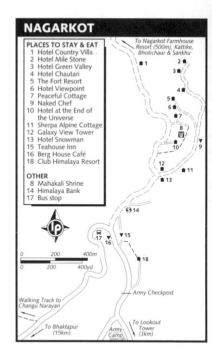

NAGARKOT

PLACES TO STAY & EAT
1 Hotel Country Villa
2 Hotel Mile Stone
3 Hotel Green Valley
4 Hotel Chautari
5 The Fort Resort
6 Hotel Viewpoint
7 Peaceful Cottage
9 Naked Chef
10 Hotel at the End of the Universe
11 Sherpa Alpine Cottage
12 Galaxy View Tower
13 Hotel Snowman
15 Teahouse Inn
16 Berg House Café
18 Club Himalaya Resort

OTHER
8 Mahakali Shrine
14 Himalaya Bank
17 Bus stop

To Nagarkot Farmhouse Resort (500m), Kattike, Bhotichaur & Sankhu

Walking Track to Changu Narayan

To Bhaktapur (15km)

Army Camp

To Lookout Tower (3km)

Army Checkpost

ing, the unplanned scatter of lodges is unattractive.

Nagarkot is very much a one-night stand, and few visitors stay longer, although you can make some pleasant strolls in the surrounding country. There are a number of walks to and from Nagarkot, including fine walks down to Sundarijal, Sankhu, or Changu Narayan in the valley, north to Chisopani or south to Banepa (both beyond the valley).

Orientation

Nagarkot is on a ridge on the eastern rim of the valley and the view extends all the way from Dhaulagiri in the west, past Mt Everest (little more than a dot on the horizon) to Kanchenjunga in the east. An easy hour's walk (4km) south from the village will give an even better 360 degree view from a lookout tower on a ridge.

Nagarkot's accommodation is spread out along the dirt track that heads north from the bus stop at the town's one and only intersection. The main group of guesthouses crowd around a hill topped by a Mahakali shrine, a 15-minute walk from the bus stop,

Curd for sale at the market, Asan Tole

Colourful dyes, Pashupatinath

Rice noodles dyed red and pink, Lampata village

Rice paper drying near Barabise

Temple, Bungamati, Kathmandu Valley

Raja's Palace, Lo Manthang, Mustang Conservation Area

Bryaga village, Manang

and many have rooms that offer Himalayan views straight from your bed. At the worst you'll just have to take a few steps outside to bring the whole panorama into view.

Places to Stay – Budget

Nagarkot has a fair selection of lodges, guesthouses and hotels, most of them far from pretty. Most are expensive for the facilities you get, but the views are priceless.

Hotel Snowman (☎ 6680146; singles/ doubles with private bathroom US$18/25, deluxe singles/doubles with view US$30/40, 50% discount), an uninspiring spot, is the first place you come to heading north from the intersection. Even with heavy discounts it's overpriced. The rooms vary from bright and spacious to tiny and poky.

Galaxy View Tower (☎ 6680122; rooms US$5-15), just where the road splits, has a wide range of rooms spread across the hillside. Most are reasonably pleasant, and have at least partial views. The best-value rooms are in the middle bracket at around US$8 to US$10.

Hotel at the End of the Universe (☎ 6610874; chalets Rs 200-500, cottage Rs 1000, modern rooms Rs 700, family rooms Rs 1000), a budget hotel close to the Mahakali shrine, is a good little place. It has some pleasant but basic bamboo-walled cottages and also some modern brick rooms with hot showers. Only the restaurant has a view. With a carpeted bench around low tables it's a popular gathering place in the evening.

Peaceful Cottage (☎ 6680077; partitioned rooms with shared bathroom Rs 300/500, standard singles/doubles with private bathroom US$12/16, deluxe US$16/24), farther down the road, has pretty good rooms, though the cheapest are little more than cells divided by plywood. The real draw is the terrace restaurant and the friendly management. Climb to the top of the tower for the best views in town.

The road that forks off to the right by the Hotel Snowman leads to a few more hotels.

Sherpa Alpine Cottage (☎ 6680015; cottages Rs 250-350), first up, is a little place that has some very ramshackle timber cottages. It's a nice setting but the outside bathrooms and cramped rooms disappoint.

Naked Chef (☎ 6680006; dorm bed US$3, singles/doubles US$14/16, deluxe US$27/35, 60% discount) has some rooms below its popular restaurant. The cheaper ones are clean, bright and good value with discounts, though they don't have views. Deluxe rooms come with a sunny terrace and there's an OK five-bed dorm in the basement.

Hotel Green Valley (☎ 6680078; rooms Rs 250-500) is at the end of the dirt road, perched on the edge of a steep slope and a fair old walk from the bus station. The building is a concrete lump, but the rooms are decent and modern, there's a good-value restaurant and the terrace has a fabulous view. The cheaper rooms offer the best value.

Hotel Mile Stone (☎ 6680088; single/ double rooms Rs 200/300, cottages Rs 200/ 400), next door to the Hotel Green Valley, is a good budget place with four cramped cottages and a couple of much nicer doubles. The cosy restaurant is good.

Places to Stay – Mid-Range and Top-End

Hotel View Point (☎ 6680123; e vpoint@ wlink.com.np; singles/doubles US$24/30, deluxe US$55/65, 35% discount) is the highest hotel in Nagarkot, and something of a blot on the skyline. The rooms are nothing special and on the small side, but the views are superb and there are lots of nice terraces to relax on.

The Fort Resort (☎ 6680149; w www.moun tain-retreats.com; singles/doubles US$65/80, 30% discount), next to the Hotel Viewpoint, is a stylish place built in a Newari style on the site of the original kot (fort). Rooms in the main building are small and have no balconies. The secluded and peaceful cottages are better value, with private balcony and huge bathrooms, though they do vary. Breakfast is included in the price. There's a nice restaurant, with mains around Rs 280.

Hotel Chautari (☎ 6680075; e keyman@ wlink.com.np; singles/doubles US$48/60, 35% discount), farther along the main road from The Fort, has rooms in the rambling old building and in much better individual cottages. Rooms are cosy but a little dowdy.

Hotel Country Villa (☎ 6680128; e hcvilla@ col.com.np; singles/doubles US$55/65, 30% discount), down from the Peaceful Cottage, has smallish rooms but with private balconies, and there's a decent restaurant.

Nagarkot Farmhouse Resort (☎ 6228087; e nfh@mos.com.np; singles/doubles with *shared bathroom US$25/40, with private bathroom US$32/50, deluxe US$42/60, 20% discount)* is in a beautiful, Newari-inspired building with just 15 rooms. It's well away from the sprawl of Nagarkot, about 1km past Hotel Country Villa on the very rough track to Sankhu, and is highly recommended. It's run by Kathmandu's Hotel Vajra, and the rates include three meals. It's a great place to get away from it all or use as a hiking base.

Club Himalaya Resort *(☎ 6680080; e club@mos.com.np; singles/doubles US$60/ 75, 15% discount)* is at the other end of the ridge, south of the bus stop. A large construction like this really does nothing for the rural ambience. Having said that, the building has been well thought out: each room has a private balcony with view, and there are also views from the stylish atrium-type lobby with its restaurant and indoor swimming pool and Jacuzzi. The rooms are large and well furnished.

Also run by the resort, the **Teahouse Inn** *(☎ 6680045; singles/doubles US$17/22)* has cheaper and smaller rooms (without views) but is still cosy and allows access to the resort's pool and Jacuzzi.

Places to Eat

There's not much choice in the food department and most people eat at their lodge.

Teahouse Inn *(mains Rs 150-225)*, a modern place with a nice terrace aimed at daytrippers (it's relatively expensive), is above the main intersection (look for the blue roof). It is an attractive building, with good views.

Naked Chef *(☎ 6680006)* is no longer run by Kilroy's of Kathmandu but for now at least the food is still some of the best in Nagarkot. The largely Continental menu is similar to Kilroy's', even down to the apple crumble and custard (Rs 145). The house speciality is chicken with cheese, mushroom and spinach (Rs 380).

Berg House Café *(breakfasts Rs 50-90)*, right by the bus stop, is a cosy little place with a good range of breakfast foods like omelettes, pancakes and crepes, as well as heavier fare.

There are a couple of basic eating houses at the foot of the viewing tower, so you can at least get a drink or something to eat after making the trip on foot from Nagarkot.

Getting There & Away

Direct buses from Kathmandu are elusive beasts and you'll probably have to get a bus to Bhaktapur and change, which is a pain, since you get dropped off at the west end of town and have to pick up the next bus in the east. Extremely crowded buses depart for Nagarkot for Bhaktapur every hour or so (Rs 10, 1½ hours). A taxi from Bhaktapur is about Rs 600 one way and Rs 900 return.

Because of the inconvenience of taking the public buses, one 'tourist' bus' runs daily from Kathmandu at 1.30pm from a stand on Lekhnath Marg, west of the Hotel Malla and near the dairy (Rs 75, three hours). Return buses depart from the Galaxy View Tower at 10am. Buses may not run out of season.

Walking to, or preferably from, Nagarkot is an interesting alternative; there are several possible routes.

HIKES FROM NAGARKOT

There are a number of hiking routes to and from Nagarkot. If you only want to walk one way it's a good idea to take the bus to Nagarkot and walk back down. The following walks are all written heading downhill from Nagarkot.

Nepa Maps' 1:25,000 *Nagarkot – Short Trekking on the Kathmandu Valley Rim* is useful, though its 1:50,000 *Around the Kathmandu Valley* is probably good enough.

To Changu Narayan

Walking down to Changu Narayan is more interesting than the walk down to Bhaktapur. From Nagarkot it is very easy to see the long spur that extends into the Kathmandu Valley. At the very end of the spur the ridgeline gives one final hiccup and then drops down to the valley floor. The beautiful temple of Changu Narayan is on the top of this final bump on the ridgeline.

The walking trail from Nagarkot parallels the road to Bhaktapur along a ridge, branching off at the sharp hairpin bend at **Tharkot** (marked on some maps as Deuralibhanjhang). Catching a bus to here from Nagarkot (Rs 5) saves you the tedious first half of the walk.

From the bend, take the dirt road heading west and take the left branch (the right drops towards Sankhu). The track climbs uphill through a pine forest for about 20 minutes until it reaches the top of the ridge and then it simply follows the ridgeline, undulating gently down to Changu Narayan. The walking trail passes through small Chhetri villages with wonderful views over the valley to the Himalaya. Finally, the shining roof of **Changu Narayan** appears above the village of Changu itself, from where a stone-paved street leads to the temple. From Tharkot it takes about one to 1½ hours to walk to the temple. See Changu Narayan Temple under Around Bhaktapur earlier in this chapter for details of the temple and hikes from here to Bhaktapur and the road to Bodhnath.

To Sankhu

From Nagarkot a dirt road leads all the way to Sankhu, offering an easy and interesting way to return to Kathmandu on foot or bike.

From Nagarkot take the northwest road down to the Nagarkot Farmhouse Resort and follow the switchbacks down to the village of **Kattike**, which has a tea house and shop. Take a left at the junction at the edge of town. You can continue all the way down this track. For a more interesting walk take a minor road that turns off sharply to the right fifteen minutes down this track. Follow this footpath for 15 to 20 minutes as it shrinks to a trail and then take a sharp left downhill past several houses to join the main track. From here it's an hour's slog to **Sankhu** and the town's east gate.

To Sundarijal

It takes two easy days or one very long one to reach Sundarijal from Nagarkot on a trail that follows the valley rim. From Sundarijal you can take the road to Gokarna, Bodhnath and Kathmandu or you can continue for another day along the rim to Shivapuri and Budhanilkantha. Some trekking agencies operate treks on this valley-rim walk, but it is also possible to find accommodation in village inns. There are many confusing trail junctions, so ask directions frequently.

The trail follows the same route as to Sankhu as far as the village of **Kattike** (about one hour) and then turns right (north) to **Jorsim Pauwa**. Walk farther down through **Bagdhara**, with its village inns, to **Chowki Bhanjyang** (about one hour). From Chowki Bhanjyang, another hour's walk will take you farther north through **Nagle** to **Bhotichaur**, which makes a good place to stop overnight in a village inn.

The walk continues by returning towards **Chowki Bhanjyang** for a short distance and taking the fork by a *chautara* (porters' resting place) uphill, then continues more steeply uphill to cross a ridge line before dropping down on the middle of three trails to **Chule** (or Jhule). From here the trail enters the **Shivapuri National Park** *(entry Rs 250)*, Nepal's most recent protected area, and contours around the edge of the valley, crossing several ridgelines running down into the valley, before dropping down to **Mulkarkha** and the trail past the reservoir and along the pipeline to **Sundarijal**. The last part of this trail to Sundarijal is the first part of the popular Helambu Trek (see the Trekking chapter).

Another variant on this hike is to continue northwest from Bhotichaur to **Chisapani**, where there are several trekking lodges (Chisapani is an overnight stop on the Helambu trek), and then the next day to hike southwest back over the ridge through Shivapuri National Park to Sundarijal.

To Banepa

The town of Banepa is outside the valley and is the major junction town on the way to Dhulikhel on the Arniko Hwy (the road to the Tibetan border). From Nagarkot, you start this walk near the lookout tower south of town at the southern part of the ridge and follow a steep descent to the southeast. Following a precise trail is difficult, but fortunately that isn't a problem – all the trails lead to Banepa. A few kilometres north of Banepa the trail passes through the old Newari town of Nala with its interesting temples (see following).

From Banepa, you can take a bus back to Kathmandu or on to Dhulikhel or Panauti.

BANEPA

Just outside the valley, the small town of Banepa is a busy crossroads, 29km from Kathmandu. Dhulikhel is just beyond Banepa, the temple town of Panauti is about 7km south, the interesting village of Nala is 4km to the northwest, and Chandeshwari, with its legendary old temple, is only 1km or so northeast – yet noisy Banepa itself is of limited interest.

There are some pleasant squares and quieter laneways in the older northwest part of Banepa. The old town square has two

Narayan temples with virtually back-to-back worshipful Garuda statues. Right beside the turn-off to Chandeshwari is a pretty tank with bas-reliefs of gods at one end.

Getting There & Away
Regular buses leave from Kathmandu's City bus station (Rs 15, two hours). Buses continue on from Banepa to Dhulikhel and farther towards Kodari on the Tibetan border. There are also a few regular services south from Banepa to Panauti.

AROUND BANEPA
Chandeshwari Temple
Only 1km or so northeast of Banepa the temple to the goddess Chandeshwari perches on the very edge of a gorge. The road out of Banepa runs gently uphill, then just as gently downhill through open fields and to a short village street, past an old tank and right to the arched entrance gate to the temple.

Legend has it that the people of this valley were once terrorised by a demon known as Chand, when Parvati, in her demon-slaying mode, got rid of the nuisance she took the name Chandeshwari, 'Slayer of Chand', and this temple was built in her honour.

The temple is entered through a doorway topped by a brilliantly coloured relief of Parvati disposing of the demon. The triple-roofed temple has roof struts showing the eight Ashta Matrikas and eight Bhairabs, but the temple's most notable feature is on the west wall, which is painted with a huge and colourful fresco of Bhairab at his destructive worst.

The temple also has a Shiva shrine complete with lingam, and Nandi and Ganesh also make an appearance. The ghats below the temple, beside the stream, are an auspicious place to die and people come here when their end is nigh.

Nala
The small town of Nala is about 4km northwest of Banepa. Nala's **Bhagwati Temple** dominates the central square of the town and is one of the very few four-tiered temples in the Kathmandu Valley. On the edge of the settlement is the Buddhist temple of Karunamaya, dedicated to Avalokiteshvara.

The old road from Bhaktapur to Banepa via Nala offers the most pleasant route if you are cycling from Kathmandu to Dhulikhel.

DHULIKHEL
☎ code 011 • pop 9,800
Only 3km southeast of Banepa (32km from Kathmandu) is the interesting small town of Dhulikhel. It's popular as a Himalayan viewpoint, in part because the road to Dhulikhel is an easier route than the steep and winding road to Nagarkot, but also because Dhulikhel is a real Newari town, not just a tourist resort. It's also a good centre for short day treks – many visitors come here to stretch their legs before setting off on longer treks.

The prime Himalayan viewpoint is the parade ground, on the ridge just southeast of the centre. An even better view can be found from the hill topped by a Kali Temple, about a 30-minute walk along the Namobuddha trail. The peaks on view stretch from Langtang Lirung (7246m) in the east, through Dorje Lakpa (6966m) to the huge bulk of Gauri Shankar (7145m) and nearby Melungtse (7181m) in the west.

A new highway from Dhulikhel to Sindhuli is being constructed with Japanese assistance and when finished will considerably shorten the travelling time between Kathmandu and the towns of the eastern Terai. What an increase in heavy vehicle traffic will do for the peaceful ambience of Dhulikhel – and the narrow and inadequately engineered Arniko Hwy back to Kathmandu – is not yet clear. Construction was put on hold in 2002 (every time the government workers laid some tarmac, Maoist rebels would creep up in the middle of the night and blow it up!) but should resume before long.

Temples
The old part of the town, west of the bus stop, is an interesting area to wander around, with some fine old Newari buildings and several interesting temples. The town's main square has a tank, the small triple-roofed **Hari Siddhi Temple** and a **Vishnu Temple** fronted by two worshipful Garudas in quite different styles. One is a kneeling stone Garuda topping a low pillar, while the second Garuda is in bright metal, more like the bird-faced Garudas of Indonesia than the conventional Nepali Garudas.

Walking in the other direction you pass the Nawarangu Guest House and the mountain viewpoint, and after 1.5km you reach the junction where the road turns right (west) to Namobuddha. Continue straight on from the

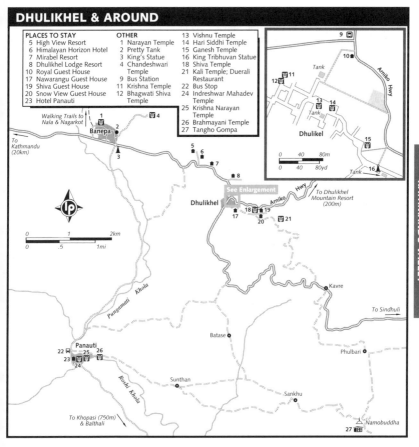

DHULIKHEL & AROUND

PLACES TO STAY	OTHER	
5 High View Resort	1 Narayan Temple	13 Vishnu Temple
6 Himalayan Horizon Hotel	2 Pretty Tank	14 Hari Siddhi Temple
7 Mirabel Resort	3 King's Statue	15 Ganesh Temple
8 Dhulikhel Lodge Resort	4 Chandeshwari	16 King Tribhuvan Statue
10 Royal Guest House	Temple	21 Kali Temple; Duerali
17 Nawarangu Guest House	9 Bus Station	Restaurant
19 Shiva Guest House	11 Krishna Temple	22 Bus Stop
20 Snow View Guest House	12 Bhagwati Shiva	24 Indreshwar Mahadev
23 Hotel Panauti	Temple	Temple
		25 Krishna Narayan
		Temple
		26 Brahmayani Temple
		27 Tangho Gompa

Walking Trails to Nala & Nagarkot

Banepa

To Kathmandu (20km)

Dhulikel

Tank

Amiko Hwy

Dhulikhel

See Enlargement

To Dhulikhel Mountain Resort (200m)

Kavre

To Sindhuli

Panauti

Batase

Phulbari

Sunthan

Sankhu

To Khopasi (750m) & Balthali

Roshi Khola

Pungamati Khola

Namobuddha

junction and dip down to a picturesque little **Shiva Temple** at the bottom of a gorge. Water flows through the site, where the main sanctum features a four-faced lingam topped with a metal dome with four *nagas* (snake deities) arching down from the pinnacle. The temple is fronted by two figures of Nandi on pillars, and kneeling devotees. To one side is a fine image of Ganesh. Below that is a tank, but this is a temple with everything – if you look around you can find images of Hanuman, Saraswati, Shiva and Parvati, lingams, tridents and much more.

Dhulikhel's final temple attraction is the **Kali Temple** high up the hill towards Namobuddha. Climb up the hill for the excellent view, not for the temple, which is of little interest. To get there, take the right branch

of the junction mentioned earlier and follow the footpaths, not the mud road. It's a 20- to 30-minute uphill walk. The decent Deurali Restaurant is just below the temple.

Places to Stay – Budget

Nawarangu Guest House (☎ 561226; singles/ doubles without bathroom Rs 120/200, with bathroom Rs 200/300), southeast of the main chowk towards the Shiva Temple, is a classic budget backpacker hangout, with cheap rooms, a cosy restaurant decorated with local paintings (for sale) and good honey pancakes (Rs 40). Part of the old building collapsed during a recent monsoon and the rebuilt rooms now offer hot water bathrooms.

Snow View Guest House (☎ 561229; doubles with shared bathroom Rs 300, with private bathroom Rs 500-700) is another couple of minutes' walk towards the Shiva Temple. It's a friendly place set in a pleasant garden with bright clean rooms, a rooftop sitting area and mountain views. Rooms are basic but comfortable; the more expensive doubles are carpeted.

Shiva Guest House (doubles with shared bathroom Rs 200-400, with bathroom Rs 600) is a tiny family-run place with only five clean, fresh rooms. The upper floor has the best views. Food comes fresh from the organic garden. It's very secluded and there's no road here; follow the signposted path one minute on foot from the Shiva Temple.

Royal Guest House (☎ 564010; singles/doubles with shared bathroom Rs 225/375, with private bath Rs 450/750) is another good place, back by the main road near the bus stand. Rooms are good value and the common bathrooms are clean. Roadside rooms can be noisy. There's a cosy **restaurant** (mains Rs 90-140) with satellite TV.

Places to Stay – Mid-Range & Top End

Dhulikhel Lodge Resort (☎ 561114; W www .dhulikhellodgeresort.com; singles/doubles US$70/80, up to 70% discount) is just off the main road, near the Dhulikhel bus stop. This large, modern but tastefully built place has comfortable rooms and superb views (try to get a room on the top floor). There's also a block of newer rooms, but some don't have the views. Discounts can make it excellent value.

Mirabel Resort (☎ 561972; e mirabel@ info.com.np; singles/doubles US$90/100, up to 50% discount), a top-end place, is a rather out-of-place Mediterranean-style resort, but it is very well done and offers the top accommodation in Dhulikhel. The rooms have views, a balcony, fridge, TV and phone.

Himalayan Horizon Hotel (☎ 561296; W www.himalayanhorizon.com; singles/ doubles US$51/55, deluxe US$62/66, 20% discount), also known as the Hotel Sun-n-Snow, is farther again from Mirabel Resort. The hotel is a bit of a monster, but it does feature traditional woodcarving, has a pleasant restaurant and garden terrace area, and all the rooms face straight out on to the Himalayan peaks. The spacious split-level deluxe rooms come with private balcony views and offer the best value, although if the other resorts are offering bigger discounts head for those.

High View Resort (☎ 561966; e hvrd@ wlink.com.np; singles/doubles US$30/40, deluxe US$60/65, 50% discount) is an excellent place 700m further down the same side road as the Himalayan Horizon and then a stiff five-minute climb up the hillside. Huge deluxe rooms come with a fireplace, bathtub, sitting area and private balcony with excellent views. The cheaper rooms are above the restaurant and much smaller but still very pleasant.

Dhulikhel Mountain Resort (☎ 561466; e dmrktm@wlink.com.np; singles/doubles US$76/78, 20% discount), a flash spot, is one of a number of upmarket places downhill from Dhulikhel towards Tibet. This one is 4km beyond the village and the Himalayan views from here are also superb. Accommodation is in luxurious thatched cottages set in a very pleasant garden.

There are several other resort-type places, all of which are pretty good and offer varying degrees of luxury.

Getting There & Away

Frequent buses to Dhulikhel leave from Kathmandu's City bus station (Rs 18, two hours). The buses skirt Bhaktapur at the eastern end of the valley and then climb over the Sanga Pass out of the valley, passing a major military checkpoint en route. The last bus back to Kathmandu is around 5.30pm.

A taxi from Kathmandu costs about Rs 800, and about Rs 550 from Bhaktapur.

The walk to Dhulikhel from Nagarkot is an interesting alternative. After watching the sunrise at Nagarkot you can walk down through Nala to Banepa, from where you can take a bus the last few kilometres to Dhulikhel (see Hikes from Nagarkot earlier in this chapter for details).

DHULIKHEL TO NAMOBUDDHA

The hike from Dhulikhel to Namobuddha is a fine leg-stretcher. It takes about three hours each way, so it makes a good day walk. The walk can be made either as a return trip from Dhulikhel or a one-way hike to the interesting village of Panauti, from where you can stay the night or, if you start early enough, return by bus to Dhulikhel via Banepa.

Namobuddha is a relatively easy trek, which can even be made during the monsoon and it's also a good mountain bike ride. Asking directions is no problem, as any Westerner heading in this direction is assumed to be going to Namobuddha. Much of the hike follows a dirt road that is currently being upgraded; it remains to be seen whether increased traffic takes away from the pleasure of the hike.

From Dhulikhel the trail first climbs up to the Kali Temple lookout (see Temples under Dhulikhel earlier in this chapter) then drops down (take the left path after the Deurali Restaurant) for half and hour to the village of **Kavre** by the new road to Sindhuli. Cross the road, take the road by some prayer flags and pretty much follow this for the next hour until you round a ridge to the village of **Phulbari**, where you can get a cold drink or cup of tea. Soon you crest a hill and in the distance you'll see a Tibetan monastery atop a hill, with Namobuddha just below it. Just before Namobuddha the main track branches right; take the left branch to the stupa.

There are several tea houses by the stupa where you can get a basic lunch. You will be asked for a donation to the site as an entry fee.

Surprisingly, there is very little known about the stupa at **Namobuddha**, but it is an important destination for Buddhist pilgrims. A legend relates that the Buddha came across a tigress close to death from starvation and unable to feed her cubs. The sorrowful Buddha allowed the hungry tigress to consume him. A marble tablet depicting the event in Tangho Gompa on the hill above the stupa marks the holy site where this event is supposed to have taken place. It's worth hiking ten minutes up to the monastery; take the path uphill to the left of the stupa.

From Namobuddha the trail to **Sankhu** descends to a track from the right side of the stupa, through forest to the temple and mini ghats of Sankhu. About an hour from Namobuddha the path splits right uphill to Batase and Dhulikhel, or left along the road past terraced fields to **Sunthan** and **Panauti**, about two hours from Namobuddha.

PANAUTI

In a valley about 7km south of Banepa (36km from Kathmandu), the small town of Panauti sits at the junction of the Roshi Khola and Pungamati Khola. Like Allahabad in India, a third 'invisible' river is said to join the other two at the confluence (see the boxed text 'Trickery & Repentance at Panauti'). A popular tradition asserts that the entire town is built on a single piece of solid stone, making it immune to earthquakes.

Panauti once stood at the junction of important trading routes and had a royal palace in its main square. Today it's just a quiet backwater, but is all the more interesting for that. The town has retained and restored (with French help) much of its traditional architecture and has a number of interesting temples, one of which may be the oldest in Nepal.

Indreshwar Mahadev Temple

The three-storey Indreshwar Mahadev Temple in the village centre is a Shiva Temple. It was originally built in 1294 over a Shiva lingam and was subsequently rebuilt in the 15th century. In 1988 an earthquake caused serious damage. In its original form it may well have been the oldest temple in Nepal – Kathmandu's Kasthamandap may predate it, but Kasthamandap was originally built as a dharamsala, not as a temple.

Trickery & Repentance at Panauti

Legends relate that Ahilya, the beautiful wife of a Vedic sage, was seduced by the god Indra, who tricked her by assuming the shape of her husband. When the sage returned and discovered what had happened he took a bizarre revenge upon Indra by causing Indra's body to become covered in yonis, female sexual organs! Naturally, Indra was somewhat put out by this and for many years he and his wife Indrayani repented at the auspicious *sangam* (river confluence) at Panauti. Eventually, Parvati, Shiva's consort, took pity upon Indrayani and turned her into the invisible river, which joins the two visible ones in Panauti. More years passed and eventually Shiva decided to release Indra from his strange predicament. Shiva appeared in Panauti as a great lingam and when Indra bathed in the river his yonis disappeared. The Shiva lingam is the one that stands in the temple.

The temple, run-down though it may be, is certainly a fine one and the roof struts depicting the various incarnations of Shiva and some discreetly amorous couples are said to be masterpieces of Newari wood-carving. The courtyard has numerous smaller shrines apart from the stone pillar to Ahilya.

To the south of the main temple is a rectangular Bhairab Temple, with three faces peering out of the upstairs windows, rather like the Shiva-Parvati Temple in Kathmandu's Durbar Square. A small, double-roofed Shiva Temple stands by the northwestern corner, while a Vishnu shrine with a 2m-high image of the god faces the temple from the west. Look for the pots and pans hanging under the roof eaves of the main temple, donated to the temple by newlyweds to ensure a happy married life.

Other Temples

On the east side of the village, at the junction of the Roshi Khola and Pungamati Khola, is the interesting **Krishna Narayan Temple** complex, with some woodcarvings of similar age to the Indreshwar Mahadev Temple (look for Krishna playing his flute on the roof struts). The riverbank stone sculptures are also of interest, but unfortunately the late 1980s were cruel to Panauti: as well as an earthquake there were severe floods, which swept away the cremation ghats at the river junction.

Across the Pungamati Khola is the 17th-century **Brahmayani Temple**; a suspension bridge crosses the river at this point. Brahmayani is the chief goddess of the village and her image is drawn around the town each year in the chariot festival.

As you enter Panauti through the northwestern gate, turn right at the first crossroads to get to a collection of interesting buildings, including the wonderfully restored municipality office, a pilgrim resthouse and a temple with some lovely golden window frames. There are lots of other temples and shrines hidden in the backstreets around here.

Special Events

Panauti celebrates a chariot festival at the end of the monsoon each year, when images of the gods from the town's various temples are drawn around the streets in temple carts. The festival starts from the town's old Durbar Square.

Every 12 years (next in 2010), the Magh Sankranti festival (in mid-January, or the Nepali lunar month of Magh) is celebrated with a great *mela* (religious fair) in Panauti that attracts large crowds of pilgrims, worshippers and *sadhus*.

Places to Stay & Eat

The best option is the **Hotel Panauti** (☎ 011-5661055; singles/doubles with shared bathroom Rs 150/300, with private bathroom Rs 300/500), about a five-minute walk south from the main western gate by the bus stand. Rooms are simple but bright, clean and comfortable (though the hot water is only solar heated) and there's a decent rooftop terrace and café.

The **Aaphno Ghar Newari Kitchen** (snacks Rs 20-75) is a friendly local hangout in the upper floor of an atmospheric *path* (pilgrims shelter), 70m inside the town's western gate. It's a great place to hang out, nurse a beer and try Newari snacks such as *chatamari* (rice-flour pancake topped with meat and/or egg) and *sekuwa* (barbecued meat). Look for the old runners of a temple chariot just below the building.

The **Indreni Café** (snacks Rs 50-120), near the western entrance to the Indreshwar Mahadev Temple, is a more tourist-oriented place with a great location in a lovely old building.

Getting There & Away

Buses run frequently between Panauti and Kathmandu's City bus station (Rs 19) via Banepa; the last bus leaves Panauti around 6pm. For Dhulikhel you'll have to change in Banepa.

See Dhulikhel to Namobuddha earlier in this section for some information on walking to Panauti.

AROUND PANAUTI

The terraced fields, villages and lush hills southeast of Panauti offer great scope for hiking and village exploration. It's a far less visited area than Dhulikhel.

The only place to stay is the excellent **Balthali Resort** (☎ 011-562896; in Kathmandu ☎ 4477510; ☑ www.balthalivillageresort.com; singles/doubles US$15/30, half board US$25 per person), perched on top of a hill above the village of the same name, with sweeping Himalayan views. The 10 rooms lack much

AROUND THE
KATHMANDU VALLEY

architectural charm, but are decent and clean. Staff there can lead you on hikes to Tamang villages like Dada Gaun, across the Rossi Khola to the Namobuddha stupa or deep into the Mahabharat range to the south.

To get to Balthali take a bus (Rs 4) or walk from Panauti to Kholpasi, past the sericulture (silk) cooperative, and then continue on foot over the Saladu Khosi for an hour or so to Balthali village.

The Southern Valley

The destinations in this section lie on four radial routes that branch off the Kathmandu Ring Rd like spokes from a wheel, making it hard to combine more than a couple of sites in one out-and-back trip. There is, however, a couple of useful connector routes that link a couple of these radial routes to make a useful loop itinerary.

The Chapagaon and Godavari routes can be combined on a bike, motorbike or foot trip. Kirtipur, Chobar and Bungamati can be combined on another bike or motorbike trip by crossing the Bagmati River by Chobar Gorge. Kirtipur, Chobar, Pharping and Dakshinkali can also be visited in one trip.

Most of these destinations are excellent day trips on a mountain bike. Many involve steep uphill stretches as you approach the valley walls – which is all the better for the return trip. Of these, the best mountain bike runs are probably the roads to Bungamati and to the Lele Valley via Chapagaon.

KIRTIPUR

Strung out along a ridge 5km southwest of Kathmandu, the small town of Kirtipur is a relatively neglected and timeless backwater despite its proximity to the capital. At one time it was associated with Patan and then became a mini-kingdom in its own right.

During the 1768 conquest of the valley by Prithvi Narayan Shah it was clear that Kirtipur, with its superbly defensible hilltop position, would be the key to defeating the Malla kingdoms, so it was here the Gorkha king struck first and hardest. Kirtipur's resistance was strong, but eventually, after a bitter siege, the town was taken and the inhabitants paid a terrible price for their courageous resistance. The king, incensed by the long struggle his forces had endured,

ordered that the nose and lips be cut off every male inhabitant in the town. Fortunately, for a small minority, he was practical as well as cruel, and those who could play wind instruments were spared.

At one time there were 12 gates into the city; traces of the old city wall can still be seen. As you wander through Kirtipur, you can see dyed yarn hanging from upstairs windows and hear the background clatter of the town's hand looms. Many of the town's 9000 inhabitants are weavers or farmers; the lower-caste people generally live outside the old city wall, lower down the hill. Kirtipur's hilltop position offers fine views over Kathmandu, with the Himalaya rising behind.

The campus of Nepal's **Tribhuvan University** (open 9am-6pm Sun-Fri), named after King Tribhuvan, stands below Kirtipur hill and has the best library facilities to be found in Nepal.

Temples

Kirtipur's ridge is actually two hills, with a lower saddle between them. The **Chilanchu Vihara** tops the southern hill and has a central stupa with four smaller stupas, numerous statues and bells, and Buddhist monastery buildings around it. The entrance to the courtyard is marked by a tree that has completely encased a small shrine.

From the rear of the stupa go right down to the *shikhara*-style **Lohan Dehar**. Continue beyond the temple, then take a left to the **Bagh Bhairab Temple**, at the bottom of the saddle where the town's two hills meet. The upper wall of this famous triple-roofed temple is decorated with the swords, machetes and shields of the Newari troops defeated by King Prithvi Narayan Shah. The temple sides are decorated with buffalo horns. The temple's principal image is of Bhairab in his tiger form and is sacred to both Hindus and Buddhists. Look for the temple's *torana* to the left of the entrance door with an image of Vishnu astride the Garuda and, below him, Bhairab between Ganesh and Kumar. To the far right of the courtyard is a fertility shrine under a tin umbrella. Animal sacrifices are made early on Tuesday and Saturday mornings. The square in front of the temple was the former royal residence and features some fine woodcarving.

From the saddle, head west through the village to a stone stairway, flanked by stone elephants, that leads to the triple-roofed **Uma Maheshwar Temple**. The elephants wear spiked saddles to keep children from riding them! Curiously, the main image of Shiva and Parvati is a standing one, not in the standard Uma Maheshwar pose. To the left of the central image of the god and his consort is a smaller image in the standard pose. The temple was originally built in 1673 and had four roofs until it was badly damaged by the earthquake of 1934.

Getting There & Away

Bus, Minibus & Taxi Numerous buses (No 21) depart from Kathmandu's City bus station (Rs 5, 45 minutes). They terminate at the university, from where you can stroll up the hill to the town itself. Alternatively, it's a short trip by taxi (around Rs 230).

From the bus park at the east entrance to town you'll notice a modern Thai-designed Buddhist temple to the left of Kirtipur's Naya Bajaar (New Bazaar) at the foot of the Kirtipur hill. From the beginning of Naya Bazaar, climb the stairway straight ahead and at the top take a right and then a left to get to the Chilanchu Vihara.

Cycling It takes around 1½ hours to Kirtipur by mountain bike, and it's quite a long, steep hill from the road to Dakshinkali. After about 1km from the Kathmandu's Ring Rd bridge over the Bagmati River turn right at the road flanked by two low, brick gatehouses. Continue up the hill for 1km or so and take the left fork where the minibuses park (take the right fork to the university). See the following entry for trekking details in the area.

KIRTIPUR TO CHOBAR

Instead of simply returning from Kirtipur to Kathmandu the same way, you can continue by foot or bike from Kirtipur to Chobar and the Chobar Gorge. The route is mostly rideable, but is also an interesting walk.

From the Chilanchu Vihara at the southeastern end of Kirtipur, head south downhill past a brick base (built with the intention of being the foundations of a stupa) to the main road around the base of the village. Head southeast to the village of **Panga**, which has a number of temples. You'll probably arrive in the northwest corner of the town so head south through the village

and then swing back to the northeast corner of the village where you'll find the road to Chobar. There are two parallel roads to Chobar village; both join at the **Vishnu Devi Mandir**, marked by a large trident. The temple has a tiny Garuda on a pillar and a small image of a reclining Vishnu surrounded by *naga* serpents. If you get lost at any point just ask for the road to Vishnu Devi Mandir.

Continue past the temple for around 30m, join a cart path to the right (south) and after a couple of minutes branch left up a cobbled path and then left again up a steep footpath past clumps of bamboo. At the next junction take a right up another path up to the first square of the interesting small village of Chobar, right on the top of the hill.

After you've visited Chobar's Adinath Lokeshwar Temple head out the east entrance past a stupa and follow the path down east and then southeast past a small quarry to the main Pharping road. A path leads down from the other side of the road to the Jal Binayak Temple and the bridge across the river. It's possible to catch a bus from here back to Kathmandu or south to Pharping.

CHOBAR

The picturesque little village of Chobar, 6km from Kathmandu, tops a hill overlooking the Bagmati River where it flows through the Chobar Gorge.

The town's main attraction is the **Adinath Lokeshwar Temple**, originally built in the 15th century and reconstructed in 1640. Inside the main sanctuary the red face of Rato Machhendranath can be seen peering out. The temple is dedicated to this popular valley deity and is sacred to both Hindus and Buddhists. Six figures of the Buddha are lined up beneath the temple's golden *torana*, but the most interesting feature is the astounding array of metal pots, pans and water containers that are fixed to boards hanging all around the temple roofs next to photos of the recently deceased. These kitchen utensils are donated to the temple by newlyweds in order to ensure a happy married life.

Getting There & Away

Buses to Pharping and Dakshinkali run by the turn-off to Chobar. See Kirtipur to Chobar earlier in this section for details of walking between Kirtipur and the Chobar Gorge via Chobar.

CHOBAR GORGE

The small Chobar Gorge is southeast of Chobar village, where the Bagmati River cuts through the edge of the Chobar hill. Down by the river, just south of the gorge, is another important temple, the Jal Binayak.

The valley's first cement factory is a more recent addition to the scenery. A high percentage of solid particles in the valley's hazy air can be attributed to this place, though there are plans to close the monstrosity.

A neat little suspension bridge spans the river here; there are fine views of the gorge on one side and the Jal Binayak Temple on the other.

Jal Binayak Temple

Just below the gorge on the riverbank stands one of the valley's most important Ganesh shrines. The triple-roofed temple dates from 1602, although there was probably a temple here even earlier. On the temple's eastern platform there is an aged and worn image of Shiva and Parvati in the Uma Maheshwar pose, which predates the temple by 500 years.

The temple's Ganesh image is simply a huge rock, projecting out the back and bearing very little likeness to an elephant-headed god. The temple's roof struts depict eight Bhairabs and the eight Ashta Matrikas (Mother Goddesses) with whom Ganesh often appears. On the lower roof Ganesh himself appears on some of the struts, with beautiful female figures standing beside him and tiny, brightly painted erotic depictions below. A bronze figure of Ganesh's 'vehicle', in this case a shrew rather than a rat, stands respectfully in the courtyard and faces the shrine.

Getting There & Away

The Chobar Gorge is usually visited en route to Pharping and Dakshinkali by road. A more interesting way to reach Chobar Gorge is to walk there from Kirtipur via the village of Chobar. See Kirtipur to Chobar earlier in this section for more details.

From the gorge you can cross the suspension bridge and follow a trail on the left up hill to a small village junction. A left here will take you the Kathmandu Ring Rd, entering Patan at Jawlakhel. A right turn will take you on a convoluted path that eventually links up with the Bungamati road.

Legend of the Chobar Gorge

Eons ago the Kathmandu Valley was the Kathmandu Lake. In that long-ago time, the hill of Swayambhunath was an island; gradually the lake dried up to leave the valley we see today.

Legends relate that the change from lake to valley was a much more dramatic one, for Manjushri is said to have taken his mighty sword and with one blow cut open the valley edge to release the pent-up waters. The place where his sword struck rock was Chobar on the southern edge of the valley and the result was the Chobar Gorge.

Countless snakes were washed out of the valley with the departing waters, but Kartotak, 'king of the snakes', is said to still live close to the gorge in the Taudaha pond, next to the road to Pharping.

PHARPING

Pharping is a thriving, traditional Newari town, 19km south of Kathmandu and surprisingly untouched by the swarms of tourists that visit Dakshinkali. The town is famous for its pilgrimage sites, whose Hindu origins have been largely superseded by the now predominant Tibetan Buddhist monasteries. The town is popular with both Tibetan and Hindu pilgrims.

The Pilgrimage Route

The best way to visit the sights of Pharping is to join the other pilgrims on a clockwise pilgrim circuit (a *parikrama* in Nepali or *kora* in Tibetan).

As you enter the town from the main road, take the first right by the football pitch and head uphill, past the large Tibetan chorten (pop inside to turn its prayer wheels), a couple of restaurants, and the Sakyapa school **Tharig Gompa** with its huge chorten. Just beyond here at the bend in the road is a Tibetan monastery signposted 'Pharping Ganesh and Saraswati Temple'. The chapel to the left is actually a Tibetan-style **Drolma Lhakhang** (Drolma is the Tibetan name for Tara, who is identified here with Saraswati), with images of Ganesh and the 21 manifestations of Tara.

To the right of this chapel is the **Rigzu Phodrang Gompa**, which is identified with the Indian sage Padmasambhava (known to

Tibetans as Guru Rinpoche), the Bodhisattva credited with introducing Buddhism to Tibet. He is clearly recognised by his curly moustache and *katvanga* (staff of skulls).

Ascend the flight of stairs between the two temples and eventually you'll come to the **Guru Rinpoche Cave** (also known as the Asura, or Gorakhnath, Cave), perched on the hill at the centre of a web of prayer flags. Take off your shoes to enter. There are great views of Pharping and the valley.

Continue out of the cave enclosure, down a flight of stairs lined with prayer flags to the **Vajra Yogini Temple**. The 17th-century pagoda-style temple is in a courtyard surrounded by relatively modern two-storey, Newari-style living quarters. The Tantric Buddhist goddess Vajra Jogini (known to Hindus as Ugra Tara) is featured in the temple's toranas.

From here, pilgrims continue east up some stairs to the Nyingmapa school **Do Ngag Choeling Gompa**, whose main chapel features a central statue of Sakyamuni flanked by Padmasambhava and Vajrasattva. From the monastery head down to the junction and branch downhill to the main road and the Amdo Dechen Restaurant (see Places to Stay & Eat) for a post-pilgrimage cup of tea.

Places to Stay & Eat
Dakshinkali Village Inn (☎ 4710053; ⓦ www.dakchhinkali.com; singles/doubles US$15/25, 20% discount), on a bluff right by the main gate which marks the start of the descent to Dakshinkali, is quiet and relaxing, with fairly basic but still cosy rooms. There's also a very pleasant garden **restaurant** (snacks Rs 80, mains Rs 130-190).

Dakshinkali Fast Food (☎ 4710041; singles/doubles Rs 200/300), across the road, is a bare-bones option with bright but slightly grubby rooms, hard beds and basic common bathrooms. The downstairs **restaurant** (Rs 50-100) is cheap and cheerful.

Asura Cave Hotel (rooms with shared bathroom Rs 250-300), in Pharping Village, is a decent restaurant with rooms on the upper floors.

Also in Parphing, **Snowland** is a good little Tibetan restaurant, but all food is made to order and so it doesn't pay to be in a hurry. The *momos* (dumplings) with soup (Rs 20) here are excellent. **Amdo Dechen Restaurant** is another good place for a cheap lunch.

Hattiban Resort (☎ 4371397; ⓦ www .intrekasia.com/out.html; singles/doubles US$52/62), perched on a ridge a few kilometres before Pharping, offers some of the best views in the entire valley. The small resort is set in a pine forest, and is reached by a rough, steep and winding 2km track from the main road, although you can leave your vehicle in the (guarded) car park at the bottom and take the resort 4WD up the track. The resort buildings are pleasant, being timber-lined, and the **restaurant** (mains US$10) has an excellent terrace. There are 24 rooms, each with balcony and bathroom. A return transfer from Kathmandu costs US$80 per vehicle.

Getting There & Away
Buses leave throughout the day for Pharping from Kathmandu's City bus station (Rs 16, two hours), or catch the No 21 bus from Kathmandu's Shahid Gate.

AROUND PHARPING
Dakshinkali
At the southern edge of the valley, in a dark, somewhat spooky location in the cleft between two hills and at the confluence of two rivers, stands the bloody temple of Dakshinkali (entry Rs 15, including parking). The temple is dedicated to the goddess Kali, Shiva's consort in her most bloodthirsty incarnation, and twice a week faithful Nepalis journey here to satisfy her bloodlust.

Sacrifices are always made to goddesses, and the creatures to be sacrificed must be uncastrated male animals. Saturday is the major sacrificial day of the week, when a steady parade of chickens, ducks, goats, sheep, pigs and even the occasional buffalo come here to have their throats cut or their heads lopped off by professional local butchers. Tuesday is also a sacrificial day, but the blood does not flow quite as freely as on Saturday. During the annual celebrations of Dasain in October the temple is literally awash with blood and the image of Kali is bathed in it.

After their rapid dispatch the animals are butchered in the stream beside the temple and their carcasses are either brought home for a feast or boiled up on the spot for a picnic in the grounds. You'll see families arriving with pots, bags of vegetables and armfuls of firewood for the big day out. Non-Hindus are not allowed into the actual compound where Kali's image resides (there is often an incredibly long queue for Hindus to get in), but it is OK to take photos from outside. Unfortunately, many tourists behave poorly, perching vulture-like from every available vantage point in order to get the goriest possible photos. However extraordinary the sights might seem, this is a religious ceremony, and the participants should be treated with respect, not turned into a sideshow.

The path down to the temple is lined with tea stalls, *sadhus*, souvenir sellers and hawkers selling offerings of marigolds and coconuts, as well as *khuar*, a sweet somewhere between cottage cheese and fudge.

Despite the carnival spirit, witnessing the sacrifices is a strange and, for some, confronting experience. The slaughter is surprisingly matter-of-fact (and you won't get to see much of it), but it creates a powerful atmosphere.

A pathway leads off from behind the main temple uphill to the **Mata Temple**, which offers good views.

A sign of the times, Dakshinkali even has its own website (w www.dakshinkali.org), which has information on this and nearby sights.

Getting There & Away Buses operate from Kathmandu's Shahid Gate (Martyrs' Memorial) and City bus station (Rs 15) on Tuesday and Saturday – the most important days for sacrifice. Although there are plenty of them, they are very crowded. On other days catch a bus to Pharping and it's an easy 1km downhill walk or ride from there.

Cycling It is an enjoyable but exhausting two-hour (20km) bicycle ride from Kathmandu. The views are exhilarating, but it is basically uphill all the way – so mountain bikes are the way to go. Tuesday is probably the better day to pick as the traffic fumes are not too thick. Make sure you get an early start, as the shrine is busiest early in the morning. There's a small charge to park your bike in the car park. The climb from Dakshinkali back up to Pharping is a killer.

Walking If you are travelling by public transport and have walked or got a lift to Dakshinkali, consider the short-cut hiking route back up to Pharping. A path on the southern side of the sacrificial compound brings you to an open picnic area. From the cooking area at the back of this area there's a steep scramble up a goat track that follows a ridge on the northwestern side of the gorge. At the top you come out on a plateau – you'll immediately see the white monastery surrounded by prayer flags on a nearby hill. Make your way through the paddy fields, on the narrow paths between the rice. It takes about 40 minutes to get to Pharping.

Sekh Narayan Temple

The Sekh (or Shesh) Narayan Temple is the centrepiece of an interesting collection of temples, pools and carvings. The crystal-clear pools – beside the road to Pharping, where it makes a sharp left-hand turn (south, coming from Kathmandu) – are often used by local women for washing clothes. The main Sekh Narayan Temple is above the pools and is sheltered under a multi-hued, overhanging cliff.

The temples and carvings have suitably diverse ages. The main temple, one of the most important Vishnu temples in the valley, was built in the 17th century, but it is believed that the cave to the right of the temple has been a place of pilgrimage for much longer. To the right of the temple is a bas-relief of Vishnu Vikrantha, also known as the dwarf Vamana. This probably dates from the Licchavi period (5th or 6th centuries).

Half-submerged in the lowest, semicircular pond is a sculpture of Aditya, the sun god, framed by a stone arch and with a lotus flower at each shoulder. This dates from the 12th or 13th century. If you are lucky you might catch devotional religious music being played in the pavilion by the pools.

Sekh Narayan is only about 1.5km from Pharping and is probably best reached by foot from the village if you haven't got your own transport. You can hail a returning bus from here to Kathmandu.

BUNGAMATI

Bungamati is a classic Newari village dating from the 16th century. It is perched on a spur of land overlooking the Bagmati River, 10km from Kathmandu, and is shaded by large trees and stands of bamboo. Fortunately, the village streets are too small and hazardous for cars. Visitors have yet to arrive en masse, so tread gently.

Things to See

Bungamati is the birthplace of Rato Machhendranath, regarded as the patron of the valley, and the large *shikhara*-style **Rato Machhendranath Temple** in the centre of the village square is his home for six months of the year (he spends the rest of his time in Patan). The process of moving him around Patan and backwards and forwards to Bungamati is central to one of the most important annual festivals in the valley. See the special section Festivals of Nepal for details.

The chowk around the temple is one of the most beautiful in the valley – here one can see the still-beating heart of a functioning Newari town. There are many chaityas and a huge prayer wheel, clearly pointing to the capacity of Newari religion to weld together elements from different religious traditions. To get to there from the bus park at the edge of the town, follow the signs for the **Newari Cultural Museum**, which is worth a quick visit for its displays of local traditional lifestyle.

Between Bungamati and Khokna, the **Karya Binayak Temple** is dedicated to Ganesh. It's not particularly interesting and Ganesh is simply represented by a stone, but the view is spectacular. To get here from Bungamati's Rato Machhendranath Temple, exit the chowk via the northern gate along a cobbled alley, past several woodcarving shops, and at the crossroads take a left. When this path meets a larger track after a couple of minutes take a left for the temple.

If you take a right at this crossroads, after five minutes you'll arrive at the village of **Khokna**. The town is not as appealing as Bungamati, as it was seriously damaged in the 1934 earthquake, but it has retained many traditional aspects of Newari life, and is famous for its mustard oil presses. There is no central square, unlike in Bungamati, but there's plenty of action in the main street, including women spinning wool. The main temple is a two-tiered construction dedicated to Shekala Mai, a mother goddess.

Getting There & Away

Buses to Bungamati leave from Patan's Lagankhel station (Rs 11, 1½ hours).

The road to Bungamati provides yet another ideal mountain-biking expedition. From Patan, continue over Kathmandu's Ring Rd from the main road through Jawlakhel. After you cross the Nakhu Khola, veer left. The right fork takes you through to the Chobar Gorge, where you can cross the Bagmati River and return to Kathmandu by a different route. It's a pleasant ride along a gradually climbing ridge to get to Bungamati.

Kite Flying in the Kathmandu Valley

No visitor to the Kathmandu Valley in autumn, around the time of Dasain, can fail to notice the local penchant for kite flying – kids on rooftops, on streets, in open spaces and in parks can be seen flying kites.

To the uninitiated, this looks like, well, kids flying kites, but there is a lot more to it than meets the eye. First and foremost is the fact that kites are flown to fight other kites – whereby downing your opponent is the objective, and this is done by cutting their line.

The way to protect yourself from the ignominy of becoming a dreaded *hi-chait* (kite with a cut line) and to make your own kite as lethal as possible is to armour the line of the kite. In the past, people used to make their own *maajhaa* (line armour) and everyone had their own secret recipe, often involving a combination of crushed light bulbs, boiled slugs and gum. The trick was to make it sharp enough to cut an opponent's line, but not so sharp that it would cut itself when wound on to the *lattai* (wooden reel). These days people use ready-made threads, which cost anything from Rs 40 for 1000m up to Rs 25 per metre for pre-armed line from India.

The other hazard that may catch the unwary is the *mandali*, a stone on a string launched by a pirate on low-fliers – the idea being they cross your string, bring down your kite and then make off with said kite!

The paper kites themselves look very basic but are surprisingly manoeuvrable, the so-called Lucknow kites being the most sought after. Prices for kites start as low as Rs 5 and go to a modest Rs 50 or so. Popular places to buy kites are Asan Tole and Bhotahiti in Kathmandu's old city.

Approximately an hour after leaving Kathmandu's Ring Rd by bicycle along the road to Bungamati, just past a restaurant, you'll come out at a viewpoint marked by a single, large tree. It's worth pausing here to take in the lie of the land. To the left lies Bungamati, and right of here comes Karya Binayak; Khokna is about 1km further right.

To get to Khokna directly from the main Kathmandu road take the road signposted to the 'Gyanadaya Residential School'.

CHAPAGAON

Chapagaon is a prosperous village with a number of shops, temples and shrines. Near the entrance to the village is a small Ganesh shrine. There are temples dedicated to Narayan and Krishna, the latter with some erotic roof struts, and there's a less interesting Bhairab shrine at the top end of the village.

Vajra Varahi Temple

This small temple complex – an important Tantric site – lies about 500m east of the main road. When you enter Chapagaon take the path on your left after the Narayan and Krishna temples. Note the disused irrigation system, with stone channels and bridges, behind the village.

The temple was built in 1665 and is popular with wedding parties and picnickers who set up shop in the forested grounds. Nonetheless, it's an interesting and atmospheric place that has probably been a centre for worship for millennia. Photography is not allowed and there's an Rs 5 parking charge.

Getting There & Away

Local minibuses leave from Lagankhel in Patan to Chapagaon (Rs 12, one to 1½ hours). By mountain bike, Chapagaon is about an hour (13km) from Kathmandu's Ring Rd (yes, that's faster than the bus!).

A useful route east of Chapagaon links up to the Godavari road and allows you to combine the Chapagaon and Godavari roads into one route. The dirt road continues east from the Vajra Varahi Temple, passing some lovely rural scenery until it finally joins a tarmac road. A left at this junction will take you past the Godavari Resort to the main Godavari road just south of Bandegaon. The dirt road makes for a nice bike trip or you can walk it in an hour and then catch a minibus up to Godavari.

AROUND CHAPAGAON

Lele Valley

The peaceful, beautiful Lele Valley seems a million miles from the hustle and bustle of Kathmandu and is in many ways untouched by the 21st (or 20th) century. You won't find many (if any) other tourists here.

Apart from touring the lovely scenery, the main thing to head for is the **Tika Bhairab**, a huge, multicoloured painting marked by a huge sal tree at the confluence of two rivers, about 5km south from Chapagaon.

Malla Alpine Resort (☎ 4262968; singles/ doubles US$61/72 plus tax), signposted at Kalitar, a few kilometres beyond Lele along a rough dirt track, is a very pleasant place operated by the Malla Hotel in Kathmandu (make a reservation there). The 18 rooms, set in eight bungalows, offer some great views, and just so you don't have to rough it too much there is also a pool, sauna, bar and restaurant.

Getting There & Away There are a couple of route options to consider if you are making a bike trip to the valley. The main road south of Chapagaon splits and offers two ways of getting to the valley, or more importantly a loop option for a return trip of around 12km. The only downer is that the main (western) branch sees lots of truck traffic heading to a nearby quarry.

A quieter biking option would be to take the Chapagaon–Godavari track east (see Getting There & Away under Chapagaon earlier) and instead of turning left when the track meets the tarmac road, take a right on the dirt track south to Badhikhel and, eventually, the Lele Valley. From here you can head west up the Lele Valley to the Tika Bhairab, and then return along the main road northwards to Chapagaon, for a 16km-ish loop.

GODAVARI

Godavari is not really a town, although there are a number of points of interest in the area, such as the Godavari Kunda, Pulchowki Mai Temple and enjoyable walks to the giant Shanti Ban Buddha or shrine of Bishankhu Narayan (see that entry later in this section).

The 22km sealed road from Kathmandu passes through the village of Godavari to St Xavier's College and a minibus parking area at the foot of the hills. Here a partially sealed road continues south to Pulchowki

Mai Temple; the main road veers left (northeast) 1km to the gardens and Godavari Kunda.

You may be stopped a couple of kilometres before town and asked to pay a spurious Rs 50 'entry fee' to Godavari, basically a village fundraiser.

Things to See

The main entrance to the **Royal Botanic Gardens** (entry Rs 100, children under 10 Rs 50; open 10am-5pm daily) is flanked by white-painted walls. Although this is a quiet and peaceful spot, few of the trees and plants are labelled, so unless you are a keen botanist you won't end up any the wiser. The entry fee is quite outrageous. The road from Kathmandu passes several large plant nurseries, highlighting the region's botanical importance and commercial viability.

A road continues past the turn-off to the botanical gardens and after 100m or so you come to the **Godavari Kunda** – a sacred spring – on your right. It's a curious spot, and although none of the architecture or sculpture is particularly inspiring, it is revered by Hindus. The hill behind the spring is covered in colourful prayer flags. Every 12 years (next in late 2015) thousands of pilgrims come here to bathe and gain merit.

Clear mountain water collects in a pool in a closed inner courtyard, flows through carved stone spouts into a larger pool and then drains down to a photogenic line of five stupas that offer a perfect picnic spot.

Pulchowki Mai Temple

If you return towards the main crossroads and take the partially sealed road to the south, the Pulchowki Mai is a couple of hundred metres past St Xavier's College and virtually opposite the main gates to an awful marble quarry. There's a three-tiered pagoda to a Tantric mother goddess flanked by a temple to Ganesh. The two large pools before the temple compound are fed by nine spouts (known as the *Naudhara Kunda*) that represent the nine streams that flow off Pulchowki.

Shanti Ban Buddha

You can see this huge golden statue of the Buddha on the hillside behind Godavari as you approach the village. To get a closer look (be warned – it looks better from a distance) and for fine views over the valley,

take the signposted road to the right at the end of Godavari village. From the turn-off it's a 15-minute walk past some lovely traditionally thatched houses.

Places to Stay

Godavari Resort (☎ 5560675; ⓦ www.god avariresort.com.np; singles/doubles US$150/165, up to 60% discount) is signposted off the road 3km before Godavari. This modern place consists of a number of attractive Newari-style buildings, on a hillside, with idyllic views over rice paddies to the Himalaya beyond. It's perfect as a quiet base for local hiking or biking. The 68 modern rooms come in bungalows or larger blocks; as ever the upper floor rooms have the best views. There's also a pool, sauna, Jacuzzi, clay tennis courts and even bowling, plus a shuttle bus to Kathmandu every two hours. Bike hire is available (Rs 600 per day) and the weekend **barbecues** (Rs 500) are popular.

There are some cheap **restaurants** in front of the Godavari Kunda that are popular with local students and make for an excellent lunch break. There are also a couple just before Godavari village itself.

Getting There & Away

There are local minibuses (No 5) and buses (No 14) between Lagankhel in Patan and Godavari (Rs 8, one hour). It would be quite feasible to ride a mountain bike – the road is good – but if you're going to make the effort, there are more interesting rides in the valley.

AROUND GODAVARI
Bishankhu Narayan

If you're looking for an excuse to get off the beaten track, the **shrine** of Bishankhu Narayan may do nicely. There's not much to see, despite the fact that it is one of the most important Vishnu shrines in the Kathmandu Valley, though the site has a timeless, almost animistic feel. A steep stairway leads up to the chainmail-covered shrine and then down into a narrow fissure in the rock, where pilgrims test their sin levels (and need for an immediate crash diet) by trying to squeeze through the tiny gap.

There are two main ways to get to the shrine. By vehicle, the unsealed road to Bishankhu Narayan takes off to the north from the undistinguished village of Bandegaon, then veers to the southeast and crosses a small stream. After 1km you come to a small village. The road forks left at the village football ground; from here it's a steep uphill climb (if in doubt keep taking the steepest path) for around 1km to reach the shrine.

The best way to the shrine on foot is from Godavari village. You'll have to ask the way, as there are several trails that wind around the contoured terraces of the valley to the shrine.

The **Bishanku Village Resort** is currently under construction not far from the shrine.

Pulchowki Mountain

This 2760m-high mountain is the highest point around the valley and there are magnificent views from the summit. It's also home to over 570 species of flowering plants and one third of all the bird species in Nepal, as well as one of the last surviving 'cloud forests' in central Nepal. Government officials say it will be declared a conservation area 'soon'. The mountain is famous for its spring flowers, in particular its magnificent red and white rhododendrons.

The unsealed road is very rough in places and you really need a 4WD or a motorbike (take care on the slippery gravel sections). You may need to register with the local army base if someone stops you.

You would need to be very keen to undertake the climb on a mountain bike, though it could certainly be done. On foot it would be a strenuous full day hike; start early in the morning, bring plenty of water and follow the footpaths from Pulchowki Mai Temple, not the main road which snakes around the mountain. It would be wise not to hike this remote route alone.

Beyond the Kathmandu Valley

While the following eight destinations are well beyond the confines of the Kathmandu Valley, they can be visited as part of an overland vehicle tour from Kathmandu in a relatively short period.

ARNIKO HIGHWAY BEYOND DHULIKHEL

The Arniko Hwy provides Nepal's overland link with Tibet and China. Past Barabise the road is particularly vulnerable to landslides

and during the monsoon sections are likely to be closed temporarily between May and August. Even when the highway is passable it's of limited use in breaking India's commercial stranglehold on Nepal, as it's still cheaper to ship Chinese goods via Kolkata (Calcutta) than to truck them through Tibet.

After Dhulikhel the road descends into the beautiful **Panchkhal Valley**, reaching the town of Panchkhal after about a 20-minute drive. About five minutes' drive beyond Panchkhal a dirt road takes off to the left, giving road access to the Helambu region.

About 8km later you arrive at **Dolalghat**, a thriving town at the confluence of the Indrawati and Sun Kosi rivers and the departure point for many rafting trips. The turn-off to Jiri is another 14km away, on the right. **Lamosangu** is a few kilometres after the Jiri turn-off, on the Arniko Hwy. North of Lamosangu is a hydroelectric plant with a tedious military checkpoint.

For a more detailed description of this route see Dhulikhel to Kodari under Touring Routes in the Mountain Biking chapter.

Barabise

Barabise is the next bustling bazaar town, the final stop for buses from Kathmandu, 102km away, and the largest (and noisiest) settlement along the road.

There's little reason to stay here, but you might find yourself caught here at the end of the day, particularly if the night time curfew continues to shut down transport options early.

Bhote Khosi Guest House (doubles Rs 200) by the bridge in the centre of town isn't bad. Other options include the **Milan Guest House** (triples Rs 150), in the south of town, right by the noisy stand for buses to Kathmandu, or the **Hotel Chandeshwori** (doubles Rs 200) in the north of town, with a decent restaurant.

Buses run frequently from different ends of town to Kodari (Rs 40) and Kathmandu (Rs 60).

Borderlands Resort

Tucked away in a bend of the Bhote Kosi River, 105km from Kathmandu, **Borderlands** (☎ 01-4425894; ⓦ www.borderlandresorts .com; twins per person US$40), offers a quiet and isolated retreat. It consists of a central bar and dining area, and a number of thatch-roofed safari tents dotted around a verdant garden. Activities offered include rafting, canyoning and trekking, and there are more sedentary pursuits such as yoga and meditation.

Accommodation includes meals and transport from Kathmandu. Packages that include activities seem to be better value; drop in to the resort's office in Kathmandu (near the Kathmandu Guest House) for more details. As a guide, two days of canyoning costs US$110 and rafting costs US$70.

The Last Resort

Another 4km towards Tibet, **Last Resort** (☎ 01-4439525) lies in a beautiful spot on a ridge above the Bhote Kosi river, 12km from the Tibet border. Access is by suspension bridge across the river, and it's here that Nepal's only bungy jump is set up. The 'ultimate bungy' is a mighty 160m drop into the gorge of the Bhote Kosi (higher than the highest bungy in New Zealand) and is proving immensely popular. The cost of the jump is US$75, which includes lunch and transport to and from Kathmandu. If you want to stay overnight at the resort the cost of the jump is US$95, which includes four meals.

The resort also offers canyoning (US$50 per day, or US$35 if already staying at the resort), as well as rafting on the Bhote Kosi, kayak clinics (US$40 per day), trekking, mountain biking and rock climbing.

Accommodation at the resort is in comfortable safari tents, with the focus being the soaring stone-and-slate dining hall and Instant Karma bar. Take mosquito repellent and a torch (flashlight). The cost of accommodation without activities is US$25 to US$35, which includes meals and transport to and from Kathmandu.

Like Borderlands, the Last Resort does a range of packages that combine any or all of the above activities, so it's not a bad idea to call into its office in the centre of Thamel (near Kathmandu Guest House) for more information.

Tatopani

The next point of interest is the **hot springs** (entry Rs 2) of Tatopani, 3km south of the Tibetan border at Kodari. Five minutes' walk north of the central bazaar, look for a turnstile and sign on the right-hand side.

You then descend some steps to the springs, which come out as a set of showers (great after a hard bicycle ride from Dhulikhel).

There is a small *gompa* above the southern edge of town and a large *mani lhakhang* (shrine housing a prayer wheel) in the centre.

Sonam Lodge (doubles Rs 80-100), in the centre of town above a shop, is basic and cheap, but that's its only redeeming feature. Dal bhaat is available.

Family Guest House (doubles Rs 250; veg/nonveg Rs 70/90), farther up the main street, is much cleaner but overpriced. It's a better place for **dinner**.

Kodari

Nepal's border town with Tibet (China), Kodari is little more than a collection of shabby wooden shanties perched perilously on the edge of the gorge on the Nepali side of the **Friendship Bridge**. It is possible to continue past the Nepali checkpoint and stop in the middle of the bridge to pose for photos on the red line drawn across the road. From here on is Tibet, which looks just like Nepal. The Chinese border post is 8km away at Khasa (Zhangmu). A Chinese visa and Tibetan travel permit is needed to progress farther than this.

Places to Stay & Eat There is a string of five or so guesthouses right by the border, all of which are the same design, have decent restaurants and charge around Rs 200 for a double. Of these the best are probably **Rumba Guest House** and **Kailash Guest House**. They are mostly used as lunch stops by groups headed to or from Tibet.

Kodari Eco-Resort & Roadhouse (☎ 01-4249104; e kodari@mail.com.np), about 1km before the border, consists of two parts. The **Roadhouse** (singles/doubles with breakfast per person US$10) on the main road has comfortable rooms let on a share basis. The Roadhouse is also the reception for the **Eco Resort** (cottage singles/doubles with private bathroom US$40/50), which is a 10-minute walk up the hill behind the road. It consists of three comfortable stone cottages (12 rooms in all) built in local style, and with excellent views of Zhangmu and the Friendship Bridge. Unfortunately, with the current slump in tourism, both places are often deserted unless you contact them in advance.

Getting There & Away Buses run frequently between Kodari and Barabise (Rs 40, two to three hours) until around 5.30pm. Buses are generally packed and most people ride on the roof. You may find a seat in a taxi or minibus headed back to Kathmandu. There's no public transport to Zhangmu on the Chinese side.

Charikot
☎ 049

If you take the turn-off from the Arniko Hwy to Jiri, the first town you come to is Charikot, a pleasant place on a ridge, with a stunning view. At the time of writing, this was Maoist rebel heartland and it was unadvisable to visit the town. Maoists blew up a public bus travelling between Charikot and Kathmandu in late 2002, resulting in the death of two passengers.

If the political situation improves, there are a couple of decent places to stay, including the **Subhechchha Hotel** (☎ 420222; rooms Rs 150-200) and the less impressive **Sagun Guest House** (doubles Rs 85) and **Laxmi Lodge & Restaurant** (rooms Rs 60-100).

The **Charikot Panorama Resort** (☎ 420245; singles/doubles US$25/35) is a comfortable mid-range place with great views, run by a Swiss-Nepali couple. Breakfast is included in the room rates. Its website carries some useful information on the area, particularly on security issues.

Jiri

Jiri, 143km from Kathmandu, is a fairly pleasant place, and has many lodges to choose from, as it's the traditional starting point for the approach trek to the Solu Khumbu region. Maoist activity in the area had made both the trek and the town off-limits as of early 2003, so check the current situation before heading out here.

If the political situation improves, there are some fine day hikes to be made from town, including a 12km circular hike to the trading town of Those Bazaar.

Sherpa Guide Lodge (doubles Rs 80), on the far side of town – farthest from the bus stop – is a good place, as is **Hotel Jirel Gabila** (doubles with bathroom Rs 80).

An 'express' bus to Jiri leaves Kathmandu at 7am (Rs 175, 10 hours). There have been problems with theft from backpacks on this bus, with ticket sellers even recommending

travellers buy an extra seat for their backpack, but this seems to have settled recently.

THE ROAD TO LANGTANG

A tarmac road heads northwest out of Kathmandu for 23km to Kakani, perched on the edge of the Kathmandu Valley with spectacular views of the Ganesh himal, and continues to Trisuli Bazaar. Beyond here the road to Dhunche deteriorates to very rough gravel, and is travelled by mountain bikers and trekkers headed for the Langtang region. A 4WD is essential.

Just before Malekhu, on the Kathmandu-Pokhara (Prithvi) Hwy, there's a bridge over the Trisuli River and the turn-off for the new road to Trisuli Bazaar. This makes an interesting circular bicycle ride a possibility, taking in Kakani, Trisuli Bazaar, Dhading and Malekhu. See the Kathmandu to Pokhara map in the Pokhara chapter for this route.

For details of Mountain Biking routes in this area see The Scar Road from Kathmandu under Touring Routes in the Mountain Biking chapter.

Kakani

Standing at 2073m on a ridge northwest of Kathmandu, Kakani is nowhere near as popular as Nagarkot, but it does offer magnificent views of the Ganesh himal and the central and western Himalaya. The road to Kakani also offers beautiful views.

Apart from looking at the view (one could argue this is enough), there's not much to do. There is a century-old summer villa used by the British embassy and a large police training college, although this does not seriously impinge on the tranquillity of the surroundings.

Although it's easy to get to Kakani on a day trip, it's worth staying overnight if you want to see the view (you stand a much better chance if you are there early in the morning before the clouds roll in).

Places to Stay & Eat The **Tara Gaon Kakani Hotel** (☎ 4290812; e taragaon@enet .com.np; singles/doubles with private bathroom US$20/25) is an old-fashioned, government-owned place that has some wonderful views. Although it is small, it's also quite comfortable, and on a clear day the views from the front lawn are superb.

Some of the rooms have views. The hotel also serves reasonably priced meals.

Kakani Guest House (*doubles Rs 250*), just before the Tara Gaon Kakani Hotel, is one of a couple of typical village lodges, and is about as basic as they come. It's friendly, however. Dal bhaat is available, but there's very little else to eat.

With advance notice you may be able to eat at the Tara Gaon Kakani Hotel.

Getting There & Away Kakani is an hour by car or motorcycle from Kathmandu, so it would be a long, though rewarding, bicycle trip. There are a number of restaurants along the way. The road is sealed almost all the way and it is a fairly gentle climb – downhill all the way home! See the Mountain Biking chapter for details of a route (The Scar Road from Kathmandu) that takes in Kakani.

Kakani is 3km from the main Dhunche road. Turn onto the broken bitumen road just before the Kaulithana police checkpoint (the first outside Kathmandu) and there is a signpost for the Tara Gaon Kakani Hotel and the police training college.

Buses for Kakani, Trisuli Bazaar and Dhunche leave counter 28 of the Kathmandu bus station on Kathmandu's Ring Rd. You can catch a Trisuli Bazaar or Dhunche bus, get off at Kaulithana (about Rs 25) and walk the 3km to Kakani.

Trisuli Bazaar

Trisuli Bazaar is a classically unattractive roadside town 68km from Kathmandu that owes its development to a large hydroelectric project on the Trisuli River, and the fact that it was once a trailhead for treks into the Langtang region. These days trekkers head straight through to Dhunche, and there are few persuasive reasons to stop.

Nawakot, a small village a few kilometres southeast of Trisuli Bazaar, has the ruins of a fortress that was built by Prithvi Narayan Shah when he was planning his campaign to take the Kathmandu Valley. It can be reached by bicycle or foot and is an interesting spot.

Places to Stay & Eat There are several thoroughly unimpressive places on the eastern side of the bridge, which you reach when you enter town, before the turn-off to Dhunche. If you continue over the bridge, there are a few dal bhaat restaurants and a couple of reasonable options. The **Trishuli Rest House** is the best of a bad lot, although the **Ranjit Hotel** is also OK.

Getting There & Away It is a spectacular drive from Kakani along a narrow, twisting road with great views, and would be an excellent long descent by bicycle. Buses leave from the Kathmandu main bus station on the ring road every 15 minutes between 6.30am and about 2.30pm (Rs 53, four hours).

Dhunche

By the time you reach Dhunche, 119km from Kathmandu, you will have been inspected by countless redundant police and army checkpoints, plus paid Rs 1000 to enter the Langtang National Park. Irritation evaporates quickly, however, because there are spectacular views of the Langtang Valley, and although the modern section of Dhunche is pretty tacky, it's definitely a Tamang town, and the old section is virtually unchanged. Many people start trekking from Dhunche, although there is a bus to Syabrubesi as well (see Langtang Trek in the Trekking chapter).

Places to Stay & Eat There are a number of decent trekking-style hotel restaurants, including the **Hotel Namaste** (*dorm beds Rs 30, doubles Rs 80*) and similarly priced **Hotel Langtang View**.

Getting There & Away The road to Dhunche is bad, but it deteriorates further if you continue 15km to Syabrubesi. The views on both stretches are spectacular. Three buses leave from the Kathmandu main bus station on the ring road at 6.30am and 7am for Dhunche (Rs 110, seven to eight hours) and at 6.30am and 7.45am for Syabrubesi (Rs 140, nine hours).

Kathmandu to Pokhara

My first journey from Kathmandu to Pokhara (a vehicular road distance of 200km) in the year 1952 lasted 10 whole days. I had to walk the entire way, since the horse put at my disposal by the government was killed on the very first day during a difficult crossing of the Thrishuli river and I myself had only very narrowly escaped death.

Toni Hagen *(Nepal)*

Today, the journey takes less than one day, and there are comfortable refreshment stops en route. For many travellers, the 206km road between Kathmandu and Pokhara, the busy Prithvi Hwy, will be their first taste of the Nepal that exists outside the Kathmandu Valley, and although for most of the way the road follows rivers at the bottom of deep valleys there are still some magical views – rock gorges and river rapids, precipitous hills, tiered rice terraces and glimpses of the Himalaya.

Migrants from around Nepal (especially the Kathmandu Valley) have been attracted by the economic opportunity, albeit minimal, offered in the roadside towns that have sprung up along the route. Most of these towns contain the usual unattractive collection of shanties and two-storey concrete boxes. There are, however, some interesting places off the main road that are worth visiting, including Gorkha, which was the original capital for the Shah dynasty, and Bandipur, an old Newari trading settlement.

The countryside is inhabited by Bahun, Chhetri, Magar and Gurung peoples. The large multistoreyed houses, especially east of Mugling, are most likely owned by Bahuns and Chhetris, but around Mugling the region is dominated by Magars, and to a lesser extent, Gurungs.

Much of the region appears relatively prosperous, although some Magar families are desperately poor. Landholdings are small, but the region seems to have avoided major problems such as overpopulation, deforestation and land degradation. The intensive, traditional forms of agriculture – based on rice cultivation and a small number of domestic animals – are quite sophisticated and sustainable.

Most travellers will tackle this journey by bus (see Getting There & Away in both the Kathmandu and Pokhara chapters for

Highlights

- Climbing to Gorkha's fort, palace and temple complex, a triumph of Nepali architecture offering superb views of the surrounding valleys and mountains
- Exploring picturesque Bandipur, a well-preserved Newari village on an ancient trade route
- Illuminating the limestone formations in the largest cave in Nepal, the Siddha Gufa near Bandipur

details). For those making the journey by bicycle, motorcycle or private car, we have provided approximate distances between points of interest. Because of diversions, landslides and roadworks, these figures are not deadly accurate but they should help you plan your next stop. The time for the journey will depend on many variables, not least being the number of accidents occurring in your path.

KATHMANDU TO NAUBISE

The road leaves from the western end of Tripureshwar Marg and runs through straggling roadside bazaars. About 15km from town, all heavy traffic stops at a police checkpoint to pay a toll at **Thankot**, and 4km later the road crosses the rim of the valley. In clear weather there are views (from east to west) of the Ganesh himal, Himal Chuli, and the twin peaks of Manaslu himal. You also look down over incredible terracing rising from the Trisuli River and the small Mahesh Khola.

The road from the rim of the valley to Naubise is in generally good condition, with the occasional bad spot. It snakes dramatically down the steep hillside in a series of switchbacks. This is a notoriously dangerous and congested section of road, and is further enlivened by the antics of the drivers (mainly trucks and buses) as they jockey for position.

At **Naubise**, about 29km from Kathmandu, the Tribhuvan Hwy joins the road after its spectacular journey from Hetauda (see both Hetauda and Daman in The Terai & Mahabharat Range chapter for details).

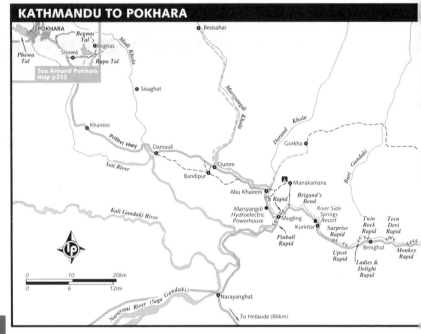

NAUBISE TO MUGLING

From Naubise, the road follows the Mahesh Khola, passing the small town of Darke, through fields of sugar cane and banana. At **Mahatibesi**, 10km from Naubise, the road crosses the Agora Khola and continues to weave 7km to the next small town of **Simle**, where river rocks are broken by the tonne and carted away to Kathmandu to build yet another high-rise. After another 7km, the Mahesh Khola joins the Trisuli River just past **Bhaireni**, and then continues 15km along the Trisuli Valley through the small villages of Belkhu and Adamghat to **Gajuritar**.

Four kilometres after Gajuritar, a bridge over the river leads to Trisuli Bazaar, superseding the old, winding, single-lane road that leaves the valley at Kakani. Another 2km brings you to the village of **Malekhu** where the valley is still attractively forested

Two kilometres after Malekhu there are a number of small restaurants, which are good places to break the journey. **Hill Top Restaurant** is a funky rotunda with a great view over the river where many rafting trips start. It is looking a little worse for wear these days, and a much better option is **Blue

Heaven Restaurant**, which is a few minutes down the hill, right on the bank of the Trisuli. Breakfast at either of these places could consist of eggs (Rs 30 to Rs 70), muesli (Rs 60), various fried snacks (Rs 40 to Rs 150), or *momos* (dumplings; Rs 80). Set lunches are available (Rs 250 to Rs 350).

At **Benighat**, 7km from Malekhu, the large Buri Gandaki flows into the Trisuli from the north, giving rafters the volume of water required for plenty of excitement. Three kilometres farther on, at tiny Bishalter, the **Lovely Panorama Restaurant** serves up reasonable food, though the **Real Highway Restaurant** 2km farther on at Charaudi is a more popular roadside eatery.

At **Kurintar**, 25km from Benighat, you will see the turn-off to the **River Side Springs Resort** (☎ 056-540129; e nangint@ ccsl.com.np; cabin singles/doubles US$50/ 60, 25% discount), a surprisingly sophisticated place that consists of a number of comfortable cabins and an airy central lodge with a restaurant serving Indian, Chinese and continental dishes; you can choose between a US$7 set menu and an à la carte menu. And there's an audacious swimming

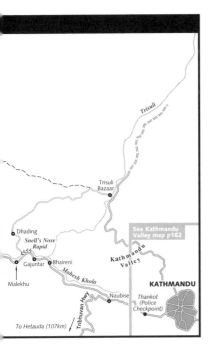

Mugling is also at the junction of the westward-flowing Trisuli River and the eastward-flowing Marsyangdi Khola, which together form the Narayani, a major tributary of the Ganges. This is the finishing point for most of the serious white-water rafting trips on the Trisuli, and the launching place for the more sedate trips down the Narayani to Narayanghat and Royal Chitwan National Park.

Most buses travelling between Kathmandu and Pokhara stop here for a meal break, so there are plenty of hawkers and hangers-on milling around. Keep an eye on your gear, and don't leave valuables on the bus.

Places to Stay & Eat
Mugling would not be a pleasant place to spend a night. There are plenty of hotels, but few are interested in having a westerner stay, since their main business is prostitution.

Machhapuchhare Hotel & Lodge (☎ 540 029; *rooms with private bathroom Rs 220*), towards the western end of town past the toll barrier (on the right-hand side coming from Kathmandu), does accommodate the occasional stranded backpacker. Avoid the noisy front rooms, and instead take one at the rear. There is a downstairs restaurant.

As well, there are literally dozens of restaurants that serve good dal bhaat for around Rs 50.

MUGLING TO ABU KHAIRENI
Leaving Mugling, a suspension bridge crosses the Narayani River just below the junction of the Trisuli and Marsyangdi. About 4km farther on you reach the **Marsyangdi Hydroelectric Powerhouse**. Water is diverted to the building you see beside the road from a dam 12km away. The road from here to Abu Khaireni winds for 6km through a narrow gorge of the Marsyangdi, and it's probably the most scenic part of the whole trip.

Abu Khaireni is at the intersection of the road to Gorkha, and is the starting point for the climb to the **Manakamana Temple**. To get to the temple, turn right off the highway on the road to Gorkha; continue for 1km until you see the Manakamana Hotel on the right; turn right and cross the suspension bridge over the river, and then keep climbing for three or four hours.

pool just a stone's throw from the river. Cabins have fan and bathroom and a small veranda. The discount is for the low-season, but always ask for it anyway.

The nearby **Manakamana Village Resort** (☎ *01-4252560;* e *om@hons.com.np; singles/ doubles US$15/20, with air-con US$20/25*) is more downmarket, lacking the atmosphere and facilities of River Side Springs. It's aimed at weekend pilgrims visiting the Manakamana Temple, but most other times it will be empty and offering a substantial discount.

The highway continues along beside the Trisuli to Mugling, passing the Manakamana cable car.

MUGLING
☎ 056
Mugling is at the junction between the most important road from the plains (from Narayanghat) and the Kathmandu–Pokhara (Prithvi) Hwy, so it is a popular stop for buses and trucks. It's 110km from Kathmandu and 96km from Pokhara, and it lies at an elevation of just 208m, making it the lowest town between the two.

Manakamana Cable Car

A few kilometres from Mugling is the Mana-kamana cable car, which whisks pilgrims up to the Manakamana Temple (one of the most popular temples in Nepal) on the top of the ridge across the Trisuli River. The cable car was built by an Austrian company and is very popular, especially on Saturday when you may have to wait for an hour or more in a very long queue to get on.

Trivia buffs might like to know the following: the trip time is eight minutes and 40 seconds, it's 2.8km in length and the vertical rise is 1034m.

Nepalis pay Rs 200/250 one way/return; for foreigners it costs US$8/10 plus 12% tax. In addition to regular passenger cars there are three freight cages, which transport sacrificial animals up to meet their maker (Rs 100 per goat!). Children under 3ft are free.

The lift operates from 9am (8am Saturday) to 5pm daily but stops from noon to 1.30pm. Hardy souls who want to climb up to the temple from the road should see Mugling to Abu Khaireni later in this chapter for details.

GORKHA
☎ 064

Gorkha, 24km north of the Kathmandu–Pokhara (Prithvi) Hwy, is accessible by a good sealed road that intersects with the highway at Abu Khaireni, 6km west of Mugling. The countryside is spectacular, and the steep approach road passes through traditional villages, such as Terho Kila Bazaar (17km from Abu Khaireni) and Biren Chowk (4km from Abu), weaving through forested valleys and past swift mountain streams with great views of the Himalaya.

Gorkha Durbar

Gorkha Durbar, a fort, palace and temple complex, is the centre point and highlight of Gorkha. Some of the building is believed to date from the reign of King Ram Shah (1606–36), but later generations have made alterations, often utilising Newari artisans. The complex is a triumph of Nepali architecture – perched like an eagle's nest high above the town in a perfect defensive position – with superb views of plunging valleys and the soaring Himalaya.

To get to Gorkha Durbar, walk north from the bus station until you come to several small temples (Vishnu, Krishna and Ganesh) surrounding a tank. Head to your right until you come to a square, to the right of which is **Tallo Durbar**, a large, square Newari-style building, built in 1835, that housed a Rana banished from Kathmandu for playing a role in one of the never-ending palace intrigues. The building is slowly being renovated and will eventually house a museum.

You pay for the impressive view from the Gorkha Durbar with a steep one-hour walk. From Tallo Durbar, return to the square and continue north. The old part of town is inaccessible to cars, so it's quite pleasant to wander the cobbled, shop-lined streets. On your left after about 100m you'll see some well-made steps heading directly up to Gorkha Durbar. If you get to the gully where village women wash clothes you have gone too far.

The hillside has a network of paths and retaining walls that must have cost a fortune to build. When you get to the big pipal tree, the path forks and although you can take either path, the one on the left offers the gentlest ascent. After about 200m there is another junction; again head to your left. It's a rewarding walk; when you get to the ridge you will be greeted with stupendous views of the Ganesh and Annapurna himal.

From the ridge, you obviously turn right to the palace, but if you turn left you soon come to **Tallokot**, a small, old fort now used as a sacrificial site. Photography is not permitted once you are inside the Gorkha Durbar complex, and this rule is strictly enforced by soldiers, so you may want to try to capture something on film from here.

Officially you are not allowed to wear leather inside the complex, so wear sand-shoes or a thick old pair of socks if you want to do some serious exploration (though the rule is not strictly enforced).

If you enter from the west, the first building on your left is the **Kalika Temple** (note the 'Star of David' window), which has some superb woodcarving. Only a special caste of Brahmin priests and the king can enter, but sacrifices are made outside.

The main palace, called the **Dhuni Pati**, has latticed windows all around the top floor but unfortunately you're not allowed to enter. Next, walk up a few steps. You'll see a **priests' house** on the left and two bells on the right. Between the latter are stairs descending to a cave where a reclusive saint named Gorkhanath once lived.

Beyond the priests' house is a four-faced **Shiva lingam**. You can descend to servants quarters and a temple on the next level below, then down again to a crude but dramatic repainted carving of Hanuman, the monkey god, and six carved steles.

From here it's another half-hour walk east to **Upkallot**, the highest point on the ridge, with the ruins of a fort, and a telecommunications tower. The views over the palace and across the Himalaya are stupendous.

Places to Stay & Eat

There are some cheap, basic accommodation options near the Gorkha bus station that offer simple meals in addition to a bed.

New Amit Lodge (☎ 420348; doubles/6-bed dorm with shared bathroom Rs 200/240) is very basic, but it's friendly, has hot water and some rooms have sensational views. A bowl of plain rice costs Rs 50; rice with meat costs Rs 85.

New Prince Guesthouse (☎ 420131; doubles/quads with private bathroom Rs 150/250) is just across the road and is much bigger with a large choice of rooms.

Gurkha Inn (☎ 420206; singles/doubles US$25/35, discount available) has a very pleasant garden setting and restaurant, and the views from the terrace are excellent. The building itself is Nepali mock-Spanish in style, and it is very pleasant and airy. The rooms are comfortably furnished.

Hotel Gorkha Bisauni (☎ 420107; singles/doubles with shared bathroom US$12/18, with private bathroom US$21/32, 50% discount) is 200m farther down the hill from Gurkha Inn. The rooms, with phone and TV, are quite comfortable, and are good value. The pleasant restaurant has an extensive menu that includes continental, Chinese and Mexican, Indian and Nepali dishes.

Gorkha Hill Resort (☎ 420326, 01-4223488 in Kathmandu; singles/doubles US$40/50) has a superb site 4km before town (800m down a dirt road to the east off the main road at Laxmi Bazaar). The ageing but well-kept resort has a very pleasant garden, and there are great views across to Gorkha. There is a 20% discount available for stand-by guests and meals cost US$5/9 for breakfast/lunch or dinner.

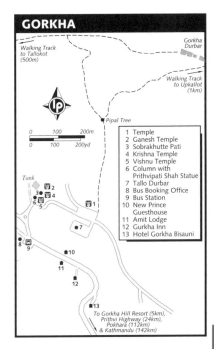

GORKHA

Walking Track to Tallokot (500m)

Gorkha Durbar

Walking Track to Upkallot (1km)

Pipal Tree

Tank

1 Temple
2 Ganesh Temple
3 Sobrakhutte Pati
4 Krishna Temple
5 Vishnu Temple
6 Column with Prithvipati Shah Statue
7 Tallo Durbar
8 Bus Booking Office
9 Bus Station
10 New Prince Guesthouse
11 Amit Lodge
12 Gurkha Inn
13 Hotel Gorkha Bisauni

To Gorkha Hill Resort (5km),
Prithvi Highway (24km),
Pokhara (112km)
& Kathmandu (142km)

Getting There & Away

The bus station is in the square in the centre of town, and the booking office for night buses is in the group of shops on the west side of the square. There are three buses a daily to and from Pokhara (Rs 80, 4½ hours), and at least seven day buses to and from Kathmandu (Rs 105, five hours). Buses from Gorkha all leave early in the morning. There are also direct buses from Gorkha to Birganj (Rs 145, six hours, four daily), Sunauli (Rs 150, six hours, one daily) and Narayanghat (Rs 50, three hours, two daily; minibus Rs 65, two hours, two daily).

If you are dropped off at Abu Khaireni, 8km from Mugling on the Kathmandu–Pokhara (Prithvi) Hwy, there are local minibuses to Gorkha (Rs 20). It's an enjoyable drive on a good road, but it's a steep climb for cyclists.

DUMRE

Dumre, 17km past Abu Khaireni, is a new town that was built after the construction of the road, and it is a typical, dirty, dusty (or muddy) roadside bazaar. Apart from being the turn-off to Besisahar, the starting point for the Annapurna Circuit Trek, it has nothing to recommend it. For trekkers it's the last place where there is a decent range of supplies at reasonable prices.

Trekkers may have to spend the night at Dumre if they arrive late.

Mustang Lodge *(singles/doubles with shared bathroom Rs 50/100)*, opposite the small roadside temple in the middle of town, has basic rooms.

Hotel Chhimkeshari *(singles/doubles Rs 60/120)* is another passable option. It's opposite the bus station.

By bus, Dumre is about five hours from Kathmandu and 2½ hours from Pokhara. Public buses leave from the Kathmandu Bus Terminal and cost Rs 90; the fare from Pokhara is Rs 50. The tourist buses that travel between Pokhara and Kathmandu cost around Rs 155.

Many people start their trek by catching shared 4WDs or trucks to Besisahar. You can expect to pay around Rs 500, although porters and local people pay less. The road is very rough and the journey can take up to five hours, though three hours is more common.

BANDIPUR
☎ 065

Straddling a dramatic ridge overlooking Dumre, and with excellent views of the Marsyangdi Valley and a broad sweep of the Himalaya from Dhaulagiri to Langtang, Bandipur is a beautiful hilltop village just to the south of the Kathmandu–Pokhara (Prithvi) Hwy.

The original settlers of the Bandipur district were Magar farmers. About two hundred years ago the village was settled by Newari traders and Bandipur became a vibrant centre for trade between the plains of India and Tibet. The prosperity of this trade is evident in the solid Newari architecture of the commercial buildings and temples. Narrow stone-paved roads pass between multistoreyed shops and houses – many of which are empty.

About 50 years ago, many of Bandipur's residents saw a brighter future down on the plains. The fertile Terai was opened up for settlement through the eradication of malaria, and trading patterns changed dramatically with the construction of roads and the introduction of trucks. Such was the downhill migration that Narayanghat is jokingly referred to as New Bandipur.

The town today is a perfect place to get a feel for Newari village life before the advent of concrete construction and fume-belching vehicles. This picturesque town is making a name for itself on the travellers' circuit thanks to the concerted effort of a few locals to preserve its charm.

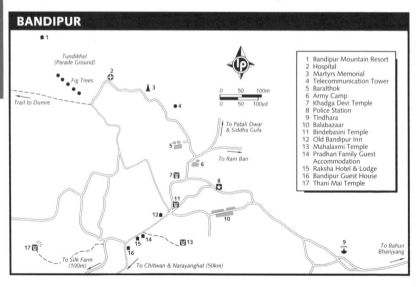

BANDIPUR

1 Bandipur Mountain Resort
2 Hospital
3 Martyrs Memorial
4 Telecommunication Tower
5 Baralthok
6 Army Camp
7 Khadga Devi Temple
8 Police Station
9 Tindhara
10 Balabazaar
11 Bindebasini Temple
12 Old Bandipur Inn
13 Mahalaxmi Temple
14 Pradhan Family Guest Accommodation
15 Raksha Hotel & Lodge
16 Bandipur Guest House
17 Thani Mai Temple

Tundikhel (Parade Ground)
Fig Trees
Trail to Dumre
0   50   100m
0   50   100yd
To Patali Dwar & Siddha Gufa
To Rani Ban
To Bahun Bhanjyang
To Silk Farm (100m)
To Chitwan & Narayanghat (50km)

Bandipur Village Walk

This short walk around the village can be made in a couple of hours of leisurely strolling and interacting with the villagers. The first few steps follow the ancient trade route through the bazaar up to the **Tundikhel**, the village parade/fair ground. This open field is bordered on the southwestern side by five large fig trees; the first and largest is a pipal (representing Vishnu), next to it there's a bar (representing Brahma), another pipal, another bar, and lastly a swami (representing Shiva). On the northeastern side there's a dramatic valley view that stretches to the Himalaya. Leaving the Tundikhel, make your way east, behind the hospital, to the Martyrs Memorial. This is a memorial to six locals who fought against the Ranas during the political turmoil that shortly followed Indian independence.

After passing the communication tower, you come to the small Magar settlement of **Baralthok**. Magars were the original inhabitants of this region and Baralthok is a common Magar surname. To your left (east) is the trail to Patali Dwar, Siddha Gufa, Dhungebari and the Rani Ban, a public forest. The army camp and police station had been abandoned at the time of writing (apparently to the delight of residents, as attention from Maoists is now directed elsewhere).

The small **Khagda Devi Temple** shares grounds with a lively little primary school and houses the sacred sword of Siddhi Mukunda Sen, king of Tanahun, the former district of which Bandipur was the capital. Once a year, on the day of Phulpati during Dasain, the sword is taken to the main bazaar in a ceremony associated with the worship of Durga. This ceremony intimately involves the Magars and blacksmith castes.

From the temple take a left turn and head east to **Tindhara** on the edge of the Rani Ban. *Tindhara* means 'three water spouts', but here there are five carved water spouts issuing clean, cool spring water from the ground beneath the forest. Opposite is a small Shiva temple carved from stone; a great place to sit and watch the comings and goings of village life. It is also a popular picnic spot for locals. Behind Tindhara, the new, Radha Krishna Temple is being built.

Backtrack to the main bazaar past the old cloth emporiums of **Balabazaar**. Many of these buildings are deserted, their owners plying their trade in Narayanghat or elsewhere in the Terai.

Things to See & Do

The architecture and the ambience of Bandipur are medieval, but much of the history is in living memory. You can walk around this friendly village yourself, but it is much more enjoyable and interesting to take a tour with Krishna Kumar Pradhan, the owner of Pradhan Family Guest Accommodation and a former teacher and local historian.

There are a few small Hindu temples – the **Khagda Devi Temple** (see the 'Bandipur Village Walk' boxed text) is just off the northern end of the small bazaar, while the **Mahalaxmi Temple** is a short stroll to the east.

For impressive views of the Himalaya, there's a short, steep walk up to **Thani Mai Temple** perched at the top of Gurungche Hill. It takes about 20 minutes to walk up the steep track that starts behind the school, southwest of the bazaar. Sunrise and sunset are spectacular, but you must take great care on the slippery track.

There is a **silk farm** an easy 30-minute walk south of the village, just off the trail that eventually leads to the Seti River. The staff don't speak much English but they'll happily show you around.

If Bandipur has a 'must see' it is **Siddha Gufa**, supposedly the largest cave in Nepal. It lies below the town, about a 1½-hour walk, and is in fact much closer to the highway than Bandipur. The cave is probably best visited when leaving Bandipur, as you can continue down to the highway at Bimalnagar, and then grab a passing bus to Dumre, 1km to the west. The lower part of the path from the cave down to Bimalnagar is somewhat overgrown and can be a bit of a scramble. The cave itself is large and long (at least 200m) and you will need a guide with a decent torch (flashlight) or lantern to fully appreciate it. The limestone formations within the cave are impressive and undamaged. Guesthouses in Bandipur should be able to arrange a guide – count on spending around Rs 300.

Places to Stay & Eat

There are a number of very basic lodges in the bazaar. Many are actually hostels for the

Notre Dame School, an English-medium boarding school in Bandipur, which attracts pupils from all over the country.

Bandipur Guest House *(☎ 520103; rooms Rs 200)*, in a funky building with a majestic, though crumbling, facade, at the south end of the bazaar, is a good budget choice. Breakfast is available for Rs 70 to Rs 100 and lunch and dinner comprise dal bhaat (Rs 100).

Raksha Hotel & Lodge and **Pradhan Family Guest Accommodation** *(rooms Rs 200)* midway along the bazaar offer similar, simple rooms and the ubiquitous dal bhaat (Rs 100).

Old Bandipur Inn *(☎ 520110; 1 night/ 2 nights US$20/30 per person)* is the pick of the accommodation. This beautifully restored building overlooking the bazaar is run by **Himalayan Encounters** *(☎ 01-4417426 in Kathmandu)*. You can include short treks and rafting in the accommodation package. The welcome, accommodation and meals are all of a high standard.

Bandipur Mountain Resort *(☎ 520125, 01-220162 in Kathmandu; singles/doubles US$40/55, full board US$45/70)*, at the western end of Tundikhel, is the other upscale accommodation in Bandipur. The resort offers 12 comfortable rooms each with views of the Himalaya. All rooms have en suite bathroom, colour TV and phone. It may be difficult to obtain accommodation without phoning ahead.

Getting There & Away

The traditional way of getting to Bandipur was the old trade route, which heads off the highway about 500m west of Dumre and emerges at the southwestern corner of Tundikhel. This is a three-hour walk up through some very pretty countryside; you may prefer to do this on the way down – or not at all.

The 7km link road up to Bandipur heads off the main highway about 2km west of Dumre, and you can ask to be dropped off to meet the local buses to Bandipur. Local buses

from Dumre to Bandipur cost Rs 15, or you can jump on a 4WD for Rs 30. To reserve a 4WD for the journey will cost Rs 300.

There is a daily bus to Narayanghat (Rs 65) via Dumre leaving Bandipur at 9am, and a daily bus to Pokhara (Rs 65) at 8.30am. Failing all that, there is an irregular trickle of tractors with large trailers bringing supplies up from Dumre; a ride on the load is far from comfortable, but you will get there.

DUMRE TO POKHARA

From the Bandipur turn-off west of Dumre it is just 16km to the district headquarters of **Damauli**, a chaotic highway town with little to recommend it. There are a couple of pleasant highway restaurants along the way: **Culture Village Restaurant & Lodge**, 11km from the turn-off, and **Green Park Highway Restaurant**, a farther 3km, are popular refreshment stops for the tourist buses.

Soon after Damauli the road crosses a large bridge over the Madi Khola, and follows the Seti River for the remaining 54km to Pokhara. Three kilometres from Damauli, the **Green Hill Restaurant** provides refreshments as does the similar **Gunadi Highway Restaurant** a farther 2km down the road. Here, the twisting highway passes through a steep, forested valley, the valley floor intensely terraced and the watercourses tamed in channels. After passing through the small villages of Tharpu and Manahi, the next town is **Khaireni**, 40km from Dumre, where a German-assisted agricultural project is based.

Nineteen kilometres after Khaireni, the road passes the turn-off to Rupa Tal and Begnas Tal, which are the second- and third-largest lakes in the Pokhara Valley. **Sisuwa** is the last place en route to Pokhara, 12km away. The highway follows the steeply eroded banks of the Seti River and the magnificent Annapurna range looms on the horizon, giving a preview of the vistas to be enjoyed in Pokhara.

Pokhara

☎ 061

Pokhara is the most popular destination in Nepal after Kathmandu. Its fame has resulted from its lakeside ambience and its proximity to one of the best trekking locations in the world – the magnificent Annapurna range. Pokhara is the gateway to some of the most famous long-distance treks in Nepal; however, there are plenty of rewarding short walks and day trips, suitable for children or weary trekkers, which can be made around the valley.

Pokhara enjoys a mild climate, clean air, snowcapped mountains reflected in a sheltered lake and an enormous number of good-value hotels and restaurants. It's ideal if you are recovering from (or gearing up for) a trek or travel in India. Its relaxed atmosphere is pleasantly removed from the hectic bustle of Kathmandu and the outright chaos of many Indian cities. Unashamedly a tourist town, Lakeside Pokhara is a travellers oasis where leisurely meals, good books and short walks can easily fill several days.

The first Western tourists to discover Pokhara were hippies in the early 1970s. Here they discovered the perfect venue for doing the things they were best at: getting stoned, eating, growing their hair, talking, and staring into the middle distance while looking cool. They came for a week and stayed for months. The world has changed since then (and so have the drug laws and visa regulations), but Pokhara retains something of the laid-back, hedonistic style of that time, although this is increasingly sidelined by the Thamel-style development threatening to overwhelm the Lakeside area.

Only foothills separate Pokhara from the full height of the Himalaya. The massive peaks of the Annapurnas loom large, though it's the photogenic and much closer Machhapuchhre, denying its mere 6997m, which dominates the skyline. The valley boasts three large lakes: Rupa Tal and Begnas Tal are slightly to the east of town, while the third and largest, Phewa Tal, is the focal point for Pokhara's tourist enclave.

Pokhara sits at 884m above sea level, about 400m lower than Kathmandu. The autumn and winter temperatures are generally much more comfortable than in often-chilly

Highlights

- Paddling around Phewa Tal enjoying the peaceful lake and the picture-perfect backdrop of the snowcapped Himalaya
- Witnessing the illumination of the majestic Annapurna panorama from the viewpoint of Sarangkot at sunrise
- Expanding your horizons on the trekking trails and the raging rivers that surround Pokhara
- Celebrating the end of a gruelling trek or white-water rafting adventure at a casual Lakeside restaurant or bar

Kathmandu, but the monsoon rains can be twice as heavy, and the humidity can often be uncomfortably high.

The Pokhara valley is chiefly inhabited by Bahuns and Chhetris, while the surrounding hills are predominantly inhabited by Gurungs. These people continue to play an important part in the Gurkha regiments, and their earnings, including pensions, have a major impact on the local economy.

As a tourist destination Pokhara is moving into the 21st century with its unprecedented, and seemingly uncontrolled development, checked only by the periodic downturns in tourism.

ORIENTATION

Pokhara is a sprawling town, stretching in a north–south direction for about 5km. Starting from the north, there's the busy bazaar area, containing the oldest part of Pokhara – the town as it was before electricity and roads. South of the bazaar is the bus station and farther south is the airport.

Most of Pokhara's local shops and businesses and the post office are around the Mahendrapul (Mahendra Bridge) in the strung-out bazaar. The campus of Prithvi Narayan University and the museums are also found here.

Farther south, and west of the bus station and airport, is Phewa Tal. It's a long uphill walk from the lake to Mahendrapul.

Starting at the southeastern end of the lake, near the airport, there's a hydroelectricity

POKHARA

To Sarangkot (500m)

To Penguin Pool (1km) & Baglung (67km)

Yamdi Khola

Pokhara-Baglung Hwy

To Mahendra Gufa & Bat Cave

Kali Khola

Bhalam Khola

▲ (1344m)

Silingebot

Seti River

To Kahun Danda (600m)

Gyarjati

Phirke Khola

Bag Bazaar

1 🏛

Nadipur

Jamunabot

Bhairab Tole

2 🏛

Khola

Orlan

Bazaar

Patan

▲ (1054m)

3 🚌 4 🏛

Phulbari

Methlan

Chaur

Gupha

Khude Pokhari

New Bazaar

Mahendrapul

5 ✉

6 ☎

See Pokhara Lakeside map p245

Tibetan Buddhist Monastery

Chipledhunga

Pode Tole

10 🏛

9 🏛

Manswara

Shreejana

8 ✚

Lakeside (Baidam)

Simalchaur

7 🏛

Chowk

Seti River

Ranipauwa

Royal Palace

Ram Ghat

Varahi Temple

11 ●

12

Prithvi Hwy

A49

Phewa Tal

Ratnapuri

13 🏛

Stadium

To Begnas Tal (12km), Rupa Tal (15km) & Kathmandu (205km)

14

15 🏛

Nagdhunga

▲ (967m)

16

Airport ✈

To World Peace Pagoda (1km)

Damside (Pardi)

Rani Ban

Pardi Dam

Pardi Bazaar

See Pokhara Damside map p243

To Tansen (110km) & Bhairawa (165km)

A48

Devi Falls

Pardi Khola

(Siddhartha Hwy)

17

Seti River

18

Tashiling Tibetan Village

To Fulbari Resort (1km)

Fusre Khola

Khola

0   500   1000m
0   500   1000yd

PLACES TO STAY
13 New Hotel Crystal
14 Hotel Mt Annapurna; Yeti Airlines
16 Fish Tail Lodge
17 Bluebird Hotel
18 Shangri-la Village

OTHER
1   Natural History Museum
2   Binde Basini Temple
3   Buses to Baglung
4   Bhimsen Temple
5   Post Office
6   Telecommunications Building
7   Bhadrakali Temple
8   Hospital
9   Tamu Kohibo Museum
10 Pokhara Museum
11 Cosmic Air
12 Bus Station
15 Gorkha Airlines

POKHARA

station. This area is often rather confusingly called Damside (although the dam and the lake are continuous), or Pardi. The tourist and immigration offices are here, and there are several hotels and a small selection of restaurants.

Finally there's the Lakeside area itself, also known as Baidam, where the majority of foreign visitors stay. Along the Lakeside road is a continuous stretch of hotels, restaurants and shops. In this book, Lakeside has been divided into three sections: Lakeside East (or Ammat) ending at the Royal Palace; Central Lakeside (or Pallo Patan) ending just before the intersection known as Camping Chowk, where the main road returns eastward to town; and Lakeside North (or Khaharey).

INFORMATION
Tourist Offices
Pokhara's **tourist office** (*☎ 535292; open 10am-5pm Sun-Thur, 10am-3pm Fri; 10am-4pm Sun-Thur, 10am-3pm Fri Nov 17-Feb 13*) is in the same building as the immigration office at Damside. Unfortunately it is of limited use – your hotel staff and any of the numerous travel agents in Lakeside will be much more informed about Pokhara and surrounding attractions.

The **Annapurna Conservation Area Project** (*ACAP; ☎ 521520, 531823; open 9am-4.30pm daily*) has a small office near Camping Chowk at Lakeside. Come here to pay the Rs 2000 entry fee to the Annapurna Conservation Area – this is important if you are trekking as the fee is Rs 4000 if you turn up at an ACAP entrance station without a permit. You will need to provide one photo and permits are issued on the spot. This is also an excellent source of information on trekking in the Annapurna region, including the latest weather and trail conditions.

Upstairs from ACAP, and open roughly the same hours, is the Pokhara office of the **Kathmandu Environmental Education Project** (*KEEP; ☎ 531823*). Check the travellers' noticeboard, pick up handy trekking information, meet fellow trekkers and chat to the friendly, dedicated staff.

Visa Extensions
For visa extensions, the **immigration office** (*☎ 521167; open 10am-4pm*) in Damside is open for applications from 10am to 12.30pm. Processing takes about two hours and you can usually pick up your passport before 4pm the same day.

Money
In Lakeside, the **Standard Chartered Bank** is convenient. Here you can make cash and travellers cheque advances against Visa and MasterCard credit cards. There are two Standard Chartered ATMs in Lakeside, one at the bank and the other a few hundred metres south near Hotel Snowland. Alternatively, there are plenty of private moneychangers strung out along Lakeside that are open seven days a week. These charge commission and/or have a less generous exchange rate than the bank.

Post & Communications
The **post office** is a long way from Lakeside in the bazaar area near Mahendrapul, but many of the bookshops at Lakeside sell stamps and will post letters and cards for a small fee.

For phone calls abroad or to Kathmandu, there's a telecommunications building east of the post office across the bridge, and there are any number of private phone centres in Lakeside. Most will allow callback for Rs 5 a minute and, where available, Internet phone services for around Rs 50 per minute. Calls are charged in one-minute 'blocks' – you will be charged for a full minute even if you have only used one or two seconds of the last minute! Get into a position where you can watch the timer.

There are plenty of email and Internet places in Lakeside. The going rate is Rs 2 per minute with a minimum Rs 20 charge.

PHEWA TAL
Phewa Tal, or Phewa Lake, is the travellers' focal point of Pokhara and the second-largest lake in Nepal. Only Rara Lake in the far west of the country is larger.

In contrast to the tourist development of Lakeside, the steep southwestern shore is beautifully forested. From Lakeside, the dense Rani Ban, or Queen's Forest, gives the still waters a deep emerald hue over which flocks of starkly white egrets take to the wing or roost in overhanging branches.

You can take to the lake in one of the brightly painted *doongas* (boats) available for rent at Lakeside. Getting out on the lake is the best way to appreciate it.

Another way to discover Phewa Tal is to walk or cycle around the lake. See Activities later for details of boat and bike hire. The traditional Lakeside villages are mainly inhabited by Chhetris, although there has been a great deal of immigration from the hills and the Kathmandu Valley. Along Lakeside are a number of *chautaras*, stone platforms designed as village meeting points and resting places for porters carrying trade goods. Their prevalence is a reminder of Pokhara's earlier incarnation as a trade-route bazaar. Building a *chautara* was one way of improving one's karma (Buddhist and Hindu law of cause and effect) for future existences.

MOUNTAINS

The wonderful Annapurna panorama forms a superb backdrop to Pokhara. You can see the mountains clearly from the lake, while from the other side of Phewa Tal, by Fish Tail Lodge, you can actually see them reflected twice in the often placid waters. Additionally, you can climb to Sarangkot or one of the other viewpoints around the valley and enjoy a closer uninterrupted view. See Around Pokhara later for details.

World Peace Pagoda

There are a couple of ways to combine a visit to the World Peace Pagoda, the large Buddhist stupa (hemispherical religious structure) on the ridge overlooking Phewa Tal, with a stroll through the Rani Ban (Queen's Forest) and a boat trip on Phewa Tal. The views from the top are well worth it. One option is to start with an early morning paddle to the village of Anadu on the western shore of the lake and then climb the steep track to the stupa. After enjoying the magnificent views of the mountains, lake and town you can return along the gentle descent through the Rani Ban to Pardi Dam and visit Devi Falls. Alternatively, as described here, start in Damside (Rs 50 taxi ride from Lakeside) and gradually ascend to the stupa through the verdant Rani Ban in the cool of the morning. Descend quickly to Anadu to catch a boat back to Lakeside – all in about two hours.

At the small footbridge below the dam where the walk starts you may pick up a guide for a small, negotiable fee. A guide is not really necessary, but they do provide companionship and ensure you take the right turns. From the bridge, head to the red-and-yellow Bhattri temple on the edge of the forest. Continue another 30m or so skirting the forest till you reach a fork in the trail. The left fork heads to Devi Falls (15 to 20 minutes). Take the right fork, which zigzags up into the forest over large stone steps.

On these low western slopes, the Rani Ban comprises a plantation of young chestnut trees. Ten minutes from the start you reach an obvious fox den cut into the high side of the track, and the spur of the ridge (crowned with an overgrown *chautara*). From here the ascent is gradual, the trail well constructed and the bird-filled canopy provides protection from the sun. Look out for the amazing vines whose 'octopus' arms spread out to reach the tops of several trees. The large nests of leaves in the upper branches belong to red army ants – best left well alone.

After about 20 minutes you enter an older, more diverse forest. This is macaque territory, and if you are lucky you will be able to observe these wary monkeys and their energetic juveniles enjoying the fruits of the forest.

Soon the trail swings to the east, or lake side, of the ridge. Here the forest is darker, the trees, festooned with ferns and epiphytic orchids, are larger and the undergrowth thicker. After 40 minutes you reach the northern boundary of Kodi village, the trail weaving between abandoned stone houses, to crest the top of the ridge. The recently constructed pagoda is only five minutes away. You are welcome to climb the steps (after removing your shoes) to take in the views and the serenity. More earthly refreshments are available at the small *bhatti* (teahouse) near the entrance.

To return by boat take the trail 100m east of the *bhatti* that heads steeply down to the lake. The trail junction is marked by the decapitated tree adorned with prayer flags. This trail is very steep and usually slippery. After 10 minutes from the top, you enter fields and pass the sign to the Raniban to Retreat. The trail forks at a *chautara*, but either fork will get you to the Fewa Resort & Lynchi Garden Restaurant, from where you head down to the Typical Restaurant. Most likely there will be a boat waiting here to take you back to Lakeside (Rs 150 to Rs 200).

The incredible **Annapurna massif** includes the Lamjung himal, Hiunchuli, Varahashikhar, Khangsar Kang, Tarke Kang and Gangapurna mountains but it is the five Annapurna peaks (called 'the Annapurnas') – Annapurna I to IV plus Annapurna South, and the magnificent Machhapuchhare – that are best known.

Machhapuchhare means 'Fish Tail'. If you walk several days west along the Jomsom Trek route (see the Trekking chapter) you will find that the mountain has a second peak, and a graceful ridge between the peaks does indeed look like a fish tail. From Pokhara, however, it's simply a superb pyramid. Machhapuchhare stands out not only because of its prominent shape and isolated position, but because it is closer to Pokhara than the other peaks. In fact, at 6997m, it is lower than the five Annapurnas. Climbing this mountain is no longer permitted.

To the west of the Annapurnas is **Dhaulagiri** at 8167m. The Kali Gandaki River, which cuts the deepest gorge in the world, flows between Dhaulagiri and the Annapurnas and predates the rise of the Himalaya. Before more precise measuring methods were available, Dhaulagiri was thought to be the world's highest mountain.

TEMPLES

Pokhara is not noted for its temples, in fact there are very few of even minor note.

In Phewa Tal there's a small island with the double-roofed **Varahi Temple** dedicated to Vishnu in his boar incarnation. While there's not a great deal to look at, it's a pleasant spot to rest weary paddling arms and observe the comings and goings of worshippers.

In the northern part of the bazaar area, right on the main road in the oldest part of town, is the small, double-roofed **Bhimsen Temple**. Very much in the Newari style of the Kathmandu Valley, it has some small erotic carvings on the roof struts.

Slightly farther north, atop a small hill with a park at its base, is Pokhara's best known temple, the **Binde Basini Temple**. The pleasant, shady setting is more impressive than the white *shikhara*-style temple itself. The temple is dedicated to Durga (Parvati) in her Binde Basini Bhagwati manifestation, and interestingly the image of the goddess is in the shape of a saligram (see the boxed text 'Saligrams' in the Trekking chapter).

MUSEUMS

Pokhara has three museums, all worth a quick look if you're in the bazaar area. **Pokhara Museum** *(SAARC/foreign Rs 5/10; open 10am-4.30pm Wed-Mon 10am-2.30pm summer; 10am- 3.30pm Wed-Mon 10am-2.30pm Fri winter)*, north of the bus station on the main road, has exhibits on local history. Most interesting are the ethnic exhibits covering rituals of village life to war medals won by Gurkhas on foreign battlefields.

Tamu Kohibo Museum *(admission Rs 20; open 10am-4pm)*, close by but on the opposite side of the Seti River, focuses on Tamu (or Gurung) culture. To get there follow the path to the Seti River that runs behind the Pokhara Museum. It heads north for a short distance before descending to a small bridge. Cross the bridge, climb the embankment then turn right at the path between two *chautaras* and descend steeply to the distinctive *kohibo* (shamanic monastery and cultural centre). The four large pillars are shaped like rice grains and represent Chyoppa, a protective deity. All aspects of the architectural design have religious significance, although it is the simple yet informative displays accompanied by excellent English descriptions that make this the pick of Pokhara's museums. Be prepared to hunt around to find someone to open the museum and issue a ticket.

At the northern end of town, on the Prithvi Narayan University campus, is the **Natural History Museum** *(Annapurna Regional Museum; open 9am-12.30pm & 1.30pm-4pm Sun-Fri)*. It has some interesting although dated exhibits on the environmental problems of the region. The natural history section has rather amateurish, life-size cement models of wildlife (you don't have to feed them) and a large butterfly, moth and insect collection. There is no entry charge, but please make a donation.

SETI RIVER

The Seti River flows right through Pokhara and in places it runs completely underground, sometimes dropping to 50m below ground level. *Seti* means 'white' and the water's milky colour comes from the soft limestone that the river cuts through.

There's a good view of this elusive river from the bridge at the northern end of the bazaar (north of Mahendrapul); an even more dramatic viewpoint can be found just beyond the airport runway. From the far side of the airport, follow the trail to the river where a footbridge crosses the canyon. The bridge is only about 10m wide but the river flows past a good 30m below, although it is difficult to actually see.

DEVI FALLS

Also known as Patale Chango, Devin's or David's Falls, this waterfall *(admission Rs 10)* is about 2km southwest of the airport on the main Siddhartha Hwy, just before the Tashiling Tibetan Village.

The Pardi Khola (Pardi Stream) is the outflow from Phewa Tal, and at Devi Falls it suddenly drops down into a hole in the ground and disappears. One of its alternative names comes from a tale about a tourist named David who disappeared down the hole, taking his girlfriend with him!

The river emerges 200m farther on and joins the Fusre Khola before flowing into the Seti River.

TIBETAN SETTLEMENTS & MONASTERY

There are a number of Tibetan settlements around Pokhara and you can see many Tibetans around the lake selling their crafts and artefacts. The **Tashiling Tibetan Village**, where Tibetan carpets are woven, is only 2km southwest of the airport.

There's also a larger settlement known as **Tashipalkhel** at Hyangja, a short drive or a one- to two-hour walk northwest of Pokhara on the Baglung road. The large monastery here is interesting, although to get to it you have to run the gauntlet past a dozen or more handicraft stalls. Also of interest is the carpet weaving centre, where you can see all stages of the process, and buy the finished article. The **community guesthouse** *(doubles Rs 150)* close to the monastery would make a good overnight stop.

The hilltop **Tibetan Buddhist Monastery** is a comparatively recent construction with a large statue of the Buddha and colourful wall paintings. Cross Mahendrapul from the bazaar area and follow the road, which is paved at first, to the monastery.

ACTIVITIES
Boating

Boating on Phewa Tal is a relaxing (or pleasantly energetic) pastime that also affords great mountain views. The colourful wooden *doongas* are available for Rs 130 to Rs 140 per hour, around Rs 300 per half-day. Rates vary slightly and are most expensive opposite the Varahi Temple, but get cheaper as you head south towards Damside. If paddling yourself is too strenuous, a boat plus boatman will cost from Rs 170 to Rs 200 per hour. You can also get rides across to the other side of the lake for Rs 250/400 one way/return.

Sail boats are Rs 200/600 per hour/half-day; pedalos are Rs 350 per hour; and kayaks are Rs 250/350/500 per hour/half-day/full day. Make inquiries at **Ganesh Kayak Shop** (☎ 522657) near Moondance Restaurant & Bar.

If you are boating near Damside, keep well away from the dam wall as currents can be strong, especially during and immediately after the monsoon.

Swimming

Swimming in the lake is good, but it's best to have a boat to fully enjoy the lake and avoid the polluted shoreline. Also, don't swim near the dam and beware of currents particularly in the monsoon season.

The swimming pool at Shangri-la Village is open to nonguests on weekends for Rs 550 all day, and this includes an excellent buffet spread (see Places to Stay – Top End). At Lakeside, Hotel Barahi welcomes nonguests to use the pool, charging Rs 200 per person (see Places to Stay – Mid-Range).

The **Penguin Pool** *(admission Rs 100; open 10am-12.30pm & 1.30pm-6.30pm summer, closed winter)*, a few kilometres from town along the road to Baglung, is a decent public swimming pool.

Walking

The Pokhara area offers some fine walking possibilities ranging from day walks, such as the climbs up to Sarangkot or the World Peace Pagoda, to three- or six-day treks. See the boxed text 'World Peace Pagoda' earlier and Around Pokhara and Short Treks Around Pokhara later for details.

Cycling

Cycling is a great way to get around Pokhara, whether you are visiting the museums, braving the bazaar or just cruising the main drag in Lakeside. The traffic is relatively light though the usual warnings about speeding and reckless drivers apply. Pokhara looks flat but actually slopes steadily uphill as you move north. If you ride a bicycle from Phewa Tal to the Binde Basini Temple at the northern end of the bazaar, you'll find it's a wonderfully long freewheel on the way back.

Good-quality mountain bikes can be hired from some of the Lakeside adventure tour operators for US$10 per day. For a guided mountain-bike tour expect to pay US$15 per day. From the roadside vendors you can hire Indian mountain bikes for Rs 200 to Rs 300 per day, and a sturdy clunker will cost Rs 100 to Rs 200 per day. You can also hire children's bicycles.

Meditation & Yoga
The more sedentary pursuits of meditation and yoga are available in and around Lakeside. You can choose from short morning and evening sessions to intensive multiday retreats.

Ganden Yiga Chopen Meditation Centre (☎ 522 923) This centre, also known as the Pokhara Buddhist Meditation Centre, in Lakeside North holds three-day meditation courses as well as daily sessions.

Nepali Yoga Center (☎ 532407, W www.yoga center.info) This centre in Central Lakeside holds daily Hatha yoga classes (Rs 400, 1½ hours) at 7.30am and 4.30pm. One-day (Rs 1000) and three-day (Rs 3000) courses, as well as individual courses, can be arranged.

Sadhana Yoga (W www.sadhana-yoga.org.np) Classes held in a building on a lovely ridge-top setting at Sedi Bagar, about 2.5km north of Lakeside. To get there head northwest along the main Lakeside road that quickly deteriorates into a deeply rutted track. Go past Green Peace Lodge to Corner Quiet View Restaurant. Here an even rougher track to Sarangkot branches to the right. Take this track and follow the signs and arrows 'To Sarangkot' painted on rocks. After a brisk 10-minute uphill walk you will find the centre. Local buses to/from Lakeside pass by the intersection hourly and cost Rs 5. You can attend for one day or sign up for a course lasting three days (Introductory), six days (Standard) or 21 days (Intensive). The cost of Rs 1100 per day includes accommodation, three meals and steam and mud baths.

Paragliding
If you feel the need to throw yourself off Sarangkot and glide with the eagles, **Sunrise Paragliding** (☎ 521174; W www

POKHARA DAMSIDE

PLACES TO STAY
10 Dragon Hotel; Skyline Airways Office
11 Tibet Resort
12 New Hotel Pagoda
15 Hotel Peaceful
16 Hotel Mona Lisa
17 Hotel Twin Peaks

PLACES TO EAT
7 Rose Garden Restaurant
9 Don't Pass Me By

13 German Bakery
14 Bamboo Garden

OTHER
1 Bus Station
2 RNAC
3 Mountain Air
4 Buddha Air
5 Bus Stand
6 Shangri-La Air
8 Tourist Office & Immigration Office

.nepal-paragliding.com), near the Lemon Tree restaurant, offers just the chance, although novices have to do tandem jumps (starting from US$50 for a 15 to 20 minute flight). It's possible to do a three-day course (US$300), a six-day course (US$600) or a nine-day course (US$900), which qualify you for solo flights.

Powered Glider Flights
Avia Club Nepal (☎ 5412830; e aviaclub@ mos.com.np), which has an office at the airport, offers exciting ultralight flights around the area ranging from 15 minutes (US$45) to one hour (US$170).

PLACES TO STAY
There are four accommodation areas in Pokhara: around the bus station and bazaar; by the airport; at Damside (Pardi); and at Lakeside (Baidam).

Damside, at the southeastern end of the lake, is popular with travellers, and many of the touts who meet the tourist buses from Kathmandu insist that this is the place to go. They will point out that the distinction between Damside and Lakeside is meaningless.

POKHARA

Damside, however, has a completely different atmosphere to Lakeside. It is a modern, rather dreary area, with few fields and trees. Many of the buildings are of the bleak, concrete, five-storey variety and there is a limited range of restaurants – most people eat in their hotels. Still, there are a couple of pleasant mid-range hotels that reward guests with great mountain views and an escape from the Lakeside scene.

At Lakeside you'll find an enormous number of budget to mid-range lodges and guesthouses. There are so many places to stay, and they change so quickly, that making individual recommendations is a chancy game. Listen to other travellers' recommendations, and if you arrive by bus avoid the clutches of the touts who will, apart from anything else, get a 50% commission from the hotel they take you to. The best thing you can do is grab a taxi to central Lakeside, have a drink and a bite to eat and then ask to leave your bag somewhere safe (most restaurants will happily do this) while you check out some hotels for yourself.

If you're staying in one of the really rock-bottom Lakeside places take care of your valuables, as theft is not unknown.

As is the case in Kathmandu, hotel rates are highly negotiable (see the boxed text 'A Note on Hotel Prices' in the Facts for the Visitor chapter) and you can often get a discount of between 25% and 50% on the advertised rates at the mid-range hotels. Bear this in mind with the prices quoted here.

PLACES TO STAY – BUDGET

Many hotels in Pokhara offer a range of rooms from dorms with shared facilities through to en suite, air-con rooms with TV and phone. Also, many mid-range hotels offer significant discounts that can make their comfortable rooms cheaper than some of the budget places (although in this category there's usually 12.2% in taxes added to the bill). Therefore there is a degree of overlap between our 'budget' and 'mid-range' categories. Remember to always check if there's a discount or a better room and always inspect a room before accepting the price.

Damside

The crucial variables here include the quality and atmosphere of the hotel restaurant, as you probably won't feel like walking into Lakeside for every meal, and which direction your room faces – the views can be impressive.

Hotel Mona Lisa (☎ 520863; en suite rooms US$5-35) has a good position by the water and the restaurant caters well for Japanese guests.

Hotel Twin Peaks (☎ 522867; e twinpeak@ fewanet.com.np; rooms US$5-30) features the Fawlty Towers restaurant. British comedy obviously impressed the ex-Gurkha owner and he has in turn impressed the British forces who sing the hotel's praises.

New Hotel Pagoda (☎ 521802; singles/ doubles with shared bathroom US$6/8, with private bathroom US$10/12), which has views and very clean rooms, is also good value.

Hotel Peaceful (☎ 520861; singles/doubles with shared bathroom US$5/8, with private bathroom US$8/12) is a small and friendly hotel with comfortable rooms.

Lakeside

Many of the budget lodges and guesthouses along the lake have similar facilities and prices. Prices tend to vary with demand. There's usually plenty of room for bargaining, especially if you plan to stay more than a couple of days. There's usually hot water in the bathrooms, though the solar-heated water in some places is barely adequate in winter. Many guesthouses have very pleasant gardens, often right in front of your room.

You can stay close to the centre of things, on or near the main Lakeside road, or opt for a quieter location either back from the main road or, for real peace and quiet and rock-bottom prices, way up at the northern end of the lake.

Lakeside East In a quiet street set back from the main thoroughfare, **New Nanohana Lodge** (☎ 522478; e nanohana_lodge@hot mail.com; doubles with private bathroom US$4-10) is a modern, clean, friendly place with good mountain views from the top-floor rooms and an inviting terrace.

Kiwi Guest House (☎ 522052; e romeo bista@hotmail.com; rooms US$5-19) has a small garden and there are good views from the hotel roof. There is a range of rooms, all of them fair value. The cheapest have shared bathroom, the most expensive have air-con and TV.

Moonlight Resort (☎ 521704; e mlight@ mos.com.np; rooms with private bathroom

POKHARA LAKESIDE

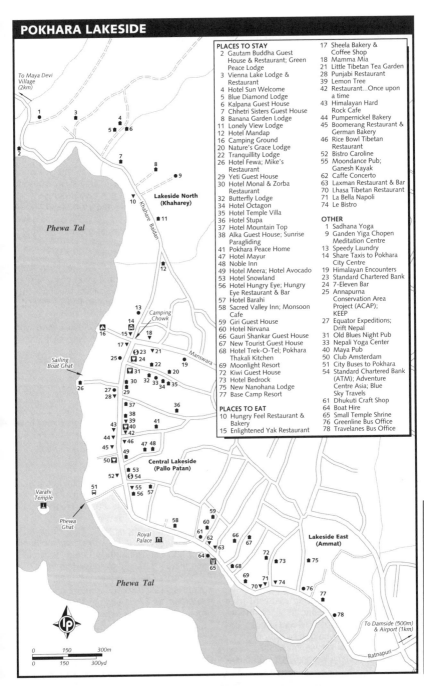

To Maya Devi
Village
(2km)

Phewa Tal

Lakeside North
(Khaharey)

Camping
Chowk

Sailing
Boat Ghat

Central Lakeside
(Pallo Patan)

Varahi
Temple

Phewa
Ghat

Royal
Palace

Phewa Tal

Lakeside East
(Ammat)

To Damside (500m)
& Airport (1km)

Ratnapuri

Manswara

Khahare Baidan

0   150   300m
0   150   300yd

PLACES TO STAY
2 Gautam Buddha Guest
  House & Restaurant; Green
  Peace Lodge
3 Vienna Lake Lodge &
  Restaurant
4 Hotel Sun Welcome
5 Blue Diamond Lodge
6 Kalpana Guest House
7 Chhetri Sisters Guest House
8 Banana Garden Lodge
11 Lonely View Lodge
12 Hotel Mandap
16 Camping Ground
20 Nature's Grace Lodge
22 Tranquillity Lodge
26 Hotel Fewa; Mike's
   Restaurant
29 Yeti Guest House
30 Hotel Monal & Zorba
   Restaurant
32 Butterfly Lodge
34 Hotel Octagon
35 Hotel Temple Villa
36 Hotel Stupa
37 Hotel Mountain Top
38 Alka Guest House; Sunrise
   Paragliding
41 Pokhara Peace Home
47 Hotel Mayur
48 Noble Inn
49 Hotel Meera; Hotel Avocado
53 Hotel Snowland
56 Hotel Hungry Eye; Hungry
   Eye Restaurant & Bar
57 Hotel Barahi
58 Sacred Valley Inn; Monsoon
   Cafe
59 Giri Guest House
60 Hotel Nirvana
66 Gauri Shankar Guest House
67 New Tourist Guest House
68 Hotel Trek-O-Tel; Pokhara
   Thakali Kitchen
69 Moonlight Resort
72 Kiwi Guest House
73 Hotel Bedrock
75 New Nanohana Lodge
77 Base Camp Resort

PLACES TO EAT
10 Hungry Feel Restaurant &
   Bakery
15 Enlightened Yak Restaurant

17 Sheela Bakery &
   Coffee Shop
18 Mamma Mia
21 Little Tibetan Tea Garden
28 Punjabi Restaurant
39 Lemon Tree
42 Restaurant...Once upon
   a time
43 Himalayan Hard
   Rock Cafe
44 Pumpernickel Bakery
45 Boomerang Restaurant &
   German Bakery
46 Rice Bowl Tibetan
   Restaurant
52 Bistro Caroline
55 Moondance Pub;
   Ganesh Kayak
62 Caffe Concerto
63 Laxman Restaurant & Bar
70 Lhasa Tibetan Restaurant
71 La Bella Napoli
74 Le Bistro

OTHER
1 Sadhana Yoga
9 Ganden Yiga Chopen
  Meditation Centre
13 Speedy Laundry
14 Share Taxis to Pokhara
   City Centre
19 Himalayan Encounters
23 Standard Chartered Bank
24 7-Eleven Bar
25 Annapurna
   Conservation Area
   Project (ACAP);
   KEEP
27 Equator Expeditions;
   Drift Nepal
31 Old Blues Night Pub
33 Nepali Yoga Center
40 Maya Pub
50 Club Amsterdam
51 City Buses to Pokhara
54 Standard Chartered Bank
   (ATM); Adventure
   Centre Asia; Blue
   Sky Travels
61 Dhukuti Craft Shop
64 Boat Hire
65 Small Temple Shrine
76 Greenline Bus Office
78 Travelanes Bus Office

POKHARA

US$9-10, with air-con US$20) is on the Lakeside road, but far enough back to offer privacy. The cheaper rooms are good though basic, and the larger rooms have better facilities (the official price for the air-con room is double that quoted here).

Gauri Shankar Guest House *(☎ 520422; singles/doubles with shared bathroom US$3/4, with private bathroom US$6/10)* has a friendly atmosphere and a small but verdant garden.

New Tourist Guest House *(☎ 521479; e ntgh2002@yahoo.com; singles/doubles from US$2/3)* is pleasant with a decent garden. Prices go up to US$10/12 for a luxury room (carpeted and with bathtub).

Hotel Nirvana *(☎ 523332; e nirvana@ cnet.wlink.com.np; rooms US$6-15, discounts available)* is immaculately clean and well maintained. There are good views from the rooftop and some of the rooms.

Giri Guest House *(☎ 524955; ground floor/upstairs rooms Rs 250/350)* is almost next door to Hotel Nirvana. The spacious rooms are clean and have attached bathrooms.

Central Lakeside The real centre of Lakeside activity is also known as Pallo Patan. Here CD shops resonate to the ubiquitous *'Om mani padme um'* and you can hire bikes, motorbikes, taxis and boats a short stroll from your hotel, and eat at any number of al fresco restaurants offering everything from anchovies to yak.

Sacred Valley Inn *(☎ 531792; e svalley@ cnet.wlink.com.np; rooms with private bathroom US$8-12)* is a popular, inviting place right opposite the Royal Palace. The rooms are large, clean and comfortable.

Hotel Snowland *(☎ 520384; e snowland@ cnet.wlink.com.np; rear wing singles/doubles US$8/20, deluxe US$20/45, super deluxe US$25/65)*, near Hotel Hungry Eye, is another long-time favourite. The budget rooms are comfortable and some have spacious bathrooms and mountain views. The front of the hotel consists of a block of modern deluxe rooms, all with a view of the lake.

The narrow road running eastward from the next *chautara* (beside the incongruous Cape Cod–style Hotel Meera) looks uninviting but it has a couple of options.

Hotel Mayur *(☎ 522285, fax 525261; lower floor singles/doubles Rs 300/350, upstairs Rs 400/500)*, is 50m or so along the lane. The

top-floor views are excellent, and the plain rooms are well kept.

Noble Inn *(☎ 524926; rooms with shared/ private bathroom US$5/8)*, right at the end of the road, is modern, if basic, with a pleasant garden and OK rooms.

Hotel Avocado *(☎ 523617; singles/doubles with private bathroom Rs 200/250, twin room with separate bathroom Rs 150)* has fairly ordinary rooms showing their age and no garden, but there are rooftop views.

The next eastward lane (just before the next *chautara*) is more pleasant, retaining some of the old Pokhara atmosphere, despite the steady march of concrete progress.

Pokhara Peace Home *(☎ 524960; rooms with private bathroom Rs 250)* is not a bad choice. It has a pleasant garden retaining a village feel.

Alka Guest House *(☎ 523357; e sunrise@ mos.com.np; doubles with shared/private bathroom Rs 200/300)* is in a good position right on the main road. The rooms (doubles only available) are at the back, well away from the road, and are good value.

Yeti Guest House *(☎ 521423; rooms with shared/private bathroom Rs 250/300)* is central but well back from the noisy road in a large garden. The rooms are simply furnished, but quite OK.

Hotel Mountain Top *(☎ 520779; e hmt pkr@mos.com.np; discounted singles/doubles from Rs 300/500)* is a four-storey concrete monstrosity, but the comfortable rooms have superb views and are not bad value considering that the low-season discounts appear to be permanent.

Tranquillity Lodge *(☎ 521030; singles/ doubles Rs 400/600)* is a pleasant hotel set in a well-tended, shady garden. Rooms are large and comfortable. Follow the eastbound road beside the 7-Eleven Bar.

Butterfly Lodge *(☎ 522892; dorm beds Rs 200, singles/doubles with private bathroom Rs 300)*, near Tranquillity Lodge, is popular and there's a decent-sized garden.

Nature's Grace Lodge *☎ 527220; w www .naturesgracelodge.com; doubles with shared bathroom US$7, doubles with private bathroom US$10-15)* is a friendly place run by the Child Welfare Scheme. There's a rooftop restaurant that makes use of the organic vegetable garden and an intimate bar.

Hotel Octagon *(☎ 526978; e hotelocta gon@hotmail.com; rooms with shared/private* *bathroom US$6/10, with discount US$4/6)* is a little farther along from Butterfly Lodge. This unusual modern place was built as a house, and the owner lets out the four large rooms on the upper floor. Consequently it has a homely feel, and it's shoes off as in any Nepali house. All the rooms are spotless.

Hotel Temple Villa *(☎ 521203; e adv@ cnet.wlink.com.np; doubles with shared bathroom US$5-10, with private bathroom US$10-20)*, next door to Octagon, is a small and pleasant lodge in a quiet location. It is clean, and the rooms are large and comfortable.

Lakeside North Things certainly become quieter, cheaper and more basic once you go north of Camping Chowk to Lakeside North (Khaharey). Before long you're out in the rice paddies and closer to the lakeshore.

For those with tents the best bet is to make a deal to camp in one of the lodge gardens. Alternatively, there's the **camping ground** *(☎ 524052; tent sites Rs 40)*, in a great spot by the lake near Camping Chowk. The facilities are very basic and there's not much shade, although it is a nice grassy site and is a good option if you have a large vehicle. There are modest charges for vehicles.

Hotel Mandap *(☎ 527088; e hotelman dap@hotmail.com; ground/top floor rooms Rs 300/450)* is a well-groomed place with lake views from the top floor and is good value.

Lonely View Lodge *(☎ 526457; singles/ doubles with shared shower and toilet Rs 100/ 150)* is a basic and friendly little place reached along a short, steep track leading from the road.

Banana Garden Lodge *(☎ 521880; singles/ doubles Rs 80/100)* is a popular budget house. Its slightly elevated position provides good views.

Chhetri Sisters Guest House *(☎ 524066; e trek@3sistersadventure.com; dorm beds Rs 200, rooms with private bathroom US$5-20)* is the newest place in this area. It is owned by three sisters who also organise female porters and guides for female trekkers. The rooms are relatively expensive, but there is a dorm option.

Blue Diamond Lodge *(rooms from Rs 120)*, along a rather rough foot track and set well back from the road, is very basic, quiet and private. You will need a flashlight (torch) if venturing out at night.

Kalpana Guest House *(singles/doubles with shared bathroom Rs 150/200)* is also back from the road, and being right among the rice fields, has a very rural ambience. It's clean, well run and good value.

Vienna Lake Lodge & Restaurant *(☎ 528 228; singles with private bathroom Rs 100, doubles Rs 150-400)*, above and behind the Hamlet Lodge, has excellent lake views. The rooms are large and spartan but reasonable, and there's a large verandah for relaxing.

Right out on a point, perched on the edge of the road 5m above the lakeshore, are a couple of small, cheap lodges, which are very popular, partly because of their superb location. A bicycle would be handy here as they are a good 20-minute walk from the nearest Lakeside restaurants and bars.

Gautam Buddha Guest House & Restaurant *(singles/doubles with shared bathroom Rs 100/150)* is a friendly though modest place where hot water comes in a bucket.

Green Peace Lodge *(☎ 532780; singles/ doubles with shared bathroom Rs 80/120, doubles with private bathroom Rs 250)* is slightly fancier and has a pleasant restaurant. The doubles with bathrooms are in a building right among the rice paddies, about five minutes north of the lodge.

Maya Devi Village *(singles/doubles with shared bathroom Rs 300/450, doubles with private bathroom Rs 500)* is ideal for those who really want to escape. It's 2km or so farther on from Green Peace Lodge, and consists of rustic, mud-and-thatch cottages and a lovely communal dining room – all surrounded by rice paddies. The local bus passes every hour or so but a bike would be ideal.

Western Shore
Fewa Resort & Lynchi Garden Restaurant *(☎ 520885; doubles with private bathroom US$15)* is set right on the shore below the World Peace Pagoda and access is by boat from Lakeside. The rooms are decent and the setting offers peace and seclusion.

PLACES TO STAY – MID-RANGE
Airport
Hotel Mt Annapurna *(☎ 520037; e lodrik@ mos.com.np; singles/doubles with private bathroom US$30/40)* is Tibetan-owned and decorated in Tibetan style. It's looking a bit tired these days and it's not great value, even with discounts. But it is convenient to the airport

and comfortable, and the staff are friendly and attentive.

Damside

Dragon Hotel (☎ 520391; e dragon@mos .com.np; singles/doubles US$40/50 plus 12% tax) is a reasonable option. Rooms come with air-con and bathroom. There's a restaurant, bar and roof garden.

Tibet Resort (☎ 520853; e tibetres@cnet .wlink.com.np; singles/doubles with private bathroom US$23/34, 30% discount) is clean, pleasant and has a big garden. Rooms are good value with the discount. This is one of the best Damside places to stay, even though you can't actually see the lake from here.

Lakeside

Although the majority of the Lakeside (Baidam) places are firmly in the budget range, there's also a fair sprinkling of mid-range, with en suite bathrooms, air-con, carpets and comfortable beds. Hefty discounting is almost guaranteed.

Base Camp Resort (☎ 521226; e base camp@mos.com.np; singles/doubles US$72/ 75, up to 35% discount), a good, modern upmarket place, is set back from the road. A number of two-storey bungalows are grouped around an attractive garden. There is satellite TV, IDD telephones and gas heating. This place is a good option if Fish Tail Lodge is booked solid.

Hotel Bedrock (☎ 524876; e bedrock@ cnet.wlink.com.np; singles US$20-40, doubles US$28-48 plus tax, up to 50% discount), large yet undistinguished, is a multistorey place with comfortable rooms, a good restaurant and a well-maintained garden.

Hotel Trek-o-Tel (☎ 528996; e trekotel@ acehotels.wlink.com.np; singles/doubles US$35/ 40) is a well-run, modern hotel with spacious, well-appointed, comfortable rooms that are the best in this price range and even better than some of the top-end places.

Hotel Hungry Eye (☎ 520908; e hungry@ mos.com.np; singles/doubles US$20/30, 20% discount), a popular survivor behind the restaurant of the same name, has rooms that are smallish without being cramped with TV, phone and fan. The rates seem to be permanently discounted, making it pretty good value.

Hotel Barahi (☎ 523017; w www.barahi .com; singles/doubles with private bathroom US$25/31, deluxe US$55/64) is a good upper mid-range option on the nearby eastbound road. It has a huge garden with a swimming pool and a wing of very comfortable deluxe rooms with air-con. There are also some older, less appealing rooms.

Hotel Meera (☎ 521031; e meera@cnet .wlink.com.np; singles US$10-15, doubles US$35-45, discount available), something of an eyesore, is a prime example of inappropriate development. Nevertheless, the rooms are appealing and the front-room views are excellent. Deluxe rooms have TV and air-con.

Hotel Fewa (☎ 520151; e mike@fewa .mos.com.np; singles/doubles with bathroom US$25/35, cottage singles/doubles US$40/ 55), one of the few hotels on the western side of the road, is superbly situated right on the edge of the lake. It is owned and run by Mike of Mike's Breakfast fame in Kathmandu. The price is not bad – you are definitely paying a premium for the location. There are also six Nepali-style cottages, which are very tasteful, and these are better value.

PLACES TO STAY – TOP END
Lakeside

Fish Tail Lodge (☎ 526428; e fishtail@ fewanet.mos.com.np; singles/doubles US$95/ 105, deluxe US$110/120, 25% discount low season) is beautifully positioned and isolated from the Lakeside development; guests are shuttled over to the hotel by a rope-drawn pontoon. The imaginatively designed buildings sit in attractive gardens (with pool) from where there are superb views of the mountains and their reflections, particularly at dawn and dusk when the mountains glow and the lake is mirror-still. The rooms have all the usual luxury mod cons but are looking a little tired. The best views are to be had from rooms 16, 17 and 18 – you will need to book well in advance. The newer wing, the Palm Court, is not really worth the extra expense as the rooms are less attractive, with limited views. There's an elegant bar and restaurant and cultural shows are held nightly (when there is sufficient patronage) at 6pm. These are open to nonguests (Rs 200).

Western Shore

Raniban Retreat (☎ 531713; e sales@raniban .com; singles/doubles with private bathroom US$45/50) is on the other side of the lake from Fish Tail Lodge, along the Panchase ridge from the Peace Pagoda, and has superb mountain views. Its stone cottages are well furnished, and the restaurant is also pretty good.

Airport Area

New Hotel Crystal (☎ 520035, fax 520234; singles/doubles US$65/75, 35% discount), almost adjacent to the airport, is a big business hotel used to dealing with groups. All rooms are well appointed, comfortable and have private bathrooms.

Bluebird Hotel (☎ 525480; e hotel@blue bird.mos.com.np; singles/doubles US$150/180), just south of the airport – and, disconcertingly, right under the approach flight path – is excellent. The rooms are spacious and have air-con and most have excellent mountain views. There's also a swimming pool and a couple of eating options. Substantial discounts are offered.

Shangri-la Village (☎ 522122; e hosan gp@village.mos.com.np; singles & doubles US$150) is signposted about 1km past the southern end of the airport. This is a very elegant, low-key place, with buildings arranged around a pool and garden. The rooms are tastefully decorated, and good use has been made of local furnishings. Rooms have air-con, TV and phone. Other facilities include a sauna and health club with massage and beauty treatments. There are excellent mountain views and the food is also good. The Rs 550 weekend brunch is excellent value, especially for nonguests as, in addition to a full buffet meal, it gives you use of the pool for the day.

Fulbari Resort (☎ 523451; e resv@fulbari .com.np; singles/doubles from US$160/170) is farther south again from Shangri-la Village, but accessed from the Kathmandu road to the east of the airport. The location is dramatic, being perched on the edge of the Seti River gorge, and the mountain views are superb. No expense has been spared in the hotel's construction; the lobby is simply stunning, but one wonders just how they ever hope to fill this 165-room, five-star place. Rooms come with all the mod cons you'd expect. Facilities include a golf course, pool, health club and tennis courts.

Elsewhere

Tiger Mountain Pokhara Lodge (☎ 01-4411225; e info@tigermountain.com; cottages per person US$100, discount available) is set on a ridge about half an hour's drive from Pokhara along the Kathmandu road, and has amazing views over Pokhara and the mountains. Accommodation consists of cottages made from local stone and slate, each with its own balcony and stunning views. The main lodge building has a bar, eating area and library. There's also a dramatically sited swimming pool. The cost includes all meals and transfers to and from Pokhara.

PLACES TO EAT

The bazaar area has restaurants serving dal bhaat (lentil soup and rice) and curries, though most travellers will want to exercise their taste buds on the ambitious offerings of the Lakeside hotels and restaurants. The eating experience has steadily improved over the years. Ingredients are being imported, skills are improving and there is now more pride in Nepali regional cuisines. At most of these places you'll find the 'try-anything' travellers menu is pretty similar: lots of Italian, Chinese, Mexican and continental dishes backed up by Indian, Nepali, Tibetan and the ubiquitous fish (from the lake) and chips!

Damside

Most people staying in Damside will eat in their hotel restaurant. If you're looking for a change of scene there's a limited choice.

Don't Pass Me By (mains Rs 100-250) is a laid-back little restaurant right on the edge of the lake, where you can sit outside and enjoy the atmosphere and the well-priced travellers' fare.

The **German Bakery** is not very German but it is a popular breakfast place and the pastries and coffee are OK for the price (Rs 30 to Rs120).

Bamboo Garden and the **Rose Garden** restaurant won't surprise you with their menus, but the evenings are very quiet and the food is as good as at any Lakeside establishment.

Lakeside

Most dining possibilities are along the main road skirting Lakeside. Competition keeps them keen and there are cocktail hours, free entertainment, cosy open fires for winter evenings and elevated terraces for people-gazing.

Starting at Lakeside East, **Le Bistro** is one of the first possibilities. It has a menu that offers just about everything; there's Mexican, Italian, Chinese, Indian and Nepali, and it does a pretty good job. The apple pie (Rs 60) is not at all bad either!

La Bella Napoli, very close to Le Bistro, has decent pizzas and pastas, and other Western dishes.

Lhasa Tibetan Restaurant is a big outdoor place with a standard 'try-anything' menu, in addition to a number of Tibetan specialities. The food is very good and the service is fairly fast. *Sha bhakley*, a Tibetan meat pie, is Rs 100, and *momos* (steamed or fried meat or vegetables wrapped in dough) are Rs 50.

Pokhara Thakali Kitchen is attached to the Trek-O-Tel and has an entrance off the side road north of the hotel. This upmarket restaurant specialises in traditional Thakali cuisine, including *kanchemba* (fried buckwheat snacks; Rs 90) and a range of generous and tasty *thalis* (all-you-can-eat set meals; Rs 150 to Rs 270). There's also a small range of exceptional Japanese dishes such as vegetable tempura (Rs 250) accompanied by soup, rice and tea.

Laxman Restaurant & Bar compliments its wide-ranging menu with the claim to have the best Indian meals in Pokhara. The vegetable biryani (Rs 95) and chicken *tikka masala* (Rs 155) are indeed excellent and the beer is cold.

Caffe Concerto has small, but arguably the best, pizzas (Rs 120 to Rs 180) in town. Add good coffee and desserts (with Italian ice cream) and cool jazz and you have one of Lakeside's better roadside cafés.

Monsoon Cafe fronts the Sacred Valley Inn near the Royal Palace and is a great little restaurant. Among the many home-style offerings the cakes and desserts are especially good. It is open from breakfast until afternoon tea.

Hungry Eye Restaurant & Bar, farther past the Royal Palace near the hotel of the same name, is a long-standing survivor. The food is reliably good (the cakes are excellent), but the service can be chaotic. Pizza starts at Rs 100 and a steak is Rs 185. There's usually a cultural show each evening.

Moondance Pub, next door to Hungry Eye, has moderate prices but good food and atmosphere. The bar is popular and there's a pool table (Rs 25), darts and other board games to while away the hours. Watch those stairs if you've had a few drinks!

Bistro Caroline, run by the same people as Chez Caroline in Kathmandu, is a swank eatery that looks a little out of place (before its time?) in Lakeside. The menu is decidedly European with prices to match: steak au poivre (Rs 380) and delicious spaghetti puttanesca (Rs 290) are examples. There's also a good wine list.

Boomerang Restaurant & German Bakery is one of a number of outdoor places on the west side of the road. It's also one of a number offering evening cultural shows. There's a nice garden dotted with chairs, tables and thatched shelters – and great views. It's a great place for breakfast (around Rs 80) or lunch, but dinner is less impressive. It has the usual eclectic menu and prices. The roadside bakery does a good trade in croissants, bagels etc.

Rice Bowl Tibetan Restaurant (mains Rs 80-200) is an inexpensive place with Tibetan and other dishes, and decent views from the top floor.

Pumpernickel Bakery, next door to the Himalayan Hard Rock Cafe, has a pleasant garden in which to sit and devour an impressive array of pastries – it is popular for breakfast (and second breakfast).

Lemon Tree by one of the large pipal trees is an elegant, moderately priced restaurant with a broad menu and excellent service. Try the cakes and fruit shakes (Rs 80) for an afternoon treat.

Mike's Restaurant at the Hotel Fewa offers the best dining location in Lakeside. The open-air terrace is right by the lake, and the food and service are usually good. The generous Mexican dishes and the exotic sandwiches (Rs 100 to Rs 140) are not cheap but they're good value.

Restaurant...Once Upon a Time claims to be the original Lakeside restaurant. The continental and tandoori items are very good and the sticky sweet apple crumble (Rs 69) is decadent. Shame about the coffee – but that applies to most places in Pokhara.

Punjabi Restaurant churns out a range of tasty vegetarian curries (Rs 60 to Rs 150) and tandoori breads.

Sheela Bakery & Coffee Shop, near Camping Chowk, is a very popular little place for budget breakfasts, with excellent chocolate croissants and buns.

Little Tibetan Tea Garden is a cosy place on the main road into Pokhara from Camping Chowk. Just so no-one feels left out, it not only does excellent Tibetan food (including that traditional favourite, Tibetan pizza!), but also throws in a few Mexican and Italian dishes. At happy hour (6pm to 8.30pm) *tongba* costs Rs 60.

Mamma Mia, on the same stretch of road as Little Tibetan, is an excellent, mainly Italian place. The pastas (Rs 80 to Rs 200) here are well worth a try.

Moving north of Camping Chowk, things get decidedly quieter; **Enlightened Yak Restaurant** has views of the lake, while **Hungry Feel Restaurant & Bakery** won't win any prizes for its name, but the views are great and the pizzas (Rs 100 plus) are OK.

At the south end of Lakeside, **Fish Tail Lodge** is a fine place for a more expensive night out. The fixed breakfast costs US$9, and the buffet lunch or dinner is US$14, although these are only laid out when there are sufficient guests. An à la carte dinner for two will probably come to at least Rs 1500. On a clear day it's worth coming over here for a drink in the garden, which has stunning views of Machhapuchhare and the Annapurnas. It's also worth noting that low-season discounting has extended to the menu.

Shangri-la Village (see Places to Stay – Top End) has a weekend buffet (Rs 550) that is popular.

ENTERTAINMENT

Fish Tail Lodge puts on a nightly **cultural programme** *(admission Rs 200)* featuring Nepali dancing. It runs from 6.30pm to 7.30pm. A number of restaurants in Lakeside, including Hungry Eye, do similar shows for free.

Club Amsterdam is a popular bar with an outdoor deck and a comfortable feel. The music doesn't quite stifle conversation and the bar attracts an eclectic crowd.

Himalayan Hard Rock Cafe on the western side of the road is the latest incarnation on this site. It seems lost in these quiet times but if traveller numbers increase...

Old Blues Night Pub has nothing very bluesy about it, but the sound system is good and loud and the pool tables are popular.

Maya Pub, another good bar, has a happy hour in the early evening with two cocktails for the price of one.

7-Eleven Bar, near Camping Chowk, is a noisy place with live Indian *ghazal* music (Urdu love songs derived from poetry) in the evenings, although purists of that art form would probably be horrified at the mauling the music receives here.

SHOPPING

Books, maps and CDs are the 'toast, butter, jam' of Lakeside shopping. Most stores sell the same range (even the same counterfeits) for the same prices – little different to Thamel. Saligrams, the fossilised sea creatures found in the valleys of the Kali Gandaki and Naryani Rivers, are popular souvenirs, but they are often overpriced. You shouldn't pay more than about Rs 150. Brightly patterned textiles and embroidered clothing are cheap and the quality matches the price. The Tibetan *thangkas* (religious paintings on cotton) may not strictly follow the traditional guidelines, but there are some skilful painters producing and selling striking designs in Lakeside.

It's relaxing to browse for souvenirs in Lakeside – even the Kashmiri carpet salesmen are laid-back. The most pressure you are likely to experience will be from the Tibetan women selling trinkets such as jewellery, prayer wheels and saligrams beside the road. They are persistent rather than pushy, and will charm and haggle like there's no tomorrow. Pokhara's large Tibetan population manufactures and sells many crafts and artefacts and carpet weaving is a major local industry.

GETTING THERE & AWAY

Some travel agencies in Pokhara offer 'through' tickets or package-deal tickets to cities in India. These are dubious value at the best of times and a number of travellers have written to us complaining of rip-offs by unscrupulous agents. These range from promises of tourist buses (there are *no* tourist buses running to/from any of the border crossings), to reserved seats that were definitely not reserved, and air-con train sleepers that turned out to be 2nd class.

See India under Land in the Getting There & Away chapter for more information.

Air

There are many daily services between Kathmandu and Pokhara. As the route is something of a cash cow, all the private companies have jumped on the bandwagon; their offices

POKHARA

are opposite the airport near Mustang Chowk and close to Damside. **Skyline Airways** (☎ 521597) is in the Dragon Hotel in Damside. The flight to Kathmandu takes about 20 minutes and costs US$63 to US$69 depending on the airline. It's probably easiest to get one of the many agents in Lakeside to do the running around for a ticket.

There are great Himalayan views if you sit on the right-hand side of the plane from Kathmandu to Pokhara, and vice versa.

Bus

The main Pokhara bus station (also known as the bus park), northeast of the airport, is a dusty (or during the monsoon, muddy) expanse of chaos. The night-bus ticket office is at the top of the steps that lead into the bus station on its northwestern edge. For day buses, head to the ticket office at the south end of the park. There are no signs in English but there are plenty of willing helpers.

To/From Kathmandu The bus trip between Kathmandu and Pokhara takes six to eight hours and most departures are early in the morning. See the Kathmandu to Pokhara chapter for sights and stopovers along the route.

Greenline (☎ 531472), with an office in Lakeside, offers a daily air-con service to Kathmandu departing at 8am. It's steep at US$10 but includes breakfast at the Riverside Spring Resort at Kurintar, about halfway. **Travelanes** (☎ 531626) also has an office in Lakeside opposite the driveway entrance to Fish Tail Lodge. The air-con service to Kathmandu departs at 7am and costs US$9 including a breakfast stop en route.

Public buses (from the bus station) cost Rs 135 (day bus departures from 5am) and Rs 155 (night); tickets for the large tourist buses start at Rs 180 and the tourist minibuses cost Rs 250. It's dubious whether the extra expense of tourist buses is worthwhile. The minibuses are quicker (often considerably scarier as a result), but the full-sized tourist buses aren't significantly different to public express buses in terms of time and comfort.

The tourist buses are, however, more convenient, as in Kathmandu they pick up and drop off at the Thamel end of Kantipath. In Pokhara, all tourist buses depart and terminate at a makeshift terminus at Mustang Chowk, between Damside and the airport. Taxis await all arrivals, and everything is pretty orderly, although there are still plenty of touts. **Blue Sky Travels & Tours** (☎ 521435), near the Adventure Centre Asia in Lakeside, runs a daily tourist bus service to Kathmandu that leaves from its front door.

To/From Royal Chitwan National Park
Public buses between Pokhara and Narayanghat (Rs 85) and Tadi Bazaar (Rs 90) depart regularly from 9.45am. Ask to be dropped off in Tadi, about 15km east of Narayanghat, where the road to Sauraha leaves the Mahendra Hwy. From Narayanghat minibuses to Tadi Bazaar cost Rs 10 and taxis to Chitrasali cost Rs 300 (although you will be asked for twice this amount at the start of negotiations). From Tadi, a 4WD to Sauraha costs Rs 30 depending on the number of passengers they squeeze in.

Tourist buses from Pokhara to Tadi cost Rs 160 and depart at 6.30am and 7.30am from the bus park in Damside. Greenline (see To/From Kathmandu earlier) also offers air-con buses on this route for US$8, including breakfast. See Royal Chitwan National Park in The Terai & Mahabharat Range chapter for more details.

To/From the Indian Border Day/night buses to Sunauli and Bhairawa near the Indian border depart from the main Pokhara bus station (Rs 175/200, nine hours), or there are day minibuses (Rs 250). Several buses depart in the morning and evening for Birganj (Rs 195, 10 hours) via Mugling on the Mahendra Hwy.

Pokhara agents may try to tempt you with the offer of tourist buses to the border. Be warned there are no tourist buses. See the Getting There & Away chapter for more details on transport to India.

To/From Trekking Routes Pokhara is the base for popular treks such as the Annapurna Sanctuary Trek, Jomsom Trek and the Annapurna Circuit, plus a number of other lesser known alternatives. See the Trekking chapter for details.

For the start of the Jomsom Trek, the Pokhara–Baglung Hwy goes all the way to Beni, so most trekkers take the bus as far as Nayapul (just before Baglung), from where it's just a 20-minute walk to Birethanti. Buses for Baglung and Beni leave the local bus station roughly every half-hour from early morning until mid-afternoon. The trip to Nayapul costs Rs 45 and takes about two hours.

To Besisahar, for the start of the Anna-purna Circuit, there are four buses daily starting at around 7.25am (last bus 12.10pm) from the main Pokhara bus station (Rs 85, five hours).

GETTING AROUND
Motorcycle
To hire a motorcycle or scooter will cost about Rs 400 per day. However, Pokhara and the surrounding roads will not be improved by the growing number of motorcycles.

Taxi
It's a long way between the bazaar and Lakeside; a taxi costs around Rs 100. It's a bit of a battle to extract fair prices when catching a taxi from Lakeside to the airport or bus station. Expect to pay as much as Rs 100. Local buses shuttle between the lake, airport and bazaar for Rs 5.

Share taxis run from Camping Chowk in Lakeside into Pokhara's city centre.

Bicycle
There are lots of bicycle rental places along the lake, by the dam and near the airport. See Activities earlier for some hire and guided-tour prices.

Around Pokhara

For those with limited time, small children or less enthusiasm for walking, the area around Pokhara has some fine walks rang-ing from half-day strolls to treks lasting from two or three days to a week.

There are several shops here hiring out and selling trekking equipment, and prices are similar to those in Kathmandu. The range of equipment is not as large however, so if you want anything out of the ordinary you are best off bringing it from home or Kathmandu.

SARANGKOT
Sarangkot, at an elevation of 1592m, is probably the most popular short excursion from Pokhara. The walk can be a good, stroll to admire the mountain views, a leg stretcher before you start out on a longer trek or the first or last hours of one of the longer treks from Pokhara.

The panoramic view includes (from left to right) a glimpse of Dhaulagiri, Anna-purna South and Hiunchuli with the bulk of Annapurna behind, unmistakable Machha-puchhare, Annapurnas III, IV and II and Lamjung himal. To catch a magical sunrise or sunset you can stay overnight at the small village near the summit, or catch an early morning taxi from Lakeside.

Sarangkot has a number of budget ac-commodation (Rs 50 to Rs 200) and eating options – such as the **New Horizon Lodge** (☎ 529363), **View Top Restaurant & Lodge**, **Lake View Lodge & Restaurant** and **Sarangkot View Point**. None of these actu-ally has mountain views, but it's only a short walk to the viewpoint, so you can climb up to Sarangkot in the evening, stay overnight and catch the view at dusk and dawn.

Sarangkot once had a *kot* (fort) the re-mains of which can be seen on the very top of the ridge just a few minutes' walk above the village. At the viewpoint if you pay a donation and sign a visitors book to enter the old fort, where there's a viewing platform.

Getting There & Away
There are a number of routes to Sarangkot, but the easiest walk is from the Binde Basini Temple in the bazaar area of Pokhara, and returning straight down from the top to Phewa Tal. Allow a full day if you are a slow walker or have kids, and avoid getting caught after sundown in the myriad of tracks on the return leg.

From the temple head west and follow the bitumen road that runs about halfway up before it turns to dirt. You can short-cut many of the sharp corners. On the way up you pass several places where women work at handlooms. It takes about two hours to walk to Sarangkot from Binde Basini Tem-ple, versus three or four hours from the Lakeside area *if* you don't get seriously lost!

By motorcycle or mountain bike, just fol-low the road all the way. It actually passes below Sarangkot and continues just below the ridge line, before a track branches off to the right leading back the 1km or so to Sarangkot.

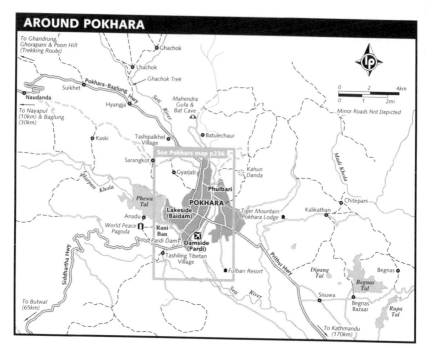

By taxi, you are taken to a point where all the taxis, minibuses, and most private cars stop, and from where it is a 30-minute walk to the viewpoint. If you have braved an early morning start from Lakeside, you will be besieged at the car park by torch-wielding guides determined to escort you to the top for Rs 100. It's not really necessary to have a guide but it makes negotiating the path in the dark much easier and quicker. Expect to pay Rs 500 for a taxi from Lakeside, regardless of whether the driver waits to drive you back or you choose to walk down.

From the top of Sarangkot it takes at least two hours to walk down to Phewa Tal. It's easy to get lost on the way up from the lake but coming down from Sarangkot is relatively straightforward. You make a very steep descent down stone stairs all the way down the hillside and through the forest. If you're exhausted when you reach the lake, there are often boatmen waiting to paddle you back to the Lakeside area.

An alternative to the routes via Binde Basini Temple or Phewa Tal is the walk from Bhairab Tole in the northern part of Pokhara's bazaar via the village of Gyarjati.

Another hour beyond Sarangkot will take you to Kaski (or Kaskikot) at 1788m. The hill is topped by a **Bhagwati temple**.

KAHUN DANDA

To the northeast of the bazaar area is Kahun Danda (*danda* means hill). It takes about three hours to walk to this popular viewpoint at 1560m and there's a lookout tower on top of the ridge. The walk starts from Mahendrapul and continues through Phulbari and up the gradual slope to the top. The remains of the 18th-century **Kanhu Kot** stand on the hilltop.

MAHENDRA GUFA & BAT CAVE

The limestone cave of Mahendra Gufa (*admission Rs 10; open 7am-6pm daily*) has very little going for it. It is simply not worth the effort. The disappointing cave is lit by electric light, so you don't need a guide, although they are available at the gate for Rs 30.

More interesting is the so-called Bat Cave (*admission Rs 10; open 7am-6pm daily*), about a 10-minute walk from Mahendra Gufa. We're not talking caped crusaders here, but real bats, thousands of them, which hang from the ceiling of the cave. The Bat Cave is unlit, so you will need a good flashlight (torch). The best option is to hire one of the would-be guides (no fixed rate) who hang around the entrance. In so doing you will ensure that this natural wonder is highly valued by the locals (though there is no evidence that tourist impact is being managed).

You could walk to the caves from Pokhara, although the route is basically through a residential area of Pokhara and not particularly interesting. Getting there by bicycle or taxi (Rs 400) is a better bet, though the road is dreadfully potholed.

RUPA TAL & BEGNAS TAL

These two lakes are the second- and third-largest in the valley, but few travellers visit them even though they're only 15km east of Pokhara.

Buses run regularly from Pokhara to Begnas Bazaar, the small market centre at the very end of the ridge that divides the two lakes. From there it's a pleasant stroll along the ridge to the other end of either lake. This trail forms the final part of the Annapurna Skyline Trek.

As this is part of a major trekking route there are a number of basic trekking lodges in the area – just wander along the ridge until you find something.

Hotel Day Break & Restaurant (doubles Rs 250) at the start/end of the trail is a good choice. The rooms are bright and spotless.

Rupa View Point (doubles Rs 200), one of the nicest lodges, is well signposted off the main trail (take the left fork 10m after leaving the road) and has views over Rupa Tal. It's a traditional family home with a couple of extra rooms that were built for trekkers, and the welcome is warm.

SHORT TREKS AROUND POKHARA

Pokhara's proximity to the Himalaya is the basis for its popularity and some of the most famous trekking routes start a short bus ride away. However, for those with less time or stamina there are a number of short treks available, including those that take in a sample of what the classic routes have to offer. You can organise camping treks to little visited regions or set out with minimum gear, hopping from teahouse to teahouse.

While these treks are short, they still go into remote and demanding country. All precautions for safe and responsible trekking apply (see the Trekking chapter and the special section, Responsible Tourism), and you should equip yourself with a suitable map. Lonely Planet's *Trekking in the Nepal Himalaya* also describes trekking options around Pokhara.

Annapurna Skyline Trek

The three- or four-day Annapurna Skyline Trek has also been dubbed the 'Royal Trek', as Britain's Prince Charles walked it many years ago. It's a fine trek to do with children as it doesn't reach any great altitude, it doesn't entail any particularly long walking days and there's always plenty to see. It's not a heavily trekked area, however, so there is no teahouse accommodation en route, except around Begnas Tal.

There are several possible variations on the route but basically the walk starts from the Kathmandu–Pokhara (Prithvi) Hwy, a few kilometres east of Pokhara, climbs up to a ridge and then mostly follows ridges with fine views of the Annapurnas before leading back down into the Pokhara Valley.

The walk passes through some small villages such as Kalikathan, Shaklung and Chisopani before it drops down to the stream that feeds Rupa Tal. The final stretch is along the ridge separating Rupa Tal and Begnas Tal, emerging on the valley floor at Begnas Bazaar from where buses and taxis leave for Pokhara.

Ghorapani (Poon Hill) to Ghandruk Loop

This five-day to week-long trek to the west of Pokhara provides excellent views of the mountains and gives a taste of the classic Annapurna routes. The walk starts at the bus stop at Nayapul (Rs 45 bus fare) on the Baglung Hwy and finishes either back at Nayapul or at Phedi. Ghorapani is reached on the second day after overnighting in Tikhedhunga or Hile on the Jomsom trail. Be very careful to stay in a group between Tikhedhunga and Ghorapani, as robbery is not uncommon. A predawn scramble up to Poon Hill (3210m) is mandatory for camera-toting mountain-watchers. The view of Dhaulagiri and the Annapurnas is awesome. The trail between Ghorapani and Ghandruk is steep and long and best broken with an overnight stop in Tadapani. Solo trekking is never encouraged, but it is important to stay in a group along this part of the trail as well – stragglers have fallen prey to violent robbery. From Ghandruk you can return to Nayapul in one day. Alternatively take two easy days via Landruk and Tolka to Phedi on the Annapurna Sanctuary trail.

Tatopani (Hot Spring) Loop

This is a four- to six-day loop combining the fabulous views of Poon Hill with the budget hot spring resort of Tatopani on the banks of the Kali Gandaki. The short option is to start at Nayapul and head straight for Ghorapani – see Ghorapani (Poon Hill) to Ghandruk Loop earlier in this chapter – spending a night in Tikhedhunga on the way. Alternatively, start in Phedi and head to Ghandruk via Tolka and Landruk. Be warned that it is a very hard slog up to Ghorapani from Ghandruk and this will add a couple more days (and considerable effort) to the trek.

From Ghorapani make the steep descent (but it's not downhill all the way!) to Tatopani. At Tatopani (which means 'hot water' in Nepali) there are riverside pools of hot spring water for which you will need a bathing costume and Rs 10. There is plenty of guesthouse accommodation – don't expect the Ritz – and an ample selection of Thamel-style restaurants and bars. The return leg is a long day following the Kali Gandaki down to Beni, from where you can take a bus or taxi back to Pokhara. Or, if you haven't had enough 'tatopani' there is another hot spring about 5½ hours northwest of Beni on the Myagdi Khola.

Ghachok Trek

This interesting two-day trek goes north from Pokhara to the Gurung villages around Ghachok. It starts from Hyangja, with its Tibetan settlement, and crosses the Mardi Khola (above its junction with the Seti River) to Lhachok, then Ghachok, before turning south and returning to Pokhara via Batulechaur.

The Terai & Mahabharat Range

When people think of Nepal, they tend to think of soaring snow-clad mountains rather than hot subtropical plains. Despite this, nearly half of the country's population lives on a narrow strip of flat and fertile land that lies wedged between the Indian border and the mountains. This is known as the Terai (sometimes spelt Tarai). Rising from the Terai are the Chure (or Siwalik) hills, the first bumps of this continental collision zone. Behind the Chures lie the broad valleys of the Inner Terai, such as Chitwan, which end abruptly at the Mahabharat Range. These foothills of the mighty Himalaya are often referred to as the Middle Hills, but this name doesn't do justice to this dramatic region of powerful rivers and deep valleys, and the equally awe-inspiring terracing, where people have carved a living out of the improbable terrain. Parts of the Terai and Middle Hills are hotbeds of Maoist activity. Be sure to follow up-to-date travel advice from your embassy.

With the Kathmandu Valley and the world's highest mountains a few hours away by bus, it is not surprising that the Terai is often just a transit zone for those travelling overland to and from India. While there is nothing here quite as startling as 8000m-high mountains, the region does have a beauty of its own and some fascinating possibilities for travellers. The most well-known spots are the magnificent Royal Chitwan National Park, famous for its elephant safaris and wildlife; Lumbini, the birthplace of the Buddha; and Janakpur, the birthplace of Sita (Rama's wife, from the Ramayana). The Middle Hills, which reach as high as 3000m, are not densely populated and there are only a handful of vehicular roads that penetrate this region. However, a few small hill towns, such as Tansen, Daman and Dhankuta, do attract travellers en route to Pokhara, Kathmandu or isolated trekking routes.

Much of the inaccessible Mahabharat Range and large sections of the Terai are still forested; the land is cut by numerous rivers, often grey and turbulent with melted snow and silt. These rivers burst from the hills onto the plains, a mere 100m above sea level yet over 1000km from the Bay of Bengal. In most parts of the Terai, Western visitors are

Highlights

- Riding an elephant on safari through the beautiful Royal Chitwan National Park in the hope of spotting a royal Bengal tiger or an Indian one-horned rhinoceros

- Contemplating the significant legacy of Buddhism in Lumbini, the birthplace of Siddhartha Gautama (the Buddha)

- Bird-watching and dolphin-spotting on the beautiful Sapt Kosi River as it flows through the Koshi Tappu Wildlife Reserve

- Mingling with thousands of Hindu pilgrims at Janakpur, with its temple to Sita and the festival of Sita Bibaha Panchami in November/December

rare, and in the farmland outside towns there is little to disturb the ancient routines of ploughing, planting and harvesting.

In general, the Terai soils are highly fertile, but there are environmental challenges facing this relatively prosperous area. Outside the national parks the native forests are rapidly disappearing and suitable land is heavily exploited. Crop yields are declining in some areas – the consequences of rapid population increase, deforestation and overworking of the land.

The Mahendra Hwy, which runs the entire length of the Terai from Mahendranagar to Kakarbhitta, was completed in 2000 and is the main artery that links the many regions of Nepal. Intersecting it are the few dramatic roads that strike north into the Mahabharat Range and those that head south to India. Most of the Terai's towns are new and unattractive, with Dickensian-looking industries on their outskirts, streets choked with buses, trucks and rickshaws, and little history or culture. The exceptions to this are the pilgrim centres of Janakpur, with its sadhus (wandering Hindu holy men) and temples, and Lumbini, which remains more significant for what it was than what it is.

Royal Chitwan National Park should not be missed, and in the cool season (November to February) it is worth travelling there during the day and seeing the country, even if you have to suffer a crowded bus. The hill

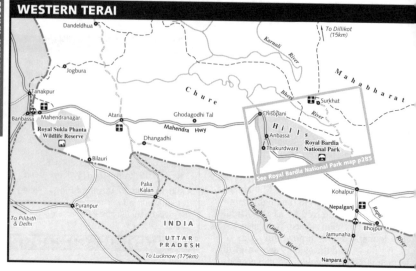

WESTERN TERAI

(Map showing: Dandeldhua, To Dillikot (15km), Karnali River, Jogbura, Tanakpur, Chure, Bheri, Mahabharat, Banbassa, Mahendranagar, Ataria, Ghodagodhi Tal, Chisopani, Surkhat, Royal Sukla Phanta Wildlife Reserve, Mahendra Hwy, Hills, Dhangadhi, Anbassa, Bilauri, Thakurdwara, Royal Bardia National Park, See Royal Bardia National Park map p285, Palia Kalan, Kohalpur, Puranpur, Nepalganj, To Pilibhit & Delhi, INDIA, UTTAR PRADESH, Ghaghara (Gogra) River, Jamunaha, Bhojpur, Rapti River, To Lucknow (175km), Nanpara)

town of Tansen makes a great stopover on the Siddhartha Hwy between Pokhara and Terai. The far western Terai (west of Sunauli/Bhairawa) is one of the least visited, least developed and therefore most interesting parts of the country.

HISTORY

Over the centuries, parts of the Terai have been under the sway of both Nepali and Indian empires. Some regions were inhabited by sophisticated agricultural and urban communities as early as 800 BC, but the empires have come and gone, and at times the countryside has been completely reclaimed by forest. Disease and war certainly played a role in the area's decline – some parts were depopulated as a result of the Muslim invasions of the 14th century, and malaria was a major problem until the 1960s.

The Terai's most famous son is Siddhartha Gautama – the Buddha – who was born in 563 BC at Lumbini. Siddhartha was the son of Suddhodana who ruled a small state from Kapilavastu. The ruins near Taulihawa, west of Lumbini, are believed to be his capital. Archaeologists have identified many successive levels of human habitation at the site (see Taulihawa & Tilaurakot later in this chapter for more details).

The Terai's most famous daughter is Sita, who is believed to have been born where

present-day Janakpur stands. The daughter of Janak, the king of Mithila (also known as Videha), Sita is famous for her faithful marriage to Rama, the hero of the Hindu epic the Ramayana, written in the 1st or 2nd century BC. The kingdom of Mithila lives on in the rich culture and language of Nepal's eastern Terai and India's northern Bihar region.

By 321 BC the Mauryan empire based at Patna in India was on the rise, and under the emperor Ashoka controlled more of the subcontinent than under any subsequent ruler until the British. Ashoka was one of Buddhism's greatest followers and missionaries, so it was perhaps inevitable that Ashoka would visit nearby Lumbini, then a thriving religious centre. In 245 BC he erected a stone pillar at Lumbini that can still be seen today. Some believe he travelled as far as Kathmandu. The next great empire to rise in the region was the Gupta empire, again originally based in Patna, which flourished between AD 300 and 600, and extended its influence to Kathmandu and beyond. In the early 13th century, invading Mughals occupied large parts of northern India, driving many Hindu refugees towards Nepal and the Kathmandu Valley.

The next (and current) Kathmandu-based dynasty, the Shah, won control in 1768 and continued to expand Nepal's borders until the kingdom was twice the size it is now,

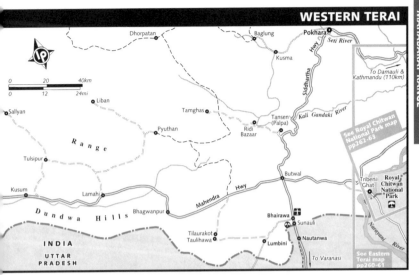

WESTERN TERAI

extending south into the Gangetic plain and east and west along the Himalaya. Eventually the Shahs and their famous Gurkha soldiers ran up against the British East India Company. In 1816, after two years of inconclusive war, the Nepalis were forced to sign a treaty that greatly reduced their territory. Land (including the city of Nepalganj) was returned to Nepal as a reward for its support for the British during the 1857 Indian Uprising (or War of Independence as it is known in India today).

Most of the Terai was heavily forested until the 1960s, although some areas were settled, and indigenous Tharu groups were widely dispersed through the region. However, the drainage and spraying programmes begun in 1954 markedly reduced the incidence of malaria, enabling mass migration south from the hills and north from India. Fertile soils and easy accessibility led to rapid development. It is now the most important and fastest-growing region for agricultural and industrial production in Nepal.

INFORMATION

There are **tourist information centres** near the borders at Kakarbhitta (☎ 023-562035), Birganj (☎ 051-522083), Bhairawa (☎ 071-520304) and Nepalganj (☎ 081-523507), as well as Janakpur (☎ 041-520755), but they are of little practical help.

Most services, including post, telephone and electricity, are more widely and efficiently available in the Terai than in the rest of the country (outside the major cities).

GETTING THERE & AWAY

The Terai is easily accessible from West Bengal, Bihar and Uttar Pradesh in India, and from Kathmandu and Pokhara in Nepal. Bus and plane services are frequent and relatively cheap. The Indian railway system runs close to the border at several points, but most people take the buses – they are much quicker and even reasonably comfortable.

Air

For details of domestic flights to/from Kathmandu and destinations in the Terai, see the Nepal Air Fares chart in the Getting Around chapter, and the relevant Getting There & Away sections for each town.

Land

Roads enter the Terai at numerous border crossings in the south. Most travellers going to or from Nepal cross at Nautanwa (India) to Sunauli/Bhairawa (Nepal), but the other crossings open for foreigners to use are Raxaul Bazaar (India) to Birganj (Nepal), Jamunaha (India) to Nepalganj (Nepal), Banbassa (India) to Mahendranagar (Nepal) in the far west, and in the extreme east of the country

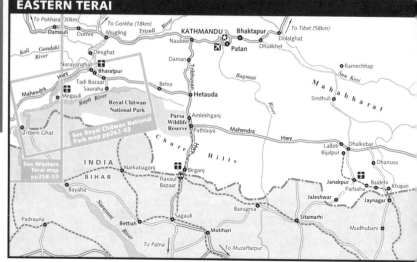

EASTERN TERAI

from Siliguri (India, near Darjeeling) to Kakarbhitta (Nepal). See the Getting There & Away chapter for details.

GETTING AROUND
Bus
Although airlines service all the major centres, most people travel by bus. This can be a serious penance, for although the price is not high in rupees, it can be in terms of comfort and sanity! The express buses (often running at night only) are usually OK, although wherever possible you should check with a local as to which are the best companies.

Unfortunately, most day buses are of the stopping-all-stations variety and they can be horrifically crowded. Bodies occupy or cling to every possible centimetre. Under these circumstances, the most comfortable place to be is the roof, although you will need to protect yourself from the elements.

Whether you travel by day or night, you will get plenty of excitement – though buses can't plummet over cliffs on the plains of the Terai, they can wind up to some pretty impressive speeds. See the Getting Around chapter for more details on bus travel.

Car
If you are travelling in a group or have the necessary funds, it is worth considering hiring a car and driver (or motorcycle) in Kathmandu to explore the Terai. When shared among a group, this is reasonably priced at around US$40 per day, plus petrol, for a small car that seats three passengers.

Bicycle
Another alternative is to ride a bicycle, preferably a mountain bike that is sufficiently sturdy to deal with rough roads. Cycling conditions are close to ideal: motorised traffic is relatively sparse on the Mahendra Hwy, there are villages at regular intervals, the climate during winter is mild and dry, and the countryside is beautiful and mostly flat.

Getting to the Terai from Kathmandu you either have to tackle the daunting Tribhuvan Hwy via Daman (at an altitude of 2322m!), or the busy and dangerous section of the Kathmandu–Pokhara (Prithvi) Hwy between Kathmandu and Mugling. Consider catching buses over these scary sections.

See the Mountain Biking chapter for more details.

Royal Chitwan National Park

☎ 056

From the 19th century, the Chitwan Valley was a centre for hunting trips by British and

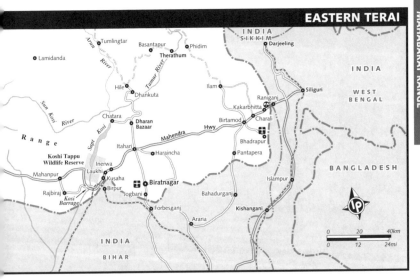

Nepali aristocrats. King George V and his son, the Prince of Wales, later Edward VIII, never made it to Kathmandu, but they did find time to slaughter wildlife in the Chitwan forests. In 11 fun-packed days during one safari in 1911, they killed 39 tigers and 18 rhinos.

Nevertheless, the occasional hunting foray did not seriously jeopardise the Terai's wildlife. In fact, the region's status as a hunting reserve probably helped protect it.

Until the late 1950s, the only settlements in the Chitwan Valley were scattered Tharu villages inhabited by people whose apparent immunity to malaria was rumoured to be the result of their heavy drinking. After malaria was largely controlled by liberal applications of DDT from 1954, land-hungry people from the hills were quick to see the potential wealth of the region and much of the jungle was rapidly transformed into farmland.

As their habitat disappeared, so did the tigers and rhinos. By 1973 the rhino population of Chitwan was estimated to have fallen to only 100 and there were just 20 tigers left. This disastrous slide was halted when a sanctuary was established in 1964, although 22,000 people were forcibly removed from within its boundaries. The national park was proclaimed in 1973 and since that time the animal population has rebounded. A census conducted in 2000 found that Chitwan contains 544 rhinos and an estimated 80 tigers, quite apart from 50 other species of mammals and over 450 different types of bird.

Today the park offers one of the finest wildlife experiences in Asia. You have to be extremely lucky to see one of its elusive tigers or leopards. However, an elephant safari is unforgettable, and you are almost certain to see rhinos, various species of deer, monkeys and numerous species of birds.

As with many national parks, the park authorities tread a delicate line between keeping the local people content and protecting the animals of the park. An often heavy-handed army presence, which involves over 1000 soldiers, has kept poaching and woodcutting to a minimum. This no doubt contributes to local resentment, and a significant problem is that the park ties up potential farming land and timber resources.

As well, the animals do not respect the park's boundaries. Rhinos wander out in November to wreak havoc on rice crops, and again in February and March when they attack mustard, lentils and wheat. Deer, monkeys and wild pigs also cause a great deal of damage. The little *machans* (lookout towers) you see in many fields outside the park are used by watchers who spend their nights in the fields waiting to scare off

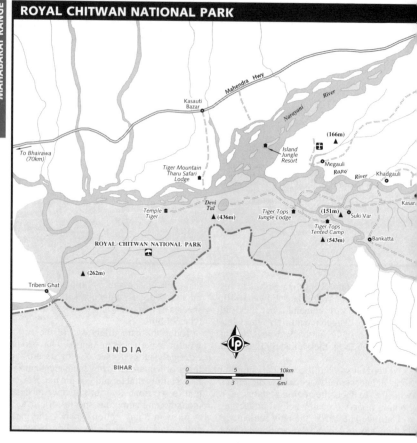

ROYAL CHITWAN NATIONAL PARK

encroaching animals. Tiger and crocodile attacks are rare, but there have been fatalities.

On the positive side, working for the park lodges provides local employment. In contrast to the expensive lodges inside the park, where much of the money goes to Kathmandu or overseas, many of the budget Sauraha lodges funnel money straight into the pockets of local families.

Numerous travel agents in Western countries, as well as in Pokhara and Kathmandu, offer package tours to the park. This is the best approach if you plan to stay at one of the expensive lodges inside the park as the package deals usually work out to be better value than the nightly 'walk-in' rate. You can also deal directly with the lodge owners through their Kathmandu offices. However, packages are both unnecessary and relatively expensive if you plan to stay in the budget lodges at Sauraha.

Many people find the two-night, three-day packages too short, because after the travelling time (six to seven hours by bus from Kathmandu or Pokhara) there is only one full day to explore. For most, a visit of two full days is sufficient, although the beautiful setting, abundant wildlife and good-value accommodation in Sauraha can easily tempt you into staying longer.

The park is easily accessible from Kathmandu or Pokhara and is en route for those heading to/from the Indian border at Birganj, as well as points east. It is only a short detour to/from western Nepal or the border at Sunauli.

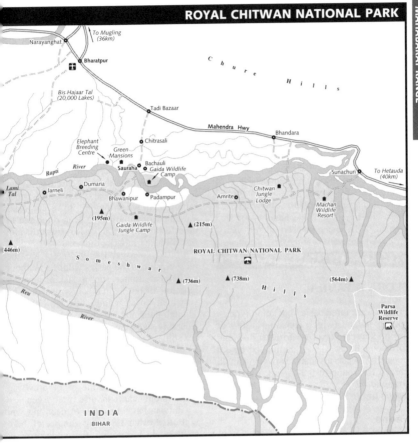

ROYAL CHITWAN NATIONAL PARK

The best time to visit Chitwan is from October to February when the average daily temperature is about 25°C. Many of the park lodges are closed during the monsoon months (May to August). Whenever you come you'll need to pack insect repellent, as there's still a small risk of malaria, and a pair of binoculars is invaluable.

GEOGRAPHY

Along most of the Terai the Gangetic plain runs to the foot of the Chure hills (which then merge with the higher Mahabharat Range), but here the Someshwar hills form the Chitwan Valley, also described as the Inner Terai, which lies between the two.

To the north the park comprises a narrow strip of floodplain along the Narayani and Rapti Rivers, a part of the Chitwan Valley and the most visited section of the park. South of this the bulk of the park encompasses the Someshwar hills, which reach a maximum height of 738m, and are largely inaccessible to visitors. In the east the Royal Chitwan National Park is adjoined by the 499-sq-km Parsa Wildlife Reserve, which is not developed for visitors but provides important additional territory for wildlife.

The park covers 932 sq km. It includes a number of *tal* (small lakes). The most interesting of these, particularly for viewing water birds, are Devi Tal near Tiger Tops jungle Lodge, Lami Tal near Kasara and Bis Hajaar Tal (literally '20,000 lakes') northwest of Sauraha.

Things Do Change

Coming on top of the downturn in tourism owing to the Maoist problem and the decline in travel generally, the flooding Rapti River inundated much of Sauraha in the monsoon of 2002. In the process of carving out a new course for the river, the floods destroyed roads and swept away less-substantial buildings. Some lodges had to be rebuilt from scratch; swimming pools were filled with mud and elaborate gardens ruined. Many lodges have been empty in the high season and some have been moth-balled, unable to trade profitably. Elsewhere, after considerable effort, lodges have reopened although prices have plummeted. Moreover, the Maoists have destroyed the telephone tower in Sauraha. The phone numbers starting with '58' were not working at the time of writing.

FLORA & FAUNA
Flora

The park has three basic vegetation types – open grassland (which constitutes 20% of the park area), riverine forest (7%) and hardwood forest (73%), dominated by sal trees. The forests also have *shisham*, kapok, *palash* (or flame-of-the-forest), pipal and strangler fig, as well as the scarlet-flowered *kusum* trees.

Fauna

Chitwan has over 43 different species of mammals; bird-watchers can try for 450 different species and butterfly-spotters have identified 67 types of butterflies at Machan Wildlife Resort. Some of the most remarkable creatures to be seen in Chitwan include elephants, rhinos and tigers.

Although you are likely to see more elephants here than any other animal, there are no wild elephants resident in the park. Chitwan's elephants are all trained Asian (Indian) elephants. Wild elephants do occasionally enter the park though. One particular male from the adjoining Parsa Wildlife Reserve regularly visits the Elephant Breeding Centre near Sauraha, with its captive audience of females!

Don't forget to bring a swimming costume. The numerous rivers in the parks have some fine swimming holes and if you're staying at one of the park lodges or in Sauraha, you'll kick yourself if you pass up the opportunity to lend a hand at elephant bath time. On a hot day in the Terai, there's no better way of cooling off than sitting on an elephant's back in a river and shouting *chhop!* If your accent is right you'll be rewarded with a refreshing cool shower!

It's the *gaida* (rhinoceros) that you will spend most time looking for in Chitwan, and with most hope of success. More than 500 rhinos live in the park and many experts consider the park too small to sustain such a number. Increasingly, rhinos are wandering outside the park and destroying local crops, and locals aren't shy about killing them when they do. In recent years a number of rhinos have been relocated to other Terai parks, notably Royal Bardia and Sukla Phanta in western Nepal.

Chitwan's royal Bengal tigers are the most elusive of the park's wildlife. Without artificial assistance, such as staking a young buffalo calf out as live bait, you would be very lucky to see a *bagh* (tiger) in Chitwan. Though their numbers have increased considerably since the park was opened, tigers are solitary creatures and they mainly hunt by night.

Chitwan is also known for more than 50 other mammals. *Chituwa* (leopards) are as elusive as tigers and the night prowling *bhalu* (sloth bears) are also rarely seen.

Chitwan has four types of deer and you will often catch a fleeting glimpse of them as they dash through the undergrowth. There's the tiny *muntjac* (barking deer), the attractive *chital* (spotted deer), the *laghuna* (hog deer) and the big *jarayo* (sambar). *Gaur*, the world's largest wild cattle, are also found in the park.

Bandar (langur monkeys) are a common sight, chattering noisily in the tree tops or scattering vegetation down below. The spotted deer often follow the langurs around, taking advantage of their profligate feeding habits. The smaller macaque monkeys are the monkeys commonly found at temples in Nepal. Freshwater or Gangetic dolphins are found in some river stretches in the park, but they are rarely seen.

There are two species of crocodiles. The marsh mugger crocodile is found in marshes, lakes and occasionally in rivers, while the rarer gharial crocodile is exclu-

Elephant Obedience School

Training an elephant takes about two years and the Chitwan elephants are usually acquired when they're eight to 20 years old, and can be expected to work until they are 40 or 50. Even the few elephants born in Nepal have to go to India to be trained. A trained elephant is not cheap to purchase or to maintain. They typically cost at least US$3000 to buy and then need to be provided with 270kg to 300kg of food a day. Their drinking capacity is just as impressive – an elephant needs more than 200L of water a day.

Keeping each elephant happy requires a support team of two or even three people. The elephant's rider or master, most commonly known as a *mahout*, is a *pahit* in Nepali. A *pahit* comes from India with the elephant and stays for three years while a local *pahit* is trained, who then stays with the elephant for life. He is backed up by one or two *patchouas* (assistants) whose main task is gathering the fodder to cater for an elephant's healthy appetite. They also assist the *pahit* when he saddles up the elephant with its *howdah* (riding platform for passengers).

sively found in rivers. The gharial, which grows to 7m in length and is a harmless fish eater, was in danger of extinction and is still rare, though with luck you will see gharial in the Rapti River if you take a canoe ride downstream. The gharial breeding centre near Kasara, the park headquarters, has had considerable success, hatching eggs and raising the youngsters to a reasonable size before releasing them into Terai rivers.

INFORMATION

The park entry fee is Rs 500 per day. If you're staying at a lodge in the park this will usually be included in the overall charge, but if you stay in Sauraha you have to pay the fee yourself. This can be arranged by most Sauraha guesthouses, or you can easily do it yourself at the ranger's office next to the park visitor centre in Sauraha, where you also book rides on government-owned elephants.

There's a **ticket office and visitor centre** *(open 6am-4pm daily)*. The visitor centre has an interesting, small museum with exhibits about the park, its wildlife, and the problems it faces. The park headquarters is farther west, inside the park at Kasara where there is a small museum of elephant skulls and a gharial crocodile breeding project.

There's no bank in Sauraha, but there are a couple of private moneychangers that accept major currencies (in the form of cash and travellers cheques).

There are a number of STD/ISD phone services in Sauraha and a couple of these also offer Internet services, although the connection is very slow (Rs 5 per minute).

For when to visit and what to bring, see the Facts for the Visitor chapter.

Dangers & Annoyances

Come prepared for Nepal's famous *jukha* (leeches). These operate in force during the monsoon and will still be waiting for unwary jungle walkers during the first month or two of the dry season. See the Health section in the Facts for the Visitor chapter for tips on how to deal with these pests.

There is also a small risk of contracting typhus fever from a tick bite. Check with your guide whether ticks are a problem, and inspect exposed skin after walking.

More obvious dangers are from the park's wild animals, particularly the rhinos. Though the risk is small the danger is real, and both tourists and guards have been wounded or killed by rhinos while on jungle walks. See the boxed text 'Warning' under Jungle Walks later in this chapter.

PLACES TO STAY

You can stay either inside the park, or at Sauraha (see Places to Stay under Sauraha later). The places inside the park are all expensive, but at Sauraha there is a range of accommodation costing from US$2 to US$50. When it comes to seeing the wildlife there's little difference between the two options.

The lodges inside the park offer the visitor considerable luxury, and well-organised wildlife-watching activities. There's also an all-encompassing safari atmosphere.

Most visitors to the park lodges arrive on package tours from Kathmandu, often as part of a larger tour of Nepal or the region. Transfer to your accommodation is usually arranged through the lodge (see Sauraha Getting There & Away later for more details).

It is necessary to book in advance. Most of the lodges have attractive individual cottages dotted around a central dining room and bar area. Some have 'tented camps' with luxurious, semipermanent tents – usually you won't have a private bathroom, but you certainly won't be uncomfortable.

The lodges generally quote a daily charge that is based on twin-share accommodation. It covers activities (including rides on their privately owned elephants) and all meals, but not park entry or the park's camping fee if you stay in a tented camp. Most also have all-inclusive packages for two or three days that include transport from Kathmandu. The only additional expenses will be for drinks and tips, and a (hefty) surcharge if you want single accommodation.

Tiger Tops Jungle Lodge (☎ 01-4411225 in Kathmandu; ⓦ www.tigermountain.com; postal address: PO Box 242, Kathmandu), which operates under the umbrella of Tiger Mountain, runs three different operations in the park. The organisation enjoys a deservedly high reputation, particularly for its excellent guides as well as its environmentally conscious approach. Tiger Tops does not expand or compromise the safari experience with unnecessary technological and consumerist trappings.

Most guests come on four-day, three-night packages that combine activities with accommodation in both the Jungle Lodge and the Tented Camp. The cost ranges from US$883 to US$1042 per person. A four-day package at the Tharu Safari Lodge costs US$527 per person. Children under 12 stay for 50% of the adult rate, and there are big discounts in the low season. However, while the accommodation is comfortable and the food good, those expecting to be pandered to with extravagant five-star luxury could be disappointed.

Jungle Lodge (closed early June-early Sept) is well known and is the original tree-top hotel. The buildings are on stilts and are constructed from local materials. The recently refurbished rooms are comfortable, with solar-powered lights and fans and solar-heated water.

Tented Camp (closed early May-early Sept) is 3km east of Jungle Lodge in the beautiful Surung Valley. There are 12 safari tents with twin beds and modern toilet and shower amenities.

Tiger Mountain Tharu Safari Lodge (open year-round) is the newest addition. Built in traditional Tharu style, the long houses are made from timber, grass reeds and mud, and are decorated with wall paintings. The rooms are attractive and comfortable; each has a single and queen-sized bed, and a bathroom. There's also a swimming pool. The lodge is actually just outside the park on the northern bank of the Narayani River.

Temple Tiger (☎ 01-4221637 in Kathmandu; ⓦ www.catmando.com/temple-tiger; postal address: PO Box 3968, Kamaladi, Kathmandu; cabins per person US$200) operates at the western end of the park, close to Tharu Safari Lodge. Accommodation consists of comfortable, elevated, individual cabins built largely from local materials, each with a private viewing area over the grasslands. Minimal forest clearance has taken place here, so the atmosphere is really one of a jungle camp. The daily rate is steep, plus you pay the park entry fee. Children aged three to 12 are charged 50% (children under three free).

Island Jungle Resort (☎ 01-4220162 in Kathmandu; ⓦ www.visitnepal.com; postal address: PO Box 2154, Durbar Marg, Kathmandu; tents/cottages per person US$100/110) is also at the western end of the park on a large island in the middle of the Narayani River. The site is superb. Accommodation consists of cottages which, although comfortable, are not particularly attractive. Packages can be considerably cheaper and very good value. There's also tented camp accommodation. Children aged three to 10 are charged 50%.

Gaida Wildlife Camp (☎ 01-4434520 in Kathmandu; ⓔ gaida@visitnepal.com.np; postal address: PO Box 2056, Kathmandu; safari tents/huts US$80/110 per person; open Oct-May) is not far from Sauraha in the only section of park north of the Rapti River.

Gaida Wildlife Jungle Camp is 8km south of the lodge at the base of the Someshwar hills. The main camp has comfortable thatched huts, and the jungle camp has safari tents. The wildlife is not particularly prolific immediately around the main camp, but is very good around the jungle camp. Package deals combine both types of accommodation as well as activities.

Chitwan Jungle Lodge (☎ 01-4442240 in Kathmandu; ⓦ www.chitwanjunglelodge.com; postal address: PO Box 1281, Kathmandu;

2-night package including transfer to/from Kathmandu US$270) is a rustic place at the eastern end of the park. Rooms are constructed in traditional Tharu style with mud walls and thatched roofs. There's no electricity, but otherwise the lodge has all the mod cons including a restaurant, private bathrooms and a very pleasant open-air bar. The forest is relatively undisturbed in this part of the park and a river with a terrific swimming (and elephant-bathing) hole runs very close by. Extra nights cost US$100 and children aged four to 11 are charged 50%. You can get there by raft for an extra US$50 per person.

Machan Wildlife Resort *(☎ 01-4225001 in Kathmandu; e wildlife@machan.mos.com .np; postal address: PO Box 3140, Kathmandu; bungalows 1st/subsequent nights per person US$125/100)* is a particularly attractive resort at the far eastern end of the park, close to the boundary of Parsa Wildlife Reserve. It offers excellent facilities including an attractive natural swimming pool and a video library of wildlife films. Accommodation is in well-designed, timber-frame bungalows with bathrooms. They are decorated with superb Mithila murals. Return transfers from Kathmandu cost US$122 by air or US$60 by car.

SAURAHA
Sauraha is just outside the park on the northern bank of the Rapti River. It lies 6km south of Tadi Bazaar (on the Mahendra Hwy). The setting is magnificent, even if much of the development is inappropriate and careless. It's a simple village that's been overrun by a boom and bust tourist industry. Outside of the tourist enclave, however, there's still ample opportunity to observe rural life – fields of verdant rice and golden mustard surround neat mud-walled houses and barns. Ox carts rumble by and there's a constant background scene of ducks, chickens and children.

A new bridge gives vehicle access from Tadi Bazaar, and it seems likely that buses will now drop you in Sauraha itself; the intrusion of buses into the village certainly won't help its character.

Be wary of being offered a free or cheap 4WD ride to a lodge in Sauraha by a tout. In theory this places you under no obligation, but in practice it's not easy to avoid staying at that particular place. If not taking the bus, you are much better off paying the standard 4WD fare (Rs 30) – hardly a king's ransom – and make it absolutely clear that you intend to check a few different places before you commit yourself.

Elephant Rides
The greatest thrill at Chitwan is the traditional elephant safari in search of wildlife; seeing a rhino from atop an elephant is an experience not to be missed. You won't want to spend your entire visit aboard an elephant, however. It is not a comfortable mode of travel and your first ride is likely to leave you with aches in muscles you did not know you had, not to mention an interesting selection of bruises! Two, three or sometimes four passengers are squeezed into a wooden-railed *howdah* (riding platform for passengers).

Government-Owned Elephants These elephants are available at Sauraha for one- to 1½-hour excursions into the park, costing Rs 1000 per person (Rs 500 for a child). At peak times the number of visitors exceeds the supply of elephants, so it's wise to turn up at the ranger's office near the visitor centre at 6am, or ask your lodge staff to get there even earlier; prebooking is not possible. Elephant safaris start at 7.30am and 3.30pm or 4pm, the prime wildlife-viewing times.

Privately Owned Elephants The lodges inside the park have their own elephants and elephant safaris are a standard activity.

Outside the park it's possible to take rides on private elephants, either arranged through your lodge or one of the two private operations, **Unique** *(☎ 580132)* and **United**, both of which have offices in Sauraha. The going rate for a two- to 2½-hour safari is Rs 550, but they are restricted to the Kumroj Community Forest, a buffer zone 30 minutes' drive east of Sauraha. The elephants are brought to Sauraha unless business is brisk, in which case transfers by 4WD to the elephants waiting in the forest is included. Wildlife sightings are usually good here, with rhinos being common, but tiger sightings are very uncommon; this is not surprising given the proximity of villages and the presence of so many people. If you only have time and money for one ride, you are much better off going into the park proper.

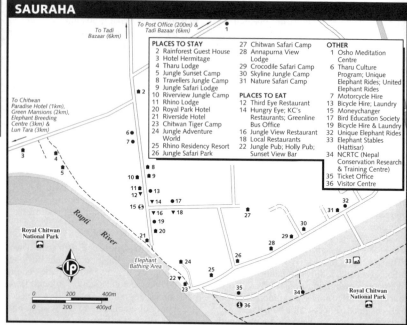

SAURAHA

PLACES TO STAY
2 Rainforest Guest House
3 Hotel Hermitage
4 Tharu Lodge
5 Jungle Sunset Camp
8 Travellers Jungle Camp
9 Jungle Safari Lodge
10 Riverview Jungle Camp
11 Rhino Lodge
20 Royal Park Hotel
21 Riverside Hotel
23 Chitwan Tiger Camp
24 Jungle Adventure
   World
25 Rhino Residency Resort
26 Jungle Safari Park

27 Chitwan Safari Camp
28 Annapurna View
   Lodge
29 Crocodile Safari Camp
30 Skyline Jungle Camp
31 Nature Safari Camp

PLACES TO EAT
12 Third Eye Restaurant
14 Hungry Eye; KC's
   Restaurants; Greenline
   Bus Office
16 Jungle View Restaurant
18 Local Restaurants
22 Jungle Pub; Holly Pub;
   Sunset View Bar

OTHER
1 Osho Meditation
   Centre
6 Tharu Culture
   Program; Unique
   Elephant Rides; United
   Elephant Rides
7 Motorcycle Hire
13 Bicycle Hire; Laundry
15 Moneychanger
17 Bird Education Society
19 Bicycle Hire & Laundry
32 Unique Elephant Rides
33 Elephant Stables
   (Hattisar)
34 NCRTC (Nepal
   Conservation Research
   & Training Centre)
35 Ticket Office
36 Visitor Centre

When booking a package tour in Kathmandu, or an elephant ride through a lodge, make sure you check whether your ride will take you inside or outside the park.

Jungle Walks

Visitors are allowed to enter the park on foot, but in order to get the most out of the experience, and for reasons of safety, it is mandatory that you go with a guide. Walks, which are often nothing more than a pleasant stroll through the jungle, can be exhilarating, but they are potentially dangerous if you meet a rhino. Most lodges (including some in Sauraha) have their own naturalists, but there are also a number of independent guides. These young locals may not have much formal training, but they're often very knowledgeable about the park's wildlife and where to find it.

Walking is the ideal way to see the park's prolific butterflies and birds, and to also see the flora close up. Jungle walks from Sauraha, which can be organised near the park ticket office, usually cost around Rs 60 per person for two hours, Rs 250 for half a day, and Rs 400 for a full day. To hire a guide, but not go in a group, will cost about Rs 250 for two hours or Rs 700 for a full day. Short walks will generally cover grassland and riverine forest; you need a day to get into the jungle. Walks can also be combined with canoe trips.

Canoeing

A canoe trip along the Rapti or Narayani Rivers is the most restful way of seeing the wildlife, particularly water birds, and with a bit of luck you may also see mugger and

---

WARNING

Tourists and guides on jungle walks have been killed by rhinos. Tigers and sloth bears can also be dangerous. Guides should brief you on safety procedures at the beginning of the walk. Many locals regard these walks as dangerous, but offer themselves as guides to remain employed – if they refuse to take tourists on guided walks they risk losing their jobs. It's a potentially risky activity (for both guides and tourists) that, upon weighing up these risks, is perhaps best avoided.

gharial crocodiles. With a great deal of luck you might catch a glimpse of a freshwater Gangetic dolphin, although they are believed to have vanished from the polluted Narayani.

Canoe trips from Saurah cost Rs 300 per person, but trips can also be combined with a walk. The standard programme is a one-hour float downriver, followed by a three-hour guided walk back to the village (costing Rs 500 to Rs 800 depending on the number in the group). National park fees must also be paid.

4WD Safaris

Animals are surprisingly unconcerned by vehicles, so a 4WD safari can be more exciting than you may expect. It also gives you a chance to get beyond the immediate Saurah area. Most 4WD drives take three or four hours (Rs 1000 to Rs 1200 plus Rs 400 for a guide). Whole-day drives cost Rs 2500 plus Rs 800 for a guide. The cost can be split between three passengers. The destination will depend on the current security status, army directions and the state of the roads after the preceding monsoon. Usually you will visit Bis Hajaar Tal, Lami Tal and the gharial crocodile breeding centre near Kasara.

Terai Culture

Staying in Saurah gives you an excellent opportunity to explore the surrounding countryside, either on foot or bicycle. Originally, the area was dominated by Tharu, but over the last decade increasing numbers of hill people have bought up the land. Many villages are now a multicultural mixture. They're full of life (and hordes of children) and give a vivid insight into the rigours and pleasures of subsistence farming. The nearest Tharu village is **Bachauli**, east of Saurah towards Gaida Wildlife Camp.

Some lodges arrange visits to nearby villages and a number organise displays of traditional Tharu dances. The stick dance, with a great circle of men whacking their sticks together, is quite a sight. In Saurah, the Tharu Culture Program performs dances each evening at 7.30pm in the high season. It's very much a tourist experience, but fun all the same. The cost is around Rs 50. Some of the more expensive lodges put on free performances for guests.

Wildlife Breeding Projects

There are two important breeding projects associated with the national park worth visiting: the Elephant Breeding Centre 3km west of Saurah and the gharial crocodile breeding centre near Kasara. Access to the Elephant Breeding Centre is by 4WD, foot or bicycle, and you need to take a canoe across the small Bhude Rapti River near the centre for a small fee. The best time to visit is after 3pm when the elephants return from the forest.

Bird Education Society

This volunteer group will be the first port of call for keen bird-watchers. The small office in the main *chowk* (intersection) is staffed by enthusiasts and sells posters, check lists (Rs 100), T-shirts and caps, with all proceeds going to bird conservation. Binoculars can be hired for Rs 10 per hour. Every Saturday morning there are bird-watching excursions that you are welcome to join.

Cycling

Bicycles are not allowed into the park proper (apparently nothing infuriates a rhino more than a bicycle), but the surrounding countryside is ideal for touring. You can hire standard Indian-made single-speed bicycles from various shops around the *chowk* in Saurah for around Rs 20 per hour, Rs 50 per half-day, and Rs 100 per full day; these are adequate for negotiating the dusty tracks as long as you are not too ambitious about the distance you want to cover.

Just wandering along the tracks east and west of Saurah is good fun. Also consider a trip to Bis Hajaar Tal, about 1½ hours northwest of Saurah. The lakes are famous for their prolific bird life. To get there, ride to Tadi, turn left (west) onto the Mahendra Hwy and continue for about 3km until you reach a signposted bridge over the Khageri Khola. Cross the bridge and take the dirt road on the left (south). After another small bridge the road forks; take the right fork and continue for about 5km. You'll see the lakes on the right.

Places to Stay

Although they can be pretty basic, the Saurah budget lodges often have an interesting clientele, are scattered around an attractive, partly traditional village, and the full range of wildlife-watching activities can also be easily organised.

There are so many lodges, and competition is so intense, that prices are ridiculously low. Many lodges have thus come to depend on 'invisible' add-on charges (commissions or service charges for organising bus tickets and wildlife-watching activities) to make a profit. Prices are sometimes inflated by ridiculous amounts, particularly since in almost all cases it's easy to organise tickets and activities yourself.

The most important variable in accommodation is the quality of the staff and your fellow travellers, both of which change, so ask other travellers for recommendations and check places for yourself. The main north–south road is busier and more developed than the east–west roads.

Budget The budget lodges are all out of the same mould; clean and simple mud-and-thatch cottages that sleep two and cost around Rs 100 for doubles. Most have a small veranda, and those with a nice garden can really be very pleasant. The mud-wall architecture keeps things surprisingly cool, and the rooms have insect screens on the windows and/or mosquito nets on the beds. Toilets and bathrooms are shared; hot water is unlikely, but this is not a major problem given the climate.

Chitwan Safari Camp & Lodge *(☎ 580078; doubles Rs 100-250)* is old-fashioned and simple. It has a pleasant garden and a quiet, but good position, handy to the park entrance, beachside strip and restaurants.

Annapurna View Lodge *(☎ 580072; 2-bed cottages Rs 100, singles/doubles with private bathroom Rs 150/300)* is another decent budget place with a nice atmosphere.

Crocodile Safari Camp *(☎ 580053; standard rooms Rs 100, doubles with private bathroom Rs 250)*, next door to Annapurna View Lodge, is similar.

Skyline Jungle Camp *(☎ 580024; cottages Rs 100, doubles with private bathroom Rs 250)*, also in this area, is a modern place with standard brick cottages or doubles. The rooms have a shady veranda.

Nature Safari Camp *(☎ 580019; rooms with shared bathroom Rs 100, with private bathroom Rs 250)*, farther along the same track as Skyline Jungle Camp, is a modern concrete construction, but the rooms and bathroom facilities are good.

Rainforest Guest House *(☎ 561435; cottage singles/doubles Rs 100/150, brick cottages with private bathroom Rs 300)*, at the northern end of town, is quiet and shady, with mud-and-thatch, or brick, cottages.

Travellers Jungle Camp *(☎ 580014; singles/doubles in row of brick cottages with bathroom Rs 200/250)* is a good family-run place with helpful owners.

Tharu Lodge *(☎ 580055; cottages Rs 100, brick cottages with private bathroom Rs 200)* is a mellow place close to the river with a nice garden and river views. It's just off the track leading to the Elephant Breeding Centre. There are standard mud-and-thatch cottages as well as brick cottages.

Jungle Sunset Camp *(cottages with shared bathroom Rs 200, rooms with private bathroom and hot water Rs 300)*, close to Tharu Lodge, is similar – mosquito nets of dubious quality are supplied. There are a number of very similar choices in this area.

Mid-Range Most mid-range places are dependent on the package trade, but they are happy to take individuals if there are vacancies. Some are good value with slightly more comfortable rooms with bathroom from around US$10/15 per single/double.

The standard package offered is three days and two nights, including transport, food, accommodation, entry fees, jungle walks, a canoe trip, an elephant ride, a performance of Tharu folk dancing and a tour of a Tharu village. Typically, the packages cost from US$100 if you travel to the park by bus, and considerably more if you travel by air or private car. It is possible to spend a good deal less if you travel independently and pay as you go. There are also combined rafting/Chitwan trips.

Rhino Lodge *(☎ 561660;* e *rhinolodge@ mos.com.np; singles/doubles with private bathroom US$9/12)*, a reputable package-oriented place, has a range of doubles; the more expensive ones are on the 2nd floor with views. The big plus is that its bar and restaurant overlook the river.

Riverview Jungle Camp *(☎ 560164; cottages Rs 400, brick cottages with bathroom Rs 650)* is a decent place, with much larger than usual double cottages or more substantial brick cottages.

Jungle Safari Lodge *(☎ 560061, 01-4416300 in Kathmandu; singles/doubles from*

US$15/20, with air-con and TV US$40/45) has comfortable cottages set in a manicured garden. The tariff includes meals and activities.

Hotel Hermitage *(☎ 580090;* **e** *hermitage@ mail.com.np)* has a river frontage and was under extensive renovation at the time of writing. Salubrious-looking double-storey town houses complete with moat suggest it is going for an upmarket crowd, but it would be worth checking out nonetheless.

Chitwan Paradise Hotel *(☎ 580048, 01- 4231183 in Kathmandu;* **e** *paradise@mos .com.np; cottages with bathroom US$15)*, farther along the road to the Elephant Breeding Centre, is nicely secluded. The cottages are roomy and set around a neat garden. Forty per cent of the profits go to NIDS, a nongovernmental organisation that supports rural communities. A bicycle would be very handy if you're staying here.

Chitwan Tiger Camp *(☎ 580060;* **e** *tiger cmp@col.com.np; doubles with shower/ bathroom Rs 300/500)* has fairly standard, bamboo-lined cottages with private bathrooms. Air-coolers are available on request. The restaurant is in an excellent position overlooking the river.

Royal Park Hotel *(☎ 580061; camp sites per person US$2, cottages US$20)* has an excellent location set in a large garden close to the river. The substantial, spacious cottages all have bathroom, fan and hot water, and beautiful slate floors. They also have wheelchair access. The cost includes breakfast. There's also an area set aside for campers. The bar here is in a great spot with limited river views.

Riverside Hotel *(☎ 561228; doubles/ triples Rs 350/750)* is a terrible eyesore down by the river. Nevertheless, it provides spacious, clean accommodation with superb river views, and the tariff includes breakfast.

Jungle Adventure World *(☎ 580064;* **e** *jaw_resort@hotmail.com; cottages Rs 700)* has a very pleasant garden setting with excellent river views. Usually catering to package groups, the comfortably furnished cottages are very good value for the walkin traveller.

Rhino Residency Resort *(☎ 01-4420431 in Kathmandu;* **e** *info@rhino-residency.com .np; doubles US$25)* is near the national park gate. Spacious air-con rooms are set in a manicured garden, and there's a swimming pool and restaurant, all surrounded by a high wall for privacy.

Jungle Safari Park *(☎ 580128, 561435; doubles RS 500)* is disconcertingly across from the bunkers of the army camp; nevertheless, the attractive brick cottages with verandas are good value.

Green Mansions *(☎ 01-4221854 in Kathmandu; 3-day, 2-night packages US$160, additional nights US$60)*, signposted about 3km west of Sauraha near the Elephant Breeding Centre, is a comfortable, low-key place. Rooms have some nice local touches, such as brass-bowl hand basins and shower bases. It's actually very nicely done, but without your own transport it's a bit far from everything.

Lun Tara *(☎ 01-4421210 in Kathmandu;* **e** *luntara@hons.com.np; singles/doubles Rs 300/650)*, is also west of Sauraha near the Elephant Breeding Centre. It is a back-tonature place with mud-and-thatch cottages which have private bathrooms. Wake up to the trumpeting of elephants and enjoy the friendly, laid-back ambience. The connection to Chitrasali and Sauraha is by horse and cart!

Places to Eat

Most lodges prepare food, and guests generally eat breakfast at their lodge. Restaurant dining is centred on the main *chowk*, where there are a handful of small, 1st-floor terrace restaurants above the shops, with limited views over the river. The food is standard travellers fare (mains Rs 90 to Rs 250), and the quality is average. Restaurants here include the **Jungle View**, **Third Eye**, **KC's** and **Hungry Eye**.

There are also a few casual places on the sandy banks of the river, including **Jungle Pub**, **Sunset View Bar** and **Holy Pub**. They are all low-key bamboo huts with tables and umbrellas. The food and prices are unexceptional (eg, pizzas Rs 125), but the position is superb, and these places are very popular at sunset.

River Sunset Restaurant, at Chitwan Tiger Camp in the park itself, also has a great position where you can sit back with a cool drink (beer Rs 120) and watch the river, the elephants and fellow tourists. The food served here is OK, too (Rs 115 for vegetarian biryani, Rs 180 for a nonvegetarian thali).

GETTING THERE & AWAY

Air

Yeti Airlines has daily flights from Kathmandu to Megauli – near the Tiger Tops, Temple Tiger and Island Jungle Resort lodges – for US$82 each way. There are also daily flights with most of the private airlines to Bharatpur (Narayanghat) for US$63 each way. The flights take around 30 minutes.

Bus

Tourist buses between Kathmandu or Pokhara and Chitwan cost from Rs 150 (six or seven hours). Any travel agent in Kathmandu or Pokhara can make a booking. Tourist buses (used by the majority of visitors) actually go to Chitrasali, the footbridge over the river midway between Tadi Bazaar and Sauraha. In Sauraha, lodges will book tickets (but beware of inflated prices) or you can book in Tadi at booking stalls near the main intersection.

Greenline (☎ 560126) has a daily air-con service in each direction for US$10 including breakfast, leaving Kathmandu, Pokhara and Sauraha (Chitrasali) at 8am – you can change at Kurintar for Pokhara.

To Sunauli on the Indian border (from Tadi), buses cost Rs 140 (five hours) and to Birganj Rs 85 (three hours).

Ordinary buses drop you in Tadi Bazaar on the Mahendra Hwy, about 15km east of Narayanghat. Minibuses (Rs 10, 30 minutes) then run from Tadi Bazaar to Narayanghat. From Tadi Bazaar it's 6km to Sauraha (Rs 30 by 4WD).

Car

Visitors to the lodges inside the park usually arrive by car from Kathmandu or Pokhara and this is usually arranged by the lodge operators. Cars typically cost around US$60, and the 160km to 180km trip (depending on where you're going) takes four to five hours.

The cars usually drop you at the turn-offs from the main road, from where your lodge vehicle will pick you up for the final trip into the park and across the river. This short trip is usually made by 4WD, although in the first month or two after the monsoon ends (September and October) the river may still be too high for vehicles and the transfer may be made by elephant. It's quite a surprise to arrive at the turn-off and find an elephant waiting for the final amble to the lodge!

If you are travelling to or from Kathmandu, try to convince your driver to take you one way via the Tribhuvan Hwy through the spectacular Daman and Hetauda section, although this will cost extra as the narrow, winding road will add at least an hour to your travel time. See both Daman and Hetauda later in this chapter for more details.

Raft

Numerous Kathmandu rafting operators offer trips down the Trisuli and Narayani Rivers to Chitwan. Most park lodges will organise a rafting trip in conjunction with your stay in the park.

Rafting trips start from Mugling, where the road to Narayanghat and Chitwan turns off from the Kathmandu–Pokhara (Prithvi) Hwy, or from farther up the Trisuli. It takes two or three days to raft down to Chitwan. Don't expect white-water thrills; this section of the river is more of a gentle drift. There are some fine views and the sandy beaches along the riverside offer great camping spots.

Prices will range from around US$30 to US$75 per day for rafting only; rafting and Chitwan trips (four nights, five days) can be as cheap as US$150. Shop around before you hand over your money; check where the rafting trip begins, what size the groups are, what activities are included at Chitwan and what transport there is from the river to your accommodation at Chitwan. See the Rafting & Kayaking chapter for more information.

Western Terai & Mahabharat Range

This section covers the towns and sights of the little-visited western Terai. From Narayanghat (see Eastern Terai & Mahabharat Range later) to Mahendranagar the Mahendra Hwy is the vital link, and it is in pretty good condition the entire way. The historic trading settlement of Tansen (Palpa) in the Middle Hills, just off the Siddhartha Hwy between Pokhara and Sunauli, is also included in this section.

BUTWAL
☎ 071

Lying at the very foot of the Chure hills and Mahabharat Range, which merge to the

THE TERAI &
MAHABARAT RANGE

north, Butwal is a busy crossroads town. The approach in from Pokhara and Tansen along the Siddhartha Hwy is dramatic; one moment you're in a narrow mountain gorge, the next you are surrounded by people, dust, rickshaws and Hindi film posters. The east–west Mahendra Hwy cuts across in the centre of town. Continue south and you cross into India at Sunauli, one of the major border posts.

If you find yourself stranded for a night, or have a couple of hours to kill waiting for a bus, it's well worth a wander through the old part of town on the west bank of the Tinau River. Walk across the main vehicle bridge, then head north through the old streets towards the hills, then cut back across the river on one of the two suspension foot and bicycle bridges.

You can check email at a small place in the Hotel Royale, which is 50m south of Traffic Chowk.

Places to Stay & Eat
There are plenty of cheap hotels at Traffic Chowk on the main road in the centre of town.

Hotel New Gandaki *(☎ 540928; doubles with shared bathroom Rs 150, with private bathroom Rs 250)*, the pick of the cheapies, has scruffy rooms.

Hotel Siddhartha *(☎ 540380; singles/ doubles with private bathroom Rs 500/700, with air-con Rs 1000/1200)* is a passably clean and comfortable hotel. The front rooms are a little noisy but the balconies give a great view of the bustling street. The attached **Nest Restaurant** is a cheap and reasonable place to eat.

Hotel Royale *(☎ 542730; singles/doubles/ triples Rs 300/450/500)*, across Traffic Chowk from the Siddhartha, is a similar budget choice with an attached restaurant.

Hotel Sindoor *(☎ 540381; singles/doubles Rs 350/500, with air-con Rs 1000/1200)* is upmarket and caters to business travellers. Though overpriced and a bit gloomy, it's clean, quiet and unquestionably the best place in town, with a good restaurant. It's on the Nepalganj road just west of the roundabout.

Nanglo West *(☎ 546184)* has secluded a branch of its fine restaurant chain in the narrow lanes of Old Butwal. Only a short rickshaw-ride from chaotic Traffic Chowk, over the Tinau Khola bridge on the Nepal-

ganj Rd, it's tucked away in an atmospheric time capsule.

Getting There & Away
All long-distance buses leave from the bus station, south of Traffic Chowk. You can book buses at the ticket counter or ask travel agent or your hotel to arrange a ticket.

There are departures for Kathmandu (day/ night/minibus Rs 155/193/240), Tansen (Rs 35), and Pokhara via Mugling (day/ night Rs 155/177, eight hours) or via Tansen (Rs 115, nine hours). Buses also depart for Nepalganj (day/night Rs 160/200), Narayanghat (Rs 75) and Mahendranagar (Rs 350).

There are also regular departures for Sunauli/Bhairawa (Rs 20).

SUNAULI & BHAIRAWA
☎ 071
Sunauli (pronounced 'so-nor-li') is a small, squalid, grubby collection of offices and hotels right on the Indian border – not a good introduction if you've just entered Nepal, but cheer up, things improve rapidly from here. Bhairawa is a somewhat more substantial town nearly 4km inside Nepal; officially its name is Siddharthanagar, but this name is rarely used.

There are three points in favour of visiting this part of the world. Firstly, Sunauli is the most popular and convenient border crossing between Nepal and northern and western India (including Varanasi, Agra and Delhi), and most prearranged bookings to or from India involve a night's stopover in Sunauli. Secondly, Bhairawa is the closest town to Lumbini, the birthplace of the Buddha. And thirdly, although Sunauli and Bhairawa are hot and featureless, they are still relaxed and pleasant in comparison to Birganj, the next major crossing point to the east.

If you are heading straight for other parts of Nepal, it makes sense to grit your teeth and stay in Sunauli (all buses depart from here). If you plan to spend a few days exploring this part of the country (well worth it, especially in the cooler months), then head for Bhairawa, which offers some better accommodation and some civility.

Orientation & Information
Both the Nepali and Indian customs and immigration offices are open 24 hours, but between about 10pm and 4am you will have to

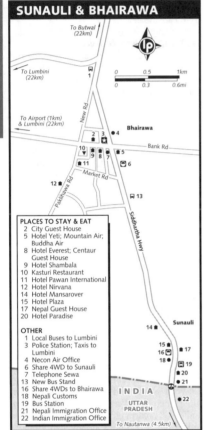

SUNAULI & BHAIRAWA

To Butwal
(22km)

To Lumbini
(22km)

To Airport (1km)
& Lumbini (22km)

Bhairawa

Bank Rd

Market Rd

New Rd

Pakilhawa Rd

Siddhartha Hwy

Sunauli

INDIA

UTTAR
PRADESH

To Nautanwa (4.5km)

0   0.5   1km
0   0.3   0.6mi

PLACES TO STAY & EAT
2   City Guest House
5   Hotel Yeti; Mountain Air;
    Buddha Air
8   Hotel Everest; Centaur
    Guest House
9   Hotel Shambala
10 Kasturi Restaurant
11 Hotel Pawan International
12 Hotel Nirvana
14 Hotel Mansarover
15 Hotel Plaza
17 Nepal Guest House
20 Hotel Paradise

OTHER
1   Local Buses to Lumbini
3   Police Station; Taxis to
    Lumbini
4   Necon Air Office
6   Share 4WD to Sunauli
7   Telephone Sewa
13 New Bus Stand
16 Share 4WDs to Bhairawa
18 Nepali Customs
19 Bus Station
21 Nepali Immigration Office
22 Indian Immigration Office

wake officials up, something they are quite accustomed to. You are free to walk across the border between the Indian and Nepali sides without going through any formalities.

There is a **tourist office** (☎ 520304) at the border, but don't expect much. There's also a bank and numerous official money-changers. Indian rupees (INRs) are accepted in Bhairawa and Sunauli (at the pegged exchange rate of Indian Rs 1 = Nepal Rs 1.60), but offload any excess before leaving as Indian rupees become harder to get rid of the farther you move from the border.

Bhairawa is a 20-minute rickshaw ride to the north. Most shops and businesses in Bhairawa are strung along Narayan Path (or Bank Rd). The Siddhartha Hwy runs along the eastern edge of town to the border.

Places to Stay & Eat

Sunauli There are about a dozen options, none of them very pleasant and all expensive for what you get. (On the Indian side there is only one very tired government tourist bungalow.)

Nepal Guest House (☎ 520877; 4-bed dorms per bed Rs 50, doubles with shared bathroom Rs 80, doubles with fan & private bathroom Rs 160 or INRs 100) has an OK restaurant, is reasonably priced and is passably clean. The rooms vary – ask to see several before you settle in.

Hotel Paradise (☎ 522777; singles/doubles with private bathroom Rs 280/400), hopefully named, is OK, but make sure you get a room on the side away from the bus station next door as buses start leaving at around 4am.

Hotel Plaza (☎ 524412; singles/doubles Rs 200/300) is reasonably clean and not bad value.

Hotel Mansarover (☎ 523686; doubles with private bathroom Rs 640, with air-con & TV Rs 1600) aims at something approaching luxury, but fails fairly dismally. It may be booked out to accommodate students from a nearby college.

Apart from the restaurants attached to hotels, there are a few small **restaurants** near the bus station.

Bhairawa More comfortable accommodation is available here than in Sunauli

Hotel Shambala (☎ 520167; Bank Rd; singles/doubles with shared bathroom Rs 200/300, with private bathroom Rs 400/450, with air-con Rs 800/1000) is not too bad. Prices are somewhat open to negotiation. There's also a decent restaurant.

Hotel Centaur (☎ 520536; Bank Rd; dorm bed with shared bathroom Rs 60, singles/doubles with private bathroom Rs 100/150) is a typical no-frills, budget place.

Hotel Everest (☎ 520317; Bank Rd; singles/doubles with private bathroom Rs 350/600) is a modern place with passably clean rooms with screened windows.

City Guest House (☎ 523481; Bank Rd; doubles with shared/private bathroom Rs 200/250), opposite Hotel Everest, is similarly passable if you find a room with intact insect screens.

Hotel Yeti (☎ 520551; e hotelyeti@wlink .com.np; cnr Bank Rd & Siddhartha Hwy; singles/doubles US$30/35, with air-con US$35/

45) is where the tour groups that occasionally pass through usually stay. It's clean, there's a decent restaurant and the prices are reasonable; 25% discounts are usually there for the asking. The hotel overlooks a main intersection (where the buses stop), so it can be a bit noisy.

Hotel Pawan International (☎ 523680; e pawanhl@mos.com.np; Paklihawa Rd; singles/doubles with air-con US$55/65) is a comfortable, glossy business hotel with the expected facilities of TV, phone and air-con.

Hotel Nirvana (☎ 520837; e nirva@ ccsl.com.np; Paklihawa Rd; singles/doubles US$95/105) is a five-star hotel that seems misplaced in scruffy Bhairawa. It's modern, clean, has air-con and is well worth the money. The restaurant here serves OK meals, and there's a bar. Ask for a discount, which may lower the price considerably – like 50%.

Kasturi Restaurant, near the corner of Bank and Paklihawa Rds, is a pleasant place with high ceilings and excellent vegetarian Indian food, but no alcohol. Dishes such as *pulau* and *korma* cost around Rs 50.

Getting There & Away

Air The Bhairawa airport is about 1km west of town. At least three airlines fly the route between Bhairawa and Kathmandu daily for US$81. The booking offices for **Buddha Air** (☎ 526893) and **Necon Air** (☎ 521244) are close to the Hotel Yeti.

Bus There are plenty of bus connections to destinations in both Nepal and India. Whether you have booked a 'through' ticket or not, be wary as everyone changes buses at the border. There are no tourist buses.

To/From India You catch buses to Indian cities from the Indian side of the border. There are direct buses to Varanasi for INRs 120 to INRs 150, depending on the degree of luxury, and the journey takes about nine hours.

There are also buses to Gorakhpur where you can connect with the Indian broad-gauge railway (INRs 60, three hours). Coming from Gorakhpur, buses leave every half-hour from 5.30am to 7pm; you'll need to catch a bus by 3pm if you want to be sure of catching a night bus to Kathmandu the same day. See the Getting There & Away chapter for more information.

To/From Other Parts of Nepal Travelling north, most buses leave from Sunauli, stopping in Bhairawa, but buses can be booked and boarded at either place. In Sunauli there's a bus booking office at the bus station; buses can only be booked on the day of departure. This office opens at 3am. In Bhairawa, buy tickets at the bus stand 500m south of the Hotel Yeti.

There are day and night buses for both Pokhara (day/night/minibus Rs 170/200/230, eight to nine hours) and Kathmandu (Rs 200/ 210/230), all travelling via Narayanghat. To Narayanghat, where you can change for Chitwan, the trip costs Rs 85.

There are also buses to Janakpur (Rs 225 at 6.10am, Rs 275 at 4pm), Biratnagar (Rs 296, 3.15pm) and Kakarbhitta (Rs 390, 4.30pm and 6.15pm).

There are plenty of local buses to Butwal for Rs 20. Taxis for Lumbini park outside the police station in Bhairawa. The charge of Rs 600 to Rs 800 for the return trip includes about two hours waiting at the site.

Getting Around

The only time you'll need transport will be to go between Sunauli and Bhairawa – four hot, flat kilometres. A rickshaw costs around Rs 50 and takes 20 minutes, or a share 4WD costs Rs 10 (Rs 80 with eight passengers!).

LUMBINI
☎ 071

Lumbini is believed to be the birthplace of Siddhartha Gautama – the founder of Buddhism, known as the Buddha or the enlightened one (see the boxed text 'Siddhartha Gautama'). This is confirmed by the existence of an inscribed pillar erected 318 years after the event by the great Indian Buddhist emperor Ashoka, and the presence of a number of ancient ruins.

Fittingly, Lumbini is an example of the ephemeral nature of human endeavour. There is not much to see and it requires much imagination to conjure up the ghosts of the past. Lumbini is not a Bethlehem or Mecca – there is no impressive architecture, no pilgrim-jammed car park, no heavily armed soldiers and no hustlers. There is, however, a tacky souvenir bazaar near the car park. Even saffron-robed monks appear unable to resist the urge to take home a memento. The Buddha in a snow dome costs Rs 110 and an electric 'enlightened' Buddha will surely trip the safety switch at Rs 150.

Allow yourself an hour or two to wander around and soak up the atmosphere. The important sights don't take long to cover – the Maya Devi Temple, the Ashokan Pillar, the Sacred Pond and the Tibetan and Theravada *viharas* (monasteries). Due to the enervating heat that afflicts this area for about nine months of the year, the site is probably best appreciated in the early morning or late afternoon, and so is worth an overnight stay.

There are grandiose plans for the development of Lumbini, with the aim of creating a place of pilgrimage and an international tourist attraction. A plan by Japanese architect Kenzo Tange was adopted in 1978, involving canals, gardens, a library and museum, monastic zones, a pilgrim lodge and a hotel. Various Buddhist countries have constructed or are in the process constructing temples and monasteries in their traditional styles in the monastic zones. Some of the best to look belong to the Burmese, Chinese, Japanese and Vietnamese.

The small village of Lumbini Bazaar is an undistinguished market town right by the main entrance to the site. It has a lively market on Monday. The rest of the time it's a peaceful corner of the Terai.

History

Ashoka visited Lumbini in 245 BC, and left a number of his famous inscribed pillars in the region. In AD 403 the region was visited by Fa Hsien, a Chinese pilgrim who described a ruined Kapilavastu and a deserted countryside.

In 636 Hsuan Tang, another pilgrim, described 1000 derelict monasteries and Ashoka's pillar at Lumbini, shattered by lightning and lying on the ground. Derelict it may have been, but the site was still known in 1312 when Ripu Malla visited, possibly leaving the nativity statue that is still worshipped in the Maya Devi Temple.

Mughal invaders arrived in the region at the end of the 15th century, and it is likely that they destroyed remaining 'pagan' monuments at both Kapilavastu and Lumbini. The whole region then returned to wilderness and the sites were eventually lost to the jungle, until the governor of Palpa, Khadga Shumsher Rana, who had a keen interest in

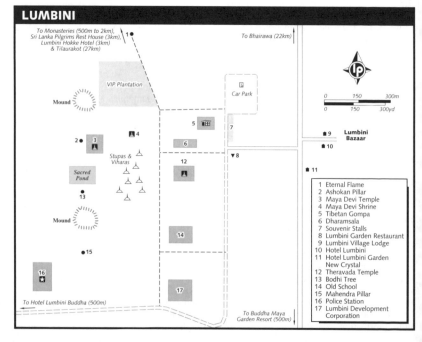

LUMBINI

To Monasteries (500m to 2km),
Sri Lanka Pilgrims Rest House (3km),
Lumbini Hokke Hotel (3km)
& Tilaurakot (27km)

To Bhairawa (22km)

VIP Plantation

Car Park

Mound

Lumbini
Bazaar

0   150   300m
0   150   300yd

Stupas &
Viharas

Sacred
Pond

Mound

To Hotel Lumbini Buddha (500m)

To Buddha Maya
Garden Resort (500m)

1 Eternal Flame
2 Ashokan Pillar
3 Maya Devi Temple
4 Maya Devi Shrine
5 Tibetan Gompa
6 Dharamsala
7 Souvenir Stalls
8 Lumbini Garden Restaurant
9 Lumbini Village Lodge
10 Hotel Lumbini
11 Hotel Lumbini Garden
    New Crystal
12 Theravada Temple
13 Bodhi Tree
14 Old School
15 Mahendra Pillar
16 Police Station
17 Lumbini Development
    Corporation

Siddhartha Gautama

The region at the foot of the Himalaya 2500 years ago consisted of a number of small republics and principalities that were vassal states to larger empires based on the Gangetic plain. Siddhartha Gautama was the son of Suddhodana (of the Sakya clan) who ruled the republic of Kapilavastu and Maya Devi (of the Koliya clan), the daughter of the ruler of the neighbouring state of Dewadaha.

It is believed that Maya Devi was 10 months pregnant when she decided to visit her parents' house in Dewadaha. On the way from Kapilavastu, her entourage had to pass through the grove of Lumbini, which was a famous beauty spot with a pond surrounded by sal trees. On the day she reached Lumbini, in May 563 BC, the sal trees were in full bloom, so Maya Devi stopped to enjoy the scene and bathe in the pond. Leaving the water, she suddenly felt labour pains. She walked 25 paces, raised her right hand and caught hold of the drooping branch of a pipal tree, and the baby was born.

Maya Devi returned to Kapilavastu where her son Siddhartha was given a sheltered, privileged upbringing. At the age of 29, while wandering in the town outside the palace walls, he came across an old man, a sick man, a corpse and a hermit. This confrontation with suffering and death impelled Siddhartha to renounce his luxurious life and to leave Kapilavastu.

He spent the next five years seeking to understand the nature of existence. Mostly he wandered as an itinerant ascetic – no doubt much like the Hindu sadhus of today – but he found that extreme self-denial did not provide him with any answers. Finally, after 49 days meditating under a bodhi tree at Bodhgaya in India he attained enlightenment. From Bodhgaya he travelled to Sarnath, near Varanasi, where he preached his first sermon.

The Buddha spent the next 46 years teaching his 'middle way'. Suffering, he taught, is a natural part of life, but suffering is caused by attachment, desire and delusion, and if these negative forces are controlled (by following the noble 'eightfold path'), it is possible to reach nirvana.

Although some people believe the Buddha visited the Kathmandu Valley, there is no firm evidence for this. Most of his preaching was undertaken in northern India and across the Gangetic plain. He died at the age of 80 at Kushinagar, near Gorakhpur, about 100km southeast of Lumbini.

Despite his disavowal of divinity, the main sites associated with the Buddha's life (Lumbini, Kapilavastu, Bodhgaya, Sarnath and Kushinagar) soon became centres for pilgrimage, and monasteries and temples sprang up. The ruins of Kapilavastu lie at Tilaurakot, 27km west of Lumbini, but Dewadaha has not been conclusively identified.

archaeology, began the excavation of Ashoka's Lumbini pillar in late 1896.

Today, no trace of the Lumbini forest remains, but the pond where Maya Devi, the mother of the Buddha, is believed to have bathed can still be seen, although in a much restored form. The brick foundations of stupas (religious structures) and *viharas* dating from the 2nd century BC can be seen around the pond. The Maya Devi Temple is built on ancient foundations, and these are the site of an archaeological dig.

Most of the surrounding countryside is dominated by extremely poor Muslim peasant farmers nowadays. There are no resident Buddhists in Lumbini.

Ashokan Pillar
Emperor Ashoka is one of the great figures of Indian history. Throughout his massive empire he left pillars and rock-carved edicts, which to this day delineate the extent of his power. These structures can be seen in Delhi, Gujarat, Orissa, Uttar Pradesh, Madhya Pradesh – and in Nepal. The pillar at Lumbini commemorates Ashoka's pilgrimage to the birthplace of the Buddha. It is 6m high, although half of it is underground.

Maya Devi Temple
Until 10 years ago the Maya Devi Temple, parts of which were believed to be over 2000 years old, stood on the spot where the Buddha is thought to have been born. A huge pipal tree, which was gradually tearing the temple apart, was believed by some to have been the tree that Maya Devi held while giving birth to Siddhartha.

In 1993 the tree was ripped out and the temple demolished to make archaeological excavations possible. At the time of writing, these were still going on. In 1995 archaeologists claim to have found a commemorative stone atop a platform of seven layers of bricks 5m below the old temple floor and dating from the era of Ashoka. Buddhist literature says Ashoka placed a stone on top of bricks at the birthplace of Prince Siddhartha – who was later called Lord Buddha. The recently discovered stone is said to be the correct distance from the nearby pool.

When the temple was demolished, the revered centrepiece of the temple, a stone carving showing the birth of the Buddha, was moved to an ugly brick structure close by (the Maya Devi Shrine). Possibly dating from the Malla dynasty (about 14th century AD), the sculpture was the centre of a fertility rite, and it has almost been reduced to formlessness by the wear of constant *puja* (offerings, prayers). One can still make out Maya Devi, with her right hand raised to hold the pipal tree branch, as she gives birth. There is also a modern marble interpretation, along with a number of small sculptures left by devotees.

Other Attractions

The pool beside the temple is believed to be where Maya Devi bathed before giving birth to the Buddha; it has been heavily restored. The foundations for a number of stupas and *viharas* dating from the 2nd century BC to the 9th century AD lie in the vicinity.

A number of monasteries to the north of the site are complete and worth visiting. The site is *very* spread out, so without your own transport you'll need to take one of the cycle-rickshaws by the main gate. The roads are bumpy so it's not exactly leisurely. The **Chinese Monastery** is the most impressive, and is something straight out of the Forbidden City; even the roof tiles were imported. Also open and worth a look are the **Burmese Monastery** and the recently completed monastery of the Indian **Mahabodhi Society**. Monasteries of Thailand, Vietnam and Korea are also under construction.

There's a small **museum** *(open 10am-5pm Sun-Thur, 10am-3pm Fri)* at the Lumbini Research Institute. Again, you'll need transport to get to it.

Special Events

A major Hindu festival is held on the full moon of the Nepali month of Baisakh (April–May), when thousands of local Hindus come to worship Maya Devi as Rupa Devi, the mother goddess of Lumbini, and to celebrate the Buddha as the ninth incarnation of Vishnu. The Buddhist celebration of the Buddha's birthday, Buddha Jayanti, is celebrated around the same time, but is more low-key. During winter, when it's not too hot, Buddhist pilgrims from the Kathmandu Valley often come to worship on Purnima (the night of the full moon) and Astemi (the eighth night after the full moon).

Places to Stay & Eat

Most people simply make a day trip from Bhairawa, but there are a couple of places to stay and eat in Lumbini.

Lumbini Village Lodge *(☎ 580258; singles/doubles Rs 250/350)* is in Lumbini Bazaar. The rooms are clean and comfortable and you can get home-style dal bhaat for Rs 65.

Hotel Lumbini *(☎ 580142; dorm beds/doubles/triples Rs 100/300/450)* is very similar, very budget and also serves basic food.

Sri Lanka Pilgrims Rest House *(☎ 580109; dorm beds Rs 100)* is about 3km north of the site, beyond the sacred flame and just off the dirt road to Tilaurakot. This odd brick place has spartan dorms in two-bed, four-bed and eight-bed configurations. It would be handy to have a bicycle if you want to travel back and forth to the site; be warned that the grounds are invaded by rowdy weekend picnickers during the cooler months.

Hotel Lumbini Buddha *(☎ 580114; rooms from around US$10)* is about 500m southwest of the site, bordering a forest. It's a very pleasant and comfortable mid-range hotel.

Buddha Maya Garden Resort *(☎ 580220, fax 580219; dorm beds US$10, singles/doubles from US$60/70)*, 500m southeast of the site, is run by the famed Kathmandu Guest House. It consists of a number of dorm rooms and very comfortable singles and doubles; there's a very good restaurant here. This represents the best value in the area – ask for a discount.

Lumbini Hokke Hotel *(☎/fax 580236; singles/doubles US$90/120 Sept-Mar, US$68/90 Apr-Aug)*, at the top of the scale, is close to Sri Lanka Pilgrims Rest House. Built with Japanese pilgrims in mind, most of the rooms have been furnished in traditional Japanese style with tatami floors, paper partitions and Japanese furniture. There are also a number of European-style rooms. All rooms have air-con and bathroom. Prices are reasonable, especially when you factor in a 25% discount. Meals (Japanese only) are US$7 for lunch or dinner.

Hotel Lumbini Garden New Crystal (☎ 580145; singles/doubles from US$90/99) is also aimed at top-end pilgrims. There are comfortable Western- and Japanese-style rooms with the expected amenities and multi-cuisine restaurant.

Lumbini Garden Restaurant, which judging by its appearance is not part of the Lumbini Development Plan, is just by the main car park. It's a modern red-brick eyesore sporting numerous large Coca-Cola ads. The prices are relatively high, but the food is OK, though service can be extremely slow.

Getting There & Away

Regular minibuses make the 22km journey from Bhairawa to Lumbini for Rs 18, but they are agonisingly slow (1½ hours). The roof is the place to be. The last bus back passes by the main entrance at about 5pm (but check). Buses leave Bhairawa from the signposted intersection with roundabout, about 500m north of the Hotel Yeti.

If you are in a group, or have the funds, it would be immensely preferable to hire a taxi-4WD (from Rs 600 to Rs 800). These prices include two hours waiting time at the site, which should be sufficient for most people.

The best method of transport for budget travellers is bicycle, although attempting this in high summer may be a bit ambitious. There are no formal rental places in Bhairawa, but if you ask around (start at your hotel, then try bicycle repair shops) something might turn up. The road to Lumbini is virtually an avenue of mango trees; beyond their shade the serene pastoral views of men and bullocks working mustard-yellow fields and women in bright saris threshing grain seem very apt for a spiritual journey.

TAULIHAWA & TILAURAKOT

Tilaurakot is now nothing more than a tiny hamlet 3km north of Taulihawa, a bustling Terai centre. Tilaurakot was once, however, capital of the republic of Kapilavastu, where the Buddha spent the first 29 years of his life.

Taulihawa is a vibrant town with the usual multicultural mix of peoples found in Terai

cities. There is a temple complex known as **Tauleshwar**, now used by Shaivites, in the centre of town.

Although even less visited than Lumbini, Tilaurakot is in many ways actually the more atmospheric of the two spots. There is a small group of farming households outside the ruins of the city walls, which, along with the moat, can be clearly discerned. The whole complex is shaded by large trees and has the peaceful atmosphere of a park.

After the discovery of Lumbini, the ruins near Tilaurakot were subsequently identified as Kapilavastu. There has been some archaeological work, which has revealed the remains of moated city walls, as well as impressive gates and the foundations for a palace complex.

The scattered foundations that can be seen within the walls give only the most minimal indication that there was once a palace here, but archaeologists have found 13 successive layers of human habitation, dating back to the 8th century BC. Today the only sign of life is a small, run-down shrine to a Hindu goddess, Somaya Mai.

The scene outside the walls could be unchanged from what Siddhartha might have seen. Timeless patterns of subsistence farming unfold along the banks of the Banganga River, and on the north side of the river there is an expanse of untouched sal forest. It is not hard to imagine Siddhartha walking out through the imposing gateway of the palace and as he wandered, seeing an old man, a sick man, a corpse and a hermit.

About 400m from the ruins, a small **museum** (open Mon, Wed-Fri & Sun) displays some of the artefacts found at the site, including coins and pottery.

Lumbini Hotel (singles/doubles Rs 80/100), on the road to Tilaurakot, is very basic but acceptably clean. There are no facilities at Tilaurakot.

There are plenty of basic **food stalls** in Taulihawa.

Getting There & Away

A road links Taulihawa with Lumbini, 27km to the east. Slow and crowded local buses link Taulihawa with Bhairawa, but a bicycle is the best method of transport.

Tilaurakot is 3km north of Taulihawa. At the end of the bitumen the museum is on the left and the ruins are 400m away down a dirt track on the right. In winter you can cross a ford over Banganga River and continue 14km due north along a dirt road through Sagar Forest, finally joining the Mahendra Hwy 35km west of Butwal and 80km east of Lamahi (also spelt Lumihi).

TANSEN (PALPA)
☎ 075

Tansen is just off the Siddhartha Hwy, between Pokhara and Sunauli/Bhairawa. Historically, it has enjoyed a strategic position on the trade and pilgrim route between the hills and the plains.

Tansen is still the administrative centre for a large region, but it sees few visitors, and is increasingly sidelined by the development on the Terai and at Pokhara.

The town sprawls over a steep ridge, and quite a few of the main streets are too steep for cars, which helps to keep some of the less pleasant aspects of the 21st century at bay. In the older sections of the town, attractive Newari buildings line cobbled streets.

Most of the surrounding countryside is dominated by Magars, but there are also Bahuns and Chhetris. Newars form the majority in Tansen itself. They migrated from the Kathmandu Valley to take advantage of trade opportunities with India that opened up in the 19th century – traditional crafts and agricultural surpluses were traded for the products of the British industrial revolution, especially cotton fabrics. Tansen is still famous for metalware and *dhaka*, the hand-woven material that is made into *topis* (Nepali hats).

There are great views over the bowl-shaped **Madi Valley** from the town, and a spectacular view of the Himalaya from the nearby hill, Srinagar Danda. There are some interesting walks in the surrounding countryside, including a day trek to the banks of the Kali Gandaki River and the vast, deserted Ranighat Durbar (Ranighat Palace). Tansen is a pleasant place to break the rough journey from Pokhara to the border at Sunauli/Bhairawa.

Information
Getup (*Group for Environmental & Tourism Upgrading Palpa;* ☎ 521341), 30m west of the Sitalpati (public square), has a very helpful tourist information office that provides

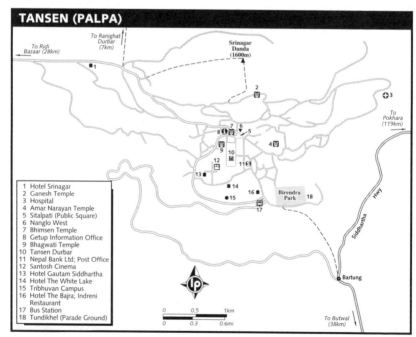

TANSEN (PALPA)

To Ranighat Durbar (7km)
To Ridi Bazaar (28km)
Srinagar Danda (1600m)
To Pokhara (119km)
Birendra Park
Siddhartha Hwy
Bartung
To Butwal (38km)

1 Hotel Srinagar
2 Ganesh Temple
3 Hospital
4 Amar Narayan Temple
5 Sitalpati (Public Square)
6 Nanglo West
7 Bhimsen Temple
8 Getup Information Office
9 Bhagwati Temple
10 Tansen Durbar
11 Nepal Bank Ltd; Post Office
12 Santosh Cinema
13 Hotel Gautam Siddhartha
14 Hotel The White Lake
15 Tribhuvan Campus
16 Hotel The Bajra; Indreni Restaurant
17 Bus Station
18 Tundikhel (Parade Ground)

0   0.5   1km
0   0.3   0.6mi

many free services, such as hotel and restaurant recommendations. Staff can organise tours of workshops where traditional metalware and *dhaka* are made. For a nominal cost, you can purchase three excellent trekking maps for short treks around Tansen. These include a short tour around the town, the classic loop to the fabulous Ranighat (see Around Tansen later), and a trek that follows the old trade route to Butwal. Getup can also organise the services of a guide.

Nepal Bank Ltd *(open 10am-3pm Sun-Thur, 10am-noon Fri)* in Bank Rd will accept credit cards and cash travellers cheques. **Pooja Communication**, near the bank, claims to have Internet access, but it is rarely working and is expensive at Rs 5 to Rs 10 per minute. At the time of writing, Getup was planning to provide Internet access for travellers – check it out.

Amar Narayan Temple
The Amar Narayan is a classic pagoda-style temple with three tiers, and is considered to be one of the most beautiful outside the Kathmandu Valley. There is some fine woodwork, with erotic figures on the roof struts and beautifully carved doors.

The temple was built in 1806 by Amar Singh Thapa, the general who annexed Tansen to Nepal. Sadhus often stay in the rest houses around the temple on their way to Muktinath, northwest of Pokhara on the popular Annapurna Circuit Trek. There's a large bat colony in the surrounding trees, and some tanks where women do their washing.

Tansen Durbar
This former palace of the provincial governor was built in a heavy-handed Rana style in 1927 and is now home to local bureaucrats. The imposing, though dilapidated, entrance gate on the eastern side of the compound is called Baggi Dhoka (Mul Dhoka). It's supposedly the biggest gate in Nepal, which allowed the governor to make a suitably impressive entrance on an elephant.

A public square known as Sitalpati lies just outside the gate; it is named after the unusual octagonal building in the centre.

Bhagwati Temple
The Bhagwati Temple, near the palace, is a rather garish construction that was unsym-

pathetically renovated after an earthquake in 1935, and again in 1974. It was built originally in 1815 to commemorate the Nepali victory over the British at Butwal.

There are some smaller temples in the vicinity dedicated to Shiva, Ganesh and Saraswati.

Srinagar Danda
Srinagar Danda is a 1600m-high hill directly north of town and a steep half-hour walk from Sitalpati. From the pine-forested top there's a spectacular view over the gorge of the Kali Gandaki River to the Himalaya – the panorama stretches from Kanjiroba in the west, all the way to Dhaulagiri, the Annapurnas, and Langtang in the east.

Places to Stay & Eat
There are some hotels around the bus station, but they're all pretty awful.

Hotel The Bajra *(☎ 520443; singles/doubles with shared bathroom Rs 100/150, with private bathroom & hot water Rs 150/250)*, just a short walk up the hill, is a much better option that is reasonably new and quite clean. The **Indreni Restaurant** here is not bad.

Farther up the hill are a couple more choices.

Hotel The White Lake *(☎ 520291; singles/doubles with shared bathroom Rs 200/300, with private bathroom Rs 400/600)* has some excellent views to the south, and the rooms are well appointed and good value. There's also a restaurant on the premises.

Hotel Gautam Siddhartha *(☎ 520280; doubles/triples with shared bathroom Rs 150/200)*, fairly close to Hotel The White Lake, is much cheaper. It is basic, but passably clean and quiet.

Hotel Srinagar *(☎ 520045, fax 520590; e srinagar@mos.com.np; singles/doubles with bathroom US$17/22)*, the most luxurious option, is about 2km away on the ridge above town, a 20-minute walk west of the summit. Although rather isolated, it's comfortable, there's a good restaurant, the views are sensational and the discount for independent travellers is 35%.

Nanglo West *(open 10.30am-8.30pm daily)* at Sitalpati is a quality restaurant and bakery with a very pleasant courtyard. The meals (Indian and continental) are reasonably priced with entrees for Rs 50 to Rs 80 and mains around Rs 200.

Almost all of the lodges around the bus station are good for a dal bhaat.

Getting There & Away

The bus station is at the southern end of the town centre. The ticket counter is hidden away in the northeast corner. There are two daily buses to Pokhara (Rs 100, five hours) leaving at 6.30am and 9.15am. To Butwal (Rs 33, two hours) there are numerous buses, the first leaving at 6.30am.

The scenery along the twisting and turning Siddhartha Hwy to Pokhara is magnificent. For cyclists and motorcyclists, there's not too much traffic and as you head to Pokhara the Himalayan peaks tantalise as they appear around curves only to disappear at the next turn. If you're coming from Pokhara, try to get a seat on the right-hand side of the bus. The road to Butwal is subject to landslides during the monsoon, and is usually in very poor condition the rest of the year, so traffic flow is often disrupted.

AROUND TANSEN
Ridi Bazaar

Ridi is a holy town, mainly populated by Newars, at the confluence of the Kali Gandaki and Ridi Rivers. The confluence of tributaries to the Ganges is always regarded as holy, and Ridi has been further sanctified by the presence of saligrams, black ammonite fossils that have a spiral shape and are regarded as emblems of Vishnu. Saligrams are found in a number of places along the Kali Gandaki, most notably north of Jomsom around Muktinath. See the boxed text 'Saligrams' in the Trekking chapter.

Although Ridi's religious popularity has declined, cremations are still relatively frequent, and pilgrims come for ritual bathing, marriage ceremonies and other rituals. Pilgrims believe that if they fast and worship for three days, and then take a ritual bath in the Kali Gandaki, all their sins will be forgiven.

The most important festival is Magh Sankranti, when pilgrims come to immerse themselves in the river. This takes place on the first day of the Nepali month of Magh (mid-January) and celebrates the gradually lengthening days and the onset of warmer weather. Worshippers also gather every Ekadashi (the 11th day after the full moon). The festival of Ridi is held in November.

The commercial part of town is across the Ridi River; the Rishikesh Temple is near the bus station. It is believed the temple was founded by Mukund Sen in the early 16th century, but the current temple dates from the 19th century. It is also believed that the statue of Rishikesh (a manifestation of Vishnu) was discovered in the river, and that the figure of the god has gradually aged from boyhood to adulthood.

It is a 13km trek from Tansen to Ridi. You can leave the road just to the west of Hotel Srinagar, and pick it up again about 7km from Ridi. Alternatively, it is 28km by road. Buses leave Tansen in the morning, cost Rs 60 and take around two hours.

Ranighat Durbar

Sometimes fancifully referred to as Nepal's Taj Mahal, Ranighat Durbar was built by Khadga Shamsher Rana in 1896. Khadga was exiled to Tansen and made governor for plotting to become prime minister. Here, he consoled himself by building a spectacular palace, supposedly in memory of his wife, Tej Kumari.

The palace is a huge, white baroque building, dramatically perched on a rocky crag above the Kali Gandaki River. It was used for 25 years as a luxurious *dharamsala* (pilgrim guesthouse) by aristocrats who ostensibly came to bathe in the Kali Gandaki, and no doubt to party and plot with Khadga. Khadga was an ambitious man, and in 1921 he made another abortive attempt to seize power only to be exiled to India. On his departure the building was stripped of its valuable furnishings, and was left to fall into ruin. As it has been largely restored, it is now looking much less forlorn than it has for years.

The trail to Ranighat begins a short distance east of Hotel Srinagar, at the edge of the pine forest. It's an attractive 7km hike down to the river and takes at least four hours each way – a very long day trip.

NEPALGANJ
☎ 081

The most important town in western Nepal, Nepalganj at times feels more Indian than Nepali. It's a border town that owes as much to trade (read smuggling) as it does to its position as a major administrative centre. It has more of an air of permanence than some border towns, and planners have had the good

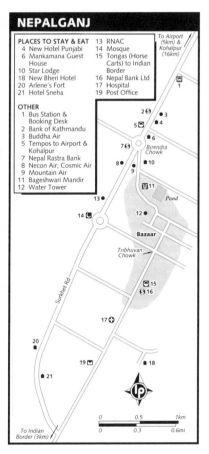

NEPALGANJ

PLACES TO STAY & EAT	13 RNAC
4 New Hotel Punjabi	14 Mosque
6 Mankamana Guest	15 Tongas (Horse
House	Carts) to Indian
10 Star Lodge	Border
18 New Bheri Hotel	16 Nepal Bank Ltd
20 Arlene's Fort	17 Hospital
21 Hotel Sneha	19 Post Office

OTHER
1 Bus Station & Booking Desk
2 Bank of Kathmandu
3 Buddha Air
5 Tempos to Airport & Kohalpur
7 Nepal Rastra Bank
8 Necon Air; Cosmic Air
9 Mountain Air
11 Bageshwari Mandir
12 Water Tower

To Airport (5km) & Kohalpur (16km)

To Indian Border

Birendra Chowk

Pond

Bazaar

Tribhuvan Chowk

Surkhet Rd

To Indian Border (3km)

An increasing number of travellers comes through Nepalganj on the way to or from western Nepal and Royal Bardia National Park, or to Jumla in northwestern Nepal. It can also be a useful back-door entry into Nepal from central Uttar Pradesh in India; Lucknow is about four hours away.

Orientation & Information

Nepalganj is about 6km north of the border. The old, vaguely interesting part of town lies to the east of the main road (Surkhet Rd) around Tribhuvan Chowk, although virtually all the hotels are on the highway.

The airport is 6km north of Birendra Chowk (with the statue) to the east of Surkhet Rd. The long-distance bus station is about 1km north of Birendra Chowk around a T-junction.

The various customs and immigration offices at the border all have different closing hours, but they are all open at least from 8am to 11am and 1pm to 5pm. There is a moneychanger at the Mankamana Guest House and at least two banks in town.

A couple of places south of Birendra Chowk on Surkhet Rd offer Internet access (with slow connections).

Things to See & Do

The old part of town has the **Bageshwari Mandir**, a garish temple to Kali. There's also a vibrant **bazaar** selling everything except kitchen sinks (although the metalworkers could probably knock one up for you). It is well worth wandering around the centre of town. The crush of people, the smells, the food, the shops, the film posters and the rickshaws give a vivid taste of the subcontinent.

Places to Stay & Eat

The cheapies are centred around Birendra Chowk.

New Hotel Punjabi (☎ 520818; singles/doubles with shared bathroom Rs 100/150, with private bathroom Rs 250/350) is one of the better choices with large, comfortable and acceptably clean rooms. The Indian dishes from the restaurant are quite passable.

Mankamana Guest House (doubles with private bathroom Rs 150), nearby, is also acceptable; bathrooms have cold water.

The hotels on Garwhari Tole, which connects Birendra Chowk with the old part of town, are somewhat quieter.

sense to run the highway to the west of the main town. Despite this, it's a distinctly unattractive place with few redeeming features.

Nepalganj is a densely crowded city, and every possible ethnic group in Nepal is represented here. There is an unusually large Muslim community, many of whom settled here to escape the violence of the 1857 Indian Uprising. The Muslim men are distinctive, with their long beards and skull caps, as are the women, some of whom dress in black and are completely veiled. The colourful throngs in the streets also include Shaivite sadhus, Tharu women (with tight bodices, bare midriffs and bright skirts), turbaned Sikhs, Bajis (Abadhi speakers from India), Bahuns, Chhetris, Newars, Magars, Gurungs, Thakuris and even Tibetans.

Star Lodge *(☎ 522257; singles/doubles with shared bathroom Rs 100/150, with private bathroom Rs 150/200)* is a basic budget lodge – gloomy but acceptable.

New Bheri Hotel *(☎ 520213; singles/ doubles with private bathroom US$8/10, with air-con US$16/20)*, offers the best value in town. The hotel is near the hospital in a quiet part of town, and has a pleasant garden. With discounts you may have to pay only half these prices. It's a good place.

There are two reasonable upper-end hotels, both south of town on the highway towards the Indian border. There are many more trees around here and the hotels are set back from the road, so there's no problem with noise and parking.

Hotel Sneha *(☎ 520119;* e *hotel@sneha .wlink.com.np; standard singles/doubles US$18/24, deluxe with air-con US$30/36)* has a range of large, clean rooms, and helpful staff. Discounts of 15% are possible. There's a restaurant here and the food is quite passable.

Arlene's Fort *(☎ 520704; singles/doubles Rs 1000/1200)* has a pleasant garden complete with water feature. The rooms are spacious and all have air-con, bathroom and TV. This is good value for a place with air-con in Nepalganj. There's also a restaurant in the garden.

Getting There & Away
Air The distinctly grubby Nepalganj airport is 6km north of town. This is RNAC's western headquarters and so there are a number of flights into the interior. RNAC flies from Nepalganj to Surkhat (US$40, Monday and Thursday), Simikot (US$92, Sunday, Tuesday, Wednesday and Friday), Kathmandu (US$103, daily), Mahendranagar (Rs 1125, Tuesday) and Jumla (US$61, Wednesday, Thursday and Friday).

Most private airlines have at least one daily flight each between Nepalganj and Kathmandu (US$106). Airline offices are all on Surkhet Rd, close to Birendra Chowk. **Yeti Airlines** *(☎ 521637, fax 520029)* flies to remote airstrips in western Nepal such as Dolpo, Bajura, Sanfebagar, Rumkum and Surkhat.

Bus There's a booking window for bus tickets just a couple of shops south of the intersection where the buses congregate.

There are private buses to Pokhara (day/ night Rs 280/350 via Mugling, 12 hours) and Kathmandu (Rs 435, 12 hours). Buses for Mahendranagar leave hourly between 5am and 11am (Rs 280, six hours). It's advisable to book at least one day in advance.

Local buses to Thakurdwara (for Royal Bardia National Park) leave at noon and 2pm, and take an interminable five hours to cover less than 100km.

Once across the Indian border, 6km to the south, there are direct buses to Lucknow (seven hours) and share taxis (INRs 150, four hours). The nearest point on the Indian rail network is Nanpara, 17km from the border.

Getting Around
There are shared *tempos* (three-wheeled minivans) from Birendra Chowk to the airport for Rs 7, or you can take a 'reserve' for Rs 50. A cycle-rickshaw costs around Rs 50, but takes up to half an hour. To get to the Indian border by cycle-rickshaw costs around Rs 30.

ROYAL BARDIA NATIONAL PARK
☎ 084
The Royal Bardia National Park *(admission per day Rs 500; open 6.30am-5.30pm, to 7pm in summer)* is the largest untouched wilderness area in the Terai. It's bordered to the north by the crest of the Chure hills and to the west by the large Geruwa River, a branch of the Karnali, one of the major tributaries of the mighty Ganges.

About 70% of the 968-sq-km park is covered with open sal forest, with the balance a mixture of grassland, savannah and riverine forest. More than 30 different mammals and 250 species of birds have been recorded in the park. The *phanta* (grass plains) are excellent for viewing wildlife. Most people will visit in the hope of seeing a royal Bengal tiger, but there are also leopards, jungle cats, mongooses, sloth bears, nilgai, langur and rhesus monkeys, and barking, spotted, hog and sambar deer. The Indian one-horned rhinoceros was reintroduced from Chitwan in 1986, and though breeding successfully the numbers are still small – 67 according to a 2000 census. Birds include numerous species of herons, storks, geese, ducks and parakeets, as well as peacocks and endangered birds such as the Bengal florican and sarus crane.

THE TERAI & MAHABARAT RANGE

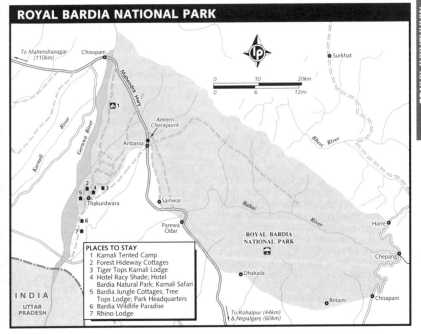

ROYAL BARDIA NATIONAL PARK

To Mahendranagar (110km)
Chisopani
Surkhat

0   10   20km
0   6   12mi

Mahendra Hwy

Amreni Checkpoint

Anbassa

Karnali River

Geruwa River

Bheri River

Thakurdwara

Sainwar

Babai

Parewa Odar

ROYAL BARDIA NATIONAL PARK

River

Harre

Chepang

Dhakaila

Betaini

Chisapani

INDIA
UTTAR PRADESH

PLACES TO STAY
1 Karnali Tented Camp
2 Forest Hideway Cottages
3 Tiger Tops Karnali Lodge
4 Hotel Racy Shade; Hotel
  Bardia Natural Park; Karnali Safari
5 Bardia Jungle Cottages; Tree
  Tops Lodge; Park Headquarters
6 Bardia Wildlife Paradise
7 Rhino Lodge

To Kohalpur (44km)
& Nepalganj (60km)

The Geruwa River rushes through a gap in the hills at Chisopani, grey with silt and snow-melt. It's home to the famous mahseer game fish, gharial and mugger crocodiles, and the very rare Gangetic dolphin.

In some ways Bardia is like Chitwan; the major difference is the degree of isolation and the limited number of visitors – of all visitors to national parks and reserves in the Terai, only 5% visit Bardia (92% visit Chitwan). This number had dropped to a trickle in early 2003 because of the Maoist and army presence, plus the closure of the upmarket Karnali Tented Camp and some other lodges.

The park is most easily visited en route to or from Delhi and western Nepal; with the completion of the Mahendra Hwy, Bardia is now more easily accessible from Delhi than Kathmandu. From Bardia it's a day's travel to Kathmandu or Pokhara, with direct buses to each.

Orientation & Information

The **park headquarters** is at Thakurdwara, about 20km southwest along a bumpy dirt road from Anbassa on the Mahendra Hwy. Anbassa is nothing more than a road inter-

section and a motley collection of temporary wooden shacks. It is about 500m south of the Amreni checkpoint, where the highway enters the park, and this in turn is 8km from Chisopani. Virtually all tourist activity is centred on the western spur of the park that takes in the forest and grasslands around the Geruwa River; the large eastern portion of the park is untouched.

There's a **park office** (☎ 429719; open 8am-10am & 2pm-5pm daily) where you can get a fishing permit for Rs 300 per rod. The national park also offers elephant rides at Rs 1000 per person from the park headquarters. The only trouble here is that you need at least 30 minutes by elephant to reach the 'core' area of the park for the best wildlife viewing. It's also possible to enter the park on foot, although you need to take an experienced guide, which your lodge can arrange. Keep in mind that walking in the park is a potentially dangerous activity, and should only be undertaken if you are accompanied by an experienced guide.

Also at the park headquarters is a small holding area for marsh mugger and gharial crocodiles that have been bred in captivity and are due to be released into the river. There's also a small **museum**.

Places to Stay & Eat

Development at Bardia is still very low-key, with just a handful of basic Chitwan-style 'jungle cottages' and a few more upmarket options primarily aimed at packaged tours. There is no electricity, but this is a perfect spot to hole up for a few days and adjust to the relaxing pace of Terai village life.

Forest Hideaway Cottages (☎ 429716; w www.foresthideaway.com; tent accommodation Rs 150, cottages with shared bathroom Rs 350-600, including breakfast), one of the best, is about 500m along the northern park boundary from the park headquarters. It is a licensed moneychanger (cash and travellers cheques, no cards), and international and local phone call facilities. There are solar-powered mud-and-thatch cottages set in a shady garden. Basic meals are available, and there's a bar. Safaris by 4WD can be arranged for Rs 1500 per person for four hours, and rafting day trips cost Rs 2000 per person. Bicycles, useful for exploring the surrounding villages, can be hired for Rs 150 per day.

Bardia Jungle Cottages (☎ 429714; cottages with shared/private bathroom Rs 250/ 400, 3-day package with full board and all activities US$130 per person) is also very good; it's right opposite the park entrance. It has a large, shady garden and good facilities, including an enclosed restaurant. The cottages are comfortable. Meals are also available here.

There are a couple of more basic places, including the **Hotel Racy Shade** and the adjacent **Hotel Bardia Natural Park**. Both have just a few mud-and-thatch cottages, and are about 500m from the park entrance.

Karnali Safari (☎ 429721; e karnali_safari@ hotmail.com; US$150 for a three-day package), in the same area as Hotel Bardia Natural Park, consists of a number of cottages and a Tharu-style central dining hall.

There are a couple more places farther south along the river, but without your own transport they can be inconvenient.

Bardia Wildlife Paradise (☎ 429715; doubles Rs 250, with private bathroom Rs 350, including breakfast) is a small place with a pleasant garden and mud-and-thatch cottages. There's also a small dining room.

Rhino Lodge (☎ 429720, 01-4416918 in Kathmandu; e rhinotvl@ccsl.com.np; cottages with bathroom around Rs 400) is about 4km from the park entrance. It consists of unattractive brick cottages set in a wide expanse of grassy garden with little shade. Accommodation prices are usually quoted in dollars.

Tiger Tops Karnali Lodge (open year-round), run by **Tiger Mountain** (☎ 01-441 1225 in Kathmandu; e info@tigermountain .com; postal address: PO Box 242 Kathmandu), which runs Tiger Tops Lodge in Chitwan, is at the top of the range. At the time of writing the lodge and tented camp were closed owing to the lack of customers, and the future of this accommodation remains uncertain. The lodge is right on the park boundary and is built out of local materials in Tharu-village style – simply outstanding. The staff are knowledgeable and helpful, without being intrusive.

The lodge also owns the only accommodation inside the park – the **Karnali Tented Camp** (camping per person US$150; closed mid-Apr–end Sept), which has a superb location overlooking the Geruwa River in the northwest corner of the park not far from Chisopani.

Getting There & Away

Mahendra Hwy is in good condition and the drive from Nepalganj takes less than 2½ hours, although local buses manage to take around five hours. It's an interesting drive past thriving villages. For Thakurdwara, there are direct buses from Nepalganj at noon and 2pm (Rs 120). Departures from Thakurdwara are at 8am and 10am.

If you are staying at Tiger Tops Karnali Lodge or Tented Camp the staff can arrange 4WD transfers from Nepalganj for US$10 per person.

Night buses for Mahendranagar from Kathmandu can drop you at Anbassa (Rs 600), though they get in between 3am and 6am. If you haven't made advance arrangements to be picked up (most places will send a 4WD for you), there's little option but to sit out the rest of the night and wait for transport. There is no electricity or telephones in Anbassa. Day buses to/from Mahendranagar are Rs 200 and take four hours.

For Kathmandu, there are numerous night buses coming from western Nepal, although it is only possible to get a reserved seat on the one from Chisopani, and your lodge will have to arrange this. It comes through Anbassa around 2pm. There are also direct night buses to Pokhara (Rs 600) and Birganj.

CHISOPANI

At the northwestern edge of Royal Bardia National Park, the Karnali River bursts out of the hills and enters the plains. Here a massive modern bridge spans the river, connecting the far western parts of the country. The single-span bridge, built by the Japanese and funded by the World Bank, is something of an engineering marvel and looks somewhat incongruous here. You may also wonder at the cost of a construction like this and whether better use could not have been made of the available funds. Still, it looks nice and it works.

The town such as it is consists of a collection of timber shacks and shelters on the western bank of the river. There are a few basic **eating houses**, and you could probably find somewhere to sleep if stuck. Surprisingly, there's a daily bus to Kathmandu that leaves at 1.30pm.

ROYAL SUKLA PHANTA WILDLIFE RESERVE
☎ 099

Sukla Phanta (*admission per day Rs 500, plus Rs 2000 per vehicle*) is smaller and more isolated than Bardia, yet is similar in some respects. In the extreme southwest of Nepal, it covers 305 sq km of riverine flood plain, which includes *phanta* (open grass plains), forest (primarily sal) and a lake, as well as the Bahini River.

The reserve is home to tigers (35 at the last estimate), leopards, rhinos (a few relocated here from Chitwan in late 2000), various species of deer (including an important colony of swamp deer, thought to number about 2000), gharial and mugger crocodiles, otters and a wide range of bird life.

The swamp deer are found in large herds and it's not unusual to see three or more herds on even a short wildlife drive in the southern part of the park in the *sukla phanta* (white grass plains). Although the deer are found in large numbers, Indian poachers are a real problem. Army guards are stationed in this part of the park, but they have to patrol by bicycle, which limits their efficacy.

This is probably one of the least visited reserves in Nepal, but if you are travelling between Nepal and India it is not too difficult to make a diversion, especially if you can afford to stay at the Silent Safari tented camp.

Information

The **rangers office** (☎ 521309) is 3km past the airport (accessible by rickshaw from Mahendranagar). It is possible to organise elephant rides for Rs 1000 per person per hour, but it's best to book in advance.

The main vehicle track within the park is closed from mid-June to mid-September.

Places to Stay

Silent Safari (☎ 521230, fax 522220; postal address: PO Box 1, Mahendranagar; tents per person US$175; open Oct-June) is the only company operating in the park. It is run by an ex-army colonel, the very personable Hikmat Bisht, who is a keen naturalist and has spent many years in and around the park. He now divides his time between the camp and his house in Mahendranagar. Visitors who come here are generally keen bird-watchers who don't mind roughing it a bit. Accommodation is in comfortable safari tents, and the price includes meals, wildlife drives and walks. Visits to local Tharu villages can also be arranged. Advance bookings are essential.

Getting There & Away

Silent Safari will pick up guests from the airport at Mahendranagar (US$10).

If you don't have a vehicle, it's possible to rent one in Mahendranagar for around Rs 4000 for a day.

MAHENDRANAGAR
☎ 099

Mahendranagar is an underwhelming village that owes its existence to the nearby border crossing at Banbassa. The locals are quite unused to dealing with tourists, so a few words of Nepali will be very useful. The surrounding countryside is inhabited by traditional Tharu communities, although there are an increasing number of hill people.

With the completion of the Mahendra Hwy in 2000, this entry point is potentially of interest to travellers coming from Delhi. However by late 2002 a couple of bridges had been attacked by Maoists, and most travellers were avoiding the region. Be sure to check on the current security situation with your embassy before entering this region.

Orientation & Information

The town is laid out to the south of the Mahendra Hwy with the bus station actually on the highway, about a 10-minute walk from the centre of the village. The main landmark is King Mahendra Square with streets one to five leading off from one side.

Mahendranagar is about 5km from the Mahakali River, which forms the Nepal–India border. The border is open 24 hours a day for pedestrians, but the barrage on the Indian side for vehicles is only open 7am to 8am, noon to 2pm and 4pm to 6pm. It's a little-used border and the crossing is straightforward and quite fast.

Places to Stay & Eat

There are a few cheap hotels on the main street.

Hotel New Anand *(☎ 522393; doubles with bathroom from Rs 400, with air-con Rs 1050)* is the best of the cheap hotels; it's friendly and has hot water by the bucket. Food is also available.

Shiv Shankar Guest House *(☎ 521447; doubles with bathroom Rs 150)*, across the road from the New Anand, is a barely passable cheap option.

Hotel Sweet Dream *(☎ 522313; doubles with private bathroom Rs 300, with air-cooler Rs 500)*, on the highway about a five-minute walk east of the bus station, is Mahendranagar's Hilton. The rooms in this recently built hotel are large and have carpets. This is pretty good value. There's also a restaurant.

Getting There & Away

Air RNAC flies to Nepalganj (Rs 1125) and Kathmandu (US$142) on Tuesday.

Bus There are daily direct buses from Kathmandu to Mahendranagar, which depart at 12.30pm. From Mahendranagar departures are around 2pm. Night/day buses cost Rs 513/480 and take 15 hours. There are also buses from Mahendranagar to Nepalganj (Rs 250, four to five hours).

To/From India Buses leave Mahendranagar roughly every half-hour for the border to the west. It's a 1km walk (or rickshaw ride) between the Nepali and Indian posts,

and then a few kilometres more to the Indian town of Banbassa.

Banbassa is on the Indian metre-gauge rail system, and the onward connections are poor. It is much better served by buses with direct connections to Delhi (nine hours), Bareilly (the nearest broad-gauge station, three hours), Nainital (seven hours), Almora (eight hours), Dharamsala (15 hours) and Agra (10 hours).

Eastern Terai & Mahabharat Range

The main east–west link across the entire Terai is the Mahendra Hwy, and access to Kathmandu is via the Tribhuvan Hwy (Rajpath) through Daman, or along the busy and popular Prithvi Hwy to Mugling and then south to Narayanghat. These highways merge at Hetauda and continue south to Pathlaiya, where the Mahendra swings east all the way to the border at Kakarbhitta; the Tribhuvan continues south to the border town of Birganj.

A number of attractive hill towns are accessible from the Mahendra Hwy, including Daman, which is between Naubise and Hetauda; Hile, Dharan Bazaar and Dhankuta (accessible from Itahari); and Ilam (accessible from Birtamod). On the plains there is also plenty to see: Janakpur is a colourful Hindu pilgrimage site and the home of Mithila art, and Koshi Tappu Wildlife Reserve is a bird-watcher's paradise.

NARAYANGHAT & BHARATPUR
☎ 056

Narayanghat is a fast-growing town on the banks of the Narayani River, just downstream from its junction with the Kali Gandaki and Trisuli Rivers. It has developed mainly because it lies at the intersection (Pul Chowk) of the Mahendra Hwy, which runs the length of the Terai, and the main road into the hills to Kathmandu and Pokhara. It is also the administrative and trading centre for the whole district. Bharatpur is contiguous with Narayanghat, and has an airport.

Although the most direct route to eastern Nepal from Kathmandu is the road from Hetauda to Naubise, most traffic goes through Narayanghat and Mugling.

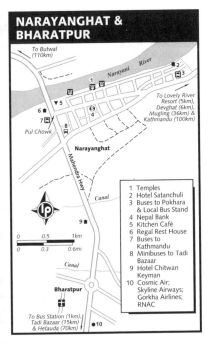

NARAYANGHAT & BHARATPUR

1 Temples
2 Hotel Satanchuli
3 Buses to Pokhara & Local Bus Stand
4 Nepal Bank
5 Kitchen Café
6 Regal Rest House
7 Buses to Kathmandu
8 Minibuses to Tadi Bazaar
9 Hotel Chitwan Keyman
10 Cosmic Air; Skyline Airways; Gorkha Airlines; RNAC

Narayanghat will, for most people, simply be a *chai* (milk tea) stop en route to Kathmandu, Chitwan or India. However, it's not a bad spot if you are exploring the Terai, and there's an interesting excursion to Devghat, a holy site northwest of town (see Around Narayanghat later).

Places to Stay & Eat
If, due to bad luck or bad management, you are forced to stay the night, there are a few choices.

Regal Rest House (☎ 520755; doubles with shared bathroom Rs 200, singles/doubles with private bathroom & hot water Rs 250/350) is right by the main intersection – very handy for buses. Don't stay here unless you can get a room at the back, as the road is very busy day and night (despite the new bus station at Bharatpur). There's also a decent restaurant here.

Hotel Satanchuli (☎ 521151; doubles/triples/quads with shared bathroom Rs 200/300/500, doubles with private bathroom & mosquito nets with/without TV Rs 400/250), near the northern bus station, is a quiet, basic place with river views from the upper floors. The rooms are a bit on the small side, but are good value.

Kitchen Café (☎ 520453; doubles Rs 600), tucked away at the southern edge of the bridge, is the best place to eat and also has two clean, comfortable rooms with private bathroom. The café makes a very pleasant escape from the mayhem out on the main road. There are tables outside in the garden, or you can eat inside. Snacks, such as vegetable *pakora*, are around Rs 50, and more substantial meals start at Rs 90.

There are also a couple of upmarket choices in Bharatpur, which are handy for the airport, and a secluded resort on the banks of the Trisuli River.

Hotel Chitwan Keyman (☎ 520200, fax 522264; singles/doubles US$36/42) is a modern place with a quiet rear garden and very comfortable rooms with air-con and TV. A 30% discount is offered. There's an air-con restaurant and bar; set meal rates are breakfast US$5, and lunch and dinner US$8.

Lovely River Resort (☎ 01-4425042 in Kathmandu; cottages Rs 500), signposted 2km off the road along a dirt track, is a few kilometres out of town on the Kathmandu road. It's very pleasantly beside the Trisuli River. Accommodation is in stone cottages and includes three meals. It even has a jet-ski, which you can ride as a passenger for Rs 200 per 15 minutes.

Getting There & Away
A number of airlines fly to Bharatpur from Kathmandu (US$63). The offices are all on the main road opposite the airport.

As Narayanghat is such a major crossroad there are buses coming and going at all hours. Some buses from Narayanghat to Pokhara leave from the bus station at the eastern end of town on the road to Mugling. Most buses to/from most Terai destinations and Kathmandu stop at the main T-junction (Pul Chowk) just to the south of the bridge.

Private buses from Narayanghat run to Kakarbhitta (day/night Rs 260/330, 10 hours), Biratnagar (Rs 205/305, nine hours), Janakpur (Rs 125/160, six hours), Mahendranagar (Rs 360/400, 12 hours), Nepalganj (Rs 225/280, eight hours), Pokhara (Rs 75, five hours) and Kathmandu (Rs 90/110, four hours). Tickets for buses can be bought from the desks set up outside the Regal Rest House.

Crowded minibuses to Tadi Bazaar (for Royal Chitwan National Park) leave from the side of the Mahendra Hwy just before the second intersection south of Pul Chowk; they cost Rs 10 and take 30 minutes. Taxis to Chitrasali (for Chitwan) cost about Rs 300 (the initial asking price is double this).

DEVGHAT

Also known as Deoghat and Harihara Chhetra, Devghat near Narayanghat is an ancient holy site that was first mentioned in the *Skanda Purana* (Skanda was the son of Shiva; this holy book expounds the doctrines and worship of Siva). It's a suitably beautiful spot, with forest-clad hills, a large sandy beach, and a number of shady shrines and temples overlooking the swirling waters where the Kali Gandaki and Trisuli Rivers meet. The confluence of rivers, particularly when they are major tributaries of the Ganges, is regarded as religiously significant by Hindus, as it is believed a third spiritual river also joins the rivers here.

Many elderly high-caste Hindus come here to quietly live out their days, and finally be cremated on the river banks, thus gaining religious merit and hopefully avoiding a stay in hell while they await reincarnation. In fact, all sorts of religious rites, including marriages, are performed at Devghat and they often involve large family groups. The atmosphere is peaceful and tranquil, not at all gloomy.

Devghat is one of the main sites for the festival of Magh Sankranti, and pilgrims come from around Nepal and India to immerse themselves in the river on the first day of the Nepali month of Magh, in mid-January. The festival celebrates the gradually lengthening days and the onset of warmer weather.

Western visitors are rare, and should bear in mind that caste-related ideas of ritual pollution may mean that some orthodox pilgrims and inhabitants are offended by any contact with westerners. Do not enter homes or temples without invitation and do not touch anything that could be holy (which means almost everything!). There is nowhere to stay, and not even a *chai* stall, so bring drinks and food.

Getting There & Away Frequent minibuses run to Narayanghat from the northern bus stop. By road, head north from town on the Mugling road for 3km, turn left on a signposted dirt road just before a police checkpoint and continue for 2km, then take the right fork and continue for another 3km. It's possible to walk along the southeastern bank of the river, but the track is a bit overgrown and it's easier to pick up and follow from the Devghat end.

DAMAN

☎ 057

Daman is 2322m above sea level, midway between Kathmandu and Hetauda. Its claim to fame is that it has, arguably, *the* most spectacular outlook on the Himalaya – there are unimpeded views of the entire range from Dhaulagiri to Mt Everest. If you have the opportunity to get to Daman, it should not be missed. There is a viewing tower with a telescope near the Daman Mountain Resort.

On the Hetauda side of Daman is a magnificent rhododendron forest (which is particularly worth seeing in spring) with great views over the Terai to India. Heading north from Daman you travel through the intensely cultivated **Palung Valley**. From here to Kathmandu, every possible inch of the hills is farmed. There are more good views of the Himalaya to enjoy before you reach Naubise on the Kathmandu–Pokhara (Prithvi) Hwy.

Places to Stay & Eat

There is a small selection of accommodation, but all budgets are catered for.

Hotel Sherpa Hillside *(singles/doubles Rs 100/200)* provides an authentic experience in a traditional building – no hot water and no toilet (there are plenty of trees). It's rustic and it's charming but importantly the rooms and bedding are kept very clean. Dal bhaat is available for a small additional cost.

There are a couple of other very basic lodges with rooms from Rs 100, such as the **Hotel Daman & Lodge** and the **Everest Hotel & Lodge**.

Daman Mountain Resort *(☎ 540387, 01-4220021 in Kathmandu; singles/doubles in safari-style double tents US$7/12, brick cottage with private bathroom US$10/18)* is a more comfortable option. The tents are under a bamboo and thatch shelter, have electric lights and OK beds. There are set meals available in the viewing tower restaurant and bar. Breakfast costs US$3 and lunch and dinner US$6. The resort accepts the equivalent in rupees.

Everest Panorama Resort (☎/fax 540382, 01-4428500 in Kathmandu; singles/doubles US$70/80), the decidedly upmarket option, is 2km on the Hetauda side of Daman, and a good bit higher. The spacious rooms all have views (although some are obscured by the large restaurant building), as well as TV and private bathroom. Hefty discounts are offered and these should be explored even when booking through the Kathmandu office. The restaurant is expensive and very good with set meals around the US$10 mark. There are mountain bikes for hire, and walks, pony rides and fishing expeditions on offer.

Getting There & Away
Daman is about two hours by car from Kathmandu and three hours from Hetauda. Unless you're on your way to/from Birganj, hiring a car (around US$80) and making a day trip from Kathmandu is probably the ideal way to get to Daman. If you have a group and the sky is clear, it would be worth it. Alternatively, this is one of the most spectacular (and most gruelling) mountain-bike routes in Nepal (see the Mountain Biking chapter for details).

From Daman a limited number of buses pass through en route between Kathmandu and Hetauda. The bus takes about four hours from Kathmandu.

HETAUDA
☎ 057

Hetauda is the starting point for a cableway that carries cement from the Terai to Kathmandu. It's quite an amazing construction, similar in concept to a ski lift. The current cableway dates from 1958 and can carry 25 tonnes per hour; it takes 15 hours for goods to travel the distance.

The town itself is of little interest, but if you want to catch a bus along the superb Tribhuvan Hwy or you need to break the journey to or from Kathmandu, there are plenty of accommodation options. Most buses heading to Kathmandu and Pokhara turn west to Narayanghat along the Mahendra Hwy. There are spectacular views on the Tribhuvan Hwy. You begin to climb into the **Mahabharat Range** the moment you leave Hetauda. The road is generally in good condition, apart from the occasional land slide,

but it's very narrow. The change from the Terai to the hills or vice versa is remarkably sudden; when you're among the cool forested hills it is almost impossible to believe the hot, dusty plains are so close. As you gain altitude, you enter magnificent rhododendron forests. The highest point on the road is 2400m, near Daman.

Places to Stay & Eat
There's a handful of cheap lodges around the bus station, but avoid these if you plan on getting any sleep.

Neelam Lodge (☎ 520900; singles/doubles with private bathroom Rs 150/200) is on the Daman road north of Mahendra Chowk in the centre of town and is the pick of the cheapies. Located beside a small temple and a chautara (stone platform for porters to rest) with a large pipal and banyan, it has clean rooms (cold water) and is good value. It's about 500m from the bus station and has an OK restaurant.

Hotel Seema (☎ 520124; e seema@mos.com.np; singles/doubles with private bathroom Rs 600/800, with air-con Rs 1500/2000), about 200m south of the chowk, is a modern place with good spacious rooms with phone and TV.

Motel Avocado & Orchid Resort (☎ 520 429; e avocado@wlink.com.np; motel singles/doubles Rs 350/500, resort singles/doubles Rs 1200/1600), on the Tribhuvan Hwy towards Daman, has accommodation in a quiet, pleasant garden with avocado trees and orchids. Rooms in an old Nissen hut are spacious, comfortable and rather idiosyncratic. They come with fans and bathroom, and rates are negotiable. There's also a three-storey wing of modern deluxe rooms with air-con. The restaurant here is very good (vegetarian curry Rs 80, chicken tikka Rs 140) and keeps interesting notebooks where cyclists and motorcyclists have recounted their travels through India and Nepal.

Getting There & Away
A few buses run the magnificent Tribhuvan Hwy to Kathmandu (Rs 100, seven hours) via Daman. The main bus station in Hetauda is southwest of the main intersection (Mahendra Chowk). Buses to Daman (Rs 70, three hours) leave from the roadside at a place called Bim Phedi bus stand, about 100m north of Motel Avocado.

A number of buses go to Kathmandu (Rs 125) and Pokhara (Rs 120) via Narayanghat and Tadi Bazaar. Buses to Tadi Bazaar take around three hours and cost Rs 40. There are numerous buses to Birganj for Rs 35.

TADI BAZAAR

In the Chitwan Valley between Hetauda and Narayanghat, the small town of Tadi Bazaar (sometimes spelt Tandi Bazaar) is a junction town for Sauraha, the budget accommodation centre for the Royal Chitwan National Park. For more details see Royal Chitwan National Park earlier in this chapter.

BIRGANJ

☎ 051

Birganj is one of the main border crossings between Nepal and India, and is also one of Nepal's most important industrial cities. This is an unfortunate combination, making it one of the most unattractive places on the planet. For much of the year the climate is oppressively hot, and during the monsoon it becomes almost unbearable.

Immigrants from around Nepal and many from India are attracted by the economic opportunities and industry and the population is growing rapidly. The local language is Bhojpuri, which is spoken on both sides of the border.

Birganj is an important entry point for travellers coming from Patna or Kolkata (Calcutta). If you are stuck in town for a while, one of the air-con hotels in the centre may be a good place to head for. Otherwise, you could hire a cycle-rickshaw (around Rs 40 an hour) and have a look around. The town has a certain gruesome fascination and there are a couple of modern temples. The most interesting is the **Bal Temple**, which is a modern Buddhist temple about 1km west of the main road.

Fortunately, there are plenty of day and night buses to and from Kathmandu and Pokhara and points south (in India) so there should be no necessity to stay more than a night in Birganj.

Orientation & Information

Birganj and Raxaul Bazaar (on the Indian side of the border) virtually run together, though it is a 60-minute rickshaw ride between the two bus stations.

BIRGANJ

To Kathmandu (185km)

New Rd

To Bus Station & Hotels (250m)

Tank

Main Rd

To Customs & Immigration (3km) & Indian Border (4km)

PLACES TO STAY & EAT
2 Hotel Heera Plaza
5 Himanchal Cabin
12 Hotel Kailas
13 Star Hotel
14 Hotel Diyalo
17 Hotel Makalu;
   Skyline Airways;
   Shangri-La Airways

OTHER
1 RNAC
3 Gorkha Airlines
4 Clock Tower
6 Maysan Temple
7 Gita Temple
8 Bal Mandir

9 Nepal Rastra Bank
10 Government Offices
11 Yeti Airlines
15 All Times Cyber Cafe
16 Moneychanger
18 Contact Point

The Birganj bus station is on the ring road at Bhanu Chowk, about 500m east of the clock tower.

There's an official moneychanger on Main Rd, and it accepts major currencies (cash and travellers cheques). Indian rupees are interchangeable with Nepali rupees in Birganj, but get rid of any excess here.

Internet access is available (Rs 30 per hour) from **All Times Cyber Cafe** (Main Rd), although there are bound to be others by now.

Places to Stay & Eat

There are a number of cheap places in the bus station area a few hundred metres east of the clock tower, but it's a noisy area and there's a good chance you won't get any sleep. Most places charge around Rs 200 for a double. Places in this area include **Park Hotel, Hotel Welcome Nepal** (☎ 524057) and **Buddha Guest House**.

There's another hotel area in the centre of town, around what was the old bus station. The really cheap places are pretty dismal but it is quieter here.

Hotel Kailas (☎ 522384, fax 522410; singles with shared bathroom Rs 100, singles/doubles *with private bathroom from Rs 200/430, rooms with air-con Rs 990)* has a range of decent rooms and a good, air-con (mercifully) restaurant with Indian and Chinese cuisine. The tandoori items are available after 6pm. The smallish singles with shared bathroom are good value. The other rooms come with TV, fan and bathroom.

Hotel Diyalo *(☎ 522370; e adarsh@atcnet .com.np; singles/doubles with private bathroom Rs 600/700, with air-cooler Rs 800/900, with air-con Rs 1600/1800)*, almost next door to Hotel Kailas, is a well-run hotel with immaculate, reasonably priced rooms. There is also a good restaurant.

Hotel Makalu *(☎ 523054; e hmakalu@ mos.com.np; Main Rd; doubles with private bathroom Rs 800, with air-con from Rs 1200)* is a very friendly, centrally located hotel with a good restaurant and bar. The comfortable rooms are good value with facilities such as phone and TV.

Hotel Heera Plaza *(☎ 523988; e giris@ atcnet.com.np; New Rd; singles/doubles Rs 700/800, with air-con Rs 1200/1400)*, midway between the clock tower and the bus station, has smallish rooms with TV, carpet and bathroom.

Star Hotel is decent, cheap tandoori restaurant between the Kailas and Diyalo hotels.

Himanchal Cabin *(Main Rd)* is a restaurant that serves South Indian food such as *dosas* (lentil and rice flour pancakes, Rs 60).

Getting There & Away

To/From India It's a 30-minute rickshaw trip (Rs 25) between the Birganj bus station and the border, and another 30 minutes (INRs 25) between the border and the Raxaul Bazaar bus station. Expect to pay INRs 90 for the five-hour bus journey to Patna from Raxaul Bazaar. The various offices on either side of the border are notionally open 24 hours, but you may have trouble finding someone before 7am and after 7pm.

To/From Other Parts of Nepal There are daily flights between Simara (the airport for Birganj) and Kathmandu with RNAC (US$48) and at least six private airlines (US$57).

There are plenty of day and night buses to and from Kathmandu, and plenty of travel agents around the bus station dealing with

tickets and bookings. Night buses leave Birganj between 7pm and 9pm daily, arriving in Kathmandu around 5am (Rs 175). Day buses leave between 6am and 10am and cost Rs 160. Tickets should be booked in advance.

There are also buses leaving for Pokhara (day/night Rs 165/195, 10 hours), Janakpur (Rs 109, five hours) and Kakarbhitta (Rs 245/276, nine hours), as well as Tadi Bazaar (for Chitwan; Rs 85, three hours).

Getting Around

Rickshaws cost around Rs 40 per hour, which is the charge to go all the way through to Raxaul Bazaar (this is recommended).

JANAKPUR
☎ 041

If you have the time and inclination to experience something of the Terai, Janakpur should be at the top of your list. Janakpur is an interesting town with temples, pools, sadhus, rickshaws and rainbow-coloured saris. It is a tourist town, but the tourists are devout Indian pilgrims, rather than Western backpackers.

Janakpur's religious significance is due to its role in the famous Hindu epic, the Ramayana. It is the legendary birthplace of Sita, an incarnation of Lakshmi, and the place of her marriage to Rama, who is one of Vishnu's most popular incarnations. At times, especially during festivals when strangely resonant vignettes from the Ramayana are played out in the streets, it can feel as if the ancient myth has come to life.

Janakpur is situated in what was once the kingdom of Mithila, a region now divided between Nepal and India. The Maithili language, which also has its own unique script, is spoken by approximately two million Nepalis – only Nepali is spoken by a greater number of people.

Janakpur is at least the third city to be built on this site, and most buildings are less than a century old. The city that was mythologised in the Ramayana existed around 700 BC, but it apparently sank back into the forest, the population perhaps wiped out by disease. Simaraungarh grew up in its place, but was destroyed by Muslims in the 14th century.

Modern Janakpur is a typical Terai town, although perhaps cleaner and less crowded than some. Narrow lanes are interspersed with temples, *kutis* (pilgrim hostels) and both *sagar*

THE TERAI & MAHABARAT RANGE

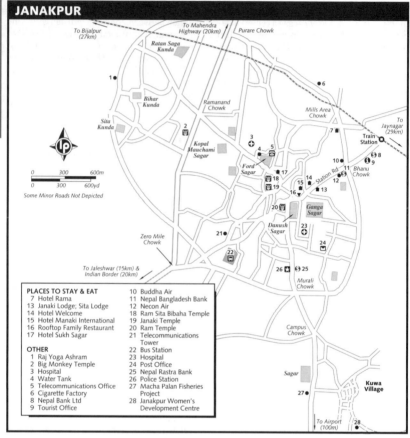

JANAKPUR

To Bijalpur (27km)
To Mahendra Highway (20km)
Purare Chowk
Ratan Saga Kunda
Bihar Kunda
Ramanand Chowk
Sita Kunda
Mills Area Chowk
To Jaynagar (29km)
Train Station
Kopal Mauchami Sagar
Ford Sagar
Bhanu Chowk
Station Rd
Ganga Sagar
Danush Sagar
Zero Mile Chowk
To Jaleshwar (15km) & Indian Border (20km)
Murali Chowk
Campus Chowk
Sagar
Kuwa Village
To Airport (100m)

0   300   600m
0   300   600yd
Some Minor Roads Not Depicted

PLACES TO STAY & EAT
7   Hotel Rama
13 Janaki Lodge; Sita Lodge
14 Hotel Welcome
15 Hotel Manaki International
16 Rooftop Family Restaurant
17 Hotel Sukh Sagar

OTHER
1   Raj Yoga Ashram
2   Big Monkey Temple
3   Hospital
4   Water Tank
5   Telecommunications Office
6   Cigarette Factory
8   Nepal Bank Ltd
9   Tourist Office

10 Buddha Air
11 Nepal Bangladesh Bank
12 Necon Air
18 Ram Sita Bibaha Temple
19 Janaki Temple
20 Ram Temple
21 Telecommunications Tower
22 Bus Station
23 Hospital
24 Post Office
25 Nepal Rastra Bank
26 Police Station
27 Macha Palan Fisheries Project
28 Janakpur Women's Development Centre

and *kunda* (large and small sacred ponds). Legend says the ponds were created by King Janak for the use of the gods who came to the wedding of Rama and Sita. They take the place of a river for ritual bathing and are also used by the local *dhobis*. Thanks to a successful development project, many ponds are also stocked with the fish that provide an important supplement to the local diet.

The town authorities have managed to keep most traffic out of the centre of town, which makes it pleasant to wander around.

It's possible to visit Janakpur on the way to/from Kakarbhitta. Although there's a small-gauge railway connecting Janakpur to the Indian town of Jaynagar, tourists are not allowed to cross the border here (see Around Janakpur later).

Orientation & Information

Janakpur is a tangle of narrow streets, so the best way to get your bearings is from the telecommunications tower southwest of the centre and the large, elevated concrete water tank to the northwest. The town itself lies to the east of the main road that runs through to Jaleshwar at the border.

The Janaki Temple (Janaki Mandir) is south of the water tank, and the bus station is southeast of the temple near the telecommunications tower. The train station is about a 20-minute walk northeast of the water tank.

There is a **tourist office** (☎ 520755; open 10am-5pm Mon-Fri Feb-Oct, 10am-4pm Nov-Jan) at Bhanu Chowk, not far from the train station. Consider ringing to check the dates for major festivals, although fluency in Nepali is usually necessary. Nepal Bank Ltd and Nepal Bangladesh Bank will cash travellers cheques.

Janaki Temple

The *mandir* (temple) to Sita (also known as Janaki) is believed to be built over the spot where her father, King Janak, found her lying in the furrow of a ploughed field. It's impressively large yet, surprisingly, you come across it from the winding Janakpur streets almost without warning.

Although it has no great architectural or historical merit – it was built in 1912 and might be described as baroque Mughal – it is nonetheless a fascinating place. There are instances of fine work, especially in some of the carved stone screens, and in the beautiful silver doors to the **inner sanctum** *(open 5am-7am & 6pm-8pm)*, which reveals a flower bedecked statue of Sita that was apparently miraculously found in the Saryu River near Ayodhya. She is accompanied by Rama and his three half-brothers, Lakshmana, Bharat and Satrughna.

During the day, there are few people in the temple – some priests, sadhus and, if you're lucky, perhaps some musicians playing in the cloisters – but it comes alive in the evenings when Sita is displayed.

Ram Sita Bibaha Temple

Virtually next door to the Janaki Temple, but built with the traditional Nepali pagoda roof, this rather bizarre temple *(admission Rs 2, camera fee Rs 5)* is built on the spot where Rama and Sita were married. The temple itself has glass walls so you can peer in at the kitsch life-sized models of Sita and Rama, his half-brothers and sisters-in-law.

Ram Temple & Danush Sagar

Located in the city's oldest quarter, to the southeast of the Janaki Temple, the Ram is another Nepali-style temple that is the centre point for the Rama Navami celebrations (see Special Events later). Immediately to its east is the Danush Sagar, which is considered to be one of the holiest ponds and is a popular pilgrimage site.

Other Temples & Ponds

There are numerous temples and ponds scattered around the outskirts of town. It is worth hiring a cycle-rickshaw to see them, although you could track them down on foot if you are feeling energetic. They're reached by brick-paved roads that meander into the paddy fields. If you hire a rickshaw, allow a couple of hours and expect to pay around Rs 100.

Start at the temple that is widely known as the **Big Monkey Temple**. This place is easy to miss as it looks like an ordinary house. It is about 100m south of Ramanand Chowk. Hanuman, the monkey god, is worshipped here in the form of a rhesus monkey, kept in a depressing cage. The previous monkey grew to 60kg before finally succumbing in 1998 to the affects of gross overfeeding and under exercising; its replacement is well on the way to following it.

Two of the most interesting and attractive ponds can be reached by following the brick-paved roads to the west. They are **Bihar Kunda** and **Ratan Saga Kunda**. The countryside is lush and tropical with coconut palms and huge trees framing the temples and ponds that are scattered across the fertile plains.

Janakpur Women's Development Centre

This women's art project *(☎ 521080; e women@mos.com.np; open 10am-5pm Sun-Fri, 10am-4pm Dec-Jan)* promotes traditional Mithila painting skills and seeks to empower local women, who live in a highly restrictive patriarchal society (see the boxed text 'Mithila Painting').

The centre is on the southern outskirts of Janakpur and incorporates aspects of traditional architecture. The beautiful site is on the edge of an interesting village, a short rickshaw ride and walk from the centre of town.

The project includes women of diverse castes and backgrounds, and the art that is created reflects this variety; wedding paintings, pregnant elephants, gods, and abstract tattoo designs are just some of the subjects portrayed. Increasingly the paintings are changing to also include scenes from the women's lives, including scenes of childbirth and marriage. In addition to paintings (acrylic on daphne paper) the women are also producing ceramics (plates and figures), papier-mache, patchwork tapestry, silk-screen prints and woven wall hangings. It is possible for visitors to see the women working and to purchase some of their striking

The Romance of Rama

The Ramayana, or romance of Rama, is among the best-loved and most influential stories in Hindu literature. Handsome Rama embodies chivalry and virtue, and his wife, the beautiful Sita, exemplifies devotion and chastity. Together with Rama's ally, the faithful monkey god, Hanuman, they are heroes and exemplars of immense popularity. Like all great mythical archetypes, they have somehow found an enduring place in the human psyche.

It's likely the legend has at least a basis in fact, and was first retold around village hearths. The Ramayana was first permanently recorded in Sanskrit, possibly as long as 2400 years ago by a sage and poet, Valmiki. Since then it has become a part of people's lives and imaginations throughout the subcontinent and, in various forms, as far as Bali, where to this day it features in puppetry and dance.

Rama was a reincarnation of Vishnu, born at the request of the gods to do battle with the ghastly demon-king Ravana, the king of Lanka (possibly Sri Lanka). He was reincarnated at Ayodhya (350km west of Janakpur) as the eldest son of a wealthy king. Handsome, virtuous and strong, he grew up as the idol of the people and especially of one of his half-brothers, Lakshmana.

In the kingdom of Mithila, good King Janak discovered baby Sita, the reincarnation of Lakshmi, lying in a furrow of a ploughed field. She too grew up to be wise and beautiful. So many men wanted to marry her that Janak set a test – a successful suitor had to bend the divine bow of Shiva. Rama, of course, drew the bow and he and Sita looked into each other's eyes and knew divine love.

Rama and his three half-brothers were married in a single ceremony – the brothers to neighbouring princesses – and there was much feasting, flowers falling from heaven, gorgeous processions across the plains and so on. But this is where things took a turn for the worse.

After returning to Ayodhya, Rama and Sita were forced to leave the palace because of the intrigues of the detestable hunchback Manthara. While they wandered in exile, Rama and Lakshmana were distracted by a golden deer, and Sita was kidnapped and carried off to Lanka by the demon-king. Imprisoned, she was forced to defend herself from the disgusting advances of Ravana.

Meanwhile, Rama and Lakshmana formed an alliance with a monkey kingdom. In particular they were served by the indomitable monkey god Hanuman. With Hanuman's loyal assistance, Sita was finally rescued and Ravana was destroyed.

Unfortunately, life didn't improve much for Sita who was forced to undergo an ordeal by fire to prove her chastity. Although Rama, now king of Ayodhya, believed her innocence, his people did not and Sita was forced into exile again. Sita gave birth to Rama's twin sons and the family was later reunited, but Sita decided she had had enough of this mortal coil and was swallowed up by the earth.

There are many versions of the story recorded in many art forms and many different languages, including English. Trying to imagine the power and subtlety of the complete story by reading this condensation is a bit like trying to imagine a tree by looking at a match.

creations at extremely reasonable prices. See also Shopping in the Kathmandu chapter.

To get there, take a rickshaw from town (Rs 25).

Special Events

On the fifth day of the waxing moon in late November/early December, tens of thousands of pilgrims arrive to celebrate **Sita Bibaha Panchami**, the re-enactment of Sita's marriage to Rama (Vivaha Panchami). This is also the occasion for an important fair and market that lasts a week. Rama's birthday (Rama Navami) in late March/early April is also accompanied by a huge procession.

Most Hindu festivals are major events in Janakpur. **Tihar** (Deepawali) is an interesting time to be here; the Mithila women repaint the murals on their houses. On the day before Holi, **Parikrama** involves a ritual walk around the town's ring road and attracts thousands of pilgrims. Holi itself can get very boisterous; women should take care.

Places to Stay & Eat

Janaki Lodge (*singles with shared bathroom Rs 125*) is a basic hotel with no English sign that has nothing more to recommend it than its cheapness. **Sita Lodge**, next door, is identical.

Hotel Sukh Sagar *(☎ 520488, fax 522488; dorm beds Rs 50, singles/doubles with private bathroom from Rs 120/220),* very close to the Janaki Temple, has large rooms that are passably clean and reasonable value. On the ground floor there's a decent restaurant for dal bhaat.

Hotel Rama *(☎ 520059; doubles from Rs 175, with air-cooler Rs 500, with air-con Rs 800),* in the northern part of town by Mills Area Chowk, has a range of rooms and prices. The cheapest are very basic and gloomy, but there are also big, airy doubles with hot water. There's a reasonable although also gloomy restaurant here with Indian, Chinese and Nepali meals.

Hotel Welcome *(☎ 520646, fax 520922; Station Rd; singles/doubles with private bathroom Rs 300/450, with air-con Rs 800/1300, suites Rs 1000/1600)* is not a bad option, despite the fact it is somewhat run-down. The rooms are tolerably grubby. On the plus side, the staff are friendly and helpful and the restaurant is good. Some of the more comfortable rooms with air-con have interesting decoration, best described as an interpretation of Mithila art. Check-out is 24 hours after check-in.

Hotel Manaki International *(☎ 521540, fax 521496),* nearing completion at the time of writing, should occupy the obvious hole in Janakpur's accommodation stakes. The three-star hotel near Janaki Chowk will offer non air-con and air-con rooms with phones and TVs.

Rooftop Family Restaurant *(Station Rd),* opposite Danush Sagar, is the best place to eat in town – good value and good food. The extensive Indian menu has ample vegetarian and nonvegetarian meals including delicious tandoori items (Rs 80 to Rs 250). Breakfast starts at 7am and the views from the outside tables are great.

Getting There & Away
Buddha Air *(☎ 041-525022)* has flights four times weekly to Kathmandu (US$69). A rickshaw to the airport costs Rs 60.

Buses to Kathmandu leave from the chaotic main bus station. There are half a dozen express night buses to/from Kathmandu that cost Rs 293 and take about nine hours. Day buses cost Rs 210. There are day buses to Birganj (Rs 109), Biratnagar (Rs 137) and Kakarbhitta (day/night Rs 198/208).

The train is only useful for sightseeing in the area (see Around Janakpur).

AROUND JANAKPUR
The fields and villages around Janakpur form a lush and magical mosaic. It's worth exploring them on foot, bicycle, rickshaw or train. Unfortunately, there are no formal bicycle-hire places, but if you ask around something may turn up. Western visitors are rare, so tread gently, and always ask before taking photos.

It doesn't really matter in which direction you go. **Jaleshwar** to the southwest on the Nepali side of the border is a completely uninspiring town, but there are some interesting villages on the way. Other possibilities include the road that runs south to the airport, which turns to dirt and continues through a number of attractive villages; the road that runs north of the cigarette factory; and also the road that runs west of Purare Chowk. **Dhanusa**, 15km to the northeast, marks the spot where Rama allegedly drew Shiva's magic bow.

Janakpur is the terminus for two train lines, one of which runs east to **Jaynagar** over the Indian border, and the other northwest to Bijalpur. However, only the first route to Jaynagar carries passengers. They are narrow-gauge trains and are very slow, so they offer an interesting if somewhat crowded method of seeing the countryside.

If you want to travel to or from Jaynagar there are three daily services in each direction, so it is easy to put together a day trip. Trains leave both Janakpur and Jaynagar at 6am, 11am and 3pm. Tickets cost Rs 44/17 in 1st/2nd class. It's about 29km (four hours!) to Jaynagar, but tourists are not allowed to cross the border into India, so you will need to get off in one of the villages along the way.

The first stop after Janakpur is **Parbaha** (1st/2nd class Rs 12/5, 8km), and there are interesting villages on either side of the tracks – you could walk back to town. Another interesting stop is **Baidehi**, about an hour (Rs 18/7, 12km) from Janakpur, where you could alight and catch the Janakpur-bound train that comes through an hour

Mithila Painting

Mithila culture is essentially a culture of the Gangetic plain, and the Hindu caste structure is strictly upheld. Most people are subsistence farmers, but land-holdings are usually very small and many families live on the edge of starvation. Many are in the grip of moneylenders or *zamindars* (landlords).

Zamindars, usually from the Brahmin (priest) or Kshatriya (warrior) castes, occupy an almost feudal role as major landowners and in their traditional role as moneylenders. Their tenant farmers and debtors are effectively serfs trapped in a system of bonded labour.

Most Mithila people live in small villages, usually with no more than around a hundred households. House walls are made from bamboo or thatch plastered with a mixture of cow dung and mud. The roofs are thatched, or sometimes tiled. Most houses have a fenced courtyard, which is also sealed with mud and cow dung.

Mithila women are raised with the expectation that they will be workers in their husband's home, and are frequently married as children. After puberty they are veiled so that their faces cannot be seen by males outside their family.

As a part of their cultural and religious tradition, the women paint striking murals on the external walls of their homes. Inside, pottery storage containers and internal pillars also carry designs. Different castes and different regions have developed distinctive styles and symbols, which are passed down from mother to daughter. Traditionally, painting and decoration is not undertaken purely to create an aesthetic result, nor is it purely cathartic or expressive. Painting largely springs from cultural and religious motives. The act of painting, as a part of a ritual, can be more important than the finished result itself, and completed paintings can act as charms, prayers and meditation aids.

Paintings often derive from Hindu mythology and can use complex symbols (sometimes with a distinct mandala-like quality), simple, apparently abstract figures (including hand stencils, peacocks, pregnant elephants and fish), or can take on a narrative quality (representing religious stories). High castes, including the Kshatriya, have developed extremely elaborate, abstract forms. Lower-caste paintings are often simpler and more realistic, but they have an energetic expressionistic style, and retain a strong sense of formal design.

Mithila paintings from Madubani in Bihar, India, have been discovered by the international art world. The most well known are the elaborate Kshatriya wedding paintings that are presented to the groom as part of the build-up to an arranged marriage.

Until fairly recently, little interest was taken in the art produced on the Nepal side of the border. This changed with the foundation of the Janakpur Women's Art Project in 1989, which has the dual aim of promoting traditional Mithila painting skills and empowering the women painters. The project is housed in the Janakpur Women's Development Centre and it's possible to visit the centre to see the women working and to buy what they produce (see Janakpur Women's Development Centre earlier for more details.)

---

later. Alternatively, you could continue as far as you are allowed, to **Khajuri** (Rs 32/12, 21km), about 8km from Jaynagar on the Nepali side of the border, and catch the afternoon Janakpur train.

KOSHI TAPPU WILDLIFE RESERVE
☎ 025

The Koshi Tappu Wildlife Reserve protects a section of the Sapt Kosi's flood plain that lies behind the Kosi Barrage. The Sapt Kosi is one of the Ganges' largest tributaries, and the Kosi Barrage is designed to minimise destructive annual floods. Most of the reserve is surrounded by high embankments that control the spread of the river and funnel it towards the barrage. Because there are so few visitors, it is an excellent place to escape the crowds for a few days.

The Mahendra Hwy skirts the reserve to the south and crosses the river at the barrage. It's a beautiful, fascinating water world. Small thatched villages perch on what little high ground there is, and wherever you look there are water birds and ponds full of flowering plants, all overwhelmed by fields of rice stretching to the horizon.

Behind the embankments the powerful river continuously changes course, and regularly floods during the monsoon, although only to shallow depths. The vegetation is mainly *phanta* with some scrub and riverine forest. Local villagers are allowed to collect grass for thatching every January, which also clears the way for easier wildlife viewing.

The reserve is home to the last surviving population of wild *arna* (water buffalo), various deer, nilgai, mugger crocodiles and Gangetic dolphins. The gharial crocodiles that were released in 1987 have not been seen since! The mugger crocs are fairly plentiful, though, and can be seen in the oxbow lakes behind the eastern embankment. The reserve is also home to more than 400 species of water birds. These include 20 species of ducks, ibises, storks, egrets, cranes and herons. Migratory species, including the sarus crane from Siberia and the ruddy shelduck from Tibet, take up residence from November to February.

The reserve mostly hosts bird-watchers between November and February, but very few people visit. There are two deluxe safari camps aimed at bird-watchers and a more basic though hardly inexpensive rest house. There's no formal budget accommodation, though there is an area where you could camp, and the helpful park staff are happy to give visitors the use of a kitchen. Most people arrive as part of a package tour and stay at the tented camps where all activities are included. If you are staying at the rest house or camping, the activities cost extra.

Information

The wildlife reserve **headquarters** (☎ 521488) is at Kusaha. There's a small information centre and museum, and a simple brochure is available from the ranger. This is where visitors must pay the daily Rs 500 entry fee.

Things to See & Do

The reserve has five elephants, which can be ridden for Rs 1000 per hour. The rides can take you beyond the grasslands to the riverine forest to see deer, nilgai and various forest birds.

Large canoes can also be arranged for trips across to the 'tappu' or islands for Rs 1500 per hour. You can split this cost between several people. The large sandy islands, which

change shape every year, are covered in tall grass and dissected by channels that become dry in winter. These channels are thoroughfares for the wild buffalo and are the best place to observe them.

The slick expanse of the Sapt Kosi runs deep and fast, and this is best appreciated from one of the rickety and leaky (but safe) boats. Keep an eye out for the rare Gangetic dolphin, and listen for the 'blow' as it rises to breathe.

Walks along the eastern embankment and around the numerous oxbow lakes can be coupled with a boat ride to the 'tappu'. Numerous water birds, raptors, parrots and others can be identified in a few minutes' stroll along the track. You may also be lucky enough to spot a basking mugger crocodile or stumble across a swamp francolin – one of Koshi Tappu's signature residents. The embankment provides a good vantage point to look down on the *phanta* where you may see wild buffalo and occasionally elephants. A guide to accompany any of these activities can be arranged at the Koshi Tappu Village Resthouse and costs US$20 per day.

Places to Stay

For those who don't mind roughing it a bit, it might be possible to stay in the home of one of the families who live near the park headquarters. This is village accommodation at its most basic. Don't expect any frills and be sensitive to the fact that this is not tourist accommodation, so people may be unfamiliar with what tourists usually expect in the way of food and facilities.

Koshi Tappu Village Resthouse (☎ 521488; *room plus 3 meals US$25 per person*) is adjacent to the park headquarters and elephant stables. The accommodation, in rustic mud-and-thatch cottages with private bathroom, is comfortable but rather expensive for what you get. Wildlife-viewing activities cost extra (US$20 per day) and the guides are not as strong in their knowledge or their English as at the upmarket lodges.

Aqua Birds Unlimited Camp (☎ 01-4413470 in Kathmandu; e aquabirds@info .com.np; *3-day, 2-night package US$198*) is a tented safari camp aimed directly at keen bird-watchers. The cost includes transfer from Biratnagar airport, all meals and guided activities, such as walks, drives, boat trips and elephant rides. The permanent tents are very comfortable and the shared bathrooms have solar hot water. The dining hall-cum-bar is spacious and the grounds have been landscaped with trees and waterholes to attract birds. The resident naturalist, Dinesh Giri, is knowledgeable and enthusiastic, and speaks good English.

Koshi Tappu Wildlife Camp (☎ 01-422 6130; e explore@mos.com.np; postal address: PO Box 536, Kamaladi, Kathmandu; singles/doubles US$225/300) is just outside the northeastern corner of the reserve, 24km north of the barrage near the tiny village of Prakashpur (accessible from Inerwa on the Mahendra Hwy). The camp is on a small waterway with excellent bird-watching possibilities from the bar! It is well set up in a pleasant established garden. Accommodation is in very comfortable tented rooms with shared bathrooms, and there's a separate dining area serving excellent meals, and a bar. There is no electricity, and therefore the evenings are illuminated by atmospheric kerosene lamps.

Tariffs include guided bird walks and an idyllic half-day rafting glide down the wide and slow-moving river. Most guests come on a package from Kathmandu, which involves flying to Biratnagar and transfers to the camp.

Getting There & Away
The turn-off to the reserve (signposted) is about 16km by road northeast of the Kosi Barrage, about 2km before the village of Laukhi. Coming from Itahari, it's about 46km to Laukhi and a further 2km to the turn-off. Any buses travelling on the Mahendra Hwy can drop you at the park turn-off, from where it is a further 3km walk or a Rs 70 rickshaw ride to the park headquarters.

For the wildlife camp, if you don't have your own 4WD, take a local bus to Inerwa on the Mahendra Hwy, and from there local buses go regularly to Prakashpur. The wildlife camp is a further 1km, which you'll have to cover on foot; ask for directions.

ITAHARI
☎ 025
Itahari is an undistinguished town at the intersection of the Mahendra Hwy and the Biratnagar to Dhankuta road. There is an interesting market held along the dusty lanes southeast of the main intersection.

There are numerous budget lodges on all axes of the intersection, but nothing salubrious.

Jaya Nepal Hotel (☎ 580113; single in twin room with shared bathroom Rs 150, doubles with private bathroom Rs 250) is about 100m along the Dharan road, beyond the roundabout. The rooms are basic but clean and that's the best description for the downstairs restaurant that does good Indian and attempts Chinese. Beware, untreated tap water is served in mineral water bottles – more for convenience than deception as there's no charge.

Getting There & Away
The bus station is unusually clean and orderly, and all the long-distance, east–west buses stop in Itahari. Many buses are bound for Kathmandu (day/night Rs 285/340) or Kakarbhitta (Rs 75). Buses to Janakpur cost Rs 155.

There are also plenty of local buses that go to Biratnagar (Rs 18, one hour) and Dharan Bazaar (Rs 15, 30 minutes). There are five buses a day leaving for Dhankuta (Rs 83, five hours).

DHARAN BAZAAR
☎ 025
Dharan Bazaar lies right at the foot of the Chure hills, and the transformation from the Terai is dramatic. It's a bustling bazaar town catering to the hill people of eastern Nepal. It has grown rapidly despite suffering a major earthquake in 1988.

There are no sights of note, but if you're heading into the mountains this will be your best chance for final purchases. A small number of trekkers bound for Hile and Basantapur come through town, and **Chatara**, the finishing point for raft trips on the Sun Kosi, is only about 15km to the west.

Places to Stay & Eat
Hotel Family Inn (☎ 520848; singles/doubles with shared bathroom Rs 100/250, with private bathroom Rs 150/400) is close to busy Bhanu Chowk in the centre of town (where the buses stop). Around the chowk there are plenty of simple restaurants serving dal bhaat and nonvegetarian curries.

Hotel Aangan (☎ 520640; singles/doubles with shared bathroom Rs 250/300, with private bathroom Rs 500/600) is one of the best options. It's about 400m west of Bhanu

Chowk along Putali Bazaar (lined with cabinet makers and carpenters). There are also more expensive air-con rooms.

There's a good **supermarket** about 50m west of Bhanu Chowk along the same road as Hotel Aangan.

Getting There & Away
Dharan Bazaar is 50km from the attractive hill town of Dhankuta. Hile, the starting point for a number of treks in eastern Nepal, is 12km past Dhankuta. The spectacular road is sealed as far as Hile, but does continue on to Therathum and is being pushed even farther. Buses to Dhankuta cost Rs 67 and take three hours. Buses to Basantapur (Rs 135, six hours) and Therathum (Rs 205, 10 hours) all go via Hile (Rs 80, three hours), cost Rs 110 and take five hours.

There are day/night buses to Kathmandu (Rs 295/350, 14 hours) and numerous buses to Biratnagar (Rs 34, two hours).

DHANKUTA
☎ 026

Although Dhankuta is only 50km by excellent road from the Terai, it seems more like a million miles away. The largest, flattest spot in the nearby vicinity is the bus station; it soon becomes quite hard to remember that expanses of waterlogged plains exist.

The town is strung along a ridge that basically runs north–south; the bus station is below the ridge. The sad remnants of the forest that once covered the hill are at the northern end of town. There's no real reason to stay here, except the colourful *haat bajar* (weekly bazaar) on Thursday. Hile is more interesting and has better walking options.

As you walk downhill (south) along the main street the road forks; the right fork goes down to the bus station – follow the left fork to a spur to see fine views of the Himalaya. The latter involves a pleasant 45-minute walk. After about 15 minutes the main track veers to the left and there is a stile over a barbed-wire fence. Climb the stile and follow the ridge line up to the left. Eventually you'll come to a small shrine. There are plenty of flowers and birds along the way and, of course, good views.

Places to Stay & Eat
There are some small, clean, basic lodges on the main street.

Shaha Lodge (☎ 520281; doubles under Rs 200) and **Naulo Lodge** (☎ 520481; doubles under Rs 200) are both very basic.

Hotel Parchaya (☎ 520425; twins Rs 100, quads Rs 200), a good option, would be a pleasant place to stay while you explored the surrounding hills. It's clean and bright and there are superb views. To find the hotel walk north up the ridge until you get to a large pipal tree in the middle of an intersection. The hotel is on the right; all rooms have shared bathroom.

Hotel Suravi (☎ 520204; singles/doubles with shared bathroom Rs 100/180, with private bathroom Rs 180/350) is the pick of a pretty basic bunch. The restaurant here is also recommended.

Puchhae Café, next door to Hotel Parchaya, is a decent little café with music and a relaxing atmosphere.

Getting There & Away
Plenty of buses travel the spectacular road from Dhankuta to Dharan Bazaar (Rs 67, three hours). Buses for Basantapur cost Rs 75 and take three hours; to Hile it is Rs 20. There are no buses beyond Therathum.

HILE
☎ 026

Hile, a scruffy, bustling, one-street bazaar town strung out along a ridge, is the starting point for Arun Valley treks (possible for individuals) and for treks to Makalu (groups only). Kanchenjunga trekkers (groups only) usually start at Basantapur. Hile is also a good base for day walks. At the time of writing, Maoist activities were restricting independent movement in this region. Though no tourists had been harmed, payments were often demanded by armed people. Check the current situation with your embassy before venturing into the trekking regions.

There are some fantastic views of the Himalaya, especially of the Makalu massif, from the ridge above the town. Walk along the Basantapur road past the army base and a few hundred metres past the army checkpoint (there's a boom across the road) you can cut up to the left onto a grassy ridge.

Nepal's ethnic map is always complicated, but at Hile it is about as complicated as it gets, with Tibetans, Bahuns, Chhetris, Magars, Tamangs, Rais, Limbus and Indians all living here.

There are several decent but basic lodges, with not much to separate them.

Doma Lodge (☎ 520574; dorm beds Rs 30, doubles with private bathroom Rs 100) is as basic as they come, but it's clean and friendly.

Hotel Himali (☎ 520340; dorm beds Rs 30, singles/doubles with shared bathroom Rs 80/120) is similar to Doma Lodge.

Hotel Hillstone (doubles with private bathroom Rs 300) near the bus stand is Hile's Hilton. Don't expect too much, but it's clean and the rooms are a decent size.

Buses to Basantapur and Therathum (about 20km beyond Basantapur and the current roadhead), depart every 45 minutes or so, cost Rs 46 and take around two hours.

There is one daily bus to Kathmandu (Rs 420, 14 hours).

BIRATNAGAR
☎ 021

The fact that Biratnagar is the second-largest city in Nepal, and an industrial centre, actually makes it sound worse than it is. It's a frenetic, bustling place with the crowds and shops you would expect of a city with several hundred thousand inhabitants. However, there's just nothing much to attract the visitor and the border crossing to the south is not open to tourists.

The countryside and surrounding villages are interesting, but difficult to explore without private transport. One possibility is to continue north along Main Rd – this veers left when you leave town. Continue westward until you reach a T-junction, and then turn right (north) along a dirt road that parallels the sealed road and continue through Sigraha and Haraincha until you reach the Mahendra Hwy to the east of Itahari.

Jute used to be grown in large quantities, and can still be seen, but the industry has been in decline for years. There are numerous ethnic groups in the region, but the most distinctive are the Tharus and Danuwars. The Danuwars are very similar in culture and appearance to the Tharu, but the women wear a distinctive embroidered sari.

Places to Stay & Eat
There's quite a range of places at varying prices. Bear in mind that anywhere on Main Rd or near the bus station will be noisy.

Kathmandu Guest House (☎ 523041; dorm beds Rs 40, singles/doubles with private bathroom Rs 130/170), near Traffic Chowk, has quiet if gloomy rooms and is a reasonable inexpensive option.

Dhankuta Lodge (☎ 522925; singles Rs 120-168, doubles Rs 200-250 with private bathroom), opposite the bus station, is gloomy but tolerable. Avoid the front rooms, which cop the bus noise.

Hotel Geetanjali (☎ 527335; Malaya Rd; singles/doubles with shared bathroom Rs 175/75, doubles with private bathroom Rs 450) is also close to the bus station and set in a pleasant garden. There's a small restaurant with Indian food on the ground floor.

Hotel Namaskar (☎ 521199, fax 523499; Main Rd; singles/doubles nonair-con Rs 300/400 or Rs 400/600 with Western commode, air-con rooms Rs 850/900) is somewhat up the scale. It's near Traffic Chowk, a 15-minute walk from the bus park. The hotel has a range of rooms. At the top price you get air-con and a private sitting room, but the cheaper rooms are clean and quite adequate, and all rooms have a bathroom. There is also a good, reasonably priced restaurant here.

Hotel Eastern Star (☎ 530798; e eastern star@brt.wlink.com.np; Roadcess Chowk; singles/doubles nonair-con Rs 700/850, with air-con Rs 1250/1450) is a very comfortable business hotel about 500m south of the bus

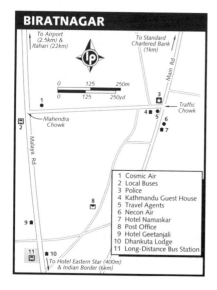

BIRATNAGAR

To Airport (2.5km) & Itahari (22km)

To Standard Chartered Bank (1km)

Main Rd

0   125   250m
0   125   250yd

Traffic Chowk

Mahendra Chowk

Malaya Rd

1 Cosmic Air
2 Local Buses
3 Police
4 Kathmandu Guest House
5 Travel Agents
6 Necon Air
7 Hotel Namaskar
8 Post Office
9 Hotel Geetanjali
10 Dhankuta Lodge
11 Long-Distance Bus Station

To Hotel Eastern Star (400m) & Indian Border (6km)

station. The rooms are spacious and have TV and phone. The restaurant does reasonable Indian, Chinese and Western dishes.

Getting There & Away
Biratnagar is serviced from Kathmandu by **Necon Air** (☎ 530177), which has four flights daily (US$87), as well as **Buddha Air** (☎ 524693) and **Cosmic Air**. There are many travel agents around Traffic Chowk

There are plenty of buses to Kathmandu, Kakarbhitta and Janakpur. Night buses to Kathmandu leave at 4.30pm to 5pm (Rs 375, 12 hours); there are also day buses (Rs 295) to Kathmandu, as well as to Kakarbhitta (Rs 95, 3½ hours), Janakpur (Rs 165), Birganj (day/night Rs 216/231, eight hours), Dhankuta (Rs 100) and Dharan Bazaar (Rs 34, two hours).

BIRTAMOD
☎ 023
Birtamod is the scruffy highway town where buses and jeeps bound for Ilam and beyond originate. There's not a great deal of accommodation. One of the best places is **Paradise Restaurant & Lodge** (☎ 540057; singles/doubles Rs 350/550), east of the main *chowk* on the southern side of the highway, opposite the line-up of Ilam-bound 4WDs. The rooms are basic, but clean and adequate, and hot water, if requested, comes in a bucket. The restaurant has a good range of Indian, Chinese and Nepali dishes and there's a daily dance programme at 5pm.

There are frequent buses running to/from Kakarbhitta (Rs 15, 30 minutes). Buses to Ilam take five hours to cover the 80km and cost Rs 80. The numerous 4WDs will take just three hours and charge Rs 120 per passenger. The road to Ilam intersects with the Mahendra Hwy at Charali, 8km east of Birtamod.

ILAM
☎ 027
Ilam is an attractive small town at the centre of Nepal's tea industry; the climate of the surrounding hills is similar to Darjeeling's. Few westerners visit, but there is some reasonable accommodation available, some tea plantations to see and it's possible to take walks in the region. At the time of writing, however, Maoist activities were restricting movement in this region. Check the current

situation with your embassy before venturing into the trekking regions.

About 40m west of Bihendra Chowk, the Sakhejung Hill Range Tea company, runs a small shop. The company's processing plant is 10km away and welcomes visitors. You need to organise your own transport, but make inquiries at the shop.

The **Nepal Rastra Bank** is 200m southwest of the *tundikhel* (parade ground) at the bottom end of town. Just follow the road that turns off the main road and runs beside the *tundikhel*.

Places to Stay & Eat
The cheapest places are around the bus station at the bottom end of the town. These can be noisy however, as buses start around 4am.

Hotel New Dish & Lodge (☎ 520626; doubles with private bathroom Rs 350) is the best of the bus station lodges. All rooms are doubles, but if you are single you can negotiate a lower tariff.

Maivalley Guest House (doubles under Rs 200) is a tolerable, cheaper option near the bus station.

Tamu Guest House (doubles Rs 180) is a bit farther away and so escapes the noise. The rooms are OK.

Danfe Guest House (☎ 520048; singles/doubles/triples/quads Rs 150/200/300/400) is set among the tea plantations, and offers real peace and quiet. Rooms are basic but clean, and all share a common bathroom. The guesthouse is a few minutes' walk from the bus station; take the stairs up at the rear corner of the station, turn right onto the track, then left at the T-junction.

Green View Guest House (☎ 520103; singles/doubles with shared bathroom from Rs 150/300, doubles with private bathroom Rs 400) is the best on offer. The rooms are large, clean and modern; most do indeed have a green view – tea plantations. The bright and airy restaurant on the 2nd floor has good Nepali and Chinese meals for Rs 35.

There's not much else in the restaurant stakes. There are a few basic Nepali **eateries** along the road between the bus station and Bihendra Chowk.

Getting There & Away
The road from the Terai is in good condition and is sealed all the way; it's also very steep and the views are spectacular (although the

good views of Kanchenjunga are only available for a short distance). Buses from Birtamod, on the Mahendra Hwy 13km west of Kakarbhitta, depart for Ilam from 7am to 1pm (Rs 80, five hours).

The road is being pushed farther into the hills beyond Ilam, and currently goes beyond Taplejung. Buses run regularly between Birtamod and Taplejung.

KAKARBHITTA
☎ 023

The sole reason for the existence of Kakarbhitta is its proximity to India. This is the border post for road traffic going to or from Siliguri and Darjeeling. In fact, it's not much more than a glorified bus stop, and it's difficult to imagine that anyone would want to stay longer than the time it takes to make a bus connection.

The surrounding countryside is attractive, however, and you can tell you're not far from Darjeeling when you see the tea plantations on the outskirts of town.

Orientation & Information

A **tourist office** (☎ 562035) is just inside Nepal, past customs on the northern side of the road (on the right if you're coming in from India). It is of little practical use.

The border is open to tourists 24 hours, but after 7pm and before 7am you may need to go searching for the Nepali officials. As you move away from the border the main bus parking area is a dusty (or muddy) quadrangle on your right, followed by the bazaar and village.

There are two banks on the Nepali side, but only the **Nepal Rastra Bank** (open 7am-7pm daily) is authorised to change money (no cards). The **Mechi Moneychanger** in the

southeast corner of the bus station changes only Indian rupees at the pegged rate.

The **post office** (open 10.15am-3.45pm) is opposite the bus park on the other side of the highway, about 20m west of the conspicuous Colour Lab. Hotel Rajat (see Places to Stay & Eat) has a 'Cyber Cafey' offering Internet connection for one to 15 minutes (Rs 30), 16 to 30 minutes (Rs 50) or 31 to 60 minutes (Rs 75).

Places to Stay & Eat

There are plenty of places to stay around the bazaar, but the quality of these is variable. If you want to get a decent night's sleep, steer clear of the places that front onto the bus park.

Hotel Shere Punjab (☎ 562477; singles/doubles with private bathroom Rs 250/400), near the bus station and the border, falls into the tolerably grubby category.

Hotel Deurali (☎ 562115; singles with shared bathroom Rs 50, doubles with private bathroom Rs 250), west of the bus park in the northernmost of the narrow streets in the bazaar, is typical of the bazaar cheapies.

Hotel Kanchan (☎ 562015; doubles with shared bathroom Rs 180, with private bathroom Rs 280, bigger rooms Rs 500), one block behind the rear of the bus park, is not a bad choice. The rooms are clean, and the restaurant serves decent food. The bigger rooms have TV and phone.

Hotel Mechi (☎ 562040; singles Rs 320-800, doubles Rs 560-1200), on the same road as the Kanchan, has a range of rooms, all with running hot water. The rooms are comfortable and there's a good air-con restaurant and a travel agency downstairs.

Hotel Rajat (☎ 562033; e hotelrajat@ jhapa.info.com.np; singles/doubles with private

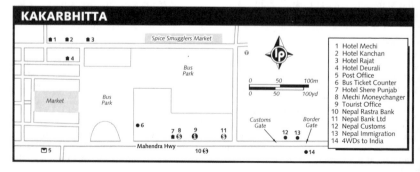

KAKARBHITTA

Spice Smugglers Market

Bus Park

Bus Park

Market

Mahendra Hwy

Customs Gate

Border Gate

0   50   100m
0   50   100yd

1 Hotel Mechi
2 Hotel Kanchan
3 Hotel Rajat
4 Hotel Deurali
5 Post Office
6 Bus Ticket Counter
7 Hotel Shere Punjab
8 Mechi Moneychanger
9 Tourist Office
10 Nepal Rastra Bank
11 Nepal Bank Ltd
12 Nepal Customs
13 Nepal Immigration
14 4WDs to India

bathroom Rs 400/600, with running hot water Rs 700/1000, with air-con Rs 800/1200) is the best hotel on offer. There are a few doubles with shared bathroom, large rooms with TV and phone, and deluxe rooms. The hotel has a decent restaurant on the ground floor and the owner is very helpful with advice for onward travel.

Most of the lodges have pretty decent restaurants serving travellers fare.

Getting There & Away

Air The nearest airport is at Bhadrapur, 10km south of Birtamod, which is 13km west of Kakarbhitta. Daily flights go to Kathmandu (US$111) with **Buddha Air** and **Necon Air**. A taxi to the airport will cost Rs 700. You can get there by local bus, first going to Birtamod where you will change buses, but it is slow.

To/From India There are plenty of land connections to destinations in both Nepal and India. Many people buy through tickets between Kathmandu and Darjeeling, but this is relatively expensive and is unnecessary. With a through ticket you travel the Kakarbhitta to Kathmandu section at night and miss the sights. Also many travellers are ripped off buying through tickets between India and Nepal. See the Getting There & Away chapter for more details.

If you are entering India, it's best to take one of the share 4WDs that line up near the border gates between 7am and 4pm. Destinations include Siliguri (INRs 35), Darjeeling (INRs 100), Kalimpong (INRs 70) and Gangtok (INRs 140). A rickshaw ride across the border costs Rs 10, but from the Indian border post of Raniganj (Panitanki) there are no share 4WDs and you must take a local bus to your next destination.

To/From Other Parts of Nepal There is plenty of competition for your business if you plan to buy a bus ticket, so it's worth shopping around. The prices won't vary, but the departure times and the quality of the buses can. Night buses can be booked at the office at the front of the bus park.

Night buses for Kathmandu and Pokhara leave between 3pm and 5pm (Rs 450, 13 hours). Not only would this be an epic and unpleasant journey, but you would also miss the views. Day buses to Kathmandu cost Rs 350. If time and weather allow, consider catching a day bus to Janakpur and stopping there; buses leave between 6.30am and 9am (day Rs 198, five hours); night buses are Rs 210. The road is quite interesting between Itahari and Janakpur; it runs across the flood plain of the massive Sapt Kosi.

There are day/night buses for Birganj (Rs 250/275, eight hours) and day buses to Biratnagar (Rs 90, 3½ hours).

The overnight buses from Kathmandu all arrive in Kakarbhitta before 11am, departing the Kathmandu Bus Terminal at 4pm and 5pm. Book a day in advance. Be very careful if catching a night bus from Kakarbhitta. The local police report many accounts of stolen luggage.

Trekking

For the people in the hills of Nepal, walking has always been the main method of getting from A to B. There were no roads leading into the hill country from the Terai or India until the Tribhuvan Hwy to Kathmandu was constructed in the 1950s. Pokhara was not connected to the outside world by road until the 1970s. Even today the vast majority of villages can only be reached on foot, although every year the roads penetrate farther into Nepal's endless ranges of hills.

The Nepali people, making their way from village to village on the well-worn trails, were only joined by Western visitors when Himalayan mountaineering came into vogue. It was the accounts of those pioneering mountaineers, who had to make their way to the base of the great peaks on foot, that inspired the first trekkers. The word 'trekking' was first applied to Nepali hiking trips in the 1960s and the enormous popularity of trekking today has developed since that time.

Trekking in Nepal means a walking trip following trails, many of which have been used for centuries. It is not mountaineering, although some of the popular trekking trails are used by mountaineering expeditions on their approach marches. Their length varies – there are popular treks around the Kathmandu and Pokhara valleys that only take a day and others that last a week or a month. You could even string a series of popular treks together and walk for months on end.

There is no question that Nepal offers some of the most spectacular and beautiful scenery in the world. Nepal has a near monopoly on the world's highest peaks – eight of the 10 highest are found here. A number of the popular trekking routes offer you wonderful views of these peaks and some visit the base camps used by mountaineering expeditions. Mountain flights may give you superb views, but there is absolutely nothing like waking up on a crystal-clear Himalayan day and seeing an 8000m peak towering over you.

The snowcapped mountains may be the most obvious scenic attraction, but there are plenty of other treats for the eye. A typical trek climbs out of the subtropical lowlands of terraced fields, oak and chestnut, through whistling stands of pine and forests of stately

Highlights

- Making the approach to Everest Base Camp, following in the footsteps of famous mountaineers

- Awakening to the uncanny stillness of the Annapurna Sanctuary as dawn reveals the awesome sight of the surrounding peaks soaring overhead

- Visiting remote mountain villages, meeting the local people and experiencing Tibetan Buddhist culture

- Witnessing the raw beauty of the ice floes; hearing the crash of avalanches and the roar of raging rivers, with a new and more spectacular view day after day

rhododendrons, until emerging through stunted birch or juniper into the treeless alpine zone at the foot of the great peaks.

Trekking in Nepal is not like hiking through an uninhabited national park. Local people are constantly passing by on the trails, usually carrying extraordinarily heavy loads of unexpected items. And along many routes there are regularly spaced villages in which to pause and find shelter. In the villages you can meet people from a diversity of ethnic groups. The warm, outgoing nature, general friendliness and good humour of Nepalis is often noted by trekkers. Religious festivals can make trekking even more enjoyable and interesting.

This chapter outlines the basic requirements for safe trekking on the mountain trails and gives an overview of the major trekking routes. For independent trekking, you will require the more detailed advice, maps and route descriptions from Lonely Planet's award-winning *Trekking in the Nepal Himalaya*.

Preparations

PLANNING

Nepal offers plenty of opportunity for treks lasting a day or less, though most are considerably longer. From Pokhara or around the Kathmandu Valley you can do a variety of two-, three- or four-day walks (see those chapters for details), but Nepal's most popular treks take at least a week. For the very popular Everest Base Camp and Annapurna Circuit Treks you have to allow three weeks. Don't take on one of these treks too lightly; the end of the first week is not the time to discover that you're not keen on walking.

When to Trek

Put simply, the best time to trek is October to May (dry season); the worst time is June to September (monsoon). This generalisation does not allow for the peculiarities of individual treks. Some people even claim that the undeniable difficulties of trekking during the monsoon are outweighed by the virtual absence of Western trekkers.

The first two months of the dry season, October and November, are probably the ideal period for trekking. The air, freshly washed by the monsoon rains, is crystal clear, the mountain scenery is superb and the weather is still comfortably warm.

December, January and February are still good months for trekking, but the cold can be bitter and dangerous at high altitudes. Getting up to the Everest Base Camp can be a real endurance test and Thorung La pass on the Annapurna Circuit is usually blocked by snow.

In March and April the weather has been dry for a long time and dust is starting to hang in the air, affecting visibility. The poorer quality of the Himalayan views is compensated for by the superb wildflowers such as Nepal's wonderful rhododendrons.

By May it starts to get very hot, dusty and humid, and the monsoon is definitely just around the corner. From June to September the trails can be dangerously slippery due to the monsoon rains, and raging rivers often wash away bridges and stretches of trail. Nepal's famous *jukha* (leeches) are an unpleasant feature of the wet season, but with care, trekking can still be possible and there are certainly fewer trekkers on the trail.

What Kind of Trek?

There are many different styles of trekking to suit your budget, fitness level and available time. You can carry your own pack and tent and rely totally on your own navigation, language skills and prior research. Or you may prefer to hire a local porter to carry your pack, or a porter and a guide to enhance the

---

Trekking in Maoist Country

At the time of writing, the Maoist uprising in rural Nepal had significantly affected most trekking routes, though the Maoists have made it clear that they are not targeting foreign tourists. While no tourists have been harmed by Maoist groups, trekkers have been asked for 'donations', ranging from Rs 1000 to US$100, when passing through areas under Maoist control.

Even in the relatively unaffected regions of Annapurna and Everest, telephone booths and ACAP posts have been destroyed and some police checkposts are no longer manned.

If the fragile cease-fire called in January 2003 holds, things may slowly get back to normal, but before undertaking *any* trek you should register with your embassy and follow its travel advice. For up-to-date information visit W www.trekinfo.com, which has links to various travel advice and news sites.

---

trekking experience. You may plan to sleep in lodges every night and forego the camping experience. To save time, many people organise a trek through a trekking agency, either in Kathmandu or in their home country. Such organised treks can be simple lodge-to-lodge affairs or magnificent expeditions with the full regalia of porters, guides, portable kitchens, dining tents and even toilet tents.

Trekking is physically demanding. Some preparation is recommended, even for shorter treks. You will need endurance and stamina to tackle the steep ascents and descents that are so much a part of trekking in the highest mountain range in the world.

On the trail you will begin to realise just how far you are from medical help and the simple comforts that are usually taken for granted. This is usually part of the appeal of trekking, but for some it is a shock to realise just how responsible they are for their own well being. A simple stumble can have catastrophic results. Even a twisted ankle or sore knee can become a serious inconvenience if you are several days away from help and your companions need to keep moving.

Independent Trekking

Independent trekking does not mean solo trekking. It simply means that you will not be part of an organised tour. The popular trekking trails have accommodation along their entire length. People have even walked the complete Annapurna Circuit without a sleeping bag, although this is asking for trouble and is definitely not recommended.

For experienced hikers, guides and porters are not necessary on the Annapurna or the Mt Everest treks. A good guide/porter will enhance your experience, but a bad one will just make life more complicated (see Guides & Porters later in this section).

There are many factors that influence how much you spend on an independent trek. In most places, dorm accommodation costs around Rs 30 to Rs 50, a simple meal

Independent Trekking with Children

A few years ago we decided to have a family holiday in Nepal. We had both travelled and trekked extensively in Nepal – without kids – and thought it would be a good place to return to with our two children – Ella aged six and Vera 2½. It turned out to be an excellent decision, although there were moments when we doubted our sanity in carting two kids halfway across the world, exposing them to all manner of bugs, not to mention the pollution of Kathmandu, just so we could see some mountains with snow on them.

One of the main goals of our trip was to do a week-long trek in the mountains. Many people we spoke to thought it was perhaps a bit of an ambitious thing to undertake with two small children, but this just made us more determined to give it a go – we could always turn back if it didn't work out. Our base point was to be Pokhara, seven bumpy and dusty but cheap hours by bus, or one easy, spectacular and not-too-expensive hour by plane (we opted for the latter) from Kathmandu.

As we were travelling on a fairly tight budget, we didn't think we could afford an organised trek where everything is taken care of for you. Instead we approached many of the trekking agencies in Pokhara, and finally settled on one that we felt had its act together sufficiently to arrange for porters and transport to the trailhead. Our plan was that we would have three porters – two to carry rucksacks, and a third to carry Vera most of the time, and Ella when she got tired of walking. As it turned out, Ella walked virtually the whole way, which was a great effort, and Vera was carried in a *doko* (a large, conical, cane basket) on a porter's back. She felt safe being up off the ground, and was emboldened enough to pull faces at trekkers and locals we passed along the trail. Her mode of travel certainly made her a curiosity to locals and foreigners alike. To wedge her in safely we sat her first in her child-pack, placed this in the basket, and then filled the gaps with sleeping bags and items of warm clothing we shed as the day wore on.

The porters were great with the kids, and although we felt a bit like a travelling show at times, it was worth hiring enough porters to free us of any major load. At around US$5 per porter per day, it was money well spent.

Overall the trek went very well, but we realised early on that we had overestimated how far we would be able to walk in one day. Once we slowed down and basically let Ella set the pace, things were fine. The walking itself was not too strenuous, largely because of our slow pace, but we did get up to 3500m, and at this altitude the children's breathing was affected. In six days we were able to comfortably walk from Birethanti to Ghorapani/Deorali on the Jomsom Trek, cut across to Ghandruk on the Annapurna Sanctuary and return to Birethanti.

Staying in the teahouses along the way was a highlight for the kids. On arrival they would disappear into the candle-lit, smoky interiors of the kitchen, and usually emerge beaming some time later, brandishing a boiled potato or some other morsel kindly given by the hard-working women of the house.

The major problem we faced on the trek was a bout of Giardia that Vera contracted, and this led to our second-biggest problem; what to do with all the soiled disposable nappies. The solution was to roll the used ones up very tightly, store them in a strong plastic bag and carry them out to a place where you can dispose of them properly. This is not as offensive as it sounds!

Some powdered flavouring helped to disguise the awful taste of iodine used to purify our water, but our two children steadfastly refused anything other than plain bottled water.

Hugh Finlay

of rice and dal around Rs 30 to Rs 50 – note that as you get farther from the road on the Annapurna Circuit and in the Everest region, prices can be more than twice as high. After a long day hiking, most people will weaken when confronted by a cold beer, an apple pie or a hot shower and these will dramatically add to your costs. Budget for US$5 to US$10 per day in the Annapurnas and Everest region, which will also cover the occasional luxury.

In almost all lodges prices are fixed and are more than reasonable. Remember this – and the real value of the rupee – before you start to get carried away with bargaining.

Guides & Porters

If you can't (or don't want to) carry a large pack, if you have children or elderly people in your party, or if you plan to walk in regions where you have to carry in food and tents, help should be considered.

If you make arrangements with one of the small trekking agencies in Kathmandu expect to pay Rs 200 to Rs 300 per day for a guide, Rs 300 to Rs 750 for a porter. The reason a guide is cheaper is that you will be buying his food – so remember to factor that in.

Finding Guides & Porters To hire a guide, look on bulletin boards, hire someone through a guesthouse or agency, visit a trekking company or check with the office of the Kathmandu Environmental Education Project (KEEP). Chhetri Sisters Guesthouse (☎ 061-524066; e trek@3sisters adventure.com) at Lakeside North, Pokhara, organises women porters and guides for women trekkers.

It's fairly easy to find guides and porters, but it is hard to be certain of their honesty and ability. Unless you have first-hand recommendations, you're best to hire someone through a guesthouse or agency. A porter or guide found at a street corner can easily disappear along the trail with all your gear even if they are carrying a slew of letters from past clients certifying their honesty.

There is a distinct difference between a guide and a porter. A guide should speak English, know the terrain and the trails, and supervise porters, but probably won't carry a load or do menial tasks such as cooking or putting up tents. Porters are generally only hired for load-carrying, although an increasing number speak some English and know the trails well enough to act as guides.

Arranging expeditions where guides, porters, tents and food are required can be very time-consuming and extremely complicated. In such cases you're definitely best off putting this in the hands of a professional.

If during a trek you decide you need help, either because of illness, problems with altitude, blisters or weariness, it will generally be possible to find a porter. Most lodges can arrange a porter, particularly in large villages or near a hill-country airstrip where there are often porters who have just finished working for a trekking party and are looking for another load to carry.

Obligations to Guides & Porters An important consideration when you decide to trek with a guide or porter is that you place yourself in the role of an employer. This means that you may have to deal with personnel problems, including medical care, insurance, strikes, requests for time off, and salary increases, and all the other aspects of being a boss. Be as thorough as you can when hiring people and make it clear from the beginning what the requirements and limitations are. After that, prepare yourself for some haggling – it's part of the process.

When hiring a porter you are responsible (morally if not legally) for the welfare of those you employ. Many porters die or are injured each year (see the boxed text 'Porters, Exploitation & IPPG') and it's important that you don't contribute to the problem.

The main points to bear in mind when hiring a porter are:

- Ensure that adequate clothing is provided for any staff hired by you. This needs to be adequate for the altitudes you intend to trek to, and to protect against bad weather. Equipment should include adequate footwear, headwear, gloves, windproof jacket and trousers, sunglasses, and blanket, sleeping mat and tent at altitude.
- Ensure that whatever provision you have made for yourself for emergency medical treatment is available to porters working for you
- Ensure that porters who fall ill are not simply paid out and left to fend for themselves (it happens!)
- Ensure that porters who do fall ill and are taken down and out in order to access medical treatment are accompanied by someone who speaks the porter's language and also understands the medical problem

TREKKING

Whether you're making the arrangements yourself or dealing with an agency, make sure you clearly establish where you will go, how long you will take, how much you are going to pay and what you will supply along the way. With a guide, agree on a daily rate for food rather than pay as you go. Arrangements where you pay for the guide or porter's accommodation and food can end up being surprisingly expensive. The amount of food a hungry Nepali guide can go through, when you're footing the bill, can be simply stunning. You need to increase the allowance at higher elevations where food is more expensive.

When you do provide equipment for porters, be sure to make it clear whether it is a loan or a gift. In reality it will be very hard to get back equipment that you have loaned unless you are very determined and thick-skinned. The porters and Sherpas have special techniques to make you feel guilty and petty when you ask for the return of equipment. If you're hiring your own porters, contact KEEP for information about the porter clothing bank, a scheme that allows you to rent protective gear for your porter.

Organised Trekking

Organised treks can vary greatly in standards and costs. Treks arranged with international travel companies tend to be more expensive than trips arranged within Nepal.

International Trekking Agencies After reading the glossy brochure of an adventure travel company, you pay for the trek and everything is organised before you leave home. The cost will probably include flights to and from Nepal, accommodation in Kathmandu before and after the trek, tours and other activities as well as the trek itself. A fully organised trek provides virtually everything: tents, sleeping bags, food, porters and an experienced English-speaking *sirdar* (trail boss), Sherpa guides and usually a Western trek leader. All you need to worry about is a day-pack and camera.

Companies organising trekking trips in Nepal include some well-known names such as Mountain Travel-Sobek, Wilderness Travel or Above the Clouds in the USA, World Expeditions or Peregrine Adventures in Australia, and Explore Worldwide in the UK. Although the trek leaders may be

Porters, Exploitation & IPPG

Porters are the backbone of the trekking industry in Nepal, and yet every year there are incidents (all preventable) involving porters suffering from acute mountain sickness (AMS), snow blindness and frostbite. Some of these illnesses have resulted in fatalities. It seems they are well down the pecking order with some trekking companies who simply don't look after the porters hired by them. This certainly does not apply to all companies, but there are plenty, especially at the budget end of the scale, who are more worried about their own profit than the welfare of those they rely on to generate that profit.

Porters often come from the lowland valleys, are poor and poorly educated and are often ignorant of the potential dangers of the areas they are being employed to work in. Stories abound of porters being left to fend for themselves, wearing thin cotton clothes and sandals when traversing high mountain passes in blizzard conditions. At the end of each winter a number of porters' bodies are discovered in the snow melt – they become tired, ill or affected by altitude, and simply sit down in the snow, get hypothermia and die. If you are hiring a porter independently, you have certain obligations to meet. If you are trekking with an organised group using porters, be sure to ask the company how they ensure the well being of porters hired by them.

In order to prevent the abuse of porters, the **International Porter Protection Group** *(IPPG;* w *www.ippg.net)* was established in 1997. The aim of both the IPPG and its sister organisation **Porters Progress** *(w www.portersprogress.org)* is to improve health and safety for porters at work, to reduce the incidence of avoidable illness, injury and death, and to educate trekkers and trekking/travel companies about porter welfare. Both organisations operate a clothing bank for porters, with branches in Lukla and Thamel. IPPG has an office in the **Himalayan Explorers Connection** *(☎ 4259275;* e *members@hec.org)* next to the KEEP office in Thamel. Porters Progress has an office farther north in Thamel (see the Greater Thamel map in the Kathmandu chapter).

experienced Western walkers from the international company, the on-the-ground organisation in Nepal will most probably be carried out by a reputable local trekking company.

Local Trekking Agencies It's quite possible to arrange a fully organised trip when you get to Nepal (and save a lot of money), but if you have a large group it's best to make the arrangements well in advance. Many trekking companies in Nepal can put together a fully equipped trek if you give them a few days notice. With the best of these companies a trek may cost upwards of US$60 or US$70 a day and you'll trek in real comfort with tables, chairs, and dining tents, toilet tents and other luxuries.

There are more than 300 trekking agencies in Nepal, ranging from those connected to international travel companies, down to small agencies that specialise in handling independent trekkers. These small agencies will often be able to fix you up with individual porters or guides. A group trek organised through one of these agencies might cost US$30 to US$50 a day. Group treks staying at village inns along the route can be cheaper still (around US$25 a day including a guide and food).

Some trekking agencies that have been recommended include:

Adventure Nepal Trekking (☎ 01-4412508, fax 4222026) Tridevi Marg, Thamel, PO Box 915, Kathmandu

Ama Dablam Trekking (☎ 01-4415372/3, fax 4416029, [e] himalaya.sales@amadablam .wlink.com.np) Lazimpat, PO Box 3035, Kathmandu

Annapurna Mountaineering & Trekking (☎ 01-4222999, fax 4226153, [e] amtk@ccsl.com.np) Durbar Marg, PO Box 795, Kathmandu

Asian Trekking (☎ 01-4424249, fax 4411878, [e] astrek@wlink.com.np) Tridevi Marg, Thamel, PO Box 3022, Kathmandu

Bhrikuti Himalayan Treks (☎ 01-417459, fax 4413612, [e] asianbht@ccsl.com.np) Nag Pokhari, Naxal, PO Box 2267, Kathmandu

Chhetri Sisters (☎ 061-524066, [e] trek@ 3sistersadventure.com) Lakeside North, Pokhara

Crystal Mountain Treks (☎ 01-4416813, fax 4412647, [e] dinesh@crystal.wlink.com.np) Nag Pokhari, Naxal, PO Box 5437, Kathmandu

Himalayan Hill Treks & River Tours (☎ 01-4520609, [e] info@hilltreks.com) Patan, PO Box 1066, Kathmandu

Inner Nepal Treks (☎ 01-4226130, fax 4224237, [e] explore@mos.com.np) Kamaladi, PO Box 536, Kathmandu

International Trekkers (☎ 01-4370714, fax 4371561, [e] nepal@intrek.mos.com.np) Chabahil, PO Box 1273, Kathmandu

Journeys Mountaineering & Trekking (☎ 01-4415092, fax 4419808, [e] journeys@mos.com .np) Baluwatar, PO Box 2034, Kathmandu

Lama Excursions (☎ 01-4220186, fax 4227202, [e] trek@lamex.wlink.com.np) Chanddol, Maharajganj, PO Box 2485, Kathmandu

Malla Treks (☎ 01-4410089, fax 4423143, [e] info@mallatreks.com.) Lekhnath Marg, PO Box 5227, Kathmandu

Mountain Travel Nepal (☎ 01-4414508, [e] info@tigermountain.com) Lazimpat, PO Box 170, Kathmandu

Sherpa Society (☎ 01-4470361, fax 4470153, [e] passang@mos.com.np) Chabahil, Chuchepati, PO Box 1566, Kathmandu

Sherpa Trekking Service (☎ 01-4220243, fax 4227243, [e] sts@wlink.com.np) Kamaladi, PO Box 500, Kathmandu

Sisne Rover Trekking (☎ 061-520893, fax 523262, [e] sisne@mos.com.np) PO Box 257, Lakeside, Pokhara

Thamserku Trekking (☎ 01-4354491, fax 4354329, [e] info@trekkinginnepal.com) Basundhara, Ring Rd, PO Box 3124, Kathmandu

Treks & Expedition Services (☎ 01-4418347, fax 4410488) Kamal Pokhari, PO Box 3057, Kathmandu

Venture Treks & Expeditions (☎ 01-4221585, fax 4220178, [e] temtig@mos.com.np) Kantipath, PO Box 3968, Kathmandu

Yeti Mountaineering & Trekking (☎ 01-4425896, fax 4410899, [e] ymtrek@ccsl.com.np.wlink .com.np) Ramshah Path, PO Box 1034, Kathmandu

Books & Maps

Books and maps are readily available in Kathmandu and Pokhara bookshops.

See Lonely Planet's *Trekking in the Nepal Himalaya* by Stan Armington for the complete story on trekking here. It has comprehensive advice on equipment selection, an excellent health and safety section, and comprehensive route descriptions not only of the popular treks covered more briefly in this book, but also of a number of interesting but less heavily used routes.

The best series of maps of Nepal is the 1:50,000 series produced by Erwin Schneider for Research Scheme Nepal Himalaya and originally printed in Vienna. Most

TREKKING

sheets are now published by Nelles Verlag in Munich. They cover the Kathmandu Valley and the Everest region from Jiri to the Hongu valley. The 1:100,000 Schneider maps of Annapurna and Langtang are available from many map shops overseas and at bookshops in Kathmandu.

National Geographic produces trekking maps to the Khumbu, Everest Base Camp, Annapurna and Langtang areas, as part of its Trails Illustrated series (Rs 950 to Rs 1050). They are generally good for the most popular treks.

The Finnish government has assisted the survey department with the production of a series of 1:50,000 and 1:25,000 maps covering most of Nepal, but they don't show all the trekking trails. They are available in some bookshops and from the Maps of Nepal outlet in Baluwatar, Kathmandu, on the road towards Bhaktapur, for Rs 80 per sheet.

There are numerous 'trekking' maps produced locally by Himalayan Map House, Nepa Maps and Shangri-La Maps. They cost from Rs 400 and are readily found in map and bookshops in Thamel. These maps are adequate for trekking the popular trails and are relatively inexpensive. Be aware that there is a great deal of repackaging going on. Don't buy two maps with different covers and names assuming you are getting significantly different maps. Check them first.

All of these maps are available at bookshops in Kathmandu and some speciality map shops overseas stock a selection. Most are available online from **Stanfords** (**W** *www.stanfords.co.uk*), **Omni Resources** (**W** *www.omnimap.com*) or **Melbourne Map Centre** (**W** *www.melbmap.com.au*).

What to Bring

Equipment It's always best to have your own equipment since you will be familiar with it and know for certain that it works. If there is some equipment that you do not have, you can always buy or rent it from one of Nepal's many trekking shops. Much of the equipment available is of adequate quality (but check items carefully) and the rental charges are generally not excessive, but large deposits are often required (usually equal to a generous valuation of the equipment itself). Never leave your passport as a deposit.

Hire rates in Kathmandu vary depending on quality. You can hire a sleeping bag (2-4 season) for Rs 25 to Rs 55, a down jacket for Rs 20 to Rs 40 and a tent for Rs 120 to Rs 150.

Thamel is the centre for equipment shopping in Nepal, though Pokhara and Namche Bazaar also have trekking equipment outlets. No longer is it easy to pick up the leftover gear from trekking expeditions, but there is a great deal of new equipment you can purchase including last-minute sundries such as iodine, sun block and led head lamps.

Some trekking gear, including sleeping bags, down jackets, duffel bags, backpacks, camera cases, ponchos and wind jackets, is manufactured in Kathmandu and sold in Thamel at very reasonable prices. Much of this locally produced gear is decorated with well-known brand names, but don't be deceived into thinking you're getting top-quality merchandise at a bargain price. Even so, most items are well made and will stand up to the rigours of at least one major trek.

Kathmandu does have a *pukka* (real) North Face showroom on Durbar Marg but ironically at the time of research it didn't have a licence to actually sell its products! Check to see if this has changed; if so, the manager promised imported gear at prices 30% lower than the US.

Approximate retail prices for new Nepali-made gear complete with fake brand names are as follows:

item	cost (Rs)
sleeping bag (2-4 season)	4000-6000
down jacket	3000
rain/wind jacket	450-1500
pile jacket	300-1000
day-pack	350-1300
expedition pack	1500-3000
duffel bag	300-450
quality socks	160-850

Clothing & Footwear The clothing you require depends on where and when you trek. If you're going to the Everest Base Camp in the middle of winter you must be prepared for very cold weather and take down gear, mittens and the like. If you're doing a short, low-altitude trek early or late in the season the weather is often likely to be fine for T-shirts and a pile jacket to pull on in the evenings.

Apart from ensuring you have adequate clothing to keep warm, it's important that your feet are comfortable and will stay dry if it rains or snows. Uncomfortable shoes or blistered feet are the worst possible trekking discomfort. Make sure your shoes fit well and are comfortable for long periods. Running shoes are adequate for low-altitude (below 3000m), warm-weather treks where you won't encounter snow, though they lack ankle support. Otherwise the minimum standard of footwear is lightweight trekking boots. Trekking boots can be bought in Kathmandu for Rs 2000 to Rs 3000, but these are generally seconds and are not recommended. The best idea is to bring your own worn-in boots.

Other Gear In winter or at high altitudes a high-quality four-season sleeping bag will be necessary. If you are going on an organised trek check what equipment is supplied by the company you sign up with. If you need to hire one, it could be grubby; check for fleas or worse.

Rain is rare during most of the trekking season, though weather patterns in the Bay of Bengal can cause massive rainstorms during autumn, and there are sure to be a few rainy days during spring. You should be prepared for rain by carrying waterproof gear, or at least a portable umbrella. The rainy season just before and after the monsoon months also brings leeches with it and it's nice to have some salt or matches to deal with them. Take a torch (flashlight) for those inevitable calls of nature on moonless nights.

Money Except in Solu Khumbu and on the Annapurna treks, changing foreign money is likely to be very difficult if not impossible. Bring enough money for the whole trek and don't count on being able to change Rs 1000 notes.

DOCUMENTS & FEES
Trekking Permits
Permits are not required for trekking in the Everest, Annapurna and Langtang regions. These three regions cover the vast majority of trekking routes taken by visitors to Nepal.

Treks in more remote areas (see table following) are camping treks that must be arranged by a trekking company; the company will arrange the permit.

area	fee ($US)
Everest, Annapurna & Langtang	No permit required
Kanchenjunga & Lower Dolpo	$10 per week for first four weeks, $20 per week after that
Upper Mustang & Upper Dolpo	$700 for 10 days, then $70 per day
Manaslu	$75 per week low season, $90 high season
Humla	$90 for seven days, then $15 per day

National Park & Conservation Fees
If you trek in the Annapurna, Manaslu, Kanchenjunga or Makalu regions, you will enter a conservation area and must pay a conservation fee; if your trek enters a national park, you must pay a national park fee.

You should buy an entrance ticket for all national parks and conservation areas in advance at the **Annapurna Conservation Area Project office** (ACAP; ☎ 4225393, ext 363; Tridevi Marg; open 9am-5pm daily, 9am-4pm daily in winter) in the basement of the Sanchaya Kosh Bhawan Shopping Centre at the entrance to Thamel in Kathmandu. You can also pay the national park fee when you arrive at the park entrance station, but you must pay the conservation fee in advance. Currently, the (once-only) fee is Rs 1000 (US$15) for national parks; Rs 2000 (US$30) for Annapurna; and Rs 1000 for Makalu-Barun and Kanchenjunga conservation areas.

Conservation fees for the Annapurna area are also payable in Pokhara at the **ACAP office** (☎ 061-532275), opposite Standard Charter Bank at Lakeside. Bring Rs 2000 and one photograph. Fortunately the permit is issued on the spot and you should accomplish the task quickly unless there is a long queue. If you arrive at an ACAP checkpoint without a permit you will be charged Rs 4000!

RESPONSIBLE TREKKING
Nepal faces several environmental problems as a result of, or compounded by, tourists' actions and expectations. These include the depletion of its forests for firewood; the

build-up of nonbiodegradable waste, especially plastic bottles; and the pollution of its waterways. Read Responsible Trekking in the Responsible Tourism section for ways to minimise your impact on Nepal's damaged ecosystem.

USEFUL ORGANISATIONS

Several organisations are attempting to deal with the environmental problems created by trekking, including the Annapurna Conservation Area Project (ACAP), which has done a great deal to encourage sustainable development in the Annapurna region. ACAP has offices in Thamel (Sanchakosh Building), Patan and Pokhara.

Two other organisations in Kathmandu offer free, up-to-date information on trekking conditions, health risks and minimising your environmental impact.

Kathmandu Environmental Education Project *(KEEP; ☎ 4259275;* w *www.keepnepa l.org; open 10am-5pm Sun-Fri)*, in Thamel, has a library, some useful notebooks with up-to-date information from other trekkers, an excellent notice board and embassy registration forms for most countries. It also sells iodine, biodegradable soap and other environmentally friendly equipment.

In the same office as KEEP is the **Himalayan Explorers Club** *(HEC; ☎ 4259275;* e *members@hec.org;* w *www.hec.org; open 10am-5pm Sun-Fri)*, which also provides information on trekking. Members can store luggage here and use the mail and email service.

The **Himalayan Rescue Association** *(HRA; ☎ 4440292;* w *himalayanhands.tripod .com)*, north of the Royal Palace in Kathmandu's Lazimpat district, runs the Trekkers' Information Centre, which has information about AMS and useful notebooks with up-to-date information from other trekkers. Lectures on altitude sickness are held at 2pm Sunday to Friday. Both KEEP and the HRA offices are excellent places to visit and advertise for trekking companions.

The slide shows held in the Kathmandu Guest House by Chris Beall, a British freelance photographer, writer and trek leader are another good source of impartial and up-to-date information in Kathmandu for independent trekking. The shows cost Rs 300 (including tea/coffee and biscuits) and you get plenty of time to ask questions at the end. If they are on you'll see posters up at the Kathmandu Guest House.

HEALTH

Acute mountain sickness (AMS) or altitude sickness is the major concern on high-altitude treks, but for the majority of trekkers health problems are likely to be minor, such as stomach upsets and blisters. Common-sense precautions are all that's required to avoid illness.

Basic rules for healthy trekking include taking care that water is always safe to drink. The best method is to treat water with iodine, as this is safe and does not require the use of firewood or kerosene to boil water. Diarrhoea is one of the comparatively minor problems that can ruin a trek so watch what you eat and ensure your medical kit has a medication such as Lomotil or Imodium (for emergencies only) and an antibiotic like Norfloxacin. The food on an organised trek is unlikely to cause any problems, but village-inn trekkers are at risk.

At high altitudes the burning power of the sun is strong, so make sure you have a pair of good sunglasses, a hat and a maximum protection sunscreen. If there is any likelihood that you'll be walking over snow, sunglasses are insufficient; you need mountaineering glasses with side pieces. Ensure that your porters also have adequate eyewear.

Many people suffer from knee and ankle strains, particularly if they are carrying their own pack. If you have a predisposition for these injuries, carry elastic supports or bandages. Lightweight, collapsible trekking poles are invaluable in this regard, providing extra support and stability especially on those knee-pounding descents. They can also come in handy when the village dogs get a bit too close. You should also carry plasters (Band Aids) in case of blisters.

Make sure you are in good health before departing as there is very little medical attention along the trails and rescue helicopters are not only very expensive but *must* be cleared for payment in advance. Your embassy can do this if you have registered with it. See Everest Base Camp Trek later in this chapter for more information on possible medical assistance along the way. In general, Himalayan hospitals can offer only very limited facilities and expertise. The

Himalayan Rescue Dog Squad (☎ *061-523267;* w *www.hrdsnrescue.org.np)* operates the largest rescue organisation in Nepal at the Riverside Hospital & Disaster Relief Unit, Shyauli Bazaar (Lamjung).

Be ever-alert for the symptoms of AMS. See Health in the Facts for the Visitor chapter for more detailed information on staying healthy while trekking.

TREKKING SAFELY

Usually, the farther you get from heavily populated centres the less likely it is that your personal safety will be threatened. Assaults in remote places are not unheard of, however. Indeed, some places have earned quite a reputation for violent assaults, almost without exception involving a solo trekker or small party of two or three. On the trails that run from Ghorapani to Tikhedhunga and Ghorapani to Ghandruk it is important to stay in a group and remain alert particularly towards the end of a long tiring day. Several basic rules should be followed: don't trek alone, don't make ostentatious displays of valuable possessions and don't leave lodge doors unlocked or valuables unattended.

See also Dangers & Annoyances in the Facts for the Visitor chapter.

Choosing Companions

You should never trek alone. It's useful to have someone to watch your pack – when you have to run off the trail into the bushes, or even when you are in a lodge and go out to the toilet. It's also good to have someone around in case of injury or illness. Women should choose trekking companions carefully and treat with caution any offer of a massage in a remote hotel.

If you do not already have a travelling companion, then you should find either a guide or another trekker in Kathmandu or Pokhara to trek with. If you're looking for a Western companion, check hotel bulletin boards or just chat with someone who sits next to you in a restaurant and perhaps your schedules and ambitions will coincide. Two websites that you can visit to find trekking companions are w www.trekinfo.com and w www.yetizone.com. Unless you have a friend to trek with, or are prepared to take a chance on finding a companion in Nepal, booking a group trek may be a good option.

Trail Conditions

Walking at high altitudes on rough trails can be dangerous. Watch your footing on slippery trails, and never underestimate the changeability of the weather – at any time of the year. If you are crossing high passes where snow is a possibility, never walk with less than three people, and carry a supply of emergency rations, have a map and compass (and know how to use them), and have sufficient clothing and equipment to deal with cold, wet, blizzard conditions.

You will be sharing the trail with man and beasts usually carrying large burdens – not for fun but to scrape a living, so show respect. If a mule train approaches, move to the high side of the trail. If you move to the outside you are at risk of being knocked over the edge. Buffalo will happily trample all over you, especially when they are moving downhill – give them a wide berth.

Register with Your Embassy

All embassies and consulates strongly recommend that their citizens register with them before they hit the trail. They have standard forms that record your name, rough itinerary, insurance details and next of kin, and can obviously speed up a search or a medical evacuation. These are usually kept at the embassy's reception desk and take two minutes to complete. You can avoid a trip to the embassy by filling in a registration form at either the KEEP or the HRA Trekkers' Information Centre in Kathmandu. These organisations regularly forward the forms to the appropriate embassies.

Rescue Insurance

Check that your travel insurance policy does not exclude mountaineering or alpinism. Although you will not be engaging in these activities on the trekking trail, you may have trouble convincing the insurance company of this fact. Check what insurance is available through your trekking company, if using one. Rescue insurance will need to cover an emergency helicopter evacuation or a charter flight from a remote airstrip. You can purchase rescue insurance from most alpine clubs in Western countries. In Nepal, **Neco Insurance** (☎ *01-4427354;* e *info@necoins.com.np; PO Box 12271, Kathmandu)* offers trekking policies. Personal accident, medical and evacuation insurance for trekkers is US$6.88 per day for the first 15 days of trekking and US$4.40 per day thereafter.

Altitude
Walking the trails of Nepal often entails a great deal of altitude gain and loss; even the base of the great mountains of the Himalaya can be very high. Most treks that go through populated areas stick to between 1000m and 3000m, although the Everest Base Camp Trek and the Annapurna Circuit Trek both reach over 5000m. On high treks like these ensure adequate acclimatisation, and the maxim of 'walking high, sleeping low' is good advice; your night halt should be at a lower level than the highest point reached in the day.

Treks

ROUTINES & CONDITIONS
Most trekkers want to get away from roads as quickly as possible, and it is still possible to leave them quickly behind. Nepali trails are often steep and taxing. The old adage that 'the shortest path between two points is a straight line' appears to have been firmly drummed into Nepalis, irrespective of any mountains that may get in the way! In compensation, the trails are often very well maintained. Busy trails up steep slopes are often flagged with stones every step of the way.

A typical day's walk lasts from five to seven hours and involves a number of ascents and descents. It's rare to spend much time at the same level. On an organised camping trek the day is run to a remarkably tight schedule. A typical pattern would be: up at 6am, start walking at 7am, stop for lunch at 10am, start after lunch at noon, stop walking at 3pm. Nepalis rise early, eat very little for breakfast, eat a large lunch in the late morning and a second meal before dark, then retire early – you will be best off following a similar schedule.

A little rudimentary knowledge of the Nepali language will help to make your trek easier and more interesting, although finding your way is rarely difficult on the major trekking routes and English is fairly widely spoken. See the Language chapter for some useful Nepali words and phrases.

Accommodation
Organised treks camp each night and all you have to do is eat and crawl into your tent. Even erecting the tent is handled by the trekking crew, who put it up for you at the site selected by your *sirdar* or group leader.

Independent trekkers usually stay in the small lodges, guesthouses or village inns that have flourished along almost all the popular trails. These lodges range from simple extensions of a traditional family home, (which can sometimes be a plywood firetrap of questionable construction) to quite luxurious places with private rooms, extensive menus and even showers. It's possible to make quite long treks relying entirely on local accommodation and food. Nevertheless, it's still a good idea to carry a sleeping bag as lodges sometimes run out of bedding at peak season, and their bedding can contain unwanted sleeping companions.

Food
On an organised trek your only concern with food is sitting down to eat it. The porters carry virtually all of the ingredients with them, and there will be a cook with well-drilled assistants who can turn out meals of stunning complexity.

Independent trekkers will find numerous places to eat along the most popular trails, although it's often wise to carry some emergency food supplies such as cheese, dried fruit or chocolate bars. On the Everest and Annapurna treks it's unlikely that you will walk more than an hour or two without coming across some sort of establishment that can offer tea, soft drinks, beer, and often a full meal. KEEP and other environmentally concerned organisations point out that dal bhaat is nutritious, easily prepared, available everywhere, and requires a minimum of fuel for preparation. You lessen your impact on the environment and usually eat better if you try to adapt to the local diet.

The standard of cuisine on the Jomsom Trek is so Westernised that it has been dubbed 'the apple pie trail' because that dish features on so many village-inn menus. It's surprising how many places even have cold beer available as well; before you complain about the price contemplate the fact that somebody had to carry that bottle of beer all the way there and will probably have to carry the empty bottle back again!

If you're going right off the beaten track and exploring remote areas like Makalu and Kanchenjunga in the east or Jumla and Dolpo in the west, you must be very self-sufficient. In these relatively untouched areas there is probably very little surplus food for sale and the practice of catering to Western trekkers has not yet developed. Village inns are rare and very rudimentary and sanitation conditions leave a lot to be desired.

CHOOSING A TREK

There are countless long treks in Nepal, some of which still see only a handful of Western walkers each year. Many of the previously off-limits areas have been opened up for trekkers in organised groups including upper Mustang, upper Dolpo, Manaslu, Humla and the Kanchenjunga Base Camp in the northeast of the country.

It is possible to do short treks in Nepal that do not reach demanding altitudes or need sophisticated equipment, years of experience and athletic stamina. Though you will find that a certain level of mental and physical fitness and sensible planning and preparation will ensure that yours is an enjoyable experience. For a selection of short treks see Short Treks Around Pokhara in the Pokhara chapter and Valley Walks and the various hiking sections in the Around the Kathmandu Valley chapter.

The six popular longer treks described in this chapter are: the Everest Base Camp, Helambu, Langtang, Jomsom, Annapurna Circuit and Annapurna Sanctuary Treks.

EVEREST BASE CAMP TREK

Duration	21 or 15 days
Max Elevation	5545m
Best Season	October to December
Start	Jiri or Lukla
Finish	Lukla

This trek takes about three weeks unless you fly in as well as out of Lukla. It reaches a significant height of 5545m at Kala Pattar, a small peak offering fine views of Mt Everest. Although the final part of the trek is through essentially uninhabited areas, small lodges operate during the trekking season so it's quite suitable for independent trekkers.

Everybody knows of Mt Everest and that's the simple reason why the Everest Base Camp Trek is so popular. The trek has a number of stunning attractions; not least of these is being able to say you've visited the highest mountain in the world. In addition there's the spectacular scenery and the outgoing Sherpa people of the Solu Khumbu, the region where Mt Everest and its attendant lesser peaks are located.

It's not until you get right into the Solu Khumbu region that the Everest trek really gets interesting. The first part of the trek is not only a hard slog, but is also pretty sparse in the breathtaking-views department. The trek doesn't follow valleys as the Annapurna treks do. Instead the Everest trek cuts across the valleys. So for day after day it's a tiring process of dropping down one side of a steep valley and climbing up again on the other. By the time you reach the base camp your ascents will total almost 9000m – the full height of Everest from sea level.

The Everest trek starts in Nepali-speaking Hindu lowlands and ends in the Tibetan-Buddhist highlands where the Sherpas are renowned for their enterprise, hard work, civic responsibility and devotion to the practice of Buddhism. In their often inhospitable land, the potato, a relatively recent introduction, is the main crop, but these days trekking and mountaineering are the backbone of the Sherpa economy. More than half the population in the region is now involved with tourism and Namche Bazaar looks more like an alpine resort than a Sherpa village.

Flights In & Out

Most Everest trekkers opt to fly one way to avoid having to repeat the difficult initial leg. This introduces its own problems as flights to Lukla are notorious for cancellations, waiting lists and short-tempered trekkers. If you have the time, walk in from Jiri and fly out from Lukla. For a shorter trip you can fly in to Lukla, trek to Everest and then fly out, again from Lukla, taking around 15 days to trek to Kala Pattar and back. From Lukla you can just visit Thami, Namche Bazaar and Tengboche, which will take about a week.

Emergency Facilities

There are small hospitals in Jiri, Phaphlu and Khunde (just north of Namche Bazaar); the HRA has a medical facility in Pheriche.

Warning

Maoist activity in the Jiri and Charikot regions has resulted in many trekkers on the access trek to the Solu Khumbu region being approached by Maoists and asked for 'donations'. Though no trekkers have been harmed, there have been several ugly confrontations when trekkers refused to pay up. Check the current situation before heading out to Jiri and, as with all treks, cooperate with both government officials and Maoists when required.

Access: Kathmandu to Jiri (via Lamosangu)

Hillary's 1953 British expedition started at Bhaktapur in the Kathmandu Valley. Today you can take the Kodari road to Lamosangu, 78km from Kathmandu, and turn off there to Jiri, a farther 110km. An 'express' bus to Jiri leaves from the Kathmandu City bus station at 7am (Rs 175, 10 hours). Keep a close eye on your luggage. See the Around the Kathmandu Valley chapter for more details on Jiri.

Day 1: Jiri to Shivalaya

The walk starts with a climb to the ridge top at 2370m then drops down to Shivalaya at 1750m. Before the Jiri road was opened the trek used to go through Those (pronounced 'toe-say'), which at that time was the busiest market town between Lamosangu and Namche Bazaar. It is still possible to walk from Jiri to Those and Shivalaya.

Day 2: Shivalaya to Bhandar

From Shivalaya you climb to Sangbadanda at 2150m, Kosaribas at 2500m, then to Deorali, a pass at 2705m. There are hotels here, or you can descend again to Bhandar at 2150m. This Sherpa settlement has a *gompa* (Tibetan Buddhist monastery) and a number of hotels. It's possible to take a short detour between Sangbadanda and Bhandar to visit Thodung at 3090m where there's a cheese factory, established with Swiss aid in the 1950s.

Day 3: Bhandar to Sete

The trail drops down to the Likhu Khola, crosses the river at 1490m, and tracks along it to Kenja at 1570m. Now the long ascent to the Lamjura Bhanjyang pass begins. The first part of the climb is quite steep, then it traverses to Sete, an abandoned *gompa* at 2575m. From here on the villages are almost all inhabited by Sherpas and have both Nepali and Sherpa names (the Sherpa village names are given in brackets).

Day 4: Sete to Junbesi

It's a long but gradual climb to the Lamjura Bhanjyang at 3530m. You're rewarded with frost and often snow along the trail in winter or with lovely flowering rhododendrons in the spring. Goyom at 3300m on your way to the pass is a good lunch stop. The pass is the highest point between Jiri and Namche Bazaar and from the top you descend to Tragdobuk at 2860m, then to the pretty Sherpa village of Junbesi (Jun) at 2675m. Junbesi has a monastery and some good hotels. It is a good place for a rest day with some interesting walks in the vicinity.

Day 5: Junbesi to Nuntala

The trail climbs to a ridge at 2980m where for the first time you can see Everest, then on to Salung at 2980m. A lower trail from Junbesi leads to the hospital and airstrip at Phaphlu and the district headquarters and bazaar at Salleri. From Salung the trail descends to the Ringmo Khola at 2570m. Then it's up to Ringmo where apples and other fruit are grown. The trail from here to Namche Bazaar was rebuilt in the 1980s and avoids many of the steep descents and ascents of the old route.

A short climb from Ringmo takes you to the 3071m Trakshindo La, then the trail drops down past the *gompa* of the same name, and on to Nuntala (Manidingma) at 2250m where there are numerous hotels offering a variety of standards.

Day 6: Nuntala to Bupsa

The trail descends to the Dudh Kosi at 1480m and crosses it to follow the other bank. The trail climbs to Jubing (Dorakbuk) at 1680m and continues over a ridge to Khari Khola (Khati Thenga) at 2070m. You should arrive in Khari Khola early enough to push on up the steep hill to Bupsa (Bumshing) at 2300m. There are several hotels on the top of the ridge and a few less sumptuous hotels at Kharte, 20 minutes' walk beyond Bupsa.

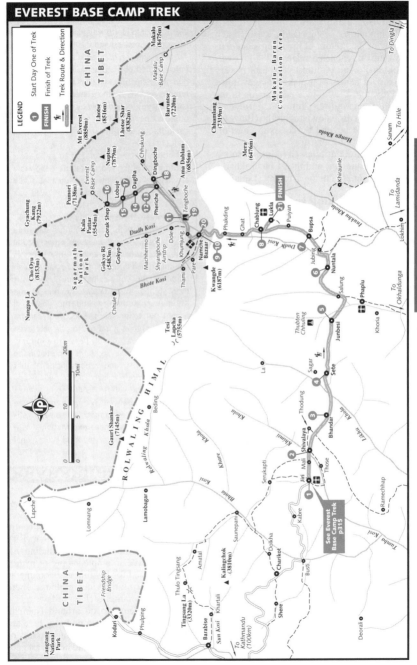

EVEREST BASE CAMP TREK

LEGEND

- **1** Start Day One of Trek
- **FINISH** Finish of Trek
- Trek Route & Direction

TREKKING

CHINA
TIBET

Makalu
(8475m)

Makalu
Base Camp

Makalu – Barun
Conservation Area

To Dingla

To Hile

Hongu Khola

To Sanam

Baruntse
(7220m)

Chhamlang
(7319m)

Lhotse
(8516m)

Mt Everest
(8850m)

Lhotse Shar
(8382m)

Nuptse
(7879m)

Chhukung

Mera
(6476m)

To Khiraunle

To Lamidanda

Everest
Base Camp

Dingboche

Ama Dablam
(6856m)

Pumori
(7138m)

Lobuje

Dughla

Pheriche

Tengboche

To Lökhim

Inkhu Khola

Gyachung
Kang
(7922m)

Kala
Pattar
(5545m)

Gorak Shep

Dudh Kosi

Phakding

Ghat

Chablung

Lukla

FINISH

Puiyan

Bupsa

Cho Oyu
(8153m)

Sagarmatha
National
Park

Gokyo Ri
(5483m)

Gokyo

Machhermo

Dole

Shyangboche
Airstrip

Khumjung

Namche
Bazaar

Pare

Jubing

Nuntala

Dudh Kosi

Nangpa La

Thami

Bhote Kosi

Chhule

Kwangde
(6187m)

Salung

To
Okhaldunga

Phaplu

Khona

Tesi
Lapcha
(5755m)

Thubten
Chhuling

Jumbesi

La

Gauri Shankar
(7145m)

Rolwaling Khola

Beding

Khuda Khola

Khola

Sagar

Sete

Thodung

ROLWALING HIMAL

Khare

Khimti Khola

Bhandar

Likhu Khola

Serukapti

Shivalaya

Mali

Jiri

Those

Ramechhap

Lamobagar

Bhote Kosi

Kosi

Saunepani

Kabre

**See Everest
Base Camp Trek
p315**

Tamba Kosi

CHINA
TIBET

Friendship
Bridge

Lapche

Lommang

Thulo Tingsang

Amatal

Tingsang La
(3320m)

Khartali

Kalinchok
(3810m)

Dolkha

Charikot

Busti

Deorali

Barabise

Sun Kosi

Khartali

Shere

Kodari

Phulping

To
Kathmandu
(100km)

Langtang
National
Park

See Everest Base Camp Trek p315

Day 7: Bupsa to Chablung

From Bupsa the trail climbs gradually, offering views of the Dudh Kosi 1000m below at the bottom of the steep-sided valley, until it reaches a ridge at 2840m overlooking Puiyan (Chitok). The trail is very narrow in places as it makes its way down to Puiyan at 2730m in a side canyon of the Dudh Kosi valley. Climb to a ridge at 2750m then drop down to Surkhe (Buwa) at 2290m. Just beyond Surkhe is the turn-off to Lukla with its airstrip.

The trail continues to climb through Mushe (Nangbug) and then Chaunrikharka (Dungde) at 2630m to Chablung (Lomdza).

Day 8: Chablung to Namche Bazaar

From Chablung the trail contours along the side of the Dudh Kosi valley before descending to Ghat (Lhawa) at 2530m. Part of this village and the old trail were washed away by floods in 1997. The trail climbs again to Phakding, a collection of about 25 lodges at 2800m. Just beyond this at Phakding, you can see signs of the devastation caused by the flooding of glacial lakes.

The trail crosses the river on a long, swaying bridge, then leads you along the river to Benkar at 2700m. A short distance beyond Benkar the trail crosses the Dudh Kosi to its east bank on a suspension bridge (built in 1996) and climbs to Chomoa.

It's a short climb up to Monjo at 2800m, where there are some good places to stay. Show your entrance ticket at the Sagarmatha National Park entrance station, then descend to cross the Dudh Kosi. On the other side it's a short distance to Jorsale (Thumbug) at 2810m, then the trail crosses back to the east side of the river before climbing to the high suspension bridge over the Dudh Kosi.

It's a steady climb from here to Namche Bazaar (Nauche) at 3480m. As this is the first climb to an altitude where AMS may be a problem, take it easy and avoid rushing.

Day 9: Acclimatisation Day in Namche Bazaar

Namche Bazaar is the main centre in the Solu Khumbu region and has shops, restaurants, a bakery, hotels with hot showers, a pool hall, a police checkpoint, a money-changer, a bank and even an Internet service. Pay a visit to the Sagarmatha Pollution Con-

---

The Yeti

Like Bigfoot in North America, the Loch Ness monster in Scotland and the elusive bunyip in Australia, the yeti or abominable snowman is much hunted but little seen. The yeti is a shy humanoid creature that lives high in the most remote regions of the Himalaya. There are countless yeti legends told by the Sherpas and other hill peoples. They tell of its legendary strength, its ability to carry off yaks and even abduct people.

Nobody has ever managed to get a clear photograph of the yeti; footprints in the snow are generally the only indication that a yeti has been by, although hastily gnawed yak bones also add to the yeti legend.

Of course, there are plenty of scientific explanations for yetis. The footprints may have been a human print or some other natural footprint that has appeared to grow larger as the snow melts. Rigorous studies have been made of the yeti scalps found in various monasteries, in particular the one at the Khumjung Monastery, and they have all turned out to be fakes. Keep your camera loaded though; a good photo of a yeti (even a small yeti) will probably be worth a fortune.

There are regular 'sightings' reported in the press every year and various incidents that have no obvious answer are sometimes attributed to the yeti. In 1998 a local woman was murdered between Mong La and Dole on the Gokyo Trek. After much intensive investigation the official police explanation was a yeti attack, and it was reported on regional radio as such!

---

trol Committee office to find out about conservation efforts being made in the region, and also visit the national park visitor centre on the ridge above town (well worth a visit).

Namche Bazaar and the surrounding villages each have an ample supply of hydro-electricity, used for lighting and cooking as well as powering the video parlours. There is a colourful market each Saturday.

There is plenty to do around Namche Bazaar and a day should be spent here acclimatising. Remember that the victims of AMS are often the fittest and healthiest people who foolishly overextend themselves.

Trekkers, Khudi Khola, Annapurna Circuit Trek

RICHARD I'ANSON

Trekkers, Langtang Valley

GARETH MCCORMACK

Manaslu himal

Trekkers, Everest Base Camp

Gauri Shanka, Nepal–Tibet border

It's important to do a strenuous day walk to a higher altitude as part of your acclimatisation, coming back down to Namche to sleep. For this purpose the long day walk to Thami (to the west) is worthwhile.

Day 10: Namche Bazaar to Tengboche

The slightly longer route from Namche Bazaar to Tengboche via Khumjung and Khunde is more interesting than the direct one. The route starts by climbing up to the Shyangboche airstrip. Above the airstrip is the **Everest View Hotel**, a Japanese scheme to build a deluxe hotel with great views of the highest mountains on earth. The hotel has had a chequered history, but is once again open, with rooms at US$135, plus an extra charge for oxygen if needed!

From the hotel or the airstrip you continue to Khumjung at 3790m and then rejoin the direct trail to Tengboche. The trail descends to the Dudh Kosi at 3250m where there are several small lodges and a series of picturesque water-driven prayer wheels. A steep ascent brings you to Tengboche at 3870m. The famous *gompa*, with its background of Ama Dablam, Everest and other peaks, was burnt down in 1989. It has been rebuilt as a large, impressive structure. There's a camping area, a number of places to stay, and during the November-December full moon the colourful Mani Rimdu festival is held here with much singing and dancing.

Day 11: Tengboche to Pheriche

Beyond Tengboche the altitude really starts to tell. The trail drops down to Devuche, crosses the Imja Khola and climbs past superb *mani* stones (carved with the Tibetan Buddhist chant *om mani padme hum*) to Pangboche at 3860m. The *gompa* here is worth visiting and the village is a good place for a lunch stop.

The trail then climbs to Pheriche at 4240m where there is an HRA trekkers' aid post and possible medical assistance. Pheriche has a number of hotels and restaurants that may feature exotic dishes left over from international mountaineering expeditions.

Day 12: Acclimatisation Day in Pheriche

Another acclimatisation day should be spent at Pheriche. As at Namche, a solid day walk to a higher altitude is better than just resting;

Dingboche and Chhukung at 4730m are possible destinations. You could also make a day trip to Nangkartshang Gompa or up past Dingboche. Either walk offers good views.

Day 13: Pheriche to Duglha

The trail climbs to Phalang Karpo at 4340m then Duglha at 4620m. It's possible to continue on to Lobuje, however, the HRA doctors at Pheriche urge everyone to stay a night at Duglha to aid acclimatisation.

Day 14: Duglha to Lobuje

From Duglha the trail goes directly up the terminal moraine (debris) of the Khumbu Glacier for about one hour then left into the memorial area Chukpilhara, before reaching the summer village of Lobuje at 4930m. The altitude, the cold and the crowding can combine to ensure less than restful nights.

Day 15: Lobuje to Gorak Shep

The trail continues to climb to Gorak Shep at 5160m. The return trip from Lobuje to Gorak Shep takes a couple of hours, leaving enough time to continue to Kala Pattar (Black Rock) – or you can opt to overnight in Gorak Shep and reach Kala Pattar the next morning. At 5545m this small peak offers the best view you'll get of Everest without climbing it.

Although there is usually accommodation at Gorak Shep it's nothing to write home about, so it's a better plan to return to Lobuje for the night. The altitude hits nearly everybody; getting back down to Lobuje or even better, to Pheriche, makes a real difference.

Day 16: Gorak Shep to Lobuje

If you want to get to the base camp then it's about six hours round trip from Gorak Shep. There's no view, so if you only have the energy for one side trip, then make it Kala Pattar. The trek to Lobuje is easy, but it seems endless because of the many uphill climbs.

Day 17: Lobuje to Dingboche

Staying the night at Dingboche instead of at Pheriche makes an interesting accommodation alternative. It's a 'summer village' at 4410m with numerous large lodges.

Days 18 to 20: Dingboche to Lukla

The next three days retrace your steps down to Lukla via Tengboche and Namche Bazaar.

TREKKING

There is extreme pressure for a seat on flights out of Lukla, so be sure to have an advance booking, and be there the evening before your flight to reconfirm (the airline offices are generally open from 5pm to 6pm, but sometimes it's 6pm to 7pm). Then be prepared for a torrid time at the airstrip as frustrated trekkers vie for the limited seats. This is especially so when flights have been cancelled for a few consecutive days due to poor visibility, and there is a huge backlog of passengers all wanting to get back to Kathmandu. Lukla has a number of places to stay including the relatively expensive **La Villa Sherpani** and the **Sagarmatha Resort**.

Day 21: Back to Kathmandu
If the gods are with you, your flight will comes in and your reservation won't have been cancelled. Then, after it took you so many days to get here by road and foot, your aircraft only takes 35 minutes to fly you back.

Alternative Routes & Side Trips
Experienced trekkers can consider taking the little-frequented Barabise to Mali route in, avoiding the Jiri road completely.

Another interesting side trip is the nine-day round trip from Namche Bazaar to Gokyo and back. This trek ends at another 'Kala Pattar' with fine, but different, views of Everest. You can even combine both Kala Pattars by crossing the 5420m Cho La, but you had better bring your ice axe and crampons and know how to use them.

A shorter side trip from Namche Bazaar is to Thami, the gateway to Tesi Lapcha and the Rolwaling himal. You can do a round trip to Thami in one very long day, but it's better to stay overnight to catch the morning views.

HELAMBU TREK

Duration	8 days
Max Elevation	3640m
Best Season	October to April
Start/Finish	Sundarijal

A one-week trek that can start and finish in the Kathmandu Valley, which does not offer superb mountain scenery but is culturally interesting. There is plenty of accommodation along the route, but you must still carry a sleeping bag.

Although not as well known and popular as the Everest Base Camp Trek or the Anna-purna Circuit, this trek offers a number of distinct advantages. The trek is easily accessible from Kathmandu. Indeed you could leave your hotel in Kathmandu and set foot on the Helambu trail within an hour. The Helambu Trek only takes a week so it is ideal for people who do not have the time for one of the longer treks. And since it stays at relatively low altitudes it also does not require sophisticated cold-weather equipment and clothing.

The Helambu Trek starts from Sundarijal at the eastern end of the Kathmandu Valley and doesn't climb above 3500m. The trek makes a loop through the Sherpa-populated Helambu region to the northeast of Kathmandu and only the first day's walk is repeated on the return trip. The trek's main drawback is that it doesn't offer fine Himalayan views like other treks, but it can be trekked on a village-inn basis as there are lodges in many of the villages along the trail. The Sherpa people of the Helambu region are friendly and hospitable, just like their kinfolk of the Solu Khumbu region.

Wherever you trek in the region, you will enter the Langtang National Park. The army is particularly conscientious about collecting the Rs 1000 park entrance fee. On this trek there are park checkposts at Magen Goth, Khutumsang and Sermathang that won't let you pass without a park permit (see Documents & Fees earlier in this chapter).

See the Helambu & Langtang Treks map later in this section for this trek.

Emergency Facilities
There is a national park radio at Magen Goth. Telephones are available at Tarke Gyang.

Access: Kathmandu to Sundarijal
Occasional buses leave from Kathmandu's City bus station to Sundarijal (Rs 20), 15km from Kathmandu, or get a bus to Jorpati, just beyond Bodhnath, and catch a Sundari-jal bus at the road junction. A taxi will cost Rs 650. At Sundarijal you enter the **Shiva-puri National Park** *(admission Rs 250)*.

Day 1: Sundarijal to Chisopani
From Sundarijal the trail starts off up con-crete steps beside the pipeline that brings drinking water down to the valley. Eventually the trail leaves the pipeline from near the dam and reaches Mulkharka, sprawling

up the ridge around 1895m, 600m above Sundarijal. There are superb views back over the valley and some tea shops on the pass for rest and refreshment.

The trail continues to climb, but less steeply, through Chisopani at 2300m then the trail drops down to Pati Bhanjyang at 1770m. Chisopani is rather like a grubby little truck stop without the trucks but the mountain views in the morning can be very fine. Take care of your possessions here; it's still rather close to the Kathmandu Valley. There are a number of lodges available at Chisopani.

Day 2: Chisopani to Gul Bhanjyang

The trail heads down to Pati Bhanjyang at 1770m, which has a police checkpoint and a number of lodges. The trail rises and falls through Chipling at 2170m. From here the trail climbs again to reach a 2470m pass before descending a forested ridge to Thodang Betini at 2250m. Continuing along the forested ridge, the trail descends to a large *chorten* overlooking the Tamang village of Gul Bhanjyang at 2140m. This is a classic hill village with a pleasant main street, several shops and a number of places to stay.

Day 3: Gul Bhanjyang to Tharepati

The trail climbs the ridge from Gul Bhanjyang to another pass at 2620m, then it's downhill to Khutumsang at 2470m, in a saddle atop the ridge. The national park office is at the far side of the village. Show your park entry permit or pay Rs 1000 if you started at Sundarijal; you will have to show your permit yet again if you are headed in the opposite direction.

The trail follows a ridge line with views of the Langtang and Gosainkund peaks through sparsely populated forests to Magen Goth (with an army checkpoint) before finally reaching Tharepati at 3640m. The trail to Gosainkund and the Langtang Trek branches off northwest from here. Tharepati has several lodges including the very nicely situated **Himaliya Lodge** on the Khutumsang side.

Day 4: Tharepati to Malemchigaon

From the pass the trail turns east and descends rapidly down a ravine to the large Sherpa village of Malemchigaon at 2530m. There are a number of lodges in the village and a very brightly painted *gompa*.

Day 5: Malemchigaon to Tarke Gyang

From Malemchigaon the trail continues to drop, crossing the Malemchi Khola by a bridge at 1920m and then making the long climb up the other side of the valley to Tarke Gyang at 2590m. This is the largest village in Helambu and the prosperous Sherpas who live here specialise, among other things, in turning out 'instant antiques' for gullible trekkers. There are a number of lodges including the pleasant **Mount View Hotel** on the Malemchi side of the village. Tarke Gyang makes a good place for a rest day or you can take a side trip up to the peak at 3771m overlooking the village. This is the end of the route down from the Ganja La.

From Tarke Gyang there is a very pleasant alternative return route via Sermathang (see Alternative Route from Tarke Gyang to Malemchi Pul Bazaar later).

Day 6: Tarke Gyang to Kiul

The circuit route back to Sundarijal leaves Tarke Gyang past the guesthouse and *mani* wall (walk to the left), then drops off the west side of the ridge in a rhododendron forest, along a broad, well-travelled path. Passing through the Sherpa villages of Kakani at 2070m and Thimbu at 1580m, the trail enters the hot, rice-growing country of the Malemchi and Indrawati valleys.

The steep descent continues to Kiul at 1280m, strung out on terraces above the Malemchi Khola. The trail is now in semitropical banana-and-monkey country at an elevation below that of Kathmandu.

Day 7: Kiul to Pati Bhanjyang

There is construction work in this portion of the valley to build a tunnel that will take water from here to the Kathmandu Valley. The trekking route is likely to be confused and dusty while construction is under way.

The trail descends along a river, crossing it on the second suspension bridge at 1190m then joins a wide trail at Mahenkal and follows it to Talamarang at 940m. The trail follows Talamarang Khola for some distance, then (it's hard to find at times) climbs steeply to Batache and then Thakani, on the ridge top, at 1890m. From here the trail follows the ridge to Pati Bhanjyang at 1770m where the Helambu circuit is completed.

Day 8: Back to Sundarijal
The final day largely retraces the route of the first day's walk.

Alternative Route from Tarke Gyang to Malemchi Pul Bazaar
An alternative route can be followed from Tarke Gyang through Sermathang and then along a ridge through Dubhachaur to join the road at Malemchi Pul Bazaar, south of Talamarang. This route is very pleasant as far as Malemchi and attracts relatively few trekkers. There are numerous lodges at Sermathang and Malemchi but the choice is limited elsewhere.

From Malemchi the final stretch is along a dusty roadway that brings you out on the Kathmandu to Kodari road at Panchkhal, from where you will have to take a bus 55km back to Kathmandu via Dhulikhel. You can usually get a ride on a bus or truck down the road from Malemchi and this route does avoid having to duplicate the final stretch from Pati Bhanjyang through Sundarijal.

(Another Helambu alternative is to start and finish from Malemchi Pul Bazaar, via Panchkhal on the main road, completing the shorter loop, which goes through Malemchi, Talamarang, Kiul, Tarke Gyang as well as Sermathang and Malemchi.)

Day 1: Tarke Gyang to Sermathang
The easy trail descends gently through a beautiful forest to Sermathang at 2620m, the centre of an important apple-growing area. Sermathang is more spread out than the closely spaced houses of Tarke Gyang; there are fine views of the valley of the Malemchi Khola to the south. If you do the trek in the reverse direction this is where you must pay the Rs 1000 entry fee to the Langtang National Park. There are lodges at Sermathang.

Day 2: Sermathang to Malemchi Pul Bazaar
From Sermathang the trail continues to descend to Dubhachaur at 1610m then steeply down to Malemchi Pul Bazaar at 880m where it meets the road. The village has a collection of lodges and village inns.

Buses run frequently along the road (known as the Helambu Hwy) from Malemchi Pul Bazaar via Bahunepati and Sipa Ghat to Banepa where you change to a bus or taxi to Kathmandu.

LANGTANG TREK

Duration	7–8 days
Max Elevation	3870m
Best Season	October to May
Start/Finish	Syabrubesi

This trek can be varied by crossing a high pass down to the Helambu region. There are fine views, interesting villages, and although there are some relatively uninhabited stretches, accommodation is available.

The Langtang Trek, offers many of the benefits of the Helambu Trek, and gives you the opportunity to get right in among the Himalayan peaks and to walk through remote, sparsely populated areas. If you want real adventure then the Langtang and Helambu Treks can be linked by high-altitude passes, via the Gosainkund Lakes or the Ganja La at 5106m (see Langtang Trek to Helambu Trek Crossings later in this section).

Langtang Lirung at 7246m is visible to the north of Kathmandu on clear days. The Langtang Trek can take up to two weeks (although a three-day approach to the heart of the Langtang Valley is suggested here) and lead to the foot of glaciers high in the Langtang Valley. The trail passes through Tibetan and Tamang villages and offers fine views of the Ganesh himal across to the northwest. Although the trek passes through lightly populated and undeveloped areas, it is still possible to stay at lodges at various points along the route. Ascending from just 541m at Trisuli Bazaar to 3870m at Kyanjin Gompa, the trail passes through an ever-changing climate and offers trekkers an exceptional diversity of scenery and culture.

The treks all enter the Langtang National Park and the army collects an Rs 1000 park entrance fee. Checkposts are at Dhunche and at Ghora Tabela. Video cameras are only allowed into the national park after paying a whopping US$1000 fee.

Emergency Facilities
There are national park radios at Ghora Tabela and Langtang, and there are tele-

phones at Dhunche and Thulo Syabru. The Yeti Guest House in Kyanjin Gompa has a satellite phone that can be used to summon a helicopter in an emergency.

Access: Kathmandu to Syabrubesi

It's 72km from Kathmandu to Trisuli Bazaar, which takes about four hours by car or six by bus. The road is paved but very winding with fine mountain views. Ranipauwa is the only large village along the route. From Trisuli, the 50km road leading to Dhunche is steep, winding and rather hairy, passing through Betrawati and Thare. There are buses at 6.30am and 7am from Kathmandu to Dhunche (Rs 110, seven to eight hours). Dhunche is a pretty village at 1950m and here you must pay the entrance fee to Langtang National Park, though it's better to buy the permit in Kathmandu before starting your trek. For more details on the road to Dhunche, see the Kathmandu Valley chapter.

There is a direct bus from Kathmandu to Syabrubesi, about 15km past Dhunche (a one-hour drive). The road descends from Dhunche, gently at first, then in a series of steep loops to a bridge across the Bhote Kosi. Syabrubesi is a string of shops and lodges along the road just past the bridge. A bus departs Syabrubesi for Kathmandu (Rs 140, nine hours) at 7am. You can book a seat in advance at a roadside ticket office.

Day 1: Syabrubesi to Lama Hotel

Start the trek from the camping area below Syabrubesi (New Syabrubesi) and trek northward past some old government buildings to a suspension bridge over the Bhote Kosi, just north of the junction with Trisuli Khola. Turn right at the eastern end of the bridge and walk into the small settlement of Old Syabru.

The trek becomes a pleasant walk through trees where langur monkeys frolic, passing a side stream and small waterfall before reaching three *bhattis* (village inns) beside a stream at Doman, 1680m. The trail then makes a steep climb over a rocky ridge to **Landslide Lodge** at 1810m, where the route from Thulo Syabru joins from above. Over the rest of the day's walk and the following morning, you will pass few settlements, but the forest abounds with birds.

It's then a long climb in forests to another trail junction with a sign pointing to Syabru (Thulo Syabru). This is a new national park trail that local people rarely use. Beyond the trail junction the trail climbs gently to **Bamboo Lodge**, a cluster of three hotels (none made of bamboo) at 1960m. Beyond Bamboo Lodge the trail crosses the Dandung Khola, then climbs to a steel suspension bridge over the Langtang Khola at 2000m.

On the north bank of the Langtang Khola the route climbs alongside a series of waterfalls formed by a jumble of house-sized boulders. Climb steeply to a landslide and the **Langtang View & Lodge** at Rimche, 2400m, and then ascend farther to Changtang, popularly known as Lama Hotel, at 2470m.

Day 2: Lama Hotel to Langtang

The trail continues to follow the Langtang Khola, climbing steeply, at times very steeply, to Ghora Tabela at 2970m, where there are fine views of Langtang Lirung. Although there is no permanent settlement here, there is the good **Lovely Lodge**; your national park entry permit will be checked again here.

From Ghora Tabela the trail climbs more gradually to Langtang at 3430m. The national park headquarters is here and Langtang and the villages around are in Tibetan style with stone walls around the fields and herds of yaks.

Day 3: Langtang to Kyanjin Gompa

It only takes the morning (passing through small villages) to climb to Kyanjin Gompa at 3870m where there is a monastery, lodges and a cheese factory. There are a number of interesting walks from the *gompa* and if you are intending to continue over the Ganja La to Helambu you should spend some time here acclimatising.

Days 4-8: Langtang Valley & Return to Syabrubesi

From Kyanjin Gompa you can climb to a viewpoint at 4300m on the glacial moraine to the north for superb views of Langtang Lirung. Day walks can also be made to Yala or farther up the valley for more spectacular views. You can return to Syabrubesi by the same route or take one of the high routes connecting to the Helambu Trek.

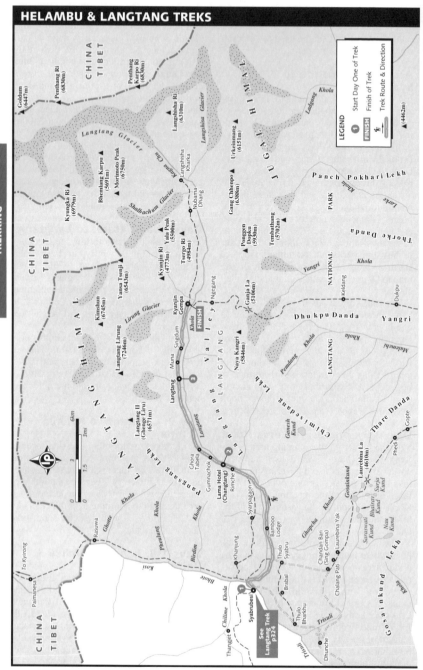

HELAMBU & LANGTANG TREKS

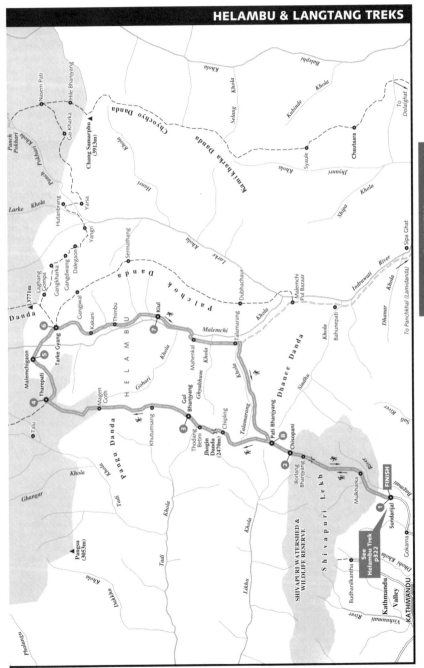

HELAMBU & LANGTANG TREKS

See Helambu Trek p322

LANGTANG TREK TO HELAMBU TREK CROSSINGS

If the weather permits, you could tackle the high route via the sacred and picturesque Gosainkund Lakes to join the Helambu Trek. And if you are a very experienced trekker, and adequately equipped with a good map, tent, stove and food, you could tackle the Ganja La.

Via Gosainkund

The trek via Gosainkund is a way of crossing between the Langtang and the Helambu Treks. Adequate preparation is necessary, but there are village inns along the route, so finding food and accommodation is not a problem in the trekking season. This route does become impassable during winter.

It takes four days to walk from Dhunche, near the start of the Langtang Trek, to Tharepati in the Helambu region. The trek can also be made from Helambu or it can be done by turning off the Langtang Trek from Thulo Syabru, and it is an excellent choice as a return route from the Langtang Trek.

Gosainkund is the site for a great pilgrimage in August each year – this is the height of the monsoon, not a pleasant time for trekking. The large rock in the centre of the lake is said to be the remains of a Shiva shrine and it is also claimed that a channel carries water from the lake directly to the tank at the Kumbeshwar Temple in Patan, 60km to the south.

Day 1: Dhunche to Chandan Bari The first day takes you from Dhunche at 1950m to Chandan Bari (Sing Gompa) at 3330m. The route from **Thulo Syabru** to the *gompa* can be confusing so take care.

Day 2: Chandan Bari to Laurebina Yak The walk climbs steeply with fine mountain views then heads for Laurebina Yak, which has lodges.

Day 3: Laurebina Yak to Gosainkund Lakes The trail drops to Saraswati Kund at 4100m, the first of the Gosainkund Lakes. The second lake is Bhairav Kund and the third is Gosainkund itself at an altitude of 4380m. There are several lodges, a shrine and numerous *paths* (small stone shelters for pilgrims) on the northwestern side of the lake.

Day 4: Gosainkund Lakes to Gopte The trail climbs from the Gosainkund Lakes to the four lakes near the Laurebina La at 4610m. It then drops down again to Gopte at 3440m where there are seasonal village inns. It was in the Gopte area that an Australian trekker became lost in 1991 and was found alive after 43 days. Nearby is the place

where a Thai International Airbus was lost in 1992 and crashed into a mountain.

Day 5: Gopte to Tharepati The final day's walk descends to a stream and then climbs to Tharepati at 3690m, where this trail meets up with the Helambu Trek.

Back to Kathmandu From Tharepati you're on the Helambu Trek and can either take the direct route south to Pati Bhanjyang and Kathmandu or east to Tarke Gyang and then complete the circuit back to Kathmandu.

Warning

The Ganja La is one of the more difficult passes in Nepal and should not be attempted without a knowledgeable guide, adequate acclimatisation, good equipment and some mountaineering experience.

Across the Ganja La

Walking from the Kyanjin Gompa at the end of the Langtang route south to Tarke Gyang in Helambu involves crossing the 5106m Ganja La. The pass is usually blocked by snow from December to March and at any time a bad weather change can make crossing the pass decidedly dangerous. The walk takes five days; between Kyanjin and Tarke Gyang there is no permanent settlement. The final climb to the pass on both sides is steep and exposed. During most of the year there is no water for two days south of the pass. You must come adequately equipped for all these complications.

JOMSOM TREK

Duration	9 days
Max Elevation	3800m
Best Season	October to May
Start	Naya Pul
Finish	Jomsom

This trek from Pokhara up the Kali Gandaki valley is among the most popular in Nepal with superb scenery, interesting people and the best trailside accommodation in the country. It takes a week to reach Muktinath, the end point of the trek. Walking back takes another week or you can fly from Jomsom. See the Annapurna Treks map later in this chapter for this trek.

Access: Pokhara to Naya Pul

Like many other treks in Nepal this one is getting shorter as roads gradually extend

Trekking Around Pokhara

Pokhara is the starting or finishing point for some of the best trekking in Nepal; the long Annapurna Circuit Trek is the most popular trek in the country.

The reasons for the area's popularity are numerous but topping the list is convenience. You can start your trek from Pokhara – there's no long, uncomfortable bus rides or problematic flights to the starting point. Also, because the Annapurna Range is so close to Pokhara you are in the mountains almost immediately.

The treks in this part of the country offer a great deal of cultural and geographic diversity; the Jomsom and Annapurna Circuit Treks both go to the north of the Himalayan watershed, into the dry desert area that is properly part of the Tibetan plateau. Finally, these treks are the best in Nepal for independent trekkers and a network of lodges and guesthouses can be found all along the main trails. The entire region is administered by ACAP, which is working to conserve the natural and cultural resources of the area.

The Pokhara area also offers a number of one-day treks or short three- or four-day treks. These are covered in the Short Treks Around Pokhara section of the Pokhara chapter. There are three popular longer treks, all of which follow the same route at some point.

The **Annapurna Sanctuary Trek** takes you right in among the mountains of the Annapurna Range to the Annapurna Base Camp. This trek takes about 10 days. The **Jomsom Trek** takes about seven days in each direction, but it is possible to fly back to Pokhara from Jomsom. Most trekkers continue a day farther to the holy temple of Muktinath. Finally, the **Annapurna Circuit Trek** takes a full three weeks and completely encircles the Annapurna Range. The last seven days of the Circuit Trek from Muktinath to Pokhara are the same as the Jomsom Trek, but in reverse.

The Annapurna Range is the centre for all of these Pokhara treks. For most of Nepal's length, the Himalaya forms the border between Nepal and China. However, the Annapurnas are different: The border is well to the north in this region, allowing the Jomsom and Annapurna Circuit Treks to go north of the Himalayan watershed, into the high-altitude desert, which is characteristic of the Tibetan plateau.

into the mountains. Eventually it will probably be possible to drive all the way to Jomsom. A road has been pushed through the hills from Pokhara to Baglung to the west. Buses leave for Baglung from the bus stop in Bag Bazaar at the northern end of Pokhara. Take the bus up the ridge to Naudanda and then down into the Modi Khola valley and get off at Naya Pul (New Bridge); the fare is Rs 45, or Rs 750 for a taxi.

Alternative Access Points It's still possible to walk all the way from Pokhara to Birethanti. You can reach Naudanda by walking through Sarangkot (see the Pokhara chapter for details) and along the ridge to Kaski, which has the ruins of a small palace, and on to Naudanda. There are fine views of the whole Annapurna Range, Pokhara and Phewa Tal from this large village. Naudanda has a choice of hotels. From Naudanda, follow the road for a bit, then turn off past Khare to Chandrakot and drop to Birethanti.

You can also avoid the long climb over the Ghorapani hill by taking the bus on to Beni farther northwest of Pokhara. From here it's a two-day walk up the Kali Gandaki valley to Tatopani.

If you want to trek the route just one way, it can save a lot of time and hassle and make the duration of your trek much more predictable to fly to Jomsom first. In this way, you avoid the predicament of being stuck in Jomsom during flight cancellations. However, you will need to account for the sudden gain in altitude if continuing to Muktinath.

Day 1: Naya Pul to Tikedungha

From Naya Pul it's a short walk up Modi Khola to the large village of Birethanti at 1000m, where you can really see how civilised this trek is. Birethanti has a bakery, bank and even sidewalk cafés! A trail north to Ghandruk turns off here. Birethanti has excellent hotels but you may want to continue farther to shorten the next day's long climb. Sticking to the northern side of the Bhurungdi Khola, the trail climbs to Hille and nearby Tikedungha at 1525m. Both Tikedungha and Hille have places to stay.

Day 2: Tikedungha to Ghorapani

From Tikedungha the trail drops down and crosses the Bhurungdi Khola, then climbs very steeply up a stone staircase to Ulleri, a large Magar village at 1960m. It continues to ascend, but more gently, through fine forests of oak and rhododendron to Banthanti at 2250m and then Nangathanti at 2460m. Another hour's walk brings you to Ghorapani at 2750m.

Only a short walk beyond Ghorapani is the Deorali pass and village (*deorali* means 'pass') with spectacular views, and this is where most people stay. An hour's climb from here will take you to Poon (or Pun) Hill at 3210m, one of the best Himalayan viewpoints in Nepal. There are hotels at Ghorapani and at Deorali. *Ghora* means 'horse' and *pani* means 'water' and indeed, long caravans of pack horses were once a regular sight here. The pack horses now go to and from Beni along the Kali Gandaki valley.

A trail also runs from Ghorapani/Deorali to Ghandruk. This part of the trek is plagued by leeches during the monsoon and there may be snow on the trail in the winter.

Day 3: Ghorapani to Tatopani

The trail descends steeply to Chitre at 2420m where there are more lodges. From here the hills are extensively terraced as the trail drops down through Sikha, a large village with shops and hotels at 1980m, and then descends gently to Ghara at 1780m. A farther steep descent of 380m takes you to Ghar Khola village where the trail crosses the river on a suspension bridge and then climbs up above the Kali Gandaki before crossing that too. There's also an ACAP checkpost.

Turning north the trail soon reaches Tatopani at 1190m. It's a busy population centre, although a monsoon flood in the late 1980s washed away a number of lodges and bathing pools, and the remainder of the village sits precariously on a shelf above the river. Tatopani offers some of the best food along the whole trail, and you can even get a cold beer to go with it. *Tato* means 'hot', so the name is earned courtesy of the hot

springs by the river. Tatopani is a popular destination for a shorter trek out of Pokhara. At the south end of the village is the trail to the hot springs and a police checkpost where you must register.

Day 4: Tatopani to Ghasa

The trail now follows the Kali Gandaki valley to Jomsom. The river cuts a channel between the peaks of Annapurna I and Dhaulagiri, thus qualifying the Kali Gandaki valley for the title of the world's deepest gorge. The two 8000m-plus mountaintops are only 38km apart and the river flows between them at a height of less than 2200m.

The Kali Gandaki valley is also the home for the Thakalis, an ethnic group noted for their trading and business expertise, particularly in running hotels and lodges not only here in their homeland but also in Pokhara and elsewhere in Nepal.

From Tatopani the route climbs across several landslides and ascends gradually to Dana at 1400m. This is where the difficult track branches off to Maurice Herzog's base camp, used for his historic ascent of Annapurna in 1950.

The trail continues to climb to Rupse Chhahara at 1560m and at one stage takes a precarious route through a steep, narrow section of the gorge. A suspension bridge crosses the river at 1620m and the trail crosses back again at 1880m, then through Ghasa, the first Thakali village, at 2120m.

Day 5: Ghasa to Larjung

A steep climb through forest takes you to the Lete Khola, then to the village of Lete at 2430m, with a superb view of the eastern flank of Dhaulagiri, and finally to Kalopani at 2530m. Kalopani has great mountain views and some comfortable lodges to view them from.

From Kalopani the trail crosses to the east side of the Kali Gandaki, before crossing back again at Larjung. This village at 2570m has interesting alleyways and tunnels between the houses, an attempt to avoid the fierce winds that often whistle down the Kali Gandaki valley.

Day 6: Larjung to Marpha

Khobang at 2580m is a village with a *gompa* above it, and the mountain views on this stretch are the best to be seen.

Saligrams

The black fossils of marine animals known as saligrams are found at several points along the Kali Gandaki, most notably in the area north of Jomsom around Muktinath, but also at Ridi Bazaar and Devghat. These ammonite fossils date back to the Jurassic period over 100 million years ago and provide dramatic evidence that the mighty Himalaya was indeed once under water.

Saligrams are considered holy emblems. They are sometimes believed to represent Vishnu, and are often held during worship and when making a puja. In Pokhara, the image of the goddess Durga (Parvati) in her Binde Basini Bhagwati form is a saligram.

You will see many saligrams on sale in Pokhara or along the Jomsom trail. Think twice before buying them; firstly, it is actually illegal to collect them, because the government is concerned about potential damage to Nepal's fossil record; secondly, they're overpriced; and thirdly, adding rocks to your backpack is never a good idea.

Tukuche at 2590m is one of the most important Thakali villages, once a meeting place for traders from Tibet. Despite the growth of tourism in this area, Tukuche is still a quieter, smaller place than it was during this era of trade.

From here the landscape changes as you enter the drier and more desert-like country north of the Himalayan watershed. It also gets windier; gentle breezes from the north shift to a gale from the south as the morning wears on. Marpha, at 2680m, virtually huddles behind a ridge to keep out of the wind. The village also has some of the most luxurious accommodation to be found along the trail which makes it a good alternative to staying in Jomsom. A government-established project between Tukuche and Marpha produces fruit and vegetables for the whole region.

Day 7: Marpha to Kagbeni

The trail continues along the valley side, rising gradually before crossing over a low ridge to Jomsom. At 2713m, Jomsom is the major centre in the region and it has facilites such as a hospital, an ACAP visitor centre and a police checkpost (where you must register and get your ACAP permit stamped). This is the last of the Thakali villages; those farther north are inhabited by people of Tibetan descent.

Jomsom has regular flights to Pokhara for US$50.

If you have time left in the day, it's worth following the trail along the river all the way to the medieval-looking village of Kagbeni at 2810m. This Tibetan-influenced settlement has a number of good lodges, and is as

close as you can get to Lo Monthang, the capital of the legendary kingdom of Mustang farther to the north, without paying a US$700 permit fee.

There is a recently built bridge and trail up the west bank of the Kali Gandaki, which provides an alternative to the original trail up the east bank.

Day 8: Kagbeni to Muktinath

From Kagbeni the path climbs steeply to rejoin the direct trail leading to Khingar at 3200m. The trail climbs through a desert landscape then past meadows and streams to the village of Jharkot at 3500m. A farther climb brings you to Ranipauwa, the accommodation area of Muktinath, at 3710m.

Muktinath is a pilgrimage centre for Buddhists and Hindus. You'll see Tibetan traders as well as sadhus (holy men) from as far away as the south of India. The shrines, in a grove of trees, include a Buddhist gompa and the Vishnu temple of Jiwala Mayi. An old temple nearby shelters a spring and natural gas jets that provide Muktinath's famous eternal flame. It's the earth-water-fire combination that accounts for Muktinath's great religious significance.

Back to Pokhara or Jomsom

From Muktinath you can retrace your steps to Pokhara, or simply trek back to Jomsom and hope to catch a flight from there. It is possible to continue beyond Muktinath and cross the Thorung La to walk the rest of the Annapurna Circuit but this long walk is better made in the opposite direction – it's a long, hard climb of 1600m ascent from Muktinath to the pass.

ANNAPURNA CIRCUIT TREK

Duration	16–18 days
Max Elevation	5416m
Best Season	October to November
Start	Besisahar
Finish	Naya Pul or Beni

It takes nearly three weeks to walk the entire Annapurna Circuit; for scenery and cultural diversity this is the best trek in Nepal. It crosses to the north of the main Himalayan range, on to the trans-Himalaya, and crosses a 5416m pass. The last week of the trek is the Jomsom Trek in reverse following the dramatic Kali Gandaki valley.

Since it opened to foreign trekkers in 1977, the trek around Annapurna has become the most popular trek in Nepal. It passes through country inhabited by a wide diversity of peoples, it offers spectacular mountain scenery and it goes to the north of the main Himalayan range to the dry Tibet-like trans-Himalaya. It also has the advantage of having accommodation available each night.

The circuit is usually walked counter-clockwise due to the steepness of the track to the Thorung La. For many people, this is too much to manage in one day. The Thorung La at 5416m is often closed due to snow from mid-December to mid-March and bad weather can move in at any time. The trail to Thorung La can be hard to find when covered in snow. Trekkers should be prepared to turn back due to the weather and altitude. Porters must be adequately equipped for severe cold and snow.

After you cross the Thorung La from Manang to Muktinath, the final seven days of the circuit trek are the same as the Jomsom Trek from Pokhara, but in reverse. Completing the Annapurna Circuit in 16 days allows for only one rest and acclimatisation day at Manang. It's very easy to slot a few additional days into the schedule.

Access: Kathmandu to Besisahar
It's a long and somewhat tedious 137km from Kathmandu to the turn-off at Dumre. From Dumre, at 440m, buses and 4WDs run regularly to Besisahar at 820m.

Day 1: Besisahar to Bahundanda
The trail drops, then follows the gentle slope of the Marsyangdi Khola to Khudi at 830m. This is the first Gurung village you reach (many of Nepal's Gurkha soldiers are Gurungs). The Khudi trail offers fine views of Himalchuli (to the northeast) and Ngadi Chuli (aka Manaslu II, and before that, Peak 29) as it climbs to Bhulbhule at 840m. You enter the Annapurna Conservation Area here and must register at the ACAP checkpoint. If you did not get your permit in advance, you will have to pay double.

The trail goes to Ngadi before reaching Lampata at 1135m and Bahundanda at 1310m. Bahundanda has a few shops, several hotels and a Public Call Office (telephone).

Day 2: Bahundanda to Chamje
From Bahundanda the trail drops steeply to Lili Bhir and then follows an exposed trail; occasionally the steep drop beside the track is hidden by thick vegetation. Ghermu Phant has a high waterfall and in Syange, at 1080m, the trail crosses the Marsyangdi Khola on a suspension bridge. The trail then follows the river to the stone village of Jagat, perched strategically in a steep-sided valley and looking for all the world like the toll station for the Tibetan salt trade that it was. The trail descends before climbing through forest to Chamje at 1400m.

Day 3: Chamje to Bagarchhap
The rocky trail follows the Marsyangdi steadily uphill to Tal at 1700m. Here the valley has been filled by ancient landslides and the river meanders through the fertile flat land before disappearing under some huge boulders. Tal is the first village in the Manang district. The trail crosses the valley floor then climbs a stone stairway before dropping down to another crossing of the Marsyangdi at 1850m. The trail continues to Dharapani at 1920m, which is marked by a stone-entrance *chorten* typical of the Tibetan-influenced villages from here northward.

Bagarchhap, at 2160m, has flat-roofed stone houses of typical Tibetan design although the village is still in the transition zone before the dry highlands. A landslide roared through the centre of this village in late 1995 and managed to wipe out much of the village, including two lodges.

Day 4: Bagarchhap to Chame
The trail, often rough and rocky, climbs to Lattemarang at 2440m and then continues

through forest of pine and fir to Kotho at 2640m. Chame, at 2710m, is the headquarters of the Manang district and its buildings include many hotels, a health post and a bank. At the entrance to the village you pass (to the left) a large *mani* wall with many prayer wheels. There are fine views of Annapurna II as you approach Chame and two small hot springs are across the river. The route crosses the Marsyangdi Khola here.

Day 5: Chame to Pisang
The trail runs through deep forest in a steep and narrow valley, and recrosses to the south bank of the Marsyangdi Khola at 3080m. Views include the first sight of the soaring Paungda Danda rock face, an awesome testament to the power of glacial erosion. The trail continues to climb to Pisang, which sprawls between 3240m and 3340m and has many lodges.

Day 6: Pisang to Manang
The walk is now through the drier upper part of the Manang district, cut off from the full effect of the monsoon by the Annapurna Range. The people of the upper part of the Manang district herd yaks and raise crops for part of the year, but they also continue to enjoy special trading rights gained way back in 1784. Today they exploit these rights with shopping trips to Bangkok and Hong Kong where they buy electronic goods and other modern equipment to resell in Nepal.

From Pisang there are two trails, north and south of the Marsyangdi Khola, which meet up again at Mungji. The southern route by Hongde at 3420m, with its airstrip, at 3325m involves less climbing than the northern route via Ghyaru, though there are better views on the trail that follows the northern bank of the river.

The trail continues from Mungji at 3480m past the picturesque but partially hidden village of Bryaga at 3500m to nearby Manang at 3570m where there are a number of lodges and an HRA post.

Day 7: Acclimatisation Day in Manang
It's important to spend a day acclimatising in Manang before pushing on to the Thorung La. There are some fine day walks and magnificent views around the village, and it's best to gain altitude during the day, return-

ing to Manang to sleep. The view of Gangapurna glacier is terrific and can even be enjoyed with a warm Khukri rum from one of the bars. Manang is a trading centre and the villagers have cottoned on to what trekkers want. You can buy film, batteries, sunscreen, Snickers bars and just about anything else a Western trekker could break, lose or crave. The Manangis' legendary trading skills are seen at their keenest here – buy with caution.

Day 8: Manang to Letdar
From Manang it's an ascent of nearly 2000m to the Thorung La. The trail climbs steadily through Tengi, leaving the Marsyangdi Valley and continuing along the Jarsang Khola valley. The vegetation becomes steadily sparser as you reach Letdar at 4250m. The night in Letdar is important for acclimatisation.

Day 9: Letdar to Thorung Phedi
Cross the river at 4310m and then climb up to Thorung Phedi at 4420m. There are two hotels here – at the height of the season as many as 200 trekkers a day may cross over the Thorung La and beds can be in short supply. Some trekkers find themselves suffering from AMS at Phedi. If you find yourself in a similar condition you must retreat downhill; even the descent to Letdar can make a difference. Be sure to boil or treat water here; the sanitation in Letdar and Thorung Phedi is poor, and giardiasis is rampant. There is a satellite phone here that you can use for US$5 per minute in an emergency.

Day 10: Thorung Phedi to Muktinath
Phedi means 'foot of the hill' and that's where it is, at the foot of the 5416m Thorung La. The trail climbs steeply but is regularly used and easy to follow. The altitude and snow can be problems; when the pass is snow-covered it is often impossible to cross. It takes about four to six hours to climb up to the pass, marked by *chortens* and prayer flags. The effort is worthwhile as the view from the top – from the Annapurnas, along the Great Barrier to the barren Kali Gandaki valley – is magnificent. From the pass you have a tough 1600m descent to Muktinath at 3800m.

Many start out for the pass at 3am. This is not necessary and is potentially dangerous

ANNAPURNA TREKS

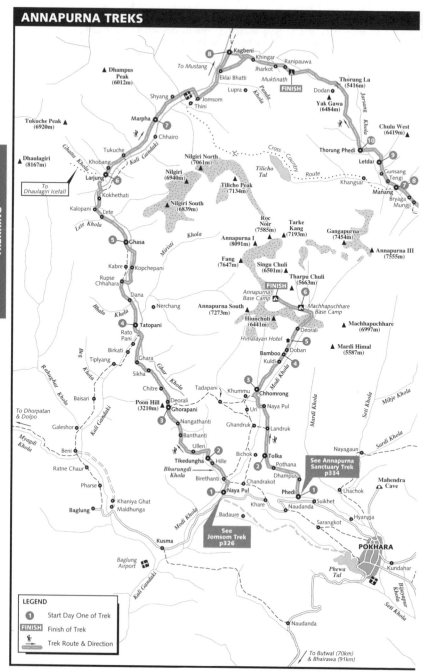

LEGEND

- ① Start Day One of Trek
- FINISH Finish of Trek
- Trek Route & Direction

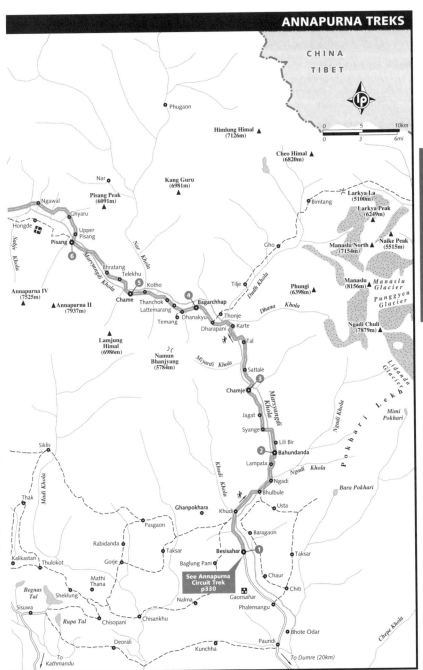

ANNAPURNA TREKS

CHINA

TIBET

TREKKING

Phugaon

Himlung Himal
(7126m) ▲

Cheo Himal ▲
(6820m)

0   5   10km
0   3   6mi

Nar

Larkya-La
(5100m)

Kang Guru
(6981m)

Bimtang

Larkya Peak
(6249m) ▲

Ngawal
Pisang Peak
(6091m) ▲

Ghyaru

Manaslu North ▲
(7154m)

Naike Peak
(5515m) ▲

Hongde

Upper
Pisang

Gho

Pisang ⑥

Bhratang
Telekhu

Tilje

Phungi
(6398m) ▲

Manaslu
(8156m) ▲

Manaslu
Glacier

Kotho ⑤

Annapurna IV
(7525m) ▲

Chame

Thanchok
Lattemarang

Bagarchhap ④

Dhana Khola

Punggyen
Glacier

▲ Annapurna II
(7937m)

Temang

Dhanakyu

Thonje
Karte

Ngadi Chuli
(7879m) ▲

Lamjung
Himal
(6986m) ▲

Dharapani

Tal

Namun
Bhanjyang
(5784m)

Sattale

Chamje ③

Jagat

Marsyangdi Khola

Siklis

Syange

Lili Bir

Bahundanda ②

Mimi
Pokhari

Thak

Lampata

Ngadi

Ngadi Khola

Bara Pokhari

Ghanpokhara

Khudi

Bhulbule

Usta

Pasgaon

Rabidanda

Taksar

Baragaon

Kalikastan Thulokot

Gorje

Besisahar ①

Taksar

Mathi
Thana

Baglung Pani

Chaur

Begnas
Tal

Sheklung

Nalma

See Annapurna
Circuit Trek
p330

Gaonsahar

Chiti

Sisuwa

Rupa Tal

Chisopani

Chisankhu

Phalensangu

Deorali

Kunchha

Bhote Odar

Chepe Khola

Paundi

To
Kathmandu

To Dumre (20km)

due to the risk of frostbite if you are hanging around waiting in the cold snow for too long. A better starting time is 5am to 6am.

Back to Pokhara

The remaining six to seven days of the trek simply follow the Jomsom Trek route but in the opposite direction.

ANNAPURNA SANCTUARY TREK

Duration	10–14 days
Max Elevation	4095m
Best Season	October to November
Start	Phedi
Finish	Naya Pul

This trek goes into the centre of the Annapurna Range, a magnificent amphitheatre of staggering scale. Glaciers and soaring peaks and an eerie atmosphere create an unparalleled mountain experience.

At one time this trek was a real expedition into a wilderness area, but now there is a string of lodges that operate during the trekking season. The return trip can take as little as 10 or 11 days but it's best appreciated in 14 days. The walk to the base camp can be tacked on as a side trip from the Jomsom or Annapurna Circuit Treks.

There are several possible routes to the sanctuary, all meeting at Chhomrong. The diversion from the Jomsom and Annapurna Circuit Treks is made from near Ghorapani to Ghandruk. See the Annapurna Treks map earlier in this section for this trek.

Access: Pokhara to Phedi

You can take a bus (15 minutes) or taxi from Pokhara a short distance along the Baglung Hwy to Phedi, a cluster of shacks. The start of the trail is outside the Dhampus Mailee Hotel.

Day 1: Phedi to Tolka

From Phedi the trail climbs to Dhampus at 1750m, which stretches for several kilometres from 1580m to 1700m and has a number of widely spaced hotels. Theft is a real problem in Dhampus, so take care.

The trail climbs to Pothana at 1990m and descends steeply through a forest towards Bichok. It finally emerges in the Modi Khola valley and continues to drop to Tolka at 1810m.

Dangers on the Trail

There is significant danger of avalanches along the route to the Annapurna Sanctuary between Doban and Machhapuchhare Base Camp. Trekkers have died and trekking parties have been stranded in the sanctuary for days, the trail blocked by tonnes of ice and snow. Always check with the ACAP office in Chhomrong for a report on current trail conditions, and do not proceed into the sanctuary if there has been recent heavy rain or snow.

There is also a theft racket throughout the Annapurna region, particularly in Dhampus and Tikedunga, but it can happen anywhere. Thieves often cut the tents of trekkers and remove valuable items during the night. Trekking groups have taken to pitching their tents in a circle like an old-time wagon train and posting a guard with a lighted lantern throughout the night. If you stay in a hotel, be sure that you know who is sharing the room with you, and lock the door whenever you go out – even for a moment (and that includes going to the toilet). The thieves watch everyone in order to decide who has something worth taking or is likely to be careless. If necessary they will wait patiently all night to make their move.

Day 2: Tolka to Chhomrong

From Tolka the trail descends a long stone staircase, and then follows a ridge to the Gurung village of Landruk at 1620m. Ten minutes from here the path splits – north takes you to Chhomrong and the sanctuary, or you can head downhill to Ghandruk.

The sanctuary trail turns up the Modi Khola valley to Naya Pul at 1340m. It then continues from Naya Pul up to Jhinu Danda at 1750m and up again to Taglung at 2190m, where it joins the Ghandruk to Chhomrong trail.

Chhomrong, at 2210m, is the last permanent settlement in the valley. This large and sprawling Gurung village has a good choice of hotels, and an ACAP office.

Day 3: Chhomrong to Bamboo

The trail drops down to the Chhomrong Khola, and then climbs to Kuldi at 2470m where there is an abandoned ACAP checkpoint. The trek now enters the upper Modi Khola valley, where ACAP controls the location and number of lodges and also limits their size. If the lodges are full, you may have to sleep in the dining room, or perhaps the lodge owner can erect a tent for you. In winter, it is common to find snow anywhere from this point on. Continue on to Bamboo at 2310m, which is a collection of three hotels. This stretch of trail has leeches early and late in the trekking season.

Day 4: Bamboo to Himalayan Hotel

The trail climbs through Bamboo, then rhododendron forests to Doban at 2540m and on to **Himalayan Hotel** at 2840m. This stretch of the trail passes several avalanche chutes. If you arrive early, it's possible to continue on to Deorali to make the following day easier.

Day 5: Himalayan Hotel to Machhapuchhare Base Camp

From Himalayan Hotel it's on to Hinko at 3100m. There is accommodation in Deorali at 3170m, on the ridge above Hinko. This is the stretch of trail that seems to be most subject to avalanches.

At Machhapuchhare Base Camp (which isn't really a base camp since climbing the mountain is not permitted), at 3700m, there is seasonal accommodation available. These hotels may not be open, depending on whether the innkeeper and the supplies have been able to reach the hotel through the avalanche area.

Be alert to signs of altitude sickness before heading off to Annapurna Base Camp.

Day 6: Machhapuchhare Base Camp to Annapurna Base Camp

The climb to the Annapurna Base Camp at 4130m takes about two hours, and is best done early in the day before clouds roll in and make visibility a problem. If there is snow, the trail may be difficult to follow. There are four lodges here, which can get ridiculously crowded at the height of the season. Dawn is best observed from the glacial moraine a short stroll from your cosy lodge.

Back to Pokhara

On the return trip you can retrace your steps, or divert from Chhomrong to Ghandruk and on to Ghorapani to visit Poon Hill and follow the Annapurna Circuit or the Jomsom Trek route back to Pokhara.

The Ghorapani to Ghandruk walk is a popular way of linking the Annapurna Sanctuary Trek with treks up the Kali Gandaki valley. It's also used for shorter loop walks out of Pokhara (see Short Treks Around Pokhara in the Pokhara chapter for more information).

OTHER TREKS

The treks described earlier in this chapter are used by the vast majority of trekkers. Yet there are alternatives that will take you to areas still relatively unvisited: Kanchenjunga Base Camps, Makulu Base Camp, Solu Khumbu to Hile, Mustang, Dolpo, and Rara Lake treks are some of these. Unfortunately, at the time of writing, all of these treks, except the Mustang trek, passed through 'Maoist country'; check with your embassy for the latest travel advice. For information on these and other treks see Lonely Planet's *Trekking in the Nepal Himalaya*.

MOUNTAINEERING IN THE HIMALAYA

The word 'Himalaya' is Sanskrit for 'Abode of Snows', and Nepal's stretch of the Himalaya has eight peaks over 8000m, including the highest of them all, mighty Mt Everest (8848m). Known to the Tibetans as Qomolangma and to the Nepalis as Sagarmatha, the world's highest place was the overpowering attraction for Nepal's first modern tourists – the mountaineers.

Most of Nepal's important peaks were conquered during the 1950s and 1960s, but this has certainly not diminished the attraction of Himalayan mountaineering. Climbing these giants today is an adventurous sporting activity; 40 years ago it required huge sponsored expeditions.

There are 14 peaks over 8000m in the world and of the 10 highest, eight are in Nepal. Some of these mountains straddle the national border and share the glory with Nepal's neighbours – Everest straddles the border between Nepal and China (Tibet) and Kanchenjunga (8598m) straddles that of Nepal and India.

History

Mountaineering became a fashionable pursuit in Europe during the second half of the 19th century. Having knocked off the great Alpine peaks, Europeans found the much greater heights of the Himalaya an obvious new challenge. An Englishman named WW Graham made a mountaineering visit to Nepal in 1883 and reached the top of a 6000m peak. He was followed by another Englishman, Tom Longstaff, who climbed Trisuli (7215m) in 1907. For the next 20 years this remained the highest summit reached in the world. An Italian attempt on K2, in Pakistan, two years later became the first of the huge Himalayan expeditions involving hundreds of porters.

The West's new-found affluence after its recovery from WWII, together with more modern equipment, vastly improved oxygen apparatus, new mountaineering skills and the reopening of Nepal, led to a golden age of Himalayan mountaineering. The pre-war failures were abruptly reversed in the 1950s, beginning with Maurice Herzog's valiant French expedition on Annapurna in 1950. His team's horrific storm-plagued struggle turned an already extremely difficult climb into an epic of human endurance, but for the first time mountaineers had reached the top of an 8000m peak. After descending the mountain they had a month-long struggle through the monsoon with the expedition doctor having to perform amputations of frostbitten fingers and toes.

The success of the 1953 British expedition to Everest began a trend towards larger and larger expeditions. The few climbers who did reach the summit from these expeditions required a huge pyramid of supporters below them. The effect on the environment was devastating as forests fell to provide firewood for the expeditions and vast amounts of mountaineering equipment and garbage were left behind. The Everest Base Camp has been aptly titled the 'world's highest garbage dump'.

Inevitably, a reaction set in, and while the checklist of important summits was methodically ticked off by huge and expensive expeditions, young climbers were perfecting a wholly different style of climbing on

The Lure of Mount Everest

During the 1920s and '30s, reaching the top of Mt Everest came to be seen as the major goal of mountaineers. Apart from the difficulties inherent in reaching such heights there were also political constraints. Nepal continued to be totally isolated, and all attempts on Everest were made from the Tibetan side.

British assaults were made in 1921, 1922 and 1924. The 1922 expedition used oxygen to reach 8326m, while the 1924 expedition fell just 300m short of the top, reaching 8572m without the use of oxygen. Apart from numerous climbers and support staff, the 1924 expedition utilised at least 350 porters. Such massive numbers of porters and support staff set a pattern that was to continue until recent years.

The discovery in 1999 of the body of British climber George Mallory frozen near the summit is a new chapter in one of the enduring mysteries of mountaineering history. In 1924, Mallory and his climbing partner, Andrew Irvine, disappeared within sight of the top. Did they reach the summit? No-one can be sure. However, Mallory did leave behind his famous explanation of mountaineering – he said he was climbing Everest 'because it's there'. Further expeditions followed through the 1920s and '30s, but no real progress was made, although the 8000m level was achieved a number of times. Maurice Wilson added his name to the Everest legend, and to the Everest death roll, when he died during a bizarre solo attempt on the mountain in 1934.

In 1951, a climber who would soon become very famous took part in an exploratory expedition to the mountain – he was New Zealander Edmund Hillary. Another name, soon to be equally famous, appeared on the list of climbers on the Swiss Everest expedition of 1952 when Sherpa climber Norgay Tenzing reached 7500m. The conquest of Everest finally took place in 1953 when the British team led by John Hunt put those two climbers, Tenzing and Hillary, atop the world's highest peak.

the peaks of Europe and North America. Getting to the top was no longer the sole aim – you had to reach the top with style.

The 'easy' ridge routes were ignored while climbers scaled the most difficult faces, combining athletic skills and high-tech equipment. British mountaineer Chris Bonington was the chief protagonist of this climbing style; his brilliant conquest of the southern face of Annapurna in 1970, followed by an expertly organised race up the hitherto unthinkable southwestern face of Everest in 1975, was a supreme example of this trend.

In 1978, the Austrian expedition to Everest put Reinhold Messner and Peter Habler on top without the use of oxygen. Once this 'impossible' feat had been achieved other climbers found they could do the same. Freed from the necessity of carting heavy oxygen cylinders up the mountains, much smaller parties could now attempt the big mountains.

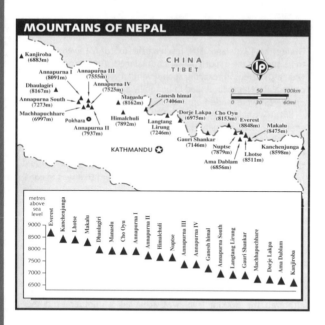

MOUNTAINS OF NEPAL

Today, mountaineering is a sport pure and simple – there's no noise made about its scientific value. In fact, the successes and failures of the various expeditions are regularly reported on the sports pages of the *Kathmandu Post*. Of course, it's also a decidedly dangerous sport; over 1300 climbers have reached the top of Everest, but about 170 climbers have died in the attempt. Some other mountains in Nepal have an even worse record: almost as many climbers have lost their lives climbing Annapurna as have managed to reach the top.

Trekking Peaks

In 2002 the Nepal government expanded the list of designated trekking peaks from 18 to 33. These vary in their level of difficulty and include significant mountaineering challenges. With respect to the mountaineering skills required, the name 'trekking peak' can be quite deceiving. The peaks are found throughout Nepal, are available for small-scale climbing expeditions, and permits usually require an established liaison in Kathmandu. It is, therefore, easiest to use an adventure travel company to organise the climb, rather than do the running around yourself.

Of the 33 'trekking peaks' the 15 peaks designated in 2002 are classified as 'A' peaks, the original 18 as 'B' peaks. Bill O'Connor's book *The Trekking Peaks of Nepal* gives a detailed description of the climb to each of the 18 traditional peaks plus the approach trek to the mountain. Equipment, applications, procedures, weather, health and other matters are also comprehensively covered. There is very little information on the new 'A' trekking peaks.

How High is Mount Everest?

Using triangulation from the plains of India, the Survey of India established the elevation of the top of Everest at 29,002ft (8839m). In 1954, the Survey of India revised the height to 29,028ft (8848m) using the unweighted mean of altitudes determined from 12 different survey stations around the mountain.

On 5 May 1999, scientists supported by the National Geographic Society and Boston's Museum of Science recorded GPS data on the top of Mount Everest for 50 minutes. Their measurements produced a revised elevation of 29,035ft (8850m). Bradford Washburn, renowned mountain photographer/explorer and honorary director of Boston's Museum of Science, said the latest data had been received 'with enthusiastic approval' by the US National Imagery and Mapping Agency and China's National Bureau of Surveying and Mapping. Nepal, however, continues to favour the 8848m elevation.

As part of the same survey, GPS readings from the South Col indicated that the horizontal position of Everest is moving steadily and slightly northeastward at about 6cm a year.

Equator Expeditions (☎ 01-4354169; W www.equatornepal.com) is one company that organises mountaineering courses and ascents of Meera and Island Peaks in the Solu Khumbu region.

Permits & Fees To climb trekking peaks, a permit is required from the **Nepal Mountaineering Association** (NMA; ☎ 01-4434525; W www.nma.com.np.; PO Box 1435, Nagpokhari, Kathmandu). The office is opposite the Biman Bangladesh Airlines office, east of the top end of Durbar Marg. Permits must be applied for in advance and are only valid for one month, although weekly extensions are available for 25% of the total fee. All people ascending trekking peaks must be accompanied by a *sirdar* (leader) who is registered with the NMA.

The fees for climbing trekking peaks depend on the group size and the classification. For group 'B' peaks the fees are: one to four people, US$350; five to eight people, US$350 for the group plus US$40 per person; nine to 12 people (the maximum group size), US$510 plus US$25 per person. For Group 'A' peaks the fees are: one to seven people, US$500; eight to 12 people, US$500 plus US$100 per person.

Mountain Biking

Ah, mountain biking! Strong wheels, knobbly tyres, a wide selection of gears and overall strength – the mountain bike is an ideal, go anywhere, versatile machine for exploring Nepal. These attributes make it possible to escape sealed roads, and to ride tracks and ancient walking trails to remote, rarely visited areas of the country. Importantly, they allow independent travel – you can stop whenever you like – and they liberate you from crowded buses and claustrophobic taxis.

Nepal's tremendously diverse terrain and its many tracks and trails are ideal for mountain biking. In recent years, Nepal has rapidly gained recognition for the biking adventures it offers – from easy village trails in the Kathmandu Valley to challenging mountain roads that climb thousands of metres to reach spectacular viewpoints, followed by unforgettable, exhilarating descents. The Terai has flat, smooth roads, and mountain biking is an excellent way of getting to the Royal Chitwan National Park. For the adventurous there are large areas of the country still to be explored by mountain bike.

The Kathmandu Valley offers the best and most consistent biking in Nepal, with its vast network of tracks, trails and back roads. Mountain biking offers the perfect way to visit the people of the Kathmandu Valley and their wealth of temples, stupas and medieval towns. A mountain bike really comes into its own when you get off the beaten track and discover idyllic Newari villages that have preserved their traditional and rural lifestyle. Even today, it's possible to cycle into villages in the Kathmandu Valley that have rarely seen a visitor on a foreign bicycle. Each year more roads are developing, opening new trails to destinations and villages that were previously accessible only on foot.

Many trails are narrow, century-old walkways that are not shown on maps, so you need a good sense of direction when venturing out without a guide. To go unguided entails some risks, and you should learn a few important words of Nepali to assist in seeking directions. It's also important to know the name of the next village you wish to reach. However, it's no simple task

Highlights

- Biking to heights that initially seem unachievable, with the world's greatest 8000m peaks looming in the distance
- Winding your way through and around the cities and towns of the Kathmandu Valley, which seem to have almost been designed with the mountain bike in mind
- Covering a distance in one day that takes several on foot, at a pace that allows intimacy with your surroundings, the people and their culture
- Exploring mountain villages reached via thrilling mountain trails

to gain the right directions, and any mispronunciations can result in misdirections. The most detailed Kathmandu Valley map is commonly referred to as the 'German map' (also Schneider and Nelles Verlag), and is widely available in Kathmandu. The maps by Karto Atelier are also excellent.

TRANSPORTING YOUR BICYCLE

If you plan to do more than use roads it may be a good idea to bring your own bicycle from home. Your bicycle can be carried as part of your baggage allowance on international flights. You are required to deflate the tyres, turn the handlebars parallel with the frame and remove the pedals. Passage through Nepali customs is quite simple once you reassure airport officers that it is 'your' bicycle and it will also be returning with you, though this requirement is never enforced.

On most domestic flights, if you pack your bicycle correctly, removing wheels and pedals, it is possible to load it in the cargo hold. Check with the airline first.

Local buses are useful if you wish to avoid some of the routes that carry heavy traffic. You can place your bicycle on the roof for an additional charge (Rs 50 to Rs 100 depending on the length of the journey and the bus company). If you're lucky, rope may be available and the luggage boy will assist you. Make sure the bicycle is held securely to cope with the rough roads and that it's lying as flat as possible to prevent it catching low wires or tree branches. Unless you travel with foam padding it is hard to avoid the scratches to the frame, but a day pack may come in handy. Supervise its loading and protect the rear derailleur from being damaged. Keep in mind that more baggage is likely to be loaded on top once you're inside. A lock and chain is also a wise investment.

EQUIPMENT

Most of the bicycles you can hire in Nepal are low-quality Indian so-called mountain bikes, not suitable for the rigours of trail riding. Quality, imported bicycles are slowly becoming available for rent through tour operators. Some of the better rental shops can supply helmets, pannier bags and luggage racks. See Getting Around in the Kathmandu and Pokhara chapters for more information on bicycle hire.

If you bring your own bicycle it is essential to bring tools and spare parts, as these are largely unavailable in Nepal. Unfortunately, carrying a complete bicycle tool kit and spares for every situation may be impractical. The established mountain bicycle tour operators (such as Himalayan Mountain Bikes or Dawn Till Dusk in Kathmandu) have mechanics, workshops and a full range of bicycle tools. Dawn Till Dusk also has a separate repair workshop near Kilroy's ·restaurant in Thamel – see the Greater Thamel map in the Kathmandu chapter.

Fortunately, what the standard local bicycle repair shops lack in spare parts and knowledge of the latest faddish equipment they make up for in their ability to improvise. For basic adjustments their standard of skill is usually high, but you still need to maintain a watchful eye on your equipment during repairs. On the trails you're on your own, so plan for all situations and be ready to improvise.

Sleeping bags, mats and tents can be hired in Kathmandu cheaply. More thin layers of clothes offer better protection and convenience than thick, bulky items. These days a greater number of mountain bike clothing items are being manufactured locally and are of good quality. They are a good buy and may save you luggage space on the way.

Although this is not a complete list, a few items that may be worth considering bringing with you include:

- bicycle bell
- cycling gloves, tops and shorts
- energy bars and electrolyte water additives
- fleecy top for evenings
- helmet
- lightweight clothing (eg, Coolmax and Gor-Tex)
- medium-sized money bag for valuables
- minipump
- spare parts (including inner tubes)
- stiff-soled shoes that suit riding and walking
- sun protection
- sunglasses
- torch (flashlight)
- warm hat and gloves
- water bottles or hydration system (eg, Camelbak)
- windbreaker

ROAD CONDITIONS

Traffic generally travels on the left-hand side, though it's not uncommon to find a vehicle approaching you head-on. In practice, smaller vehicles give way to larger ones, and bicycles are at the bottom of the hierarchy, and will definitely come off second best if they mess with Tata trucks! Nepali roads carry a vast array of vehicles: autorickshaws, tempos, buses, motorcycles, cars, trucks, tractors…Once you've thrown in a few holy cows, wheelbarrows, dogs, wandering children and chickens all moving at different speeds and in different directions you have a typical Nepali street scene. In the past few years the introduction of newer and faster vehicles has added a new element of risk – speed.

The centre of Kathmandu, unfortunately, is a very unpleasant place to ride because of pollution, heavy traffic and the increasingly reckless behaviour of young motorcyclists. If you are sensitive to traffic fumes, consider bringing some sort of mask.

Extreme care should be taken near villages as young children play on the trails and roads. Local pedestrians seem to have a philosophy of 'others can watch out for me', thus they (and drivers) rarely look and appear to have little awareness of surrounding traffic. The onus seems to fall on the approaching vehicle to avoid an incident. On the trails, animals should be approached with caution. Don't even try to predict what a buffalo, dog or chicken will do. A good bicycle helmet is a sensible accessory, and you should ride with your fingers poised on the rear brake lever.

A few intrepid mountain bikers have taken bicycles into trekking areas hoping to find great riding. What they have discovered is that these areas are generally not suitable for mountain biking and they carry their bicycles for at least 80% of the time. Trails are unreliable, and are subject to avalanche and frequent obstacles. In addition, there are always trekkers, porters and local people clogging up the trails. Bicyclists just add one more problem to these heavy-traffic areas in peak season. To say 'I did it' may be enough, but there are other equally great locations that can be ridden. Courtesy and care on the trails should be a high priority when biking.

Riders who have taken bicycles to such places as the Everest Base Camp or around the Annapurna Circuit will know of the long carries. If you decide to indulge in such a bicycle trek, have a good shoulder pad and be thoughtful of others sharing the trail so that opportunities for future cyclists are preserved. While mountain bikes are being banned from many trails around the world, Nepal remains mainly unrestricted, and this is a great attraction of biking here. Some regions are under review, however. The issue is whether trekkers are being hindered by mountain bikers.

TRAIL ETIQUETTE
Arriving in a new country for a short time where social and cultural values are vastly different from those of your home country does not allow much time to gain an appreciation of these matters. So consider a few pointers to help you develop respect and understanding. For more information, see Cultural Considerations in the Responsible Tourism special section.

Clothing
Tight-fitting Lycra bicycle clothing might be functional, but is a shock to locals, who maintain a very modest approach to dressing. Such clothing is embarrassing and also offensive to Nepalis.

A simple way to overcome this is by wearing a pair of comfortable shorts and a T-shirt over your bicycle gear. This is especially applicable to female bicyclists, as women in Nepal generally dress conservatively.

Safety
Trails are often filled with locals going about their daily work. A small bell attached to your handlebars and used as a warning of your approach, reducing your speed, and a friendly call or two of *'cycle ioh!'* ('cycle coming!') goes a long way in keeping everyone on the trails happy and safe. Children love the novelty of the bicycles, the fancy helmets, the colours and the strange clothing, and will come running from all directions to greet you. They also love to grab hold of the back of your bicycle and run with you. You need to maintain a watchful eye so no-one gets hurt.

Conservation
When it comes to caring for the environment, the guidelines that apply to trekkers also apply to mountain bikers. For more detailed information, see Responsible Trekking in the Responsible Tourism special section.

ORGANISED TOURS
A small number of companies offer guided mountain-bike trips. They provide high-quality bicycles, local and Western guides, helmets and all the necessary equipment. There is usually a minimum of four bicyclists per trip, although for shorter tours two is often sufficient. For the shorter tours (two to three days) vehicle support is not required, while for longer tours vehicles are provided at an extra cost.

Tours start at around US$30 for a day trip, US$50 per day for three to four days, and around US$80 per day for long, fully catered trips of up to 21 days. Companies can also organise customized group tours.

The following companies have good-quality imported mountain bikes that can also be hired independently of a tour. Any others fall a long way back in standards and safety.

Dawn Till Dusk (☎ 01-4418286, fax 4412619, ⓦ www.nepalbiking.com) Kathmandu Guest House compound, Thamel
Himalayan Mountain Bikes (HMB)
Kathmandu: (☎ 01-4437437, fax 4410988, ⓦ www.bikingnepal.com) Part of Adventure Centre Asia (ⓦ www.adventurecentreasia .com), Northfield Café entrance, Thamel
Pokhara: (☎ 061-523240) Adventure Centre Asia, Central Lakeside
Massif (☎ 01-4439468, ⓦ www.massif mountainbike.com) Across from La Dolce Vita Restaurant, Thamel

TOURING ROUTES
The Scar Road from Kathmandu

The Scar Rd can be considered one of the Kathmandu Valley's classic mountain-bike adventures. It's got the lot and offers a challenging ride for all levels of experience. It's a 70km round trip, which for the average bicyclist will take around six hours.

Leaving Kathmandu, head towards **Balaju**, on the Ring Rd only 2km north of Thamel, and onto the Trisuli Bazaar road. At this point you start to climb out of the valley on a sealed road towards **Kakani**, 23km away at an altitude of 2073m. The road twists and turns at an even gradient past the **Nagarjun Forest Reserve**, which provides the road with a leafy canopy. Once you're through the initial pass and out of the valley, the road continues northwest and offers a view of endless terraced fields to your left. On reaching the summit of the ridge, take a turn right (at a clearly marked T-junction), instead of continuing down to Trisuli Bazaar. (If you go too far you reach a checkpoint just 100m beyond.) At this point magnificent views of the Ganesh himal (*himal* means a range with permanent snow) provide the inspiration required to complete the remaining 4km of steep and deteriorating blacktop to the crown of the hill just past the Tara Gaon Kakani Hotel in Kakani, for a well-deserved rest.

It is possible to spend the night at this hotel, or at one of the basic village inns, so as to take advantage of sunrise and sunset from this great spot. (See Kakani in the Around the Kathmandu Valley chapter for details.)

After admiring the view from the hotel's garden terrace or a road-side tea shop, descend for just 30m beyond the gate and take the first left on to a 4WD track. This track will take you through the popular picnic grounds frequented on Saturday by Kathmandu locals. Continue through in an easterly direction towards **Shivapuri**. The track narrows after a few kilometres near a metal gate on your left. Through the gate, you are faced with some rough stone steps and then a 10-minute push/carry up and over the hilltop to an army checkpoint. Here it's necessary for foreigners to pay an entry fee of Rs 250 to the Shivapuri National Park. Exit the army camp, turning right where the Scar Rd is clearly visible in front of you. You are now positioned at the day's highest point – approximately 2200m.

Taking the right-hand track you start to descend dramatically along an extremely steep, rutted single trail with several water crossings. The trail is literally cut into the side of the hill, with sharp drops on the right that challenge a rider's skill and nerve. As you hurtle along, take time to admire the view of the sprawling Kathmandu Valley below – it's one of the best.

The trail widens, after one long gnarly climb before the saddle, then it's relatively flat through the protected Shivapuri watershed area. This beautiful mountain biking section lasts for nearly 25km before the trail descends into the valley down a 7km spiral on a gravel road. This joins a sealed road, to the relief of jarred wrists, at **Budhanilkantha**, where you can buy refreshments. Take a moment to see the Sleeping Vishnu just up on your left at the main intersection. From here the sealed road descends gently for the remaining 15km back into the bustle of Kathmandu via Lazimpat.

Kathmandu to Dhulikhel

This two- or three-day circular tour takes you through a classic selection of valley sights. The first day from Kathmandu to Dhulikhel, an interesting hilltop town at 1500m, is 32km; the second day is 58km.

From Thamel, head east out of town in the direction of Pashupatinath and once on the Ring Rd proceed towards Tribhuvan Airport.

Proceed along the northern fringe of the Pashupatinath complex, and look for the trail running to the northern end of the airport runway. From the northeast corner of the runway, ask for directions to the 'Pepsi' and from there head almost due east into the town of Bhaktapur.

If you stay on the Ring Rd instead, follow the western boundary of the airport past the very end of the airport runway to the south. Here the road descends just after branching left followed by a straight run through to the edge of Bhaktapur and the beginning of the Arniko Hwy. A basic map of the area will assist you here.

The Arniko Hwy was built by the Chinese and carries an enormous amount of traffic. The minor roadway running parallel to the highway to the north, via Thimi and into

MOUNTAIN BIKING

Bhaktapur, is a much nicer route. To find the old road, take the first left off the main highway onto a narrower sealed road that heads back towards the airport on its east side. At the next main intersection (1.8km on), turn right before continuing on to complete the 16km to the medieval town of **Bhaktapur**.

You could spend time in this wonderfully preserved kingdom, but if you intend to drive straight through, bear in mind that you'll have to pay Rs 750 to transit through the old town. Continue through the town to the eastern gate, join a tarmac road and then continue straight on, bearing southeast.

The tarmac ends and the road continues in the form of a compacted track towards the rural village of Nala. This route is an excellent alternative to the Arniko Hwy and takes you through a beautiful corner of the valley. The track climbs gradually, and becomes progressively steeper near the top. A gentle 3km downhill gradient brings you to rural **Nala** with its pretty temples.

From Nala head right, via the Bhagwati Temple, and continue for a couple of kilometres to **Banepa**. Turn left and continue along the sealed main road for a further 5km to **Dhulikhel**, which is visible on your right-hand side as you approach, after passing through a truck and bus checkpoint. This completes the first day.

For more information on Dhulikhel and the other towns mentioned here, see the Around the Kathmandu Valley chapter.

Dhulikhel to Namobuddha & Kathmandu The trail to Namobuddha is a popular detour from Dhulikhel, and offers superb trail riding with spectacular views of the Himalaya. See Dhulikhel to Namobuddha in the Around the Kathmandu Valley chapter for a description of the route. From Panauti you join a sealed road that's a flat run along the valley to the main road at **Banepa**. From this point you can return to Kathmandu, 26km via the Arniko Hwy, or ride the 3.5km back to Dhulikhel. The loop from Dhulikhel via Namobuddha is 37km; if you return to Kathmandu it's a total run of 58km via Namobuddha.

Dhulikhel to Kodari

From Dhulikhel, it is possible to continue 82km along the Arniko Hwy to the Friendship Bridge that marks the Tibetan border at Kodari (1500m). This is a three- or (more likely) four-day return trip from Dhulikhel.

Dhulikhel to Lamosangu From Dhulikhel you immediately begin an adrenaline-filled descent (almost 900m) into the **Panchkhal Valley**, on a slick sealed road, with majestic views of the Himalaya adding to a thrilling ride. A couple of short climbs interrupt the descent as you cycle to **Dolalghat**, a popular starting point for Sun Kosi rafting trips. On the downhill watch for overtaking buses on the blind corners.

From Dolalghat (60km from Kathmandu) there is a short 2km climb, and after 20km you cross the bridge over the Indrawati River and climb out of the Panchkhal Valley to join the Bhote Kosi, on your left, which you follow for the rest of the journey. Owing to landslide damage there is a mixture of surfaced and unsurfaced roads. Traffic can be quite heavy along this section. This is a delightful on-road trip with interesting sights, and is also the road to Jiri, a popular starting point for the Everest Base Camp trek. The road climbs at a gentle gradient as it follows the river.

A couple of kilometres past the turn-off to Jiri is Lamosangu, 27km from Dolalghat. **Lamosangu** provides a far more pleasant place to spend the night than Barabise due to the fact that fewer buses stop here. About here you have several options in choosing your next overnight stop. Your choice will depend largely on your progress on the bicycle. Lamosangu is 87km from Kathmandu while Barabise is 90km. A much more upmarket destination is **Borderlands resort**, a farther 13km from Barabise, on a dirt road. A few kilometres farther is the **Last Resort**, another good spot to stay. Many find these riverside safari camps a high point of this ride. See Arniko Highway Beyond Dhulikhel in the Around the Kathmandu Valley chapter for more on accommodation options in this area.

Lamosangu to Kodari & Tatopani The next day's ride continues past **Barabise** where the road changes into a compacted dirt track with a top layer of dust. Recent roadwork along here has improved things, but still the dust cover is transformed into choking clouds when buses pass; in wet weather it all turns to mud. Care should be taken during heavy rains as this section of the road is particularly susceptible to landslides. The valley's sides begin to get steeper and it gradually changes into a beautiful gorge with spectacular waterfalls.

The track climbs practically the entire 27km to **Tatopani** and a farther 5km to **Kodari** at the edge of the Friendship Bridge and the border with Tibet. As it climbs from Tatopani to the Friendship Bridge, this section of the ride is probably the most beautiful. It is possible (but dependent on border guards) for border junkies to cycle beyond the bridge and climb a rough and steep track to the Chinese customs checkpoint (8km), just outside of **Khasa** (Chinese: Zhangmu), which is visible from the bridge. It should be possible to return as far as Borderlands or Lamosangu the same day, taking advantage of a mainly downhill ride. Otherwise, you can stay in Tatopani and visit the hot springs there. Again, see the Around the Kathmandu Valley chapter for information on accommodation.

Tatopani to Dhulikhel The ride back to Dhulikhel is 43km and includes the long climb out of Dolalghat, for which you should allow plenty of time. An option here is to jump on a local bus with your bicycle. Depending on how you feel after the climb, you can stay in Dhulikhel or complete the trip by returning the 32km to Kathmandu.

The Rajpath from Kathmandu

The Tribhuvan Hwy (or Rajpath as it is popularly known) was the first highway to connect Kathmandu with the rest of the world. The road switchbacks 150 spectacular kilometres between Kathmandu and Hetauda. Most traffic from the Terai and India uses the highway that runs to the west between Narayanghat and Mugling – which, although longer, is actually quicker. The Rajpath has a great mixture of light traffic and magnificent scenery, culminating at Daman with an incomparable Himalayan view. It is a classic ride over a 2488m pass on a rough sealed road.

The ride begins on the Kathmandu–Pokhara (Prithvi) Hwy, which gives the only access to the valley. After leaving the valley, the highway descends to **Naubise**, at the bottom of the Mahesh Khola valley, 27km from Kathmandu, where the Rajpath

intersects with the Kathmandu–Pokhara (Prithvi) Hwy. Take the Rajpath, which forks to the left and is well signposted for Hetauda. Start a 35km climb to **Tistung** at a height of 2030m. You climb through terraced fields, carved into steep hillsides. On reaching the pass at Tistung you descend for 7km into the beautiful Palung Valley before the final steep 9km climb to Daman, at a height of 2322m.

This day's ride (almost all climbing) takes between six and nine hours in the saddle. Thus, with an early start it is possible to stay in **Daman**, which will give you the thrill of waking up to the broadest Himalayan panorama Nepal has to offer. On a clear morning you can see from Dhaulagiri to Everest, a view worth the pedal. The following day the road climbs a farther 3km to the top of the pass, at 2488m. At this point, you can savour the very real prospect of an exhilarating 2300m descent in 60km!

As you descend towards the Indian plains, laid out before you to the south, notice the contrast with the side you climbed, as the south side is lush and semitropical. With innumerable switchbacks and a bit of speed you should watch out for the occasional bus and truck looming around a blind corner. The road eventually flattens out after the right turn to cross a newly constructed bridge and the first main river crossing. The rest of the journey is a gently undulating route alongside a river; a farther 10km brings you to **Hetauda**. (See Hetauda in The Terai & Mahabharat Range chapter for details on accommodation.) After a night's rest, you can continue along the Rajpath towards India or turn right at the statue of the king in the centre of town and head towards Royal Chitwan National Park.

Hetauda to Narayanghat & Mugling

Hetauda is just to the east of Royal Chitwan National Park, which has a wide selection of accommodation, both in the park and in the town of Sauraha, as well as a great range of activities. See Royal Chitwan National Park in The Terai & Mahabharat Range chapter for more details. You are prohibited from riding inside the park, but are allowed to ride directly to your resort.

This is vastly different riding from that of Kathmandu, or the other rides described in

MOUNTAIN BIKING

this chapter, and in the summer months (say May to September) it can be a very hot ride. From Hetauda, as you cycle along the flat, smooth road towards Narayanghat enjoying the lush subtropical scenery, watch for resort signposts on your left. Machan Wildlife Resort's turn-off is 40km from Hetauda, and the resort is reached after a farther 4km of beautiful trail riding with three river crossings. Alternatively, a farther 23km from the Machan turn-off brings you to the Chitwan Jungle Lodge turn-off. A farther 14km brings you to **Tadi Bazaar** and the turn-off for **Sauraha**, reached by an interesting 6km-long 4WD track.

From **Narayanghat**, on the banks of the Narayani River 20km from Sauraha, you can return to either Kathmandu or Pokhara via Mugling. Although some may say this section from Narayanghat to Mugling is best avoided on a bicycle because of heavy bus and truck traffic, it is nonetheless a very beautiful section of road to ride, and traffic during many times of the day can be light. The alternative is to catch a bus. If you're heading to Pokhara (96km) it may be a good idea to miss the busy highway between Mugling and Pokhara by catching a bus in Mugling. Here, the road is much improved and vehicles travel a lot faster in what are still quite dusty conditions.

Kathmandu to Pokhara via the Prithvi Highway

A surprisingly large number of bicyclists show an interest in this ride. No doubt the scenery of great Himalayan vistas, the Trisuli River, quaint townships, numerous bridge and river crossings and changing landscapes add to its attraction. The fact that you can escape a bus ride and arrive in Pokhara safely on your own two wheels is a big plus. The downside is that you are almost guaranteed to see the remains of a truck or bus crash any time you travel this road. The message is pretty obvious – take care on this notorious stretch of road.

After leaving the valley on the Kathmandu–Pokhara (Prithvi) Hwy at **Thankot**, the highway descends to **Naubise**, at the bottom of the Mahesh Khola Valley, 27km from Kathmandu, where the Rajpath intersects with the Prithvi Hwy.

Following the thrilling, if not hair-raising, descent (watching for oil slicks after on-the-spot truck repairs), you are on your way for either one long day or two comfortable days of biking to Pokhara. **Mugling** is about the halfway mark at 120km. It's a largely downhill run from Kathmandu so you can reach here comfortably within four to five hours. At Mugling you'll find all the food and supplies you need, plus accommodation for an overnight stay. Just before Mugling, at **Kurintar**, is the idyllic **River Side Springs Resort**. Here you can get good food, a comfortable bed and use of a huge swimming pool. There are also lots of simple food stops along the way at some very scenic spots. See the Kathmandu and Pokhara chapters for details.

To make Pokhara in a day takes around 12 to 14 hours of steady biking, so an early start is needed if you decide to go for it. It's a good idea to calculate the daylight hours available during the season you make this trip. Approaching and entering Pokhara after dark is not advised.

From Mugling you keep to the right as you exit the town and within 300m you will cross the Trisuli River bridge. The second half of your journey to Pokhara is mostly uphill, but still offers some excellent downhills. From Mugling there's overall altitude gain of about 550m over 96km. Again there are numerous roadside cafés and food stops to keep the carbohydrates supplied. The final approach to Pokhara, with the Annapurna Ranges as a backdrop, certainly adds some inspiration after a long day of biking.

Around Pokhara

Pokhara is famous for its beauty, relaxed atmosphere and spectacular views of the Annapurnas and Manaslu himal, as well as the splendour of the unclimbed Machhapuchhare. The surrounding area provides excellent opportunities for trail riding around lakes and rivers and towards the mountains. The riding, however, is less consistent or contiguous than that around Kathmandu, and this means shorter trips. The area is also less populated than the Kathmandu Valley, so although there are fewer trails, villages and temples to explore, the rides are more tranquil and the traffic is hardly noticeable.

Pokhara to Sarangkot & Naudanda

The ride to Sarangkot, visible directly north from Pokhara Lakeside, provides an excellent, challenging day trip. This is in fact the bicycle leg of the Annapurna Triathlon.

Leave early and ride along Lakeside (towards the mountains) to the last main intersection and sealed road. Turn right; this is the road that returns to central Pokhara. After 2km you turn left and continue straight on (north). This intersection is the Zero Km road marker. After a farther 2km there is a smaller sealed road to the left, signposted as the road to Sarangkot. This winds its way along a ridge into **Sarangkot**, providing outstanding views of the Himalaya, which seems close enough to reach out and touch. After 6km a few tea shops mark a welcome refreshment stop just where the stone steps mark the walking trail to the summit. From here it's a 4WD track that closely hugs the edge of the mountain overlooking Phewa Tal. Continue until you join a Y-intersection that doubles back sharply to the right and makes the final climb to Sarangkot Point.

From this point you could also continue straight ahead, riding the narrower motorcycle trails leading to Kaski and Naudanda. After the Sarangkot turn-off the trail soon begins to climb to **Kaski**, towards the hill immediately in front of you. The section to Kaski takes around 30 to 60 minutes, and you may need to push your bicycle on the steeper section near the crown of the hill. Over the top you follow the trail through to Naudanda. You are now at around 1590m, having gained around 840m altitude from Pokhara. The trail is rocky in parts and will test your equipment to the extreme, so do not consider riding this trail on a cheap hire bicycle.

The view from the ridge at **Naudanda** is spectacularly beautiful. Dhaulagiri, Manaslu, the Annapurnas and Machhapuchhare create a classic Himalayan panorama, especially on a cool, clear morning. To the south you can look down over Pokhara and Phewa Tal.

Naudanda to Beni & Pokhara Having reached Naudanda from Sarangkot Point you have the choice of continuing west or east. Heading west, the sealed Pokhara–Baglung Hwy continues along the spine of the ridge and connects Pokhara with Lumle (a popular starting point for trekking in the Annapurnas). If you choose to head towards **Lumle** and on to **Beni** you have a mostly downhill run on sealed roads except for the last 10km into Beni. Riding on to Birethanti may be a good option if Beni is too far. This is an initial 5km up followed by a 20km switchback downhill. There are nice lodges in **Birethanti** (walk in from Birat) for an overnight stop before you return to Pokhara.

From Naudanda it is 32km to Pokhara. You can either return via the Sarangkot trail (described earlier in this chapter) or follow the highway back. The latter starts with a twisting 6km descent into the Madi Khola Valley. The highway has an excellent asphalt surface and descends gently as it follows the river, allowing an enjoyable coast almost all the way back to Pokhara.

This chapter was originally written by John Prosser. For the past two editions it has been updated by Peter Stewart, who again provided his expert advice for this 6th edition.

MOUNTAIN BIKING

Rafting & Kayaking

Nepal has earned the reputation of being one of the best places in the world for rafting and kayaking. Its mountain scenery has drawn trekkers as well as climbers for many years; these same mountains shape an incredible variety of white-water challenges for paddlers.

A series of the world's most outstanding river journeys are found here, ranging from steep, adrenaline-charged mountain streams to classic big-volume wilderness expeditions. The combination of spectacular rivers, mountain scenery and a rich cultural heritage makes Nepal an obvious river-runner's destination.

No other country has such a choice of trips on wild rivers with warm water, a subtropical climate (with no bugs!) and huge beaches with white sand that are ideal for camping.

There has been a continuous increase in the number of kayakers coming to Nepal and it is justifiably recognised as a mecca for boating. Some companies offer trips that cater specifically to kayakers, where you get to explore the river with rafts carrying all your gear and food, and often camp near choice play spots.

The opportunities for kayak expeditions are exceptional. Apart from the rivers discussed later in this chapter, of note and at the right flows are the, Madhi Khola, Tamba Kosi, Karnali headwaters, Thuli Bheri, Balephi Khola and tributaries of the Tamur.

PLANNING

Anyone who is seriously interested in rafting and kayaking, and especially anyone contemplating a private expedition, should get hold of *White Water Nepal*, an excellent guidebook by Peter Knowles, with David Allardice as the consultant on rafting. It should be possible to get copies of the book in Kathmandu. It has very detailed information on river trips, with 60 maps, river profiles and hydrographs, plus advice on equipment and health; in short, it has all the information a prospective river-runner could want.

Anyone who plans to raft or kayak independently should contact local rafting companies to get some up-to-date information. Himalayan rivers are dynamic, and their

Highlights

- Winding along the Sun Kosi through the beautiful Mahabharat Range in eastern Nepal
- Journeying down the Karnali, the longest and largest river in Nepal, with awesome, challenging rapids and plenty of wildlife
- Experiencing a full-on adrenaline rush rafting the Bhote Kosi, the steepest river rafted in Nepal
- Sharing a peaceful moonrise over a picturesque river with your friendly fellow river-runner

rapids change every monsoon. **W** www.raft nepal.com offers an excellent overview of rafting options across Nepal, as well advice about other extreme sports.

When to Go

The best times for rafting are September to early December, and March to early June. From early September to early October, and May to June, the rivers can be extremely high with monsoon run-off. Any expeditions attempted at this time require a very experienced rafting company with an intimate knowledge of the river and strong teams, as times of high flows are potentially the most dangerous times to be on a river.

From mid-October onwards, the weather is settled, and this is one of the most popular times to raft. In December many of the rivers become too cold to enjoy unless you have a wetsuit, and the days are short with the start of winter – the time to consider shorter trips. The summer season from March to early June has long hot days and lower water flows to begin with, which generally means the rapids aren't as powerful. The rivers rise again in May with the premonsoon storms and some snowmelt, then it's high-water time again.

From June to August, the monsoon rains arrive. The rivers carry 10 times their low-water flows, and can flood with 60 to 80 times the low-water levels, making rivers much more difficult. Few rivers should be attempted at flood levels. There is a definite relationship between volume, gradient and difficulty. River levels can fluctuate dramatically at any time, although as a general rule weather patterns in Nepal are quite stable.

Learning to Raft

For many people a rafting trip in Nepal will be their first white-water experience. There are many different kinds of rafting trips, and it is important to select a river that suits your interests and ability. The style of trip, the difficulty of the river and the length of time you have are all factors to consider.

Any raft can be paddled, or rigged with an oar frame and rowed. With an oar frame, the guide normally sits in the middle and rows, while the other passengers enjoy the scenery – and hold on through the rapids. With a paddle raft the guide sits at the back calling instructions and steering, while the crew provides the power. Most active people prefer the teamwork of paddle rafting. With a strong team a paddle raft can probably run harder rapids than an oar raft, and the sense of achievement cannot be compared.

Learning to Kayak

Nepal is an ideal place to learn to kayak and there are quite a few learner kayak clinics on offer with different companies. Teaching yourself to kayak is fraught with problems. At the very best you'll learn horrendous techniques that will yield little satisfaction and will probably have to be relearned later. At the very worst you'll hurt yourself. A qualified instructor is highly recommended.

For the communication required to teach, the best instruction clinics tend to be staffed with both Western and Nepali instructors. Kayak clinics normally take about four days, which gives you time to get a good grounding in the basics of kayaking, safety and river dynamics.

Permits

For certain rivers, rafting permits are not required. There's a list of rivers where rafting is permitted (including all the rivers under River Routes later in this chapter), but this is constantly being expanded, so it's best to check the situation when you arrive.

Equipment

If you go on an organised rafting trip everything should be arranged for you. Normally, all specialised equipment is supplied, as well as tents. A few tips:

- quality equipment is important, for both safety and comfort
- modern self-bailing rafts are essential
- good life jackets and helmets are mandatory on any white-water trip
- modern plastic and alloy paddles are preferable to locally made wooden ones
- ask how old all the equipment is
- roll-top dry bags will keep your gear dry even if the raft flips
- waterproof camera containers will allow you to take photos all the way down the river

Usually you will only need light clothing, with a warmer change for nights. A swimsuit, a sunhat, sunscreen and light tennis shoes or sandals (that will stay on your feet) are all necessary, but can be bought in Kathmandu. Overnight trips require a sleeping bag, but these can easily be hired. Temperatures on some rivers vary, so check with the company you are booking with – they will recommend what to bring. In winter you will need thermal clothing for running rivers.

Most airlines will carry short kayaks on the same basis as surfboards or bicycles; there's no excess baggage charge, so long as you are within the weight limits. If you are a group, negotiate a deal at the time of booking. If there are only one or two of you, just turn up, put all your bulky light gear in the kayak, with heavy items in your carry-on luggage, and smile sweetly! If you phone the airline in advance they have to quote the rulebook and start talking air cargo, which is expensive.

SAFETY

Safety is the most important part of any river trip. Safety is a marriage of the right technical skills, teamwork, planning and local knowledge. Unfortunately, there are no minimum safety conditions enforced by any official body in Nepal. This makes it very important to choose a professional rafting and kayaking company. It seems that not all rafting companies are created equal.

If you choose an organised trip, ask what first-aid gear, supplies, spare parts and repair equipment are carried. It's important that the guides are capable of dealing with any situation that occurs; more so if it is a long wilderness expedition. Many a trip has gone astray because of lack of preparation, not having the right equipment, or insufficient training to deal with the variety of situations that can arise.

This section outlines some of the factors you should consider in ensuring a safe trip, and is based on the experience of many international guides. For more information on choosing a safe company, see Organised Tours later in this chapter.

River Grading System

Rivers are graded for difficulty on an international scale from class 1 to 6, with class 1 defined as easy-moving water with few obstacles, and class 6 as nearly impossible to negotiate and a hazard to life. Anyone who is in reasonable physical shape and isn't afraid of water can safely go on rivers graded class 1 to 3. For more difficult and exciting class 4 rivers, you should be active, confident in water, and have rafting experience. Class 5 is a very large step up from class 4; expect long continuous sections of powerful white water, strenuous paddling, steep constricted channels, powerful waves and the possibility of overturning a raft. Swimming in a class 5 rapid poses a significant risk.

Nepal has a reputation for extremely difficult white water, which is well justified at times of high water flow (during the monsoon), but at most flows there are many class 3 and 4 rivers. There are also many easier class 1 and 2 rivers where you can float along admiring the scenery and running a few small rapids.

Raft Numbers

There should be a minimum of two rafts per trip. If anyone falls out of a raft the second raft can help with the rescue (the victim is known as a 'swimmer'). In higher water, three rafts are safer than two. Many experts also agree that one or two safety kayakers can replace the second raft, though the kayakers need to be white-water professionals with the training, skill and experience not only to run the most difficult rapids on the river, but also to be able to perform rescues in these rapids. Kayakers may also teach you to kayak on the easier sections of some rivers. Among safety kayakers, there is no substitute for skill; having more kayakers along does not necessarily mean a safer trip if these people are

not capable and experienced. Good safety kayakers are invaluable on steeper rivers where they can often get to a swimmer in places no other craft could manage a rescue.

Check how many people have booked and paid for a trip, as well as the maximum number that will be taken.

Raft Guides

The most important aspects of rafting safety are both the skills and judgment of the raft guides and the teamwork of the group on the trip. The person leading the trip must be a qualified guide with a minimum of 50 days of rafting experience. This person should also have done at least five previous trips on the river on which they are guiding. All raft guides should have done the river before.

If possible, speak with the guide who will lead the trip to get an impression of the people you will be spending time with and the type of trip they run. Ask them about their previous experience. Overseas experience or training allows the guides to keep up with the latest advances and safety training. Kayaking experience adds additional depth to a guide's skills. All guides should have a current first-aid certificate and be trained in cardiopulmonary resuscitation.

Many Western river guides have worked in Nepal, shared ideas, strengthened local skills and improved the standard of trips. They pioneered many of the runs that have now become classics. However, all international companies running trips in Nepal, including those that supply their own experienced Western leaders, must run trips in association with local companies. There is rightly a strong sense of pride among Nepali rafters, and reputable companies with reliable guides will seek international accreditation such as the Swiftwater Rescue Technician (SRT) qualification. Himalayan rivers are some of the most powerful rivers run commercially in the world, and expedition guides need to be of the highest standards. The standard of the best Nepali guides is world class, but there are budget outfits where guides do not have river-rescue or first-aid qualifications yet they are leading multiday wilderness trips in Nepal.

On the River

Your guide should give you a comprehensive safety talk and paddle training before

Phoksundo Lake, Shey Phoksundo National Park

White-water rafting, Upper Marsayangdi River

Indrawati River near Sipa Ghat village, Helambu region

Trekkers, near Deurali, with Annapurna South in the background

Pilgrims, Ghasa

Bridge over the Dudh Kosi, below Namche Bazaar

you launch off downstream. If you don't get this it is probably cause for concern.

- Listen to what your guide is telling you. Always wear your life jacket in rapids. Wear your helmet whenever your guide tells you, and make sure that both the helmet and jacket are properly adjusted and fitted.
- Keep your feet and arms inside the raft. If the raft hits a rock or wall and you are in the way, the best you'll escape with is a laceration.
- If you do swim in a rapid, get into the 'whitewater swimming position'. You should be on your back, with your feet downstream and up where you can see them. Hold on to your paddle as this will make you more visible. Relax and breathe when you aren't going through waves. Then turn over and swim at the end of the rapid when the water becomes calmer. Self rescue is the best rescue.

ORGANISED TOURS

There are about 100 companies in Kathmandu claiming to be rafting and kayaking operators. A few are well-established companies with good reputations, and the rest are newer companies, often formed by guides breaking away and starting their own operations, and sometimes people with very little experience of rivers. Although these new companies can be enthusiastic and good, they can also be shoestring operations that may not have adequate equipment and staff. Most of the small travel agencies simply sell trips on commission; often they have no real idea about the details of what they are selling and are only interested in getting bums on seats. To further confuse the situation, there are also sometimes complicated subcontracting arrangements between companies. It is immensely preferable to deal with the rafting company directly.

If a group has recently returned from a trip, speak to its members. This will give you reliable information about the quality of equipment, the guides, the food and the transportation. Question the company about things such as how groups get to and from the river, the number of hours spent paddling or rowing, where the camps are set up (near villages?), food provided (rafting promotes a very healthy appetite), who does the cooking and work around the camp, the cooking fuel used (wood isn't convenient or responsible), what happens to rubbish, hygiene precautions, and night-time activities.

Many companies have a photo file or video in their office, which can give you an impression of the equipment, safety and how trips are operated. Ask a lot of questions.

If your time is limited you may choose to book a trip before you leave home. However, all the operators accept bookings in Kathmandu. Booking in Kathmandu gives you the opportunity to meet your fellow rafters and guides before you make a commitment. Trips depart on a regular basis (there's at least one long trip a week during the season), and the best companies will refer you to a friendly competitor if they don't have any suitable dates.

Rafting trips vary from quite luxurious trips where you are rowed down the river and staff do everything for you (pitch camp, cook and so on), to trips where you participate in the running of the expedition including pitching tents, loading the rafts and helping with the cooking. The quality of the rafting equipment is another variable, and can make a huge difference to the comfort and safety of participants.

Trips range in price from US$15 to US$60 a day, and generally you get what you pay for. At US$15 you don't get much at all. It is better to pay a bit more and have a good, safe trip than to save US$100 and have a lousy, dangerous trip. Bear in mind that trips in Nepal are generally less than half the cost of similar trips in the USA, so in relative terms all the prices are extremely reasonable. If you plan to do a more difficult trip it's particularly important to choose a company that has the experience, skills and equipment to run a safe and exciting expedition.

With the constant change in rafting companies it's difficult to make individual recommendations; the fact that a company is not recommended here does not necessarily mean it will not deliver an excellent trip. Nonetheless, the following companies have been recommended for their professionalism.

Prices for rafting tours range from US$30 to US$60 a day.

Equator Expeditions (☎ 01-4354169, W www .equatornepal.com) in Thamel, Kathmandu; also in Pokhara. This company specialises in long participatory rafting and kayaking trips as well as kayak instruction.

Himalayan Encounters (☎ 01-4417426, e rafting &trekking@himenco.wlink.com.np) Kathmandu Guest House compound, Thamel, Kathmandu;

also in Pokhara. This company is associated with Encounter Overland, and has earned a solid reputation through many Trisuli and Sun Kosi trips.

Himalayan Wonders (☎ 01-4414049, e himalayan@wonders.wlink.com.np) Namche Bazaar Bldg, near Bandari Photo Shop in Thamel, Kathmandu. This reliable company is at the budget end of rafting.

Raging River Runner (☎ 01-4430259, e ragriver@ccsl.com.np) Jyatha, greater Thamel. A recommended budget company.

Ultimate Descents Nepal (☎ 01-4419295, w www.udnepal.com) Adventure Centre Asia, near Northfield Café, Thamel. Specialises in long participatory rafting trips as well as kayak instruction and clinics on the Seti River.

Ultimate Rivers (☎/fax 01-4439526, e rivers@ultimate.wlink.com.np) Next to the Kathmandu Guest House. Ultimate Rivers is associated with the New Zealand company Ultimate Descents International (w www.ultimatedescents.com) and specialises in participatory rafting and kayak instruction.

CHOOSING A RIVER

Before you decide on a river, you need to decide what it is that you want out of your trip. There are trips available from two to 12 days on different rivers, all offering dramatically different experiences.

First off, don't believe that just because it's a river it's going to be wet 'n' wild. Some rivers, such as the Sun Kosi, which is a full-on white-water trip in September and October, are basically flat in the low water of early spring. On the flip side, early spring can be a superb time to raft rivers such as the Marsyangdi or Bhote Kosi, which would be suicidal during high flows. The Karnali is probably the only river that offers continually challenging white water at all flows, though during the high-water months of September and May it's significantly more challenging than in the low-water months.

There is much more to rivers than just white water, but the climate in Nepal being what it is, many companies will promote whichever river they're running at the time as the pinnacle of white-water excitement. Not all companies run all rivers, especially the more technical and demanding ones, and some companies shouldn't be running any rivers at all, but such is life. Buyer beware.

Longer trips such as the Sun Kosi (in the autumn), the Karnali and the Tamur offer some real heart-thumping white water with the incredible journeying aspect of a long river trip. With more time on the river, things are more relaxed, relationships progress at a more natural pace, and memories become entrenched for a lifetime. Long after the white water has blurred into one white-knuckled thrill ride, the memories of a moonrise over the river and friends you inevitably make will remain. River trips are much more than gravity powered roller-coaster rides; they're journeys traversed on very special highways. For many people they become a way of life.

If a long trip is simply impossible because of financial or time constraints, don't undervalue the shorter ones. Anyone who has ever taken a paddle-raft or kayak down the Bhote Kosi (at any flow) would be hard pressed to find anything better to do with two days in Nepal. There are also medium-length options that are perfect for people who want to experience river journeying but have limited time.

The Future of River-Running in Nepal

In the past 15 years, a number of rivers have stopped flowing freely because of construction of hydroelectric projects. Nepal sees hydro development as a means of stimulating economic growth. If this is done responsibly, with consensus among the river-running community and other concerned parties, then there will still be many world-class river runs. But under the present government this may not be the case. A new river project on the Marsyangdi – to take water out at Philesangu and drop it back in at Bhote Odar – has made the Marsyangdi a series of shorter sections. There are projects planned for the Karnali, Arun and Bhote Kosi Rivers. The Nepal River Conservation Trust (NRCT) was formed by a group of concerned river guides in 1995 to raise awareness of the plight of Nepal's rivers, to lobby governments and to promote responsible use of rivers. The NRCT trains river guides in best environmental practice and organises river restoration projects. Contact the **NRCT** (☎ 01-350794; w *www.nepalrivers.org; PO Box 12346 Kathmandu)* for more information.

RIVERS OF NEPAL

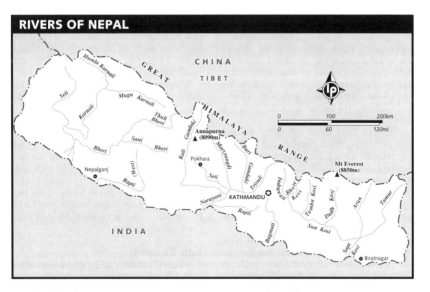

RIVER ROUTES

This section describes the main commercially rafted rivers in Nepal. It is by no means a complete list, and private boaters who have the experience, equipment and desire to run their own expeditions are best advised to consult the aforementioned guidebook, *White Water Nepal*.

Karnali

The Karnali is a gem, combining a short trek with some of the prettiest canyons and jungle scenery in Nepal. Most experienced river people who have paddled the Karnali find it one of the best all-round river trips they've ever done. In high water, the Karnali is a serious commitment, combining *huge*, though fairly straightforward, rapids with a seriously remote location. At low water the Karnali is still a fantastic trip. The rapids become smaller when the river drops, but the steeper gradient and constricted channel keep it interesting.

Being the longest and largest river in all of Nepal, the Karnali drains a huge and well-developed catchment. Spring snowmelts can drive the river up dramatically in a matter of hours – as the river rises, the difficulty increases exponentially. The river flows through some steep and constricted canyons where the rapids are close together, giving little opportunity to correct for potential mistakes. Pick your company carefully.

The trip starts with a long, but interesting, bus ride to the remote far west of Nepal. If you're allergic to bus rides, it's possible to fly to Nepalganj and cut the bus transport down to about four hours on the way over, and two hours on the way back. From the hill town of Surkhet a lovely two-day trek brings you to Sauli, from where it is a two-hour trek to the Karnali River. Once you start on the Karnali it's 180km to the next road access at Chisopani, on the northern border of the Royal Bardia National Park.

The river section takes about seven days, giving plenty of time to explore some of the side canyons and waterfalls that come into the river valley. Better-run trips also include a layover day, where the expedition stays at the same camp site for two nights. The combination of long bus rides and trekking puts some people off, but anyone who has ever done the trip raves about it. Finish with a visit to the Royal Bardia National Park at the end for what is an unbeatable combination.

Sun Kosi

This is the longest river trip offered in Nepal, traversing 270km through the beautiful Mahabharat Range on its meandering way from the put-in at Dolalghat to the take-out at Chatara, which is far down on the Gangetic plain. It's quite an experience to begin a river trip just three hours out of Kathmandu, barely 60km from the Tibetan border, and end the trip looking down the hot, dusty gun barrel of the north Indian plain just nine or 10 days later. Because it's one of the easiest trips logistically, it's also one of the least expensive for the days you spend on a river.

The Sun Kosi starts off fairly relaxed, with only class 2 and small class 3 rapids to warm up on during the first couple of days. Savvy guides will take this opportunity to get teams working together with precision, as on the third day the rapids become more powerful and frequent, and those on highwater trips find themselves astonished at just how big a wave in a river can get.

While the lower sections of large-volume rivers are usually rather flat, the Sun Kosi reserves some of its biggest and best rapids for the last days. At the right flow it's an incredible combination of white water, scenery, villages, and quiet and introspective evenings along what many people consider to be one of the world's great 10 classic river journeys.

Upper Sun Kosi

Not to be confused with the Bhote Kosi, which finishes at Lamosangu, the upper Sun Kosi is a fun 20km stretch of easy class II water and beautiful scenery. From Khadichour to Dolalghat the river is crystal blue, with brilliant beaches on which to picnic. It's a great place for a short family trip or learner kayak clinics.

Trisuli

With easy access just out of Kathmandu, the Trisuli is where many commercial trips operate. This is the cheapest trip available in Nepal – if you sign on to a US$15-a-day raft trip, this is where you'll end up.

What makes the Trisuli so cheap is also what makes it one of the least desirable rafting trips in the country. The easy access is provided by the Prithvi Hwy, which is the only highway connecting Kathmandu and India, and it runs right alongside the river. During most flows the rapids are straightforward and spread well apart. The large number of companies operating on the river drives the prices down, but it also detracts considerably from the experience of the trip. Beaches are often heavily used and abused, with garbage, toilet paper and fire pits well assimilated into the sand. This, combined with the noise and pollution of the highway, makes the Trisuli a less than ideal rafting experience.

It's not all bad news though. During the monsoon months the Trisuli changes character completely as huge run-offs make the river swell and shear like an immense ribbon of churning ocean. There are fewer companies running at this time of the year, and the garbage and excrement of the past season should by now be well on its way to Bangladesh as topsoil.

The best white water is found on the section between Baireni and Mugling, and trips on the Trisuli can be combined with trips to Pokhara or Chitwan.

Kali Gandaki

The Kali Gandaki is an excellent alternative to the Trisuli, as there is no road alongside, and the scenery, villages, and temples all combine to make it a great trip.

The rapids on the Kali Gandaki are much more technical and continual than those on the Trisuli (at class 3 to 4 depending on the flows), and in high water it's no place to be unless you are an accomplished kayaker experienced in avoiding big holes. At medium and lower flows, it's a fun and challenging river with rapids that will keep you busy for three days.

This is one of the holiest rivers in Nepal, and every river junction on the Kali Gandaki is dotted with cremation sites and aboveground burial mounds. If you've been wondering what's under that pile of rocks, we recommend against exploring. Because of the recent construction of a dam at the confluence with the Andhi Khola, what was once a four- to five-day trip has now become a three-day trip, starting at Baglung and taking out at the dam site. At very high flows it will probably be possible to run the full fiveday trip to Ramdhighat by just portaging the dam site. This option would add some great white water and you could visit the wonderful derelict palace at Ranighat, which is slowly being restored. It is a fantastic place to stop and also have a look around.

If you are able to raft to Ramdhighat on the Siddhartha Hwy between Pokhara and Sunauli, you could continue on to the confluence with the Trisuli at Devghat. This adds another 130km and three or four more days. The lower section below Ramdhighat doesn't have much white water, but it is seldom rafted and offers a very isolated area with lots of wildlife.

Seti

The Seti is an excellent two-day trip in an isolated area, with beautiful jungle and plenty of easy rapids. Beware of companies who market this as a hot white-water trip. While it's a beautiful river valley well worth rafting, it's not a white-water bonanza.

This is the perfect river in which to learn to kayak. The water is warm and the rapids are class 2 or 2+. There are a few reputable companies running courses on the Seti.

The logical starting point is Damauli on the Kathmandu–Pokhara (Prithvi) Hwy between Mugling and Pokhara. This would give you 32km of rafting to the confluence with the Trisuli River. This is an excellent trip for learner or intermediate kayakers.

It is possible to raft a higher section, starting at Dule Gouda, which would add another 30km, but considering the quality of the rapids it probably isn't worth it. Beware if you decide to try the upper section of the river, as it disappears underground above Dule Gouda! Perhaps this is what they refer to as class 6.

Bhote Kosi

Just three hours from Kathmandu, the Bhote Kosi is one of the best short raft trips to be found anywhere in the world.

The Bhote Kosi is the steepest river rafted in Nepal – technical and totally committing. With a gradient of 80ft per mile (24m per 1.6km), it's a full eight times as steep as the Sun Kosi, which it feeds farther downstream. The rapids are steep and continual class 4, with a lot of continual class 3 in between.

The normal run is from around 95km northeast of Kathmandu (north of Barabise) to the dam at Lamosangu. The river has been kayaked above this point, but a raft trip here would not be recreational. At high flows several of the rapids become solid class 5, and consequences of any mistakes become serious.

This river is one of the most fun things you can do right out of Kathmandu and a great way to get an adrenaline fix during the low water months, but it should only be attempted with a company that has a lot of experience on the Bhote Kosi, and is running the absolute best guides, safety equipment and safety kayakers. Most trips are two days, but usually the whole river is rafted on the second day, so if you are already up there then it can be done as a day trip.

Camping on the Bhote Kosi is limited, with few good beaches, so some companies have created river camps and resorts between Barabise and Tatopani (see the Around the Kathmandu Valley chapter for details). Rafting the Bhote Kosi out of one of these camps means you get a bit more river time and can relax at the end of a day's rafting or kayaking in pristine surroundings and comfort. The environmental impact of trips is limited by staying at fixed camps, and the camps create local employment and business. These camps and resorts also offer other activities, so you can mix and match what you do.

Marsyangdi

The Marsyangdi was one of the best whitewater runs in the world; unfortunately a hydro project has severely affected this world-class rafting and kayaking river. It is still possible to have a two-day run on the rapids before reaching the dam. The trip starts with a bus ride from Dumre to Besisahar. From here it is a beautiful trek up to the village of Ngadi, with great views of the Manaslu and the Annapurnas ahead of you the whole time. Some companies are trying to resurrect what they can from the changes by combining a short three-day trek with the two-day rafting trip.

From Ngadi downstream to the end of the trip at the dam side above Phaliya Sangu, it's pretty much solid white water. Rapids are steep, technical and consecutive, making the Marsyangdi a serious undertaking. Successful navigation of the Marsyangdi requires companies to have previous experience on the river and to use the best guides and equipment. Rafts must be self bailing, and should be running with a minimum of weight and gear on board. Professional safety kayakers should be considered a standard safety measure on this river.

Tamur

Newly opened and seldom run, this river combines one of the best short treks in

Nepal with some really challenging white-water action. The logistics of this trip make it a real expedition, and while it is a little more complicated to run than many rivers in Nepal, the rewards are worth the effort.

Most expeditions begin with a stunning four-day trek from Basantapur up over the Milke Danda Range to Dobhan. At Dobhan three tributaries of the Tamur join forces, combining the waters of the mountains to the north. The first 16km of rapids is intense, with one rapid feeding into the next, and the white water just keeps coming after that. The best time to raft the Tamur is probably when flows are at medium, which is between mid-October and mid-November.

Other Rivers
The **Bheri**, which is in the west, is a great float trip with incredible jungle scenery and lots of wildlife. This is one of the best fishing rivers and can be combined with a visit to the Royal Bardia National Park.

The **Arun** from Tumlingtar makes an excellent three-day wilderness trip, although the logistics of getting to the starting point are pretty complicated. The **Upper Seti** just outside Pokhara makes an excellent day trip when it is at high flows.

A plethora of rivers in Nepal could be rafted and kayaked, but getting government permission is another matter. Things change quickly and capriciously in this part of the world, and the best advice is to check local information sources (several of them) to see what's running.

This chapter was originally supplied by David Allardice with additional information from Ravi Fry; it was updated by Megh Ale.

Language

It's quite easy to get by with English in Nepal; most of the people the average visitor will have to deal with in the Kathmandu Valley and in Pokhara will speak some English. Along the main trekking trails, particularly the Annapurna Circuit, English is widely understood.

However, it's interesting to learn at least a little Nepali and it's quite an easy language to pick up. Nepali is closely related to Hindi and, like Hindi, is a member of the Indo-European group of languages. For a more in-depth guide to the language, get a copy of Lonely Planet's *Nepali phrasebook*.

Although Nepali is the national language and is used as a lingua franca (linking language) between all the country's ethnic groups, there are many other languages spoken. The Newars of the Kathmandu Valley, for example, speak Newari; other languages are spoken by the Tamangs, Sherpas, Rais, Limbus, Magars, Gurungs and other groups. In the Terai, bordering India, Hindi and Maithili, another Indian language of this region, are often spoken (see the table on this page for a breakdown of first language spoken in Nepal).

Even if you learn no other Nepali, there is one word every visitor soon picks up – *namaste* (pronounced 'na-ma-stay'). Strictly translated it means 'I salute the god in you', but it's used as an everyday greeting encompassing everything from 'Hello' to 'How are you?' and even 'See you again soon'. It should be accompanied with the hands held in a prayer-like position, the Nepali gesture equivalent to Westerners shaking hands.

Studying Nepali

Peace Corps and other aid workers pick up a working knowledge of the language very quickly and there are language courses available that will enable you to get by with just four to eight weeks of intensive study. See the Courses section in the Facts for the Visitor chapter for details. The best source-book for the serious language student is *Teach Yourself Nepali* by Michael Hutt and Abhi Sabedi, which concentrates on both written and spoken Nepali.

Languages of Nepal

Language	% of Total Population
Nepali	50.3
Maithili	11.9
Bhojpuri	7.5
Tharu	5.4
Tamang	4.9
Newari	3.4
Rai	2.4
Magar	2.3
Abadhi	2.0
Limbu	1.4
Gurung	1.2
Sherpa	0.7
Other	8.6

Pronunciation

Vowels

a	as the 'u' in 'hut'
ā	as the 'ar' in 'garden' (no 'r' sound)
e	as the 'e' in 'best' but longer
i	as the 'i' in 'sister' but longer
o	as the 'o' in 'sold'
u	as the 'u' in 'put'
ai	as the 'i' in 'mine'
au	as the 'ow' in 'cow'

Consonants

Most Nepali consonants are quite similar to their English counterparts. The exceptions are the so-called retroflex consonants and the aspirated consonants. Retroflex sounds are made by curling the tongue tip back to touch the roof of the mouth as you make the sound; they are indicated in this guide by an underdot, eg, ṭ, *Kaṭhmaṇḍu*.

Aspirated consonants are sounded more forcefully than they would be in English and are made with a short puff of air; they are indicated in this guide by an **h** after the consonant, eg, **kh**, *khānuhos* (please). You should ensure that you don't confuse the Nepali aspirated combinations **ph** and **th** with their English counterparts in words such as 'phone', 'this' and 'thin'. In Nepali, **ph** is pronounced as the 'p' in 'pit', and **th** is pronounced as the 't' in 'time'.

Both retroflex and aspirated consonants are best learned by having a native speaker demonstrate them for you. You could start with *Kaṭhmaṇḍu*, which contains both retroflex and aspirated consonants.

Greetings & Civilities

Hello/Goodbye.	*namaste*
How are you?	*tapāilai kasto chha?*
Excuse me.	*hajur*
Please (give me).	*dinuhos*
Please (you have).	*khānuhos*
Thank you.	*dhanyabad*

Unlike in the West, verbal expressions of thanks are not the cultural norm in Nepal. Although neglecting to say 'Thank you' may make you feel a little uncomfortable, it is rarely necessary in a simple commercial transaction; foreigners going round saying *dhanyabad* all the time sounds distinctly odd to Nepalis.

Basics

I	*ma*
Yes. (I have)	*chā*
No. (I don't have)	*chhaina*
OK.	*theekcha*
Where?	*kahā?*
here	*yahā*
there	*tyahā*
good/pretty	*ramro*

Do you speak English?	*tapāi angreji bolna saknu hunchha?*
I only speak a little Nepali.	*ma ali nepāli bolchhu*
I understand.	*ma bujhchu*
I don't understand.	*maile bujhina*
Please say it again.	*pheri bhaṇuhos*
Please speak more slowly.	*tapāi bistārai bolnuhos*
I don't need it.	*malai chahiṇa*
I don't have it.	*ma sanga chhaina*
Wait a minute.	*ek chhin parkhanos*

Getting Around

bus	*bus*
taxi	*taxi*
boat	*nāu*
ticket	*tikaṭ*

How can I get to ...?
   ... kolāgi kati paisā lāgchha?
Is it far from here?
   yahābata ke tādhā chha?
Can I walk there?
   hiḍera jāna sakinchhu?

Signs

खुला	Open
बन्द	Closed
प्रबेश	Entrance
निकास	Exit
प्रबेश निषेध	No Entry
धूम्रपान मनाही छ	No Smoking
मनाही, निषेध	Prohibited
शौचालय	Toilets
तातो	Hot
चिसो	Cold
खतरा	Danger
रोक्नुहोस	Stop
बाटो बन्द	Road Closed

I want to go to ...
   ma ... jānchhu
Where does this bus go?
   yo bus kahā jānchha?
How much is it to go to ...?
   ... jāna kati parchha?
I want a one-way/return ticket.
   jāne/jāne-āune tikaṭ dinuhos.
Does your taxi have a meter?
   tapāi ko taxi mā meter chha?

Accommodation

Where is a ...?	... *kahā chha?*
guesthouse	*pāhuna ghar*
hotel	*hoṭel*
camp site	*shivir*
lodge	*laj*

What is the address?
   thegānā ke ho?
Please write down the address.
   thegānā lekhunuhos
Can I get a place to stay here?
   yahā bās paunchha?
May I look at the room?
   kothā herna sakchhu?
How much is it per night?
   ek rātko, kati paisā ho?
Does it include breakfast?
   bihānako khāna samet ho?

room	*kothā*
clean	*safā*
dirty	*mailo*
fan	*pankhā*
hot water	*tāto pāni*

Around Town

bank	*baink*
... embassy	*... rājdutāvas*
museum	*samgrāhālaya*
police	*prahari*
post office	*post afis*
stamp	*tikaṭ*
envelope	*kham*
tourist office	*turist afis*

What time does it open/close?
kati baje kholchha/banda garchha?
I want to change some money.
paisā sātnu manlāgchha

Internet

Is there a local Internet cafe?
ya·hā inṭarneṭ kyah·phe chha?
I'd like to get Internet access.
ma·lai inṭarneṭ cha·hi·yo
I'd like to check my email.
imel chek gar·nu·par·yo
I'd like to send an email.
imel pa·ṭhau·nu·par·yo

Shopping

Where is the market?	*bazār kata parchha?*
What is it made of?	*kele baneko?*
How much?	*kati?*
That's enough.	*pugyo*
I like this.	*malai yo ramro lagyo*
I don't like this.	*malai yo ramro lagena*

money	*paisa*
cheap	*sasto*
expensive	*mahango*
less	*kam*
more	*badhi*
little bit	*alikati*

Trekking

Which way is ...?
... jāne bato kata parchha?
Is there a village nearby?
najikai gaun parchha?
How many hours/days to ...?
... kati ghanṭā/din?
Where is the porter?
bhariya kata gayo?
I want to sleep.
malai sutna man lagyo
I'm cold.
malai jado lagyo
Please give me (water).
malai (pani) dinuhos

way/trail	*sāno bāṭo*
bridge	*pul*
downhill	*orālo*
uphill	*ukālo*
left	*bāyā*
right	*dāyā*
cold	*jāḍo*
teahouse	*bhatti*

Food & Drink

| I'm a vegetarian. | *ma sākāhari hun* |
| What is this/that? | *yo/tyo ke ho?* |

food/meal	*khāna*
bread (loaf)	*(pau) roṭi*
rice/cooked rice	*chāmal/bhāt*
meat	*māsu*
green, leafy vegetable	*sāg*
vegetable (cooked)	*tarakāri*
lentils	*dāl*
egg	*phul/anḍā*
fruit	*phala*
sugar	*chini*
salt	*nun*
pepper	*marich*
curd	*dhai*
milk	*dudh*
tea	*chia*
drinking water	*khāna pāni*

Health

Where can I find a good doctor?	*rāmro dākṭar kaha pāincha?*
Where is the nearest hospital?	*yahā aspatāl kahā chha?*
I don't feel well.	*malāi sancho chhaina*
I have diarrhoea.	*dishā lāgyo*
I have altitude sickness.	*lekh lāgyo*
I have a fever.	*joro āyo*
I'm having trouble breathing.	*sās pherna sakdina*

| medicine | *ausadhi* |
| pharmacy | *ausadhi pasal* |

I have ...	*malāi ... lāgyo*
asthma	*damko byathā*
diabetes	*madhu meha*
epilepsy	*chāre rog*

Times & Dates

| What time is it? | *kati bajyo?* |
| It's one o'clock. | *ek bajyo* |

minute	*minet*
hour	*ghantā*
day	*din*
today	*āja*
yesterday	*hijo*
tomorrow	*bholi*
now	*ahile*
week	*haptā*
month	*mahinā*

| What day is it today? | *āja ke bār?* |
| Today is ... | *āja ... ho* |

Monday	*som bār*
Tuesday	*mangal bār*
Wednesday	*budh bār*
Thursday	*bihi bār*
Friday	*sukra bār*
Saturday	*sani bār*
Sunday	*āita bār*

Emergencies

Help!	*guhār!*
It's an emergency!	*āpaṭ paryo!*
There's been an accident!	*durghaṭanā bhayo!*
Please call a doctor.	*dākṭarlai bolāu-nuhos*
Where is the (public) toilet?	*shauchālaya kahā chha?*
I'm lost.	*ma harāye*

Numbers

0	*sun·ya*	शून्य
1	*ek*	एक
2	*dui*	दुइ
3	*tin*	तीन
4	*chār*	चार
5	*panch*	पाँच
6	*chha*	छ
7	*sāt*	सात
8	*āṭh*	आठ
9	*nau*	नौ
10	*das*	दस
11	*eghāra*	एघार
12	*bā-hra*	बाह्र
13	*te-hra*	तेह्र
14	*chau-dha*	चौध
15	*pan-dhra*	पन्ध्र
16	*so-hra*	सोह्र
17	*satra*	सत्र
18	*a-ṭhāra*	अठार
19	*un-nais*	उन्नाईस
20	*bis*	बीस
21	*ek kais*	एककाईस
22	*bais*	बाईस
23	*teis*	तेईस
24	*chau bis*	चौबीस
25	*pach·chis*	पच्चीस
26	*chhab·bis*	छब्बीस
27	*sat·tais*	सत्ताईस
28	*aṭ·thais*	अट्ठाईस
29	*u·nan·tis*	उनन्तीस
30	*tis*	तीस
40	*chālis*	चालीस
50	*pachās*	पचास
60	*sā-ṭhi*	साठी
70	*sat-tari*	सत्तरी
80	*a-si*	असी
90	*nab-be*	नब्बे
100	*ek say*	एक सय
1,000	*ek hajār*	एक हजार
10,000	*das hajār*	दस हजार
100,000	*ek lākh*	एक लाख
200,000	*dui lākh*	दुइ लाख
1,000,000	*das lākh*	दस लाख

Glossary

Beware of the different methods of transliterating Nepali and the other languages spoken in Nepal. There are many and varied ways of spelling Nepali words. In particular the letters 'b' and 'v' are often interchanged.

ACAP – Annapurna Conservation Area Project

Aditya – ancient *Vedic* sun god, also known as Surya

Agni – ancient *Vedic god* of the hearth and fire

Agnipura – Buddhist symbol for fire

AMS – acute mountain sickness, also known as altitude sickness

Ananda – the Buddha's chief disciple

Annapurna – the goddess of abundance and an incarnation of *Mahadevi*

arna – water buffalo

Ashoka – Indian Buddhist emperor who spread the Buddhist religion throughout the subcontinent

Ashta Matrikas – the eight multi-armed mother goddesses

aunsi – new moon

Avalokiteshvara – as Gautama Buddha is the Buddha of our era, so Avalokiteshvara is the *Bodhisattva* of our era

avatar – incarnation of a deity living on Earth

bagh chal – traditional Nepali game

bahal – Buddhist monastery, usually two storeys high and built around a courtyard; many of these buildings are now used as schools

bahil – simpler version of a *bahal*

bajra – see *vajra*

ban – forest or jungle

bandar – langur monkeys

bandh – the severest form of strike where all shops, schools and offices are closed and vehicles don't use the roads; see also *julus* and *chakka jam*

bazaar – market area or market town

betel – mildly intoxicating concoction of areca nut and lime, which is wrapped in betel leaf and chewed

Bhadrakali – Tantric goddess who is also a consort of *Bhairab*

Bhagavad Gita – *Krishna*'s lessons to Arjuna, part of the *Mahabharata*

Bhairab – the 'terrific' or fearsome Tantric form of *Shiva* with 64 manifestations

bhalu – sloth bears

bhanjyang – mountain pass

bhatti – teahouse or village inn

Bhimsen – one of the Pandava brothers, from the *Mahabharata*, seen as a god of tradesmen

Bhote – high-altitude desert valleys north of the Himalaya bordering Tibet; Nepali term for a Tibetan

bodhi tree – a pipal tree under which the Buddha was sitting when he attained enlightenment, also known as 'bo tree'

Bodhisattva – a near-Buddha who renounces the opportunity to attain *nirvana* in order to aid humankind

Bön – the animist religion of Tibet prior to Buddhism

Brahma – the creator god in the Hindu triad which includes *Vishnu* and *Shiva*

Brahmin – the highest Hindu caste, said to originate from *Brahma*'s head

bright fortnight – two weeks of the waxing moon, as it grows to become the full moon; see also *dark fortnight*

Buddha – Awakened One; the originator of Buddhism; also regarded by Hindus as the ninth incarnation of *Vishnu*

chaitya – small *stupa*, which usually contains a *mantra* rather than a Buddhist relic

chakka jam – literally 'jam the wheels', in which all vehicles stay off the street during a strike; see also *bandh* and *julus*

chakra – *Vishnu*'s disc-like weapon, one of the four symbols he holds

Chandra – moon god

chautara – stone platforms around trees, which serve as shady places for porters to rest

Chhetri – the second caste of Nepali Hindus, said to originate from *Brahma*'s arms

chirag – ceremonial oil lamp

chituwa – leopards

chorten – Tibetan Buddhist *stupa*

chowk – (pronounced choke) historically a courtyard or marketplace; these days used more to refer to an intersection or crossroads

dal – lentil soup; the main source of protein in the Nepali diet

dal bhaat tarakari – staple meal of Hindu Nepalis, consisting of lentil soup, rice and curried vegetables

Dalai Lama – incarnation of a *Bodhisattva* and the spiritual leader of Tibetan Buddhist people

danda – hill

dark fortnight – two weeks of the waning moon, as the full moon shrinks to become the new moon; see also *bright fortnight*

Dattatreya – deity who is thought of as an incarnation of *Vishnu*, *Shiva*'s teacher, or the Buddha's cousin

deval – temple

Devanagari – Sanskrit Nepali script

Devi – the short form of *Mahadevi*, the *shakti* to *Shiva*

dhaka – hand-woven cotton cloth

dharamsala – resthouse for pilgrims

dharma – Buddhist teachings

dhoka – door or gate

Dhyani Buddha – the original Adi Buddha created five Dhyani Buddhas, who in turn create the universe of each human era

doko – basket carried by porters

doonga – boat

dorje – see *vajra*

durbar – palace

Durga – fearsome manifestation of *Parvati*, *Shiva*'s consort

dyochen – a form of temple enshrining Tantric deities

dzopkyo – male cross between a *yak* and a cow; also zopkiok

dzum – female offspring of a *yak* and a cow; also zhum

ek – Nepali number one; a symbol of the unity of all life

freaks – 1960s term from the overland era for the young Western travellers who could be found congregating in Bali, Kabul, Goa and Kathmandu

gaida – rhinoceros

gaine – itinerant musician

ganas – *Shiva*'s companions

Ganesh – son of *Shiva* and *Parvati*, instantly recognisable by his elephant head

Ganga – goddess of the Ganges

ganja – hashish

Garuda – the man-bird *vehicle* of *Vishnu*

Gautama Buddha – the Buddha of our era

Gelugpa – one of the four major schools of Tibetan Buddhism; its adherents are sometimes referred to as the *Yellow Hats*

ghanta – Tantric bell; the female equivalent of the *vajra*

ghat – steps beside a river; a 'burning ghat' is used for cremations

ghee – clarified butter

gompa – Tibetan Buddhist monastery

gopi – cowherd girl (*Krishna* had a lot of fun with his gopis)

gufa – cave

guhya – vagina

Gurkha – Nepali soldiers who have long formed a part of the British army; the name comes from the region of Gorkha

Gurkhali – British army name for the Nepali language

Gurung – western hill people from around Gorkha and Pokhara

haat bajar – weekly bazaar

Hanuman – monkey god

harmika – square base on top of a *stupa*'s dome upon which the eyes of the Buddha are painted; the eyes face the four cardinal directions

hathi – elephant

himal – range or massif with permanent snow

hiti – water conduit or tank with waterspouts

hookah – water pipe for smoking

howdah – riding platform for elephant passengers

incarnation – a particular life form; the form mortals assume is determined by *karma*

Indra – king of the *Vedic gods*; god of rain

Jagannath – *Krishna* as Lord of the Universe

Jambhala – god of wealth; look for his money bag and his attendant mongoose

janai – sacred thread, which high-caste Hindu men wear looped over their left shoulder

jatra – festival

jayanti – birthday

jhankri – faith healers who perform in a trance while beating drums

Jogini – mystical goddesses, counterparts to the 64 manifestations of *Bhairab*

jukha – leech

julus – a procession or demonstration; see also *bandh* and *chakka jam*

Kali – the most terrifying manifestation of *Parvati*

Kalki – *Vishnu*'s 10th and as yet unseen incarnation during which he will come riding a white horse and wielding a sword to destroy the world

Kalpa – day in the age of *Brahma*

Kam Dev – *Shiva*'s companion

Kamasutra – ancient Hindu text on erotic pleasures

karma – Buddhist and Hindu law of cause and effect, which continues from one life to another

Kartikkaya – god of war and son of *Shiva*, his vehicle is the cock or peacock; also known as Kumar or Skanda

Kaukala – a form of *Shiva* in his fearsome aspect; he carries a trident with the skeleton of *Vishnu*'s gatekeeper impaled upon it; this act was the result of banning *Shiva* from *Vishnu*'s palace

KEEP – Kathmandu Environmental Education Project

Khas – Hindu hill people

khat – see *palanquin*

khata – Tibetan prayer shawl, often presented on introduction to an important Buddhist

khola – stream or tributary

khukuri – traditional curved knife of the *Gurkhas*

kinkinimali – temple wind bells

kosi – river

kot – fort

Krishna – fun-loving eighth incarnation of *Vishnu*

Kumari – living goddess, a peaceful incarnation of *Kali*

kunda – water tank fed by springs

kutis – pilgrim hostels

la – mountain pass

lama – Tibetan Buddhist monk or priest

lathi – bamboo staves used by police during a protest

lingam – phallic symbol that represents *Shiva*'s creative powers

machan – a lookout tower used to view wildlife

Machhendranath – patron god of the Kathmandu Valley and an incarnation of *Avalokiteshvara*

Mahabharata – one of the major Hindu epics

Mahadevi – literally 'Great Goddess', sometimes known as *Devi*; the *shakti* to *Shiva*

Mahayana – the 'greater-vehicle' of Buddhism; a later adaptation of the teaching which lays emphasis on the *Bodhisattva* ideal, teaching the renunciation of nirvana in order to help other beings along the way to enlightenment

mahseer – game fish of the Terai rivers

Malla – royal dynasty of the Kathmandu Valley responsible for most of the important temples and palaces of the valley towns

mandala – geometrical and astrological representation of the world

mandir – temple

mani – stone carved with the Tibetan Buddhist chant *om mani padme hum*

Manjushri – the god who cut open the Chobar Gorge so that the Kathmandu Lake could become the Kathmandu Valley

mantra – prayer formula or chant

Mara – Buddhist god of death; has three eyes and holds the *wheel of life*

math – Hindu priest's house

mela – country fair

naga – serpent deity; the nine nagas have control over water, and are often seen over house entrances to keep evil spirits away

Nagpura – Buddhist symbol for water

nak – female *yak*

namaste – traditional Hindu greeting (hello or goodbye), often accompanied by a small bow with the hands brought together at chest or head level, as a sign of respect

Nandi – *Shiva*'s *vehicle*, the bull

Narayan – *Vishnu* as the sleeping figure on the cosmic ocean; from his navel *Brahma* appeared and went on to create the universe

Narsingha – man-lion incarnation of *Vishnu*

Newari – people of the Kathmandu Valley

nirvana – ultimate peace and cessation of rebirth (Buddhism)

om mani padme hum – sacred Buddhist *mantra*, which means 'hail to the jewel in the lotus'

padma – lotus flower

Padmapani – literally 'Lotus in Hand'; a manifestation of *Avalokiteshvara* as he appears in many Nepali religious buildings, holding a tall lotus stalk

pagoda – multistoreyed Nepali temple, which was exported to China and Japan

palanquin – portable covered bed usually shouldered by four men; also called a *khat*

Parvati – *Shiva*'s consort

pashmina – goat wool blanket or shawl

Pashupati – *Shiva* as Lord of the Animals

path – small raised platform to shelter pilgrims

phanta – grass plains

pipal tree – see *bodhi tree*

pith – open shrine for a Tantric goddess

pokhari – large water tank

prasad – food offering

prayer flag – each carries a sacred *mantra* that is 'said' when the flag flutters

prayer wheel – cylindrical wheel inscribed with a Buddhist prayer or *mantra* that is 'said' when the wheel spins

Prithvi – *Vedic* earth goddess

puja – religious offering or prayer

pujari – priest

puri – town

purnima – full moon

Qomolangma – Tibetan name for Mt Everest; literally 'Mother Goddess of the World' (also spelt Chomolongma)

rajpath – road or highway, literally 'king's road'

raksha bandhan – yellow thread worn on the wrist that is said to bring good fortune

Ramayana – Hindu epic

Rana – of the hereditary prime ministers who ruled Nepal from 1841 to 1951

rath – temple chariot in which the idol is conveyed in processions

Red Hats – name given collectively to adherents of the Nyingmapa, Kargyupa and Sakyapa schools of Tibetan Buddhism

sadhu – wandering Hindu holy man; generally a *Shaivite* who has given up everything to follow the trail to religious salvation

sagar – large sacred ponds

Sagarmatha – Nepali name for Mt Everest

sal – tree of the lower Himalayan foothills

saligram – a black ammonite fossil of a Jurassic-period sea creature which is also a symbol of *Shiva*

Saraswati – goddess of learning and creative arts, and consort of *Brahma*, who is often identified by her lute-like instrument

seto – white

Shaivite – follower of *Shiva* whose face is covered in ashes with three horizontal lines painted on the forehead, and who carries a begging bowl and *Shiva*'s symbolic trident

shakti – dynamic female element in male–female relationships; also a goddess

Sherpa – of the Buddhist hill people famed for stalwart work with mountaineering expeditions; literally 'People from the East'; with a lower case 's' sherpa means trek leader

Sherpani – female *Sherpa*

shikhara – Indian-style temple with tall corncob-like spire

Shitala Mai – ogress who became a protector of children

Shiva – the most powerful Hindu god, the creator and destroyer

sindur – red vermillion dust and mustard oil mixture used for offerings

sirdar – leader/organiser of a trekking party

STOL – short take off and landing aircraft used on mountain airstrips

stupa – hemispherical Buddhist religious structure

Sudra – the lowest Nepali caste, said to originate from *Brahma*'s feet

sundhara – fountain with golden spout

tabla – hand drum

tahr – wild mountain goat

tal – lake

Taleju Bhawani – Nepali goddess, an aspect of *Mahadevi* and the family deity of the *Malla* kings of the Kathmandu Valley

Tantric Buddhism – form of Buddhism that evolved in Tibet during the 10th to 15th centuries

Tara – White Tara is the consort of the *Dhyani Buddha* Vairocana; Green Tara is associated with Amoghasiddhi

teahouse trek – independent trekking between village inns

tempo – three-wheeled, automated minivan commonly used in Nepal

Thakali – people of the Kali Gandaki Valley who specialise in running hotels

thali – literally a plate with compartments for different dishes; an all-you-can-eat set meal.

thangka – Tibetan religious painting on cotton

third eye – symbolic eye on Buddha figures, used to indicate the Buddha's clairvoyant powers

thugpa – traditional thick Tibetan meat soup

tika – red sandalwood-paste spot marked on the forehead, particularly for religious occasions

tole – street or quarter of a town; sometimes used to refer to a square

topi – traditional Nepali cap

torana – pediment above temple doors, which can indicate the god to whom the temple is dedicated

Tribhuvan – the king who in 1951 ended the *Rana* period and Nepal's long seclusion

trisul – trident weapon symbol of *Shiva*

tumpline – leather or cloth strip worn across the forehead or chest of a porter to support a load carried on the back

tunal – carved temple strut

tundikhel – parade ground

Uma Maheshwar – *Shiva* and *Parvati* in a pose where *Shiva* sits cross-legged and *Parvati* sits on his thigh and leans against him

Upanishads – ancient Vedic scripts, the last part of the *Vedas*

urna – the bump on the forehead of a Buddha or *Bodhisattva*

vahana – a god's animal mount or *vehicle*

Vaishnavite – follower of *Vishnu*

Vaisya – caste of merchants and farmers, said to originate from *Brahma*'s thighs

vajra – the 'thunderbolt' symbol of Buddhist power in Nepal; *dorje* in Tibetan

Vajra Jogini – a Tantric goddess, *shakti* to a *Bhairab*

Vasudhara – the wife of *Jambhala*, the god of wealth; she rides a chariot drawn by a pig

Vedas – ancient orthodox Hindu scriptures

Vedic gods – ancient Hindu gods described in the *Vedas*

vehicle – the animal with which a Hindu god is associated

vihara – Buddhist religious buildings and pilgrim accommodation

Vishnu – the preserver, one of the three main Hindu gods

wheel of life – this is held by *Mara*, the god of death; the wheel's concentric circles represents the Buddha's knowledge and the way humans can escape their conditioning and achieve *nirvana*

yab-yum – Tibetan term for Tantric erotica

yak – main Nepali beast of burden, a form of cattle found above 3000m

yaket – Tibetan wool jacket

yaksha – attendant deity or nymph

Yama – *Vedic god* of death; his messenger is the crow

Yellow Hats – name sometimes given to adherents of the *Gelugpa* school of Tibetan Buddhism

yeti – abominable snowman

yogi – yoga master

yoni – female sexual symbol, equivalent of a *lingam*

zamindar – absentee landlord and/or moneylender

Thanks

Spafford Ackerly, Magnus Ahrenberg, Husain Akbar, Juan Antonio Alegre, Jim Allen, Louise Amandini, Ryan Anderson, Wayne & Jean Andreen, Mark Anstiss, Martijn Antonius, Dan Atkinson, Neil Atkinson, Frans Attevelt, Susan E Ball, S R Barker-Damste, Sebastien Barrette, Dr Wolfgang Bayer, James Beattie, Emily Becca, Inger-Anne Becker Wold, Geoff Beckett, Lisa Bell, Marie Bell, Kristina Bellach, Nicki Beltchev, Kim Belz, Shua Ben-Ari, Sven Berger, Mark Berry, Rick Bevan, Shimon Bigelman, Gino Bilardo, Jennie Billson, Matthew Bird, Alice Birnbaum, Rebecca Blackwell, C Boeckenhauer, Thomas Boedeker, Chhedup Bomzan, Johnny Boruch, Bernhard Bouzek, Susan Boysal, Nancy Breckenridge, Mario Brendel, Tom Brichau, Keri Bridgwater, Dawn Bright, Graeme Brock, Tom Brooks, Alden Brown, Ryan Bruce, Mark W Bryant, Esther Buis, Brigadier C Bullock, Katja Bunnik, Alex Burns, Arnout Burns, Lori Burnside, Enzo Caffarelli, Sue & Chris Campion, Laurent Chamuleau, Isabel Chappat, Ruth Cheesley, Radim Chomic, Matthew Claydon, Stephen Clemmet, Yael Cohen, Derrick Cook, Chris Courtheyn, Clement Cousin, Nicholas Covelli, Nick Cox, E C Craven, Tim & Marika Crosby, Ana Paula Curiacos, Paul Daman, Amanda Davies, Barrie Davies, Yigal Dayan, Koen De Boeck, J De Vries, Erika DeCarlo, Marie-Pierre Degoulet, Heather Deller, Sandy Denize, W Derkx, Scott DeRuiter, Kirk & Jenn DesErmia, Annemarie Dijk, Nick DiNardo, Louise Diracles, John Dixon, Peter Docktree, Sarah Docktree, Sara Doherty, Inga Domke, Laszlo Dora, Amy Douglas, Andrea Doukas, Dennis Dowling, Russell Downey, Magdalena Dral, Randell Drum, Jeremy Durston, Frazer Egerton, Natalya Eliashberg, Navyo Eller, Ariel Erez, Robin & Linda Erickson, Charlotte Evans, Horace Fairlamb, Jeff Faris, Eric Feigenbaum, Mauricio Fernandez, Andree Fernee, John Fernyhough, Steve Fisi, Luke Fletcher, Mark Follett, Sarah Franklin, Walter Fraser, Michael Freiberg, Elina Freitag, Bernd Friese, Penny Gardner, Sean Geiger, Daniel Gerster, Bob Gibbons, Paul W Gioffi, Katia Giraud, Rosie Gleser, Detlev Goebel, Martha & Donald Goldman, Mark Gray, Mona Gray, Lara Green, Michael Green, Vivienne Green, Heather Griffin, Henk Groeneveld, Dr Hans Guggenheim, Bob Guyett, Mike & Karen Hadwen, Thomas Hagen, Tina Hall, Elliott Halter, Scott Hansing, Deb & Tony Harrip, David Harris,

Nicole Havranek, Dr Silke Heidrich, C Hertogh, Russell Heywood, E M Hill, Josie Hill, Alan Hodgson, Patrick Holland, Steve Hollins, Anni Holm, Wendy Hoogervorst, Susanne Hoorn, Sarah Hornby, Tony Horrigan, Katherine Howard, Tony Howard, Nadine Hudson, Luke Huges, Cordelia Hughes, Laura Hughes, Jaana Ilkko, Bob & Ann Isaacson, Alene Ivey, Amy Jackson, Will Jackson, Sonya Jakos, Brandy James, Rae James, Mark Jansch, Anthony Jenkins, Adriana Jenkins-Fitzgerald, Anna Jinnedal, Lisa Joffe, Robin Johnson, Jillian Johnston, Peter & Ulrika Jonell, Ard Jonker, Russell Jutlah, Boris Kaeller, Sandra Kanders, Costi Karayannis, Eileen Kardos, Judith Karena, Pius Karena, Sheena Karim, Andrew Keba, Birgit Keil, Chris Kelly, David Kelly, Sandie Kemp, Bridget Kendrick, Lin Ketchell, Alex Kettles, Noa Kfir, Sina Khasani, Jae Hoon Kim, Simone Klik, Thomas Korostenski, Thirsa Kraayenbrink, Alexis Kruger, Tessie & Dennis Kuiper, Marie Kvamme, Alexandra Kwiatkowski, Jan Laan, Simon Ladley, Helga Langer, Wolf Langer, Adrian Lanigan, Kelly Lapinskas, Cheryl Larden, Lotte Larsen, David F Latchford, Suzy Lebasi, Jenni Lee, Bert Leegmaat, Bert Leffers, Igor Lekuona, Rose Leone, Pamela Levine, Viridian Light-Hart, Tim & Theresa Lloyd, Peter Lockley, Margaret Lorang, Catherine Lowell, Katie-Jo Luxton, Katryna Lynch, Donna Mackey, Morag Maclean, Mario Magoga, Christine Maier, Rene Mairis, Bernie Major, Hitesh Makwana, Ram Malis, Tanja Mammen, Lisa Manley, Richard Manley, Annie Manning, Dannen Mannschreck, Robert March, Celeste Marsh, John Martin, Luigina Mascherpa, Klaus Maurer, Claire May, Matt McCabe, Monika McCallum, Rosemary McDermott, Bronwyn McEwen, Serge McGregor, Barbara Meinhardt, Julie Midgley, Rachel Miles, Karral Miller, Ron Miller, Kevin & Rhona Millgate, Claire Monaghan, Zoe Moore, Kath Morrell, Lee Morris, Stephan Muis, Sue Muldenhall, Jorand Nadege, Susan Naus, Jonny Nease, Jakhan Nguyen, Masha Nikiforov, Danielle Noyce, Jen O'Neal, David Osrin, Rogerio Paglerani, Jodi Pallett, Dick Palmer, Andy Parker, Julie Parker, Colin Parsons, Benita Pasch, Carlo & Emanuela Paschetto, Sruti Patel, Adam John Pattersol, Lisa Patterson, Scott Patterson, Luca Patti, Mario Pavesi, Cheryle Payton-Todd, Chris Peake, Wendy Pearce, Suzanne Pearson, Ada Yu Pei-Ying, Edward Pelgrim, Sherpa Pemba, Shyam Penubolu,

Daniela Peters, Ngoc Phan, Hilda Phillip, Daniela Pichleritsch, Becky & Bob Pine, Simon Piney, Luise Poggensee, Sue & Abe Pollak, Klaus Pott, Lucy Potter, Ivy & Richard Preddy, Belinda Price, Marjolein Prins, Sian Pritchard-Jones, Emma Pritchett, Angela Pucillo, Matthias Pusch, Mark Quinlan, Cameron Raine, Meriel Randerson, Michael Ranger, Claire Ranyard, Tom Ratcliffe, Sandy Ratner, Chris & Sherry Rauh, Hillol Ray, Ben Ridder, Rhymer Rigby, Reg Roberts, Alex Robertson, Erin Robertson, Katie Rodd, Anna Rogers, Hendrik-Jan Rogge, Rachely Romem, Amit Rosner, Alan Ross, Joshua Ross, Joyce Maples Rowlatt, Martine Roy, Paul Ruijgrok, Mary Ryan, Henryk Sadura, Carrie Sands, Mario Santens, Joseba Sanz, Jill Sazanami, Renato Scapolan, Bart Schalkx, Vivian Schatz, Matthias Schermaier, Monica Schmitz-Salue, Jerry Schwartz, Greg Schwendinger, Douglas Scott, Stephen Scott, Virender K Sharma, Ray Sharrock, Daniel Sher, Caryl Sherman, Leigh Sherpa, Dana Shields, Margaret Sinclair, Megha Singh, Bob Skinner, Lee Smith, Scott Michael Smith, Craig Snow, Pierre Soete, David Soucy, Simon Spence, Lucinda Squires, Henrik Stabell, Todd Stehbens, Mareike & Lena Steinmann, Nicole Stiechler, Magnus Stomfelt, Jeroen Struik, Cornelius Suchy, John & Lynn Sullivan, Rob & Jodie Swales, Balazs Szasz, Ramon Tak, Ineke & Jacqueline Tamis, Mirja Tapanen, Joyce Tapper, Gabriele Tellgmann, Jeff Thaldorf, Christina Themar, David Thomas, Georgina Thomas, Lauren Thompson, Dr Quyen To Do, Michael Trabuio, Louise Trethewey, Sheri Tsai, Fredrik Tukk, Imogen Turner, Rachel Tyler, Jessica Uppelschoten, Laura Upton, Michel J van Dam, Peter Van den Bossche, Jeanette van der Burgh, Miriam van der Gugten, Robert van der Plas, Anne van der Waerden, Werner Van Dessel, Aljie Van hoorn, Paul Van Mechelen, Berry van Oers, Robert van Opstal, Erwin van Veen, Remko van Yperen, Darryl & Tania Vance, Ian Veinot, Elwin Verheggen, Susie Vickery, Ineke Visser, Reto Wagner, Karin Waibl, Bob Walbers, Karen Wallace, Mark Wallem, Yau Wan-Kong, Luke & Hannah Watson, Jimmy Wattkins, Fiona Watts, Martina Weber, Michel Weber, Dan Weene, Jules Wehberg, Lukas Weilenmann, Frank Wheby, Elizabeth White, Linda White, Pamela White, Paul White, Ricard Wihstrom, Jeanette Wijnhoven, Tomasz Wilanowski, Teresa Williams, Lee Wing Kin, Tom Wislon, Kris Wolmer, Ian Wolstenholme, Susan Wood, Tonia & Daniel Wood, Berber & Jan-Joris Woudstra, John Yau, Leesa Yeo, Ling Sing Yeun, Rita Pema Yhonjan, Galia Zacay, Linda Zespy, Maike Ziesemer, Alon Zilberman, Birgit Zwick

LONELY PLANET

ON THE ROAD

Travel Guides explore cities, regions and countries, and supply information on transport, restaurants and accommodation, covering all budgets. They come with reliable, easy-to-use maps, practical advice, cultural and historical facts and a rundown on attractions both on and off the beaten track. There are over 200 titles in this classic series, covering nearly every country in the world.

 Lonely Planet Upgrades extend the shelf life of existing travel guides by detailing any changes that may affect travel in a region since a book has been published. Upgrades can be downloaded for free from **www.lonelyplanet.com/upgrades**

For travellers with more time than money, **Shoestring** guides offer dependable, first-hand information with hundreds of detailed maps, plus insider tips for stretching money as far as possible. Covering entire continents in most cases, the six-volume shoestring guides are known around the world as 'backpackers bibles'.

For the discerning short-term visitor, **Condensed** guides highlight the best a destination has to offer in a full-colour, pocket-sized format designed for quick access. They include everything from top sights and walking tours to opinionated reviews of where to eat, stay, shop and have fun.

CitySync lets travellers use their Palm™ or Visor™ hand-held computers to guide them through a city with handy tips on transport, history, cultural life, major sights, and shopping and entertainment options. It can also quickly search and sort hundreds of reviews of hotels, restaurants and attractions, and pinpoint their location on scrollable street maps. CitySync can be downloaded from **www.citysync.com**

MAPS & ATLASES

Lonely Planet's **City Maps** feature downtown and metropolitan maps, as well as transit routes and walking tours. The maps come complete with an index of streets, a listing of sights and a plastic coat for extra durability.

Road Atlases are an essential navigation tool for serious travellers. Cross-referenced with the guidebooks, they also feature distance and climate charts and a complete site index.

ESSENTIALS

Read This First books help new travellers to hit the road with confidence. These invaluable predeparture guides give step-by-step advice on preparing for a trip, budgeting, arranging a visa, planning an itinerary and staying safe while still getting off the beaten track.

Healthy Travel pocket guides offer a regional rundown on disease hot spots and practical advice on predeparture health measures, staying well on the road and what to do in emergencies. The guides come with a user-friendly design and helpful diagrams and tables.

Lonely Planet's **Phrasebooks** cover the essential words and phrases travellers need when they're strangers in a strange land. They come in a pocket-sized format with colour tabs for quick reference, extensive vocabulary lists, easy-to-follow pronunciation keys and two-way dictionaries.

Miffed by blurry photos of the Taj Mahal? Tired of the classic 'top of the head cut off' shot? **Travel Photography: A Guide to Taking Better Pictures** will help you turn ordinary holiday snaps into striking images and give you the know-how to capture every scene, from frenetic festivals to peaceful beach sunrises.

Lonely Planet's **Travel Journal** is a lightweight but sturdy travel diary for jotting down all those on-the-road observations and significant travel moments. It comes with a handy time-zone wheel, a world map and useful travel information.

Lonely Planet's eKno is an all-in-one communication service developed especially for travellers. It offers low-cost international calls and free email and voicemail so that you can keep in touch while on the road. Check it out on **www.ekno.lonelyplanet.com**

FOOD & RESTAURANT GUIDES

Lonely Planet's **Out to Eat** guides recommend the brightest and best places to eat and drink in top international cities. These gourmet companions are arranged by neighbourhood, packed with dependable maps, garnished with scene-setting photos and served with quirky features.

For people who live to eat, drink and travel, **World Food** guides explore the culinary culture of each country. Entertaining and adventurous, each guide is packed with detail on staples and specialities, regional cuisine and local markets, as well as sumptuous recipes, comprehensive culinary dictionaries and lavish photos good enough to eat.

LONELY PLANET

OUTDOOR GUIDES

For those who believe the best way to see the world is on foot, Lonely Planet's **Walking Guides** detail everything from family strolls to difficult treks, with 'when to go and how to do it' advice supplemented by reliable maps and essential travel information.

Cycling Guides map a destination's best bike tours, long and short, in day-by-day detail. They contain all the information a cyclist needs, including advice on bike maintenance, places to eat and stay, innovative maps with detailed cues to the rides, and elevation charts.

The **Watching Wildlife** series is perfect for travellers who want authoritative information but don't want to tote a heavy field guide. Packed with advice on where, when and how to view a region's wildlife, each title features photos of over 300 species and contains engaging comments on the local flora and fauna.

With underwater colour photos throughout, **Pisces Books** explore the world's best diving and snorkelling areas. Each book contains listings of diving services and dive resorts, detailed information on depth, visibility and difficulty of dives, and a roundup of the marine life you're likely to see through your mask.

LONELY PLANET

OFF THE ROAD

Journeys, the travel literature series written by renowned travel authors, capture the spirit of a place or illuminate a culture with a journalist's attention to detail and a novelist's flair for words. These are tales to soak up while you're actually on the road or dip into as an at-home armchair indulgence.

The range of lavishly illustrated **Pictorial** books is just the ticket for both travellers and dreamers. Off-beat tales and vivid photographs bring the adventure of travel to your doorstep long before the journey begins and long after it is over.

Lonely Planet **Videos** encourage the same independent, tough-minded approach as the guidebooks. Currently airing throughout the world, this award-winning series features innovative footage and an original soundtrack.

Yes, we know, work is tough, so do a little bit of deskside dreaming with the spiral-bound Lonely Planet **Diary** or a Lonely Planet **Wall Calendar**, filled with great photos from around the world.

TRAVELLERS NETWORK

Lonely Planet Online. Lonely Planet's award-winning Web site has insider information on hundreds of destinations, from Amsterdam to Zimbabwe, complete with interactive maps and relevant links. The site also offers the latest travel news, recent reports from travellers on the road, guidebook upgrades, a travel links site, an online book-buying option and a lively travellers bulletin board. It can be viewed at **www.lonelyplanet.com** or AOL keyword: lp.

Planet Talk is a quarterly print newsletter, full of gossip, advice, anecdotes and author articles. It provides an antidote to the being-at-home blues and lets you plan and dream for the next trip. Contact the nearest Lonely Planet office for your free copy.

Comet, the free Lonely Planet newsletter, comes via email once a month. It's loaded with travel news, advice, dispatches from authors, travel competitions and letters from readers. To subscribe, click on the Comet subscription link on the front page of the Web site.

LONELY PLANET

Guides by Region

L onely Planet is known worldwide for publishing practical, reliable and no-nonsense travel information in our guides and on our Web site. The Lonely Planet list covers just about every accessible part of the world. Currently there are 16 series: Travel guides, Shoestring guides, Condensed guides, Phrasebooks, Read This First, Healthy Travel, Walking guides, Cycling guides, Watching Wildlife guides, Pisces Diving & Snorkeling guides, City Maps, Road Atlases, Out to Eat, World Food, Journeys travel literature and Pictorials.

AFRICA Africa on a shoestring • Botswana • Cairo • Cairo City Map • Cape Town • Cape Town City Map • East Africa • Egypt • Egyptian Arabic phrasebook • Ethiopia, Eritrea & Djibouti • Ethiopian Amharic phrasebook • The Gambia & Senegal • Healthy Travel Africa • Kenya • Malawi • Morocco • Moroccan Arabic phrasebook • Mozambique • Namibia • Read This First: Africa • South Africa, Lesotho & Swaziland • Southern Africa • Southern Africa Road Atlas • Swahili phrasebook • Tanzania, Zanzibar & Pemba • Trekking in East Africa • Tunisia • Watching Wildlife East Africa • Watching Wildlife Southern Africa • West Africa • World Food Morocco • Zambia • Zimbabwe, Botswana & Namibia
Travel Literature: Mali Blues: Traveling to an African Beat • The Rainbird: A Central African Journey • Songs to an African Sunset: A Zimbabwean Story

AUSTRALIA & THE PACIFIC Aboriginal Australia & the Torres Strait Islands •Auckland • Australia • Australian phrasebook • Australia Road Atlas • Cycling Australia • Cycling New Zealand • Fiji • Fijian phrasebook • Healthy Travel Australia, NZ & the Pacific • Islands of Australia's Great Barrier Reef • Melbourne • Melbourne City Map • Micronesia • New Caledonia • New South Wales • New Zealand • Northern Territory • Outback Australia • Out to Eat – Melbourne • Out to Eat – Sydney • Papua New Guinea • Pidgin phrasebook • Queensland • Rarotonga & the Cook Islands • Samoa • Solomon Islands • South Australia • South Pacific • South Pacific phrasebook • Sydney • Sydney City Map • Sydney Condensed • Tahiti & French Polynesia • Tasmania • Tonga • Tramping in New Zealand • Vanuatu • Victoria • Walking in Australia • Watching Wildlife Australia • Western Australia
Travel Literature: Islands in the Clouds: Travels in the Highlands of New Guinea • Kiwi Tracks: A New Zealand Journey • Sean & David's Long Drive

CENTRAL AMERICA & THE CARIBBEAN Bahamas, Turks & Caicos • Baja California • Belize, Guatemala & Yucatán • Bermuda • Central America on a shoestring • Costa Rica • Costa Rica Spanish phrasebook • Cuba • Cycling Cuba • Dominican Republic & Haiti • Eastern Caribbean • Guatemala • Havana • Healthy Travel Central & South America • Jamaica • Mexico • Mexico City • Panama • Puerto Rico • Read This First: Central & South America • Virgin Islands • World Food Caribbean • World Food Mexico • Yucatán
Travel Literature: Green Dreams: Travels in Central America

EUROPE Amsterdam • Amsterdam City Map • Amsterdam Condensed • Andalucía • Athens • Austria • Baltic States phrasebook • Barcelona • Barcelona City Map • Belgium & Luxembourg • Berlin • Berlin City Map • Britain • British phrasebook • Brussels, Bruges & Antwerp • Brussels City Map • Budapest • Budapest City Map • Canary Islands • Catalunya & the Costa Brava • Central Europe • Central Europe phrasebook • Copenhagen • Corfu & the Ionians • Corsica • Crete • Crete Condensed • Croatia • Cycling Britain • Cycling France • Cyprus • Czech & Slovak Republics • Czech phrasebook • Denmark • Dublin • Dublin City Map • Dublin Condensed • Eastern Europe • Eastern Europe phrasebook • Edinburgh • Edinburgh City Map • England • Estonia, Latvia & Lithuania • Europe on a shoestring • Europe phrasebook • Finland • Florence • Florence City Map • France • Frankfurt City Map • Frankfurt Condensed • French phrasebook • Georgia, Armenia & Azerbaijan • Germany • German phrasebook • Greece • Greek Islands • Greek phrasebook • Hungary • Iceland, Greenland & the Faroe Islands • Ireland • Italian phrasebook • Italy • Kraków • Lisbon • The Loire • London • London City Map • London Condensed • Madrid • Madrid City Map • Malta • Mediterranean Europe • Milan, Turin & Genoa • Moscow • Munich • Netherlands • Normandy • Norway • Out to Eat – London • Out to Eat – Paris • Paris • Paris City Map • Paris Condensed • Poland • Polish phrasebook • Portugal • Portuguese phrasebook • Prague • Prague City Map • Provence & the Côte d'Azur • Read This First: Europe • Rhodes & the Dodecanese • Romania & Moldova • Rome • Rome City Map • Rome Condensed • Russia, Ukraine & Belarus • Russian phrasebook • Scandinavian & Baltic Europe • Scandinavian phrasebook • Scotland • Sicily • Slovenia • South-West France • Spain • Spanish phrasebook • Stockholm • St Petersburg • St Petersburg City Map • Sweden • Switzerland • Tuscany • Ukrainian phrasebook • Venice • Vienna • Wales • Walking in Britain • Walking in France • Walking in Ireland • Walking in Italy • Walking in Scotland • Walking in Spain • Walking in Switzerland • Western Europe • World Food France • World Food Greece • World Food Ireland • World Food Italy • World Food Spain **Travel Literature:** After Yugoslavia • Love and War in the Apennines • The Olive Grove: Travels in Greece • On the Shores of the Mediterranean • Round Ireland in Low Gear • A Small Place in Italy

LONELY PLANET

Mail Order

Lonely Planet products are distributed worldwide.They are also available by mail order from Lonely Planet, so if you have difficulty finding a title please write to us. North and South American residents should write to 150 Linden St, Oakland, CA 94607, USA; European and African residents should write to 72-82 Rosebery Ave, London, EC1R 4RW, UK; and residents of other countries to Locked Bag 1, Footscray, Victoria 3011, Australia.

INDIAN SUBCONTINENT & THE INDIAN OCEAN Bangladesh • Bengali phrasebook • Bhutan • Delhi • Goa • Healthy Travel Asia & India • Hindi & Urdu phrasebook • India • India & Bangladesh City Map • Indian Himalaya • Karakoram Highway • Kathmandu City Map • Kerala • Madagascar • Maldives • Mauritius, Réunion & Seychelles • Mumbai (Bombay) • Nepal • Nepali phrasebook • North India • Pakistan • Rajasthan • Read This First: Asia & India • South India • Sri Lanka • Sri Lanka phrasebook • Tibet • Tibetan phrasebook • Trekking in the Indian Himalaya • Trekking in the Karakoram & Hindukush • Trekking in the Nepal Himalaya • World Food India **Travel Literature**: The Age of Kali: Indian Travels and Encounters • Hello Goodnight: A Life of Goa • In Rajasthan • Maverick in Madagascar • A Season in Heaven: True Tales from the Road to Kathmandu • Shopping for Buddhas • A Short Walk in the Hindu Kush • Slowly Down the Ganges

MIDDLE EAST & CENTRAL ASIA Bahrain, Kuwait & Qatar • Central Asia • Central Asia phrasebook • Dubai • Farsi (Persian) phrasebook • Hebrew phrasebook • Iran • Israel & the Palestinian Territories • Istanbul • Istanbul City Map • Istanbul to Cairo • Istanbul to Kathmandu • Jerusalem • Jerusalem City Map • Jordan • Lebanon • Middle East • Oman and the United Arab Emirates • Syria • Turkey • Turkish phrasebook • World Food Turkey • Yemen **Travel Literature**: Black on Black: Iran Revisited • Breaking Ranks: Turbulent Travels in the Promised Land • The Gates of Damascus • Kingdom of the Film Stars: Journey into Jordan

NORTH AMERICA Alaska • Boston • Boston City Map • Boston Condensed • British Columbia • California & Nevada • California Condensed • Canada • Chicago • Chicago City Map • Chicago Condensed • Florida • Georgia & the Carolinas • Great Lakes • Hawaii • Hiking in Alaska • Hiking in the USA • Honolulu & Oahu City Map • Las Vegas • Los Angeles • Los Angeles City Map • Louisiana & the Deep South • Miami • Miami City Map • Montreal • New England • New Orleans • New Orleans City Map • New York City • New York City City Map • New York City Condensed • New York, New Jersey & Pennsylvania • Oahu • Out to Eat – San Francisco • Pacific Northwest • Rocky Mountains • San Diego & Tijuana • San Francisco • San Francisco City Map • Seattle • Seattle City Map • Southwest • Texas • Toronto • USA • USA phrasebook • Vancouver • Vancouver City Map • Virginia & the Capital Region • Washington, DC • Washington, DC City Map • World Food New Orleans **Travel Literature**: Caught Inside: A Surfer's Year on the California Coast • Drive Thru America

NORTH-EAST ASIA Beijing • Beijing City Map • Cantonese phrasebook • China • Hiking in Japan • Hong Kong & Macau • Hong Kong City Map • Hong Kong Condensed • Japan • Japanese phrasebook • Korea • Korean phrasebook • Kyoto • Mandarin phrasebook • Mongolia • Mongolian phrasebook • Seoul • Shanghai • South-West China • Taiwan • Tokyo • Tokyo Condensed • World Food Hong Kong • World Food Japan **Travel Literature**: In Xanadu: A Quest • Lost Japan

SOUTH AMERICA Argentina, Uruguay & Paraguay • Bolivia • Brazil • Brazilian phrasebook • Buenos Aires • Buenos Aires City Map • Chile & Easter Island • Colombia • Ecuador & the Galapagos Islands • Healthy Travel Central & South America • Latin American Spanish phrasebook • Peru • Quechua phrasebook • Read This First: Central & South America • Rio de Janeiro • Rio de Janeiro City Map • Santiago de Chile • South America on a shoestring • Trekking in the Patagonian Andes • Venezuela **Travel Literature**: Full Circle: A South American Journey

SOUTH-EAST ASIA Bali & Lombok • Bangkok • Bangkok City Map • Burmese phrasebook • Cambodia • Cycling Vietnam, Laos & Cambodia • East Timor phrasebook • Hanoi • Healthy Travel Asia & India • Hill Tribes phrasebook • Ho Chi Minh City (Saigon) • Indonesia • Indonesian phrasebook • Indonesia's Eastern Islands • Java • Lao phrasebook • Laos • Malay phrasebook • Malaysia, Singapore & Brunei • Myanmar (Burma) • Philippines • Pilipino (Tagalog) phrasebook • Read This First: Asia & India • Singapore • Singapore City Map • South-East Asia on a shoestring • South-East Asia phrasebook • Thailand • Thailand's Islands & Beaches • Thailand, Vietnam, Laos & Cambodia Road Atlas • Thai phrasebook • Vietnam • Vietnamese phrasebook • World Food Indonesia • World Food Thailand • World Food Vietnam

ALSO AVAILABLE: Antarctica • The Arctic • The Blue Man: Tales of Travel, Love and Coffee • Brief Encounters: Stories of Love, Sex & Travel • Buddhist Stupas in Asia: The Shape of Perfection • Chasing Rickshaws • The Last Grain Race • Lonely Planet ... On the Edge: Adventurous Escapades from Around the World • Lonely Planet Unpacked • Lonely Planet Unpacked Again • Not the Only Planet: Science Fiction Travel Stories • Ports of Call: A Journey by Sea • Sacred India • Travel Photography: A Guide to Taking Better Pictures • Travel with Children • Tuvalu: Portrait of an Island Nation

LONELY PLANET

You already know that Lonely Planet produces more than this one guidebook, but you might not be aware of the other products we have on this region. Here is a selection of titles that you may want to check out as well:

India
ISBN 1 74059 421 5
US$27.99 • UK£16.99

Tibet
ISBN 1 86450 162 6
US$19.99 • UK£12.99

Nepali Phrasebook
ISBN 1 74059 192 5
US$7.99 • UK£4.50

China
ISBN 1 74059 117 8
US$29.99 • UK£17.99

Trekking in the Nepal Himalaya
ISBN 1 86450 231 2
US$19.99 • UK£12.99

Healthy Travel - Asia & India
ISBN 1 86450 051 4
US$5.95 • UK£3.99

Available wherever books are sold

Index

Abbreviations

CA – Conservation Area
HR – Hunting Reserve
NP – National Park
WR – Wildlife Reserve

Text

Boxed Text

Bold indicates maps.

MAP LEGEND

CITY ROUTES

Freeway	Freeway		Unsealed Road
Highway	Primary Road		One-Way Street
Road	Secondary Road		Pedestrian Street
Street	Street		Stepped Street
Lane	Lane		Tunnel
	On/Off Ramp		Footbridge

HYDROGRAPHY

	River, Creek		Dry Lake, Salt Lake
	Canal		Spring; Rapids
	Lake		Waterfalls

REGIONAL ROUTES

	Tollway, Freeway		Primary Road
	Primary Road		Secondary Road
	Secondary Road		Minor Road

BOUNDARIES

	International		State
	Disputed		Fortified Wall

TRANSPORT ROUTES & STATIONS

	Train		Cable Car, Chairlift
	Underground Train		Walking Trail
	Metro		Walking Tour
	Tramway		Path
	Bus Route		Pier or Jetty

AREA FEATURES

	Building		Market
	Park, Garden		Sports Ground
	National Park		Campus
	Cemetery		Plaza

POPULATION SYMBOLS

○ CAPITAL	National Capital	● CITY	City	● Village	Village
◉ CAPITAL	State Capital	● Town	Town		Urban Area

MAP SYMBOLS

▪	Place to Stay	⌂	Cave	⚑	Monument	⊠	Shopping Centre
▼	Place to Eat	⊟	Cinema	ⓒ	Mosque	⌂	Stately Home
●	Point of Interest	⌂	Embassy, Consulate	▲	Mountain	⚲	Stupa
⊞	Airfield	⚓	Fountain	⌂	Museum	⊠	Swimming Pool
⊠	Airport	⊞	Gompa	⊟	Pagoda	⊟	Taxi
⊝	Bank	⊞	Hindu Temple	)(	Pass	⊞	Telephone
⊕	Border Crossing	⊕	Hospital	⊙	Petrol/Gas Station	⊕	Tourist Information
▪	Buddhist Temple	⊠	Internet Cafe	⊞	Police Station	⚲	Trail Head
⊟⊟	Bus Terminal, Stop	⚡	Lookout	⊟	Post Office	⊟	Transport (General)
⌂	Camping Ground	龕	Monastery	⊟	Pub, Bar	⊟	Wildlife Reserve

Note: not all symbols displayed above appear in this book

LONELY PLANET OFFICES

Australia
Locked Bag 1, Footscray, Victoria 3011
☎ 03 8379 8000 fax 03 8379 8111
email: talk2us@lonelyplanet.com.au

UK
72-82 Rosebery Ave, London, EC1R 4RW
☎ 020 7841 9000 fax 020 7841 9001
email: go@lonelyplanet.co.uk

USA
150 Linden St, Oakland, CA 94607
☎ 510 893 8555 TOLL FREE: 800 275 8555
fax 510 893 8572
email: info@lonelyplanet.com

France
1 rue du Dahomey, 75011 Paris
☎ 01 55 25 33 00 fax 01 55 25 33 01
email: bip@lonelyplanet.fr
www.lonelyplanet.fr

World Wide Web: www.lonelyplanet.com *or* AOL keyword: lp
Lonely Planet Images: www.lonelyplanetimages.com